The Structure of Social Inequality

The Structure of
Social
Inequality

BETH ENSMINGER VANFOSSEN

State University of New York at Brockport

Little, Brown and Company

Boston Toronto

Alex Inkeles, Series Advisor

Library of Congress Catalog Card No. 78–70850

First Printing

Published simultaneously in Canada
by Little, Brown & Company (Canada) Limited

Printed in the United States of America

To Ross and Margaret

who gave the first lessons

Preface

IN THIS TEXT, I have attempted to accomplish two related tasks: (1) to present the best information that empirical research has been able to provide about the structure of social inequality; and (2) to use the best that sociological theory offers to interpret those empirical findings so that their significance is revealed. The text was written for courses in social stratification and inequality, with the upper-level undergraduate student in mind as the primary reader.

The theoretical perspective of this text is the outgrowth of my own development. As a student in the 1950s, I was taught the functionalist perspective on social inequality, and it was with that framework in mind that this book was begun. But before the manuscript was finished, I had become convinced of the powerful utility of a conflict perspective. Gradually, the completed chapters were rewritten to reflect the new insights, and the unwritten chapters were replanned. The odyssey I took from one theoretical stance to another was difficult, and it was exciting. It was not one I travelled alone. Its path was taken by many of us in the discipline of sociology as we were profoundly affected by the events and issues of the

1960s — the civil rights movement, the Vietnam War, the failure of the War on Poverty, and the emergence of the women's movement. These events suggested that there is a substantial element of domination and coercion involved in the normal relationships between races, classes, sexes, and nations, and further that such domination is stable and well-entrenched.

As I made the intellectual transition from one perspective to the other, the functionalist argument that the basic explanation for social inequality is the outcome of society's need to motivate talented workers to fill important jobs seemed increasingly weak. The related assumptions that income rewards the talented, that a primary effect of the education system is to sort out the able from the unable, and that the function of the prestige system is to establish reverence for those who carry on essential and vital tasks also began to seem questionable. I became aware of research reports that indicated, for example, that there is no relationship between the size of the income received by American workers and their measured intelligence (one presumed index of talent), that some able people are not very educated while some of the educated are not very able, and that in many occupations educated workers perform no better than less educated ones (although they are paid more). Studies of values suggested that prestige is accorded to those who are powerful rather than to those who perform vital tasks.

On these and other issues, a conflict perspective that focuses on the reasons for domination seemed more applicable to the understanding of structured social inequality than a functionalist theory that focuses on the societal utility of highly rewarded positions. The conflict perspective suggests that inequality emerges out of a struggle for dominance over scarce and valued goods and services. Dominant groups use economic and political resources in attempting to maintain their control. Their superordination is made easier by compatible ideologies which are transmitted by schools, families, and mass media; and by the cooperation of agencies of social control such as lawmakers, the courts, and the police. While the conflict perspective does not entirely supplant the insights provided by other points of view, it does lead to new ways of looking at old realities, new ways that are exciting because they explain those realities so well.

The thinking of twentieth-century scholars of social stratification has until recently been based on functionalist assumptions, and for this reason the incorporation into this text of insights from the conflict perspective has required certain innovations, both of topic and of analysis. Two chapters on the economics of inequality and one on its political sources demonstrate a shift of emphasis from traditional texts that have chapters on neither. The conflict perspective also encourages a focus on structural sources of inequality rather than on social-psychological sources. To look at how political and economic elites are able to perpetuate a system of privilege, or how occupational groups strive to increase their income, for example, becomes more productive and thus more interesting than to examine the dynamics of how individuals rank and value one another.

Whatever innovation has occurred has had to be based on the empirical information available to us about the realities of wealth, power, and status. The time is no more when polemical contrasts between one theory and another suffice. While students want to sample different sociological perspectives on why inequality exists and how it is maintained, and they can become excited about the divergent policy implications of, say, functionalism as contrasted to conflict theory, they also want to see how we know that the nature of the phenomenon is what we claim it to be. They want to know such things as how much structured inequality really exists in modern industrial society, what is the probability of eliminating poverty, and, also, what are their own chances of getting ahead.

The book is divided into three parts. The first presents major theoretical perspectives and concepts. Following an introductory chapter that acquaints the student with the field and defines basic concepts, the ideas of Marx, Weber, Parsons, and Lenski are used to illuminate the discussion of functionalism and conflict theory. While the virtues of both of these competing theoretical positions are discussed, the basic paradigm employed in the text is a conflict model which emphasizes the relationship between institutions and the structuring of classes.

The second part deals with those institutions, particularly as they have developed in complex societies. The effects of industrialization upon a class system are explained to present the larger context. Following are chapters on the major institutional determinants (the economic and political structures) and supports (education, the family, and ideology and prestige) of stratification systems in complex societies, emphasizing American society. The origin of social mobility in a changing occupational structure and the reactions of people to their own social mobility are outlined in the final chapter of Part Two.

Part Three shifts the focus to the consequences of structured social inequality for individuals and families, and the relationships among social strata. For the purpose of analysis, four major strata are discussed: the privileged and managerial, the lower white-collar, the blue-collar, and the poverty strata. The emphasis is on the ways in which the meaning and quality of life of people is affected by their location in an inequality structure. The final brief chapter addresses questions of value and policy. From what we know, what can we say about what should be done? This chapter departs from conventional treatments by speculating about and evaluating alternative structures.

While writing is essentially a lonely task, an author is lucky to be surrounded by those who give encouragement and ideas. Anthony Turrittin was delightful to work with as co-author of the chapter on social mobility.

Several people read parts of this manuscript in various stages of its development. Because their responses were influential in its shaping, I wish to acknowledge the help given by Margaret Ensminger, Robert Potter, Henry Mather, and Edwin Rhyne. Their comments were most helpful. David J. Gray suggested and convinced me that a final chapter on implications would be worthwhile. Two other people were especially significant. Leonard Pearlin gave invaluable advice and support at a crucial time in the development of thought. Alex Inkeles was a most perceptive critic, turning around several matters of style and orientation. I am grateful also to those anonymous reviewers who took the time to make detailed and pointed criticisms. I followed many of their suggestions. Gloria Condoluci gave superb assistance in the preparation of the manuscript. Finally, I wish to acknowledge the wise advice and direction given by two editors, Frank Graham and Katherine Carlone, who were very efficient and supportive as well.

Contents

Two

Determinants of Inequality   55

Contents

Three

**The Correlates and
Consequences of Inequality**   281

One

Introduction

1 SOCIAL INEQUALITY

EVEN FOR THE BEGINNING sociology student, the presence of gross inequalities in power, wealth, and privilege in the United States does not need much documentation. A simple drive across the countryside or into the cities shows shacks that abut landscaped homes, slums that surround high rises. Less familiar is the extent to which inequality pervades the institutions of society and affects everyday affairs. From the moment we are born to poor or rich parents, or to those of moderate means, our lives are patterned by differences in wealth and power and by the rules restricting access to the things we desire. To average citizens, the mechanisms of distribution are normally invisible; as members of various strata, we are insulated from people in other circumstances whom we may not want to see. Yet, without our awareness, inequality affects health and wealth, training and occupation, experience and happiness. It influences whom we marry, where we live and how well, with whom we eat and relax, what kind of illnesses we will get and how often, and what we read and think.

Many people do not wish to acknowledge the importance of social

2

stratification. It is easy for them to suggest that although there are obviously great differences in income or wealth among individuals, happiness or love or health belongs to anyone. It is one purpose of this text to elucidate the extent to which even these important components of life are unequally distributed. For example, let us examine the distribution of happiness and health. A survey of 2,006 adults in Illinois found that people who make more money and have completed more years of schooling are more likely to say that they are happy (Bradburn and Caplovitz 1965). Of course, respondents might say to an interviewer that they are happy when they are not, and maybe there is some reason that the more affluent consistently misreport their emotional states. We are inclined to be suspicious of such findings.

Yet, Bradburn and Caplovitz's findings are congruent with researches employing other measures of well-being. An analysis of National Opinion Research Center data that used complicated scales of variables found that the higher the social class position of the 3,100 men in the sample, the greater was their sense of being in control of the forces that affected their lives, the less beset by anxiety they were, and the more independent they considered their ideas to be (Kohn and Schooler 1969). Another study asked 2,300 people in Chicago to agree or disagree with ten statements about their feelings of worth (Pearlin 1974). These statements were incorporated into a measure of self-esteem that is very strongly related to family income, as shown in Table 1.1. While nearly three-fifths of those whose family income was over $25,000 felt good about themselves, less than one-fourth of those with incomes under $8,000 did so. The higher their stratification position, the more likely it is that individuals will feel pleased with their situation and themselves. High status rewards them

Table 1.1

Self-esteem and family income

	1972–1973 family income			
Self-esteem	Less than $8,000	$8,000 to $16,000	$16,001 to $24,000	More than $24,000
High	24%	38%	44%	58%
Moderate	21	23	29	18
Low	55	39	27	24
Total	100%	100%	100%	100%
Number	(571)	(947)	(325)	(149)

Source: From L. T. Pearlin, "Social Origins of Stress," 1974. Unpublished study, National Institute of Mental Health, Washington, D.C.

not only with greater material resources and social prestige, but with a greater probability of psychological satisfaction as well.

If we look at health statistics, similar conclusions emerge. The lower one's social status, the more likely one is to get sick and to have chronic illnesses (U.S. National Center for Health Statistics 1965), and the less likely one is to seek care by physicians and hospitals (Bierman 1961), to receive quality care in hospitals (Linden 1967), and to go to dentists (Kriesberg 1972, p. 476). These differences in health care ultimately affect mortality rates. Occupants of the poorer strata die at earlier ages than occupants of the more affluent strata (Antonovsky 1972). They are also more likely to die at the hands of public violence, on death row (E. H. Johnson 1957), and in war. Table 1.2 reveals the higher casualty rates experienced by sons of the poor in the Korean War. Similar trends have been found relative to death rates in the Vietnam War (Zeitlin et al. 1973).

These assorted facts are consequences of the inequalities of economic, political, and status resources in American society. When we look at them together, many questions come to mind. Why do some people live a life of abundance and power, while others can only barely survive? What are the determinants of an individual's chances for success, and how are these related to distributive structures? What is it like to be a really poor individual, a common man, or an influential figure? How much do large

Table 1.2

Korean War casualty rate indexes, by median income of census tract, Detroit, Michigan

Median income	Casualty rate index
Under $2,500	14.6
$2,500–2,999	10.8
$3,000–3,499	9.1
$3,500–3,999	8.6
$4,000–4,499	7.5
$4,500–4,999	6.6
$5,000–5,499	5.8
$5,500 and over	4.6

Source: Reprinted from *Social Forces* 34 (December 1955). "Social Stratification and Combat Survival" by Albert J. Mayer and Thomas Ford Hoult. Copyright © The University of North Carolina Press.

organizations, such as corporations or professional associations, influence the distribution of wealth and income? It is the purpose of this text to attempt to answer such questions. We are particularly interested in the social inequality inherent in the stratification systems of modern industrial societies. We want to know not only what are the consequences of social stratification, but also what are its causes. In order to cover these kinds of topics, we have divided this book into three parts. Part 1 discusses theories of stratification, particularly conflict theory and functionalism. Part 2 considers the determinative institutions (such as the economic and political systems) and the supportive institutions (such as the family and education). In Part 3, the consequences of social stratification in the United States are reviewed — consequences for the upper crust and the destitute poor, as well as the working people. Before proceeding further, we need to clarify the words we will be using.

Definitions and Dimensions

SOCIAL STRATIFICATION AND SOCIAL INEQUALITY

"Social stratification" is one subtype of a more general phenomenon called "social inequality." Thus, it is useful first to explore the more general term, *social inequality,* which may be defined as any evaluated social distinction among individuals or groups. The informal ranking of members of a motorcycle gang by their degree of influence over the gang's activities exhibits social inequality, as does the prestige distinction between airline stewardesses and diner waitresses. In fact, the term *social inequality* is so general that it applies as equally to the minute differentiations within a small group of friends as it does to the elaborate ranks, rules, and rituals of a classic kingdom. Slavery and communism, caste and class, private clubs and political states — all provide examples of inequality.

At base, social inequality grows out of the process of *social differentiation,* which is the perception of differences in individuals, social positions, or groups.[1] Physical attractiveness, athletic ability, or achievement, as well as any other quality or role considered to be important in the culture, can serve as the criterion for social differentiation. It is found in all societies, from the simplest to the most complex.

The significance of social differentiation is that when it is combined with its twin process, *social evaluation,* social inequality emerges. Social

---

[1] Most definitions stress the differentiation of positions rather than of individual attributes. Dennis Wrong (1959, p. 73), for example, equates social differentiation and the division of labor. Mayer and Buckley (1970, p. 4) and Barber (1957, pp. 1–3) define social differentiation as the division of roles and positions.

evaluation is the assignment of relative value to the characteristics that are differentiated. It is a common process; people tend to approve or disapprove, to develop preferences, and to judge (Davis 1948, pp. 47–48). Listen to students leaving a class that has just had a heated discussion. Invariably, their comments reflect evaluations of this or that person's argument, motives, or intellect. As the human mind perceives and classifies, it also tends to evaluate.

This is not to suggest that differentiation is always followed by evaluation. For example, as Heller (1969) points out, in American society the position of adolescent is generally not considered superior to that of infant, merely different. Yet, in their ordinary interactions, people spend a great deal of time in creating, adjusting, and applying personal value systems to the ranking of the actions and appearance of others.

We are now ready to define the relationship of social inequality to social stratification. Social inequality, the result of the evaluation that often accompanies social differentiation, is found in most human relationships and settings. Social stratification, on the other hand, exists only when social inequality becomes structurally patterned and intergenerationally transmitted. To indicate the stability and permanence of such a form of inequality, *social stratification* can be usefully defined as the institutionalization of power arrangements that perpetuate intergenerational patterns of economic, political, and prestige inequalities among collectivities (Pease et al. 1970, p. 128). The patterns are reinforced by the major institutions of the society — the economy, family, religion, and education. In a stratification system, the alignments of strata or classes become permanent and are perpetuated from generation to generation. Because of this institutionalization and rigidity, stratification differs in both a qualitative and a quantitative sense from the inequality of prestige found in simpler systems.

Stratification tends to develop when an economic system becomes sufficiently productive that it produces a sizable surplus of goods beyond those needed for bare survival (Lenski 1966). Usually a system of formal government develops concurrently. The state conveniently provides the political means whereby the surplus goods (wealth) are gathered together and redistributed into the hands of the powerful. Sometimes taxation is the means, while at other times property laws serve the purpose. The struggles to use government in that way make up a recurrent plot in history. Once economic inequality has taken hold in a society, political control is utilized to maintain and perpetuate the privilege. Wealth may then become very unequally distributed, classes may emerge, kings and courts may top off an elaborate hierarchy, and slaves may be captured to do the dirty work.

Is stratification universal and, therefore, perhaps inevitable? An important question it is, because if stratification is inevitable, then its elimination — which Karl Marx predicted and about which the New Left has dreamed — cannot occur. As for the answer, stratification scholars themselves disagree. Absurd as it may seem, their disagreement revolves around definitional problems. If stratification is defined as existing whenever *any* form of social differentiation and evaluation is present, then it can be considered to be universal. In all societies that have been studied, there is at least a minimal degree of prestige ranking of individuals and roles. If, however, it is defined (as above) to include the notion of institutionalized and relatively permanent hierarchical arrangements of strata, then the evidence suggests that it exists mainly in the more economically advanced societies.[2] As shown in Table 1.3, based on Murdock's world ethnographic sample of 565 cultures, 59 percent of the agricultural societies — in contrast to just 1 percent of the simplest hunting and gathering societies — had complex class systems. Since more productive societies came into being only ten thousand years or so ago, we can conclude that for the major part of human history most people have lived in relatively egalitarian societies. According to this definition, then, social stratification is a recent development in the human saga.

STATUS AND ROLE

Status is among the most popular words in the sociological vernacular. It has been defined in a number of different ways: (1) position in society; (2) position in a hierarchy; (3) any social category; (4) any quality indexed by objective characteristics such as income or occupation; (5)

---

[2] An example of the first position is Barber's statement (1957, pp. 2–3) to the effect that social stratification is the structure of differential rankings "that seems to occur in all societies" and is the product of the interaction of social differentiation and social evaluation. The classic statement by Kingsley Davis (1949, p. 366) takes an intermediate position: "Looking at the cultures of the world one finds that no society is 'classless,' that is, unstratified. There are some primitive communities so small that no class strata appear, the social organization resting almost entirely on age, sex, and kinship, but even here chieftainship, individual prowess, and clan or family property introduce an incipient stratification. As soon as greater size and complexity are attained, stratification unmistakably appears." Buckley counters (1958, pp. 370–71): "But Barber fails to include the central notion of strata in his definition of stratification and thus, like Davis and Moore, ignores the distinction between stratification and differentiation." Buckley maintains that the essential difference between a stratified and a nonstratified society lies in the ease with which intergenerational mobility may take place: In the nonstratified society a person's initial position at birth would not be correlated with his or her adult social position, but in the stratified there would be such a correlation, giving rise to castes, estates, or classes. The majority of modern definitions include the ideas of patterned inequality and permanence of intergenerational continuity. (See, for example, Roach et al. 1969, p. 11; Heller 1969, p. 4; and Mayer and Buckley 1970, pp. 5–9.)

Table 1.3

Type of economy, percentage distribution by degree of stratification[a]

Type of economy	No strati- fication	Wealth distinc- tions important	Presence of nobility	Complex class system	Total	No.
			Degree of stratification			
Hunting and gathering	70	17	12	1	100%	(133)
Horticultural	53	11	25	11	100%	(223)
Pastoral	26	31	33	10	100%	(76)
Plow agricultural	9	17	15	59	100%	(115)

Source: Calculated from *Cross Tabulations of Murdock's World Ethnographic Sample* by Allan D. Coult and Robert W. Habenstein (Columbia, Missouri: University of Missouri Press, 1965).

[a] The eighteen economies on which there is no information have been eliminated from the calculations.

prestige; and (6) a collection of rights and duties (Vanfossen 1960). Because of these diverse definitions, Burchard in 1959 suggested that the use of the concept *status* was a fad; he predicted its demise. Yet, by the 1970s, it still had not lost its popularity. The classical definition, and the one adopted here, was made by Ralph Linton in 1936: "A status . . . is a position in a particular pattern" (p. 113). Every individual may have many statuses, since each individual participates in a number of patterns.

A status may be a position in a hierarchy of a relatively closed social system such as a corporation, a military establishment, or a government bureaucracy. It may also be a position in a more general sense, such as an age, sex, or family status. If it exists because of the biological characteristics of an individual and is assigned to that individual independently of achievement, it is an *ascribed status.* If it exists as a result of individual choice or effort, it is an *achieved status.* Being a princess or a diabetic is an ascribed status; being a policewoman or an alcoholic is an achieved one. Statuses are generally tied up with *roles,* or expectations of behavior appropriate to the concept of the status. Although it should be recognized that a status typically receives a particular prestige rating, it seems conceptually more precise to denote the degree of respect given to positions or groups by the term *prestige* and to avoid using *status* to mean *prestige* (as in "status seekers").

SOCIAL CLASS

The concept of *class,* more germane to the study of stratification, has been given two contradictory meanings. One meaning, which Wrong (1959) calls the "nominalist" definition, regards classes as any arrangement of categories of people who possess certain differentiated attributes in common — all people who work as professionals or managers, for example. They do not necessarily form social groups, feel class-conscious, or behave in a distinctively different manner from the adjacent strata.[3] In this usage, "social class" is virtually synonymous with "social strata"; "class" exists whenever there are patterned economic, political, or prestige differentiations.

The other meaning, the "realist" position, emphasizes the group nature and class consciousness of the classes.[4] A class system is present when the strata exhibit noticeable boundaries (in terms of interaction patterns, exclusivity, and degree of self-consciousness), which still are not as clearly distinct and rigid as those of a caste system. Because this definition distinguishes a more highly crystallized system of discrete groups from a continuum system that lacks breaks between strata, it is our preferred definition. Formally, we may define *social class* as a group of people with similar economic conditions and life styles who interact with each other, maintain exclusive boundaries, are conscious of their common group membership, and are separated by clearly obvious degrees of social distance from other groups. Essential ideas of the definition above are: (1) a class is clearly set off from other classes by distinctive economic conditions that set the parameters of living style, as well as by evident differences in behavior and attitudes; (2) class consciousness is well developed, on the part of both the members of the class and those who belong to other classes; and (3) the classes maintain boundaries through exclusive limitations on social interaction, intermarriage, and upward mobility into the class.[5]

[3] For examples of nominalist points of view, see Barber (1957, p. 76); Lenski (1966); and Dahrendorf (1959).

[4] Most of the classical theorists — Marx, Schumpeter, Weber — accepted realist definitions. For examples of modern uses of realist class conceptions, see Cuber and Kenkel (1954, pp. 12–13); Wrong (1959); Centers (1949); Rose (1958); Nisbet (1959); A. Miller (1954, p. 343); and Matras (1975, p. 90).

[5] For similar discussions of class, see Ossowski (1966) and R. Brown (1965, p. 134). After reviewing the conceptual "ambiguity" of the term class, Ossowski (1966, p. 92) concludes that there are four main characteristics of a class system: (1) the vertical order of social classes; (2) a distinctness of permanent class interests; (3) class consciousness; and (4) social distance between classes.

SOCIAL MOBILITY

Societies can also be classified on the basis of how much social mobility occurs. *Social mobility,* as used in this sense, is the movement of any individual or social group from one position to another. It is usually conceptually differentiated into two types: horizontal and vertical mobility (Sorokin 1959, p. 133). *Horizontal* mobility is movement from one position to another of the same rank (that is, social, political, or economic standing) or from one location to another. Change of occupation from one blue-collar job to another blue-collar job is an example of horizontal mobility. If the horizontal mobility involves movement among occupational categories without change in status (say, from machinist to fireman), the movement is said to be from one *situs* to another (Benoit-Smullyan 1944). We are only incidentally interested here in horizontal mobility. What is more crucial to a study of social stratification is *vertical* mobility, the movement from one position to another one of differing rank (as, for example, when a mail carrier becomes an accountant).

Vertical social mobility may be gained by individuals who separately infiltrate the stratum above or below their point of origin — for example, Joe Jones, the son of a banker, becomes an auto mechanic; or it may be achieved by whole groups whose prestige or power or wealth has changed, as has happened to Irish Catholics in America. Much of the high rate of mobility characteristic of the United States in the last hundred years (and also of the Soviet Union, Bulgaria, Sweden, France, or any other nation that has recently industrialized) results from group mobility. As the number of white-collar and skilled labor jobs has increased in response to industrialization, and as the number of farming and unskilled manual jobs has declined, whole sections of the population of young adults have entered occupations that were unavailable to their parents.

A society in which vertical mobility is difficult or rare is termed a *closed* society, while one in which it is common and relatively easy is called an *open* society. In a totally closed society, mobility would be nil and individuals would remain for all of their lives in the same social positions, positions they would hold by virtue of their *ascribed statuses,* such as family or caste membership. In a totally open society, persons would enter occupations on the basis of *achieved statuses* or individualistic characteristics, such as their preferences or inclinations. Every individual would have an equal chance of acquiring a particular social position, being unhampered or unaided by birth, family position, or differential access to education.

In reality, the extremes of these types are not characteristic of any known society. No society is completely devoid of economic, political, or occupational mobility. Likewise, no society is so open that there are no barriers between strata or impediments to stratification without regard to social origin. Nevertheless, societies can be ranked by the degrees of mobility present in them. A society with *slavery* represents one of the more extreme forms of a closed society. The distinguishing feature of a slave system is that slaves are *owned* by other persons (Finley 1960, p. 145). It results when strangers are brought into a society for use in economic production and are legally defined as property (Sio 1965).

Even among societies with slavery, there are variations in the amount of slave mobility that is possible. In ancient Greece or Rome, slavery was based not on race, but on heritage or nationality, and often occurred when one society conquered another in war. Because everyone was a potential slave, the idea of "natural slavery" never gained ground. In nineteenth-century America, however, race became the basis for slave status, resulting in a sharper distinction between slave and free person than in ancient society (D. B. Davis 1966). It came to be viewed as proper and fitting that Negroes be slaves because of their race. While freed slaves could be rapidly mobile in ancient Rome or Greece, the status of freed Negroes in America remained low due to the threat they posed to the ideology of racial inferiority (Heller 1969, p. 55).

A *caste* society allows a little more mobility, particularly the mobility of caste groups, but still has a quite fixed arrangement of strata. Of present-day societies, India, Sri Lanka, and Pakistan most closely approximate the ideal form of the caste society. A person is born into his or her caste and has little expectation or desire to become a member of a different caste. Castes themselves may become mobile through subdividing, such as when a caste that chauffeurs automobiles splits into two castes, one that drives Volkswagens and another that drives Rolls Royces. (As this example indicates, castes commonly are associated with certain traditional occupations.)

Contact between castes is minimal and highly regulated. Certainly, one would not wish to marry outside his or her caste, nor even to develop important friendships. But sometimes members of different castes must come into contact with each other, particularly in the performance of occupational duties. In that event, the interaction is highly impersonal and ritualistic, and it symbolizes the superordinate-subordinate nature of the relationship.

Castes are highly stratified in their access to valued resources, with the upper levels being more favored. In addition, objective inequities of the castes are often ideologically justified by the belief that each caste has a certain quality of ritual purity. In India, for example, the elaborate rules of etiquette governing social distance between the castes come primarily from these beliefs, which view contact with inferior castes as polluting. Religious beliefs also support caste patterns. One of the central tenets of Hindu religion, the belief in transmigration, maintains that souls are reborn after death in an endless series of reincarnations. It is the duty of

11

individuals in their present life to carry out the requirements of their occupation and to observe the moral laws of their particular caste. If they do not, after death their souls will be reborn in a lower caste. Excellence in the performance of caste duties, on the other hand, results in rebirth in a higher caste. Thus, it is believed that members of the untouchable caste are individuals who have failed their duties in previous lives. Their low status and destitute situation are justified; they "get what they deserve." Individual social mobility is disapproved in such a system as being immoral (Gupta 1968).

The *estate* society, similar to the caste society in many ways, still contains slightly higher rates of social mobility. An estate is a legally defined segment of the population of a society that has distinctive rights and duties established by law (Lenski 1966, p. 77). The term often is used when describing the stratification structure of medieval Europe, where social organization revolved around a specific type of land tenure.

The typical strata of the European estate society consisted of a royal family and a landholding, hereditary, military aristocracy at the top, who had authority over priests and secular nobility, themselves quite powerful. These top groups maintained economic dominance by their ownership of the land, which provided the major source of subsistence. Less privileged were the merchants and craftsmen, who yet were more powerful than the peasants and unfree serfs who tilled the soil. The church provided solace for the poor and also upheld the legitimacy of the inequitable system by promising the poor a better life in the hereafter.

In an estate society, each estate has rights and duties defined by law. Individuals are born into an estate, but can legally change their estates under certain circumstances, as when the king confers aristocratic status upon a commoner by making him a lord or when a serf is released from the legal responsibility to his master. Estates are less rigid than castes, though social mobility between estates is difficult and limited. A member of an estate also has more rights than a slave, who has little right to the products of his or her own labor, to physical protection, or to religious services (Mayer 1955; Bergel 1962).

Finally, the *class* society has more mobility than any of the forms just mentioned, yet it, too, maintains a stable stratification system. Unlike the slave, caste, and estate systems, which are founded on an agricultural economic base, the class society results from industrialization and is characteristic of all industrial societies, communist as well as capitalist. The higher rates of social mobility in class societies result in large part from the changes in occupational structure that accompany the industrialization process and open up higher-level jobs. Educational requirements are established for those jobs, and the youth in class societies are encouraged to acquire the education necessary to meet the requirements. In contrast to the caste society, in which individual striving is viewed as immoral, the class society highly values achievement and mobility.

Many young people do indeed achieve a higher occupational rank, and thus a higher income, than their parents. Nevertheless, the mobility of any one individual tends to be minor and limited, and those from privileged families get extra boosts in the competition. There is a greater appearance of mobility than actually exists, and that which does exist does not diminish the overall and striking inequalities in wealth, income, and power among the population.

Class societies tend to have a powerful and wealthy elite composed of economic and political leaders and, occasionally, leaders of other institutions; an upper-middle stratum of professionals and scientists who provide the technical expertise for running the industries; a middle stratum of lower-level white-collar workers and skilled blue-collar workers who do much of the record keeping and manipulating of machines; and a semiskilled and unskilled laboring stratum that provides the muscles. Income, power, and wealth are unequally distributed to these classes, but an achievement ideology tends to convince people that this is as it should be, achievement being equated with role performance in highly rewarded occupations.

CRITERIA OF STRATIFICATION

It has become common in the mass media to refer to categories of people by such expressions as "upper-middle-class" or "working-class." As we get down to more precision in the study of social stratification, we need to ask, What criteria are being employed when such labels are used? What does it mean to be called "upper-middle-class"? Is income more important than the life style or moral character of a person in locating him or her in a stratification system? Is Mr. Jones "upper-middle" if he earns over $15,000 and under $50,000 per year? Or is it that he goes sailing in the summer and skiing in the winter, or that he has a career as a research chemist, or that he listens to Bach rather than country and western, or that he makes love with the lights on, or that he has a graduate degree? These questions point to an issue of some standing in stratification research: What are the important dimensions of stratification?

One of the classical theorists of nineteenth-century sociology, Karl Marx, believed that the *economic dimension* is of paramount importance. Economic conditions structure the nature of classes, and one must look at an individual's relationship to the production process to understand his or her class position. In capitalist society, Marx believed, one class owns the means of production, while another class provides the labor that is the major instrument of production. Using the example above, we categorize Mr. Jones as "upper-middle-class" because he is a research chemist. His role in production is the dictating characteristic. While he has some privilege because his job is more pleasant and remunerative than other laboring jobs, he still works for the owners of the chemical industry, serving them in their drive for profit.

To label a person using this economic criterion, we would look at that person's wealth, income received, and occupation. To explore the economic dimension in a broader sense, we would be interested in how economic power is used to distribute valued resources and services in the society and what economic roles the different classes play.

Although Marx stressed economic conditions, he was not guilty of a rigid economic determinism, as it is often believed. He also recognized the role of political inequalities, and he pointed out that ideologies and beliefs are important props of the class structure. Yet, Marx did not explicitly outline other forms of inequality as determinants of classes. This task was left for a contemporary of Marx's, Max Weber, who suggested that two other very important dimensions of stratification focus on power and prestige.

First, the *political dimension* revolves around the use of power (when a group is able to get what it wants even against the wishes of others). In labeling Mr. Jones, we would want to know how much access he has to the political process. Can he call up a senator and get laws passed favoring his corporation? It also would be significant to know how much authority he has over others in the occupational world. Does he direct a division of twenty supervisors, each of whom likewise directs twenty people? Or is he ordered around by each one of twenty supervisors above him? In the broader sense, we would be interested in which groups are able to get their way when there is conflict of interest and what are the processes by which decisions are made in favor of one group rather than another.

Weber also stressed a *prestige dimension,* which is one of respect and disrespect, of honor and dishonor. It is a subjective dimension, for it focuses on how people evaluate each other. To assess Mr. Jones, we might try to find out his reputation. How respected is he relative to other people? Or we might note the prestige rating of his occupation.

Weber's analysis concentrated heavily on the subcultures formed when people of similar prestige standing and similar economic and political condition interact on the basis of a common life style. This easily becomes conceptualized as an additional dimension: *group membership and life style.* Weber wished to differentiate categories of people who are similar merely in economic characteristics from groups of people who practice common life styles and who form a community. The latter he called "status groups." Members of status groups share three components: a societal component of prestige or honor; a group component of a certain life style; and an individual component of self-esteem (Nicholls and Van Til 1973, p. 22). To investigate this dimension, we would want to know Mr. Jones's "patterns of consumption, dress, speech, attitudes and patterns relating to focal points of interest in the culture, such as sex, morality, religion, the family, patriotism, education, the arts, sports, etc." (M. Gordon 1963, p. 19). We would check out Mr. Jones's associations — whom he joins for lunch, visits, and marries. It would also be helpful to know that he goes skiing rather than snowmobiling, prefers sailing to powerboating, and attends a concert rather than a boxing match.

The definitions outlined in this section have emerged out of decades of discussion among stratification scholars. It is useful at this point to indicate what is the nature of the discussion, how biases have affected research topics, and where the state of empirical evidence now leads us. The following section briefly sketches the major ideas and controversies of the twentieth century that have led to the current state of knowledge.

Stratification Studies within American Sociology

HISTORY

It may come as a surprise to discover that the systematic study of social stratification was undeveloped before 1940. One would expect the early twentieth-century American sociologists to have analyzed social stratification as thoroughly as they did other subjects. They certainly were familiar with the discussions of social class in the writings of Plato and Aristotle. They probably were acquainted as well with other social thinkers, such as Confucius, Cicero, John of Salisbury, Thomas Aquinas, Ibn Khaldun, Hobbes, Locke, and Rousseau, who discussed at length the unequal distribution of wealth, power, and honor among the citizenry. In attempting to account for this peculiar oversight, recent chroniclers suggest that the early sociologists were not very sensitive to inequality because such concerns would have been inconsistent with the ideologies prevailing in America at the time (Page 1969; Pease et al. 1970). Along with other Americans, the sociologists writing between 1900 and 1940 believed that the United States was the land of equal opportunity for all, that the natural evolutionary forces of a private economy would continue to limit the harshness of stratification, and that only the unfit would remain poor (Pease et al. 1970, p. 128). In 1924, E. A. Ross, one of the more important sociologists of the period, dismissed the poor by suggesting that "the hopelessly poor and wretched are . . . the weak and incompetent who have accumulated at the lower end of the social scale because they or their parents have failed the tests of the competitive system" (p. 128). The social climate of the time did not make American sociologists aware of the

15

socially created structures that maintain economic, political, and social inequalities independent of the abilities of people. Rather, the prevailing values blinded theorists to the realities of class, as Reissman indicates:

> The antiaristocratic heritage, an antiradical philosophy, a frontier psychology, and a secularized Protestant ethic all were so deeply ingrained in the American value system that the realities of a class system could never come through to public awareness. Added to these beliefs were the facts of a rapidly expanding industrial system, the growth of cities, massive immigration, all of which hid some of the more obvious class differences and at the same time heightened the opportunites for social advancement (1959, p. 30).

This example of how cultural values influence the scientist's view of reality highlights a problem continually faced by stratification scholars: political beliefs influence theories of inequality, and theories of inequality carry political implications. Even the social theorist who is thoroughly committed to an objective, value-free analysis of the real world finds it exceedingly difficult to construct a theory of society that does not in one way or another reflect a value position and imply a political stance.

It is in this context of the interplay of social values and social thought that we should view the development of sociology's study of inequality. In the early twentieth century, while European sociologists such as Simmel, Weber, Michels, and Pareto began to explore the implications of a Marxian emphasis on conflict and domination, American sociologists, perhaps because they were suspicious of "foreign" doctrines of revolutionary activity (Gordon 1958, p. 8), leaned toward a view of society as harmonious and integrated. In fact, they were moving close to the position that American society is classless (Page 1969, p. 250). Such sociologists as Ward, Sumner, Small, Giddings, Cooley, and Ross, while recognizing the significance of class divisions and conflicts in community life, constructed theories that were compatible with the anticlass elements of American democracy and with the social virtues of that "classless segment of society — the middle class" (Page 1969, p. 250). In 1909, Cooley was optimistic that "under conditions which a country of opportunity, like the United States, affords, great masses of people rise from poverty to comfort, and many of them to opulence" (p. 295). We now know that the rates of social mobility in 1909 were not higher than they are now, which means that they were only moderate and that the great masses of people rose only slightly, if at all. But the presence of the western frontier, the absence of an aristocracy, and the continual waves of immigrants in the United States made it seem as if America were indeed a land of opportunity. The intellectual climate reflecting this optimism was what Pease and associates have labeled "evolutionary liberalism," the view that nebulous classes emerge as a consequence of individual mobility (1970, p.

128). The contrasting view, "structural realism," which maintains that distinct classes emerge as a consequence of socially created arrangements that maintain economic, political, and social inequality, has until recently played only a minor role in the development of the American sociology of inequality.

An interest in class finally began to develop during the 1930s, influenced perhaps by the Great Depression, the effects of which were too devastating to be ignored, and by the emergence of organized labor and the development of socialist parties. A growing number of studies dealing with socioeconomic status, occupation, educational level, income, and amount of rent began to explore empirical relationships, and there was some discussion of the concept of "class." By the 1940s, contributions to stratification research began to accelerate. These were preoccupied with predominantly middle-class concerns, such as prestige hierarchies, consumption patterns, viability of the American dream, individual mobility, and empirical tests of middle-range propositions. As Bottomore put it (1966, p. 105), "The underlying conception was that of . . . a middle-class society in which some people were simply more middle-class than others."

The middle-class emphasis led to a concentration on the invidious comparisons that people make of each other ("prestige") to the exclusion, unfortunately, of an accompanying interest in the economic and political structures on which prestige is based. An exception was an early study by Lynd and Lynd (1937), which focused on the economic power of the "X family" in Muncie, Indiana. But the Lynds' book, while influential, did not prevent the development of an emphasis on the subjective aspects of social inequality. Sociologists embraced Weber's concept of "status groups" and ignored his position that economic classes and political groups are equally important. The emphasis on prestige perhaps would never have developed if it had not been for the publication in the 1940s of a series of studies of Newburyport, Massachusetts, which were conducted by William Lloyd Warner and his associates. These were particularly concerned with status reputation and the ways in which different classes live. They focused on the prestige hierarchy as the essence of inequality, which was seen to consist not so much of economic and political inequalities as of differences in values and life styles. The Warner studies had a tremendous impact on the study of stratification following the war. They suggested that class and status can be measured and, thus, studied in a scientific way. They stimulated a large number of further investigations of the class structures of local communities (Pfautz 1953). In this sense, they performed a valuable service to the field of stratification, in spite of what later came to be defined as their unbalanced perspective.

In the period following World War II, two trends developed. One was the increasing use of empirical research. The other was a continuing debate over "functionalism" — whether the stratification system ensures that

17

the most competent and able members of the society will fill the most important positions. Studies of community power structures and vertical mobility started to appear, while concern over concepts, the number of dimensions of inequality, and the fluidity and shape of the class structure were reflected in the literature. The works of this period began the formation of some of the conceptual and methodological tools used in present-day work. Research expanded to cover national systems as well as local community systems; the multidimensionality of class determinants was recognized; and interest shifted from description to the search for causes and the testing of hypotheses. Yet, the underlying assumptions still emphasized a middle-class perception of inequality.

It was not until poverty and institutional racism were "rediscovered" in the 1960s that the emphasis began to shift from the study of prestige to power. Poverty researchers found that "cultural deprivation" explanations of the poor were only "blaming the victim," while radicals pointed out how little is known about the foibles and vulnerabilities of the rich. Some called for study of the processes by which resources such as income and health care are distributed among the people and of the ways in which influence and wealth are used to accumulate privilege. Power-elite researchers began to investigate the military-industrial complex, and quantitative sociologists began to find that differences in individual income are unrelated to intelligence or training. Growing recognition of the importance of the economic and political aspects of institutionalized social inequality in the 1960s did not entirely supplant earlier concerns, but it produced a viable competitive perspective. Many of the issues reported in this text reflect the growing encounter between the older functionalist perspective and the newly reemerged emphasis on domination and coercion.

CURRENT CONTROVERSIES

Where are we now? The accumulation of empirical findings since World War II has settled many issues, but it has also raised further questions. The controversies have been summarized by Rossi (1976). One concerns the processes of social mobility and questions whether American society is basically an open one, in which the best people get to the top, or a more closed one, in which equality of opportunity is limited. We do know that formal education plays an important role in adult "status attainment." But, these educational experiences are hardly independent of the status positions of parents. Furthermore, there are other causes of status attainment that have not yet been identified and probably come from the influences of larger groups — businesses, labor unions, professional associations, and government agencies — on the allocation of prestige, power, and income.

We do know that the rates of social mobility in this century have been high, a fact that seems to indicate a relatively open stratification system. But the high rates of mobility are due more to those alterations in the occupational structure resulting from a changing technological environment than to the absence of ascriptive influences. Upper-middle-class families have simply not produced enough children to fill all the white-collar positions created by industrialization. In addition, the high rates are not much higher than the rates of mobility in other countries that were assumed to be more status- and class-ridden. Finally, it is clear that the elites of America come from elite backgrounds and, in that sense, America is run by an establishment.

We were surprised to learn from the studies of occupational prestige that politicians rate very high in the United States and that intellectuals are more revered than industrial captains. We were also amazed that ratings of occupational prestige are extremely stable over time and place and that the hierarchy found in the United States differs little from that found in Tanzania, Japan, or Great Britain. The general consensus on occupational prestige lends support to the view that occupational inequalities are at the heart of the social stratification system and that inequality is widely recognized.

A further controversy, Rossi pointed out, revolves around the role of education. It started with Hollingshead's classical study (1949) of how the faculty in the Morris, Illinois, high school acted as gatekeepers in allowing middle-class adolescents through to their diplomas and closing the door on working- and lower-class adolescents. Since that early study, the results of years of research have definitely established that while the net effect of educational attainment on adult prestige and income is not very high, it is clearly higher than any other studied relationships, particularly for white males. Education seems to affect what kind of job a person can get and thus where he or she will be located in the stratification system. Yet it has also become clear that education is often unrelated to the skills needed on the job. While medical schools may prepare persons to become doctors and law schools prepare persons to become lawyers, for a large proportion of occupations the skills learned in schools are not those used on the job. Nor does educational attainment correlate very highly with measures of general intelligence. It is increasingly apparent, then, that except for the most highly technical and professional occupations, education serves more as a credential than as an indicator of job performance skills. It is widely used by employers as a screening device because everybody accepts its legitimacy, because it is cheap to apply, and because it is easy to identify.

In spite of these controversies over mobility and education, the picture of the American social stratification structure that is beginning to emerge is one in which things are run by several ruling elites who wield tremendous power because of their influence over the major institutional structures. It is one in which strong ascriptive forces operating along racial, ethnic, and sexual lines are disguised behind the operation of institutions that appear to be universalistic in style. It is one in which most people are allocated minor and impoverished roles in the system, but they do not seem to be bothered by that. They are basically satisfied because they are more impressed by the small amounts of relative affluence and mobility they have gained in their individual life histories than they are disturbed by the grossly inequitable distributions of status, income, and power that persist unchanging across the total society.

Currently, several theoretical issues are still unresolved. While some students of stratification are investigating the economic and political aspects of institutionalized inequality, others are restating the prestige thesis. As Pease et al. (1970, p. 133) point out, the latter use an updated version that asserts that society is evolving from a middle-class to a middle-mass society. The processes of urbanization, industrialization, professionalization, and bureaucratization, they believe, have made American society so homogeneous that the idea of a stratified political and economic order is no longer applicable. What matters now is not the amount of money individuals have, but the taste and style they show in spending it. In their concluding remarks on the ideological currents in American stratification literature, Pease et al. (1970, p. 137) fault the prestige theorists:

> Sociologists who view stratification as a matter of individual occurrences rather than social structure, who study consumption to the neglect of distribution and production, who study the labor market but not the credit and commodity markets, who emphasize status, . . . neglect wealth, define power as being outside stratification, and . . . fail to see "race relations" . . . and poverty in the context of stratification confirm Robert Lynd's observation that when it comes to matters of class stratification, "the social sciences tiptoe evasively around the problem."

The issues mentioned in this quote are the issues examined in the following chapter on the competing claims of functional and conflict theories of inequality. The functionalist paradigm accommodates an emphasis on prestige, while conflict theory stresses wealth and power. We review there the arguments that lead to our preference for the conflict perspective.

2 THEORIES AND THEORISTS

SINCE ARISTOTLE, social philosophers have addressed and struggled with the problem of why social inequality exists. They have attempted to explain and justify the striking contrasts they observed around them in the social and economic standing of members of a society — the parallel existence of powerful and wealthy people alongside the weak and the poor. Beggar and nobleman, charwoman and lady, all have lived within the same social system. The contrasts were striking, but their causes were more obscure. While thoughtful people for centuries have reflected on the consequences of inequality, only a few have analyzed the processes by which it is brought about and the mechanisms by which it is maintained.

This chapter deals with the more recent attempts that have been made by social scientists to understand social stratification. The goal is to find an analytical framework that best explains it and identifies its important causal variables. Is stratification mainly the inevitable result of the authority hierarchies that accompany a complex division of labor? Does it merely emerge out of values consensually held by the people? Or is it a result of coercion and power exerted by a ruling elite? In sociology, these types of questions have been addressed by two major and contrasting theoretical paradigms. The first, functionalism, argues that inequality is necessary for the efficient functioning of the society, and it exists because it meets crucial societal needs. The second, conflict theory, maintains that society is made up of groups that compete for scarce and valued resources. Inequalities occur when certain groups achieve dominance over other groups.

The dialogue between the advocates of these two perspectives at times becomes intense, not only because scientists tend to be committed to the ideas they support, but also because political implications are so readily aroused in the discussion. People who basically favor the way the social and economic rewards are distributed may find it appealing to believe that inequality exists because it recruits talented people to important jobs. Those who wish a redistribution of rewards may find it easy to be convinced that inequality exists because the wealthy survive only by controlling the property produced by the poor. Political preferences are invalid as criteria for the evaluation of social science theory, but they do lend interest to the work of theory building.

Social theory has always carried political implications. Through the ages, the predominant tendency of philosophers has been to define the existing structure of social relationships as natural and therefore, by implication, good. Thus, more frequently than not, a society's body of mythologies, concepts, and secular explanations has been consistent with and supportive of the power and authority arrangements that exist. In India, for instance, the traditional belief has been that individuals are innately unequal and therefore are born to the caste appropriate to their worth. It is then only through the performance of the proper duties of their caste in this life, through staying in their place, that they can eventually reach salvation by being reborn in higher castes (Barber 1957). During the Middle Ages, the concept of the "divine right of kings," which meant that the status and power of the king and his retinue result from the will of God, lent religious sanction to the class system.

Although a supporting justification of class and power arrangements has been most common, there has also been significant development off and on of the "radical antithesis" (Lenski 1966, p. 5). Ideologies of dissent and change challenge the prevailing world view. It was the ideas of the Enlightenment during the eighteenth century, for example — the skepticism of supernatural religions, the criticism of divine-right monarchy, the exaltation of human reason — that provided the intellectual preconditions for the French Revolution in 1789. Later, Marxism had political appeal because it predicted an inevitable overthrow of the propertied class. Ideologies contain explanations of social stratification. Theories of social stratification have implications for ideologies.

Our task in this chapter is to examine the two theoretical perspectives, their critiques, and the attempts that have been made toward a synthesis. In the process of outlining the paradigms, we look briefly at the ideas of the major theorists associated with each one. Finally, we construct the model that guides the focus of the rest of the book.

The Functional Explanation of Stratification

The most widely accepted theoretical paradigm in sociology is what is commonly labeled *functionalism*. In order to understand its interpretation of stratification, we need first to understand its broader outlines. Having origins in the organic models of ancient intellectual history, functionalism was developed in the writings of such early sociologists as Comte, Spencer, and Durkheim and such anthropologists as Radcliffe-Brown and Malinowski. Functionalism views societies as integrated systems held in equilibrium by certain patterned and recurrent processes. Every society, or social system, has certain needs ("functional prerequisites") that must be satisfied if the system is to survive. Every society must reproduce itself, for example, and must protect its members against the elements, resolve internal conflicts, and produce the goods necessary for subsistence. In order to meet these needs, every society is composed of a number of inter-related and interdependent parts, such as the economy, religion, and the family. Each part contributes to the successful functioning of the whole: the economy produces food and other essential goods; government resolves conflicts between parties; the family reproduces and prepares the young to be productive adults. Functionalism as a theory thus seeks to explain social systems by looking at how the parts of the system satisfy the requirements for its continued existence.

In a relatively stable social system, the parts become interdependent. Therefore, if one part undergoes change, then the other parts must also change. If the economy shifts from predominantly agricultural to industrial, then the family form will usually shift from a community-based extended family unit to the more mobile nuclear family unit. Because of the tendency of the parts to readjust to each other following change, the social system is sometimes considered to be in "dynamic equilibrium."

Against this backdrop of concepts of needs, prerequisites, and functioning parts, it is hardly surprising that functionalists came to see stratification as a necessary feature. W. Lloyd Warner in 1949 stated the position that many later functionalists adopted:

> When societies are complex and service large populations, they always possess some kind of status system which, by its own values, places people in higher or lower positions. . . . This happens primarily because, to maintain itself, the society must coordinate the

efforts of all its members into common enterprises necessary for the preservation of the group, and it must solidify and integrate all these enterprises into a working whole (p. 8).

Warner was thus a spokesman for the idea that stratification meets the societal need for coordination, yet he spent little effort in his own research in further elaborating that theme. Instead, the task was taken up shortly by other functionalists, particularly Talcott Parsons and two of his students, Kingsley Davis and Wilbert E. Moore.

In Parsons's writings, the focus of attention is on the role of the collective consensus. While Parsons acknowledged that stratification serves the societal goals of maintaining order and coordinating activities, he did not mean to suggest that stratification is consciously created by societies for the purpose of meeting those goals. Rather, its creation is related to another feature of social systems, the common values shared by the members of the society. On the basis of common values, individuals and roles are evaluated and they are ranked. The ranking forms the basis of social stratification. A reward-punishment process provides rewards for those people who meet the standards of the value system and punishment for those who do not. Some rewards that may be employed to bring about conformity are esteem, acceptance, and response. In this way, differences in prestige among a people come to reflect the collective evaluations made of individuals and roles.

When Parsons discussed particular stratification systems, the emphasis he placed on the relationship of values to inequality is readily evident. For example, he suggested that in America achievement goals are dominant, and productive activity in the economy is most valued. The two main goals of the people, then, are possession of money, on the one hand, and of "reputation," on the other. Other values fall in line. Thus, science is important because it is tied to technology. The universities are important because they supply the scientists and other professionals. "Equality of opportunity" to receive health care and education is important because it maximizes productive achievement (Parsons 1953). The result is that Western society is organized around the work people do. This fact is significant for the study of stratification because the occupational structure is the source of two functional bases of hierarchy: (1) the differentiation of levels of skill and competence involved in the many different functional roles and (2) the centralization of leadership and authority necessitated by organization (Parsons 1954, pp. 326–27). The value system makes work significant, and work requires hierarchy.

In Parsons's view, then, stratification exists because people evaluate and rank each other and the roles that others play in the system. They agree about what is important because they have been socialized to the society's common value orientations. It is this agreement that leads to the prestige hierarchy. Functionally, stratification is necessary to the successful operation of the society because it coordinates activities, allocates workers to positions, and minimizes conflicts. Society is integrated, stable, and rather smoothly functioning; stratification plays a major part in ensuring that stability.

Although Parsons is generally regarded as the most influential functionalist in American sociology of the twentieth century, it was two of his students, Kingsley Davis and Wilbert E. Moore, who presented the strongest case for the functional explanation of stratification. In a persuasive paper written in 1945, they argued that in societies of any complexity, an extensive division of labor must exist to accomplish the tasks required for maintenance and survival. But not all positions and roles are of equal difficulty, nor do all require the same talents and motivations. Furthermore, societies are frequently faced with a shortage of labor and personnel and must find some way to encourage those with superior qualities to enter into the more important and difficult positions as well as to motivate the occupants of positions at all levels to perform their duties satisfactorily. These problems can be solved by the unequal distribution of rewards.[1]

Consider, for example, the need in the United States for leaders in governmental, business, military, and educational fields, people who must early in their careers undergo extensive training and postpone gratification of personal wants in order to become properly qualified. After their training is over, they often carry considerable responsibility and continue a life of self-discipline and deferment of gratification. According to the functionalist explanation, talented individuals are willing to do all this in order to become generals or senators or college presidents because they anticipate that they will receive a high income, considerable respect from their peers, and a sense of accomplishment. In their classic statement of the functionalist explanation of stratification, Davis and Moore wrote:

> [A society] must thus concern itself with motivation at two different levels: to instill in the proper individuals the desire to fill certain positions, and, once in these positions, the desire to perform the duties attached to them.... If the duties associated with the various positions were all equally pleasant to the human organism, all equally important to societal survival, and all equally in need of the same ability or talent, it would make no difference who got into which positions.... But actually it does make a great deal of

[1] Davis and Moore classified the rewards that a society has at its disposal as being of three types: the things that contribute to sustenance and comfort (economic incentives); the things that contribute to humor and diversion (aesthetic incentives); and the things that contribute to self-respect and ego expansion (symbolic incentives).

difference who gets into which positions, not only because some positions are inherently more agreeable than others, but also because some require special talents or training and some are functionally more important than others.... Social inequality is thus an unconsciously evolved device by which societies insure that the most important positions are conscientiously filled by the most qualified persons. Hence every society, no matter how simple or complex, must ... therefore possess a certain amount of institutionalized inequality (1945, pp. 242–43).

THE CRITIQUES OF THE FUNCTIONALIST EXPLANATION

As logical and consistent as it seems, the Davis-Moore hypothesis did not remain unchallenged. It took eight years for the publication of a rebuttal to appear, a paper by Melvin M. Tumin that stimulated a debate that has still not entirely subsided.[2] Although much of the critical reaction was repetitive and redundant, certain theoretical and empirical difficulties of the functionalist theory immediately began to appear as the countercomment developed. One of the most important criticisms centered around the observation that *there is no way to prove or disprove the theory because it is impossible to measure functional importance* (Tumin 1953, p. 388; Reissman 1959, p. 90; Tausky 1965, pp. 135–36). How can the functional importance of a task be determined? What criteria shall we use to decide which positions are more important? If we use the values of the culture as the criteria, then we are only reflecting value judgments. If we use the prestige of an occupation as a measure of its importance, we involve ourselves in circular reasoning. Is it really clear that positions with high prestige are more important to societal maintenance and survival than those with low prestige? Is it really clear that the physician ultimately is more necessary than the garbage collector? The disastrous consequences of garbage collection strikes for health are well known. The plagues of Europe that sometimes decimated a third of the population were in part due to inadequate garbage disposal. Is the steel company executive more important than the steel worker? One could not operate without the other. The general without the foot soldier could win no wars. In the current state of the social sciences, we cannot with confidence determine which roles make the greater contribution to societal survival (Huaco 1963, p. 804).

The functionalists respond that although it is indeed difficult to establish functional importance, there are three independent clues (Davis and

[2] See, for example, Tumin 1953; Buckley 1958; Fletcher 1956; Gordon 1958; Moore 1963; Parsons 1953; Schwartz 1959; Simpson 1956; Reissman 1959; Tumin 1963; Wrong 1959; and *American Sociological Review* 24 (February 1959): 82–86.

Moore 1945, p. 244n). One is the degree to which a position is functionally unique, there being none other that can perform the same function satisfactorily. The highest positions in religion, politics, the economy, and education are not easily interchangeable, for example. But here the critics point out that in many cases a unique position does not seem to be important. The village idiot and the court jester were unique positions in medieval society. Indeed, the more important the position, the greater is the pressure to develop alternatives for securing its performance and the less likely is it to be unique (Grandjean and Bean 1975).

A second clue, according to functionalists, is the degree to which other positions are dependent on the one in question. Many people are dependent on the decisions of the president of a corporation or a university. But here the critics respond that even if we could develop a measure of positional dependency, its empirical relevance to functional importance (the degree of contribution to the preservation of a system) is still undemonstrated (Huaco 1963). For example, all positions in a modern army are dependent on the position of supply sergeant, perhaps more so than on captain or lieutenant, yet the supply sergeant is not rewarded highly, nor is his functional importance clear in comparison to that of the captain or lieutenant.

The third clue is the degree to which occupations are interchangeable (Stinchcombe 1963). An example is the suggestion that the physician can do the work of the garbage collector, but the garbage collector cannot do the work of the physician. Because the physician is not interchangeable, his or her societal importance is greater. But note that the garbage collector and the physician both are equally unequipped to do the work of the astrologer or the Talmudic scholar. How then does their functional importance compare with that of the physician? Highly specialized skills are not easily interchangeable, but the mere fact of specialization does not therefore make the skill essential for societal survival.

To assess functional importance there must be an independent definition of societal survival (a concept equal in vagueness to "functional importance"), and also there must be criteria that allow measurement of the degree of contribution to societal survival of one role vis-à-vis any other role (Huaco 1963, p. 804). These we do not have. The logical difficulty with the functionalist explanation is that it is untestable. It does not enable one to deduce statements from it which, if false in the light of evidence, would lead one to modify or reject the hypothesis (P. Cohen 1968, p. 51).

Grandjean and Bean (1975) argue that the concepts of supply and demand, borrowed from the field of economics, are more productive concepts for explaining reward differentials than is functional importance. Assuming, as do Davis and Moore, that the supply of labor is quite elastic over time (that is, high rewards draw workers to positions for which the supply of personnel is inadequate) and that demand is inelastic (because demand is primarily determined by functional importance), they are able to show that rewards are affected much more by supply factors such as talent and training than by the demand factor of functional importance. This suggests the need for paying greater attention to the processes that control the avenues to training for different positions and to the salience of power and conflict in the determination of rewards.

But let us suppose for the moment that our subjective impressions of the importance of a position do actually reflect its importance to societal survival. (Several research reports have assumed this, equating "importance" with judgments of importance made by students.) In this case, a second criticism is made: *There is an imperfect correlation between the reward of a position and the importance of it.* Some highly rewarded positions do not really contribute much to the welfare of the society, while some very important positions receive only a moderate reward. Who could claim that the contribution of television heroes, athletes, and speculators to the well-being or functioning of the society is worth thousands or millions of dollars more than the contribution of schoolteachers, social workers, or farmers? A popular comic-strip writer earns more income than a state senator; a top business executive receives many times more income than does an American president; and physicians earn in their lifetime one-and-a-half times as much as physicists and engineers and twice as much as chemists, college professors, and psychologists. The positions of highest responsibility in government, education, judiciary, and religion are financially not highly rewarding in the American system (although there is considerable reward for some of these positions in terms of prestige and power). And there exist some positions that are well rewarded but do not seem to contribute much at all to the society — for example, the valet or kept woman, the rich playboy or gangster boss.[3] They are rewarded out of proportion not only to their functional importance, but also to the relationship of the supply and demand for occupants of the position or to the difficulty of training. As Simpson puts it, "It is hard to believe that a motion picture star, or a tobacco executive whose income is a reward for persuading the public to smoke one cigarette rather than another, must be paid fifty or a hundred times as much as a schoolteacher in order to insure an ample supply of actors and tobacco executives" (1956, p. 133).

In addition, how do we know how unequal the rewards must be to enable the society to survive? Lenski estimates that the salaries of corporate executives in the United States (generally, from $50,000 to over $500,000), which are basically determined by the executives themselves,

---

[3] Simpson 1956, p. 132. There are some who would argue, however, that such occupations as prostitute and personal servant *do* serve some functions to the larger society. Along this line, see the discussion of the functions of political bossism in Merton 1949, pp. 71–81.

are far larger than what they need to be to attract capable personnel; he argues that the salaries for public officials and managers of public utilities and railroads, which are subject to much greater governmental scrutiny, are substantially lower without resulting in a decline in proficiency (1966, pp. 352–57). Grandjean and Bean argue that the high rewards going to the limited supply of famous athletes and movie stars results from their profit-making capabilities, not from their importance to society as a whole (1975, p. 551).

Even if some differential reward is necessary to induce people to become trained for difficult jobs, some critics maintain that the sacrifices undergone during training are not extreme enough to merit the continued unequal rewards of the position. Thus, Tumin speculates that the higher reward that is received for the first ten years after completion of graduate school is sufficient compensation for the tribulations of graduate study. Furthermore, as in the case of the college student, it may be the parents — rather than the individual — who make the sacrifices. Tumin maintains that even during training there is differential reward accruing to the individual (1953, p. 390).

The functionalists reply that their theory was never meant to suggest that there is a perfect correlation between the importance of the position and the reward for it, nor that every specific occupation receives an appropriate reward (other factors, such as tradition or scarcity of personnel may reduce the correlation); it suggests only that the reward must merely be enough to ensure that the position will be filled competently (Davis and Moore 1945, p. 253; Wrong 1959, p. 774). Unimportant roles may be highly rewarded, provided that they do not compete so successfully with important roles that they reduce the quantity or the quality of candidates for the more important roles below some minimum level.

A third major criticism points out that *the correlation between the presence of talent and its use is imperfect*. Much talent and ability goes unrecognized and undeveloped. The more rigidly stratified a society is, the less chance does that society have of discovering any new facts about the talents of its members or of motivating the children of the under-privileged classes. In American society, for example, opportunity to exercise one's abilities is frequently denied to black, poor, and female children. Motivation and opportunities for training are related more to family origin than to the presence of ability. In this respect, a stratification system may be dysfunctional, promoting unfavorable self-images, inhibiting development of the individual, and preventing the free circulation of people with ability into difficult or important positions (Tumin 1953, p. 393; Gordon 1958, p. 168; Huaco 1963, p. 803). It may actually prohibit those of superior native talent from performing tasks that are monopolized by the upper classes. In fact, some argue that in view of the large amount of blundering and ineptitude in highly remunerated positions, it is clear

29

that the "most important" positions are not always filled by the more qualified persons (C. Anderson 1974, p. 82). Bottomore suggests that "it would be a more accurate description of the social-class system to say that it operates, largely through the inheritance of property, to ensure that each individual maintains a certain social position, determined by his birth and irrespective of his particular abilities" (1966, p. 11).

But the functionalists counter that their explanation or stratification does not claim that all features of the system are functional, nor does it deny that inequality of opportunity exists. The theory is concerned with the stratification of *positions* and not of *individuals:* "It is one thing to ask why different positions carry different degrees of prestige, and quite another to ask how certain individuals got into those positions" (K. Davis 1949, p. 369).

A fourth criticism points out that *unequal rewards are not the only means for motivating people to fill important positions.* Alternative mechanisms for allocating people to positions and for developing talent may be possible. "Major value orientations" could focus on public service, perhaps, instead of profit or individualistic competition. As Wesolowski puts it, "It is very doubtful . . . if ever differences of prestige and differences of income were 'functionally necessary' for the filling of positions in stabilized societies where statuses were ascribed. And it should be remembered that societies of this type have been predominant throughout by far the greater part of history" (1962, p. 28). Or one may suggest that the pleasure of being in a position of authority over others may be sufficient to encourage talented individuals to enter important occupations (Wesolowski 1962, p. 35). Others have argued that the more complicated the occupation, the greater is the intrinsic satisfaction in pursuing it, and so *less* formal reward should be necessary to attract occupants.

Another of the most persistently applied criticisms of the functional perspective on inequality is the complaint that functional theories are basically supportive of the status quo because they imply that any scheme of stratification is somehow the best that could be had and that the prevailing distribution of rewards is functionally necessary and therefore the most desirable (Simpson 1956, p. 133; Tumin 1953, p. 388; Dahrendorf 1958a, p. 124). The slightest jump of logic makes it a close relative of the concept of the "survival of the fittest." Those at the top justly receive rewards for doing their important jobs, it seems to say. They are there because they have the talent to be there, and the difference between their wealth and that of the poor is legitimate because it is essential. According to this point of view, functionalism is a form of justifying myth that is perpetuated by intellectuals and that rationalizes inequality; it is an ideology that explicitly legitimates a capitalist system.

Finally, the critics point out that *functionalism is in some ways unrealistic as a theoretical model;* it assumes that members of a social system

rationally calculate an individual's contribution (Simpson 1956, p. 137);
it infers that social systems are always well integrated (Cohn 1960;
Dahrendorf 1959, p. 161); and it includes no theoretical categories by
which change can be accounted for, even though change is more prevalent than stability (Dahrendorf 1959, pp. 161–62; Reissman 1959, p. 94).

In spite of these difficulties, there have been several attempts to find
support for the Davis-Moore hypothesis. These generally have used some
form of the occupational prestige rating scale as their source of basic data.
Svalastoga (1959), for example, assumed that prestige is a social reward
accruing to the incumbent of an occupation. He sought to test the Davis-
Moore hypothesis that prestige is related to the functional importance and
difficulty of a job. Using number of subordinates as a measure of functional importance and level of schooling as a measure of difficulty, he
found the multiple correlation between these two measures and prestige
to be .92. While this may be consistent with the Davis-Moore assertion
that rewards (prestige) encourage indviduals to undertake training (formal education), one might question the assumption that number of subordinates measures importance (rather than authority or power, for instance) or that educational level measures training and difficulty (rather
than class certification).

Another set of prestige studies are those which make international comparisons. In 1956, Inkeles and Rossi compared the prestige rankings of
occupations of six highly industrialized societies (the United States, Germany, Great Britain, New Zealand, Japan, and the Soviet Union). If it
is true, as Davis and Moore suggest, that prestige is one form of reward
related both to the functional importance of a job and to its difficulty,
then one would expect to find similar prestige ratings for an occupation
in the different countries even though such countries might differ in
history, culture, and tradition. This turned out to be so. In all cases,
the professions, high government posts, and top industrial positions occupied the highest places in the prestige hierarchy; semiskilled and unskilled positions consistently fell near the bottom. (Twelve of the fifteen
correlation coefficients were above .90 and only one was below .80.[4])
Does this mean that occupational roles cross-culturally perform similar
functions and therefore are similarly rewarded? Occupational differentia-

---

[4] A coefficient of correlation is a statistic which indicates the degree to
which two variables are related. It ranges from + 1 to 0 to − 1. A correlation coefficient of 0 indicates that there is no relationship at all. A coefficient of + 1.0 indicates the two variables are very highly related, that is, as
one increases, the other increases (an obvious example is the high relationship between individual income and amount of goods purchased). A correlation of − 1.0 indicates that the two variables are very highly related, but as
one increases the other decreases (the relationship between income and the
number of yearly trips to the welfare office). A "multiple correlation"
measures the simultaneous relationships among a number of variables.

tion, one might infer, is functional, and thus the inequality associated with it is functional. But that judgment is not conclusively supported. It can as reasonably be argued that prestige, rather than being a motivational factor that brings about the assignment of people to positions, merely reflects the hierarchies of power established as a result of other forces, such as dominance or economic inequities. The consistent rankings of occupations, if this were true, could be seen to be a product of consistent occupational patterns of access to power or control.

Another attempt to assess empirically the validity of functionalist theory discovered that the incomes of corporals, captains, and diplomats rise at a greater rate during times of war than the incomes of comparable civilian occupations. Arguing that positions that are more directly involved in the war attain greater functional importance than civilian counterparts, Abrahamson (1973) concluded that his data "conform to the functional hypothesis." The evidence, however, is ambiguous. The same data can be found to be consistent with conflict theory (Vanfossen and Rhodes 1974). Elites wish to wage war, so they pump money into the military sector. One could even argue, as did Mills, that the military is influential in persuading the society to go to war. This money is necessary to provide bombs, ships, and incomes for an increased number of foot soldiers. Is it also necessary to motivate the captains and generals to acquire the necessary skills and to perform their jobs? Most corporals, captains, and generals were already trained, belonged to the service, and were performing their jobs before the funds were increased. Conflict analysis would suggest that the reason the incomes of officers rise during times of war is that collectively they have sufficient influence over the distribution of the increased resources accruing to military activities that they can siphon some of it into their own pockets.

In spite of its empirical problems and the many criticisms pointing out the difficulty of testing the theory, the functional perspective on inequality has retained many supporters. In spite of the vagueness of the concepts of "functional importance," "societal survival," and "functional necessity," researchers continue trying to find empirical support for the functional theory of inequality (Abrahamson 1973; Grandjean and Bean 1975; Land 1970). Dennis Wrong even suggests that "critics of the authors' thesis have succeeded in showing that there are a great many things about stratification that Davis and Moore have failed to explain, but they have not succeeded in seriously denting the central argument that unequal rewards are functionally necessary in any and all societies with a division of labor extending much beyond differences in age and sex" (1959, pp. 772–73). But how can a "central argument" be dented or not when its major propositions are elusive to measurement? Until adequate measures of the concepts are created, the theory remains in the realm of the unverifiable. It serves as a perspective, but it remains to be validated.

The problems of measurement pointed out in the scores of scholarly papers debating the Davis-Moore hypothesis between 1950 and 1970 were temporarily overshadowed when functional theory was placed in even greater threat, after 1965, by the increasing popularity of conflict theory. Constituting an alternative model of the way in which society operates, conflict theory presented a radically different perspective on social stratification.

The Conflict Theory of Stratification

Whereas functionalists think of society as a relatively stable system of interdependent and interacting parts held together through integrative value consensus, the conflict theorists think of society as a system of perpetually conflicting and divergent special interest groups, associations, or classes that are held together through compulsion, constraint, and domination. Functionalism views conflict and change as abnormal, whereas conflict theory views conflict and change as ever present, inevitable, and expected (Dahrendorf 1958a, p. 174). The functionalists claim that stratification exists because it is necessary to society's operation; the conflict theorists say that stratification is caused by the domination and exploitation of one interest group by another and is perpetuated by the holders of power in attempts to maintain and increase their influence. Classes emerge, according to conflict theory, because in the struggle for dominance, some groups are able through inheritance or force to acquire sufficient economic and political resources to develop and solidify a privileged position. Power acquired in one segment, such as the economy, is useful for the acquisition of power in other segments, such as the polity. Since the domination is based on coercion, resistance by the subordinated is always potential. This is why the dominant group attempts to legitimate its privilege through ideology and myth. What appear to be society's common values, according to conflict theory, are really the values of the privileged strata.

The intellectual tradition of the conflict perspective runs from Machiavelli and Hobbes to Marx and Weber. It adopts a basically cynical stance about human society (Collins 1975, pp. 56–61). This emerges from the belief that human behavior is best explained in terms of how individual self-interests are acted out in a material world of threat and violence. Social order is seen to be based on organized coercion.

The basic insight of the conflict perspective is that while human beings are sociable animals, they often come into conflict over scarce resources such as food or fertile land (Collins 1975, p. 59). Conflict is of many types, including violent conflict, which is always a potential resource of domination. But being coerced is an inherently unpleasant experience, and therefore any use of coercion calls forth further conflict in the form

33

of antagonism to being dominated. "Add to this the fact that coercive power, especially as represented in the state, can be used to bring one economic goods and emotional gratification — and to deny them to others — and we can see that the availability of coercion as a resource ramifies conflict throughout the entire society" (Collins 1975, p. 59).

As a model of human action, a conflict perspective can be used to interpret many social patterns. Collins suggested that there are several general analytic principles to be followed when applying conflict theory to concrete situations:

1. Think of people as animals maneuvering for advantage, susceptible to emotional appeals, but steering a self-interested course toward satisfactions and away from dissatisfactions.
2. Look for the material arrangements that affect interaction: the physical places, the modes of communication, the supply of weapons, devices for staging one's public impression, tools, and goods. Assess the relative resources available to each individual: their potential for physical coercion, their access to other persons with whom to negotiate, their sexual attractiveness, their store of cultural devices for invoking emotional solidarity, as well as the physical arrangements just mentioned.
3. Apply the general hypothesis that inequalities in resources result in efforts by the dominant party to take advantage of the situation.
4. For the origin of ideals and beliefs, look to the groups which have the resources to make their viewpoint prevail.
5. Compare empirical cases; think causally; look for generalizations. Be aware of multiple causes — the resources for conflict are complex (1975, pp. 60–61).

Many of the ideas underlying these generalizations come from Karl Marx and Max Weber, two nineteenth-century philosophers, economists, and sociologists. An understanding of stratification theory is not complete without a review of their class paradigms, which continue to inspire the imaginations of men and women.

THE CONFLICT THEORY OF KARL MARX

One of the most influential conflict theorists was Karl Marx (1818–1883), whose impact on modern world thinking has been profound. Politically engaged and passionately advocating involvement for change, he saw his own ideas to be both descriptions of reality and prescriptions for revolution. At age thirty, he set down in the often quoted words of the *Communist Manifesto* a theme that was never abandoned as he matured:

> The history of all hitherto existing society is the history of class struggles. Freeman and slave, patrician and plebeian, lord and serf, guild-master and journeyman, in a word, oppressor and oppressed,

stood in constant opposition to one another, carried on an un-interrupted, now hidden, now open fight, a fight that each time ended, either in a revolutionary re-constitution of society at large, or in the common ruin of contending classes (Marx and Engels 1964, p. 57–58).

At the base of Marx's thought was the belief that conflicts between labor and management — or, to use the Marxist vocabulary, between the proletariat and the capitalists — are the major facts of modern societies, which reveal the essential nature of these societies and allow us to predict their historical development (in particular, their self-destruction and their evolution into new economic forms). Human history is characterized by the struggle of human groups characterized as oppressors and oppressed, which tend to become polarized into two, and only two, blocs.

The basis for classes comes from the differing relations that people have to the means of production. This idea recognizes that in each economic system there are a limited number of work roles. A person can raise food, produce goods, oversee the work of others, or sell goods, among other possibilities. Marx conceived of a class as consisting of those people who perform analogous roles in the productive process and who have become aware of their mutual problems. They not only have similar jobs, but they also have similar interests, and these interests are at variance with the interests of other classes.

In all societies, then, classes are shaped by the mode of production. That is why, Marx believed, in order to understand society one must first understand its economic structure. He distinguished between the economic base, or "infrastructure," as it has come to be called, and the other institutions of society, the "superstructure." The economic base is the most important in shaping the groups and events in history. It consists of two kinds of relationships. One is the "forces of production," which are all those features contributing to a given society's capacity to produce — features such as scientific knowledge, technological equipment, and organization of labor. The other is the "social relations of production," a term that is only vaguely defined in Marx's writings, but refers in general to the practices governing property, such as the distribution of wealth and income. Above the economic structure rises the "superstructure," which includes all the other institutions of society, such as the legal and political institutions, as well as the society's ways of thinking, its ideologies, and its philosophies.

Marx traces the history of presocialist systems through five modes of production: primitive communism, ancient society (slavery), feudalism, Asian systems, and capitalism. In primitive communism, the small amount of property that exists is communally and publicly owned. There are no classes. But, when an economic system becomes more productive, private ownership of economic resources begins to emerge. Whoever gains control of the means of production gains thereby an enormous source of economic and political power. The owners are able to appropriate the surplus products and perpetuate their wealth intergenerationally, leading to their further differentiation from the rest of the population (Marx 1961, pp. 115–22).

The ancient mode of production is characterized by slavery, the feudal mode by serfdom, and the capitalist mode by wage earnings. All three are forms of one individual's exploitation by another. The Asiatic mode, however, is characterized by exploitation not by those classes which possess the instruments of production, but by a bureaucratic class representing the state. As Aron points out, some neo-Marxists have speculated that the demise of capitalism, rather than leading to the classless society (as Marx predicted), might lead to the spread of the Asiatic mode of production, in which the state would dominate all, throughout the world (Aron 1968, vol. 1, p. 122).

THE EMERGENCE OF CAPITALISM AND LABOR EXPLOITATION   Marx was most interested in the capitalist mode of production. Based on the expansion of the division of labor and the ascendancy of private property, capitalism emerged out of feudalistic roots. Through a series of revolutionary changes, the basis of production switched from land to capital. The rise to power of those who control capital, the emergent bourgeoisie, developed progressively from the sixteenth century on. As the new economic form of capitalism became entrenched, it led to the creation of the two great classes, the bourgeoisie and the proletariat.[5] The capitalists (the bourgeoisie) use the natural resources, labor, technology, and capital that they control for the purposes of accumulation of profit. But the masses (the proletariat) have only their labor to sell to the capitalists, who gain control of the products produced by that labor and the money brought by the sale of the products.

In this way, the capitalists appropriate the value produced by the workers. The workers are first managed and then exploited. To describe it, Marx here put forth a "labor theory of value": The real value of a product is determined by the monetary equivalent of the labor time needed for its production. Because all products and activities are viewed

---

[5] Marx did note the existence in capitalism of other strata, such as landowners, white-collar workers, and the peasantry, but he considered these to be transitional classes that would eventually disappear as salient categories. Certain other strata, such as higher-level managers, are not really significant as classes under capitalism, Marx believed, because they identify politically with the ruling class. The marginal "lumpenproletariat" — the thieves, criminals, and vagabonds — likewise are of minor interest because they are unintegrated into the division of labor, thus standing at the outskirts of the class system.

36

in terms of their exchange values, labor-power itself then becomes an item of exchange, a commodity. To realize a profit from the buying and selling of goods, the buyer must find a commodity that sells for more than it costs. Labor-power is one such commodity. That is because labor-power creates value above and beyond the cost of its production (the cost of feeding, housing, and maintaining workers and their families). Once purchased (hired), laborers produce goods that, when sold, not only pay for their maintenance, but also give a profit to the capitalists. In this sense, their work consists of "necessary labor," which provides for their subsistence, and "surplus labor," which gives profit to the capitalists. Increases in their productive powers enrich the capitalists' pockets, but not their own. Exploitation occurs as the gap grows between the value the workers create and the value they receive.

Widespread alienation is the result. Because labor is a "life activity," a "living purposeful activity," the transformation of labor-power into a commodity alienates workers from their own nature. They are alienated from the work process itself because the work has become only a means of obtaining the wage necessary to maintain their existence. They also become alienated from themselves. As they lose power over the products of their labor, they lose the sense of meaning that work can bestow. Economically, physically, and psychologically, they are drained of important human satisfactions, and their lives tend to lose any sense of meaning and power.

TECHNIQUES OF BOURGEOIS CONTROL   Once capitalism becomes entrenched, there are forces that promote the stability of the class structure and others that encourage its alteration or demise. In fact, in Marx's view, all economic systems contain contradictory forces vying against one another, inevitably and eventually leading to class alteration. In capitalism, for example, overproduction leads to unemployment and stagnation, and affluence is made possible by poverty. While the bourgeoisie strengthens and maintains its exploitative position, the conditions of life experienced by the working class deteriorate. These and other contradictions lend an inherent instability to the class system, because they eventually stimulate the oppressed class to resist the means of its oppression. Yet, for long periods of time, the ruling class may be successful in maintaining its dominance.

To maintain dominance, the ruling class relies on certain structural features of the society. One such feature is the coincidence of the economic and political institutions. The exercise of government can be of utmost importance in perpetuating class inequality. In fact, according to Marx, the state is nothing more than that form of organization that the economic elite adopts for the guarantee of its property and interests. It is a committee for the administration of the interests of the bourgeoisie as a whole. It is the organized power of one class for oppressing another. The bourgeoisie is able to use the state for such purposes because power derives from wealth, and the capitalist class controls most of society's wealth.

The state is not the only means available for the perpetuation of economic classes. The economic system is supported and sustained by all the secondary institutions that constitute the superstructure. Law and government, art and literature, science and philosophy, family and ideology — all are mobilized to serve the interests of the ruling class. Ideology, for example — that body of beliefs that defines the nature of the universe and the actions that should be taken relative to it — generally justifies the inequality of wealth and power and makes it seem just and fair. As Marx wrote, "The ideas of the ruling class are in every age the ruling ideas, i.e., the class which is the dominant *material* force in society is at the same time its dominant *intellectual* force. The class which has the means of material production at its disposal, has control at the same time over the means of mental production" (Marx 1961, p. 78). The important point about the supportive role played by the superstructure is that basic changes cannot be brought about through its manipulation, for the real basis of power lies within the economic system, not within ideology, the government, or the educational institution. The superstructure ordinarily maintains order against the conflicting forces that inevitably arise.

SOURCES OF CLASS CHANGE   Yet, enormous potential for change is inherent within capitalist society. One of the most important sources of change derives from class conflict. Workers become increasingly antagonistic to the bourgeoisie both because of a struggle for economic advantage and because of the alienation of the workers from their work. To end the exclusion of the proletariat from political power, the first step is that the polarization between the bourgeoisie and the proletariat must be transformed into a movement. This is brought about when the workers recognize their common interests and common class opponent. At first, the workers, divided by competition, are not aware of these. They may even identify with the bourgeoisie ("false consciousness"). Until the workers become aware of their mutual interests, they merely remain in the status of a class aggregate. But when they begin to develop a network of communication, a concentration of numbers of people, the recognition of a common enemy, and some form of social organization, they begin to become conscious of their common fate and to organize to further their own interests. They become a class united to action for its own ends. Class conflict becomes prevalent. In time, the workers may overthrow the bourgeoisie in a violent revolution and establish a temporary ruling class of the proletariat, which either solidifies its position or evolves into a new bourgeoisie. In the final stage of the dialectic, the proletariat abolishes capitalist private ownership of the means of production, eliminates class differences, and creates a classless utopian society in which all people are workers. Until the classless society is created, however, each successive form of economic organization sows the seeds of its own destruction through the polarization of classes and eventual revolution of the masses against the propertied classes.

Marx's conflict theory, then, is a sociology of the class struggle. Central ideas are that modern society is an antagonistic society; classes are the main forces in the historical drama of capitalism; the class struggle is the moving power of history and leads to a revolution; revolution is followed by a dictatorship of the proletariat, which in turn is followed, as the state withers away, by the abolition of all classes in the classless society (Aron 1968, vol. 1, p. 161).

Applying the Marxian scenario to our question — why does stratification occur? — we find the following assertions. (1) Classes develop when an economic institution produces sufficient economic surpluses that wealth can be appropriated as private property from the producers by a minority of "nonproducers" who own and control the means of production. (2) The economic power so acquired is used by the owners to dominate and exploit others who have no access to the property. (3) For the most part, the dominant group takes advantage of the state, philosophy, religion, and education to induce conformity to a system that serves its interests. (4) The dominant groups perpetuate myths to rationalize their domination; ideas are thus tools of domination. (5) Those who are deprived do not object to their deprivation because they are either unaware or unorganized. (6) Built-in contradictions within any mode of production, however, as well as the ever present potential for the development of proletarian class consciousness, create conditions that ultimately bring about class conflict and change. Conflict, exploitation, struggle, and change — these are key words of Marxian analysis.

THE CONFLICT THEORY OF MAX WEBER

Although Max Weber (1864–1920) is considered by many to have engaged in a polemic with Marx in much of his work, he actually shared with Marx a conflict orientation. Weber focused not on society as a whole, but rather on the groups formed by self-interested individuals, groups that struggle with each other for advantage. But he believed that what is at any one time defined to be in a person's self-interest is highly variable and is socially defined by political or religious points of view. Social life thus rests on a polytheism of values in conflict; the individual must choose among them. It is Weber's emphasis on the multidimensionality of inequality and, indeed, of all social life that most strikingly differentiates his theory from Marx's.

Rejecting a theory of history that ties inequality to mode of production alone, Weber focused on three sources of stratification: economic class, social status, and political power. Economic classes arise historically only as the institution of the market develops, an institution in which exchange of goods and services is undertaken for profit. Economic classes emerge out of the unequal distribution of economic power, particularly the control of property. Here, Weber reads much like Marx. Nonowners cannot compete for the highly valued goods, which are monopolized by the owners. Those lacking property thus have only their services to offer in exchange for subsistence, while the propertied can transfer their holdings to capital for the purposes of entrepreneurship. " 'Property' and 'lack of property' are, therefore, the basic categories of all class situations" (Weber, in Gerth and Mills 1946, p. 182).

Status inequality is based on prestige distinctions. Status is "every typical component of the life fate of men that is determined by a specific, positive or negative, social estimation of honor" (Gerth and Mills 1946, p. 187). In contrast to members of classes, individuals who possess similar prestige ratings tend to form groups. A status group, Weber believed, develops not out of access to the means of production, but rather out of consumption patterns and life styles, which are limited only by the person's income. What style of life people choose is affected by their interests, which in turn are related to their values and education. People come to recognize others who share their life style. They associate and form social bonds. They begin to exclude others. They may even form negative attitudes about other groups, considering them, for example, "uneducated" or "dirty and lazy." They visit within their own status group and urge their children to marry within it. In such ways they draw subtle social boundaries between themselves and others.

Weber suggested that status groups are characterized by competition and emulation, not conflict, as Marx believed. They compete for honor — their demands for deference are successful, however, only when recognized by others. High-ranking groups try to promote their favored status by monopolizing status symbols and restricting membership.

Weber maintained that there is significant overlap between economic stratification and prestige stratification. Typically, "stratification by status goes hand in hand with a monopolization of . . . material goods. . . . Besides the specific status honor, which always rests upon distance and exclusiveness, we find all sorts of material monopolies" (Weber, in Gerth and Mills 1946, pp. 190–91). Yet, while the status order is generally highly dependent on the economic order, it does have a certain causal power of its own. He pointed out that during the nineteenth century, for example, the newly rich had less prestige than the aristocracy because they possessed neither the lineage credentials nor the manners that were necessary for social acceptance by those whose wealth had been in the family for some generations.

Inequality of power exists when groups are able to influence action in favor of their interests.[6] "In general, we understand by 'power' the chance of a man or of a number of men to realize their own will . . . even against the resistance of others" (Weber, in Gerth and Mills 1946, p. 180). Power is an aspect of most, if not all, social relationships. Two particularly important types of power are, first, that which comes from economic control or a position of monopoly and, second, that which comes from a position of authority that allocates the right to command and the duty to obey. These two may combine and reinforce each other. The example Weber used to illustrate the merging of economic power and authority was a large central bank that dominates its debtors because of its monopolistic position in the credit market. It uses its legitimate position of authority to accumulate advantages not inherent in the authority structure. The borderline beween the two types is fluid. Thus, "any type of domination by virtue of . . . [economic] interests may . . . be transformed gradually into domination by authority" (Weber, in Roth and Wittich 1968, p. 943).

Weber was greatly interested in the interplay of ideas and interests. Like Marx, he rejected the notion that ideas are in themselves politically efficacious; rather, there must be some interested group behind them to make them effective. To survive, an idea must gain an affinity with the interests of special strata. "Not ideas, but material and ideal interests, directly govern men's conduct" (Weber, in Gerth and Mills 1946, p. 280). However, ideas not only thrive on self-interest, but they also help define self-interest. "Very frequently the 'world images' that have been created by 'ideas' have, like switchmen, determined the tracks along which action has been pushed by the dynamic of interest. 'From what' and 'for what' one wished to be redeemed . . . depended upon one's image of the world" (Weber, in Gerth and Mills 1946, p. 280).

Like Marx, Weber believed that ideas play an important role in the legitimation of vested interests, the "fictitious superstructures" that serve as tools for self-justification. (Unlike Marx, Weber included the interests of the proletariat and the socialists among the vested interests that could be furthered by ideological assertion.) Because human fates are not equal, those who are more favored feel the need to justify their own advantage as "deserved," while claiming that others' disadvantage is their own "fault." Thus, groups develop myths about their own superiority, myths that in a stable system of domination are generally accepted by the less privileged strata. For example, the rich may claim that their wealth is

[6] In Weber's famous essay, "Class, Status and Party" (in Gerth and Mills 1946), the third dimension of stratification is clearly associated with the political order. Thus, class, status, and party are three kinds of power — economic, social, and political. However, it is usual to read Weber's concept of "party" as political power and to call it "power" alone without specifying its reference to the political order.

a reward for industriousness and ambition or that it is essential for reinvestment and business growth. It is only when "the class situation has become unambiguously and openly visible to everyone as the factor determining every man's individual fate, that [the] very myth of the highly privileged about everyone having deserved his particular lot...[becomes] one of the most passionately hated objects of attack" (Weber, in Roth and Wittich 1968, p. 953).

MARX AND WEBER COMPARED Weber and Marx share perspectives to a greater extent than most historians of social theory have since been willing to acknowledge.[7] They agreed on the following points. (1) Human beings are importantly motivated by self-interest. (2) Human society is characterized by group conflict. (3) The propertyless have fewer resources for serving their self-interests than do the propertied. (4) The economic institution is of fundamental importance in shaping the other institutions of society. (5) The dominant groups perpetuate myths to rationalize their domination; ideas are thus tools of domination. (6) Only when class inequalities become patently obvious are the underprivileged likely to attack the rationalizing myths.

They also differed in several ways: (1) Marx made his predictions of societal evolution specific, but Weber denied any form of unilinear evolution. (2) Marx saw the role of ideas to be reflective of vested interests, whereas Weber asserted that ideas may shape what people value. (3) Marx believed that the base of inequality is economic and the state is subsidiary; Weber thought that the bases of inequality are multidimensional and that the state could be a source of power independent of business. (4) In Marx's projected utopia, the state would be subservient to society; Weber was pessimistic that in the future the power of the state and other forms of bureaucratic influence could be reduced. (5) They concentrated on different issues: while Marx developed a more extensive account of the preconditions of class consciousness, Weber discussed at greater length the nature of the status and power dimensions; while Marx analyzed at length the market base of capitalism, Weber emphasized the role of ideas (especially religion) in the emergence of capitalism. Even though these differences exist, and though their judgments of the relative influence of different institutional segments vary, clearly they share a basic conflict perspective.

Marx, in particular, has been roundly criticized. His ideas were considered by some to be too dangerous to be ignored and were considered by others to be too oversimplified to stand for an accurate reflection of real-

---

[7] See Jere Cohen et al. 1975 for the argument that Parsons's interpretation of Marx was partly responsible for the current views on Weber and Marx.

ity. We deal with the most important of the criticisms in the next section. But first it is useful to sketch the propositions of conflict theory in general, which are different at some points from Marx's propositions.

MODERN CONFLICT THEORY IN BRIEF

Not all conflict theorists accept every point made by Marx; nor do modern conflict theorists agree among themselves on all principles. Yet a general theme emerges, even though many specific generalizations must still be subjected to empirical test. The general theme consists of several propositions.

1. *Social inequality emerges as the result of domination or constraint of one or more groups by other groups.* At least six sources of domination have been identified.

A. *Competition for scarce goods and services.* Those who can control the surpluses gain power and prestige (Marx 1961, pp. 115–19; Weber, in Gerth and Mills 1946, p. 182; Lenski 1966, p. 44), because possession of one resource enables one more easily to acquire possession of another resource.

B. *Ownership or control of property.* In capitalistic and agricultural societies, dominance emerges out of ownership or control of property (Marx 1961; Lenski (1966),

C. *Unequal marketability of occupations.* Those occupations which rank high in marketable skills (professional, managerial, athletic) can demand greater material and symbolic advantages than those which are low in such skills (Parkin 1971, pp. 21–23). This proposition appears similar to the Davis-Moore explanation. There is a crucial difference, however. The Davis-Moore theory postulates that "society" offers rewards on the basis of the "importance" of the task. The interpretation suggested here postulates that the size of the rewards are related to the bargaining power that the subject group can summon. Part of this power may be a perception by those who determine salary that the occupation is "important." It may depend on other factors as well, however, such as the ability of the occupational incumbents to restrict entry into the occupation (through apprenticeship systems, high educational requirements, and required certification), thereby reducing supply, or to create increased demand for its services (as when beauticians advocate short hairstyles or dentists recommend straight teeth).

Anderson points out that physicians in the United States are rewarded highly not because they are in possession of some rare and difficult talent that exists in such small quantities that the country must pay them highly. Rather, they receive high incomes because admission to a college of medicine is difficult to gain, except for a privileged few. He contrasts this situation with that in Sweden, where the state-controlled medical system has been producing doctors and dentists at such an accelerated pace that unemployment has become a problem. "As a result the Swedish taxpayers see their medical professionals paid less than American medics, while at the same time receiving more extensive medical benefits" (1974, pp. 85–86). Whatever specific mechanisms are used to elevate the rewards received by one occupational group relative to others, they are part of a bargaining process, a competitive struggle over the question of who gets how much.

D. *Unwillingness of the majority to band together for political purposes.* "An organized minority, acting in concert, will forever triumph over a disorganized majority of people without common will or impulse" (Mosca 1844, p. 19). Isolation and apathy lead to powerlessness.

E. *Oligarchical processes in organizations.* As Michels (1949) postulates in his "iron law of oligarchy," action requires organization, but organization requires the delegation of tasks, responsibilities, and powers to a few leaders. The result is a concentration of skills and prerogatives; the leaders tend to become independent of the rank and file, and their power is consolidated. The self-perpetuating power of the leaders is strengthened further by the political indifference and submission of the masses. The aims of the organization become subverted and more conservative.

F. *Unequal distribution of authority.*[8] The fact that authority relations are dichotomous, consisting of those who command and those who obey, is in any given association the cause of the formation of two groups. Those who are in the subordinate statuses will be interested in changing the status quo. Thus the emergence of overt conflict is a latent possibility in any authority relationship. The conflict's form and intensity and the kind, speed, and depth of any change that may be brought about by the conflict are determined by variable conditions (Dahrendorf 1958b and 1959; Burnham 1941).

2. Because inequality is based on dominance and coercion, *the potential for opposition, resistance, and hostility on the part of the subordinated groups is always present.* Often opposition is scattered and unorganized, as when the subordinated groups are unaware of their mutual interests or when they are divided among themselves by competing interests or crosscutting ethnic, racial, or religious loyalties. Yet passivity can never be taken for granted.

3. *Conflict most frequently occurs over the distribution of scarce resources, such as property or power.* Ruling classes are particularly sensi-

---

8 One objection to this postulate is raised by Parkin, who suggests that authority conflicts refer to cleavages within formal or bureaucratic organizations, but not to cleavages at the societal level. The lines of authority cutting across each formal organization do not interlock to form a major cleavage cutting across society. Therefore, authority relations do not adequately explain society-wide social inequality. See Parkin 1971, pp. 45–46.

tive to encroachments in these areas and are most likely to use counter-measures when their economic or political dominance is challenged.

4. Contrary to Parsons's notion that inequality emerges out of common values, conflict theorists maintain that *what appear to be common values are really the values of the elite, the purpose of which is the legitimation of the arrangement of power.* The dominant groups are generally able to establish a value system favorable to them. For example, with reference to the criteria of evaluation used to establish the prestige of occupations, those particular criteria that emphasize technical expertise, training, skill, and responsibility give professionals and managers the highest esteem. But other criteria could as reasonably be employed — the amount of physical effort involved, for example, or the danger or dirtiness of the tasks performed. These would favor blue-collar and unskilled workers (Sackrey 1973). The prestige system, thus, predominantly reflects the valuation of dominant class members and rests on the fact that those who control the major agencies of socialization are either members of the privileged class or are employed by the privileged class (Domhoff 1967). Because of the successful socialization conducted by dominant group members, major segments of the subordinate class endorse a prestige system that puts a negative evaluation on their own class.

5. Since class relationships are exploitative, *members of the dominant class are faced with crucial problems of social control of the subordinate classes* (Parkin 1971, p. 48). A number of mechanisms, however, may exist or be employed to bring about the acquiescence of the lower classes.

A. *Force.* Ultimately, behind the many laws or practices benefiting the dominant group lies the threat of physical coercion. If people do not do what is expected of them, they may be faced with physical punishment or with deprivation of property, rights, or reputation. The fact that crimes against property, which are usually committed by the lower classes (robbery, burglary, auto theft), are much more likely in the United States to be punished than those committed by dominant group members (embezzlement, price fixing, graft and bribery in government) (Sutherland 1940) can be seen as the use of force to keep the subordinate group in line. After setting up ownership of property as one of the prime sources of prestige and honor, the privileged classes use the threat of force to discourage others not so privileged from taking one of the sources of their honor or acclaim.

B. *Value legitimation.* The constraint of the subordinate classes is made much easier if they willingly accept the privileged position of the dominant group. Belief that the privileged are bright and talented and that the poor cheat and are lazy makes the system of rewards seem just and, in this way, legitimates the values of the dominant class. But value legitimation can be used as the primary source of control *only* if the values receive widespread acceptance throughout the society. In heterogeneous societies, the diversity of subgroups results in the possibility for substantial challenge of the supportive ideologies. Most commonly, consensus and coercion exist side by side in the system of social control (Parkin 1971, p. 49). Compared with the value legitimation, force is relatively inefficient as a control mechanism because it is more expensive and arouses resentment.

C. *Social mobility.* So long as there are significant opportunities for social mobility, many individuals who are economically deprived by the system of social inequality will accept its basic assumptions with the hope that they, too, or their children may eventually achieve a "better life" (Parkin 1971, p. 49). Those who remain immobile will tend to blame their own lack of ability or ambition rather than the structure of inequality (Lane 1962; Chinoy 1956).

D. *Low expectations.* The expectations of members of the subordinate groups may be kept low by the educational system, the community, peer groups, and parents (Sewell, Haller, et al. 1970). Tracking programs, vocational schools, and separate curricula for "college-oriented" and "non-college-oriented" youth are examples of sanctioned programs that communicate to working-class youth that they should not expect to develop in the same way as middle-class or upper-class youth. To the extent that such socialization programs are successful, members of the subordinated groups will agree to the inequality of wealth and opportunity.

Conflict theory, then, approaches the subject of social inequality from an entirely different point of view than does functionalism. Davis and Moore were concerned with the question, "Who shall do the important work?" and they answered, "The talented and the trained." In contrast, Gumplowicz asked, "Who shall do the dirty work?" and his answer was "The despised and the defeated" (Svalastoga 1964, p. 533).

THE CRITIQUE OF CONFLICT THEORY

With the exception of criticisms of Marxism, conflict theory has in no way received the same degree of critical attention that greeted functionalism in American sociology. This is in part because conflict theory has never been the dominant paradigm and in part because it is less developed than is functionalism. The critique of conflict theory is found in scattered sources. The major thrusts are as follows:

1. *Conflict theory is difficult to test empirically.* As Chapter 5 will discuss, the concept of power is elusive. How can "dominance" and "coercion" be measured? Perhaps it can be easily shown that when a society goes to war, its economy prospers, but this would in no way prove that the economic elite caused the war. The proof must come from evidence of actual steps that an elite might have taken and of the effects of those steps. But evidence is difficult to amass; sometimes dominance is exerted

46

unconsciously, and when it is conscious, it is likely to be used in a secretive manner. The aeronautical firm that bribes a nation's politicians in order to receive favorable contracts does not call in reporters to observe the transaction. Because dominance is hidden from view, our perceptions of it often rest on inferential observations. The exact relations of interdependence between business, the government, the military, and the professions are somewhat elusive to the outsider. Even if actions or ideologies are found to be in the interests of the ruling class, proof that the ruling class created them must still be established (Roach and Roach 1973). Some valuable research has been done (and is presented in later chapters), but for the most part, social scientists have a wide open field of empirical work yet to do in determining exactly how, under what conditions, and in which ways is dominance established and perpetuated (Turner 1974, p. 124).

2. *Conflict theory too easily leads to the inference of conspiracy.* Critics who argue this point suggest that dominance largely emerges out of unorganized and unconscious processes. They object to the image of the smoke-filled room that conflict theorists sometimes promote. If there is an establishment, it is an unconscious and inadvertent one.

3. *Conflict theory explains change, but its positing of ruling-class dominance does not adequately explain the overwhelming persistence of social order.* Stability is more common than change. Conflict theorists reply that the pervasiveness of order is overestimated by the critics, because in fact change is more prevalent than stability. In any case, they would suggest, discussions of mechanisms of social control are sufficient to explain stability.

4. *Conflict does not always occur in bipolarized form across the entire society* (Turner 1974, p. 80; van den Berghe 1963). It is not always between the ruling class and the rest of the people, but may be within the ruling class,[9] or among the less privileged strata, or between one segment of the ruling class and one segment of the underprivileged classes. That is, numerous coalitions and divisions are possible. In addition, there are often conflict groups in society besides social classes, which themselves may be in substantial agreement on many issues (Dahrendorf 1959). Be that as it may, conflict theorists reply, it is still fruitful to see class relationships as a form of dominance.

5. *Conflict does not always lead to change.* Indeed, it may contribute to social order by reaffirming values, resolving disagreements, or reasserting power (Simmel 1956; Coser 1956, p. 73).

6. *Marxism,* as a subtype of conflict theory, *has its own particular problems.* Because these criticisms are so extensive, and because Marx has

[9] For research that finds that conflict is more intense within the "dominant" class than between this and the "subjected" class, see Lopreato 1968, pp. 70–79.

been such an influential thinker, it is useful to examine in some greater detail the dialogue between his critics and his defenders.

THE CRITICISM OF MARXIAN ANALYSIS

The weaknesses of Marx's model are well publicized. Some of the reservations deal with aspects of Marx's economic theory, which are of little relevance to our discussion. Several, however, strike at the core of Marxian class analysis.

The most common objection made by critics, many of them neo-Marxists, is that societies are more than mere reflections of economic interests (Turner 1974, p. 80). Inequality is influenced as well by other relatively autonomous institutions, such as the state, the military, or education (Ossowski 1963; Dahrendorf 1959). This point was first made by Max Weber, who particularly stressed that power and status are equally important forms of inequality. Other critics have maintained that political power, in particular, is an independent phenomenon and not exclusively a product of economic forces, as Marx viewed it. Dahrendorf, for example, argued forcefully that the coincidence of economic conflict and political conflict has ceased to exist in what he terms the postcapitalist societies. "Increasingly, the social relations of industry, including industrial conflict, do not dominate the whole of society but remain confined in their patterns and problems to the sphere of industry" (Dahrendorf 1959, p. 268). Others suggest that political forces have even become dominant over economic forces. As a Polish sociologist, the late Stanislaw Ossowski, put it:

> There are other reasons why the nineteenth-century conception of social class, in both the liberal and the Marxian interpretations, has lost much of its applicability in the modern world. In situations where changes of social structure are to a greater or lesser extent governed by the decision of the political authorities, we are a long way from . . . classes conceived of as groups determined by their relations to the means of production (1963, p. 184).

Ossowski was in particular describing societies, such as the Soviet Union, in which the rule of a single party has allowed a highly unequal ordering of income and rank to develop. Marx was able to foresee neither the emergence of a dictatorship of a party, as found in modern communist nations, nor the welfare state politics of modern capitalist nations, where there is substantial control by government over the economy and the nature of social classes (Bottomore 1966, p. 34).

A second criticism is that many of Marx's predictions for the future development of capitalism have not been borne out. He did not anticipate the emergence of labor unions, the rise of corporations, or the influence of government in regulating and directing the economy. He underestimated the potential size and significance of the middle class in playing a mitigating role between the upper and lower classes. He overemphasized the potential intensity of class consciousness and class conflict. Marx's predictions for the progressive misery of the proletariat have not been substantiated. Instead, the workers in advanced capitalist countries are wealthier and possibly more contented than previously, whereas it is in the underdeveloped and the recently industrialized nations that revolutions are more common. The idea that a classless society will emerge out of the dictatorship of the proletariat is unrealistic, some claim. In addition, critics suggest that the eventual disappearance of the state in the industrial society is improbable. In any highly complex society, there must be some agency to coordinate activities. Even in the planned economy, centralized organizations must make the fundamental decisions implied by the very idea of planning (Aron 1968, vol. 1, p. 171).

As with functionalism, the criticisms of Marxian analysis served more to modify the theory than to discredit it. Modern neo-Marxists retain the emphasis on class conflict, production forces, property relations, class consciousness, and infrastructure and superstructure. After reviewing the criticisms, Aron comments:

> Personally, if I want to analyze a society, whether it be Soviet or American, I often begin with the state of the economy, and even with the state of the forces of production, and then proceed to the relations of production and finally to social relations. The critical and methodological use of these concepts to analyze a modern society, or perhaps any historical society, is unquestionably legitimate (1965, vol. 1, p. 155).

Zeitlin (1967) provided a useful tool for modern researchers by making a checklist of factors that Marx took into account. He suggested that students who wish to understand a particular society should consider first the economic order, and the effect of changes in it on such important variables as relationships at work, distribution of workers, and unemployment rates. Then they should locate the main economic classes and determine their objective economic interests, level of class consciousness, and degree of class conflict. They should consider the roles of the other institutions to the power elite, the coalitions among classes and parties, and the degree of powerlessness of the subordinate classes. It is Zeitlin's conclusion that questions such as these, together with the general premises of Marx's theoretical approach, are what make his work relevant to contemporary social science inquiry.

The criticisms of Marxian analysis, and the criticisms of conflict theory in general, have not so much demolished conflict theory as modified it, in the same way that functionalist theory was modified by its criticisms. The movement of each theory away from the extremes and toward the center has led some students of stratification to suggest that a synthesis is due.

Attempts to Reach Synthesis

Functionalism and conflict theory clearly present radically differing perspectives of social inequality. Functionalists stress consensus and integration, while conflict theorists stress coercion and discord. Roach et al. have contrasted the two views on the major issues in stratification theory:

The functional view	*The conflict view*
1. Stratification is universal, necessary, and inevitable.	1. Stratification may be universal without being necessary or inevitable.
2. Social organization (the social system) shapes the stratification system.	2. The stratification system shapes social organization (the social system).
3. Stratification arises from the societal need for integration, coordination, and cohesion.	3. Stratification arises from group conquest, competition, and conflict.
4. Stratification facilitates the optimal functioning of society and the individual.	4. Stratification impedes the optimal functioning of society and the individual.
5. Stratification is an expression of commonly shared social values.	5. Stratification is an expression of the values of powerful groups.
6. Power is usually legitimately distributed in society.	6. Power is usually illegitimately distributed in society.
7. Tasks and rewards are equitably allocated.	7. Tasks and rewards are inequitably allocated.
8. The economic dimension is subordinate to other dimensions of society.	8. The economic dimension is paramount in society.
9. Stratification systems generally change through evolutionary processes.	9. Stratification systems often change through revolutionary processes.[10]

Neither the functional model nor the conflict interpretations can at the present time be shown to be more empirically valid. The problems they concentrate on, the problems of order and change, are important, and each model has its appealing features in explaining them. Dahren-

[10] Roach, Gross, Gursslin, *Social Stratification in the United States,* © 1969, p. 55. Reprinted by permission of Prentice-Hall, Inc., Englewood Cliffs, New Jersey.

dorf (1959) suggests that the two models present complementary, rather than alternative, views and that we should choose between them only for the interpretation of specific problems. Functionalism explains how highly talented people are motivated to spend twenty-five years of study to become surgeons; conflict theory explains how surgeons utilize their monopoly on their vital skills to obtain greater rewards than necessary to ensure an adequate supply of talent. Other scholars suggest that a synthesis of the two models is desirable, and several attempts at synthesis have been made (Ossowski 1963; van den Berghe 1963; Williams 1966; Horowitz 1962; Lenski 1966). These attempts usually take the form of statements such as "every society has order, yet every society has conflict," or "the forces that produce order also provide the preconditions for change." Van den Berghe (1963) notes that both perspectives look at societies as systems of interrelated parts, both share an evolutionary notion of social change, and both are essentially equilibrium models (but see Frank 1973, pp. 62–73, for a rebuttal).

The most important attempt at synthesis to date was made by Lenski (1966, chap. 2). He started with propositions about human nature: People are social beings obliged by nature to live with others as members of society. Lenski here is stating the relatively obvious fact that social life is essential not only for the survival of the species, but also for the maximum satisfaction of human needs and desires. Yet, this does not mean that human beings are consistently altruistic in their relations with each other, especially in regard to power and privilege. Lenski's second proposition argues that when people are confronted with important decisions in which they are forced to choose between their own (or their group's) interests and the interests of others, they nearly always choose the former, although they may try to hide this fact from themselves and others. Self-interest comes into play particularly relative to the objects people want, most of which are in short supply. Thus, a struggle for rewards will be present in every human society. But, people are unequally endowed by nature with the attributes necessary to carry on these struggles. Yet while such natural inequalities do affect the effectiveness with which different people engage in their struggles, they are not the primary source of inequality. Finally, Lenski suggests that people are creatures of habit and are influenced by custom, which fact goes a long way toward explaining the stability of existing systems of stratification. In his attempted synthesis, Lenski clearly leans toward an emphasis on power and struggle, while incorporating the idea that survival depends on cooperation among humans.

Our Basic Paradigm

The debate between functionalists and conflict theorists would be essentially a scholastic discussion except for the fact that any further investigation is guided by the theoretical model that one chooses. A model suggests concepts, leads to certain areas of investigation rather than others, and influences interpretations of the data so collected. Its use must be made explicit. As Barber puts it, "Each sociologist carries in his head one or more 'models' of society and man which greatly influence what he looks for, what he sees, and what he does with his observations by way of fitting them along with other facts, into a larger scheme of explanation" (quoted in Chambliss 1973, p. 2).

The model to be employed in the remaining chapters of this text, although incorporating elements of both functionalism and conflict theory, is basically a conflict model with systemic assumptions. The precedents for its propositions are found in many sources, but particularly in the works of Marx, Weber, and Lenski. See Figure 2.1 for its diagrammatical representation. The first assumption to be made is that human beings, when given a choice, will tend to act in terms of their own interests or the interests of the group with which they identify (Marx 1967; Weber

Figure 2.1

The basic paradigm: stratification in advanced societies

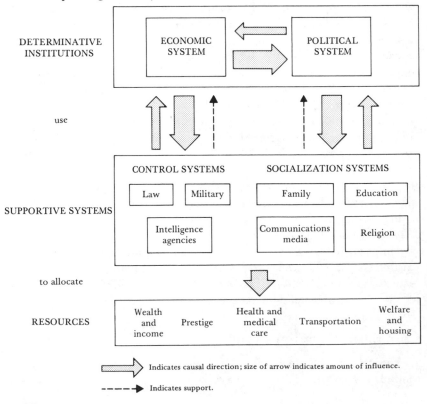

in Roth and Wittich 1968; Lenski 1966). What is defined by them to be in their interests is varied. It may be consistent with major value themes already extant in the culture — themes that are disseminated by religious precepts, major ideologies, or educational emphases and that provide world images, as Weber noted. But, despite the diversity of possible definitions of self-interest in a society with an economy that produces a surplus (material and nonmaterial), definitions of self-interest or group interest usually include the acquisition of or control over scarce and valued goods and services (Lenski 1966, p. 31). Since scarce objects are not available to all, the individual's or group's access to them is heavily dependent on commandeering other bargaining resources.

It is further assumed that in highly productive and therefore highly specialized modern societies, the economic institution (as compared to the state, the educational system, or the church) sets the basic form that social stratification will take. It determines the elaborateness of the division of labor and the degree of hierarchy in the occupational world; it is causally related to the level of productivity, the possibilities for exchange with other societies, and the amount of surplus; it is the locus of the resources of land, capital, and labor; it includes the distribution of wealth and income; and it is the scene of the work that men and women do and thereby of their occupational differentiation. The accumulation of its products — goods, services, and wealth — provides tools of power, manipulation, and influence. Common value orientations may play a role in stability, as Parsons suggested, but to understand stratification one must first understand the distribution of economic resources.

However, the economic structure is not the only determinant of social stratification. There are other sources of power, particularly those which come from the political institution, the legitimated control institution that arbitrates conflicts and employs force to enforce the decisions so made. That political maneuverings are intertwined with the maneuverings of the economic elite is obvious; for instance, the American government has done little to redistribute wealth in spite of the efforts of labor. The economic elite is most likely to attempt to influence the workings of the state when its interests are directly affected. Yet evidence of significant interlacing does not disprove that the state can act as an autonomous or semiautonomous force. The degree to which and the circumstances in which it acts autonomously are subject to empirical investigation.

The other major institutions — the family, religion, education, communications media, law — primarily play supportive roles to the stratification system set up by the economic and political elites. Some of these (the law, the police, and the military) enforce stratification through the threat of force. Others (the family, education, communications media, and religion) bring about acquiescence to the stratification system through socialization and value indoctrination. The educational system, in

53

addition, plays a structural role by allocating individuals to adult roles, barring some from the more highly rewarded occupations and allowing others access to them. Stability comes about through the integrative interlacing of the determinative and supportive institutions, which together structure the allocation of resources such as wealth, health care, welfare, and housing. Change comes about as subordinated groups gain in access to manipulative resources and thus shift the balance of power. The causes of changes in resource access are many. (For example, changes in technology or occupational monopolization can bring about changes in the distribution of access.)

Status groups emerge from the identification of individuals with others on the basis of characteristics that they consider important. These characteristics are varied. They usually involve economic position, but may also be based on religious affiliation, education, ethnic background, race, sex, or any other historically salient feature. The affiliations and networks that people establish because of such identifications form the structure of the status groups. Such groups are concerned with maintaining the level of prestige they have come to expect and, occasionally, with increasing it.

The interplay between the economic institution and the other sources of social stratification are made more obvious when examined in a historical context. Under conditions of orderly evolutionary change, one generation's raw struggles over power and wealth are transformed into the next generation's institutionalized and legitimated hierarchies of inequality. The process of legitimation of power won through conflict requires the mobilization of the supportive institutions. These institutions, acting in concert with the coercive influence of political dominance, ordinarily provide the order and conservative stability that mark the normal day-to-day operations of the society. Yet the supportive institutions can be mobilized for change. The second generation's membership includes subordinated and powerless status groups who have the potential for fighting and resisting their own subordination. A small gain in access to manipulative resources can lead to larger gains in a multiplicative fashion. Eventually, the supportive institutions may be employed for their benefit in the struggle. Part of our search, then, must be the search for the conditions that prompt radical, rather than conservative, responses on the part of the subordinated groups.

In the next part, we thus must deal with two questions: (1) Within the determinative institutions, what are the circumstances under which dominance is established, how does it come about, and how is it enforced? (2) What are the circumstances in which the supportive institutions and subordinated groups play supportive roles, and what are the circumstances in which they become radical?

Two

Determinants of Inequality

3 INDUSTRIALIZATION AND THE OCCUPATIONAL STRUCTURE

NOT ALL SOCIETIES have social classes, wealth and poverty, or kings and chiefs. Some are remarkably equalitarian, at least by standards we employ today. In many hunting and gathering societies, for example, the material possessions of the whole tribe could be contained in one U-Haul truck. In many, there are no specialized occupations — only tasks differentiated along age and sex lines. In many, leadership rests only tentatively on the persuasive abilities of the more capable and respected hunters.

There is, in fact, enormous variation among historical societies in the kinds and extent of stratification structures they contain. Some societies have nine or ten unequal castes or social classes, while others have none. Power may be wielded by an informal, democratic council of community adults or by an elaborate political hierarchy of nobles, gentlemen, retainers, and royalty. In the Indian fishing villages on the northwest coast of Canada, it was considered honorable to destroy wealth blatantly in great *potlatch* ceremonies. But in other times and places, it has seemed more worthy to be poor but religious, or poor but intellectual. The variety is almost endless.

The variety is not completely meaningless and random, however. If we group societies by their dominant economic form, their stratification systems begin to fit an orderly pattern. In essence, societies with subsistence economies tend to be equalitarian, while those with vast economic surpluses tend to have elaborate class hierarchies. It is only when an economy can produce the tools and resources necessary for the subordination of one group by another that a class structure can emerge. For example, a highly developed agricultural society can readily adopt slavery, but hunting and gathering societies have neither the political and material tools of force to maintain a slave class in submission nor the food surplus to support such a large population. History tends to confirm the observations of both Marx and Weber that classes emerge only when private property replaces communal property, that is, when surpluses are given over to private control.

Twentieth-century cultural evolutionists, such as Leslie White (1943), have suggested that the emergence of classes is a natural part of a trend toward the greater cultural complexity that follows technological complexity. These developments, in turn, are based on increases in the potential energy that can be used. The simpler economies produce less energy than the more developed economies. White calculated that a society that derives all its energy from human labor produces no more than .05 horsepower per person. An industrial society such as the United States produces over 13 horsepower per person — the equivalent of 100 human slaves for each American. White believed that the use of nonhuman sources of energy, such as animal or machine power, increases the energy per capita that can be utilized and, therefore, the cultural complexity.

White's idea was pursued by Sahlins, who looked at the effects of productivity on the stratification structures of fourteen Polynesian cultures. He found that among Polynesian societies lowest in productivity, as in Pukapuka, Ontong Jave, Tokelau, and the Marquesas, either there is no significant stratification or there are only distinctions of wealth that are not crystallized into hereditary classes. In Polynesian societies with the greatest productivity, on the other hand, such as Easter Island, Hawaii, and Mangaia, there is hereditary aristocracy and slavery. He concludes, "other factors being constant, the greater the productivity, the greater the amount of stratification" (Sahlins 1958, p. xi).

The Philippines evidence seems supportive of White's belief that the amount of available energy leads to the complexity of stratification structures. It appears to be a usefully simple theory, supported by data. Yet, a suspicion emerges: Is it really all this simple? *Why* should a higher level of energy expenditure lead to a more complex culture? What about the roles of conflict, oppression, and domination? How do these common human states, so integral a part of many class structures, relate to the supply of energy? What are the mechanisms by which a society with a more complicated technology evolves a more complicated class structure? White's thesis does not seem to go deep enough for our purposes, nor does it offer many clues to the internal dynamics of the relationship to which it points.

A further contribution to a theory of economic stratification has been developed by Lenski (1966). Returning to the ideas of Marx and Weber, Lenski has argued that power and privilege come about through the control of the economic surpluses. Lenski suggested that there are two major "laws of distribution" in effect:

First Law of Distribution: Individuals will share the product of their labors to the extent required to ensure the survival and continued productivity of those others whose actions are necessary or beneficial to themselves.

Second Law of Distribution: Power will determine the distribution of nearly all of the surplus possessed by a society (1966, p. 44).

In societies where there is little surplus, the criterion of distribution is the "need for survival" (Lenski 1966, p. 44; also see Polanyi 1944, p. 46). Goods and services are distributed largely on the basis of need. There is virtual equality of possessions, because there are not many possessions to go around.

But prestige is one resource that members of even the poorest society can grant unequally to the more valued members of society. Prestige differentiation does in fact develop in all societies. By itself, however, prestige differentiation cannot lead to social stratification, because it is not something that can be stored, accumulated, and passed on to one's children, as can material goods. Consequently, a hereditary class based on prestige inequality cannot be established.

When technological and agricultural advances create an abundant economic surplus, an increasing proportion of the available goods become distributed on the basis of "power." The more powerful individuals, often part of an established ruling class, take over and accumulate a disproportionate amount of the surplus for their own ends. A common way by which this is done is through taxation. In modern industrial societies, it is also done through property laws regulating the distribution of "profits." Once the surplus has been accumulated, it can be passed on to the children of the wealthy. Political power also is often passed on, as when sons become king.

Inequality bears a relatively simple, one-to-one relationship to personal skills and abilities in primitive hunting and gathering societies. It is only when the economy increases in complexity that stratification becomes institutionalized and entrenched. The peak of this development is reached in agrarian societies, in which hereditary differences of power and prestige become the most marked. A cross-cultural comparison of concrete societies substantiates these observations. Recall Table 1.3, which showed that

59

about two-thirds of 133 hunting and gathering societies have *no* stratification system and that only 1 percent have a complex class system. At the same time, less than one-twelfth of 115 agrarian societies *lack* a stratification structure, while over half possess complex class systems.

What neither Marx, nor Weber, nor White anticipated is that the tendency toward greater stratification with greater complexity does not hold for industrial societies. In these most complex societies, Lenski found a significant decrease in political and economic inequality, constituting a "reversal in a major historical trend" (the reasons for which are discussed in the next section). This reversal and the other relationships between inequality and economic system are graphically illustrated in Figure 3.1, which shows Lenski's estimate of the range of inequality possible for each economic type.

Economic Structure and Social Stratification

In order to see more clearly the distributive dynamics involved in these processes, let us briefly examine each economic type singly, looking at how its economic parameters influence its stratification system. A brief description of each of the major forms of economic structure that Lenski discusses should be sufficient to illustrate the processes of allocation.

Figure 3.1

Degree of social inequality by type of society

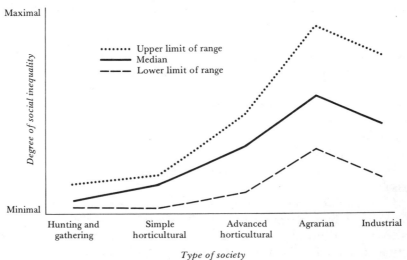

Source: From *Power and Privilege: A Theory of Social Stratification* by Gerhard E. Lenski. Copyright © 1966 by McGraw-Hill, Inc. Used with permission of McGraw-Hill Book Company.

HUNTING AND GATHERING SOCIETIES

Hunting and gathering economies are the oldest known to humankind. During most of the time human beings have existed, from their beginnings two million years ago until about 9000 B.C., all groups were hunters and gatherers. Even today, hunting and gathering societies are found in all parts of the world.

Survival in a hunting and gathering society is nearly always at a minimal subsistence level. The people have to depend on the natural availability of game and plants in the area since they do not produce their own food. But the yield from hunting and gathering is so low that the quest for food is the full-time occupation of all able individuals. Life expectancies are short, and the size of the population is small, ordinarily not more than fifty people.

The division of labor in a hunting and gathering society is very simple, restricted mainly to a division by age and sex. Coupled with the small size of the population, a simple division of labor means that the internal differentiation among the tribesmen is very limited (in comparison, for example, to the differentiation possible in a society with 200 million people).

Because of the limited internal differentiation among the populace, formalized structures such as political hierarchies do not exist. Instead, the social organization consists primarily of self-sufficient family groups or loose confederations of families, which are the main sources of political control. The greatest degree of political specialization to be found is government by council; there is usually no permanent status of chief. Leadership moves from one individual to another depending on the activity. Prestige is granted to those who possess the greatest personal skills and ability. The benefits of higher social status cannot be transferred from one generation to the next because there are little wealth and no hereditary roles. In addition, government by coercion is impossible because the leader lacks a loyal corps of specialists in violence to carry out orders (Lenski 1966, p. 106). As a result of their occupational simplicity, lack of wealth, and small size, hunting and gathering societies are the most equalitarian societies to be found on earth.

THE DEVELOPMENT OF AGRICULTURE

During most of the time that the species *homo sapiens* has existed, people have been hunters and gatherers. Utilizing this limited technology, they survived the climatic and environmental changes associated with the advent and decline of four glacial epochs. But about ten thousand years ago, following the end of the last glacial period, an "agricultural revolution" began to take place, one which altered the nature of human life drastically. Resulting from the discovery that plants and animals can be domesticated, an effective food-producing technology emerged and was

61

followed in several thousand years by the first urban societies and in less than ten thousand years by the industrial revolution. With the domestication of plants and animals, vast new dimensions of cultural evolution became possible. Living became more certain, populations increased and concentrated, food surpluses allowed some of the population to work at tasks other than food production, and communities became stationary.

The typical sequence of events following the adoption of agricultural practices is as follows. Agriculture, a more productive type of economy than hunting and gathering, changes a migratory population to a sedentary one by tying the people to the land. Because the method of securing food is more efficient, more people can eat, and populations tend to increase. Because a single person can harvest larger crops, some other people are relieved of the necessity of growing food. They become craftsmen, and occupational specialization develops. The division of labor becomes more elaborate, and goods can be produced for trade. Because there are surpluses, wealth in property and goods is accumulated. In these ways, food surpluses permit both a high degree of occupational specialization and a class structure based on economic differentiation.

Historically, the domestication of plants and animals was a gradual process that occurred several times independently in different parts of the world. It was always preceded by a period of intensified food collection ("incipient agriculture") during which a knowledge of the habits of the plants and animals of the area became very developed. (Full domestication occurs when seeds, roots, or shoots are deliberately planted or stored for use during the next year. It requires preparation of the soil as well as foresightedness.) The first successful domestication of food probably took place around 8000 B.C. in the "fertile crescent," a semicircular area in southwestern Asia in the valleys of the Tigris and Euphrates rivers. The skills of farming and animal husbandry eventually spread to all parts of the world.

The simpler forms of farming, which depend on human labor to cultivate the land, are called *horticultural* forms. It is only when animal power or mechanical devices are used to work the land that the economy is classified as *agrarian*.

HORTICULTURAL SOCIETIES

Designating the simplest type of agricultural society, *horticulture* is the term applied to the cultivation of domesticated plants by human energy and without the use of the plow. The digging stick is the most frequently used implement for working the soil, although occasionally the hoe or spade is employed. Cultivation is always very shallow, and usually new fields must be cleared and cultivated every few years as the old fields undergo soil exhaustion. Nevertheless, a food surplus is produced — not a great one, yet one sufficient to free part of the population for other kinds of labor. Surplus goods are produced, and some degree of wealth accumulation is possible. Horticulturists today are found primarily in South America, Africa south of the Sahara, and Oceania. Their average community size is one hundred to two hundred people, but they may have communities as large as three thousand.

Because of the increased opportunity for specialization, it is in the horticultural societies that we see the first development of social and political inequality. Full-time political occupations emerge, and quite frequently there even develops a staff of subordinates who support the headman, thereby encouraging the continuance of his reign. The chief serves the function of collecting and redistributing the economic surplus. As a by-product, he is likely to gain prerogatives such as distinctive clothing, deference, receipt of taxes, and exemption from labor.

In Lenski's view, this development of full-time political offices in simple horticultural societies is very significant because it "represents an important early step in the direction of stabilizing, solidifying, and institutionalizing systems of social inequality" (1966, p. 132). However, the specialization of political functions is still too elemental to allow an intergenerational transmission of ruling-class power. Leaders of simple horticultural societies do not have enough staff, wealth, or coercive power to last without the support of the population. Therefore, personal skills and persuasive abilities are still requisites for leadership. There are compelling reasons for the chief to convince the tribe that he has their best interests in mind (Malinowski 1932, p. 97).

The situation is a little different in the *advanced* horticultural societies, which often develop quite complicated class systems. An advanced horticultural society is one in which the economy is so productive that great wealth and material resources are often produced. If these are gathered from the producers and redistributed to an elite class, vast inequities in power can develop.

The productivity of the advanced horticultural society usually comes from a technology superior to that of the simple horticultural society. The advanced horticultural societies use metal hoes, which are far superior to the digging stick. Of most significance is the fact that metal hoes turn up the soil to a greater depth than digging sticks, exposing more nutrients. The practice of metallurgy also leads to better weapons and a greater variety of other tools. In addition, advanced horticultural societies frequently utilize the techniques of irrigation, terracing, and fertilization. Their technology, superior to the type previously discussed, allows for even greater leisure time and economic surplus.

Advanced horticultural societies are larger than simple horticultural societies, the advanced occasionally reaching a size of three to four million. Horticultural kingdoms in Africa and the Mayan, Aztec, and Incan civilizations in the New World are typical examples. The economic surplus produced may be sufficient to support political and military machines, which in turn lead to empire building and the formation of dynasties. Occupational specialization becomes marked; states develop and grow in power; military conquests supply slaves and greater wealth; complex social organizations emerge to carry on the affairs of the state and the military. Trade, commerce, and taxation become important activities.

In many of these societies, the kings, who are regarded as gods, are able to wield great power because they are supported by a staff of chief ministers and subordinates. For example, in writing about the advanced horticultural kingdoms of Africa, Murdock (1959) indicates that the institution of "African despotism" has the following characteristics of political structure: monarchical absolutism, ownership of all territory by the king, divine kingship, ritual isolation of the king, insignia of office, capital towns, royal courts, court protocol, harems, queens, territorial bureaucracy, ministers of state, titles, security provisions, electoral succession, anarchic interregnums, and human sacrifice. In such a situation, the reign of the headman no longer has to depend on his popularity with the people. In fact, he can become quite abusive and still not lose his control.

AGRARIAN SOCIETIES

In spite of the fact that stratification may be quite complex in the advanced horticultural societies, the greatest extremes of inequality are to be found in agrarian societies, which cultivate land by use of the animal-drawn plow. A plow is much more efficient than the digging stick, because heavier soils can be cultivated, larger areas can be prepared for sowing, planting can be accomplished in a shorter period of time, and soil can be turned up to a greater depth. Its use frees even larger proportions of the population for manufacturing and other activities. Villages become more stable because land can be used for generations. Occupational specialization and trading are accentuated.

In agrarian societies, a symbiotic relationship tends to develop between the urban centers and the outlying rural areas and villages. Food and resources are supplied to the cities by rural areas in return for religious, military, educational, and commercial services. The farmer becomes dependent on the specialist who prepares the tools, and the specialist is dependent on the trader and the miner. As the villages grow into cities, "organized military forces, armed with superior metal weapons...[are] required to protect both the wealth of the city and its dependent territory and to ensure the control of trade routes and natural resources" (Beals and Hoijer 1965, p. 400). Wars between empires or nations, sometimes worldwide in scope, become more costly and are carried on by highly specialized armies supported by the plow's surplus.

As the division of labor extends, social stratification becomes pronounced. Marked class differentiation results. Evidence in support of this generalization comes from Murdock's Cross-cultural Survey, which reveals that all but one-fourth of the agrarian societies so referenced had systems of nobility and/or complex classes (see Table 1.3), while 50 percent of them were characterized by advanced levels of statehood (compared to 15 percent of the horticultural societies and 1 percent of the hunting and gathering societies) (Vanfossen 1969, Table 2).

Lenski's opinion is that the primary source of social inequality in agrarian societies results from the institutions of government. The state becomes "the supreme prize for all who ... [covet] power, privilege, and prestige. ... By the skillful exercise of the powers of state, a man or group could gain control over much of the economic surplus, and with it at his disposal, could go on to achieve honor and prestige as well" (Lenski 1966, p. 210). For this reason, intrigues and power struggles among the upper echelons of the class hierarchy are almost continuous and tend to reflect the self-interest of the conflicting parties.

Agrarian societies, then, tend to contain the prerequisites for an elaborate system of stratification: sufficient food supplies to support a complicated division of labor, a surplus of goods that can be accumulated and passed on from generation to generation, stability of population, and the means to apply force (metal for weapons, for example).

Lenski (1966, pp. 210–84) describes the typical stratification structure of an agrarian society in terms of the following nine classes, which can be found in such societies as Ottoman Turkey, Mughal India, imperial Rome, nineteenth-century China, ancient Egypt, and medieval Europe:

1. The ruler, extremely powerful and very wealthy. For example, in England by the end of the fourteenth century, "English kings averaged £135,000 a year.... This was almost forty times the income of the richest member of the nobility, and was equal to 85 percent of the combined incomes of the nearly 2,200 members of the nobility and squirearchy as reported in the tax on income in 1436" (p. 212).
2. The governing class, ordinarily about 2 percent of the population. By virtue of their position, its members receive at least a quarter of the national income. In some cases the governing class comes from the feudal nobility, and in other cases it consists of nonhereditary bureaucratic officials. There frequently is a struggle for power between the rulers and the governing class, but the outcome of the struggle ordinarily has little effect on the lives of the common people.
3. The retainer class, about 5 percent of the population. It consists of such service groups as personal servants to the rulers, tax collectors, professional soldiers, and officials, who provide "badly needed numerical support for the ruler and governing class in their efforts to maintain their essentially exploitative position in society" (p. 246). They also mediate between the governing class and the common people, do

much of the actual work of collecting the economic surplus, and deflect hostility away from the upper classes.

4. The merchant class, important to the development of commerce. Originally from humble origins, its members gain in wealth and power as its position becomes solidified.

5. The priestly class, highly variable in nature. Frequently it provides moral legitimation for the rulers and governing class.

6. The peasant class, a majority of the population, which bears the main burden of supporting the state and the privileged classes. Peasants are taxed heavily, frequently subscripted into forced labor, sometimes subjected to cruel and inhuman treatment, and almost always required to live at a minimal subsistence level with little more than the bare necessities.

7. The artisan class, a very poor and low status group. Only occasionally is this group able to raise its social standing through apprenticeship systems and guilds.

8. The unclean and degraded classes, such as the untouchables of Hindu society. Found especially in the Orient, they work at offensive occupational tasks, such as tanning.

9. The expendables, including petty criminals, outlaws, beggars, and itinerant workers and comprising about 10 to 15 percent of the population. An agrarian society typically produces more people than it can support without either taking away the privileges of the upper classes or simply ignoring the needs of some of the populace. The latter must support themselves however they can.

Lenski's conception of the proportion of the population and the range in status of these various classes is portrayed in Figure 3.2. Notice that the relative size of the unskilled groups is large in comparison to the size of the governing group and its supporters. A middle class of skilled and trained experts hardly exists, for it is not needed. Instead, what is needed are bodies to till the soil and produce the handicrafts. This means that most people in the agrarian society lack access to or monopoly over resources of skill or training with which to bargain for the economic surpluses. Only those who have gained political power through their supporting roles to the governing class are able to command a share of the wealth. Enormous economic inequalities exist because a ruling class mobilizes political and legal as well as economic means to control wealth, while the bulk of the population has few political or economic resources with which to demand a greater share.

SEXUAL INEQUALITY IN NONINDUSTRIAL SOCIETIES

An examination of the status of women in nonindustrial societies shows that it is not necessarily true that *sexual* equality is most evident in hunt-

Figure 3.2

The relationship among classes in agrarian societies

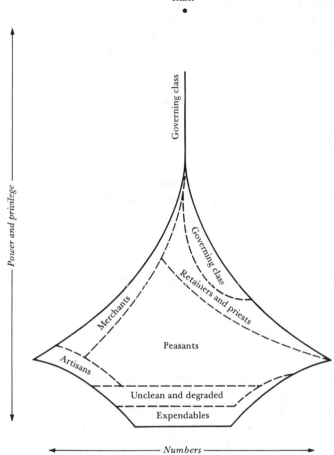

Source: From *Power and Privilege: A Theory of Social Stratification* by Gerhard E. Lenski. Copyright © 1966 by McGraw-Hill, Inc. Used by permission of McGraw-Hill Book Company.

ing and gathering societies and least evident in agricultural societies, as we have found to be true with *social* equality. Nevertheless, economic principles continue to govern the position of women. Friedl (1975) has proposed a concept for which considerable empirical support can be found: It is the right to distribute and exchange valued goods and services to those not in a person's own family that confers power and prestige in all societies. A person's role in production is important, because those who work to produce the goods have a greater chance of being assigned the control over distribution of those goods (producers do not automatically gain such control, however). Male dominance in any society, then, is a consequence of the frequency with which men have greater rights than women to distribute goods outside the domestic group.

There are four patterns of sexual division of labor in hunting and gathering groups that result in different patterns of sexual inequality: (1) both men and women forage for plants for themselves, and there is very little hunting of game; (2) groups of men and women communally hunt animals and gather food; (3) men hunt animals and women gather foodstuffs; and (4) only men hunt and gather. In the first two of these, women provide half or more of the subsistence, and their status tends to be equal to that of men. Because men and women each control some of the resources and services required by the other, both men and women have considerable autonomy, and those of each sex have the basis for acquiring self-esteem. Male dominance in the other two, when it exists, develops primarily out of male control of the distribution of meat. In all societies of which we have record, only men have hunted large game. This is significant because protein is usually considered valuable. Since societal norms require that hunters share their protein with the whole tribe, and since only men hunt, only men have the opportunity to gain the respect and esteem of others by acting publicly as generous hosts and by validating their skill as hunters of valued food. Male dominance is greatest where hunting is the sole source of food, as among the North Alaskan Eskimo, and it is the least, virtually nonexistent, where men and women work together in the major tasks of acquiring and distributing food, as in the Washo of the Sierra Nevada.

It is in the horticultural societies that female equality is most likely to be found (Sanday 1973). The only monopolies possessed by men in horticultural societies are those of clearing the fields and of waging war. Both sexes often participate in the planting, weeding, harvesting, and transporting of crops. There is great variation in the patterns of domestic exchange, because there is no single division of labor whereby men must produce one kind of food or crafts and women another. The most common patterns of sexual division of labor are: (1) men clear the fields, and both men and women raise the crops; (2) men clear the fields, and women raise the crops; (3) men clear the fields and cultivate the crops as well, while women help out.

While it is in the horticultural societies that the position of women most closely approaches equality with men because they participate in control of the fields and of the products (Schlegel 1972), male dominance occasionally develops, particularly when men are engaged in frequent warfare. Friedl (1975, p. 135) suggests that men are the ones responsible for warfare because a population can survive the loss of men more easily than that of women. The male monopoly over warfare often leads to control over the allocation of land. Men rather than women clear the land and, thus, often control it, because new lands are frequently on the border of the territories of other peoples with whom warfare is a potential threat. The consequence is that men, by their control of warfare and land allocation, are more deeply involved than women in economic and political alliances, which are extradomestic and which require for their maintenance the distribution and exchange of goods and services.

The status of women is likely to decline appreciably in agrarian societies. The male monopoly over warfare and thus over political affairs becomes entrenched with the development of the state. In addition, the advent of the plow, which may require intensive labor input, often results in the decreased participation of women in food-producing activities. Sanday (1973) has shown that the percentage of subsistence activities that women perform drops on the average from 45 percent in horticultural societies to 29 percent in agrarian ones. Michaelson and Goldschmidt (1971) have shown that the less women participate in agricultural activities, the more they are dominated by men. Women's declining productivity ultimately leads to their exclusion from the major political and economic spheres of activity.

The minor role of women in production may even decline as an agrarian society industrializes. In the agrarian society, women are at least involved in the manufacture of goods and services (clothing and food processing, for example). As industrialization takes place, however, production shifts almost entirely to factories, which are at first staffed by men. Women's roles become almost trivial if they remain in the home, confined largely to socialization of the young before the educational system takes over and to physical maintenance. This was clearly evident in the United States before World War II. Since then, as more women have entered the labor market, the balance of power between the sexes is being challenged. Even in this case, however, equality is confined primarily to domestic affairs, because women are excluded from top occupational and political positions that control the extrafamilial distribution of resources.

INDUSTRIAL SOCIETIES

THE IMPACT OF INDUSTRIALIZATION ON INEQUALITY In the agrarian society, increased productivity leads to a greater degree of stratification. Surprisingly, while productivity is increased even more in the industrial society, relative inequality of wealth and services is somewhat less than in the agrarian. According to Lenski's estimates, in agrarian societies the top 1 or 2 percent of the population usually receives at least half of the total income of the nation, whereas in industrial societies the top 2 percent receives only about 15 percent of the national income (1966, pp. 309–10). Additional comparisons have been made by economists. Examine Table 3.1, for example, which ranks countries in descending order of per capita

69

incomes (a measure of productivity). Drawing an arbitrary line at Japan shows that the top 5 percent in the more developed countries receive 20 percent or less of the income, while in the less developed countries the share of the top 5 percent averages above 20 percent.

These findings do not mean that industrial societies have achieved equality of income and wealth. The gaps between the rich and poor in modern affluent nations are enormous, in spite of the fact that these nations are best able to eliminate gaps. Thus, for example, the richest quintiles of the population of such societies as Sweden, the United Kingdom, West Germany, Japan, and the United States have incomes five to eight times greater than the poorest quintiles (Thurow and Lucas 1972, p. 4). Nevertheless, "while it is true that the upper classes still benefit disproportionately from the actions of government in every industrial society, it is also true that the masses of ordinary citizens benefit to an extent undreamed of in the agrarian societies of the past, or even in those which still survive" (Lenski 1966, p. 310).

Table 3.1

Distribution of before-tax income within countries, around 1965

Country	Percentage share of income earned by	
	Top 5%	Bottom 40%
United States	15	18
Australia	14	20
Sweden	18	14
France	25	10
United Kingdom	19	15
Japan	15	15
Puerto Rico	22	14
Argentina	29	17
Mexico	29	10
Chile	23	15
Lebanon	34	7
Philippines	28	13
Brazil	38	13
Zambia	38	16
Pakistan	20	18
Sri Lanka	18	14
India	20	20
Tanzania	43	13
Sudan	17	15

Source: Adapted from Paukert, F., "Income Distribution at Different Levels of Development: A Survey of Evidence," *International Labour Review* (Geneva, ILO), Vol. 108, Nos. 2–3 (August–September 1973), Table 6.

The notion of decreased relative inequality in the industrial society over the agricultural one is further substantiated by a detailed cross-cultural investigation made by Robert W. Jackman (1974, 1975), who compared sixty Western and Third World countries on income equality, nutritional and health benefits, and social insurance programs. He found that inequality of income and welfare is definitely less pronounced in the more affluent industrial nations than in the poorer agricultural nations. As a society shifts from agrarian to industrial, an equalization process begins. But it proceeds only up to a point. That is, the continuing maturity and growth of an industrial system beyond a medium level of advancement apparently impede any further equalization. The effect is curvilinear. In the later phases of economic development a threshold is reached whereby the effects of industrialization on social inequality become progressively weaker (R. Jackman 1975, chap. 3). Thus, for example, income is no more equally distributed in the most productive countries — the United States, Canada, and the United Kingdom — than in less productive industrial countries such as Argentina and Israel.

Figure 3.3 is a graph illustrating how income equality is related to a

Figure 3.3

Effects of economic development on income equality in sixty nations

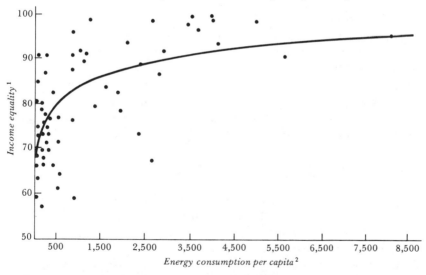

Source: Adapted from Robert W. Jackman, *Politics and Social Equality: A Comparative Analysis* (New York: Wiley, 1975), Figure 3.3. Copyright © by John Wiley & Sons, Inc. Reprinted by permission.

[1] The higher the score of a country, the greater the degree of income equality within it.

[2] Expressed in kilograms of coal equivalents. This indicates "industrial output and sheer economic size."

country's productivity (as measured by energy consumption per capita). Notice that the industrialization process is a diminishing force leading to greater equality as industrialization becomes advanced. This suggests that the pressures that increase equality in the earlier stages of industrialization result from basic changes in the access of the middle masses to important resources and from changes in the division of labor, but that these forces eventually become exhausted as the industrial economy matures.

Why does inequality decline in the industrializing society? Why is there a reversal of the relationship between productivity and inequality that is manifested in the transitions from hunting and gathering to agricultural economies? Any such attempt to identify causes of distributional changes must necessarily be based on a simplified view of a development process. Nevertheless, several hypotheses have been suggested.

The first claims that as wealth increases enormously, *an elite can make economic concessions in relative terms without suffering any loss in absolute terms* (Lenski 1966, pp. 314–15). At the same time, such concessions reduce worker hostility by allowing the middle and lower ranks a greater share in the economic surplus. These concessions are made by allocating greater income returns to those at the middle and bottom levels of the occupational hierarchy, which improve their lots considerably (without appreciably diminishing the wealth and power of those at the top).

The redistribution of wealth is made partly through the processes of government (Baster 1970). R. Jackman found that governments of wealthier countries are able and are also more likely to allocate larger absolute expenditures for nondefense purposes, an action that in the long run reduces inequality (1975, p. 163). In particular, those parts of the public expenditures which are social insurance programs (for example, old age programs, family allowance plans, and unemployment insurance programs) may redistribute wealth so that the economic well-being of those at the lowest economic levels is raised by protecting them against unemployment, poor health, and so forth.

Concessions to the workers in the form of public expenditures also pacify the less privileged, it has been suggested. The reduction of worker hostility is an important function of welfare systems (Piven and Cloward 1971). Welfare programs in the United States and Britain were instituted in the early stages of industrialization to take care of the masses of indigent people who were displaced by the commercialization of agriculture. These systems were continued as industrialization matured because they were useful in quieting discontent and regulating the size of the work force. When unemployment is high and civil disorder increases, relief arrangements are initiated or expanded to ensure political stability. When the civil turbulence subsides, the relief system contracts, expelling those who are needed to populate the labor market. While not redistributing wealth in any substantial way, unemployment and welfare programs give minimal subsistence to large numbers of people who otherwise might be disgruntled with the economic system.

A second hypothesis concerning inequality and industrialization claims that in the complex technological and occupational structures of industrial societies, *the ruling classes must increasingly rely on the expertise of scientists, technicians, and professionals.* These specialists and highly trained workers at the middle levels are not interchangeable without effort, which improves their bargaining position. The managing faction must be interested in the goodwill of the labor force, because technological efficiency requires the initiative and cooperation of the workers (Lenski 1966, p. 314). Thus, because the middle class in the industrial society is large and conducts much of the managing functions of the economic system, it can demand a greater share of the wealth and prestige, while in the agrarian society it is very small and has relatively little bargaining power. At the same time, because a greater proportion of the workers in the industrial society are skilled, they can insist on greater return for their effort. In the agrarian society, much of the work requires relatively low levels of skill. When combined with an oversupply of labor, this lack of skill means that laborers have few resources to bargain with.

The third hypothesis states that *development of highly effective methods of birth control limits population growth,* which, if unchecked, can drain off the capital reserves necessary for economic growth. If unchecked, numbers tend "to increase up to the carrying power of the economy except as limited by the development of tyrannical political systems" that divert the economic surplus to the elite at the expense of further population increase (Lenski 1966, p. 315). R. Jackman's data substantiate that rapid population increase does indeed contribute to heightened inequality levels (1975, pp. 47–49).

Whatever the reasons, it is clear that industrialization has a profound effect on social stratification. Its overall productivity is so great that the absolute gap between top and bottom increases enormously. Yet, it gives more power to the middle class and reduces the relative gap between the top and the bottom. In addition to these effects on economic distribution, industrialization has a number of other consequences for social organization.

THE SOCIOECONOMIC IMPACT OF INDUSTRIALIZATION Industrialization has drastically altered the nature of human life only in the last one hundred years. Its impact has perhaps been even greater than that of the agricultural revolution. Associated social and economic changes are still taking place, and we have yet to see the truly mature industrial society that represents the final stage of the process of industrialization.

The origins of the industrial revolution are relatively obscure; however, one can detect throughout the history of human existence a slowly accumulating base of knowledge and invention that ultimately provided the foundation for the industrial society. The beginnings of mathematics were established in Babylonia, ancient Greece, and Arabia. The water-wheel was developed in the sixth century, the stirrup in the eighth, the horse collar and the rudder in the ninth, and the windmill in the twelfth. The invention of printing in the fifteenth allowed the rapid dissemination of information. Science became significant in the seventeenth century, followed by accelerating technological change in the nineteenth. The nineteenth century also included the development of complex social organization around the activities of science. Research and development became so institutionalized by the twentieth century that the rate of change of both knowledge and technology increased enormously (Boulding 1964, pp. 7–8).

Changes in other areas of social organization as well as in the fields of science and technology likewise provided impetus for the transition. An early example is the change in commercial practices between 1400 and 1700, which set the stage for later financial innovations. The market expanded in scope from local and regional to worldwide, while the increased demand for products was satisfied by the new entrepreneurs who bought raw materials, distributed them among craftsmen, and found markets for the finished products. By the time of the disintegration of serfdom and the guild system in the eighteenth century, the labor supply had developed both mobility and adaptability, two characteristics that are prerequisite for industrial growth.

The spread of industrialization in Europe was a comparatively slow process. England and Belgium experienced industrialization around 1760, but they were not followed by France until nearly a century later nor by Germany until well after the middle of the nineteenth century. It was not until the mid-twentieth century that the industrial revolution reached China and India. Some countries in South America, Africa, and Indonesia are only now beginning to make an industrial transition.

Industrialization of agrarian societies has always been followed by significant developments and changes in a number of areas. Technological changes that have accompanied the emergence of industrial society include the use of new materials (iron and steel, for example), the application of additional energy sources such as electricity and petroleum, the use of new machines that permit increased production and require less human energy, the emergence of the factory system, the development of transportation and communication, and the application of scientific principles to industry.

Nontechnological changes have been fully as significant to the growth of industrialism. One of the most important has been the freeing of a large portion of the labor force from the necessity of farming by improvements in the efficiency of agriculture. In the United States in 1820, for example, 72 percent of all workers were employed in agricultural occupatons, but by 1967 the percentage had dropped to 4 (U.S. Bureau of the Census, 1964c, 1968a). Released from the necessity of farming, workers move to the cities, where they find employment in industry and related occupations. As a consequence, industrial societies are predominantly urban societies. Thus, in 1790 only 5 percent of America's population lived in urban areas, whereas by 1960 this percentage had grown to 70.

Economic changes accompanying industrialization have included a wider distribution of wealth; the development of commercial capitalism, which encourages the entrepreneur; the availability of investment capital; and the shift from land as the chief source of wealth to industrial production. Ownership has tended to pass from individuals and partnerships to joint stock companies (corporations). Control of industry has become somewhat divorced from ownership, and a new class of professional managers has emerged to direct the huge industrial bureaucracies. The scope of knowledge has expanded considerably. At the same time, a much larger proportion of the populace has become educated. Some commentators have regarded the "knowledge explosion" in industrial societies to be a precursor of a new "post-industrial society," in which educated scientists and professors become the center of a new knowledge-based power elite (see Bell 1973, for example). While this idea has not been fully accepted by social scientists, they are more in agreement with Bell's contention that power has become distributed over wider segments of the population and that government has taken on a greatly expanded function of regulating business and labor.

Social changes that have followed industrialization are extensive also. Individuals become less dependent on their kin groups for survival. The family structure tends to change from the extended family group and large household, which characterize agrarian communities, to the small nuclear family living alone in an apartment in the city or in a single-family dwelling in the suburbs. The average number of children per family is much smaller in the industrial society because children are not economically productive; indeed, for the most part they put a drain on the family's resources for support during the many years they spend in the educational system. On the whole, emphasis in the industrial society is placed on achieved status rather than on hereditary placement. The basis for assignment to a class position becomes less the position of the family and more the individual's placement in the occupational structure.

Industrialization and Bureaucratic Power

These technological and economic changes have been accompanied in most industrial societies by extensive changes in social organization, two of which are quite significant for our analysis of the causes of stratification in the industrial society. One is the emergence of bureaucracy as a dominant organizing mode. The other is the increased elaboration and importance of the occupational hierarchy.

THE RISE OF BUREAUCRATIC POWER

We use the term *bureaucracy* here not in the pejorative sense of an inefficient and bumbling organization characterized mainly by red tape, but as a neutral term to denote a way in which people are organized to carry out activities. A bureaucratic organization has the following characteristics, as Weber (in Gerth and Mills 1946) pointed out in his classic essay on the subject:

1. A systematic division of labor, often with a high degree of specialization. Each individual has specific, limited duties to perform.
2. Complementing this specialization is the requirement of thorough and expert training, which means that many positions in the bureaucracy are occupied by professionally or technically qualified specialists.
3. A formal status hierarchy. As Weber noted, "The principle of hierarchical office authority is found in all bureaucratic structures" (p. 197). Each official takes orders from those above and, in turn, gives orders to those below.
4. Structured, written communication channels in the form of official documents. There is a need for files, records, accounts, and internal communications, which keep the entire organization functioning. The presence of such paperwork makes necessary the employment of many clerks, "a staff of subaltern officials and scribes of all sorts" (p. 197).
5. An elaborate system of rules, regulations, and procedures, which outline the rights and duties of the occupants of bureaucratic positions and which guide the day-to-day functioning of the organization.

The classic discussion of bureaucracy was made by Max Weber, whose insights "provided a framework for a systematic theory of formal organization" (Blau et al. 1966, p. 179). Weber considered the consequences of organizing people by a bureaucratic model to be profound. He viewed bureaucratization to be a subtype of a more general process of "rationalization," whereby logical, calculated rules and procedures are substituted for spontaneous, traditional, informal methods. In fact, he believed the rationality of the modern capitalist enterprise to be the single most important factor distinguishing it from more traditional economic forms (Giddens 1973, p. 46). Weber disliked the organization of activity according to rational criteria because he believed that human values were being subverted for the sake of technical proficiency. However, Weber also believed that bureaucracy is the most efficient way to coordinate large numbers of people for the accomplishment of complex tasks. (Consider how difficult it would be to mail a letter from New York City to Hawaii if there were no postal and transportation bureaucracies.) Precision, speed, continuity, reduction of friction, and economy — all are characteristics of bureaucracy.

The bureaucratic mode of organizing people is not new. Bureaucracies existed in ancient Egypt, Rome, the thirteenth-century Roman Catholic church, and China. What is new is the broad extent to which modern activities are carried out under bureaucratic auspices. Many important activities — as diverse as defense, education, and manufacturing, for example — are conducted in bureaucracies. The Pentagon, American Telephone and Telegraph, and state university systems are familiar to everyone.

Underscoring the breadth of activities conducted by bureaucracies is the enormous power they have come to command in modern society. Consider business corporations as one example. Although there are some 11 to 12 million business "enterprises" in the United States, economic assets are concentrated mostly in the hands of the largest 500 or so corporations. A mere 100 firms account for 58 percent of net profits generated by manufacturing (Means 1970, p. 25), employ 45 percent of manufacturing employees (*American Almanac* 1970, Tables 341, 730), make nearly 40 percent of new capital expenditures, and own about half of all assets used in manufacturing (*American Almanac* 1972, Tables 727, 728; Means 1970, p. 14). The high concentration of economic power means a high concentration of capital as well. The two largest corporations, Exxon and General Motors, have combined revenues exceeding those of the states of California and New York, and in combination with Ford and General Electric, their revenues exceed those of all farm, forest, and fishing enterprises (Galbraith 1973, p. 43). The revenues of General Motors alone are greater than those of Japan, Italy, Poland, Canada, and Sweden (Lee and Johnson 1973, p. 32).

The 100 largest corporations carry on a major portion of the nation's business. Exxon, General Motors, Ford, Texaco, and Mobil, the top 5, exhibit the subtle, but pervasive influence that the leading corporations exercise on the economic fates of all Americans. The power of these corporations, discussed further in Chapter 5, inevitably affects the economic well-being of a large proportion of the general population. For example, a decision to automate throws blue-collar workers into unemployment, while opening up white-collar jobs for those with more training. The shutdown of factories can affect the economic health of entire communities. In 1975, the 4 largest employers — General Motors, Ford, International Telephone and Telegraph, and General Electric — fired 200,000 employees (*Fortune* 1976, p. 317). As Anderson describes it,

> the power of the corporate elite substantially influences what the nation's vast resources are used for, what kinds of jobs are available, how many jobs are available, where jobs are available, how much jobs will pay, what kind of education will be needed, how much

profit will be returned in dividends and how much retained, what will be invested in, what people can afford to buy, what the quality of their purchases will be, and how soon they must or think they must buy again (1974, p. 194).

Bureaucracies extend and rigidify social inequality. They extend inequality by creating a more elaborate hierarchy of authority than would exist otherwise, and they rigidify the inequality so produced by setting up rules and rewards to support that system of authority.

Once established, bureaucracy is among those social structures that are the most difficult to destroy (Weber, in Gerth and Mills 1946, p. 228). As Weber suggests, it is the means of transforming community sentiments into rationally ordered societal action. It is superior in power to every resistance of mass action. Its power transcends that of the individual bureaucrat, who is entrusted to specific tasks. Only those at the top are able to change the direction of bureaucratic momentum.

The hierarchy of authority in bureaucracies enables the people at the top to control the workers not at the top. The control factors were enumerated by Bowles and Gintis (1976, p. 55), who were particularly interested in the dominance enjoyed by employers in capitalist enterprises (a generalization that holds for other kinds of bureaucracies as well). They maintain that control is exerted through the organization of the productive process itself. Labor is arranged hierarchically within the corporate bureaucracy and is ordered by an elaborate authority system. A meritocratic ideology (one that promotes rule based on "merit") justifies the inequities of authority. The power of workers is reduced further by internal cleavages of race, sex, and education. Bowles and Gintis point out that currently about two-thirds of American paid workers are employed in either corporate or state bureaucracies, where "control over work processes is arranged in vertical layers of increasing authority with ultimate power resting nearly exclusively in the top echelon of owners and managers" (1976, p. 61).

Control over lower-level workers in a bureaucracy is facilitated by the hierarchical organization of labor and by the fragmentation of tasks, which divides the workers on different levels against one another. Maximizing the social distance between hierarchical levels by hiring on the basis of educational credentials, social class, life style, race, sex, and age diffuses worker solidarity further. Not only is the total power of workers vis-à-vis employers thereby reduced, but superiors also become alienated enough from workers to act only in the interests of the organization and according to the dictates of their own superiors (Bowles and Gintis 1976, pp. 83–84).

The employer's goals thus are served by maintaining and increasing the social distance between groups of workers. For example, while employers generally resist wage demands whenever possible, under pressure they sometimes do accede to demands of workers, but mainly to those demands that are nonthreatening to their security of control, that increase the social distance between groups of workers, or that acknowledge the legitimacy of the allocation of roles in the organization.

> Thus it is not surprising that some workers themselves often demand (and are granted) higher wages or privileges which de facto exclude other groups of workers on the basis of educational credentials, racial and sexual characteristics, and artificially maintained skill differences. Such demands are relatively cheap and help to enforce the internal stratification and fragmentation of worker solidarity (Bowles and Gintis 1976, p. 84).

The hierarchy of bureaucracy must be legitimated by drawing on general cultural values; otherwise, it might appear unjust and be overthrown. It is for this reason, Bowles and Gintis suggest (1976, p. 82), that a superior must always have a higher salary than a subordinate, whatever the conditions of relative supply of the two types of labor. It is for this reason that in the United States, with its characteristic racial and sexual prejudices, blacks and women cannot be placed above whites or men in the line of hierarchical authority. It is for this reason that young people do not ordinarily boss old people and the less educated do not have authority over the more educated.

THE OCCUPATIONAL HIERARCHY

The inequality of authority that is reinforced by the bureaucratic mode of organization goes hand in hand with the hierarchy of occupations. Occupations can be ranked both by the attitudes of people and by the degree of advantage inherent in them. Some occupations give a higher income, entail more pleasant duties, involve more exercise of power, allow more fringe benefits, and are more conducive to a sense of self-worth than are others. These tend to be the ones near the top of the bureaucracies, so their privilege is reinforced. Consider these examples:

A service station attendant must take orders from his immediate boss and from the station owner. He works in the cold and rain as well as in the heat of summer. He performs the routine and dirty tasks of filling gas tanks, washing windows, and changing tires, often for a grumpy public. For this, he is paid a minimum wage that is less than adequate to support his family. His wife does not wish to work outside the home because they cannot afford child-care services for their three children, yet she occasionally works part-time as a night janitor in a nearby department store, which is about the only job her six years of schooling qualify her for. The

79

husband also often takes a second job during his off hours just to cover the most essential expenses. The family's status in the eyes of others is not particularly high, and they are used to being ignored and unnoticed.

The family of the bricklayer attached to a large construction company fares somewhat better. His union has been able to bargain for a better wage for him, and he has some job security, and some fringe benefits. His wife, who has a high school diploma and who could find a job as a typist, does not work while her children are younger, and it is a source of pride to herself and her husband that the family can survive economically without her working. The bricklayer has more dignity on the job than does the filling station attendant, because others respect his skills and they see that he is making a living wage. He has more leisure, because he does not need to moonlight at a second job. He receives more respect from his children. Still, he and his wife are not able to save a great deal of money, and it is doubtful whether they will be able to afford to send their children to college.

The chemist working for a leading corporation earns a considerable salary, never worries about unemployment, receives long vacations, and occupies a position of respect in the community. His wife has a career as a high school administrator. They send their one preschooler to a quality day-care center, and their other two children attend private schools. The chemist belongs to the Rotary Club, and they both are patrons of the local art museum. They enjoy a high sense of self-worth, and others listen to their opinions.

As these examples illustrate, in modern industrial societies, occupational conditions have a strong impact on the quality of human existence. A person's occupation affects his or her authority and autonomy on the job, economic survival, social relations, health and emotional well-being, child-rearing attitudes, and a host of other characteristics. This impact is maximized in the industrial societies, where the hierarchy of occupations has achieved greater complexity than in any other type of economic system. In industrial societies — and in all systems where the influence of ascribed statuses has declined — a person's adult status is determined more by his or her occupation than by any other single variable (including income!). Examining how occupations are arranged will be worth our while. It is instructive to look first at the nature of the occupational hierarchy (which jobs are more privileged and which are less?), then at cross-cultural similarities in the occupational distribution, and finally at the distribution of jobs in the United States.

THE MEASUREMENT OF OCCUPATIONAL INEQUALITY   The first problem encountered in the attempt to understand the occupational hierarchy involves measurement. Occupations as such have no inherent scalar properties, as do incomes or educational achievements. Some way of classifying occupations that makes sense relative to inequality must be used. The simplest classification scheme is that which divides jobs into white-collar and blue-collar categories. Although this dichotomy has been used in mobility studies, it grossly oversimplifies the reality of occupational stratification. An early attempt to make more meaningful distinctions was made in 1897 by William C. Hunt of the Bureau of the Census, who placed all workers into the categories of proprietor class, clerical class, skilled worker class, and laboring class. Several other occupational classification schemes were devised in the late 1800s, but each had its particular weaknesses.

Finally, Alba M. Edwards constructed an eleven-category classification that was used in the 1940 and 1950 censuses and set the basic model for all subsequent classifications developed by the Bureau of the Census. The 1960 census incorporated a related detailed occupational classification containing 479 categories condensed into eleven major occupational groups. These groups are listed in Table 3.2. The class designations on the right in the table are those traditionally appointed labels that correspond to the various occupational classifications.

There has been some question among stratification students as to the degree of accuracy of even an eleven-part occupational breakdown in portraying social rankings of modern Americans. One of the problems is that some occupational categories are too broad to delineate consistently one social stratum rather than another. For example, the category of "salesworkers" includes sellers of computers and heavy industrial machinery, whose qualifications include college degrees and technical knowledge and who make incomes in the top 1-percent bracket, as well as retail salespeople in the local clothing store, who may have completed one year of college and who receive a below-average income. "Farmers" is another category including people of widely varying levels of affluence and privilege. Even those categories which are more internally consistent — such as "professionals" — include a range of status positions (from nightclub dancer to Supreme Court judge, for example).

The occupational scales devised in the last thirty years have concentrated on a large number of specific occupations in order to avoid the oversimplifications of two-, four-, or eleven-part classifications. The most important scale was one developed by North and Hatt at the National Opinion Research Center (NORC) in 1947, which measures the relative prestige standing of ninety occupations. To create this scale, the researchers asked respondents their opinion of the "standing" of each of the ninety occupations. From the answers, scores ranging from 0 to 100 were attached to the occupations, which could then be ranked in order of perceived importance. (See Chapter 7 for a fuller discussion of the methodology used by NORC, and see Table 7.1 for the results). In general, the

Table 3.2

Occupational classifications of the U.S. Census, with income and educational medians for males in each category, 1971

Occupational classifications	Income[a]	Education[b]	Traditional class labels used by social scientists and journalists
Professional, technical and kindred workers	$12,518	16.5	Upper and Upper-Middle Classes
Managers, officials, and proprietors, excluding farm	12,721	13.0	
Sales workers	10,650	13.2	Lower-Middle Class, White-Collar Class
Clerical and kindred workers	9,124	12.6	
Craftsmen, foremen, and kindred workers	9,627	12.1	Working Class, Blue-Collar Class, Upper-Lower Class
Operatives and kindred workers	7,915	11.3	
Service workers, excluding private household	7,111	12.1	
Private household workers	n.a.[c]	n.a.[c]	Low-Income Group, Poverty Class, Lower Class, Lower-Lower Class
Farmers and farm managers	4,308	11.9	
Laborers, except farm	6,866	10.0	
Farm laborers, foremen	3,752	8.1	

[a] Income is median earnings of full-time male workers in 1971, from U.S. Bureau of the Census, "Money Income in 1971 of Families and Persons in the United States," *Current Population Reports,* series P-60, no. 85, Table 55.

[b] Education is years of school completed by employed males twenty-five to sixty-four years old in March 1972, from U.S. Bureau of the Census, "Educational Attainment: March 1972," *Current Population Reports,* series P-20, no. 243, Table 4.

[c] Not applicable, because the number of male private household workers was considered by the census bureau to be too small for meaningful analysis.

highest ratings were given to the occupations of government officials and professionals. Clerical workers and skilled laborers received middle ratings; unskilled laborers and service workers received the lowest ratings.

Some very important work has been done using occupational prestige scales such as the one developed by NORC, work that has increased our understanding of the occupational prestige hierarchy. But prestige is only one form of inequality, and some sociologists later became curious about how the prestige of an occupation is related to other characteristics of the occupation, particularly its economic power and control over resources. Recent attempts to measure occupational inequality, then, have focused on multidimensional indexes ranking specific occupations according to their average yearly incomes and to the educational accomplishments of their incumbents. It is argued that measures of income and education tap two separate aspects of social status — livelihood and social interests — and that therefore a scale that measures both of them would be more valuable. The average level of education completed indicates the level of formal training required. Average income levels indicate the rewards of occupations. A way of measuring and scoring the interaction of these two variables would go a long way toward revealing the inequities of training and reward inherent in the occupational structure.

The best-known of the multidimensional indexes is Duncan's Socio-Economic Index (SEI), which scores the detailed occupational categories of the U.S. Bureau of the Census so that they are highly correlated with the prestige scores of the North-Hatt NORC occupational prestige scale (see Duncan 1961; Blau and Duncan 1967). A scale that can be used in conjunction with census data is, of course, very useful.[1] In the initial stage of the scale construction, Duncan selected forty-five of the occupations rated in the NORC scale. Data on two variables for each of the forty-five occupations were obtained from the 1950 census of population: the percentage of male workers with four years of high school or a higher level of educational attainment and the percentage of males with incomes of $3,500 or more in 1949 (both characteristics subsequently were age-standardized). The variables were weighted so that the overall score of an occupation would approximate its NORC prestige score.[2]

The correlation between the NORC prestige scores of the forty-five occupations, on the one hand, and the educational and income measures, on the other hand, turned out to be .91, implying that "five-sixths of the variation in aggregate prestige ratings was taken into account by the combination of the two socioeconomic variables" (Blau and Duncan 1967, p. 120). This seemed to justify assigning similarly weighted scores on the basis of income and educational standing to a large number of the occupational titles used in the census in order "to give near-optimal reproduction of a set of prestige ratings" (Blau and Duncan 1967, p. 119).

A less well known occupational scale is Bogue's Index of Socioeco-

---

[1] This type of scale was first developed by Canadian social scientists. See Charles (1948) and Blishen (1958).

[2] The formula $X_1 = 0.59X_2 + 0.55X_3 - 6.0$ provides the index score for an occupation, where X_1 is the percentage of "excellent" or "good" ratings received by an occupation in the prestige survey, X_2 the proportion of men in the occupation with 1949 incomes of $3,500 or more, and X_3 the proportion of men in the occupation with four years of high school or higher educational attainment.

nomic Achievement (SEA), which is interesting because it was designed to measure *relative* inequality (Bogue 1969). It is a ratio scale with a zero point and equal intervals; this design allows the absolute and relative differences between categories to be examined. For example, consider the breakdown of SEA scores by occupation:

Occupation	SEA score
Professional workers	39
Managers	37
Sales	29
Craftsmen	27
Clerical	26
Operatives	23
Service workers, farmers, and farm managers	20
Laborers	18
Private household workers	14
Farm laborers	12

Bogue observes that whereas managers and professionals stand apart from the rest by a rather wide margin, and farm laborers and private household workers are considerably below all the rest, the intermediate groups are clustered together with average differences of only two or three points. Craftsmen (traditionally classed as blue-collar workers) have an SEA score about equal to that of sales and clerical workers. Finally, workers who change from being farm laborers or private household workers to being operatives improve their status by almost 100 percent, but those who change from operatives to sales or clerical workers improve their status by only 13 percent (1969, pp. 442–43). These findings suggest that there is a wide gap between the highest status levels and the middle status levels, that a smaller gap exists between the lowest and the middle, and that the various middle levels are not clearly differentiated from each other at all, but rather merge and blend.

Bogue computed the SEA scores for over four hundred occupational categories utilized by the 1969 census. For most of the occupations, the value of the educational component differed little from the value of the income component, indicating perhaps that most people are paid salaries consistent with the average salaries received by their education-age group, regardless of the occupation.

This last generalization does not hold for all the occupational groups, however; leaders of business receive a larger income than their educational level would lead us to suspect, whereas farmers, laborers, and private household workers receive less. Bogue hypothesized that the "economic dominance" of an occupational group occurs when individuals are in a unique position to divert the flow of income to themselves and that "economic subordination" occurs when the group is less powerful. Those occupations that are clearly economically dominant (receive at least $1,000 more income per year than one would expect on the basis of their educational attainment and age) include physicians, bank managers, lawyers, airplane pilots, professors of statistics, dentists, physicists, economists, railroad conductors, real estate brokers, stock and bond sales personnel, photoengravers, tool and die makers, and operatives in the manufacture of photographic equipment and petroleum refining.

Occupations that are economically subordinate (receive at least $1,000 less than one would expect on the basis of educational attainment and age) include the clergy, college professors, librarians, nurses, religious workers, social workers, public school teachers, farmers, file clerks, secretaries, hucksters and peddlers, shoemakers, former members of the armed forces, auto attendants, laundry and dry cleaning operatives, truck drivers, and operatives in the manufacture of floor coverings and wood products (Bogue 1969, p. 456).

The economically subordinate occupations are primarily either intellectual, moral, and service occupations or operative and craftsmen occupations in the less economically powerful parts of industry, frequently those that are not unionized. A number of them are occupations filled mainly by women. Several occupations receive incomes so far below what would be expected that one suspects they are objects of economic exploitation: nurses, elementary teachers, library attendants, hospital attendants, fishermen and oystermen, kitchen workers, farm owners and tenants, laborers in food canning, and farm laborers.

Both the Duncan and the Bogue scales indicate considerable occupational inequality in the United States, as this is measured by income and educational differences. The causes of this inequality and the processes by which an individual comes to occupy a particular niche in the hierarchy are taken up in later chapters. It is sufficient to note here that there is a wide range of economic and educational characteristics associated with various jobs and that those occupations that receive the most respect in American society also tend to be the ones that require more restrictive educational credentials for entry and that give greater monetary reward to their incumbents.

CROSS-CULTURAL SIMILARITIES IN OCCUPATIONAL PRESTIGE   One important result of the creation of measures of occupational inequality by sociologists such as North and Hatt, Duncan, and Bogue is that inequalities in different countries can be compared. The NORC prestige scale in particular has been used to make such comparisons. Originally, the sociologists conducting cross-cultural research expected to find major differ-

Table 3.3

Correlations between prestige scores (or ranks) given to comparable occupations in six national studies

	U.S.S.R.	Japan	Great Britain	New Zealand	United States	Germany
U.S.S.R.		.74	.83	.83	.90	.90
Japan			.92	.91	.93	.93
Great Britain				.97	.94	.97
New Zealand					.97	.96
United States						.96
Average correlation	.84	.89	.93	.93	.94	.94

Source: From Alex Inkeles and Peter H. Rossi, "National Comparison of Occupational Prestige," *American Journal of Sociology* 61 (1956). Copyright © 1956 by The University of Chicago. Reprinted by permission of The University of Chicago Press.

ences from nation to nation in how occupations are ranked. They were well aware of the wide diversity of stratification systems revealed by historical analysis. So they were somewhat surprised to discover that all modern complex societies have similar configurations of occupational roles. This was first indicated in a comparison of the prestige rankings of occupations in six industrial countries made by Inkeles and Rossi in 1956. In each country, a sample of the population had been asked to rank the relative "importance" of a list of occupations, as a sample of Americans had been asked by the NORC. The six countries were the United States, Germany, Great Britain, New Zealand, Japan, and the Soviet Union — all highly industrialized, but differing somewhat in culture, social structure, and history. When the rankings from the various countries were statistically correlated, Inkeles and Rossi found remarkable similarity from country to country in the evaluation of occupations. These results are shown in Table 3.3. Twelve of the fifteen coefficients of correlation were above .90, and only one was below .80.[3]

The American and German occupational prestige hierarchies were more similar to those of other nations, while the hierarchies of Japan and the Soviet Union, the two most recently industrialized nations, were less

[3] For an explanation of correlation coefficients, see Chap. 2, n. 4. In the Inkeles-Rossi research, what are being correlated are the rank orders of occupations according to their prestige ("perceived importance"). So, if the rankings of two countries are highly correlated, then an occupation considered to be important in one country will be considered important in the other. Doctors will be near the top of the ranking in both cases, and street sweepers will be near the bottom.

similar. But in all cases, the professions, high government posts, and top industrial positions occupied the highest places in the prestige hierarchy; semiskilled and unskilled positions consistently fell near the bottom. Inkeles and Rossi interpreted the extremely high level of agreement in occupational ratings to be a product of industrialization:

> a great deal of weight must be given to the cross-national similarities in social structure which arise from the industrial system and from other common structural features, such as the national state.... there is a relatively invariable hierarchy of prestige associated with the industrial system, even when it is placed in the context of larger social systems which are otherwise differentiated in important respects (1956, p. 339).

From other sources, however, came additional surprises: Cross-national comparisons of occupational prestige ratings are similar not only when highly industrialized nations are compared, but also when industrialized nations are compared with agricultural societies. D'Souza (1962) found a .98 correlation between the rankings made by Indian students and those made by British students; another correlation made between the rankings of 939 high school students in Indonesia and those of the Inkeles-Rossi study was reported to be .90 (Thomas 1962). Tiryakian (1958) computed a correlation of .94 between the ratings of adults in four rural communities and the one urban community of the Philippines and the ratings of the six industrialized nations.

Finally, overall summaries of all the intercorrelations show high similarity of occupational prestige across nations. Hodge, Treiman, and Rossi (1966) found an average correlation of .91 between United States ratings and those of twenty-three other nations. In a comparison of sixty nations, the largest sample yet, Treiman (1977) found an overall correlation of .83 between the United States ratings and those of the other nations. Treiman also used a statistical computation showing the average correlation of *all* countries with each other. This turned out to be a little lower, but still very high: .79, as compared to the Inkeles and Rossi correlation of .91 (p. 93). It indicates that when more countries are included in the sample (thus increasing the chances of getting a country with a less similar occupational ranking), the correlation drops, but it still is quite substantial.

The similarity ratings seem to exist across population subgroups within a nation as well as across nations. Rankings are similar regardless of the social class of the rater, his or her region, or place of residence (North and Hatt 1947; Treiman 1977). The cultural distinctiveness of the country does not seem to matter, either. Treiman classified fifty-five societies into eight cultural categories — the intercorrelation among categories remained high at .81.

In spite of the overwhelming stability of occupational prestige hierar-archies across time and space that these researches have revealed, there are several types of minor variation. One is related to industrialization. Industrialized societies tend to be more similar to each other than to non-industrialized societies (albeit the correlations with the latter are still quite high). The differences between the industrialized and nonindustrialized nations in occupational prestige are mainly found in the ranking of blue-collar jobs (Hodge et al. 1966; Treiman 1977). While the reasons for this have not been explored, it has been speculated that blue-collar work can be organized in a wider variety of ways than can white-collar work. All nation-states need bureaucratic superstructures to handle the affairs of state, and this need produces similar managerial and professional roles at the tops of the political and economic hierarchies. The organization of blue-collar work, however, is more variable, depending on the nature of the technology. A shoemaker in a highly industrialized society, for exam-ple, is a worker in a shoe factory, while the one in a more traditional country is an independent craftsman (Treiman 1977, p. 131).

Even within industrialized societies, manual jobs are more likely than nonmanual jobs to vary from country to country. In the Eastern Euro-pean socialist countries in particular, skilled manual positions have come to have a higher social status than the lower white-collar positions (Parkin 1971, pp. 156–58; Penn 1975; Treiman 1977). The history of these coun-tries suggests that political intervention based on ideological principles played a major role in structuring inequality. Following communist sei-zures of power, there occurred radical reforms in the educational system, implementation of equalitarian income policies, and expropriation of landed estates and factories, all serving, as Parkin (1971, p. 143) noted, "to alter substantially the former balance of class advantages." These re-forms did not bring about equality (as the studies of occupational rank-ings reveal), but they did serve to increase the status of blue-collar jobs.

Treiman (1977, pp. 144–45) points out that the elevation of the pres-tige of manual work in the socialist countries is supported by "structural arrangements" — that is, by higher wages and better working conditions — at the same time that the wages and the prestige levels of clerical work-ers are downgraded relative to the rest of the world as a whole. The important point he makes is that it is not the ideological differences be-tween socialist and nonsocialist countries alone that led to the differences in the prestige of clerical and manual jobs, but rather the ideological dif-ferences *supported by* differences in wages and working conditions. Differ-ences in privilege lead to differences in prestige.

In general, then, it seems evident that occupations are rated in a basi-cally similar way throughout the world. Those occupations that are professional and higher managerial tend to be in the top positions, fol-lowed by technical, semiprofessional, and lower managerial occupations, then by lower white-collar and skilled blue-collar jobs, and finally by unskilled service and laboring jobs. To give an idea of the prestige ordering of occupations, Table 3.4 presents the internationally standardized prestige scores of fifty common occupations.

Why do these similarities in occupational rankings exist? A number of interpretations have been offered. The functionalist explanation, you will recall, suggests that occupational roles cross-culturally perform similar functions and therefore are similarly rewarded. For example, everywhere a leader or set of leaders — president, king or queen — is needed to maintain order, and so everywhere these individuals are encouraged to perform by being rewarded with higher prestige. Conflict theory, by contrast, emphasizes power — similar occupational roles in different cultures tend to have similar levels of access to power, and therefore they tend to be similarly held in awe by others. The king, for example, is able to appoint and to behead, so he is considered "important."

Table 3.4

Internationally standardized prestige scores of fifty common occupations

Occupation	Prestige score	Occupation	Prestige score
Physician	77.9	Mechanic, repairman	42.8
University professor	77.6	Shopkeeper	42.4
Lawyer, trial lawyer	70.6	Printer	42.3
Head of large firm	70.4	Typist, stenographer	41.6
Engineer, civil engineer	70.3	Policeman	39.8
Banker	67.0	Tailor	39.5
Airline pilot	66.5	Foreman	39.3
High school teacher	64.2	Soldier	38.7
Pharmacist	64.1	Carpenter	37.2
Armed forces officer	63.2	Mason	34.1
Clergyman	59.7	Plumber	33.9
Artist	57.2	Sales clerk	33.6
Teacher, primary teacher	57.0	Mail carrier	32.8
Journalist	54.9	Driver, truck driver	32.6
Accountant	54.6	Bus or tram driver	32.4
Civil servant (minor)	53.6	Miner	31.5
Nurse	53.6	Barber	30.4
Building contractor	53.4	Shoemaker, repairer	28.1
Bookkeeper	49.0	Waiter	23.2
Traveling salesman	46.9	Farm hand	22.9
Farmer	46.8	Street vendor, peddler	21.9
Electrician	44.5	Janitor	21.0
Insurance agent	44.5	Servant	17.2
Office clerk	43.3	Street sweeper	13.4
Garage mechanic	42.9		

Source: From Donald J. Treiman, *Occupational Prestige in Comparative Perspective* (New York: Academic Press, 1977), Table 7.2. By permission.

A further contrast in views has been held by culturalists and structuralists. The culturalists, the most outstanding example being Parsons, argue that cultural features of a society, and especially its common value orientations, determine the relative prestige of occupations. If a society values war, its soldiers will be revered. Structuralists, such as Inkeles and Rossi, counter that structural arrangements determine both the values and the occupational prestige structure. Industrialization produces certain common problems and common tasks, which lead to common evaluations of occupations that meet those needs and perform those tasks.

Most interpretations start out with a discussion of the division of labor. Treiman (1977), for example, points out that a division of labor into specialized tasks is efficient. Some tasks can be better performed by individuals with particular personal traits. In addition, most tasks require learned skills. For these reasons, any society developed enough to support specialists will evolve a division of labor. In general, the larger the society, the more highly developed will be that division of labor (Blau 1973, pp. 258–70).

Treiman further argues that the same complement of occupational roles is found in all complex societies, primarily because all societies face certain problems that must be solved, certain "functional imperatives" (Aberle et al. 1950) that must be met, if they are to survive. Consider these problems. In every society food must be grown, so farmers are needed. In addition, tools, clothing, housing, and other goods must be manufactured, so craft specialists emerge. Next there must be some mechanism for exchanging and distributing goods, so commercial and trading specialists develop. All societies must have the actions of their members coordinated and order maintained, so political roles come into play. In addition, the culture in all societies must be transmitted and expanded, so educators, scientists, and engineers are needed.

Second, Treiman (1977, p. 8) suggests, complexity carries its own "organizational imperatives." Some social roles require other roles, and some depend on others. In the complex society, for example, large-scale organizations require directors to coordinate tasks and clerks to keep records. They cannot exist without managers and secretaries.

Stratification emerges out of an occupational structure, Treiman maintains, because the specialization of functions into distinct occupational roles inherently gives rise to differential control over scarce and valued resources. These resources are of three main types: (1) resources of knowledge and skill; (2) resources of control over economic assets; and (3) resources of authority — that is, legitimated control over the activities of others (Weber 1947, p. 152). Treiman comments:

> We can expect that in all societies intellectual or "professional" roles will require the greatest skill and knowledge and achieve the

greatest monopoly of crucial expertise, that owners and managers of land or capital will exercise the greatest economic power, and that political officials, together with managers of other enterprises, will exercise the greatest direct authority over the actions of others (1977, p. 16).

The occupational differences in access to resources eventually give rise to differences in privilege. This occurs for a variety of reasons. In some cases, people in occupations that monopolize valued skills, such as physicians in the United States, can drive up the price paid for their services. In addition, once an occupational group has gained superior control over resources, it will often use that control to maximize its advantage. For example, it may manipulate the political system to secure special rights and privileges; it may use its control over capital to create opportunities for the accumulation of personal wealth or to set its own salaries; or, if its members are organized and monopolize essential skills, it may use collective bargaining to acquire advantages.

> In short, occupational groups are able to convert their command of scarce resources — skill and knowledge, economic power, and authority — into material advantage both by virtue of the superior market position command of these resources provides and by virtue of the ability to directly manipulate the system that such power creates. For this reason, there is a general consistency in the skill, economic control, authority, and material reward hierarchies of occupations in all societies, and a similarity in these hierarchies across societies (Treiman 1977, p. 19).

The theory just outlined, building on a long tradition of thought coming from scholars such as Weber, Parsons, and Lenski, incorporates parts of both functionalist and conflict theory. A division of labor exists because it is functional. But that division of labor gives rise to power differentials among occupations. In the struggle for dominance, powerful occupations come to enjoy the greatest privilege.

THE AMERICAN OCCUPATIONAL STRUCTURE   Many of the generalizations developed in the previous sections are supported by a more detailed analysis of a specific country. When they are applied to a particular nation — say, the United States — their implications for the individual become clearer. They suggest how the prevailing trends and forces of a historical era determine the kinds of jobs available, the nature of work to be done, and the opportunities for mobility that are available, all of which impinge upon the life of the individual very directly.

Consider the distribution of work in the United States. About 20 percent of the male workers are skilled craftsmen and foremen (carpenters, tool and die makers, machinists, electricians, mechanics and so forth) and another 20 percent are semiskilled operatives who assemble goods in factories, operate machines, drive trucks, and so on. These two groups perform most of the productive work. They are directed by a group of managers, officials, and proprietors, who constitute 14 percent of the male work force. "Thus roughly 50 percent of the total [male] employed labor force is engaged in occupations pertaining to the performance of technical, nonagricultural tasks that result in the production of some good or service desired by the population" (Bogue 1969, p. 265).

Besides these groups is a very large professional and technical group, comprising 14 percent of the total, which provides professional services, teaches the upcoming generation, and conducts the research required to maintain improvements in products and services. These are followed in size by clerical workers, who operate computers and office machines and keep records, as well as service workers who provide services to businesses and individuals, maintain law and order, and see to it that the public is accommodated in places of public use. The number of persons engaged in agricultural endeavors is relatively small. The remainder of the labor force is made up of unskilled workers, who are busy moving, lifting, and carrying tools and materials, and of private household workers such as caretakers, gardeners, and chauffeurs. The employment of females is somewhat different from that of males. There is a greater concentration of females in clerical and service occupations, and less are employed in managerial and craft occupations. In addition, a sizable percentage of women work outside the employed labor force at rearing and maintaining the young. See Table 3.5 for a statistical summary of the occupational distribution.

Young people entering the job market are channeled into one or another of the job categories just described. The probabilities that they will enter any one category are related to the proportionate size of that category, which in turn is related to economic and historical trends.

Correspondingly, the history of the occupational structure in the United States has been one of shifts and adjustments, as the economy has moved from predominantly agricultural to early industrial and, more recently, to advanced industrial stages. During these transitions, some occupations have expanded, some have diminished, and others have been created. The increasing need for more highly educated and trained personnel has meant an overall opening of higher-level positions, providing considerable opportunity for upward social mobility.

The most important shift has been the dramatic increase in the proportion of professionals and other white-collar workers, accompanied by a decline in the number of farmers and laborers. This has meant that the middle class has expanded, while the laboring category has shrunk. When

Table 3.5

Percentage distribution of persons in major occupational categories in the United States in 1970, by sex

Major occupational group	Male		Female	
White-collar workers	41.3		61.1	
Professional and technical workers		14.1		15.1
Managers and proprietors		14.3		4.6
Clerical workers		7.2		33.9
Sales workers		5.7		7.5
Manual and service workers	53.8		37.3	
Manual workers	47.0		15.8	
Craftsmen and foremen		20.4		1.1
Operatives		19.4		14.3
Laborers		7.2		0.4
Service workers	6.8		21.5	
Private household workers		0.1		5.0
Service workers		6.7		16.5
Farm workers	4.9		1.6	
Farmers and farm managers		3.3		0.3
Farm laborers and foremen		1.6		1.3

Source: U.S. Bureau of Labor Statistics, 1970, table A–19.

the American economy made the first transition from a predominantly agricultural society in the 1800s to an industrial one in the 1900s, the proportion of people involved in what Colin Clark (1952) calls the "primary extractive" occupations — agriculture, fishing, forestry, and mining — declined tremendously (from 75 percent in 1820 to 8 percent in 1960), while the proportion involved in the secondary industries of basic manufacturing increased.

In the second transition, from an early industrial stage to one of advanced industrialization, the economy shifted toward a greater dominance of the "tertiary industries," those which provide services (such as trade, finance, transportation, health care, recreation, education, and government). Increasingly important in this stage are the activities of large-scale corporate organizations. Corporations need managers, clerical workers, scientists, and technicians, in addition to the workers who carry out the actual manufacturing. All of these occupational groups have expanded in size since 1940. They are filled by people who in earlier days would have become farmers or unskilled laborers.

In effect, the shift from an agricultural to an industrial economy has seen the movement of people from the farms to the cities, from work requiring less education and skill to that requiring more, and from self-employment to wage and salaried employment for larger organizations. In the 1800s and early 1900s, it was relatively easy for uneducated immigrants, farm children, and offspring of the poor to get jobs at manual labor — but increasingly this avenue has been closed off. Today, people whose interests and experiences direct them toward declining occupational categories such as farm work and unskilled labor are more likely to face unemployment and to receive a low income than those whose occupational abilities are more in demand.

Many children of farmers and laborers have responded to the shifts just described by getting the training necessary for skilled blue-collar and clerical jobs. At the same time, some of the children of skilled laborers, clerks, and salespersons have moved into professional and managerial occupations, via educational channels. The overall result has been fairly high rates of social mobility during the last half-century (see Chapter 6).

Whether or not such opportunities for mobility will continue to be available to today's and tomorrow's children is anyone's guess. However, it is clear that mobility opportunity in the United States is primarily due to the presence of shifts in the distribution of occupations (Hauser et al. 1975a). That the economy has now reached a point at which the current distribution of jobs fits well the future needs for personnel seems entirely plausible. If so, we can anticipate increasing competition for the higher-status jobs and retarded opportunities for social mobility at all levels.

Summary

Referring back to the basic paradigm put forth at the end of Chapter 2, we can now support the proposition that the economic institution sets the basic form that social stratification takes. This does not mean that the economic system determines all aspects of stratification — there is indeed considerable variation among societies even of the same general economic type. It does mean that the nature and range of feasible forms of social organization are influenced and limited by the level of technological development.

When the division of labor is simple and the economic surpluses are small, social inequality takes the form of prestige differentiations that never result in hereditary classes. Only when surpluses increase to a medium level, as in the agrarian society, is it likely that permanent patterns of strata inequality will develop and be perpetuated by institutional systems. The economic surpluses, when concentrated within an elite group, provide the means for mobilizing the labor force to carry out the decisions of the elite. The development of the state facilitates the transfer of economic dominance into political dominance. Then, there emerge powerful ruling groups that tend to become entrenched and stabilized.

The supportive institutions of religion, education, family, and ideology help to legitimate the stratification and to prepare new members for participation in it. Less privileged strata receive material and status rewards depending on their importance to the elite and on their capacity to demand rewards. (This explains in part the diminishing of inequality as a society industrializes on an agrarian base. Classes other than the elite gain in bargaining resources as white-collar and blue-collar skills increasingly become an integral part of industrial production.)

In the industrial society, stratification is extended, rigidified, and reinforced by the bureaucratic mode of organization, which institutionalizes a hierarchy of authority (and, correspondingly, a hierarchy of privilege). Because the basis of individual class placement shifts from family membership to occupational ranking, the individual's involvement in the job structure and in bureaucracies is of considerable importance to his or her class placement. In the next chapter, we continue our analysis of economic stratification by examining the extent of economic inequality in the United States and the way in which incomes are determined.

4 ECONOMIC RESOURCES IN THE UNITED STATES

IN THE PRECEDING CHAPTERS we have seen that the nature of class in any society can be fully comprehended only with an understanding of how and to whom economic resources are distributed. It has been emphasized that the institutions of society create and sustain the practices by which some people become wealthy while others are kept poor. This chapter describes the consequences of those institutional practices, as revealed in the distribution of wealth and income among individuals. Three types of economic inequalities are examined: (1) inequalities in *wealth* — assets such as capital, land and property — which is concentrated within the "propertied" class; (2) inequalities of *income* — the flow of money that comes from wages, salaries, and profit — which provides the subsistence for most laborers; and (3) inequalities of *transfer payments* — the economic support provided by the society for those who are nonparticipants in the economic system. We concentrate particularly on wealth and income in the United States, although information on other societies is included for comparison purposes. In the final section we discuss the sources of income inequality, applying the perspectives of the functionalist and conflict theories.

96

The Distribution of Economic Resources: Wealth

It may seem a truism that the person who possesses wealth is advantaged. However, because there are those who dispute the luxury of being rich by pointing out the equally obvious fact that money does not bring happiness, or that the rich are not free, let us mention certain benefits that accrue to the wealthy. First, and obviously, the wealthy person is advantaged because she or he can secure the essentials for survival that the society has to offer — shelter, food, and health care. Affluent Americans on the average spend more money on food than do the less affluent. They are more likely to receive health care and more likely to receive health care that is high quality. They are quite likely to own a home or two. Money for essentials is not a worry. As *Fortune* describes the attitude toward spending shared by its sample of people who live on high incomes: "The affluent do not spend frivolously or riotously, but they do spend casually. Nobody seems to keep a budget" (Main 1968).

Second, the economically advantaged are also able to acquire those possessions that contribute to diversion, comfort, and a sense of well-being. The 257-foot private yacht owned by a wealthy businessman (described in Tobias 1975) — with its year-round crew of thirty-one, its sixteen bathrooms and thirty touch-tone telephone extensions, its walk-in freezer for the several hundred pounds of meat flown in for every weekend cruise, and its gold-lettered Cartier stationery at $1.75 per sheet — undoubtedly contributed to the comfort and diversion of its owner and his guests and probably enhanced his sense of well-being as well.

Third, if one is wealthy, large numbers of people can be mobilized to satisfy one's wishes. In fact, it is partly through the purchase of the labors and loyalties of others that economic advantage leads to political advantage. In this way, wealth becomes an important source of power in society, particularly political power.

Finally, in addition to these important survival and instrumental uses, wealth generally bestows honor. It wins the respect of others by coming to signify in the minds of many the importance of the person who possesses it. From the individual's point of view, as Veblen (1934) argued, wealth may be desired because the esteem of others leads to self-esteem. This suggests that one reason Americans consume goods is that they wish to win the respect of others and thereby to maintain their own self-respect. Goods become a symbol of money in American culture, money becomes a symbol of social worth, and social worth becomes a basis of self-esteem. As one of *Fortune*'s respondents put it, "When I go to buy a car I want a car of quality make. . . . It signifies success and good living to others as well as myself" (Main 1968).

In recognition of the importance of wealth and income in a money-based society, the question of how much wealth various segments of the population *should* command easily becomes an ideological and political issue. Some argue that if everyone has the necessities of life, it really does not matter that a few individuals live in luxury. What harm is caused by the Rockefeller family's control of billions of dollars, as long as no one is starving? It is also occasionally suggested that the existence of a small, very wealthy class of leaders, industrialists, and successful professionals not only sets a good example for others, but also creates quality goods, new products, artistic innovations, and cultural activities. Besides, those people who work harder and sacrifice more to achieve economic success *should* receive greater rewards than those who sit idle. Moreover, concentrations of capital are needed to spur further economic growth through research, development, and investment.[1] We see in these arguments the policy implications that sometimes emerge from a functionalist explanation of stratification. Because stratification serves very useful purposes, it should not be substantially tampered with.

The counterarguments suggest that the extremes of wealth are not justified by hard work and responsible activity. The magnitude of existing inequality is considerably out of proportion to the degree of contribution, sacrifice, and work load of the favored classes. Moreover, many people who work hard and are responsible are rewarded with no wealth at all. It is pointed out that the possession of wealth in itself provides a source of income that is unrelated to human accomplishment. Much wealth results not from the individual's own achievement, but from accidents of birth or from advantages gained because of social origin. While concentrations of capital may be necessary for research and development, the wealthiest corporations possess amounts of capital far greater than their research and investment needs. The surplus capital is ultimately distributed as dividends to those individuals who already were wealthy enough to own stock. Finally, some argue that it does indeed matter that the Rockefeller family is worth billions, even if no one starves, because they use their wealth, as do other wealthy families, to make and enforce decisions affecting the economic fates of everyone else. Besides, it is unjust for one small segment of society to experience such enormous advantages at the expense of others.

These views, basically rooted in conflict theory, recommend alterations of the system of stratification on the grounds that it is not only exploitative, but also dysfunctional. Some suggest a totally equal distribution of wealth, because only then will the greatest number of individuals in society experience the most satisfaction and only then will power be effectively decentralized (Kuznets 1962; Peckman 1969, p. 22). Others merely

[1] These arguments are well presented in Jouvenal 1967, pp. 6–13; Meade and Hitch 1967, pp. 1–5; and Pigou 1967, pp. 134–39.

advocate the elimination of the extremes of wealth and poverty, which means that no one suffers unduly.

Strong value judgments often come into play when these issues are debated in ordinary conversation, which tends to degenerate from rational discussion because of the intensive emotions evoked. Insight is more likely if the debaters are aware of the dimensions of wealth and income inequalities and of the processes that bring them about. To promote that insight, the following sections outline the facts of who and how many are rich and poor and how they came to be that way.

THE EXTENT OF INEQUALITY OF WEALTH

Although it is difficult to construct an overview of the distribution of wealth, government surveys indicate a pronounced concentration of wealth among a few. In 1960–1961, one such survey found that the richest 20 percent of families and individuals possesses 76 percent of the wealth of the United States (Federal Reserve System 1966). Further, a mere 5 percent of the households owns 50 percent of the wealth. This wealth consists of assets such as businesses or professions, investments in securities and real estate, money held in trusts, oil royalties, patents, homes and automobiles, and money in checking and savings accounts. Most consumers, even some with substantial incomes, have very little wealth at all — roughly 10 percent either have no equity in any assets or are actually in debt (they have "negative equity"); 16 percent have equity ranging from $1 to $999. Nearly two-thirds own assets worth less than $10,000 — enough for the average family to cover furniture, clothes, a television set, a secondhand car, and a little emergency money in the bank. See Figure 4.1 for a graphic portrayal of these facts.

SOURCES OF WEALTH

From figures on sources of income, we learn that the richer segments of the population are likely to be "capitalists": the major part of their subsistence is derived from their incomes from stocks, bonds, and property holdings (that is, their income from dividends, interest, and capital gains). In order to substantiate this generalization, Ackerman et al. divided all taxpayers into three categories according to their source of income: (1) "small businessmen" — farmers, self-employed professionals, and those who own unincorporated businesses; (2) "wage-earners" — those whose incomes result exclusively from wages and salaries; and (3) "capitalists" — individuals who receive income in the form of dividends and capital gains (1971, pp. 27–28). The results, shown in Table 4.1, do indeed indicate that the wealthier the individual, the more likely he or she is to receive income from dividends and capital gains increases. Thus, those taxpayers whose taxable incomes exceeded $100,000 received only 15 percent of their income from wages and salaries, while the bulk of it,

Figure 4.1

Wealth of consumer units, by amount of wealth, 1962

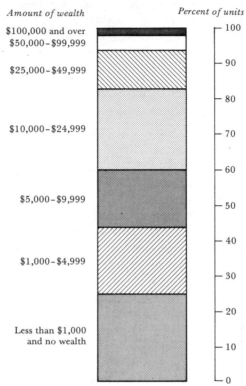

Source: U.S. Office of Management and Budget, 1973; Federal Reserve System, 1966, Table 5/16.

67 percent, came from dividends and capital gains. These figures reveal clearly that the 1 percent of the population that owns 25 percent of the total wealth are property owners whose wealth is invested in stocks, bonds, loans, and real estate (Smith and Franklin 1974).

The occupational histories of the very wealthy are instructive. It has been estimated that some two thousand to three thousand of the top wealth holders earn salaries of $50,000 to $1 million through their jobs as executives in large corporations. Another two thousand to three thousand are independent entrepreneurs with small businesses or highly paid professionals, such as surgeons who perform expensive operations. An even smaller number are popular entertainers or athletes who receive large rewards during brief careers of stardom (Lundberg 1968). But these are

Table 4.1

Source of income of taxpayers by size of taxable income

	Percentage receiving taxable income of			
Source of income	Under $20,000	$20,000– 50,000	$50,001– 100,000	Over $100,000
Wage and salary	87	51	34	15
Small business	9	31	32	13
Capitalist holdings	3	15	28	67
Other (pensions and annuities)	1	3	6	5
Total	100	100	100	100

Source: Summarized in F. Ackerman et al. "Income Distribution in the United States," *Review of Radical Political Economics,* Vol. 3, 1971. Reprinted by permission.

not the wealthiest of the wealthy, and most of these are not millionaires. For the most part, the fortunes of these categories of people are small in comparison to those of the wealthiest. That is, most of the wealth holders identified in government surveys fall in the lower brackets of the wealth distribution. It is among the top 1 percent of the population that we find the multimillionaires. Their wealth has two major origins: (1) speculation in such fields as oil, insurance, and real estate; and (2) inheritance.

Some of these "centimillionaires" were identified in a 1968 *Fortune* (p. 156) study. Although the list is now somewhat out-of-date, it serves to illustrate the occupations and sources of wealth. At the top of the list, possessing wealth of $300 million to over $1.5 billion were oil speculators such as J. Paul Getty, H. L. Hunt and his son N. Bunker Hunt, and R. E. Smith; and business heads such as Edwin Land of Polaroid, William McKnight of Minnesota Mining and Manufacturing, and Charles Mott of General Motors. In the total list, some families were represented more than once: the Rockefellers, Mellons, Schaifes, du Ponts, Fords, and Whitneys had more than several family members on the list. Speculators represent about half the top wealth holders. They tend to come from prosperous middle-class origins, but because they do not inherit any great reserves of capital, they have to build their fortunes during their own lifetimes. Both J. P. Getty and Howard Hughes inherited substantial amounts, but added greatly to their inheritance through investment. Lundberg summarizes *Fortune*'s descriptions of thirty-five individuals who acquired their wealth since World War I (1968, chaps. 4 and 5). The majority, including such multimillionaires as H. L. Hunt, Joseph P. Kennedy, and C. W. Murchison, became prosperous through real estate operations or oil prospecting. Very few were builders, inventors, or creators of new industries; few became wealthy through manufacturing or banking, the preserves of the old rich. Many of them had limited formal education, and there is little evidence that the college graduates made use in their careers of what they learned in college (Lundberg 1968, p. 109). Many of them created their fortunes by taking advantage of special government shelters over oil, insurance, and real estate. For example, Clint Murchison, whose father owned the First National Bank in Athens, Texas, started his fortune by buying up $50,000 in oil leases of land on which a wildcat oil strike was rumored at a poker game; the following day he unloaded the leases for more than $200,000. With this initial capital, he was able to buy and trade oil companies, eventually expanding his holdings to life insurance companies, bus and transit lines, a publishing house, a glass company, and a railroad.

Building a fortune in one lifetime is possible, as the above cases attest, but a more common way to acquire wealth is to inherit it. Estimates of the percentage of top wealth holders who have inherited their wealth range from 50 to 60 percent, and some suggest that nearly *all* of the 0.5 percent of the wealthiest multimillionaires inherited their assets.

In these cases, large extended *families* become meaningful units of analysis. The du Pont family, for example, which numbers 1,600 in all, includes 250 people who are financially elite. The combined wealth of 4 of the du Ponts has been estimated to be between $600 million and $1.2 billion. *Fortune* was able to identify 45 individuals holding $75 million or more who belong to prominent families having a history of successful investment (Lundberg 1968, chap. 4). These families attempt to invest their resources so that the total holdings are increased. On the death of the parent generation, the holdings are usually divided among the surviving family members, but in many cases family members combine their fortunes to form dynasties of wealth. Four members of the Mellon family, for instance, control between $1.6 billion and $2.8 billion, which they have invested in stock concentrations in Aluminum Corporation of America, Gulf Oil Company, Bethlehem Steel Corporation, Pittsburgh Coal Company, and others. As we point out in the next section, because of the large size of the fortunes involved, inherited family wealth plays no small role in the running of corporate affairs.

USES OF WEALTH

For the truly wealthy, there are no economic barriers to the placement of children in elite preparatory schools and universities, the purchase of luxurious homes, the participation in expensive recreational activities, frequent travel abroad, and the acquisition of other material goods that fit the stereotyped life style of the rich. As Rose Kennedy put it, "Obviously not everybody in the world has two very nice houses, a couple of boats, a tennis court, a swimming pool, and a Rolls Royce or two in the family."

Wealth, of course, can purchase these things. Less apparent to the common eye are those more far-reaching uses of wealth, the economic investments that protect and increase the wealth holdings. Over half of the wealth owned by the top 1 percent of wealth holders is invested in corporate stocks and bonds; one-fifth is in land and buildings; only 10 percent is in cash, either in checking or saving accounts (data calculated from Smith and Franklin 1974). Wealth is primarily used to control property and capital resources rather than to purchase goods for personal consumption. This usage naturally allows the wealth holders to have considerable influence in business and industry. There is continuing debate among social scientists about the relative influence of wealthy families compared to corporate managers in controlling corporate business (with estimates of the percentage of the largest corporations that are run by management rather than families ranging from 20 to 90; see Zeitlin 1974 and Allen 1976 for discussion); but there is little doubt that wealthy families still have a noteworthy impact on corporate action.

For the average American, however, wealth is limited to the ownership of a home, an automobile, and a few personal possessions. For the average American, economic assets come only from income, not from dividends and capital gains from invested wealth.

The Distribution of Economic Resources: Income

To understand the economic resources possessed by the majority of the population, we need to turn from wealth and look at income data. Yet, the latter give a misleading picture of economic inequality, because *the inequality resulting from the distribution of income is far less than that resulting from the ownership of wealth* (see Figure 4.2, p. 104). While the wealthiest 20 percent of all families receive only 41 percent of all family income, they own 76 percent of all assets; likewise, the poorest 20 percent has 6 percent of total income, but only 0.2 percent of the private assets. This is one reason that changes in income taxation (or other forms of income redistribution) can only minimally affect the distribution of wealth in the society.

Although the greatest inequalities are found in the possession of wealth, *there are striking disparities also in the distribution of income.* In 1974 around 12 percent of all Americans — 24.3 million people — lived in poverty (less than $5,034 for a nonfarm family of four); at the same time, 22 percent of all families received incomes of over $20,000, which is sufficient for considerable economic comfort (see Figure 4.3 and Table 4.2, pp. 105–106). The average income of the richest 5 percent of all families was twenty-two times that of the poorest 5 percent of all families.

In terms of international comparisons, the United States has neither the greatest nor the least inequality of income. According to a major study

Figure 4.2

*Distribution of wealth: consumer units ranked by
wealth, income, and age, 1962*

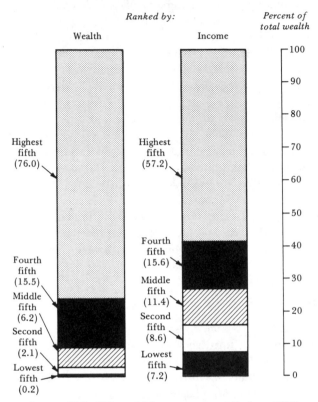

Ranked by: *Percent of
total wealth*

Wealth   Income

Source: U.S. Office of Management and Budget, 1973;
Federal Reserve System, 1966, Tables 5/15 A and B.

of comparative data on income distribution made by the Organization for
Economic Cooperation and Development, France stands out as the Western country in which the largest gap exists between rich and poor. This
fact created a stir in France when it was first published in 1976 because
it provided ammunition to the battle then being fought over French
wages and prices by giving unwitting support to the French left, which
had argued that income was unfairly distributed, and to a claim made by
the West German chancellor that communists were active in countries
where there had been inadequate social gains, such as France. According
to the study, Australia and Japan are the least unequal countries in pre-
tax inequality, and France is joined by the United States as the most unequal countries. In posttax distributions, however, as shown in Table 4.3
(p. 107), the three most equalitarian countries are Sweden, the Nether-

Figure 4.3

Distribution of family income by race, in the United States, 1974

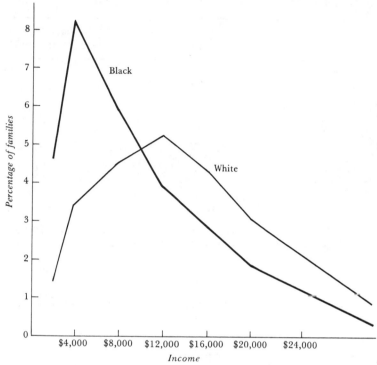

Source: U. S. Bureau of the Census, "Money Income in 1974 of Families and Persons in the United States," *Current Population Reports,* series P–60, no. 101, Table 25.

lands, and Norway, and the least are Germany, France, and Spain (Farnsworth 1976).

TRENDS IN THE INEQUALITY OF INCOME

There has been an overall increase in the standard of living of the American people since the depression of the 1930s. The median (middle) family income increased between 1950 and 1974 from $3,319 to $12,836 (U.S. Bureau of the Census 1974). Even when price inflation is taken into account, these figures show a rise of 387 percent in family buying power. However, it should be noted that when the overall standard of living rises, it is more difficult for the poor to survive with incomes that would have been adequate during earlier periods. For example, as automobile ownership increases, public transportation declines; as telephones become common, it is hard to job hunt without one; when more can

105

Table 4.2

Distribution of income of families and unrelated individuals in the United States, 1974

Income	Percentage of families	Percentage of unrelated individuals
Under $3,000	5.5	34.9
$3,000 to $6,000	12.1	26.9
$6,000 to $9,000	13.5	16.6
$9,000 to $12,000	14.9	10.0
$12,000 to $15,000	14.1	5.5
$15,000 to $20,000	18.1	} 4.9
$20,000 to $25,000	10.3	
$25,000 to $50,000	10.4	1.0
$50,000 and over	1.1	0.2
Median income	$12,836	$4,439

Source: U.S. Bureau of the Census, "Money Income in 1974 of Families and Persons in the United States," *Current Population Reports,* series P–60, no. 101, calculated from Table A.

afford indoor plumbing, privies become illegal; and so forth. As Jencks et al. put it, the "cost of living" is the cost of participating in the social system, and this cost tends to be at least half the average income (1972, pp. 5–6). In 1972 those who could not meet that cost included nearly 9.6 million families (17.4 percent of the total). Thus, there is a strange paradox that population pockets are created in which considerable economic anguish can be experienced even as the overall level of life style improves. For this reason, to get a true picture of the well-being of a nation's people, one must look at changes in levels of inequality as well as in overall standard of living.

Claims that inequality is either increasing or decreasing escalate every so often into public debate. One optimistic and egalitarian belief places great faith in progressive taxation, a system whereby higher-income groups pay higher rates of taxes. The belief is that this has resulted in a radical redistribution of income, with the rich getting poorer over time and the poor getting richer. The facts are not exactly consonant with that belief. Changes in the distribution of wealth and income in the United States over the last fifty years are difficult to measure,[2] yet several conclusions can be drawn from available data. *Between 1917 and 1930 there was no*

[2] For instance, there are differing measures of the income-receiving units as well as of the income itself. The use of families rather than individuals tends to understate inequality, and failure to take account of nonmoney income tends to exaggerate inequality.

Table 4.3

International comparisons of income inequality: distribution of after-tax income

Country	Percentage received by the poorest 10 percent of households
France	1.4
Spain	1.5
Australia	1.6
Canada	1.6
United States	1.7
Britain	2.4
Norway	2.4
Sweden	2.6
Japan	2.7
Germany	2.8
Netherlands	3.2

	Percentage received by the richest 10 percent of households
Sweden	18.6
Netherlands	21.6
Norway	21.9
Britain	23.9
Canada	24.7
Australia	25.2
United States	26.1
Japan	27.8
Spain	28.5
France	30.5
Germany	30.6

Source: From Clyde H. Farnsworth, "In France, the Income Disparity Is Great," *New York Times,* September 10, 1976, p. D1. © 1976 by The New York Times Company. Reprinted by permission.

change in the share of income received by the top 5 percent of the population, which received around 25 percent of the total income in that time period (H. Miller 1966, p. 19; Thurow and Lucas 1972, pp. 41–42). *But inequality of income began to decrease in the 1930s* and declined somewhat during the years of the depression and World War II. The diminishing in income inequality during this period was the result of (1) the tremendous reductions in business and property incomes during the depression; (2) the narrowing of wage differentials between low-paid workers and higher-paid skilled workers and salaried employees as a result of wage controls and labor controls when "full employment" was reestablished during the war (Solow 1960, p. 104); (3) the institution of a very progressive income tax (more progressive than the current income tax) that converted a regressive tax system into a mildly progressive tax system (Kuznets 1962; Thurow and Lucas 1972); and (4) the increase in employment of married women, which increased the incomes of the lower- and middle-income families (Lydall 1959, p. 23). (Nevertheless, some economic historians believe that the data overestimate the decline in income inequality [Smolensky 1971, pp. 95–96]. They point out that the statistics do not take account of capital gains and income supplements in the form of expense accounts, automobiles, and stock options, which accrue to a much greater extent to individuals at the upper end of the income distribution than to those at the lower.)

Since the war, income inequalities have continued at nearly constant levels. Even though all income groups receive more income than before, there has been no appreciable narrowing of the income gap between the rich and the poor in the last thirty years. In this time period, the richest 20 percent of all families received about 41 percent of the total personal money income, while the poorest 20 percent received only about 6 percent. Thus, the leveling that started with World War II has played out, and the income gap is being closed very little, if any. One convenient way to portray these trends is to rank all families by size of income and then to divide the ranking into fifths. Figure 4.4 shows that when the average income of each fifth is compared to the overall average, there was very little relative change between 1947 and 1971. The stability of shares is remarkable.

There is also little empirical justification for the fairly widespread belief that a radical redistribution of income has been brought about by progressive income tax legislation passed in 1941. The higher-income groups have been able to avoid severe taxation by shifting their incomes away from a taxable fixed-salary basis to incomes gained from tax-free interest, capital gains, inheritance trusts, bonds, and other low-tax investments. Deductions and exemptions further erode the progressiveness of the tax rates.

"Tax reforms" frequently benefit the wealthy. The Tax Reform Act of 1969, for example, reduced the average tax rate for those people with incomes in the $9,000–$10,000 adjusted gross income bracket by .01 percent and the rate for those with an adjusted gross income of $1 million or more by 23 percent (Pechman 1971, pp. 298–99). Income taxes fall most heavily on the middle-income groups, and sales and social security taxes bear most heavily on the lower-income groups. The net result is that the distribution of income of all classes is practically the same after

Figure 4.4

Ratio of the mean income of each fifth of families to the mean income of all families, 1947–1971 (families ranked by size of income)

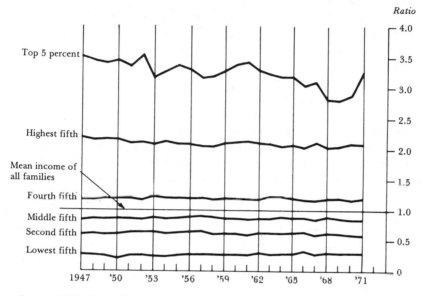

Source: U.S. Office of Management and Budget, 1973, Chart 5/9.

taxes are collected as it is before (Pechman and Okner 1974; Thurow 1961, chap. 4; Kolko 1962, pp. 32–33).

SOURCES OF INCOME

The income receivers are the people who make the economic system go. They are not the ones who make the final decisions, but instead are those who carry on the everyday affairs of the industries and the service institutions. Their salaries and wages are, for the most part, predetermined and preset; they are employed by others and thus are subject to being fired by others. They sell their services and their labors and receive a wage in return.

Their incomes come from their work, which can be divided into several major categories, ranked by size of income. See Table 4.4, which gives the average earnings of the most prevalent occupations in 1970. The males fall into several main categories — professional, managerial, lower-white-collar, blue-collar, and laboring. The occupations with the highest incomes, which we might term "upper-income professionals," are lawyers and judges, physicians and dentists, and airline pilots. Closest to these in income are "managers and administrators," who are mainly middle-level managers in large corporations, heads of school systems, top-

109

level managers in smaller businesses, and owners of smaller businesses. Earning only slightly less than managers are "middle-income professionals" — accountants, architects, engineers, social and physical scientists, and professors.

Then there seems to be an income gap. Considerably below these three groups in income are "lower-white-collar" workers — schoolteachers, engineering and health technicians, and salesmen. Following them closely are skilled laborers — carpenters and plumbers, mechanics and machinists. Earning only slightly less than skilled laborers are clerical workers — bookkeepers and postal clerks.

Another gap separates lower-white-collar and skilled laborers from the semiskilled workers — the operatives such as meat cutters and textile workers and the truck and taxicab drivers. These are separated by another income boundary from laborers, farmers, and service workers (cooks and guards). Finally, receiving the lowest incomes by far is a relatively small group of farm laborers and private household workers.

The ranking of the occupations held by women is basically similar to that for men, yet women make far less in income than men on the average; this is a striking fact revealed by the occupation-income data. The highest-paying category for women, professionals, receives lower incomes than the male semiskilled occupations. Within the professional category, the highest-paying occupations for females are computer specialists, mathematicians, and social scientists, but even these make less than male skilled laborers. The sexual and racial discrimination hinted at in Table 4.4 is explored more fully in later sections of this chapter.

Table 4.4

Income of the labor force, by occupation, sex, and race, 1970

Occupation	Median earnings of total (1969 dollars)	Median earnings of blacks (1969 dollars)
Male	7,610	5,194
Professional, technical, and kindred workers	10,735	7,763
Accountants	10,627	8,447
Architects	13,447	10,433
Computer specialists	11,193	9,565
Engineers	13,149	10,444
Aeronautical and astronautical	14,766	12,228
Civil	12,675	9,262
Electrical and electronic	13,361	11,180
Mechanical	13,436	9,924
Lawyers and judges	15,000+	12,914
Life and physical scientists	12,155	9,752
Chemists	11,740	9,799

Table 4.4 (continued)

Occupation	Median earnings of total (1969 dollars)	Median earnings of blacks (1969 dollars)
Physicians, dentists, and related practitioners	15,000+	14,380
Dentists	15,000+	15,000+
Pharmacists	12,175	10,993
Physicians, medical and osteopathic	15,000+	15,000+
Health technologists and technicians	7,368	6,932
Religious workers	6,232	5,118
Social scientists	13,356	11,045
Social and recreation workers	7,925	7,581
Teachers	9,151	7,878
College and university	11,313	9,004
Elementary and prekindergarten	8,013	7,521
Secondary	9,002	7,991
Engineering and science technicians	8,680	7,321
Draftsmen and surveyors	8,415	6,751
Electrical and electronic engineering technicians	9,374	8,618
Technicians, except health, engineering, and science	11,364	7,913
Airplane pilots	15,000+	8,974
Writers, artists, and entertainers	9,444	6,589
Managers and administrators, except farm	11,277	7,439
Buyers, purchasing agents, and sales managers	11,612	7,520
School administrators	13,256	11,393
Specified managers and administrators, public administrators	10,634	9,253
Other specified managers and administrators	9,970	6,573
Managers and administrators, n.e.c., salaried	12,196	7,660
Managers and administrators, n.e.c., self-employed	8,857	5,611
Sales workers	8,451	5,425
Insurance agents, brokers, and underwriters	10,024	7,207
Real estate agents and brokers	10,295	7,869
Sales representatives, manufacturing industries	11,488	7,273
Sales representatives, wholesale trade	9,576	6,623
Sales clerks, retail trade	5,532	4,511
Salesmen, retail trade	7,848	5,965
Salesmen of services and construction	9,177	6,066
Clerical and kindred workers	7,265	6,157
Bank tellers and cashiers	3,860	4,440
Bookkeepers and billing clerks	7,417	6,439
Mail handlers and postal clerks	7,976	7,536
Craftsmen and kindred workers	8,172	5,920
Apparel craftsmen and upholsterers	6,422	5,161
Bakers	6,956	5,871

Table 4.4 (continued)

Occupation	Median earnings of total (1969 dollars)	Median earnings of blacks (1969 dollars)
Cabinetmakers	6,514	4,770
Construction craftsmen	7,660	5,120
Carpenters	7,001	4,545
Excavating, grading, and road machine operators	7,314	4,945
Electricians	9,334	7,151
Masons and tile setters	7,644	5,230
Painters, construction and maintenance, paperhangers	6,156	4,826
Plasterers and cement finishers	7,123	5,384
Plumbers and pipe fitters	8,997	5,546
Foremen, n.e.c.	10,070	7,721
Linemen and servicemen, telephone and power	8,893	6,153
Locomotive engineers and firemen	11,292	8,252
Mechanics and repairmen	7,597	5,999
Air conditioning, heating, and refrigeration	8,103	6,128
Aircraft	9,196	7,805
Automobile, including body	6,887	5,580
Radio and television	7,393	6,104
Metal craftsmen, except mechanics	8,816	6,992
Machinists and job and die setters	8,368	6,866
Sheetmetal workers and tinsmiths	8,665	6,663
Tool and die makers	10,086	8,033
Printing craftsmen	8,581	6,418
Compositors and typesetters	8,341	6,327
Pressmen and plate printers, printing	8,428	6,431
Stationary engineers and power station operators	8,855	7,332
Operatives, except transport	6,730	5,582
Assemblers	6,947	6,391
Checkers, examiners, and inspectors, manufacturing	7,996	6,889
Garage workers and gas station attendants	2,768	3,801
Laundry and drycleaning operatives, n.e.c.	4,791	4,384
Meat cutters and butchers	7,467	5,906
Mine operatives, n.e.c.	7,281	5,655
Packers and wrappers, except produce	5,319	4,727
Painters, manufactured articles	6,780	5,935
Precision machine operatives	7,894	6,761
Sawyers	4,966	3,332
Stationary firemen	7,915	6,376
Textile operatives	5,241	4,363
Welders and flamecutters	7,625	6,600
Other metalworking operatives	7,060	6,704
Other specified operatives	6,380	5,257
Miscellaneous and not specified operatives	6,901	5,698

Table 4.4 (continued)

Occupation	Median earnings of total (1969 dollars)	Median earnings of blacks (1969 dollars)
Transport equipment operatives	6,903	5,431
Bus drivers	6,682	7,024
Taxicab drivers and chauffeurs	5,113	5,127
Truck drivers and deliverymen	7,049	5,231
Laborers, except farm	4,617	4,207
Construction laborers	5,155	4,366
Freight, stock, and material handlers	4,535	4,553
Other specified laborers	4,019	3,503
Miscellaneous and not specified laborers	5,021	4,583
Farmers and farm managers	4,822	1,749
Farm laborers and farm foremen	2,570	1,862
Paid farm laborers and farm foremen	2,619	1,866
Unpaid family workers	1,559	1,484
Service workers, except private household	5,100	4,359
Cleaning service workers	4,679	4,220
Food service workers	2,935	3,657
Cooks, except private household	3,986	4,729
Busboys and dishwashers	1,389	1,671
Health service workers	4,425	4,595
Personal service workers	5,112	4,327
Protective service workers	7,997	6,810
Firemen, fire protection	9,488	8,409
Guards and watchmen	5,885	5,782
Policemen and detectives	8,962	8,391
Private household workers	1,891	1,945
Female	3,649	3,008
Professional, technical, and kindred workers	6,034	6,172
Accountants	5,818	6,078
Computer specialists	7,763	7,438
Librarians	6,009	6,414
Mathematical specialists	7,177	8,080
Life and physical scientists	7,526	7,498
Registered nurses, dietitians, and therapists	5,586	5,487
Registered nurses	5,652	5,687
Dietitians	4,431	3,992
Therapists	(NA)	(NA)
Health technologists and technicians	5,182	5,252
Social scientists	7,678	7,845
Social and recreation workers	6,166	5,812
Teachers: College and university	6,346	6,269
Elementary and prekindergarten	6,439	6,573
Secondary	6,723	6,832
Other teachers	2,283	4,897
Engineering and science technicians	5,417	5,220
Technicians, except health, engineering, and science	5,040	5,707
Writers, artists, and entertainers	4,187	4,728
Actors and dancers	3,975	4,120

Table 4.4 (continued)

Occupation	Median earnings of total (1969 dollars)	Median earnings of blacks (1969 dollars)
Authors, editors, and reporters	5,476	6,251
Managers and administrators, except farm	5,495	5,235
Buyers, purchasing agents, and sales managers	5,530	5,486
Restaurant, cafeteria, and bar managers	3,777	3,293
School administrators	7,600	9,461
Managers and administrators, n.e.c., salaried	6,011	5,648
Wholesale and retail trade	5,411	4,448
Managers and administrators, n.e.c., self-employed	3,886	3,201
Wholesale and retail trade	3,640	2,898
Sales workers	2,238	2,635
Demonstrators, hucksters, and peddlers	1,048	1,747
Insurance, real estate agents, and brokers	4,835	4,247
Sales clerks, retail trade	2,226	2,553
Salesmen, retail trade	2,949	2,715
Clerical and kindred workers	4,232	4,152
Bank tellers	4,190	4,382
Bookkeepers	4,480	4,642
Cashiers	2,429	2,791
Counter clerks, except food	3,027	3,030
Enumerators and interviewers	1,557	2,701
File clerks	3,460	3,667
Office machine operators	4,547	4,674
Payroll and timekeeping clerks	5,164	5,531
Receptionists	3,396	3,680
Secretaries	4,798	4,704
Stenographers	5,213	5,371
Telephone operators	4,252	3,896
Typists	4,046	4,204
Operatives, except transport	3,635	3,342
Assemblers	4,133	3,881
Bottling and canning operatives	2,727	2,636
Checkers, examiners, and inspectors; manufacturing	4,357	3,939
Dressmakers and seamstresses, except factory	2,644	3,015
Laundry and drycleaning operatives, including ironers	2,907	2,921
Graders and sorters, manufacturing	3,077	3,031
Packers and wrappers, except produce	3,566	3,312
Sewers and stitchers	3,390	3,261
Textile operatives	3,903	3,395
Transport equipment operatives	2,574	3,152
Laborers, except farm	2,988	2,929
Farmers and farm managers	2,277	1,810

Table 4.4 (continued)

Occupation	Median earnings of total (1969 dollars)	Median earnings of blacks (1969 dollars)
Farm laborers and farm foremen	1,087	778
Paid farm laborers and farm foremen	1,112	779
Unpaid family workers	810	673
Service workers, except private household	2,320	2,727
Cleaning service workers	2,294	2,436
Chambermaids and maids	2,060	2,217
Food service workers	1,806	2,228
Cooks, except private household	2,150	2,291
Health service workers	1,637	2,110
Waiters and food counter workers	2,974	3,682
Nursing aides, orderlies, and attendants	3,263	3,454
Practical nurses	4,236	4,773
Personal service workers	2,748	2,688
Hairdressers and cosmetologists	3,067	2,557
Private household workers	986	1,152
Private household workers, living in	1,829	2,403
Private household workers, living out	948	1,123

Source: U.S. Bureau of the Census, U.S. Census of Population: 1970, Detailed Characteristics, final report, PC (1) D1, United States Summary.

As revealing as figures on wealth and income distributions may be, the picture of economic inequality is completed only after we look at how well those people fare who cannot or do not receive wages and salaries and who own no income-producing property.

Economic Support for the Unemployed: Transfer Payments

As the American economy changed from an agricultural to an industrial one, the economic dependence of the members of society on employment within the industrial occupational structure increased. Very few Americans now find it a viable option to own or rent land to raise their own food and produce their own goods. The fact of the current economic dependency of citizens raises the question, What happens to those individuals who are unable or are prevented from working for wages or salaries? We are thinking here of those who are too old (or too young) to receive salaried employment, the physically or mentally disabled and infirm, those responsible for child care, and those unemployed by labor layoffs, shutdowns, or recessionary conditions. One adaptation employed by most modern societies is a system of transfer payments, defined by the International Labor Organization (1954, p. 11) as measures that protect

115

the public from the economic stress occurring as a result of stoppage of earnings in sickness, unemployment, or old age and after the death of the main earner; that make available public medical care as needed; and that subsidize families bringing up young children.

Industrial societies to a greater or lesser degree provide "transfer payments" or "social insurance programs" to support those who receive no subsistence income from employment. Of seventy-six nations studied, for example, two-thirds had work injury programs; over half had programs to deal with sickness, old age, invalidism, and death; and about one-third had family allowance plans and unemployment insurance programs (Cutright 1965, p. 539). As suggested in the previous chapter, the relationship between the energy consumption level of a society and its expenditures on social insurance programs is curvilinear (Jackman 1975; Pryor 1968, p. 52). While the proportion of public moneys spent on social insurance programs tends to increase when an economy shifts from agrarian to industrial, such proportions are extremely varied among industrialized nations (Pryor 1968, p. 145). In comparison to other countries, and in spite of its wealth, the United States expends a relatively small proportion of its gross national product on social insurance programs (6.7 percent in 1962), less than half the percentage in France, Germany, and Italy. In fact, its expenditure rate is the lowest of seven capitalist nations sampled by Pryor (1968, p. 145).

Yet, the American public is inclined to believe that too much public money is being spent on welfare and "social programs" (National Opinion Research Center 1975). As the statistics are presented by the government, it does appear that enormous proportions of federal funds are being spent for transfer payments. Thus, one reads in the *Social Security Bulletin* that total social welfare spending is 18 percent of the gross national product and 55 percent of total government expenditures (Skolnick and Dales 1974). Closer examination reveals the misleading nature of the categories, however. "Social welfare," as used in this context, refers to all governmental expenditures that are not for military purposes or administrative overhead. It includes support for education, highways, housing, medical research, social security programs, health and medical programs, veterans' pensions, and unemployment insurance. If we eliminate state and federal support of schools and expenditures on health and medical care, only 34 percent of the social welfare budget remains. From another perspective, welfare payments per se (public assistance) are only 2.2 percent of the gross national product and 7.2 percent of the total federal and state government expenditures.

The major transfer programs in the United States had their origins in the Great Depression of the 1930s (Fried et al. 1973, pp. 69–71). The widespread unrest resulting from the unemployment and destitution of that period led to new programs that attempted to protect people from income losses beyond their control. The predominant philosophy guiding the engineering of the programs was that benefits paid should not be charity, but should be earned rights based on past contributions. As a result, social security, railroad retirement, and unemployment insurance systems all are financed from payroll taxes and provide benefits related to past wages. However, public assistance programs for the needy people who could not work also were established. It was believed that these programs would wither away as the economy prospered and social insurance programs matured. They did not wither away, but grew and changed. The work-ethic philosophy remained, however, with three dominant results: (1) the "earned right" programs have been much more popular than the "welfare" programs, although the difference between them is mainly a fiction; (2) the aged and disabled poor have been treated far more generously than people who have low incomes for other reasons; and (3) the problem of poverty has not disappeared (Fried et al. 1973, p. 70).

Who benefits from the transfer payments and services that the government provides? Many of the programs benefit the rich and middle classes far more than the poor. This is particularly true of social security, education, and housing programs. Social security payments, the largest of the expenditures, benefit the old (who might otherwise be poor), but particularly the old from the more affluent classes, who have paid smaller proportions of their incomes into the program, but receive larger benefits, and who are more likely to live to old age anyway (Glenn 1968). Expenditures for education, the next largest category, likewise are disproportionately used to pay for the education of the middle classes. Housing expenditures include tax breaks for homeowners (favoring the rich) and building programs for low-cost housing that are carefully designed to guarantee a profit by banks, developers, and real estate speculators (Harrington 1975, p. 17).

Public assistance payments, however, do tend to help the poor. They consist of money payments and social services to the aged, the blind, the disabled, and needy families with dependent children. Most families who receive public assistance are those with incomes of less than $4,000 per year (1972) (U.S. Bureau of the Census 1973, P–60, no. 90). Even so, a majority of those who are in severe need do not receive public assistance. Thus, of the 2.5 million families and individuals who had incomes of less than $1,000 in 1970, some 59 percent received no transfer payments at all (Projector and Bretz 1975, Table 4). It has been suggested that the really poor are less likely than the moderately poor to receive public assistance because they are ignorant of the public funds available to them, because they assume they would be ineligible or have been denied assistance before, or because they are afraid or ashamed to apply (Piven and Cloward 1971, pp. 150–51).

117

In sum, transfer payments in the United States do help, to a limited extent, a little over half of the neediest families. They are more likely to go to people in the bottom half of the income distribution, particularly to the aged and disabled, than to the more affluent, as shown by Table 4.5. Yet, notice in the table that 20 percent of the examined transfer payments go the richest 40 percent of the families. *These transfer payments do redistribute family income, but only to a limited and minor extent.* Table 4.6 shows that the reduction of income inequality that comes about as a result of transfer payments is only minor, and it is a reduction that is helped not at all by taxation (Fried et al. 1973, Table 3.5).

In sum, in the United States, currently one of the most economically productive societies in the world, wealth holdings of capital, property, and cash are concentrated among a very few families and individuals. The concentration of wealth is relatively stable over time and is protected by property laws and taxation procedures. The bulk of the population subsists on salaries and wages, which also are distributed unequally. Some of the remaining individuals, who are unable to participate in economic exchanges, receive limited support through transfer payments.

Sources of Income Inequality

In this section we consider how income inequalities come about. All of us are aware of such inequalities, some of them very puzzling. Why do sales representatives for the manufacturing industries make $2,000 more than sales representatives for the wholesale trades? Why do airplane pilots make three times as much as bus drivers? Why do electricians make more

Table 4.5

*Percentage distribution of cash transfers[a]
received by families, 1972*

Income quintile	Percentage distribution
Lowest 20 percent	40.2
20 to 40	26.8
40 to 60	13.1
60 to 80	10.3
80 to 100	9.6
Total	100.0

Source: Edward R. Fried et al., *Setting National Priorities: The 1974 Budget* (Washington, D.C.: the Brookings Institution, 1973), Table 3.5. Copyright © 1973 by the Brookings Institution.

[a] Transfers include old age, survivors, and disability insurance, unemployment compensation, public assistance, and veterans' benefits.

Table 4.6

Combined effect of federal individual income and payroll taxes and transfer payments on distribution of income, 1972

	Percentage distribution		
Income quintile	Total income before taxes and transfers	Total income after income and payroll taxes	Total income after taxes and transfers[a]
Lowest 20 percent	1.7	1.8	6.3
20 to 40	6.6	7.0	9.1
40 to 60	14.5	14.8	14.6
60 to 80	24.1	24.4	22.8
80 to 100	53.1	51.9	47.1
Total	100.0	100.0	100.0

Source: Edward R. Fried et al., *Setting National Priorities: The 1974 Budget* (Washington, D.C.: the Brookings Institution, 1973), Table 3.5. Copyright © 1973 by the Brookings Institution.

[a] Transfers include old age, survivors, and disability insurance, unemployment compensation, public assistance, and veterans' benefits.

than plumbers, who make more than carpenters? In taking up the issue, we are returning to the question raised in Chapter 2: Why does inequality exist? We are concerned not only with inequality among specific occupational groups or among individuals with different talents, but also with inequalities between broad groups. Why do whites earn more than blacks and men more than women?

It is important for two reasons that the causes of income disparity be identified. One is that the incomes that people earn bear very directly on a whole host of life chances. While the differences in the paychecks people bring home may seem insignificant when compared to the wealth controlled by the very rich, they nevertheless can loom very large to those people who never expect to have much money, whose horizons are limited to spreads of a few thousand dollars, and for whom small raises may make a great difference in the ease and comfort of living. Several thousand dollars may be the margin separating the people who are able to live comfortably from those who are on the economic brink. The other reason we need to understand the reasons for income inequality is that until we know the underlying conditions, we will be unable to create firm and effective policies to bring about desired changes.

Social scientists have only recently begun to explore these questions empirically. Their research usually has been guided by one of two major perspectives on income inequality. One, which we call "individualistic explanations," concentrates on the characteristics of individuals, such as training, ability, or work motivation, that influence their placement in the occupational structure. This explanation is not foreign to the conventional wisdom that holds that the poor are poor because they are lazy and wasteful and that the rich are rich because they are hard-working, enterprising, and talented (Feagin 1975). Similar interpretations are given by "human capital" economists, who believe that a person's income reflects the degree of training he or she has received and that this income is merely sufficient to compensate for the costs of this training (A. Atkinson 1975, p. 82). Likewise, sociologists who are functionalists, although not claiming that there is a one-to-one correlation between training and reward, do suggest that many high-income receivers are people of talent and training who have been lured into societally important positions.

"Structural explanations," on the other hand, assume that income inequality results from the workings of social and economic forces external to the individual, such as the supply of laborers and the corporate demand for them, governmental regulation of wages, or the bargaining power of unions and employers' associations. The average citizen, though more inclined to individualistic explanations, gives a structural explanation when he or she agrees that low wages in certain industries or exploitation by the rich are causes of poverty (Feagin 1972). A structural explanation also is inherent in conflict theory, which suggests that incomes reflect group differences in economic dominance.

The two types of explanations are not necessarily incompatible. Thurow and Lucas demonstrated a combining of the two in their testimony to the U.S. Senate on income distribution:

> One set of factors determines an individual's relative position in
> the labor queue; another set of factors, not mutually exclusive of
> the first, determines the actual distribution of job opportunities
> in the economy. Wages are paid based on the characteristics of the
> job in question and workers are distributed across job opportunities
> based on their relative position in the labor queue (1972, p. 2).

The remainder of this chapter examines the research findings that bear on each stance.

Individualistic Explanations: "It's in the Person"

An individualistic explanation looks for the sources of income inequality in the characteristics of individual income receivers. It would suggest that Attorney Jones receives a higher income than paralegal aide Smith because Jones increased his value — his human capital — by going to law school. Individualistic explanations focus on those characteristics which make the individual a more desirable or productive worker. In particular, training, ability, and experience are usually mentioned.

120

The belief that incomes are primarily related to education and ability is well entrenched in the folk wisdom as well as in social science literature. Yet, if we record the incomes of a sample of workers and match these with their educational levels and measures of mental ability, does a strong association actually emerge? Surprisingly, as we will see in the following section, it emerges only to a limited extent and then only for education, not for measured intelligence. Bright people are not particularly likely to be affluent. If they are educated, it helps; yet all college seniors are aware that some of their cohorts will walk into jobs paying $20,000, while others will land jobs paying less than $10,000.

Two sociologists, Bibb and Form (1977), made a careful study of the 1972 wages of 1,004 full-time blue-collar workers. They were particularly interested in the relative influence of a person's education, vocational training, experience, and employment history on his or her income. As it turned out, all of these characteristics together account for almost one-fifth of the variation in incomes of their sample. A similar analysis was conducted by Wachtel and Betsey (1972). Let us look at these factors more carefully.

EDUCATION AND INCOME

Census data on the earnings received by individuals who have completed various levels of education seem to show that the more degrees a person has, the higher will be his or her income. Males with an eighth grade education in 1975, for instance, had a median income of about $6,515; only 9 percent of this group was able to draw incomes of over $15,000. College graduates, on the other hand, had a median income of about $14,350, and 46 percent received over $15,000 (U.S. Bureau of the Census 1977). Granted, a high level of formal education completed does not guarantee a high income. Of the college graduates just mentioned, one-fifth had incomes of less than $8,000. Yet education may well serve as a minimum requirement for entry into many occupations that bring higher incomes.

For several decades, these data on average incomes convinced social scientists that a person's training is the key factor in determining his or her economic remuneration. On the basis of such information, young people were advised to go to college, or at least to finish high school, in order to be able to support themselves in a middle-class fashion in adulthood. The advice was perhaps not ill founded, but it was incomplete. That the causal chains are more complicated than a simple "education yields income" nexus became clear only as sociologists and economists applied to the income data a set of statistical techniques called regression analysis. These revealed that the amount of income an adult male receives is not related very closely to the education he has gained. According to the calculations made, an additional year of elementary or secondary school generally increases future income only about 4 percent; an additional year of college, about 7 percent; and an additional year of graduate school, about 4 percent (Jencks et al. 1972). All in all, if you choose a group of white men of various ages and educational attainments, the differences in their education will explain only about 7 percent of their differences in earnings (Mincer 1974, p. xiv; Jencks et al. 1972).

Nor is income related to social class origins or mental ability (Jencks et al. 1972; Sewell and Hauser 1975). But it is slightly related to occupational prestige. If individuals have completed above-average educational levels, they are able to translate this into earnings if they use their credentials to enter jobs that pay above average. That is, it is not the case that educated workers are directly rewarded for their superior knowledge; rather, they are rewarded if they are able to enter the higher-status occupations. It has been suggested that employers assume that education serves as a proxy for such traits as reliability and learning potential, and thus employers prefer to hire more educated applicants, even when formal education has little bearing on the skills needed for the job (Doeringer and Piore 1966, pp. 132–33; Taussig 1928, pp. 97–98, 100; Weisbrod 1962, p. 112; Chamberlain 1965, p. 22; Siegel 1971, pp. 290–91; Stolzenburg 1975, pp. 302–03).

AGE, EXPERIENCE, AND INCOME

Age is an ascribed characteristic, while experience is an achieved one, but they tend to have similar effects on income. Of the two, experience seems to be the more important influence (Wachtel and Betsey 1972; Fuchs 1971). There are several typical life-cycle patterns. Young men, for example, are more likely to have part-time employment, to be less skilled, or to be beginners in the occupational structure. By the middle years, the typical male worker has acquired seniority rights and gains promotions. By the time he is fifty, he has usually reached the peak of his earning power, and from that time until he is ready to retire, his earnings stabilize or decline, particularly if he is a blue-collar worker. The working pattern for women is more likely to involve peak periods of employment in the early twenties and then again in the forties and fifties. It was in looking at the incomes of women that Mincer and Polacnek (1974) confirmed that years of experience are more predictive of income than is age. The never-married women, who typically have longer work experience, earned higher incomes on the average than the married women, whose work experience is more often interrupted.

MENTAL ABILITY AND INCOME

It is a common popular belief some people have higher incomes than others because they are more intelligent. This common belief is not supported, however, by statistical data on such measurements of intelligence as tests of mental performance (IQ tests). Mental ability "accounts for" only 2 percent of variation in income (Jencks et al. 1972, Figure B–2). Obviously, mental performance hardly affects in a direct way the income one can expect to receive.

There is a slight indirect relationship that operates through the effect of mental performance on education, which in turn affects occupational status, which affects income. But the effects are small. Jencks comments: "Neither family background, cognitive skill, educational attainment, nor occupational status explains much of the variance in men's incomes. Indeed, when we compare men who are identical in all these respects, we find only 12 to 15 percent less inequality than among random individuals" (1972, p. 226).

What does explain income differentiation? The kind of research we have just been examining has looked at the personal characteristics of individuals — their intelligence, their education, their experience — and has not found an adequate answer. Jencks et al. speculate that it might be "luck" that explains the differences in income: "chance acquaintances who steer you to one line of work rather than another, . . . whether bad weather destroys your strawberry crop, whether the new superhighway has an exit near your restaurant . . ." (1972, p. 227). But their research ignored many other variables besides luck that we might think of, and as we shall see, some of them explain considerable variation in income. Because individualistic explanations typically examine the backgrounds and attributes of people, and not the characteristics of the occupational structure or economic institution, they lead one to overlook how these latter structures influence income.

Structural Explanations: "It's in the System"

Structural explanations are not necessarily in conflict with individualistic explanations; rather, they approach the understanding of income inequality from a different perspective. They focus on the actions of groups (such as whites and males, for example) toward other groups (such as blacks and females) in setting incomes and on the overarching features of the economic structure that create the limitations within which the labor market operates. As Thurow and Lucas (1972) noted, the labor market must be considered separately from the talents of the laborers, even though it has been the latter that has captured the attention of many economists (particularly the "human capital" theorists) and sociologists (particularly the fuctionalists).

That groups are treated differently in the wage-determination process is suggested when we examine the wages of blacks and women in comparison to white males. A person's race and sex are important to income because these characteristics influence what occupation the person will have. It indicates that different groups are channeled into different types of jobs. The processes by which certain categories of people are encouraged to follow the routes to remunerative occupations while other groups are discouraged are structural processes. That doctors tend to be white, Anglo-Saxon, Protestant males is no accident. That cleaning personnel tend to be immigrants, ethnics, blacks, and women likewise is no accident. We need to look at characteristics of the system, not of individuals, to understand these phenomena.

RACE AND INCOME

Almost as important as education and experience in the determination of income, according to the Wachtel-Betsey analysis, is one's racial identification. Race is not an achieved status, and it gives no indication of a person's ability or productivity, yet it apparently is a personal characteristic that affects income. In the labor queue, a black stands behind an equally qualified white. This shows up first of all in family income figures. In 1974 the median family income for whites was about $13,360 while that for blacks was $7,810, or only 58 percent of the former. It shows up also in individual income figures, as represented in Table 4.7. In every category of employment, blacks earn less money. This is in part because they hold the lowest-paying jobs in that category. As Herman P. Miller pointed out: "They are clerks instead of managers, laborers instead of bricklayers, machine operators instead of toolmakers. But that is only part of their disadvantage. They often receive lower pay even when doing exactly the same work as whites. White men earn more simply because they are white, regardless of the job" (1964, p. 102).

As shown in Table 4.8, the income differences between whites and blacks exist even when they have completed the same levels of education.

Table 4.7

Median incomes by sex and race of workers with year-round full-time jobs, 1973

	Sex	
Race	Male	Female
Black	$7,953	$5,595
White	$11,800	$6,598
Ratio of black to white	.67	.85

Source: U.S. Bureau of the Census, "Money Income in 1973 of Families and Persons in the United States," *Current Population Reports,* series P-60, no. 97, table 60.

The differentials are so large and so universal at all educational levels that they clearly reflect the patterns of discrimination characteristic of hiring and promotion practices in many segments of the economy (National Advisory Committee 1968, p. 256). One study, taking account of the effects of family background, education, mental ability, number of siblings, and occupation, concluded that at least one-third of the difference in average income between blacks and whites "arises because Negro and white men in the same line of work, with the same amount of formal schooling, with equal ability, from families of the same size and the same socioeconomic level, simply do not draw the same wages and salaries" (Duncan 1968, p. 108). For the black man, there are serious flaws in the assertion of the Horatio Alger, rags-to-riches, success ideology that all one needs to succeed is hard work and ambition.

SEX AND INCOME

A similar situation faces women. Simply stated, fully employed women earn only about $6 for every $10 earned by fully employed men. This does not represent much of an improvement over Biblical times, at least according to Leviticus 27, wherein it is indicated that adult females were worth thirty shekels and adult males fifty shekels. In fact, in modern times, the earnings gap has widened, even in the midst of feminist activity. For year-round full time workers in 1973, the female median income was 57 percent of the male median income, a drop from 63 percent in 1956 (U.S. Bureau of the Census 1975, P–60, no. 97, Table 60).

Such differences hold even when comparing men and women with the same education. Women who have five or more years of college education and who work full-time earn on the average about 65 percent of

Table 4.8

Median income for all males, twenty-five years old and over, by race and education, 1973

Years of schooling	Black male	White male	Ratio of black to white
Elementary, less than 8 years	$3,338	$4,820	.69
Elementary, 8 years	4,930	6,511	.76
High school, 1–3 years	6,513	8,967	.73
High school, 4 years	8,284	11,074	.75
College, 1–3 years	8,643	11,937	.72
College, 4 or more years	11,294	14,908	.76

Source: U.S. Bureau of the Census, "Money Income in 1973 of Families and Persons in the United States," *Current Population Reports,* series P–60, no. 97, table 58.

what comparable men earn. That happens to be a little less than what full-time male workers with only high school diplomas earn, but a little more than what a male high school dropout can bring home (U.S. Department of Labor 1977, p. 3).

Likewise, if we group men and women by their occupational categories, the story is about the same: The earnings of fully employed women lag significantly behind those of men. Women fare best, relative to men, in professional occupations, in which they earn about 68 percent of what men earn. They fare worst in sales occupations, in which they earn only about 40 percent of what men earn.

As is true for blacks, the most important source of income inequality of the sexes is the fact that women tend to be employed in lower-paying jobs than those of men. Most women wind up in what economist Marina Whitman calls the "employment ghetto" of women's work: jobs as waitresses and seamstresses, secretaries and bookkeepers, nurses and teachers. Although they are represented in highly paid occupations, over 73 percent of women workers are employed as salespersons, clerks, semiskilled factory workers, or service workers (compared to 36 percent of the men) (U.S. Bureau of the Census, *Statistical Abstracts*, 1975, Table 589). These differences exist in spite of the fact that women in America receive about the same amount of education as do men.[3]

Even when women are employed in the same jobs as men, they are paid less. For example, full-time female Class A computer operators earned $168 per week in 1972, compared to $178 earned by males. The weekly salary differential between the earnings of female and male Class A accounting clerks ranged from $6.50 to $42.50. The patterns of earnings in institutions of higher education provide another example. Salaries of male and female full professors differ by around $1,000, and a similar gap exists for assistant and associate professors (U.S. Department of Labor 1971).

Testimony in a $2-million sex discrimination suit brought against a publishing company in 1977 provides further illustrations (Lyons 1977). A perusal of company files by a labor consultant for the complainant revealed a number of interesting comparisons. Two assistant supervisors were hired at the same time, the woman at $105 a week and the man at $128. Both received excellent evaluations, and the woman received a local businesswoman-of-the-year award. When the woman's supervisor retired, the male employee became supervisor at $261 a week, and the woman remained at $209. The man could not run the department and was transferred, and the woman then became supervisor at $255. In an-

---

[3] U.S. college women reading this passage may be interested to know that nearly one-fifth of employed women who have completed four years of college labor as service workers, private household workers, sales or clerical workers, or factory operatives.

other case, two employees started in the same job at $60 a week and had similar performance ratings. Eventually, the man had been moved into another department, making $261, while the woman remained where she had started, at $179. These cases illustrate unequal pay for equal work and discriminatory promotion opportunities. In addition, the testimony brought out that the most common form of discrimination was for women and men to be placed in different career routes from the time of their initial job placement. Women were generally routed along a clerical path. Years later, women with superior education, work experience, and job performance could be found in jobs similar to ones in which they started, at pay rates below those of men with equal or poorer qualifications. (For corroboration based on a study of wage rates in three firms, see Cassell and Doctors 1972; also see Malkiel and Malkiel 1973).

Discrimination such as described in these case studies is not due to differences in education, experience, and training. When Featherman and Hauser (1976, p. 480) compared workers' actual salaries with what they would be expected to earn on the basis of achievement and background characteristics, they found that the average woman came out with about $5,824 less income than the average man. Sex discrimination per se apparently plays a substantial role; after controlling for personal characteristics such as experience, education, migration, marital status, and number of children, one economist concluded that discrimination accounts for approximately 78 percent of the wage differential between white males and females and 94 percent of that between black males and females (Oaxaca 1973, p. 704; also see Suter and Miller 1973).

LABOR MARKET FORCES

The statistics on the incomes of blacks and women suggest that some groups have been more successful than other groups in demanding high pay from corporations and clients. A number of structural forces operating on the determination of wages have been identified.

Bibb and Form (1977) focus on three major structural variables. First is the stratification of industrial establishments. At the top are large capital-intensive oligopolistic firms (General Motors and Exxon, for example) that earn high profits. Their managers command the highest salaries (the president of General Motors earned over $1 million in 1977). Their employees can command the highest wages because they belong to large and powerful unions. At the bottom are "periphery" establishments, which have few material and organizational resources. These firms are small, geographically scattered, and labor-intensive. They have many competitors, uncertain profits, and the lowest wage scales because they operate in free markets (dry cleaning establishments, for example).

In general, there seem to be five types of labor markets whose special characteristics influence wages (Huber 1974, pp. 108–09, from Miller and Form 1964, pp. 452–55). Managers of large corporations operate in a *self-controlled market,* whereby top executives make decisions on incomes. They assign themselves large salaries and bonuses, which remain high even when losses are high. Doctors, lawyers, plumbers, and carpenters operate in a *traditional market.* Here, the practitioners have monopolized certain skills that require a long time to learn. Incomes derive from fees and take into account the clients' ability to pay. The most important factor affecting income is control of entry into the occupation, as is the case, for example, in the medical profession (Friedman and Kuznets 1954, p. 394). *Administered markets* affect white-collar workers in bureaucracies, where salaries are nicely graduated. The salaries tend to be lower than those for people with similar levels of training in other markets because bureaucratic salaries are supported by public taxation. In a *contested market,* labor unions bargain with industrial management, raising wages perhaps as much as 10 percent (H. G. Lewis 1963, p. 91), although the data on this point are still inadequate. Poor people, such as small retailers, farm laborers, or domestic and casual workers, typically operate in *free markets,* in which wages and skill levels are low, wages reflect supply and demand, and custom and union organizations are almost nonexistent. These variations among markets reflect the differential power of occupational groups. Poor workers are those who are forced to accept low-paying employment because of ascribed characteristics such as race, age, ethnic background, or sex or because of a lack of credentials to cross the barriers into more powerful occupations.

A second important structural variable is the stratification of groups, in terms of their organizational power to extract high wages from management. Significant here is the extent to which the members of the occupation possess scarce skills that are in high demand and the extent to which the workers are cohesively organized.

In some occupations, the size of the supply of labor and the intensity of demands for people to fill occupational slots influence how much income is offered. If there is great demand but few laborers, then the salaries will go up, as is true for medical doctors in the United States. When an industry develops the desire for computers to handle its accounts and to coordinate its expansion, there is a demand for computer programmers and systems analysts. Until enough people become trained in computer technology, the salaries of those who have prior experience remain inflated. On the other hand, when an occupation becomes flooded with applicants, or when the need for a certain skill drops, as is currently true of elementary and secondary teaching, then salaries become depressed, because there is an excess of teachers.

Workers are often organized through large formal organizations such as unions or employers' associations. Union membership in the United

States now is about one-third of the nonagricultural labor force. Unionization typically has been high in mining, construction, manufacturing, and transportation, but much lower in agriculture, the distributive trades, and the government sector (A. Atkinson 1975, p. 99). Do unions make any difference? The desire of unions to get wages up may be counterbalanced by the desire of employers to keep wages down, and their powers may balance. But it has in fact been determined that when labor is unorganized, it is more susceptible to receiving lower incomes than it would receive under conditions of perfect competition. A well-known study by Lewis, based on an analysis of the average earnings of employees in heavily unionized industries, concluded that "the average union-nonunion relative wage was approximately 10 to 15 percent higher than it would have been in the absence of unionism" (1963, p. 5; for similar results, see Penceval 1974, p. 205; Weiss 1966; Boskin 1972).

Professional associations also attempt to affect the salary levels of their members. Friedman and Kuznets (1954) investigated the role that medical associations have played in raising the cost of physicians' labor by restricting the number of M.D.'s produced by medical schools. H. G. Lewis (1963) estimated that airline pilots have been able through their professional associations to elevate their wages by some 21 to 34 percent.

The third variable is the location of the labor force in the community stratification system. Groups that are disadvantaged by ethnicity, race, and sex are denied access to better-paying jobs by purposeful social action on the part of employers, unions, and other dominant groups, which justify their exclusionary actions with an elaborate economic and stratification ideology. This is accomplished in part through the existence of what economists have called "primary" and "secondary" labor markets. Workers are channeled into one or the other of these on the basis of their objective characteristics. Blacks and women are more likely to be looking for jobs in the "secondary market." Jobs in this market involve little on-the-job training, high job insecurity, and poor promotion opportunities (Doeringer and Piore 1971). For example, consider the advancement potentials of the typical jobs that women are employed in: clerks, typists, waitresses, and service workers. White males, on the other hand, are more likely to look for jobs in the "primary market," jobs characterized by employment stability, good working conditions, and mobility opportunities. Baran and Hyer summarized their study of the dual labor market in Chicago:

> Segregation in the Northern labor market has been as efficient a mechanism for subjugating Negroes to second-class status as segregation in housing and education. In Chicago the process of allocating jobs to white workers is so effectively separated from the process of allocating jobs to Negro workers that year after year the

differentials between white and Negro workers are maintained. At the same time, a large segment of the Negro labor force is relegated to the role of an urban peasantry destined to live off welfare payments and white paternalism. The Negro labor force, unlike those of other large ethnic groups, has not been allowed to assimilate into the metropolitan labor market. . . . Negroes in Chicago are still systematically restricted in both the skills they may acquire and the extent to which they can utilize any given level of skills (1971, p. 100).

Some economists suggest that employers benefit when there are categories of people, such as blacks, women, and immigrants, who are effectively eliminated from competition for higher-paying jobs. When these people have great difficulty in entering the more desirable occupations, they provide a ready pool of laborers who are willing to work for low wages. This is the "crowding hypothesis," which argues that the major reason for the low wages of women workers (or black workers) is that by being denied access to many occupations, they are crowded into a limited number of remaining occupations (Bergmann 1971). Because women must compete for a small number of jobs, the supply of labor for these occupations is artificially enlarged, and the remuneration is therefore less than it otherwise would be. At the same time, men in many occupations are protected from competition by women workers, so the supply of labor in men's occupations is artificially reduced, and their wages are therefore higher than they otherwise would be. Reduction of discrimination would lessen the competition for female-dominated occupations and increase the competition for male-dominated occupations, resulting in pay increases in the former and decreases in the latter (Stevenson 1975, p. 75). That this process does in fact operate has been suggested by at least two studies (Stevenson 1975; Bibb and Form 1977).

OVERALL RESULTS

That structural characteristics are indeed important was confirmed in both the Bibb-Form and the Wachtel-Betsey studies. Bibb and Form used as their measures of structure the standing of individuals on the following variables: characteristics of the firm in which the individual is employed (comparing wages given by firms in the primary industrial sector to those in the peripheral sectors), location of residence (because the highest-paying industries are located in the major metropolitan areas), skill level of the occupation (because craftsworkers are known to be able to control their work environments more effectively than the less skilled), union membership (because unions are attracted to industries that are easier to organize and have higher profit margins), and sex ("because we believe that both the market and occupational groups respond particularistically to women's subordinate estate") (1977, p. 981).

The results of their study indicate that structural variables are far more important in determining blue-collar income than are the personal characteristics of education, vocational training, experience, and employment history. Fifty percent of the variation in incomes is related to structural variables, while only 18 percent is related to human capital variables. Particularly important are the sex of people, where they are located, whether they belong to a union, and which sector they are employed in. These are important even when the effect of personal characteristics has been eliminated. That is, a worker in manufacturing will earn more than a worker in wholesale trade even if he or she is of equal educational attainment, vocational training, and experience. In concrete terms, the analysis showed on the basis of 1972 income data that to be male increased one's income by about $4,000; to be employed in the primary sector, by almost $2,000; to be located in a major metropolitan area, by about $1,200; and to belong to a union, by $1,100.

The results of the study by Wachtel and Betsey are similar. They included race as a variable and found that race is an important predictor of income, more important even than sex. In both of these studies, income differentiation based on "human capital investments" are minor in comparison to the differentiation based on sex or race. The low wages of blacks and women result not from their education or their labor force experience, but from their restriction to sex- and race-segregated jobs. White males gain from this restriction by having freer access to the better-paying jobs (see Bergmann 1971 and Villemez 1977 for evidence).

Conclusions on Structural and Personal Characteristics

What does this information now tell us about the sources of income inequality? The functional theory of stratification argues that income inequality is one device that helps to ensure that able people are attracted to important and difficult jobs. The human capital theory within economics in similar fashion contends that the inherent productivity of workers and, thus, their job chances are based on the degree to which they have improved their own capital potential by investing in their own education and training (see Thurow 1970 and 1969; Mincer 1970). The policy implication is that income inequalities can be lessened by improving the productive potential of the individual. Job training programs for the unemployed and educational programs for the poor are two frequently suggested remedies to low income.

Conflict theory, as proposed by sociologists, and the similar structuralist school in economics argue that incomes are determined by power imbalances within the economy and among groups and by characteristics of the labor market. The struggle between unions and employers' associations, the degree of control over important resources held by an industry or region, the historical development of wage inequities, the job discrimination against blacks and women — these and other structural properties of the economic system are vitally important in the processes of income determination. These theories imply that income inequalities could be lessened by controlling wages and prices; by making more uniform the variations in income across industries, communities, and regions; by regulating wage rates themselves, rather than by changing individuals; or by increasing the power of low-paid occupational groups.

According to the Bibb and Form study, the structural and personal characteristics together explain about 55 percent of the variation in earnings. Considered separately, structural characteristics are far more important, explaining about 50 percent of the variance in earnings.

The structural explanation seems more valid. Education and ability are the only variables that directly relate to the functionalist argument. Differences in ability, however, as measured by tests of mental performance, do not lead to differences in income variation, as we have seen. Education does indeed show a moderate correlation with earnings. Yet, the functionalist argument still does not receive resounding support by this fact. The influence of education on income is too insignificant. Education explains only about 7 percent of the differences in earnings in two studies (Mincer 1974, p. xiv; Jencks 1971) and only 8 percent in another (Sewell and Hauser 1975, p. 79). Clearly, the main factor creating income inequality is not society's need to encourage educated people to take high-paying jobs. Education does affect income, but there are so many intervening influences in the path between educational attainment and income that the relationship is grossly obscured. The chances of achieving a high income are increased not only by achieving an education, but also by getting into a well-paying occupation in a well-paying industry in the right part of the country — and by being white and male. Income inequality seems to be based more on the denial of privilege to certain groups and occupations and on the differential advantages of specific industries and locales than it does on the training that individuals have undertaken.

Economic Inequality in the United States: An Overview

The American economic system is an industrial system operating on the basis of modified capitalistic principles and practices. Mass production, utilizing a highly developed technology and a factory system, is the most important method of producing goods. The division of labor is highly specialized and is organized largely by hierarchies of authority (bureaucracies).

132

Corporate assets and capital are largely concentrated in the hands of the five hundred or so largest corporations, which dominate the economic arena. Apart from the wealth possessed by corporate entities, individual wealth likewise is concentrated among a few. Twenty percent of the population owns 76 percent of the country's individually owned wealth, which consists predominantly of stocks, bonds, and real estate.

The income received by individuals also is distributed unequally, as the top 20 percent of the families receives 41 percent of the income, while the bottom 20 percent receives about 5 percent. Twelve percent of families live in abject poverty, while another 30 percent find subsistence a constant struggle. Incomes are distributed much the same after taxation as before. Transfer payments in the form of social security payments, unemployment compensation, and public assistance redistribute income to a very minor degree. The resulting configuration can be usefully pictured as consisting of five distinct economic classes:

1. The top wealth holders: those who own assets over $100,000, whose incomes are derived primarily from the return on capital investments or from top managerial positions in large corporations, and who have considerable access to economic power through corporate holdings.
2. The directors (professional and managerial income receivers): those who are employed as professionals and managers or who own their own medium-sized or small businesses, who receive incomes between $20,000 and $100,000, and who direct the workings of the economy although they lack ultimate control. Privileged through property and education, they are the most affluent of the income receivers.
3. Lower white-collar and skilled labor income receivers: the first phalanx under the professional-managerial class. These individuals make average incomes between $10,000 and $20,000, carry out the orders of the directors, but also organize others.
4. The semiskilled income receivers: those who take in incomes of $5,000 to $10,000. Individuals in this stratum lack economic wealth and economic power.
5. The unskilled income receivers: selling their labor for the lowest rates, these people receive $1,000 to $5,000 on the average, take orders from others, and lack any wealth assets. Also within this category would fall those families or individuals who live in poverty because they have no income at all or have only limited income from transfer payments, subemployment, or low-wage work.

These classes could be grouped as in Figure 4.5, in which the size of the gaps between classes represents the differential economic power of the classes relative to each other. The power of the top group is so large that its distance from the next highest class must be truncated rather

Figure 4.5
Economic classes in the United States

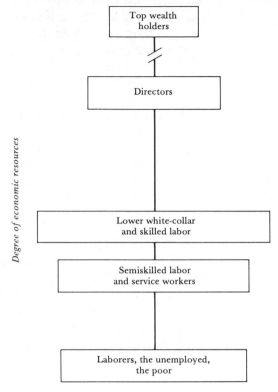

than using the approximately forty pages of space that it would take to portray its proportional economic power.

Differences in income can be attributed only in part to personal characteristics possessed by individuals. Although race, sex, experience, and schooling do play some role in assigning individuals to different income levels, just as important in the determination of income inequalities, perhaps even more so, are occupational monopolies, dual labor markets, and the power of workers' and employers' associations. The functionalist theory of stratification, which proposes that inequality exists to reward those of talent and training, does little to explain the empirical facts that schooling is only moderately related to income and that mental ability is not related at all. The actual complexity of the process of income determination is instead pointed up by the influence on income inequality discovered in such variables as industry type, region, degree of unionization, occupation, race, and sex. Conflict theory suggests that income rewards become patterned and habitual, but originally are set through a bargaining process influenced by the power that can be summoned by the competing groups. The bargaining process is affected by such factors as availability of alternative sources of labor, control of occupational entry channels, tradition, and interest group organization and cohesion.

In a sense, different principles of resource determination apply to what we are here differentiating into two main categories, the very wealthy and the majority. The very wealthy are often able to preserve their wealth by using it to ensure its perpetuation: to expand investments, to loan money for interest, to influence laws and regulatory practices, and generally to provide services for large profits. Members of the majority, on the other hand, exchange their labor for wages or salaries that provide internal differentiation, but are not large enough to give them resources for propulsion out of the wage-and-salary system and into economic autonomy and self-perpetuation. Generally unaware of the tremendous wealth controlled by the most affluent, the bulk of the population tends to identify with those who are slightly more affluent and thus tends to strive for advancement within the income structure, rather than challenge its inequities.

There is little evidence that economic inequality in the United States is substantially less now than it was earlier or than it is today in other industrial countries. The evidence is unequivocally clear that pronounced economic stratification is an entrenched, stable, and pervasive part of the fabric of American life.

The interrelations of economic and political influence play important, although often invisible, roles in determining the distribution of scarce and valued resources. Why and how corporations and wealthy individuals are able to gain cooperation from political leaders in order to accumulate and preserve wealth is considered in the next chapter.

5

DETERMINANTS OF INEQUALITY: POWER AND POLITICAL DOMINATION

IN THE LAST CHAPTER, we saw that wealth is possessed by a small number of families, while the rest of the people have little wealth and must survive on their incomes, which also are apportioned unequally. In modern American society, a few are very rich while many are barely getting by. Transfer payments help the poor a little, but the true function of welfare may be more to control the labor market than to eliminate poverty. Economic inequality is pronounced, and it has been that way for a long time.

Why do the poor, the almost-poor, and the middle-class people not rise up to protest the accumulation of wealth and privilege by a very few? Why do they not organize to confiscate the riches and redistribute them among themselves? They have the advantage of numbers, being at least two-thirds of the population by any measure. Why they accept their own relative deprivation without complaint and, to some extent, even further it by accepting compatible value systems and making accommodating political choices is not immediately understandable.

A major intent of this chapter is to address this question by discussing the ways in which social inequality is conserved, the techniques and ideologies that are used by the powerful to maintain their privilege, and the controls placed on the less privileged that encourage their acquiescence. Inequality is shaped by the interplay between those in power, who try to impose their values and interests on the total society, and those who are imposed on. The latter occasionally react by mobilizing their own power resources (Hoerning 1971, p. 8), but ordinarily they do not.

In this chapter, we are not interested in outlining all that is known about power. The fact that power is the focus of an entire discipline — political science — serves to illustrate the enormity of the subject. It is, however, important for us to explore how power is used to maintain social stratification and how the consequent political inequality reinforces economic and social inequality.

The first basic problem, then, is this: How do the economic and social elites gain power? What techniques of domination do they use, what are their tools of coercion, and how are the less privileged persuaded to cooperate in their own deprivation?

The second basic problem is, Are the people who are economically and socially privileged also politically privileged? This is an empirical question, which has been answered in the affirmative (even though the exact degree of correspondence is still being debated by power researchers). The three types of inequality tend to correspond: Rich families tend to have a lot of political clout, and they tend to be admired and respected. Poor families tend to be powerless, and they tend to be ignored or disdained. It is the correspondence of these three forms of inequality that leads to the stability of a system of social stratification, for the three reinforce each other.

To develop the answers to these questions, we begin by defining power. Then we outline the nongovernmental as well as governmental areas of power, describe the tools of control and of protest, and finally examine the issue of which groups have power. In all, the overriding interest is in the interface between social stratification and the power structure.

What Is Power?

DEFINITIONS

"Power" is one of those concepts that refer to intangible processes. We are certain of its existence only after something has occurred. When person A is able to get what she wants in spite of the objections of persons B and C, we are likely to assume that person A has power. Since it is a concept that refers to processes or events (and makes causal assumptions about who or what brings about those events), its referent — power relations — is difficult to measure.[1] Like so many of the phenomena studied by social scientists, power cannot be directly observed. We infer its existence when social actions consistently fall into patterns that reveal that some groups get their way in spite of contrary wishes of other groups.

The *Oxford English Dictionary* defines power as the "ability to do or effect something or anything, or to act upon a person or thing" and also as the "possession of control or demand over others; control, influence, authority." The notion of causal force is obvious in both of these definitions. Simply, we define social power as the ability of one party (either an individual or a group) to affect the behavior of another party.[2] But in order to study power, we must attempt to observe the influence of groups on others. When General Motors opposes automobile safety legislation being considered in the U.S. Congress, and the legislation that results is watered down, we begin to speak of the "power" of General Motors. We ask, In what ways was influence exerted, why was the legislation diluted, who talked to whom, and what kinds of leverages were applied?

TYPES OF POWER

Further conceptual distinctions are useful. The use of power can be conceived of as consisting of two types of control: authority and influence. Authority is legitimated power; the governed consent to being governed. They agree that a designated person or group should have limited power over them. In the United States, for example, Congress has authority to design automobile legislation in any way it wants because it has been delegated that power by the governed.

Authority rests upon accepted values (Bierstedt 1950, p. 733). When a judge exercises her authority by sentencing a murderer to ninety-nine

[1] There is hardly another concept within sociology that is more troublesome: "There is an elusiveness about power that endows it with an almost ghostly quality. . . . We 'know' what it is, yet we encounter endless difficulties in trying to define it" (Kaufman and Jones 1954, p. 205).

[2] Many definitions of power state that it is a *potential* or *probability* that one can control the actions of others, a potential that may or may not be realized. Weber's definition of power — "the chance of a man or of a number of men to realize their own will in communal action even against the resistance of others who are participating in the action"—is the classic example of this type (Weber, in Gerth and Mills 1946, p. 180). But this kind of definition introduces a methodological weakness, as Polsby (1963, p. 60) points out: "The assertion that any group 'potentially' could exercise significant, or decisive, or any influence in community affairs is not easy to discuss in a scientific manner. How can one tell, after all, whether or not an actor is powerful unless some sequence of events, competently observed, attests to his power?" Terry Clark attempts to avoid this problem by defining *power* as potential and *influence* as the exercise of power that brings about changes in a social system (1963, p. 54).

years or a businessman by firing a worker or a professor by giving a failing grade, it is agreed by most others that they have the "right" to do so — the power is legitimated. Occasionally, authority is challenged, and consensus breaks down or erodes. The legal system of judgeships may become open to debate, labor unions may demand the right to determine firing practices, and students may protest the system of grading. But in the usual course of events, authority structures depend on the value consensus and acquiescence of those who are being controlled. Even governments that come into being through the use of coercive force, as in a revolution or a military coup, can become stabilized only after they have achieved consensual legitimation.

Legitimate power tends to be restrained power. It is institutionalized and regulated by formal procedures for the giving and executing of commands. Inherent in the procedures are norms as to who may occupy the authority positions, exactly what powers are allocated to them, and who may be controlled. For example, a professor has the right to give assignments and grades, but not to supervise the student's personal life. Authority, thus, is limited.

Influence is another matter. It is the control that results from applying informal techniques such as persuasion and manipulation. Perhaps the General Motors lobbyists were effective talkers when they took certain members of Congress to lunch, or perhaps they made campaign pledges or even offered bribes. They probably used one or another of the three major techniques of influence (Goldhamer and Shils 1939, pp. 171–72). The most dramatic technique is force (or the threat of force), the physical manipulation of the subordinated individual or group, as exemplified by imprisonment or military conquest. In effect, the message is, If you do not shape up in the way I want you to, there will be damage to your possessions, your psyche, or your body. Organized crime firebombs the home of a businessman who has been reluctant to contribute protection money, or the judge sentences the auto thief to jail for twenty years. Both are messages of power.

The second technique of influence is domination, which can be defined as the influencing of behavior by making explicit to others what is wished, as when commands or requests are issued. Consider the wife whose husband told her she could not work at a paying job, and so she consequently remains a housewife; or consider the aspiring junior executive who transfers her family to a less desirable section of the country because her boss asked her if she would be willing to work at a new plant that will be opening up there. The husband in the first example dominated the wife by issuing an order; the boss in the second dominated by making a request. The result was the same — both actions brought about the desired behavior in others.

A third form of influence is manipulation, which is the influencing of behavior without making explicit what is wished. Propaganda and advertisements are tools of manipulation. Getting people to do what one wants by perpetrating useful myths or by encouraging compatible values are other tools. At the time this book was being written, a leading manufacturer of photographic equipment was being sued by a small competitor for the illegal use of monopolistic practices. Simultaneously, the larger company was providing propaganda as a "public service" — a slide show on the virtues of the free enterprise system and the dangers of governmental interference.

As these examples indicate, power is a factor in all relationships between people. We are more familiar with its uses in person-to-person relationships, such as between parent and child or between lovers. But the most far-reaching uses of power occur within the framework of large institutions. Individuals as individuals ordinarily are not very powerful. Of course, certain persons may be exceptionally influential by virtue of their personal charisma or vitality, but in most circumstances the power of an individual comes primarily from the position he or she holds in an organization. The organization is the basic entity, because it is the unit that controls the resources that mobilize people. When the individual no longer fills the office, he or she no longer controls the resources. A president who retires becomes powerless.

Legitimated and nonlegitimated power sometimes coexist. The first kind of power, which we have termed "authority," is limited. Often, however, a person uses a position of authority to exert nonlegitimated dominance. In actual situations, it is observationally difficult to separate authority from nonlegitimate power because the two tend to merge. A person may use a position of authority to exert control that is not inherent in the basic definition of that office, as when a president gets the FBI to wiretap his enemies for damaging information or persuades the CIA to give false reports about the progress of a war. The tendency and possibility of using an authority position to gain nonlegitimated powers is one reason that holders of top executive positions carry so much weight.

FUNCTIONS OF POWER

Americans tend to be suspicious of power. The thought that a small, unified, and powerful group of people conspires to direct national policy in its own interests is disturbing to some. They are likely to notice the close cooperation between business and government in regulating the economy, the unwillingness of local, state, and federal governments and powerful interest groups to respond to major social problems such as poverty, racial discrimination, and urban decay, or the heightened concentration of wealth that occurs when cross-industry conglomerates are created. They are likely to complain of an "establishment" that dictates policy for the rest of the nation (N. Crockett 1970, p. vii). Many Americans have an uneasy awareness that the realities of power are not consistent with democracy, as it is usually described. In Galbraith's words, "Power obviously presents awkward problems for a community which abhors its existence, disavows its possession, but values its exercise" (1952, p. 30).

Yet, many are quick to point out that the use of power (influence, authority, or domination) is necessary in many circumstances. The functionalists argue that every society must have a means for establishing and maintaining order. Conflicts must be resolved, and priorities must be ranked. In addition, in order to achieve societal goals, people must be organized; the actions of diverse individuals must be coordinated. Even in the small preliterate society, someone has to decide when planting should begin or whether a neighboring tribe is to be attacked. There must be directing and coordinating roles, what J. Porter terms "power roles." Porter states the functionalist position:

> Whenever human beings find themselves together they begin very quickly to establish a set of ordered relationships so that they are able to make some predictions about how other people are going to behave. Everyone in society has a set of expectations about how others will behave. Without ordered relationships which provide expectations it would be impossible to live. Among these ordered relationships are those which grant the right to a few people to make decisions on behalf of the group. Managing directors, archbishops, ministers of the Crown, union presidents, executive secretaries, and so forth act for and speak on behalf of a group's membership (1965, p. 202).

Conflict theorists counter that power exists because institutional roles permit some people to coerce others (Wrong 1964) and that the political institutions are so interlocked with the economic that they become the instruments of certain social classes or dominant elites. As P. Cohen suggests,

> The implication . . . is that power serves those who have it and it also affords them the opportunity to hold on to it and to pass it on to others of their choosing. A further implication is that if decision-makers were truly responsible to their supporters, they would not really have power over them at all; nor would the exercise of power be necessary, for administrative decisions would reflect the demands of those on whose behalf they are administered. The ideological overtones in this debate are scarcely concealed (1968, p. 62).

The most realistic stance, perhaps, is a synthesizing stance. There is a need for order, and there is a need for coordination. For these reasons, all societies that are too large for order and coordination to result from informal means of social control, such as group consensus or common values, will have to adopt authority systems that direct and coordinate people. Yet, the very existence of authority systems provides the opportunity for some persons to utilize power in their own interests and against the interests of others. The degree to which this is true is probably affected by the nature of the controls on the authority elites. The designs of some institutions are more conducive to the concentration of elite power than the designs of others. The consolidation of power among a small privileged elite may also be affected by the kinds of interrelations possible among institutions. Interlocking directorships, for example, which occur when someone on the board of directors of one organization (say, a bank) is also on the board of another organization (say, an insurance company), lead to a concentration of information and control and, thus, power among a very few.

What Are the Arenas of Power?

One of the characteristics of power that makes it so difficult to study is its diversity (Barber 1957, p. 235). It is in many different arenas that people influence people and that institutions dominate other institutions. Power may be political, economic, religious, scientific, sexual, or ideological. Power exists in all social institutions that have been created to accomplish desired tasks. The economic and the political institutions are two that most readily come to mind. In modern societies, there are in addition several other institutions in which large numbers of people are organized to perform complicated tasks: the military, the mass media, and educational organizations, for example. The existence of cohesive groups of people coordinated by hierarchies of authority to accomplish those activities which are desired by their leaders and managers creates considerable potential for the exercise of power.

Consider the diagram in Figure 5.1. Illustrated are those arenas of power operative in modern industrial societies which are particularly related to the creation and maintenance of social stratification. The most obvious arena of power, the one everyone thinks of first, is the governmental sphere. The state is the formal, legitimated, recognized institution that sets goals for the society, arbitrates disputes between competing groups, regulates conflicts, and makes the formal rules according to which the citizens are supposed to live.

But the nongovernmental arenas of power are at least as important as, if not more than, the governmental arenas. We must acknowledge the dominance of economic endeavors and the important socialization roles of the mass media, education, and religion. Each type has its own characteristics and results. In the economic realm, for example, ownership of property leads to power because owners have been given the right to con-

Figure 5.1

Arenas of power

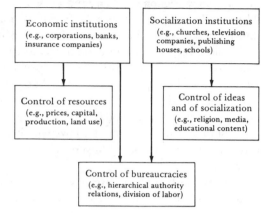

GOVERNMENTAL POWER

NONGOVERNMENTAL POWER

State

Control of rules

Activities of rule-makers
(e.g., legislators, chiefs of
state, regulatory agencies)

Activities of rule-enforcers
(e.g., police, army, surveillance
agencies, judges, lawyers,
prison personnel)

Economic institutions
(e.g., corporations, banks,
insurance companies)

Socialization institutions
(e.g., churches, television
companies, publishing
houses, schools)

Control of resources
(e.g., prices, capital,
production, land use)

Control of ideas
and of socialization
(e.g., religion, media,
educational content)

Control of bureaucracies
(e.g., hierarchical authority
relations, division of labor)

trol the use of things. Political power, by contrast, comes from a recognized right to set public policy. It is reinforced by military and police groups that control the weapons of force. Other institutions play important socialization roles. Religion, the mass media, and education exert moral and ideological persuasion. Let us look at the nature of power in these arenas a little more carefully.

GOVERNMENTAL POWER: THE MAKING OF RULES

There are two basic types of activities in the deployment of governmental power. One is the making of rules. Here legislators pass laws, regulatory agencies establish standards, courts interpret laws, and executive bodies issue orders. Rules include laws on who owns what, who can be taxed, who gets the collected taxes, who is subsidized, and so forth. The making of rules is the first step in the legitimation of inequality. The process of doing so is often bloody.

For example, the concept of the divine right of kings to own and possess the wealth took a century of warfare to establish and two centuries to destroy. It became accepted after the Norman conquest of England in 1066, when the feudal system of land tenure was introduced. Under this system the title to all land, which was the main source of wealth in those days, was vested in the king. This was a form of private property, because the king owned the land as an individual. The king's subjects could hold land as tenants, but could not own it. The king and nobles gave military protection to the lesser subjects and granted them the right to the crops raised on certain lands in return for labors performed in the cultivation of other lands. There was a continual struggle between those who benefited from the existing system of land ownership and those who did not share in its benefits. Feudalism declined with the rise of towns and a money economy, when land ceased to be the only form of wealth. The middle-class merchants, who began to amass large amounts of money, and the townspeople increasingly challenged the power of the king.

In more recent times in capitalist countries, the concept that individuals have an inviolable right to own private property — in conjunction with a laissez-faire policy that holds that government should stay out of economic transactions — sets the ideological climate consistent with the emergence of business. Today there are thousands of laws governing the ownership and use of property, laws which by and large favor the property owner over workers, buyers, or renters who must deal with the property owner.

The establishment of property laws and other procedures regarding taxation, subsidization, and social welfare programs usually is controversial because so much is at stake. An inequitable outcome is fostered when the people who are empowered to make the rules about property tend to come from a particular social stratum, represent a particular vested interest, or feel sympathetic to one sector of society rather than another. Such a situation exists more frequently than not, and it is relatively easy to demonstrate. Zweigenhaft (1975) surveyed the backgrounds of members of the U.S. Congress, who, of course, are frequently involved in decisions regarding the distribution of scarce resources. He found that the typical senator or representative is a white, Protestant male lawyer; his father, who was probably either a lawyer or a successful businessman, had the resources that allowed the son to attend a prestigious East Coast college before returning home to get his law degree. Twenty percent of the members of Congress belongs to the social upper class, and one in three is or approaches being a millionaire. Zweigenhaft suggests, "Such examples, and the more systematic information that could be provided on such matters as tax loopholes and weak or nonexistent laws to protect workers and consumers, provide little evidence that the American Congress has the broad powers of empathy that are necessary when Americans of many social, religious and ethnic backgrounds are missing from the legislative chambers" (1975, p. 128).

Similar statistics have been gathered about Supreme Court justices, diplomats, heads of governmental agencies, and high-ranking members of the executive branch of American government. Of all U.S. presidents, vice-presidents, and Cabinet members of the century and a half after 1789, only 2 percent were manual laborers or small farmers by occupation, and barely 25 percent were the sons of such workers (H. D. Anderson 1935). The generalization that political leaders are drawn disproportionately from upper-status occupations and privileged family backgrounds has been substantiated for most modern nations, including Great Britain, Italy, West Germany, Yugoslavia, the Soviet Union, and nations in Asia, Africa, and Latin America (see Putnam 1976, pp. 22–25, for a review of the research).

There are many ways in which special interests come to be disproportionately represented when rules are being made. Not only do members of Congress tend to come from the business and professional segments of society, but the congressional committees that do the work of Congress also are stacked with individuals representing particular interests. The House Agriculture Subcommittee on Tobacco is filled with representatives from tobacco-producing states; the Senate Minerals and Fuels Committee is loaded with senators from states in which large segments of the labor force are engaged in extractive industries; urban states are overrepresented on the Housing and Urban Affairs Subcommittee; and the Senate Armed Forces Committee is filled with senators from states that would suffer a loss if there were a 20-percent cutback in armament expenditures (Lieberson 1971).

In addition to the rule-making power that resides in the formal legislative bodies, rules also are made by regulatory agencies in many modern governments. In the United States, for example, control of thermal pollution has been entrusted to the Atomic Energy Commission, automobile safety to the Department of Transportation, drug purity to the Food and Drug Administration, and occupational standards to the Department of Labor (M. Bernstein 1972). Such agencies, on both state and federal levels, are institutions designed to be "power equalizers," that is, to protect consumer interests by regulating various aspects of big business. Yet, in actual functioning, such regulatory agencies often develop a sympathetic orientation toward the views and interests of the groups they are supposed to regulate.

The coincidence of interests between the regulatory body and the object of its regulation exists in part because of concentrated lobbying by the latter. Even more important, perhaps, is the cross-flow of personnel between the two groups (Serber 1975). The professional staff member of the regulatory agency often can look to a later career within the regulated industry. At the same time, industry experts frequently are recruited by the agencies. In these cases, as Nader and Serber indicate (1976, p. 283), the regulatory agency is not "bought off" in the way that police may be by narcotics dealers or underworld syndicates. Rather, influence is established by making the regulators feel that they are a privileged and personal part of the social milieu of the industry, rather than a part of the public.

In essence, the making of rules in any society reflects the differential power of special interest groups, particularly those which have become so well organized that they are able to influence the policies made to affect

145

all people (Quinney 1970, p. 12). It is out of the making of rules that there are established legal codes that favor one group over another and that define which acts will be regarded as criminal. The citizens must follow the rules, even when a rule discriminates against some groups or perpetuates inequality (as it often does, since rules tend to favor the dominant interest groups in society).

GOVERNMENTAL POWER: THE ENFORCING OF RULES

If citizens do not follow the rules, they are penalized by the personnel involved in the second governmental activity, the enforcement of the rules. Nonconformists are tracked down, and punishments for their violation of rules are levied against them. This activity provides the muscle to the making of rules, which might be otherwise ignored. Its far-flung influence is illustrated by examples of rule enforcement agencies: the courts with their attorneys, judges, bailiffs, and so forth; the surveillance groups, such as the American FBI and CIA, which keep an eye on "'subversive political groups" who advocate the overthrow of the elite; and the police network, from police chiefs directing search nets for kidnappers of wealthy children to county sheriffs' deputies who keep an eye on petty thieves and people who let their dogs run loose.

Any social class, special interest group, or family that can influence either or both of these two activities of government toward its own interest has gained an advantage. A class that has its own members elected to Congress or appointed to executive office, for example, has achieved a political advantage of the first order, for here it can influence the basic rules on which social order is established. If those who control a great deal of wealth can get rules passed that legitimate their control (say, laws sanctifying "private property"), then they have won most of the battle of maintaining their privilege. It also helps, however, to have friends among the rule enforcers. If a special interest group or social class can ensure that the courtrooms are staffed by judges and lawyers who were born into that group or class, a secondary level of support is established that is particularly useful when something goes awry on the primary, or rule-making, level.

The enforcement of rules is necessary if the rules are going to be effective. The proceedings are of interest to us because, even at this level, class bias is manifested and the system of stratification is reinforced. In the courts, class bias occurs when law reflects the differential power of special interest groups. In Anglo-American law, for example, the landlord usually has the legal advantage over the tenant, and the seller is favored in a buyer-seller relationship. The poor are more likely to be tenants and buyers than landlords and sellers. Many laws are designed to protect property privileges, and because of this fact alone, those who are most prone to violate the rules are those without property. The prisons are full of the poor.

Class bias also occurs when the treatment of lawbreakers varies by the class position of the offender. Police tend to be more suspicious of the poor and the black (Bayley and Mendelsohn 1972). At every level of law enforcement, the underprivileged person is likely to be treated more harshly than the privileged. For the same crime, one is more likely to be arrested (Wolfgang and Cohen 1970), put in jail if arrested, refused bail, brought to trial, found guilty, and sentenced to prison. The rich also receive more sympathetic treatment in the legal process. Rich defendants, but not poor ones, possess sufficient resources to hire good lawyers, pay bail, establish impressive community connections, express themselves well, and perhaps even bribe officials. The crimes of the rich are more likely to be handled informally, outside the criminal courts, and to be disposed of through fines.

Many other ways in which the underprivileged groups of society are selectively penalized by the criminal justice system have been documented. The ways are often unconscious by-products of the functioning of the system. That the poor are less likely than the affluent to present an impressive demeanor, speech, dress, and life history to judges and juries is true, but this is not anyone's conscious plan. Nevertheless, if such disabilities were consistently to work to the disadvantage of the powerful, we could anticipate that legal procedures would be altered somehow. Political inequality means a disadvantage not only in the ability to get others to do what one wishes, but also in the ability to avoid being done to.

Finally, class bias results because crimes of the affluent are handled differently from crimes of the poor. When people from the more comfortable backgrounds break laws, as they often do in connection with their businesses or occupations, they tend to be dealt with relatively leniently. A person who steals a television set worth $100 is far more likely to go to jail than a person who evades paying taxes of that amount. A simple but illegal price-fixing arrangement may cost customers more than thousands of burglaries, yet the price fixers are likely not to be apprehended or, if caught, they are likely to receive light sentences. For example, the seven defendants in the 1961 trial of executives involved in the price fixing of electrical products were fined and sent to jail for thirty days (Geis 1977). More recently, a prominent lawyer who had stolen $2.5 million received a sentence of five years' probation. His judge remarked that the crime did not involve any violence, and that "while it is just as much a crime to steal from the rich as from the poor, it remains true that the defendant's crime seems not to have subjected anyone to severe privation, or perhaps any privation." Hearing of this, another lawyer complained because he had received a two-year prison sentence for embezzling over $1 million. Of 1,000 people convicted of bank embezzlement in 1977, in fact, only one-fourth were sent to jail (Goldstein 1978).

These types of white-collar crimes are particularly likely to be committed by corporate officials in pursuing the goals of the corporation. Sutherland (1971) studied the known crimes of the seventy largest industrial and commercial corporations in the United States over a ten-year period. Every corporation had received at least one adverse decision, and 90 percent had received more than one. Their crimes included restraint of trade, infringements, unfair labor practices, misrepresentation in advertising, and rebates. Only 159 of the 980 cases were tried in the more opprobrious criminal courts, the others being settled in the less public commissions or in civil courts, which are, of course, less humiliating. For punishments, the corporations were most likely to receive fines (a penalty that is not usually devastating to the financial solvency of the corporation), and occasionally officials were sentenced to days in jail. White-collar crime — the crime of the educated, the affluent, and the powerful — exists, but it is not particularly likely to receive strong sanction. Society's attention and society's outrage are focused instead on the crimes of the poor. In this sense, the political power of the criminal justice system is employed in ways that correspond to the inequalities of power found in other institutions.

NONGOVERNMENTAL POWER

Control of people and things takes place in other institutions also. It is useful for the sake of analysis to divide the other institutions into two main branches, economic institutions and noneconomic institutions. Within both of these branches are bureaucracies that within themselves manifest hierarchies of authority, make rules to govern people, and support power inequities through their reward and punishment systems.

In addition, the elite of the economic institutions are able to employ the resources of property and capital at their command to persuade others to work for them or to do their bidding. The power resting in the noneconomic institutions is more subtle. The elite of these institutions must rely heavily on the persuasive influences of socialization messages to have their effect. A bishop can get people to work for his causes when they subscribe to the message of the church. Persuasion, education, socialization, indoctrination, and manipulation are the tools of power more likely to be employed by the mass media, the churches, and the schools. The power of the economic elite, by contrast, lies in their access to the resources of survival and physical subsistence, which in the final analysis may be more compelling.

THE ECONOMIC INSTITUTIONS   Of most importance in understanding the economic power in modern industrial nations is the recognition of the

148

power of corporations. In modern American society, for example, there are hundreds of thousands of small businesses, but the most powerful type of economic enterprise is the corporation. As evidence, it has been estimated that the 200 largest corporations hold over half of all assets of manufacturing companies. Large corporations have become economically dominant in the United States only in the last eighty years (Mueller 1970; Fusfeld 1972). Three major merger movements since 1900 resulted not only in the concentration of control over manufacturing production in single industries, but also in the development of large conglomerates that control activities across several industries.

The increased concentration has been paralleled by an increase in the power that corporations wield. As Williams put it, "The fact that in the United States the great majority of decisions concerning investment and production, as well as consumption, are made by . . . officers of nongovernmental corporations marks the American economy as basically capitalistic. The growth of giant corporations has *centralized* the making of economic decisions, but it has not *socialized* it" (1970, p. 178).

The power of large profit-oriented corporations is exerted on many issues. Corporate control over certain areas is fairly obvious. Just by knowing the nature of capitalism, we would expect corporations to have considerable power over the setting of prices, the supply of products and services, and the regulation of wage and employment practices. But corporate control extends beyond these production-related concerns. Control of the broader environment is attempted by large corporations, because it is very much to their long-term advantage to make that environment predictable and stable. If consumer demand, taxes, and government regulations, as well as prices and labor costs, can be made predictable, then long-range plans can be adopted and executed. Consequently, corporations attempt to ensure that the consumer wants the product, that adverse government action is prevented (either directly or indirectly), and that costs can be balanced by prices (Galbraith 1973, p. 39).

That these goals are not automatically reached is in part due to the fact that other sectors of society also have some power. State and federal governments administer taxes, legislate monetary and fiscal policies, direct credit and capital flows, and limit the use of air, water, and land. Unions moderate the wage-setting power of corporations, competition among corporations sometimes decreases the control of any particular one, and foreign businesses exert an independent force. Corporations thus are restricted to some extent by governmental policies and regulations, environmental limitations, international relations, and labor unions.

Nevertheless, there are a number of actions that corporations can take in their attempts to structure the environment as they would like it. Advertising helps create and sustain consumer demand for products. Government can be influenced: The contribution of funds to the campaigns of political candidates, the employment of lobbyists and lawyers to influence legislative bodies, and the allocation of personnel to important positions in regulatory agencies, military bureaucracies, and foreign policy posts can have enormous effect. It is relatively easy to balance costs by prices, as corporate managers generally are free to administer prices as they see fit, particularly if the government can be convinced to avoid price controls. Wages are more subject to control by unions since they frequently are established through collective bargaining. Yet, wage increases generally only keep pace with the increases in the cost of living, and so the percentage of corporate income that goes for wages remains about the same.

The overall result is that the American economic system is to a very significant degree dominated by large corporations that control much of the country's wealth. In the attempt to secure a stable environment, corporations make decisions touching on many broader aspects of modern life, including depletion of natural resources, employment and growth in the economy, international relations, civil rights, public works, and conditions affecting minorities and the poor. As economist Fusfeld interprets it, the net effect is that many decisions of significance are made by "a small group of men who are responsible only to themselves, who select their successors, and whose organizations continue for an indefinite time" (1972, p. 3).

STRATEGIES OF ECONOMIC INFLUENCE   There are a number of strategies that corporations can employ in attempting to offset those other sectors of society which have some say-so about the corporate environment. That the American people pay enormous governmental subsidies to the oil and gas business attests to the effectiveness of such strategies. There are many, and a few of the more obvious deserve mention.

A chief strategy of corporate influence over government is through the influencing of the appointment and election of political figures. For example, the Tobacco Institute, an organization established by the tobacco industry, lobbied vigorously in 1974 for the appointment of a Kentucky senator who was sympathetic to their interests to the Senate Commerce Committee. He was appointed and within two years became chairman of a subcommittee that had oversight jurisdiction over the Federal Trade Commission — which at the time was waging a lawsuit against the advertising practices of tobacco companies (M. Jensen 1978).

A second strategy is the financing of political campaigns. Political campaigns are very expensive, and big business has been one of the more generous contributors to their financing. In 1968, three hundred corporate directors of the top fifty military contractors donated $1.2 million to election campaigns (C. H. Anderson 1974, p. 225). Even after it was ruled illegal for companies to contribute to national political campaigns, the practice continued. R. J. Reynolds, for example, was found to have used some $190,000 in company funds between 1968 and 1973 for domestic political contributions (M. Jensen 1978).

A third strategy is lobbying. The better financed and organized a lobby is, the stronger its effect on governmental policy. This is one reason that wealthy interests have the advantage over poorer interests. Most lobbying is done by business, and it is probably most effective when it is geared to blocking legislation rather than creating it (Ziegler 1965, p. 109).

A fourth strategy is to form research organizations or policy groups that attempt to gain the ear of politicians. An example of a particularly important group that has been heeded by political figures is the Committee for Economic Development (CED), an elite organization whose highly selective membership is acquired by invitation only. In 1968 the CED recruited representatives from many of the largest corporations, including General Electric, General Motors, Westinghouse, Standard Oil of New Jersey, Socony-Mobil Oil, IBM, Procter and Gamble, Ford, ITT, and U.S. Steel. CED's interests are thus those of multinational corporations, interests that include an economic environment promoting national economic growth, control of inflation, and protection of foreign investment (Prewitt and Stone 1973, p. 68). It is in these kinds of organizations that big business leaders discuss and resolve their differences on major policy matters. Their conclusions tend to be heeded by the federal politicians who believe that the health of multinational corporations such as IBM, ITT, and Ford must be a high priority item; otherwise, they feel, the effects on employment, wage levels, shareholder income, and so forth would be adverse. As Prewitt and Stone suggest:

> It is therefore incumbent on government officials to arrange policies
> that will result in the maintenance of business confidence and en-
> courage the large firms to invest, employ large numbers of people,
> and transact a considerable volume of business with supplier and
> customer firms. . . . Government's failure to at least acknowledge
> the policy preferences of the large economic interests would shatter
> this business confidence and have disastrous results. As a result,
> what develops is such perceived mutuality of interest between high
> government officials and those elite clubs that are the authentic
> voice of big business that the latter's voice is extremely influential
> in the exercise of political power in the areas of business concern
> (1973, pp. 68–69).

Another strategy is the offering of money to key lawmakers, more commonly termed bribes. The extent of this strategy is unknown, since bribes are made in secret. That it is a significant strategy is revealed by a federal study that showed that 337 indictments of public officials on bribery and extortion charges were made in 1976 alone. Of 1,598 public officials indicted between 1970 and 1976 on corruption charges, 1,081 were convicted (Rawls 1977).

There are other strategies, but the ones cited are sufficient to illustrate the point that the great wealth controlled by the modern corporation enables it to exert an influence on policy decisions far beyond the scope of influence it enjoys merely by controlling prices, wages, and products.

THE SOCIALIZATION INSTITUTIONS   The power of other institutions, such as education and the communications systems, comes from their socialization role. The first thing that a new revolutionary government does is to gain control of the communication systems — radio and television stations, and the press. Not much later, it gains control of the schools. These sources of influence are used to convince the people of the legitimacy of the new power elite. In times of greater stability, control does not need to be so blatant, but it is there, nevertheless. In the United States, schools teach the values of the free enterprise system and shape personalities that can take the orders and show the discipline desired by the managers of factories. Television convinces people to buy more and more products. Churches avoid looking at the causes of poverty and, instead, counsel people to look within themselves for the sources of sin. The socialization institutions affect the values and beliefs of people, which can become either supportive or antagonistic to privileged classes, but usually are supportive.

When we deal with the question posed at the beginning of the chapter — why do the poor and middle-class people accept so willingly the accumulation of wealth and privilege by a very few? — the answer must include a reference to the socialization of the public. Force and coercion can only do so much. The rules of property, discussed in the previous section, and the authority to use force, which is given to rule enforcers, control the population to some extent. In addition, loyalty can be encouraged through salary, promotion, and prestige incentives. But rules and force alone are inefficient techniques of social control. Life is much more peaceful if the members of the less privileged strata accept, even endorse, their own economic and political circumstances.

To the managers of bureaucracies and the owners of property, it may seem important that members of the middle strata in particular be supportive of the stratification system and that they be loyal to their higher-ups, because they are involved in many of the nitty-gritty aspects of running the show. There is evidence that white-collar and blue-collar workers do indeed provide strong moral support for inequality in many countries, even when their economic interests logically might lead them into contrary frames of mind. In the United States, for example, middle-class whites have become the mainstay for resisting the economic integration of blacks. While it may be employers who benefit from a segregated labor market, it is the actions of middle-class whites that perpetuate residential and educational segregation of the races, thereby indirectly promoting economic segregation. Also among middle-income people can be found strong antipathies toward the poor, blaming them for their deprivation ("the poor are lazy") or denying that they even exist ("people on welfare are cheaters"). Reform proposals aimed at redistributing wealth or elevating the economic level of the poor often encounter strong resistance from the middle class (Feagin 1975). Even in their view of their own class location, middle-income people often support inequality. They may not like where they are, but the common solution proposed is not to alter the system somehow, but instead to alter their own positions within it. The desire to "get ahead," to "make something of oneself," reveals a basic acceptance of the structure in which one wishes to get ahead.

The ideological acquiescence of the masses is potentially more problematic to the dominant groups in democracies than in totalitarian countries, since democracies are designed on the model that all citizens should participate in the political process and that all interests should be represented. As it usually works out, however, in democracies the underprivileged are not politically involved. In the United States, for example, the lower the income or education of the person, the less likely he or she is to vote, campaign, join a political party, write letters to members of Congress, or belong to a special interest group (Almond and Verba 1963). Consequently, political participation is carried out mainly by two kinds of groups: those fairly permanent and organized pressure groups and lobbies which want something from the government, and those transitory groups which are unhappy about a specific government action and organize perhaps only to protest. "As a result legislation in America tends to favor the interests of businessmen, not consumers, even though the latter are a vast majority; of landlords, not tenants; of doctors, not patients" (Gans 1973, p. 133).

It is probably not anyone's conscious desire that the less privileged become politically inactive or that the politically active come to support the status quo. Nevertheless, these outcomes are one consequence of socialization, particularly that carried on by the schools. Ziegler and Peak (1970) wrote of the ways in which the educational system helps create docile, contented citizens. Of basic importance is the school's avoidance of controversial issues. Students in the classroom are easier to manage if the authority structure is not challenged; challenge might result if controversy were presented. One review of social studies texts (Hunt and Metcalf 1943, p. 230) found that such texts did not discuss shortcomings in the free enterprise system, they avoided the topic of race and ethnic relations, and they suggested that there are no classes in America. More recent texts are not much different, according to Ziegler and Peak. They generally ignore social class, sex, and religion; present ethnocentric views

153

of American government; paint a totally unreal picture of the political process; and relate jingoistic perceptions of the relationship of the United States to other nations. Ziegler and Peak further suggest that the goals of education gradually have become dominated by concern with control of behavior, creation of respect for authority, and establishment of orderly behavior. Because of this concern, schools are somewhat effective in preparing students to become obedient workers in the factories and bureaucracies, but they do not particularly encourage students to become discriminating and informed voters or political activists.

Similar interpretations have been made of the socialization role of religion, although at times religion becomes a radical force for change and certainly some church people sacrifice a great deal to further radical ideals (James Reeb, a Unitarian minister, was fatally beaten by four white men in Selma, Alabama, before the 1965 civil rights march on Montgomery, for example). For the bulk of the religious population, however, American religion supports the status quo more than it challenges it. Class-linked denominational affiliations minimize awareness of social and economic inequities and encourage the development of ideologies that rationalize and maintain the class positions of the congregations. Upper- and upper-middle-class churches, for instance, are not likely to advocate a basic restructuring of the distribution of wealth. Middle-class churches may look down on the ways of the immoral rich, but they value the propriety and respectability of the "common man." Lower-class churches place greater stress on the hope of a rewarding afterlife, which could be just as available to the poor, perhaps even more so since it is believed that money corrupts. As Demerath puts it in his comparison of "the church" (predominantly middle- and upper-class) and "the sect" (predominantly lower-class): "On the one hand, the *church* caters to those who are firmly integrated into society by providing justifications for secular values and pursuits. On the other hand, the *sect* serves the disenfranchised by providing an escape to a community that is set apart from the secular world" (1964, p. 178).

At the leadership level, challenge of the system of inequality by the religious institution is deemphasized as a result of the belief of ministers and pastors that their role is more to deal with personal problems and vices than it is to preach about social issues and ills. Stark et al. (1970) found in their survey of Protestant ministers in California that most sermons rarely touched on controversial and moral issues. Although significant differences in this respect existed between the doctrinal "traditionalists" (the predominant category) and the more liberal "modernists," the majority of pastors avoided the subject of racial problems in 1968, the year that Martin Luther King was assassinated, the Kerner Commission issued its report on racism, the ghettos erupted in rioting and burning, and Biafrans starved by the tens of thousands. Less than one-third discussed world or national poverty, world peace, or capital punishment. They did try to provide moral comfort for those who were distressed, point out the existence of sin, illustrate the type of life that a Christian should lead, and uphold Christian standards. The traditionalist clergy in particular were silent on all issues except those considered relevant to personal vices, such as crime and juvenile delinquency, drug use, alcoholism, and sexual conduct.

Parishioners and laypersons likewise show little inclination to advocate change because of religious beliefs. Milton Rokeach concluded on the basis of his national sample of over one thousand adults that church members who place a high value on salvation are conservative, anxious to maintain the status quo, and unsympathetic to the black and the poor:

> They had reacted fearfully or even gleefully to the news of Martin Luther King's assassination, they are unsympathetic with student protests, and they do not want the church to become involved with the social or political issues of our society. Considered all together the data suggest a portrait of the religious-minded as a churchgoer who has . . . a tacit endorsement of a social system that would perpetuate social inequality and injustice" (1970, p. 58).

AN EPILOGUE   Before leaving this section on how institutions instill acquiescence in the less privileged, the reader should be reminded that sources of resistance do occur. The socialization institutions would not have to be so concerned with conformity and loyalty if everyone were convinced of the rightness of the social order. As discussed below in Chapters 7 and 9, resistive ideologies do exist in most societies. In the United States they are particularly likely to be adopted by the poor, the young, the less educated, and the blacks (Feagin 1975). In addition, while the upper-middle class generally is one of the most conservative classes politically, within it there is a substratum of radical and liberal intellectuals from educational, social service, and artistic circles, which commonly provides the leadership for radical social and political movements (Hamilton 1972). Since members of this subgroup occupy influential positions within the socialization institutions, and the former groups can be organized for political action, the activity of both may on occasion become threatening to those who benefit from the status quo.

The presence of active dissenters within the society may call forth a reaction from the rule enforcers. For example, a 1976 study by the U.S. Senate of the activities of American intelligence agencies revealed that major steps had been taken in the 1960s to watch and discredit civil rights groups, antiwar groups, socialist groups, and feminist groups. The Federal Bureau of Investigation was found to have created files on more than 500,000 citizens, opened 250,000 letters, listed 26,000 citizens for detention in case of emergency, and harassed private citizens.[3] Particularly scrutinized by the FBI were the National Association for the Advancement of Colored People, antiwar groups, the John Birch Society, and the Socialist Workers Party. Martin Luther King, Jr., recipient of the Nobel Peace Prize, was considered by the FBI to be "the most dangerous and effective Negro leader in the country," and it was feared that he might "abandon his supposed 'obedience' to white liberal doctrines" (nonviolence) and "unify and electrify the 'black nationalist movement' " (quotes from FBI documents).

The FBI took actions to defuse the political activities of these groups. It opened files on every member of Students for a Democratic Society (SDS) and every black student union. Its efforts to counteract Martin Luther King, Jr., included attempts to destroy his marriage and the sending of an anonymous note that King interpreted as a suggestion that he commit suicide. FBI agents were directed to discredit New Left student demonstrators against the Vietnam War by such tactics as publishing their photographs, using "misinformation" to notify members falsely that events had been cancelled, and writing "telltale" letters to students' parents. The FBI further was found to have tapped phones and opened the mail of dissident groups, to have written letters to spouses in order to destroy marriages, to have incited conflict among rival groups, to have influenced employers to fire political activists, and to have provoked investigations by the Internal Revenue Service.

The effectiveness of the actions of either the dissidents or the FBI is difficult to assess. Blacks gained a number of legal victories during the civil rights movement, particularly relating to voting rights and public accommodations, but little advancement was made on the crucial economic issues of employment and job security. The Vietnam War ended eventually, but only after the nation's majority had been opposed to it for a number of years. King was assassinated in 1968, the New Left disintegrated during the early 1970s, and public opinion polls of the middle 1970s revealed a popular shift to the right.

Nevertheless, recent political history does illustrate that there are in modern industrial nations a number of arenas of power and a number of strategies of control. Although research findings on international comparisons must still be viewed as tentative, at least one study of power in twenty-five industrial societies finds that although democracy itself has little effect, inequality *is* reduced when democratic socialist parties gain seats in the legislatures. The author (Hewitt 1977) concludes that his finding "encourages optimism about the possibilities of political action to reduce inequality."

[3] For a review of the major findings of the U.S. Senate Select Committee on Intelligence Activities, see *New York Times,* April 29, 1976.

We now turn to the second basic problem of this chapter: Which groups have power? Are the people who are economically and socially privileged also powerful? Is there a power elite? If so, what is its composition and what kind of power does it wield?

Who Has Power? The American Case

Political scientists and sociologists have suggested two main models of power: pluralist and elitist. Both accept the idea that some concentration of power is functional and inevitable in a large, complicated, and heterogeneous society. "Pure democracy," in the sense that every member of the society could have an equal say in all decisions, is not very feasible. Not only would there be enormous logistic difficulties in arranging a system whereby every person could vote on every issue, but there also is the problematic fact that most people are neither very interested nor very informed on public issues.

The disagreements between the elitists and the pluralists revolve rather around the questions of which groups or individuals are actually involved in policy making; whether the people at the top form a cohesive unit; among how many groups power is distributed; and what level of access to decision making is held by subordinate groups.

THE ELITIST CONCEPTION OF POWER

The elitist model maintains that the decisions of basic importance in most modern industrial societies are made by a small, autonomous, and omnipotent group of business, military, and political leaders, a "managerial elite" who exert enormous power by virtue of their control over bureaucratic organizations and over human, technological, and material resources. These elites routinely interact together at lunch, at business meetings, and in clubs. Their children may even intermarry. However, the elites do not necessarily come from the upper class or from any other social class. Rather, they have gained power through their control over the most important bureaucracies in the society.

The elitist model evolved from an earlier tradition of thought exemplified by Marx, Pareto, Mosca, Weber, Michels, and Veblen. There are a number of subvarieties of elitist theories, which are outlined below.

AN ELITE OF ECONOMIC LEADERS An appealing idea because of its simplicity (the "haves" control the "have-nots") and also because of its historical Marxian development, the identification of the power elite with the corporate rich has been a popular idea. A classic statement appeared in James Burnham's 1942 publication of *The Managerial Revolution.* Burnham assumed that an elite gains a dominant position in any society through its control over the chief means of production. Control means not only that the elite will prevent others from gaining access to the means of production, but also that it will receive preferential treatment in the distribution of goods and services. Thus, according to Burnham, "the easiest way to discover what the ruling group is in any society is usually to see what group gets the biggest incomes" (1942, p. 57). More recently, Kolko (1962, pp. 68–69) asserted that the concentration of economic power in a very small elite allows that elite to guide industry toward ends compatible with its own interests.

Most advocates of this point of view assume that wealth brings power, usually exercised indirectly, and that the wealthy use their riches to influence the political, economic, educational, and religious institutions.

One who argues that an economic elite rules in part through the support given it by the political institution is Ralph Miliband, who suggests in *The State in Capitalist Society* (1969) that the capitalist class is able to rule because of the state's commitment to capitalism. The state, for example, serves capitalism by helping to defend against foreign capitalist interests. It stifles ideological challenge by outlawing anticapitalist parties and by using repressive trials to quell left-wing dissenters. Miliband also believes that the structure of bureaucracy helps maintain capitalism. Recruitment and promotion procedures select upper-level bureaucrats whose philosophies range from strong conservatism on one end to weak reformism on the other. Further, interchange of personnel between the business sectors and the bureaucracies that are supposed to regulate them creates a cozy business-government link.

Miliband argues that capitalists use their money to achieve political legitimation. For example, they dominate the means of communication, using advertising not only to encourage the sale of products, but also to connect the value of the free enterprise system to other socially approved values and norms. Other institutions help in furthering capitalist goals, Miliband argues. The schools teach capitalist values to their students; universities discourage teaching that affronts capitalism (while allowing the presence of a few "eccentrics" in order to show that there is freedom of expression). The employment of academic personnel as consultants for business and government increases the connection between academia and capitalism. Universities also teach the ideologies, values, and purposes of capitalism as well as management skills. This is not because a conspiracy exists, but because teachers themselves are in favor of capitalism.

AN ELITE OF BUSINESS, MILITARY, AND POLITICAL LEADERS   The most influential proponent of this point of view, and by far one of the most formidable exponents of elitist theory, is C. Wright Mills, who contends in *The Power Elite* (1956) that significant decisions in American society are made by a relatively small, autonomous, and omnipotent group of individuals who comprise a power elite. The most powerful roles are centered at the tops of the economic, military, and political institutions. The "commissars," "chief executives," and "warlords" who occupy these strategic command posts make vital decisions of major consequence. They affect slump and boom; they decide on war and peace.

In American society, Mills maintains, the power of individuals who occupy the "institutional command posts" of the society cannot be explained in terms of their native talents or psychology, but rather must be interpreted in the economic and social context of the particular institutions of society that they control. Power inheres not in the individual, but in the role.

The power elite is supported by secondary-level subordinates (including members of Congress) who carry out the decisions of the power elites. In themselves, these members of the middle level constitute a drifting set of stalemated, balancing forces. Underneath these two levels is the third level — the powerless, undifferentiated, and apathetic masses who are controlled by the elite through effective use of propaganda, flattery, and deception.

Although the power elite is not an aristocracy or a unified social class, in Mills's view its members do have a psychological and social base for unity, which rests on psychological similarity, social intermingling, and coinciding interests. They know one another, see one another socially and professionally, take each other into account in their decision making, and are more or less aware of themselves as a social group. Yet they do not come from a single social class, for their origins are somewhat diversified. Many do come from the upper class, but others are from the upper-middle class — from the upper third of the income and occupational pyramids, from fathers of the professional and business strata, and from urban Protestant backgrounds.

Mills identifies the power elite with the upper class, but he defines class in economic terms and thus is referring to the rich and the occupationally powerful, rather than to a purely social class. He sees America as having fallen under the sway of these power-oriented leaders who, by occupying pivotal positions in strategic institutions, seek to further their own class self-interests. Because of the absence of formal legal restraints and a system of checks and balances, the power elite is characterized by an irresponsibility that Mills terms the "higher immorality." Mindless, intellectually mediocre, amoral commanders of power unequalled in human history, elite members hold positions of organized irresponsibility within the American system.

Mills is not the only elite theorist who is disturbed by what he sees. Others are disquieted by the idea that the power elite rules in its own self-interest and is unresponsive to the wishes of the populace and to the interests of minority groups. They suggest that the majority of the people has little input to the decisions of the powerful minority. This is true regardless of the democratic mechanisms that have been built into government or of the presence of ideologies concerning the rights of the majority (Michels 1949). Indeed, the existence among the elite of what Meisel (1957) calls the "three C's" — group consciousness, coherence, and conspiracy — allows the elite to reinforce its own position relative to other groups, increasing social distance and restricting entry.

According to Mills, the power elite in the United States has emerged as a result of specific historical circumstances. Particularly significant was the coincidence of interest during the last half-century between those who controlled the major means of production and those who controlled the newly enlarged means of violence. Also important historically were the decline of the professional politician, the rise to political command of the corporate chieftains and the professional warlords, and the absence of any genuine civil service of skill and integrity, independent of vested interests.

Since World War II, a number of additional trends have contributed to elite control. These include the increasing importance of corporate conglomerates and the lessening importance of small business, which enhance the power of corporate managers; the inability of state and local governments to handle the problems of an urban, industrialized society, which enhances the power of federal politicians; and the widening impact of foreign relations on domestic policy, which enhances the power of military leaders. As Mills explains it, World War II brought about the increasing involvement of the government in the economy as well as the expanded role of the military.

The cold war was particularly important in legitimizing the ascendancy of the power elite. It was the cold war that inhibited a genuine and public debate of alternative political decisions and led to the decline of policy-coherent parties connecting the lower and middle levels of power with the top levels of decision. It also was the cold war that focused attention on international problems and encouraged expansion of the military. These developments led to a coincidence of interests between military and corporate needs, resulting in a permanent war establishment supported by a privately incorporated economy inside a political vacuum. As each of the three domains — the economic, the political, and the military — became enlarged and centralized, the consequences of its activities became greater, and its traffic with the others increased.

AN ELITE OF MEMBERS OF THE UPPER CLASS   This point of view has been referred to as the "class model of power" (see Alford 1975 for discussion). It suggests that "the ruling class" is the upper class, which may or may not include members of a managerial elite. While accepting that groups may compete, as the pluralists argue, or that organizational elites control enormous resources, as other elite theorists maintain, the class theorists add further that such conflicts seldom challenge the basic control wielded by the ruling class. The major social institutions — the courts, police, legislative bodies, schools, and so forth — are organized to perpetuate the dominance of the historically evolved ruling class. Consequently, demands of special interest groups or of bureaucratic elites are not likely to question the disproportionate allocation of the social product to that class. Conflicts and struggles go on, but without mounting a basic challenge to the rule of the upper class.

One of the leading proponents for the class conception is Domhoff, who argues in *Who Rules America?* (1967) that an upper social class runs the country. This national upper class is made up of rich businessmen and their families, who are closely knit by such institutions as stock ownership, trust funds, intermarriages, private schools, exclusive clubs, and corporate directorships. Because of the strategic role played by the upper class in the economic and political structures, Domhoff asserts that the aims of the American power elite are necessarily those of members of the upper class. He comments:

> On top of the gradually-merging social layers of blue and white collar workers in the United States, there is a very small social upper class which comprises at most 1% of the population and has a very different life style from the rest of us. Members of this privileged class . . . live in secluded neighborhoods and well-guarded apartment complexes, send their children to private schools, announce their teenage daughters to the world by means of debutante teas and debutante balls, collect expensive art and antiques, play backgammon and dominoes at their exclusive clubs, and travel all around the world on their numerous vacations and junkets (1974, p. 3).

They also command unrivaled power and wealth, which are used to maintain their cultural hegemony.

In his research, Domhoff tended to use the *positional approach,* which locates the centers of power by identifying the holders of important positions in the political and economic hierarchies of a society. (Its main defect as an approach is that the formal leaders are not always the ones who make the decisions. See Freeman et al. 1963 for a discussion.) He used this approach because he believed that it is impossible to find out directly who is most powerful, given the complexity and secrecy surrounding actual decision making. Thus, we must make inferences from information about which groups dominate the institutions in which the decisions are made.

Once Domhoff had identified position holders, particularly at the federal and national level, he looked at their background to see if they be-

161

long to an upper class. His method of determining their upper-class membership was to see if they were listed in the *Social Register,* if they or their forebears had attended an elite private preparatory school; if they or their forebears were members of an exclusive gentlemen's or ladies' club; if they had a millionaire father who had attended a private school; or if they were married to an upper-class person.

On the basis of this research, Domhoff found that the upper class does indeed own a disproportionate share of the wealth, receive a disproportionate amount of the country's income, and contribute a disproportionate number of people to the controlling institutions and key decision-making groups of the country. For example, he found that many of the leaders of major institutions are upper-class people. As many as 53 percent of the corporate directors of the leading banks, insurance companies, and industrial corporations are members of the upper class, according to his criteria. Most of the remaining 47 percent, Domhoff contends, occupy positions in institutions that are "controlled by the upper class." Likewise, Domhoff's research suggests that in the shaping of public opinion, many of the organizations that influence American thought — such as foundations, the Council on Foreign Relations, the Foreign Policy Association, the National Association of Manufacturers, the Council on Economic Development, the major universities, and the mass media — are headed, run, or owned by members of the upper class.

Domhoff also explored the influence of the upper class within the federal government itself. The upper class, he found, provides the major financial support for both the Republican and Democratic parties; dominates the Departments of State, Treasury, Defense, Commerce, and Labor; contributes many of the top level personnel for the president's "inner circle" and the diplomatic corps; controls the regulatory agencies; and influences the choice of federal judges. The majority of Cabinet members come from the upper class (Domhoff 1967, pp. 97–102), and so do the heads of agencies such as the CIA (1967, p. 127). The leaders of a number of other agencies, such as the military and the regulatory agencies, are selected or shaped by the upper class (1967, pp. 107, 125, 129).

Even those individuals who are *not* in the upper class but who are now or were previously employed by an institution controlled by the upper class can be considered to be participants in the control by the upper class. Thus, an upper-middle-class professor at Harvard (which is controlled by the upper class) who serves as a presidential adviser provides evidence of the connection between the upper class and the governing elite. In accounting for the 47 percent of the corporate directors of the leading banks, insurance companies, and industrial firms who are *not* members of the upper class, Domhoff dismisses them as a threat to his central thesis by claiming that they are "co-opted" by the upper class because of their positions in hierarchies *controlled* by the upper class. The largest number of this group are the hired executives who "are being assimilated into the upper class." The rest of the non-upper-class directors — the "experts," the college presidents, the former military men, and the corporate lawyers — in the main are cooperative with the interests of the upper class, he contends. The assumption is made that if an agency or institution is headed by a member of the upper class, then the actions of the agency are thereby controlled by the upper class. For example, because eight of the thirteen secretaries of defense since 1932 have been listed in the *Social Register,* Domhoff believes that the upper class controls the Department of Defense.

Through direct representation in top institutional positions, through control of policy-making bodies, or through co-optation of middle-class advisers and assistants, the upper class is able to control the operations of the economy, the government, education, and the mass media. For a diagrammatic representation of what Domhoff believes are the major links in the chain of influence, see Figure 5.2.

COMMUNITY STUDIES SUPPORTING THE ELITIST MODEL   An elitist view of power also has been suggested by research on community power struc-

Figure 5.2

Domhoff's representation of the power elite policy-making process

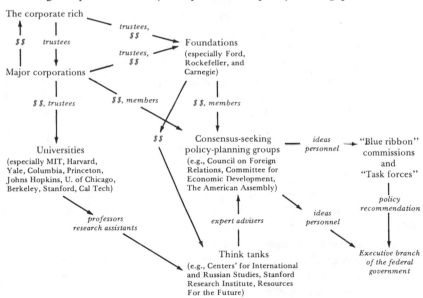

Source: From William Domhoff, "State and Ruling Class in Corporate America," *The Insurgent Sociologist,* Vol. 4, no. 3 (Spring 1974), p. 9. Reprinted by permission.

tures. While these researchers do not necessarily indicate how power functions on the national level, it is useful nevertheless to review them because they heavily influenced the models of power that were subsequently developed and tested by social scientists to describe a national power structure.

An early study of community power in the elitist tradition was conducted by Robert and Helen Lynd in the 1920s and 1930s on "Middletown" (Muncie, Indiana). In Middletown, they reported (1937), basic decisions were made by a small power elite consisting predominantly of wealthy business owners and executives and by a few key professionals. The Lynds found that the "X family," a wealthy manufacturing family of five brothers, had a virtual monopoly of all aspects of decision making and manipulation. The X family originally came to Middletown with the gas boom, began with modest capital, and became millionaires; when its second generation became socialized to upper-class position and norms, it became a part of the hereditary upper class. As Protestants trained in the school of rugged individualism and as patrons of the arts, education, religion, civic activities, and a long list of philanthropies, they were exemplars of the American dream of success.

The X brothers' industry (the making of glass fruit jars) happened to thrive during the depression, and this success made the family far more influential locally than ever before. By virtue of their financial liquidity, they were able to cushion the local impact of the depression at a number of points. Business-class control became concentrated.

The power of the X family was exerted in a number of domains. In banking, the brothers served on the board of directors of the one bank in town, thereby controlling the credit available to other industries. In legal services, the X family retained interests in Middletown's best law firms. In industry, although not seeking deliberate financial control of other industries, they commanded sufficient prestige and banking power that their influence was substantial. In retailing, the brothers maintained interests in the leading furniture store, two dairies (which squeezed out a competitor by pressing X milk into use in local institutions supported by X charity), and a brewery in a neighboring city. In transportation, they owned Middletown's interconnecting trunk railways. In residential patterns, the X family created an exclusive suburb on the northwest section of town and developed a state teachers' college and high school there. In education, an X brother was president of the school board; another brother was the school attorney; and it was said that the X state teachers' college was controlled in its larger policies and in occasional small details. In religion, their theologically conservative point of view was encouraged among the ministers and congregation by the X's generous financial aid to the churches. In the press, the X family controlled the local newspaper. In politics, they injected just enough control to ensure a tolerable tax rate, an open-shop town, and control over the numerically dominant working class, without interfering with other political issues. The control exerted by the X family, according to the Lynds, was not so much the result of conscious, coordinated planning among the members of the family as it was the result of unconscious, well-meaning, and "public-spirited" actions, as the business community interprets that concept.

Whereas the Lynds found that Muncie, Indiana, was dominated by a single large family, several decades later Floyd Hunter (1953) found that Atlanta ("Regional City"), Georgia, was controlled by a small, cohesive economic elite. For this research, which constituted his doctoral dissertation, Hunter used the *reputational approach,* which identifies powerful persons by discovering their reputation among others. (Its defect is that we cannot know how reliable the judgments of others are. See Wolfinger 1960 and Polsby 1962 for critiques.) Hunter obtained lists of 175 community leaders from community organizations such as the League of Women Voters and the Chamber of Commerce and then asked fourteen "experts" to select the top forty leaders. Then he interviewed the top forty and asked them to name the top ten among the forty. In both these steps Hunter found a large measure of agreement among the judges.

More than half of the forty elite leaders whom Hunter was able to identify were businessmen of commercial, financial, or industrial interests. Of the remainder, six were professionals, four were government personnel, two were labor leaders, and five were social leaders. Hunter concludes that "the pattern of business dominance of civic affairs in Regional City is a fact." These businessmen did not occupy formal political positions, yet they had determining voices in almost every decision of significance to the community. Decisions were made by a relatively small number of people unknown to the general public and were carried out by a large understructure of subsidiary personnel. Although different constellations of the top forty made decisions on different questions, depending on the issue, there were considerable overlapping and informal communication between all of them: "On specific projects one leader may allow another to carry the ball, as a leader is said to do when he is 'out front' on a project which interests him. On the next community-wide project another may carry the ball. Each may subordinate himself to another on a temporary basis, but such a structure of subordination is quite fluid, and it is voluntary" (1953, p. 67).

The leadership group itself was divided into cliques and crowds. Decisions were frequently made at informal and formal meetings, and committees worked out the details. No civic groups nor associations were considered to be important in policy determination, and most presidents of such groups remained in the understructure of the power hierarchy. One gets the picture of a small group of policy makers who devoted considerable amounts of time to interaction among themselves as a group, but who carefully maintained their exclusive status in a number of ways. They allowed lower-level civic leaders to voice their opinions, but the latter's wishes usually went unheeded. The bulk of the population had little to say about the direction of basic economic, political, or community decisions. The leaders tended to protect themselves from too many demands by channeling policy execution through the understructure.

Briefly, the overall picture of power in Atlanta that Hunter presents is one with four levels: the first level consists of the policy makers themselves, the industrial, commercial, and financial owners and top executives of large enterprises; the second level consists of officials, vice-presidents, public relations men, and small businessmen; the third level includes the civic organization personnel, the newspaper columnists and radio commentators, the petty public officials, and selected organization executives; and the fourth level includes such professionals as ministers, teachers, social workers, and personnel directors. The first two levels set policy, while the third and fourth levels are involved in carrying out decisions:

> The roles defined for the under-structure of power personnel are carefully defined in keeping with the larger interests. Their movements are carefully stimulated and watched at all times to see that their various functions are properly performed. Stability of relationships is highly desirable in maintaining social control, and keeping men "in their places" is a vital part of the structuring of community power (1953, pp. 108–109).

THE PLURALIST CONCEPTION OF POWER

The pluralists do not dispute the contention of the elitists that power is concentrated or the idea that certain economic or social groups may exert control out of proportion to their numbers. Rather, the pluralists stress that power is exerted by a multitude of interests—some dominant on certain issues, others more powerful on other issues — with one interest group being held in check by the opposing forces of conflicting groups. The pluralist model assumes that power is dispersed among a number of organizations, special interests, and voters. Modern societies are seen as being fractured into many special interest groups intermittently presenting demands that then are mediated and compromised through the political process. Groups apply pressure on those issues that interest them, but remain inactive on issues not relevant to their interests. Power goes to those who win in a particular struggle. (For examples of pluralist thought, see Latham 1965; Riesman 1961; and Truman 1951.)

The interest groups are not equal in power, and they employ varying techniques for exercising influence on the decisions important to them (Polsby 1963). Because there are so many groups, each one can be viewed as operating within a small sector of society. Nationally, then, the top level of power consists of "veto groups," a diversified and balanced plurality of interest groups, each of which is primarily concerned with protecting its jurisdiction by blocking the efforts of other threatening groups.

In the pluralist view, as in the elitist view, the structure of power in modern industrial nations is seen to have been shaped by historical forces. As society became more differentiated and the division of labor became more elaborate, individuals found it increasingly difficult to control the forces that governed their lives. The entrenchment of people around specific activities led to the emergence of interest groups that attempt to influence the political process (Bentley 1949; Truman 1951). These interest groups compete with each other for favorable dispositions of privilege and power. However, their competition does not proceed on equal bases; some groups have more influence on the outcomes than others.

The pluralist view of power, thus, is in direct contrast to the elitist view. Whereas elitists see the top level of power as consisting of a somewhat unified power elite, the pluralists see it as composed of veto groups. Whereas elitists stress that the power elite determines the outcome of the really important issues, the pluralists believe that who exercises power varies with the issues (and that most groups are inoperative on most issues.) Whereas the elitists argue that the power elite is a reflection of the coinciding interests of crucial institutions, the pluralists see the existence of an amorphous power structure that reflects a diversity of conflicting or differing issues. Whereas the elitists assert that the structure of power particularly favors the economic elite and also often the political and military elites, the pluralists assume that no one group or class is decisively favored over another.

The classic community study demonstrating the pluralist model was conducted by Robert Dahl (1961) on New Haven, Connecticut. Dahl used a *decision-making approach* to the study of power, which attempts to discover power by examining the history of specific decisions to see who made the basic choices and by looking at particular issues to see what persons were involved in different areas of power. Dahl selected three issue areas (party nominations, public education, and urban redevelopment) to study the decision-making process. Using direct observation, testimony of informants, news releases, speech texts, and reports, he traced the stages in the decision and identified the key personnel. Such an approach concentrates on what has been done, not what could be done. (A major defect is that the investigator has to choose which issues to study and he or she may not select the ones which are crucial to a power elite. In addition, it is difficult to get at behind-the-scenes maneuvers or long-term subtle influences when using this approach.)

In New Haven, Dahl found that the political influence that he was able to observe was rather widespread. The economic elite was involved in only one issue — urban redevelopment — and even on this issue only ten of the twenty-six people who exerted any real leadership were economic leaders. Likewise, Dahl found little evidence that members of the social elite were involved at all: The "social notables" held only two of five hundred elective offices, and they were only eight out of fifty persons who exerted influence in the issue areas.

Dahl concluded that the use of influence was specialized; that is, individuals who were influential in one sector of public activity tended not to be influential in another sector. Further, the social backgrounds of individuals in one sector of activity tended to be different from those in other sectors. In the issue of urban redevelopment, the twenty-six actors who were successful in initiating or vetoing policy came from a broadly based coalition of civic leaders, municipal bureaucrats, and the mayor. In public education, sixteen actors were involved, including the mayor, certain members of the school board, and members of the school bureaucracy. On the issue of party nominations, thirteen actors were involved, most of them being members of the two parties. In each area, different actors appeared, their roles were different, and the kinds of alternatives from which they had to choose were different. Altogether, fifty different persons or groups were involved in policy making, but only five of these were involved in more than one issue area. Over half of the fifty were public officials rather than social or economic notables. Evidence of a covert structure of economic leaders, integrated and operating behind the scenes, failed to turn up in the entire two years of research.

Dahl maintained, then, that power is tied to issues, and issues can be fleeting or persistent. American society is divided by a number of small special interest groups that have widely differing power bases. The claims of small, intense minorities are usually attended to, making it unnecessary for entire classes to mobilize because the preferences of class members are satisfied in piecemeal fashion. Groups become involved in an issue when they feel a need to defend or extend their values. (The corollary is just as important: Potentially powerful groups will not intervene when their power positions are not at stake. This generalization is said to explain why business groups will not throw their resources into every question that arises. See Spinrad 1966, p. 224.)

KELLER'S "STRATEGIC ELITES" A problem with using Dahl's research for information about the American power structure is that it may be misleading to generalize from a community study to the national scene (Prewitt and Stone 1973). Mills, for one, readily conceded that pluralism is an adequate descriptive model on the middle levels of power, but he argued that on the major national issues the pluralist model falls short. Thus, to Mills it is irrelevant whether the city of New Haven is best described by the pluralist model.

This objection is avoided by Keller (1963), who maintains that even on the national level there are a number of counterbalancing elites who are the heads of institutionally related hierarchies. They are recruited on the basis of "individual motivation and capacity" and represent the diversity of the hierarchies they head. These elites include not only political, economic, and military leaders, but also moral, cultural, and scientific leaders. Elite position is related to the achievement of high educational qualifications, specialized training, and technical excellence, although original wealth and high social status are quite helpful. While privileged birth can give many advantages and ethnic, religious, familial, and club memberships are important, they are not sufficient to ensure continued high status from generation to generation (Keller 1963, p. 261).

Keller supported the thesis that American elites are recruited on the basis of merit, rather than social background, by citing studies that show that the leading military officers, scientists, church officials, intellectuals, politicians, corporate executives, civil servants, diplomats, Supreme Court justices, journalists, and film stars are middle-class individuals, as shown by statistics indicating that they were raised in the homes of business or professional men in comfortable economic circumstances.

In Keller's view, strategic elites emerged in the historical movement from small undifferentiated and classless societies to those where occupational diversity results in the emergence of social classes. The hereditary transmission of class status is important in feudal and estate societies, but in the industrial society there is an increasing need for leaders who possess knowledge and expertise, and thus there is a decline in the importance of birth as the major criterion of selection and succession (Keller 1963, pp. 66, 219). The emergence of an elite that acquires its position because of managerial competence rather than inherited class status has developed in American society, in Keller's view, because the increasing size and complexity of industrial society require a meritocratic leadership: "Power has become less arbitrary and personal and is increasingly shared among various groups and institutions. . . . Today, no single elite has absolute power. . . . [and] none can hold power forever. . . . At best, strategic elites are temporary aristocracies over whom the public . . . exercises considerably more control than it did in the past" (1963, pp. 277–78).

The division of labor among the strategic elites means that no single one claims a long-term superiority over the rest. The struggles for power engage rival elites and also cooperating elites. One elite may temporarily dominate other elites, but this cannot last for long, because no single elite can execute all types of collective undertakings.

CRITIQUE AND EVALUATION

What are we to make of the disparate views of power in America presented by the pluralist and elitist models? They both are plausible, and aspects of both have been supported by research. Yet their assumptions

169

are fundamentally opposed, and their policy implications are divergent. In this section, the criticisms that have been leveled at each one are reviewed.

CRITIQUE OF THE PLURALIST VIEW   The pluralist approach has intuitive appeal. Complicated industrial societies like the ones in which most of us have grown up do seem to have many different conflicting groups. Any day's *New York Times* is full of this issue or that issue, and the same side does not always win. Many struggles do not seem to affect most of us.

Critics suggest that this is illusory, however. They agree with the pluralists that many conflicts are highly specialized; yet they make two important qualifiers to the pluralist thesis. The first is that while many conflicts do not involve elite interests, those which do are usually settled in the interests of the elites. Let there be welfare "reform," propertied people might reason, so long as it does not challenge the basic concepts supporting private property or change tax policies favorable to the well-heeled. Thus, Weinstein (1969) has shown that it was the big business interests in the early 1900s that supported social welfare reforms and even conservative trade unions in order to avert state socialism. In this they were bitterly opposed by smaller manufacturers and by the socialists, but they were able to prevail. Weinstein indicates that

> few reforms were enacted without the tacit approval, if not the guidance, of the large corporate interests. And, much more important, businessmen were able to harness to their own ends the desires of intellectuals and middle-class reformers to bring together "thoughtful men of all classes" in "a vanguard for the building of the good community." These ends were the stabilization, rationalization, and continued expansion of the existing political economy, and, subsumed under that, the circumscription of the Socialist movement with its illformed, but nevertheless dangerous ideas for an alternative form of social organization (1969, pp. ix–x).

The second qualifier is that pluralist theory is ahistorical, in that it ignores the built-in advantages held by some people because of their strategic location in an ongoing society with a particular economic and cultural history (Mankoff 1970). There are, indeed, many groups struggling, but some groups never even get to the point of struggle because they recognize their powerlessness. Further, of those who do, a few have greater access to the resources that count — political, economic, and military — because of advantages that they have accrued historically. As a result of the decision in New Haven on which Dahl reported, for example, hundreds of families were displaced and black neighborhoods were destroyed by the urban redevelopment program. These groups had opposed the program, but had been unsuccessful in winning their position. (Some of

170

them later were plaintiffs in a multimillion-dollar class action suit against the mayor and police department for engaging in illegal surveillance and wiretapping during the conflict.) In this case, the historical events leading to black powerlessness and the significance of such events to a theory of pluralist control are unexamined by the decision-making approach.

There also have been criticisms of the pluralists' favorite methodology, the decision-making approach. In this method, formal interviews with decision makers are conducted in order to find out why and how decisions are made. Invariably, the interviewees indicate, in the words of Prewitt and Stone (1973, p. 83), "that they were dispassionate, listened carefully to both sides of the issue, were (possibly) subjected to some pressure from affected interests but did not succumb to any blandishments. Further, all decisions, it will usually be reported, were made in public." Then such studies suggest that policy decisions reflect the interests of all involved groups and that they are not made in secret. Unfortunately, it is hard to believe that individuals of great power do not meet privately or make decisions at meetings to which the public is not privy.

Critics also point out that in any study of decision making, the choice of issues to study is subjectively determined, replication is difficult, and covert aspects of decision making are not revealed. Elitists argue that the decision-making approach may select issues that are of secondary importance or may not be salient to certain powerful elites, thus ignoring the more stable, but latent, patterns of decision making. They also suggest that the pluralists' concentration on controversial issues may fail to uncover evidence of those subtle influences of the power elite which are not elevated into public consciousness. The "nondecision," the issue that is never raised because someone has been able to keep it out of the limelight, may be just as important (Bachrach and Baratz 1963).

A careful reading of Dahl's own work raises some interesting questions along these lines. Dahl indicated that the mayor and the development administrator, neither of whom came from an upper class, were the two main developers and initiators of the urban redevelopment plan in New Haven in the 1950s. But the plans were approved by a Citizens Action Commission (CAC) composed of "the biggest set of muscles in New Haven," in the words of the mayor. The members of the CAC were considered muscular "because they control wealth, ... industries, ... banks, ...[and] labor." They evaluated all the urban redevelopment plans. While Dahl makes a big point of the fact that the mayor and his associate initiated the plans, remarks made by the muscles of the community indicate that the plans were not against their interests. As one commission member told Dahl, the proposals of the mayor and the development administrators would be presented to the commission, which "oftentimes would slant the [proposals] the way we felt the business community would react to certain things and the way we felt the approach should be made"

171

(Dahl 1961, p. 131). Then, "the CAC helps set the atmosphere in the community so they're receptive to these things the city administration is trying to do." The mayor wanted redevelopment because it would build his political career; the members of the CAC wanted it because getting rid of the "decay" of the downtown business district was essential for the success of many businesses. (For a reexamination of New Haven's power structure that supports the elitist perspective, see Domhoff 1978.)

A slightly different set of criticisms has been made of Keller's view of "strategic elites." In particular, her theory does not explain what happens when the various elites clash (Prewitt and Stone 1973, p. 126), nor does it recognize that not all elites are equal in power. For example, entertainment elites are relatively powerless. In addition, the theory overlooks any distinctions between a ruling elite and its supporting staff. Some suggest, contrary to Keller's thesis, that almost all politicians, scientists, and civil servants are part of a supporting staff because they do not make important decisions, but only carry them out.

Similarly, the theory of strategic elites does not appreciate that most nonbusiness elites must operate in the environment of the business world. Very little that is done by any elite does not require business support and approval.

Keller's assertion that the strategic elites come predominantly from middle-class backgrounds (and therefore represent the ascendancy of merit) is ambiguous. An elite who has a "professional or business" background is not necessarily from the middle class, as Keller suggested, but may be from the upper class. The main examples of elites from lower-middle-class origins that Keller presents are groups that some would attest to be least likely to possess real power — movie stars, church leaders, and journalists. The majority of certain other elites are clearly from "socially advantaged" families (Supreme Court justices, U.S. senators, and diplomats, for example.)

CRITIQUE OF THE ELITIST VIEW   The pluralists have their complaints also. Concerned with the "erroneous caricature" of American society given by the elitists, Arnold Rose presented an elaborate defense of the pluralist position and critique of the elitist in his book entitled *The Power Structure* (1967). While he agreed that there is a power structure in every organized activity of American life and at every level and that within each power structure a small number of people hold the largest amount of power, it seemed equally evident to him that modern American society contains many power elites, each powerful mainly within its own domain. These elites do not necessarily cooperate. The collusion between business and government that Mills wrote about seemed exaggerated to Rose, who stated that the relationship between the economic elite and the political authorities has been a constantly varying one of strong influence, cooperation, division of labor, and conflict. Each influences the other to some extent, and each operates independently of the other to a large extent. As examples of the competition between business and government, Rose pointed out that the government has set various restrictions and controls on business and has heavily taxed business and the public to carry out purposes deemed to be for the general good. On the other hand, business leaders use lobbyists, "business representatives" in legislatures, contributions to campaign funds, publicity designed to influence public opinion, and other techniques to influence government. Rose acknowledges that members of the business community do influence government more effectively than most nonmembers, not only because they can afford lobbyists and advertisements, but also because they are more educated, more knowledgeable, more articulate, and more activist than average citizens. Nevertheless, the economic elite has its greatest successes in influencing government when there are no counterpressures, such as in their relations with government purchasing agents and the independent regulatory commissions.

Rose claimed that it is fallacious to think of either the economic elite or the political elite as being unified, as Mills suggested, because neither one is a monolithic unit acting with inner consensus. Consider government, for example. Rose, himself a former state senator, argued that while the federal government has been gaining ascendancy over the state and local governments, and while the office of the president has been gaining power at the expense of Congress, it is far from true that Congress and the state governments are powerless. Congressional action is not only important to the outcome of key national issues, but it is also frequently independent of the wishes of an economic elite (as was true, Rose suggests, when Congress passed the social welfare legislation in the 1930s).

Perhaps we should note that an important point overlooked by Rose on this issue is that government often acts as if it cannot afford to institute business policies that jeopardize economic stability and growth (Prewitt and Stone 1973, p. 97). If it jeopardized "business confidence," it might deter new investment and product development. A substantial drop in military procurement could also gravely affect business confidence and well-being. Rose does not examine the degree to which there is a perceived mutuality of interest between the political elite and the large corporations.

Rose does acknowledge, in agreement with Mills, that there are *some* areas for which a small group tends to make decisions. The major area of small-group control of national policy is foreign policy. Particularly influential are the CIA, the foreign policy "experts" in the universities and such organizations as the Foreign Policy Association and the Council on Foreign Relations, and the military-supplies industrialists who exert their wishes through military leaders.

173

In the area of economics, the influence of business leaders is exercised most on issues affecting production, distribution of wealth, and consumption (to some extent) and very little on other issues. But even this influence is curtailed by conflicts within the economic elite, one of the most important being that between representatives of big business and small business. Recent examples of such a cleavage within the Republican party itself were the split between Robert Taft and Dwight Eisenhower and that between the Goldwater and the Scranton-Rockefeller forces. Rose contends that foreign policy decisions are made not by the economic elite, but by the executive branch and their advisers, and then are ratified in a general way by public opinion, as expressed in the vote for the president. (It must be pointed out here that Mills never asserted that the power elite is agreed on everything; he noted that factions do exist. He argued, nevertheless, that the internal discipline and community of interests binding the power elite together are more powerful than the divisions within it.)

The methodological approaches of the elitists also have come under fire. The reputational approach, such as Hunter used, which identifies powerful persons by discovering their reputation among others, has been criticized for relying on the evaluations of judges (Wolfinger 1960). How do we know that such evaluations are not heavily affected by bias, misconception, and distortion? Arbitrary choice of informants can bias the findings from the outset, while encouraging influentials to talk about influentials introduces a circularity. In addition, it has been charged, the reputational approach may uncover potential power rather than real power, folklore rather than knowledge, and status rather than power (Wolfinger 1960; Polsby 1962). Finally, the assumptions that power is related to high socioeconomic position and that power resides in a single monolithic structure are built into the methodology, resulting in findings that support the elitist theory (Polsby 1963; Dahl 1958).

The positional approach, used by those who assume that power accrues to the institutional position, also has been criticized. The argument is that office holders are not necessarily the real leaders (as reputational studies show) (Schulze and Blumberg 1957), nor are the formal leaders always involved in decision making (Freeman et al. 1963).

Domhoff's position that the power elite is a ruling class because its members come from the upper class also has come under attack. Critics contend that the fact that some people in high positions come from the upper class is insufficient evidence of a ruling upper class. They argue that it cannot merely be assumed that upper-class individuals always act in the interests of the upper class or that non-upper-class individuals are sympathetic to the goals of the upper class. A real test of these assumptions would require spelling out what are the goals of the upper class, to

174

what degree these goals are uniform, and what interests actually govern the making of decisions.

Furthermore, it is far from obvious that overrepresentation by one particular interest group in the dominant positions in the society leads to decisions in favor of that group regardless of the actions or interests of other, underrepresented groups (Oh 1969). That members of the upper class can and will somehow work in unison to further their "class interests" remains to be seen. As some point out, "On the contrary, it has been shown that on matters of minimum wage, antitrust, unionization, medicare, and other social welfare measures the interest of the upper class has been undermined consistently ever since the early New Deal days" (Oh 1969, p. 401).

In addition, some maintain that the important divisions within the economic sectors and the substantial competition between the various types of business establishments militate against a unified policy on the part of the upper class. This idea lead one reviewer to point out that Domhoff did not specify exactly what is meant by the "control" that the upper class wields:

> The corporate economy is not a single machine to be steered at will, but rather a congeries of semi-competitive institutions whose activities impinge on each other. Certainly individual boards of directors control the course of their corporations . . . but it is difficult to see what is meant by the "collective" control of the upper class when each board of directors is out to undercut . . . the income and prerogatives of the boards competing with it. . . . the "control" of the upper class need consist in no more than maintaining the general compass setting that steers us toward social, economic, and political objectives compatible with the maintenance of property as the basis of the social order. . . . In a word, the identification of an upper class and the demonstration that it occupies the seats of power do not allow one to make essential predictions as to the future course of American national behavior (Heilbroner 1968, pp. 15 16).

CONCLUSIONS

We suspect there is an element of truth in all these models, and that is one reason that the controversy has not yet been resolved. But perhaps it is not necessary to resolve all the competing claims before making some conclusions about power. Certain principles are accepted by proponents of both models. Both acknowledge that power in modern industrial societies is concentrated. Both accept the idea that business and governmental interests maintain a strong degree of political dominance. They both acknowledge that upper-class interests are disproportionately represented among decision makers, that a number of groups are relatively unrepresented among decision makers, that a number of groups are not well represented in the political process, that the distribution of wealth and power is concentrated among a very few, and, further, that such concentration has been relatively stable over time. The elitists agree with the pluralists that on the middle levels of power, conflicts may reflect the struggles of a number of competing groups. Both would accept the functionalist position that in all societies there is a need for coordination — and particularly so in societies with a complex division of labor. Out of coordination emerges authority hierarchies and, thus, inequalities of power. Furthermore, complex societies are heterogeneous, so there are a number of groups that differ in their goals. Age and sex, racial and ethnic, occupational and social class groups all may have competing or conflicting interests in the distribution of scarce goods and services.

Both models agree on the above propositions. In addition, we recognize that certain claims of each model seem to be valid. The ideas of the elitist and pluralist models that fit empirical descriptions have been summarized by several authors (Eitzen 1974, pp. 139–40; Putnam 1976, pp. 22–26). The following propositions of the elitist position fit the realities of power in the United States:

1. The federal government has, over time, assumed more and more power, thereby lessening the power of state and local governments.
2. The executive branch has tremendous power in foreign affairs, which in the immediate past has resulted in decisions to send military forces to various places, to fight undeclared wars, and to use the CIA for political intervention in the internal politics of other nations.
3. Wealthy people have great influence in Congress and in the executive branch. This influence is maintained through a variety of techniques, including campaign contributions, control of political parties, occasional bribes, and appointment or election to political office.
4. The leaders of the major institutions are almost universally wealthy and probably have some interests in common, such as preserving the economic status quo, protecting American interests abroad, and encouraging economic expansion.
5. Political leaders are drawn disproportionately from upper-status occupations and privileged family backgrounds. This is true not only in the United States, but also in Great Britain, Italy, and West Germany, in the Third World countries of Asia, Africa, and Latin America, and also in communist countries such as the Soviet Union and Yugoslavia, although to a lesser extent.
6. The social backgrounds of administrative elites are at least as exclusive as those of political leaders. Around two-fifths of the bureaucratic

managers in a number of different countries come from the upper-middle and upper classes.

7. Economic and other elites are usually drawn from even more privileged backgrounds than are political and administrative elites. This is particularly true in capitalist economies such as West Germany, Japan, Canada, Venezuela, Great Britain, and the United States. Evidence on the origin of elites in communist countries is less clear, yet some suggest that it is probable that the social origins of the Soviet industrial managers are higher than those of the Soviet political leaders (Brzezinski and Huntington 1964, p. 138).

The propositions of pluralist theory that seem to fit reality are as follows:

1. There are many separate power structures, and each operates generally within its own sphere of influence. The AFL-CIO is dominant in labor, the AMA in medicine, the NAM for large business concerns, and so forth. Within each of these spheres there is a hierarchy of power.

2. But the various power structures are unequal in power. While the economic elite is probably the most powerful overall, at times shifting coalitions may effectively counterbalance the unequal power of the corporate rich.

3. Elites are not all-powerful. Elites are further limited by the policy priorities and political procedures already established in the society. As Prewitt and Stone (1973, p. 233) suggest, political elites in the United States are not powerful enough to call off elections; political elites in the Soviet Union are not powerful enough to reject the metaphors of communism; political elites in South Africa are not powerful enough to suddenly introduce programs of racial justice. In addition, pressure groups at times can exert influence on the elite. When the mistakes of an elite group are especially devastating, mass public action, organized by a counterelite, can hasten "elite circulation." (However, the infrequency and ineffectiveness of such opposition should be noted.)

The evidence accumulated so far points strongly in the direction of elite theory. Not only are elites well entrenched in modern America, as they are in most industrial nations, but they also are more immune from popular control than the rhetoric of democracy implies. As Prewitt and Stone (1973) clearly indicate, the nation talks a more democratic game than it plays.

It is clear that the elites of the public and private spheres have used power and bureaucracies to evade responsibility as well as to gain efficiency. There is a community of interest between the economic and political elites, and there are an interchangeability and overlapping of roles among them. The government is quite concerned about maintaining a

177

favorable environment for business. There are a number of institutions — foundations, think tanks, the CIA and FBI, and the institutes — that coordinate the actions of the political and economic leaders.

Yet elite theory does not tell us how much power these elite have with respect to any given social policy, and it does not tell us what social goals they will pursue. It does indicate that many social policies, if they do not directly further the wishes of the economic and political elites, are at least compatible with them.

6 SOCIAL MOBILITY AND THE STRUCTURE OF INEQUALITY

A RECENT ADVERTISEMENT in *Esquire* appealed to its male readers by congratulating them: "Now that you've made it, you deserve Crown Royal." The writer of this ad recognized what research has more laboriously shown: Important values for Americans are achievement and success. Seventy-seven percent of the people surveyed in a small New York City poll indicated that "getting ahead in life" was personally important to them (Mizruchi 1964). How they viewed success varied. Lower-income people were more likely to stress owning a home and "having a good, steady job" (material, economic responses) as symbols of success, whereas the higher classes were more likely to stress non-materialistic goals, such as "having a good education." Nevertheless, for both groups, obtaining the symbols of achievement valued by others who were considered important constituted a basic part of their views of the appropriate goals of living. Success — fostered by a glorification of the individual, rooted in the Puritan ethic of efficiency and hard work, and justified by popularized versions of laissez-faire economics — is perhaps

Written in collaboration with Anthony Turrittin.

second to no other source of personal motivation in the United States.[1]

There are many ways of living that could be defined as successful. One of the most common is the pursuit of an occupation "better" than that held by an individual's parents. In theory, upward social mobility in an occupation is a potential avenue of class advancement for all (except those born into upper-class families). For most, to find employment or a life's work that receives greater rewards than those to which one is accustomed — income, prestige, or a sense of self-worth, for example — is a quite significant way of pursuing the success goal, and this process can become highly meaningful to the individual. In reality, however, most people are not very mobile; they end up in occupations and life styles very similar to those of their parents. To justify their own situations, they may find it necessary to reject the success ideology or to define it in such a way that their lack of mobility seems worthwhile.

In the two chapters following this one, we discuss the ideologies that favor social mobility and the educational processes that facilitate it. In this chapter, we are concerned with how many people actually become socially mobile, to what degree, and with what consequences.

The Measurement of Social Mobility

OCCUPATIONAL RANK

Some people believe it is easy to improve yourself if you want to badly enough. Others argue that getting ahead depends on luck or contacts and that average men and women are going to be left behind even if they are ambitious. As sociologists, we would like to check out the propositions implicit in these popular beliefs, but in trying to address such issues, we are immediately faced with a question: How are we going to identify when and how much mobility has occurred?

The concept of mobility is an extreme abstraction, which must be given dimensions before research can be carried out. Mobility assumes movement from one position to another, and thus it assumes placement on some kind of scale. To measure it, we must be able to construct a linear gauge according to which individuals or groups can be scored or located.

Three dimensions of inequality that lead us to such a scale were suggested by Weber: economic resources, power, and prestige. It is possible to make these abstract hierarchies more concrete by measuring limited indicators of inequality, such as income and property, political influence, occupational prestige, or community esteem (Haller and Portes 1973, pp.

---

[1] There is a substantial literature on the success theme, including Mills 1951, chap. 12; Chinoy 1955, chap. 1; Clark and Woodward 1966; Wyllie 1966; Werner 1970; Huber 1971; and Chenoweth 1974.

51–52). This has been done with income (H. P. Miller 1966, for example), general wealth (Lampman 1962), and reputational prestige in the community (Warner and Lunt 1941; Lehman 1969; Walteron 1971).

However, the most commonly used index of social inequality in social mobility research is occupational rank. It is commonly used for several reasons. First, a person's position in the occupational structure is correlated with many other behaviors and characteristics — economic and political attitudes, child-rearing practices, and emotional stability, for example. In addition, while occupation is not identical with economic or social status, it is highly correlated with both income and education. In fact, most sociologists consider occupational prestige to be the most representative summary measure of a person's social standing within the context of modern societies (Haller and Portes 1973, p. 54).

Second, information on occupation is relatively easy to obtain. Unlike income, which is a touchy topic for many people, occupation is freely discussed by most if they are asked. In fact, questioning about occupation is so common, for example, at get-acquainted socials or cocktail parties that someone who is asked about his or her occupation in an interview usually shows little hesitation in answering. Third, occupational rankings tend to be consistent across communities and over periods of time. Finally, occupational rank provides a measure of class position that is independent of the person's own subjective evaluation. For these reasons, the ranking of occupation has become the preferred method of measuring social status.[2] The development of quantitative indexes of occupational status has enabled social mobility research to achieve a high level of precision and to uncover important relationships among a large number of variables.

Having narrowed the problem of measurement of social mobility to the problem of the measurement of occupational mobility, we still face the question of how to measure occupations, which, one might point out, are really only job classifications for different kinds of labor. Obviously, occupations must somehow be ranked and scaled. There have been two approaches to the development of a socioeconomic classification of occupations (Blau and Duncan 1967, p. 118). One follows the work of census statistician Alba M. Edwards (1943) by ranking major occupational groups. Professionals stand above managers, managers stand above clerical workers, and so forth. The other, a more recent development, derives scores for occupations by examining the education and income levels of workers in each occupation (Charles 1948; Blishen 1958; Bogue 1963; U.S. Bureau of the Census 1963). These scores have been correlated with ratings by people of the "general standing" or "prestige" of particular occupations. (See Chapter 7 for a fuller discussion.) That is, a socio-

[2] For a criticism of studying mobility by limiting the concept to occupational mobility, see Strauss 1971.

economic index of occupations is established by assigning weights to the income and educational characteristics of an occupation so that its resulting score places it on a scale similar to its placement by the prestige ranking. This index, more popularly known as the Duncan Socioeconomic Index (SEI), after Duncan's original work (1961) in developing it, has been extensively used in mobility studies.

Once a scoring system has been devised, it is a relatively simple matter then to determine how much occupational mobility has taken place. The most commonly used method is to ask a nationwide sample of adult males, first, what were the occupations of their fathers when they were growing up and, second, what are their own occupations. A comparison of a father's occupation with his son's occupation indicates whether or not the son's job is in a different prestige category than the father's and, if so, how different it is.

THE EXCLUSION OF WOMEN FROM MOBILITY STUDIES

We use the words *fathers* and *sons* above, because most of the mobility studies have employed exclusively male samples. The relative inattention in stratification research to the status location of women has been based on several assumptions (Acker 1973): (1) the family is the unit in the stratification system; (2) the social position of the family is determined by the status of the male head of the household; (3) females live in families; therefore, their status is determined by that of the males to whom they are attached; (4) the female's status is equal to that of her man; (5) women determine their own social status only when they are not attached to a man; and (6) the fact that women are unequal to men in many ways and are differentially evaluated on the basis of sex is irrelevant to the structure of stratification systems. Although these assumptions can be challenged (Acker 1973, pp. 938–40), the fact of their having been made has resulted in the treatment of status hierarchies as male hierarchies and of occupational distributions as male distributions.

The disregard of the occupational status attainment of women increasingly appears unwise as more and more women seek employment outside the home (they currently make up 40 percent of all workers), as many women seek careers in their own right, and as some women choose not to be housewives and mothers and, instead, to become full-time workers. Several of the assumptions that Acker details can be challenged. The first one, that the family is the basic unit of stratification, is limited, because not all persons live in families. In 1974, 25 percent of persons over eighteen years of age in the United States were unattached individuals.

The second assumption, that the social status of the family is always determined by the status of the male head of the household, is clearly not accurate. It has been determined that the perceptions of others of the status of a family are influenced by the wife's characteristics. Sampson and Rossi (1975, p. 208) report that while their respondents considered a husband's occupation to be the most influential to their perceptions of the family's status, the wife's occupation still was considered. The husband's occupation was twice as important as his wife's, and his education was considered to be only slightly more important. Whether education or occupation is used, the wife's characteristics do contribute to the social status of the family. Sampson and Rossi continue, "This finding seems to weaken the arguments in favor of using only the head of the household's characteristics when information about a spouse is available" (1975, p. 213).

When the wife's contributions to the economic status of the family are considered, similar conclusions can be drawn. Nearly 6.8 million families in 1974, more than 12 percent of the total, were headed by women. In the remainder, those in which there is an adult male, women frequently bring resources to the family, including employment income. In 1972, in only 36 percent of families did the wife not earn income; and in the other 64 percent, wives contributed an average of one-fourth of the family income (U.S. Department of Labor 1975, p. 139).

If female status is not entirely determined by the status of the male head of the household, then it becomes important to examine the mobility patterns of females as well as those of males. In the last decade, studies of female social mobility have begun to appear. Most of these compare the process of status attainment experienced by women to studies of the process experienced by men. In the section below, we examine first the male patterns of mobility and then the emerging evidence on female patterns.

Social Mobility in the United States

MOBILITY PATTERNS OF AMERICAN MEN

It is optimistically asserted by many and cynically denied by a few that America is the land of opportunity, where anyone with ability and drive can get ahead. A corollary follows from that: "anyone who can't make it doesn't deserve to." Success is a widely expressed theme, ambition is considered desirable, and elite status is explained with the rationale that people in those positions get there as a result of their own efforts. But what facts can we ascertain about the equality of opportunity? How many Americans are upwardly mobile, how many are downwardly mobile, and what are the conditions and characteristics that promote mobility?

In 1962, the Bureau of the Census, working in collaboration with two sociologists, Peter Blau and Otis Dudley Duncan, secured data on the lifetime occupational mobility of a representative sample of about twenty thousand men between the ages of twenty and sixty-four. These data were later analyzed in great detail by Blau and Duncan (1967) in *The American Occupational Structure*. The data show that there *is* a great deal of mobility in the United States, but most of it covers a very *short distance*. Because this is an important conclusion, let us examine more closely how it was reached.

A summary of the 1962 census data on the occupations of sons as related to the occupations of their fathers is provided in Table 6.1. This type of table is called an outflow, supply, or destination table because it shows how many sons of various social origins (social origin being equated with the occupations of the fathers) reach different occupational destinations. For example, 41 percent of the sons of professionals became professionals themselves, and over 26 percent of the sons of laborers became operatives.

The next table (Table 6.2) shows the occupations of fathers and sons from another perspective. This type of table is called an inflow or recruitment table since it shows the various social origins of men in particular occupational categories. This table shows, for example, that 15.3 percent of men who were professionals in 1962 had professionals as fathers and 18.7 percent had craftsmen as fathers.

How much mobility appears to exist is affected by the number of occupational categories allowed in the table. If only two categories are used, such as white-collar occupations and blue-collar occupations, then mobility seems very limited, indeed. A man who moves from an unskilled laboring job to an operative job, for example, is not recorded as being mobile because he has not moved into the white-collar category. As the number of categories are increased, however, the amount of mobility measured also increases, as smaller and smaller mobility moves are recorded. Tables 6.1 and 6.2, from published census reports, include only eight categories. But when Blau and Duncan (1967) used the census data to do their research, they used seventeen categories. We should be alert to the variations in amount of mobility reported by different researchers that are due to their differing choices of numbers of categories.

What conclusions can be drawn from Tables 6.1 and 6.2? First of all, it seems clear from Table 6.2 that occupational mobility has been a widespread phenomenon in American society. Three out of four employed American males in 1962 were working at occupations in a different category from those of their fathers (using eight occupational prestige levels as the mobility base). One-fourth were characterized by "self-recruitment"; that is, their occupations were on the same level as those of their fathers.

Second, occupational mobility is more likely to occur over short distances than over long distances. Except for the sons of farmers and laborers, it is uncommon for a son to have an occupation that is three or more occupational categories above or below his father's category. While

184

Table 6.1

Occupation of son, by father's occupation, for the United States, 1962

Father's occupation	Son's occupation, percent									Total (number in thousands)
	Professionals	Managers	Clerical and sales workers	Craftsmen	Operatives	Service workers	Laborers	Farmers and farm managers	Total	
Professionals	41.0	17.5	15.9	8.7	10.3	3.1	1.9	1.6	100.0	1,633
Managers	21.6	34.1	16.2	13.9	8.5	2.5	1.9	1.3	100.0	4,001
Clerical and sales workers	23.4	24.4	19.5	14.2	9.9	4.5	2.5	1.6	100.0	2,516
Craftsmen	13.0	16.5	12.5	29.4	17.5	5.1	4.8	1.2	100.0	6,274
Operatives	11.7	12.2	11.0	23.9	25.9	5.9	7.5	1.9	100.0	5,242
Service workers	10.1	14.2	15.2	20.9	20.0	11.1	6.3	1.3	100.0	1,626
Laborers	5.9	8.0	11.6	22.5	26.3	9.1	14.2	2.4	100.0	2,210
Farmers and farm managers	5.0	11.2	7.0	19.8	21.0	5.5	8.9	21.6	100.0	10,470
Total (%)	12.9	16.2	11.8	20.8	18.6	5.5	6.5	7.7	100.0	33,972

Source: Figures calculated from U.S. Bureau of the Census, 1964, Table 1. Eliminated are 5,997,000 males whose occupations were not reported or who were not in the experienced civilian labor force.

Note: Any occupational category contains a range of positions in it. The professional category, for example, ranges from "singer in a nightclub" with a prestige score of 26 to "federal court judge" with a score of 83 (Treiman 1977, Appendix D). There is, then, some overlapping of the scores of specific occupations across the categories. Nevertheless, most occupations within a category cluster around the average (which for professionals is 59). Because of this clustering, the patterns of mobility found in the table, although based on the grouping of related but not identical occupations, are the same patterns that would be found if occupations were not grouped at all.

185

Table 6.2

Occupation of father, by son's occupation, for the United States, 1962

Father's occupation	Son's occupation, percent								
	Professionals	Managers	Clerical and sales workers	Craftsmen	Operatives	Service workers	Laborers	Farmers and farm managers	Total
Professionals	*15.3*	5.2	6.5	2.0	2.7	2.7	1.4	1.0	4.7
Managers	19.8	*24.7*	16.2	7.9	5.4	5.4	3.4	2.0	11.6
Clerical and sales workers	13.5	11.1	*12.2*	5.1	3.9	6.2	2.9	1.5	7.4
Craftsmen	18.7	18.8	19.6	*26.1*	17.3	17.4	13.6	2.8	18.5
Operatives	14.0	11.6	14.5	17.7	*21.4*	16.7	17.8	3.7	15.5
Service workers	3.0	4.2	6.2	4.8	5.4	*9.7*	4.6	0.8	4.7
Laborers	3.0	3.2	6.4	7.1	9.2	10.8	*14.1*	2.0	6.5
Farmers and farm managers	12.0	21.2	18.4	29.3	34.7	31.1	42.2	*86.2*	31.1
Total (%)	100.0	100.0	100.0	100.0	100.0	100.0	100.0	100.0	100.0
Total (number in thousands)	4,370	5,517	4,000	7,067	6,331	1,857	2,220	2,622	33,972

Source: Figures calculated from U.S. Bureau of the Census, 1964, Table 1. Eliminated are 5,997,000 males whose occupations were not reported or who were not in the experienced civilian labor force.

186

it is true that 3 percent of the professional sons tabulated in Table 6.2 had fathers who were unskilled laborers, nearly half of them had fathers who were themselves professionals or who had had jobs in the closely related managerial, sales, or clerical categories. Similarly, the craftsmen sons, of whom only one-fourth had craftsmen fathers, came mainly from closely located operative or farming backgrounds (two occupational groups that are related to skilled labor in the nature of their work). These three groupings account for the origins of 73 percent of the skilled laborers.

Third, upward mobility is more prevalent than downward mobility. Over half (56.4 percent) of the sons had been upwardly mobile, while less than one-fifth (18.6 percent) were downwardly mobile. Table 6.3 indicates the direction of mobility taken by sons in each occupational category. It can be observed that the higher the son's present occupational status, the more likely it is that he has experienced upward mobility; over four-fifths of the professionals in 1962 came from less prestigious social origins. A major proportion of these high rates of upward mobility is related to economic changes, particularly the increased need of an advanced industrial economy for personnel at the upper status level (scientists, technicians, and managers, for instance) and the decreased need for farmers and unskilled laborers. The two occupational groups that expanded proportionately the most between 1910 and 1960 were profes-

Table 6.3

Upward and downward mobility among eight occupational categories for males in the United States, 1962

Son's occupational category	Son's occupational category in comparison with father's category (percent)		
	Moved up	Moved down	Remained the same
Professionals	85	——	15
Managers	70	5	25
Clerical and sales workers	65	23	12
Craftsmen	59	15	26
Operatives	49	29	22
Service workers	42	48	10
Laborers	42	44	14
Farmers and farm managers	——	14	86
Total	56	19	25

Source: Figures calculated from the data presented in Table 6.2. Read the chart this way: "Of the sons who are professionals, 85 percent have been upwardly mobile and 15 percent were stable, compared to their fathers."

sionals (particularly salaried professionals) and managers, while the three that contracted the most were farmers, farm laborers, and nonfarm laborers. The expansion near the top and the contraction near the bottom created an upward flow of manpower and a chain reaction of short-distance movements throughout the occupational structure.

Table 6.4 summarizes what has happened to the sons of fathers in various occupational groups. It shows, for example, that 24 percent of the sons of professionals became blue-collar workers and that 42 percent of the sons of craftsmen became white-collar workers. One pattern becomes clear: Within each of the two major occupational groupings — white-collar and blue-collar — the highest prestige levels were the least mobile, while those at the bottom were most mobile. Sons of clerical and sales workers tended to become managers or professionals, for example, and sons of service workers became craftsmen, operatives, or white-collar workers.

A fourth conclusion is that expansion and contraction of traditional occupational groups accounts for some patterns of mobility. Every occupational origin above the level of construction craftsmen sends more than one-fifth of its sons to only two occupations — salaried professionals and managers (which have been expanding rapidly while reproducing at lower rates than the rest of the population) (Blau and Duncan 1967, p. 38). In addition, every occupational group has recruited more than 10 percent of its members from sons of farmers (for blue-collar categories the proportions are between 20 and 30 percent). This is due both to the rapid decline of the previously populous farming population and the exceptionally high fertility of farmers.

Fifth, proprietorship represents one source of rigidity in the overall occupational structure. The three occupational groups that manifest the most occupational inheritance and self-recruitment are those which entail self-employment — independent professionals, proprietors, and farmers. Proprietorship apparently discourages sons from leaving the occupations of their fathers and makes it difficult for other men to move into this category as well (Blau and Duncan 1967, p. 41).

Sixth, the education that a son receives is particularly important in determining his adult socioeconomic status. The impact of education on occupational attainment is in fact greater than the impact of social origin (Blau and Duncan 1967, p. 169; Blau and Duncan 1965; Duncan and Hodge 1963); the variables are closely related, however, since social origin influences educational achievement. In this sense, education is the major means by which fathers affect the occupational chances of their sons.

The more education a son receives, the greater is the likelihood that he will be upwardly mobile. The proportion of men in the Blau and Duncan data who experienced some upward mobility increases from 12 per-

Table 6.4

Upward and downward intergenerational mobility, by occupational categories, for males in the United States, 1962

Father's occupational group	Change in category by son, in comparison with father's category (percent)					
	Moved down, from white-collar to blue-collar	Moved up, from blue-collar to white-collar	Remained in father's category	Moved up one category	Moved up two categories	Moved up three or more categories
Professionals	24.0	—	41.0	—	—	—
Managers	26.8	—	34.1	21.6	—	—
Clerical and sales workers	33.1	—	19.5	24.4	23.4	—
Craftsmen	—	42.0	29.4	12.5	16.5	13.0
Operatives	—	34.9	25.9	23.9	11.0	23.9
Service workers	—	39.5	11.1	20.9	20.9	39.5
Laborers	—	25.5	14.2	9.1	26.3	48.0
Farmers and farm managers	—	—	21.6	8.9	5.5	64.0

Source: Calculated from the data presented in Table 6.1. White-collar includes the occupational groupings of professionals, managers, and clerical and sales workers; blue-collar includes craftsmen, operatives, service workers, and laborers.

cent of those who received no schooling to 76 percent of those who had gone beyond college (1967, p. 157). Downward mobility, on the other hand, does not show such a linear relationship to education; the curve is more U-shaped. About 2 percent of the least educated experience extreme downward mobility, while about 12 percent of those with one to three years of college and about 2.5 percent of the most highly educated do so. This indicates that men with an intermediate amount of education (beyond grammar school, but not through four years of college) are more likely to experience considerable downward mobility, probably because "their education is not quite commensurate with [their]...high social origins to overcome the danger of downward mobility inherent in a high starting point, unless this danger is neutralized by superior education" (Blau and Duncan 1967, pp. 159–60). The best educated have the qualifications to live up to their high social origins, while the least educated have less high origins to live up to.

A seventh conclusion holds that the occupational status of blacks in America is rather strongly limited by discrimination. True, many blacks are handicapped in their occupational attainment by having economically poorer parents, less education, and inferior early career experiences compared to whites. But even when these handicaps are statistically controlled — by asking what is the achievement of blacks when they have the same origins, the same education, and the same first job as whites — Blau and Duncan find that their occupational chances are still consistently inferior to those of whites.

The disadvantaged position of blacks is likewise revealed by the mobility data: Although one might expect to find higher rates of upward mobility among blacks, given their overall lower starting point, actually the data show that nonwhites are more likely to be downwardly mobile and less likely to be upwardly mobile (Blau and Duncan 1967, pp. 208–13), a fact that partially explains the widening gap in income between blacks and whites in the United States (discussed in Chapter 4). The likelihood of moving up a considerable distance from social origins increases with increasing education for both blacks and whites, but for the blacks the increment in upward mobility brought about by higher education is small, except for the college-educated.

Thus, education is not as effective a route upward for blacks as it is for whites unless the former go to college. Even when blacks receive college education, the socioeconomic status of their occupations tends to be lower than that of whites (Blau and Duncan 1967, pp. 210–13). The more education a nonwhite person receives, the further does his occupational status fall behind that of whites of comparable education. Acquiring an education is simply not as profitable for blacks. Blacks who do achieve advanced levels of education must be imbued with strong values about the virtues of education. These data suggest that many highly educated blacks, who had to have considerable motivation to overcome low social origin and obstacles to educational achievement and who then suffer comparative racial discrimination in the competition for high-status jobs and high income, are likely to experience intense feelings of relative deprivation. These mobility data thus provide some quantitative sense of the cost to blacks of white discrimination in the job market.

A final conclusion is that rates of social mobility probably have increased only slightly, if at all, over the last fifty years. We say "probably," because it is difficult to judge the degree to which rates of mobility have changed over time. The problem is that the various studies that have been made of different time periods are not directly comparable due to sampling and other methodological difficulties. If ever the myth of America as a land of opportunity is to be evaluated objectively, a great deal of work must be done to determine quantitatively the patterns of occupational mobility in the nineteenth century and the first half of this century.

Historians have only recently begun to undertake this kind of research, as there emerged a new interest in the social history of ordinary people as revealed in long neglected institutional records. A full history may never be known, since ordinary people have not left much of a written record of their personal experiences and their opinions of their times. Still, by reconstructing family histories through records found in archives — the census, birth, death, and marriage records, assessment and tax records, school, prison, and institutional records — one can gather a great deal of information on family size, marriage patterns, occupational histories, geographic movement, causes of death, and even wealth acquired.

The historian Stephan Thernstrom has been particularly interested in historical patterns of occupational mobility and has now published two important studies, one (1964) of the small Massachusetts city of Newburyport (about thirteen thousand in population in 1880) and the other (1973) of Boston. Using census records, he attempted to trace all men first listed as laborers in the censuses of 1850 and 1880 and thereby to examine movement of this lowest-prestige occupational group up the occupational ladder. Comparing his findings with a number of other studies, mainly those in the twentieth century, Thernstrom writes:

> In the United States today the climb upward from the bottom
> rungs of the social ladder is not often rapid or easy, but *it never
> was,* if the experiences of the working-class families of nineteenth
> century Newburyport are at all representative. Few of these men
> and few of their children rose very far on the social scale; most of
> the upward occupational shifts they made left them manual work-
> men still, and their property mobility, though strikingly wide-
> spread, rarely involved the accumulation of anything approaching

191

real wealth. This was not the ladder to the stars that Horatio Alger portrayed. . . . It was, however, social advancement of a kind immensely meaningful to men whose horizons of expectations were not those of an Alger hero (1964, p. 223).

Thernstrom has since published results of a similar study of Boston, focusing here on men from all occupational groupings. Random samples of men were drawn from local records from 1880, 1910, 1930, and 1958, and each person was traced through the city directories and tax records for as long as he could be found in the records. Thernstrom was impressed by the stable levels of upward and downward movement when he compared the various time samples. For example, fully 43 percent of sons born in 1850 to unskilled and semiskilled laborers eventually obtained white-collar occupations; for those born in 1880 the proportion becoming white-collar was 46 percent (1973, Table 5.3, p. 89).

Unfortunately, Thernstrom's Boston study is marked by serious sampling deficiencies (see Alcorn and Knights 1975; and Thernstrom 1975), and his conclusions regarding constant levels of occupational mobility opportunity are not well substantiated by his data. His study of Newburyport also has been faulted, because Newburyport was probably atypical of the times and cannot be used as a clear guide to what was happening in the rest of America. Only 10 percent of the 1880 unskilled and semi-skilled fathers had sons who became white-collar. Thernstrom attributes this low proportion to the economic stagnation of Newburyport at that time and to the fact that the working class of that period was heavily of recent Irish ethnic origin. It should be noted that in both Newburyport and Boston there was very heavy out-migration from these cities between pairs of censuses examined, so much so that the mobility patterns and achievements of those who stayed probably differed markedly from those men who were geographically mobile. High geographic mobility was typical of the manual class for every period studied by Thernstrom.

In sum, base-line information on past patterns of mobility is needed to evaluate present levels and is sorely missing. Historians have begun to assemble some interesting data about this, but no national data is available from the early period of industrialization and urbanization. Thernstrom's study, which attempts to provide relevant time-series data for one city, is a step in the right direction.

The methodological problems plaguing studies such as Thernstrom's do not exist for studies covering the period since World War II. As shown in Table 6.5, surveys taken at four different times since then indicate that there was no marked change in the mobility rates between 1947 and 1962, although the overall rate increased slightly by about 4 percentage points. Between 44 and 49 percent of the sons were mobile in that period. Certainly there is no evidence of an increasing rigidity of the

Table 6.5

Occupational mobility of males in four national samples

Father's occupation	Son's occupation (percent)															
	Nonmanual				Manual				Farm				Total			
	1947	1952	1957	1962	1947	1952	1957	1962	1947	1952	1957	1962	1947	1952	1957	1962
Nonmanual	70.8	64.7	66.5	70.9	25.1	34.0	30.5	27.5	4.1	1.3	3.0	1.6	100.0			
Manual	35.1	31.1	30.5	36.1	60.9	67.1	67.7	61.4	4.0	1.8	1.8	2.5	100.0			
Farm	23.0	22.0	22.1	23.2	39.1	44.3	51.5	55.2	37.9	33.7	26.4	21.6	100.0			

Summary of measures of mobility:	1947	1952	1957	1962
Inheritance	55.6	52.6	51.5	51.5
Observed mobility	44.4	47.4	48.5	48.5
Structural	19.2	26.9	27.0	23.1
Circulation	19.1	15.8	16.8	15.4
Chain	6.1	4.7	4.7	10.0
Full-equality model	67.0	67.6	67.0	64.6
Total number (all occupations)	1,153	747	1,023	33,972

Source: Data for the 1947, 1952, and 1957 samples are adapted from Elton F. Jackson and Harry J. Crockett, Jr., "Occupational Mobility in the United States: A Point Estimate and Trend Comparison," *American Sociological Review* Vol. 29, 1964, Table 4, p. 14. Reprinted by permission. Percentages for the 1962 sample were calculated from the U.S. Bureau of the Census "Lifetime Occupational Mobility of Adult Males, March 1962," *Current Population Reports,* series P-23, no. 11 (Washington, D.C.: U.S. Government Printing Office, 1964), Table 1. Eliminated were 5,997,000 males whose occupations were not reported or who were not in the experienced civilian labor force.

Note: This chart shows that in 1957, for example, 66.5 percent of the sons whose fathers had nonmanual occupations themselves had nonmanual occupations.

class structure, as some have claimed (Hertzler 1952), but there has been no marked improvement, either.

The mobility typical of that period was due in part to changes in the occupational distribution. For example, after the war, there occurred a dramatic decline in farming, on the one hand, and a rapid growth in the white-collar occupational sector, on the other hand. Many farmers' sons thus experienced a kind of "forced" mobility, especially into the ranks of blue-collar workers, while the expansion of white-collar jobs opened up opportunity for many sons of blue-collar fathers. This kind of upward intergenerational occupational mobility is called *structural mobility,* and it can be estimated by comparing the marginal frequencies of the standard mobility table, such as Table 6.5. (The proportions of structural mobility and other summary measures of mobility are shown at the bottom of Table 6.5). As shown in the table, over the four postwar mobility surveys, about one-quarter of all men could be characterized as having become upwardly mobile because of structural change.

Based on the standard mobility table, several other kinds of summary measures of mobility can be crudely estimated. As shown at the bottom of Table 6.5, total *observed mobility,* the total of upward and downward movement, varied from approximately 44 percent to 49 percent. This observed mobility is considerably below the amount that would be expected on the basis of chance. On the basis of a full-equality model — each son having an equal opportunity to be mobile — levels of mobility should have varied from about 65 to 68 percent in the postwar studies.[3]

A second summary measure is *circulation mobility,* which occurs as a result of the mutual exchange among the occupational categories, as when upward mobility is balanced by downward mobility. Circulation mobility is generated, for example, when some sons of white-collar fathers take blue-collar jobs, permitting an equal number of sons of blue-collar fathers to move into white-collar work (a process of exchange). Only from 15 to 19 percent of men in the four postwar surveys experienced the reciprocal upward and downward movement termed circulation mobility.

An additional kind of mobility, *chain mobility,* occurs when the occupational slot vacated by a son moving upward is filled by a son from a lower social origin, whose occupational slot in turn is filled by another, yet lower son (Turrittin 1974). Only 5 to 10 percent of the sons in the four postwar surveys experienced mobility from this source.

Finally, the summary measures at the bottom of Table 6.5 show the degree of occupational inheritance, indicated by the percentage of sons who remained in their fathers' occupational category. Because of the simplified system of occupational categories used in Table 6.5 (grouping all sons into only three divisions), this proportion is quite high, inheri-

[3] The frequency distribution of the full-equality model is calculated in the same way as the expected frequencies are computed for a chi square statistical analysis of a contingency table.

194

tance being equal to just over 60 percent in each of the postwar studies.

We have seen that occupational mobility is greatly affected by historical changes in the distribution of various types of work. Recent work by Hauser and associates (1973, 1975a, 1975b) indicates that occupational mobility in the United States is due largely to changes in the occupational structure rather than the accessibility of opportunity. In agreement with the findings already reported above, the analysis of Hauser et al. of the occupational mobility of males in 1952, 1962, and 1972 finds that during these time periods the total rate of occupational mobility increased, upward mobility increased, downward mobility decreased, and the relationship between occupational positions of fathers and sons became less strong. *However,* these shifts appear to be entirely due to shifts in the occupational structure. The historical tendency toward upward mobility among men in the United States is neither uniform nor inevitable (1973, p. 309). It is produced by the expansion of higher-level occupational groups, such as professionals and managers, and the depletion of lower-level groups, such as service workers, laborers, and farmers:

> Despite the many social changes in the United States in the last
> two decades, it is a more favorable occupational structure, and only
> that, which has sustained or improved the mobility opportunities of
> American men. In light of this finding, it may be discomforting to
> ponder the social consequences of economic, technological or demo-
> graphic impediments to further upgrading of the occupational
> structure (1975a, p. 597).

MOBILITY PATTERNS OF AMERICAN WOMEN

Recent research on women's occupational mobility has examined the extent to which women's social mobility and status attainment resemble men's. Most of the research has attempted to apply to women a male-based model of status attainment, which postulates that the socioeconomic status of a boy's family influences how much education he will get, which in turn influences the prestige level of the job he gets. This model is able to predict 35 percent of the variation in the occupational prestige scores of men.

Several studies have applied Blau and Duncan's method (1967), discussed above, to data on the occupations of women. They found that the occupational status distributions of men and women are essentially similar, except that more males than females are in occupations of very high prestige, such as doctor, lawyer, and engineer[4] (Treiman and Terrell

[4] These studies all use a scale of status based on male education and income levels. One report suggests that if female education and income levels are used in conjunction with the male levels to form a people's status scale, then the status of women is about 10 points lower, on the basis of a 100-point scale. See Alice Henry 1978.

1975; McGlendon 1976). The finding of similar prestige structures for men and women disguises the extent to which women workers are channeled into a very few occupations. The occupational system is, of course, highly differentiated by sex; some jobs are performed mostly by women and other jobs mostly by men (Oppenheimer 1970). Women tend to be concentrated in clerical and service work and men in managerial, craft, and laboring work. In 1973, more than two-fifths of all women workers were employed in ten occupations — secretary, retail trade sales worker, bookkeeper, private household worker, elementary school teacher, waitress, typist, cashier, sewer and stitcher, and registered nurse. Each of these occupations employed more than 800,000 women. Male employment showed much less occupational concentration. The ten largest occupations for men employed less than 20 percent of all male workers (U.S. Department of Labor 1975, pp. 91–92). Because women are offered employment in such a narow range of jobs, the effect is to limit the opportunity for women for advancement and self-development and to reduce competition with men so that men's mobility chances are not materially threatened.

Although the prestige distributions of male- and female-dominated occupations are similar, wages are by no means comparable. The jobs that women occupy pay poorly relative to their educational requirements. In fact, job for job, women are on the average paid less than men doing the same work, and, in addition, jobs dominated by women pay less than similar jobs dominated by men. One effect of the wage differential for many women is the maintenance of economic dependency on a husband for material subsistence. The fact that families headed by divorced women, widowed women, and single women are far more likely to be poor than those in which a male head is the sole wage earner is an indication of the disadvantage that unattached women face in achieving self-sufficiency. (Female-headed families had a median income of $8,795 in 1973, for example, compared to an income of $13,675 for the male-headed families in which the wife did not work. See U.S. Department of Labor 1975, pp. 140–41.)

If we look at those women who do work in the labor market, we find that the factors that affect the status of the jobs they enter are essentially similar to the factors that affect male status attainment. Amount of schooling strongly influences occupational prestige, and parental socioeconomic status affects amount of schooling. The main difference is that how far a girl goes in school is affected to a greater extent by her parents' socioeconomic level and less by her mental ability. Apparently, sons are sent to college and graduate school more often than daughters, particularly if their families have modest financial resources (Almquist 1977, p. 848). Another difference is that how much education a girl's *mother* had, whether she worked outside the home, and what occupation the mother held influence her daughter's occupational status (Rosenfeld 1978; Treiman and Terrell 1975, p. 182). In fact, the effect of the mother's occupation is relatively more important than the father's in predicting the daughter's occupational attainment (Rosenfeld 1978, p. 45).

Fewer similarities show up when black men and women are compared. Recall the Blau and Duncan finding that education is less predictive of the black male's occupational prestige than of the white male's. But this is not true for women. The schooling that black women receive is strongly related to their occupational status. Poorly educated black women are most disadvantaged relative to other groups, but highly educated black women are almost as able as highly educated white women to translate their educational achievement into occupational prestige achievement. (But, as is true for white women, that does not mean that the highly educated black women receives as much income as does her husband.) The process of status attainment thus is quite different for black husbands and wives.

In looking at the mobility of women, we need to consider also those women who do not work in the labor force. What about the mobility processes of housewives and mothers? Making the assumption that the status of such women is identical to that of their husbands, several researchers have looked at the social origins of women (measured by their father's occupational status) in comparison to the occupational status of their husbands. They have found that women tend to marry men from similar social origins. Therefore, women's mobility (as indicated by their husband's status attainment compared to their father's status attainment) tends to be similar to that of men. In fact, women's status mobility through marriage is more similar to men's than is women's status mobility through their own occupations (Tyree and Treas 1974). But this finding may be an artifact of the measurements and lack much substantive meaning. The measurement of female mobility through marriage uses the same outcome indicator (the man's occupation) as does measurement of male mobility. Its initial origin indicator (father's occupation) is similar to that used in studies of male mobility (male's father's occupation) because there is a correlation between the status of a wife's father and the status of her husband's father. The two kinds of measured mobility are similar because the technological and social forces that affect a male's chances for mobility also affect a husband's chances for mobility.

The picture that emerges is one in which some girls go to college if their parents (and particularly their mothers) were educated, while the others only finish high school. As adults, a number of them enter a limited number of occupations, whose social statuses are correlated to the level of schooling that the women received, but which provide them with significantly lower wages than the jobs occupied by comparable males. Their mobility possibilities are mainly those of entering occupations of moderately (but not extremely) high social prestige, which do not pay particularly well by male standards, or else those of marrying a husband from a similar class background whose mobility chances equal those of other men. In two ways, women are thus not in full competition with men: If they choose to be housewives, they do not compete in the labor force; if they do enter the labor force, they are restricted to occupations with no opportunity for advancement or with advancement to only higher women's positions.

Mobility in Other Nations

Americans tend to believe that there is more opportunity for social mobility in the United States than in other countries. That is one of its virtues, many believe. Whether or not this is really true is a matter to be decided by empirical investigation. Certainly, we might anticipate finding cross-cultural differences in the ease with which people can get ahead, in the barriers facing them, and in their access to elite positions of power.

Comparisons between nations with respect to mobility are difficult to make, particularly because mobility data for different periods of time are not available for a variety of nations, and because even for single nations mobility data are often scarce. Furthermore, where occupational mobility data do exist, there are often weaknesses in the sampling methods employed in obtaining the data. Nevertheless, those sets of data which seem to be relatively comparable reveal somewhat similar rates of mobility for industrial nations. Lipset and Bendix (1964, pp. 13–17), for example, attempted to overcome difficulties in making comparisons among countries having different occupational and economic structures by looking only at how many people cross over from "manual" to "nonmanual" jobs and vice versa. They compared rates of intergenerational occupational mobility (based on a comparison of the occupations of fathers and sons) for six industrialized nations — the United States, Germany, Sweden, Japan, France, and Switzerland. Their figures on the proportion of all sons of manual workers who moved up to middle-class positions and on the proportion of all sons of middle-class fathers who moved down to manual occupations revealed three facts. (1) All of these countries are characterized by a high degree of total mobility; from one-fourth to one-third of the population move from working-class to middle-class in one generation or vice versa. (2) Total mobility rates in these countries are much the same, ranging from 23 percent for Switzerland to 31 percent for Germany (five of the six countries are within the narrow range of 27 to 31 percent); there is little difference, then, among various industrialized nations in the total rate of occupational mobility between the blue-collar and the white-collar classes. (3) However, when the direction of the mobility is examined, the similarity between nations diminishes; for example, with respect to downwardly mobile nonmanual workers, the figures range from Germany's 32 percent to Switzerland's 13 percent. Lipset and Bendix concluded that the overall high levels of social mobility are the result of industrialization and that such levels are likely to be prevalent in all societies that have attained a certain level of economic advancement (1964, Table 2.1).

In a later summarization of data on mobility, Lenski (1966) obtained the following percentages on the amount of upward and downward mobility across the manual-nonmanual line in nine nations in the advanced stages of industrialization: [5]

Nation	%
United States	34
Sweden	32
Great Britain	31
Denmark	30
Norway	30
France	29
West Germany	25
Japan	25
Italy	22

This kind of data convinced Lenski that industrial societies have generally high rates of mobility. He argued that in contrast to agrarian societies, whose net mobility is downward, industrial societies are historically different. They experience net upward mobility, brought about by radical transformations of the occupational structure through technological change, the effective use of birth control (which keeps family size small), and the decline in the role of ascriptive status in job allocation. Lenski goes so far as to claim that rates of upward mobility are probably rising in industrial societies, though this claim is poorly documented and still remains a disputed issue. Further analysis by Hazelrigg (1974) found an inverse curvilinear relationship between the degree to which a son's occupation is determined by his father's occupation and an energy-consumption measure of industrial development. This would suggest that

[5] Summarization of data is from Gerhard Lenski 1966, p. 411. Omitted from the list are the results of studies based on nonnational surveys, surveys employing questionable procedures, and surveys of nations that cannot be classified as advanced industrial. The median for the less industrialized nations (Puerto Rico, India, Brazil, Hungary, and Finland) was found to be 25 percent, compared to 30 percent for the more advanced industrial nations.

as industrialization increases, the impact of paternal origin on mobility decreases, until finally the point is reached at which additional industrial growth has very little influence on mobility patterns. The Lipset-Bendix thesis thus stands challenged and open to modification (see F. L. Jones 1969 for a critique).

Another way to compare nations is in terms of mobility into the highest-prestige occupational categories, contrasting the access to this elite stratum of sons of white-collar fathers to that of sons of blue-collar fathers. In his international comparison of occupational mobility, S. M. Miller (1960) found that no nation had much movement into the highest occupational levels from the manual strata, that overall high rates of upward mobility do not necessarily indicate a high rate of mobility into elite occupations, and that there were major differences between nations with regard to manual-to-elite mobility. For example, whereas 1.5 percent of Italian manual workers entered elite occupations, the proportions for France and the United States were 2.6 and 7.8 percent, respectively. The advantage of middle-class sons was apparent, for movement from this category into elite occupations was 7.5 percent for Italy, 11.4 percent for France, and 19.8 percent for the United States. The inheritance of elite occupational status varied from 62 percent in France to a low of 26 percent for Italy; the figure for the United States was 53 percent (S. M. Miller 1960, Tables 5 and 11). The mobility of lower- and middle-class persons into the elite strata, then, is not necessarily related to the amount of mobility across the manual-nonmanual line. Many societies contain a great deal of mobility back and forth between the blue-collar and the white-collar strata, while the elite is effectively sealed off from penetration by lower groups (Tepperman and Tepperman 1971).

In comparing occupational mobility across nations, Lipset and Bendix were surprised at the high and similar levels of mobility for industrialized nations. They used this finding to attack one facet of the myth of American exceptionalism, the belief that the United States possesses a more open class system and, thus, greater occupational mobility than do European countries. Industrialization, not degree of openness, they held, was more significant for mobility. In reaching such a conclusion, however, they glossed over very marked differences in directions of movements between industrial nations. S. M. Miller (1960, pt. E), for example, found four different patterns of occupational mobility for industrialized nations.

It is not clear in what sense industrialism generates upward mobility, and how industrialization as a process produces a uniform mobility outcome has yet to be clearly specified. International similarities and differences in occupational mobility patterns, while apparent in survey research data, do not lead to any obvious causal explanations. A great deal more research is called for.

The Process of Getting Ahead in America

What we can conclude, in short, from the statistics presented above is that there is considerable social mobility in the United States, but most of it is short range and is made possible by changes in the occupational structure. There have not been enough sons of higher-status parents to fill all the positions opening up, so some sons of lower-status parents have moved up. Which sons, and why did they move up and not others? Given the *structural* conditions of the immediate past, what are the characteristics of *individuals* and the facilitating experiences those individuals have had that led to (or impeded) their social mobility?

Sociologists have so far identified only about half of the influences on American children affecting the kind of occupation that they will be allowed to enter as an adult. The other half is still unknown. What sociologists *have* looked at are the influences of parental class and educational attainment. In the United States, both are important, particularly education. Blau and Duncan's analysis of the life histories of 20,700 men (1967), for example, found that original family class position affected the amount of education they received and that the amount of education affected the kind of occupation they entered as adults. Blau and Duncan (p. 202) were even able to quantify these influences: 18 percent of the variation in the adult occupational status of the men in their sample was related to variation in their social origins; 24 percent was due to the education the men had achieved; and 57 percent was due to everything else (not measured by their study).

But what determines how much education a person is likely to get? This question is addressed in some detail in Chapter 8. Suffice it here to indicate that educational attainment is influenced by a number of preceding variables: original social class; race; sex; measured mental ability; academic performance; the influence of peers, parents, and teachers; and levels of educational and occupational aspiration. Together these variables explain a large proportion of the variation in educational attainment (Duncan et al. 1972; Sewell, Haller, and Ohlendorf 1970; Sewell and Hauser 1975; Jencks et al. 1972). For the child who wants to get ahead in America through education, it helps to be born to high-status parents, to belong to a privileged race and a privileged sex, to get good grades, to have encouraging friends and teachers, to have high aspirations, and to go far in school.

Social origins and educational attainment explain only about half of the variation in the occupational status of adult men. Beyond these factors, there are a number of other conditions that encourage high adult status, but we do not know what they are. A number have been suggested — luck, pull, marriage, connections, choice, demonstration of loyalty to a powerful person, personality, perseverance, labor force factors. These, and any others one might dream up, have been unexamined. Perhaps such personal characteristics as athletic ability or beauty are important. More likely, as we saw in Chapter 4 in our discussion of the determinants of income, a number of the other conditions are impersonal forces — labor market factors, regional influences, discriminatory practices — which are beyond the control of the individual, but by which he or she is affected.

THE FAILURE OF THE AMERICAN DREAM

In America, the belief in the possibility of upward mobility helps to dampen individuals' discontent with their current social status because it encourages them to hope for improvement. Those who can believe that it is possible and desirable for themselves or their children eventually to rise in status will be less resentful of their current, "temporary" position and less inclined to develop a hostile class consciousness.

The complex of beliefs that foster such optimism grew out of the eighteenth-century ideal that "all men are created equal" and has evolved to mean that all people should have equal *rights* and equal *opportunities*. It holds that the social and economic status of individuals should be determined not by descent, but by achievement. It also asserts that there is great opportunity for social mobility, that anyone can succeed if he or she tries hard enough, that people get what they deserve, and that one can move from the bottom to the top of the class structure if only he or she has the ambition and the talent.

Huber and Form (1973, pp. 88–99) found that the majority of Americans accept such an ideology. Their respondents indicated a belief that America is the land of opportunity and that if one works hard, one will get ahead. Yet Huber and Form also found that lower-income whites and blacks have more doubts about these statements than the higher-income strata. On the basis of interviews with 354 rich, middle-income, and poor people, they concluded that there is far from universal acceptance of the tenets of the American ideology of opportunity, even when these tenets are phrased in the most general and vague terms (Rytina et al. 1970, pp. 703–16). The support of the ideology is strongest among those who profit most from the system that the ideology explains and defends. Thus, rich people are more likely than poor people (and particularly poor blacks) to think that there is equality of opportunity in gaining an education and a good income, in running the government, and in getting fair treatment from the law.

The doubters are being more realistic: The American dream of equality of opportunity does not really present an accurate picture of the facts. Opportunity is not equal. It is restricted in access by familial, educational, social, racial, religious, ethnic, sexual, and other background characteristics of the individual. Many jobs, particularly in the working class, are dead-end; there are no avenues for advancement. A substantial minority, the black Americans, occupy a semicaste status. The majority of whites either have inherited their social class position or have been mobile to only a minor degree. Yet the ideology defines success as a result of character and failure as a result of personal inadequacy.

Inevitably, many people are not going to be socially mobile in any important sense, and some will not see their hopes and ambitions realized. What happens when individuals, imbued with the success motive, do not advance? How do they react to the fact that their own lives do not fit the American dream? There have been several investigations of the psychological dilemma that occurs when the promises of the American dream are not met by the realities of economic inequality.

Ely Chinoy (1955) studied the careers of auto workers, which are particularly relevant to the question because in the auto industry it is rare and difficult to attain middle-class status through promotion from the bench. Wages are compressed in a narrow range, as 50 percent of the workers earn within fourteen cents an hour of each other. Reactions to the absence of opportunity, Chinoy found, were varied, but they fit several patterns. Some workers tried to maintain the illusion of advancement by defining their jobs in the factory as temporary and by incessantly talking of their out-of-the-shop goals and expectations. But eventually even these had to face up to the fact that they were likely to remain factory workers for the rest of their lives. Other workers showed evidence of self-deprecation, guilt, and lowered self-regard. "I guess I'm just not smart enough" was the reaction of a thirty-eight-year-old machine operator.

Most of the workers whom Chinoy studied tried to rationalize their status as factory employees and to justify more limited ambitions. They did *not* explain their failure to rise in terms of forces beyond their control or structural barriers to mobility. Instead, they redefined advancement to mean the achievement of goals in which they were interested (security, small promotions within the factory, or a gradual accumulation of personal possessions), by projecting their hopes and aspirations upon their children, or by emphasizing other values (happiness or moral integrity, for example). Chinoy comments:

> Since these defensive measures are only partially effective, it seems probable that there remains among these workers a deep and substantial undercurrent of guilt and self-depreciation. . . . Both self-blame and the defensive rationalizations against self-blame, however, contribute to the maintenance of both existing economic institutions and the tradition of opportunity itself. To the extent that workers focus blame for their failure to rise above the level of wage labor upon themselves rather than upon the institutions that govern the pursuit of wealth or upon the persons who control those

institutions, American society escapes the consequences of its own contradiction. . . . The social order is thus protected, however, only at the psychological expense of those who have failed (pp. 129–30).

In a related study, Robert E. Lane (1959) conducted intensive interviews on the subject of equality with fifteen working-class males whose reactions to the lack of advancement were similar to those found by Chinoy. Most of them accepted the view that if a man does not succeed, it is his own fault. They tended to believe that people deserve their status, that the upper classes should be upper, and that the lower classes get no less than what they are worth.

Lane's respondents adjusted to their own stationary situation by reducing the importance of the struggle, either by limiting their outlook, or by denying its significance, or by resigning themselves to it. Some found ways of elevating the status of the working class by believing that workers possess greater happiness, power, and even income than members of other strata. Another device for dealing with their subordinate position was to emphasize spiritual and moral qualities.

Lane suggested that the greater the emphasis in a society on the availability of equal opportunity for all, the greater becomes the need for individuals to rationalize their own status. Those whose low status threatens their sense of self-esteem will particularly want to define status as just and proper. Lane also speculated that when there is a considerable emphasis on opportunity in the society, there will be a tendency for those of marginal status to denigrate those lower than themselves.

Both of these studies point to the problems generated for the less successful by a social ethic that emphasizes individual achievement. For the high school dropout, the middle-aged man in a dead-end job, or the laborer thrown out of work by automation, the tendency to denigrate oneself may be avoided by revising goals, rationalizing, or becoming resigned to one's status. To some observers, this fact becomes a powerful argument for decreasing the emphasis placed on individual achievement or for developing alternative mythologies that explain away or rationalize failure. Others suggest that the public should be educated to the structural limitations on upward mobility so that people will not be fooled into believing that advancement is more common than it is. Of course, this could well lead to heightened class consciousness and possibly increased class hostilities.

THE CONSEQUENCES OF MOBILITY FOR THOSE WHO HAVE MADE IT

The potential for psychological harm exists not only for those who are in dead-end jobs, but also for those who have indeed been able to get ahead. The stables and the mobiles alike risk emotional impairment, although of different nature.

Here we ask, What are the personal consequences of growing up in one social stratum, but of living adult life in another social stratum, characterized by different conditions, responses, and attitudes? Is it easy, from a psychological point of view, to reject the old and adapt to the new? Early writers (Sorokin 1927, pp. 522–25) speculated that upward social mobility is a disruptive process, requiring the individual to leave behind family and friends and to accept social isolation. Later writers (Tumin 1967, for example) were more specific in suggesting that the consequences of mobility include overconformity, political conservatism, lower levels of family cohesion, belief in an open class structure, anti-integrationist attitudes, and feelings of familial rejection.

Several of these ideas have not received empirical support. Hopkins (1973) concludes in a review of the research on political attitudes that upwardly mobile American men are no more likely to be politically conservative than other members of the middle class. Jackman (1972) finds in examining data from a national sample of adults that mobile persons are no less likely to feel politically and personally efficacious than the people in their new status group. Hodge and Treiman (1966) report that upwardly and downwardly mobile men are neither more nor less prejudiced against blacks than those in the classes of their origin and destination. Vorwaller (1970) found similar results concerning associational memberships.

On the other hand, other research does indicate that there may be certain social and psychological consequences for the upwardly mobile. Kessin (1971), in his review of research, concludes that detachment from parents is a likely outcome of upward mobility. Aspiring boys have a tendency to feel rejected by their parents (Dynes et al. 1956), to identify with nonfamily persons (Eulau and Koff 1962; Simpson 1962; and Ellis and Lane 1963), to have conflict with their parents over their careers (E. Ellis 1952) and their values (Himes 1952), and to be detached from the family (Levine and Sussmann 1960; and Douvan and Adelson 1958). Overall, it appears that mobility, actual or anticipated, tends to be accompanied by parent-child estrangement.

In addition, it is perhaps likely that when mobility represents a major status change, the upwardly mobile person experiences difficulties in relating to peers. The research is somewhat inconclusive on this point. Ellis and Lane's study (1967) of very mobile male students at Stanford University showed them to be difficult to get to know, socially isolated, and not active in extracurricular activities. Crockett (H. 1962) also found lower "affiliation-need" scores among upwardly mobile boys. On the other hand, Curtis (1959) was unable to observe any differences in interaction rates with friends, neighbors, and work associates between mobiles and stables. Further, Curtis (1963) found that upwardly mobile persons tend to retain friends from their former strata.

In Kessin's study (1971) of 546 adult males in a Washington, D.C., suburb, it was found that the men who had been upwardly mobile by two or more status levels (out of a possible four) are less likely than other people to have friends in the community or to socialize with relatives and are more likely to feel anxiety and to experience psychosomatic symptoms of stress. The downwardly mobile men, on the other hand, were *more* involved than the average person in community and family relationships. They also seemed to have better mental health, as this is measured by anxiety and psychosomatic symptom scores.

Obviously, behavioral and attitudinal consequences of mobility are not clear-cut. It does appear that extremely upwardly mobile persons do associate less with their parents and neighbors and also feel greater anxiety. Downwardly mobile persons are not as negatively affected psychologically as it has sometimes been suggested; in fact, their involvement in community life and their mental health may be benefited.

Social Mobility, Equality of Opportunity, and Inequality of Result

We began this chapter by noting the dominance of the value of success in American life. Americans believe that it is important to get ahead in life and that it is possible for anyone with ability and ambition to do so. They also believe that there is equality of opportunity — that those with ability and ambition *can* get ahead. After many pages of reports of empirical results, what can we now say about the presence of equality of opportunity in America? There has been considerable social mobility in America. It is usually short-distance mobility, and it is due to changes in the occupational structure. How do these facts relate to the American egalitarian ethic?

In dealing with this complex question, we take up a topic about which there is considerable controversy and debate. How one regards the interplay of mobility, education, and income is not simply a matter of establishing the facts. Since there have been public policies regarding education and income for many years, assessing the facts includes assessing the outcome of long-established policies and institutions.

The strong egalitarian theme in America has two ideological roots. Both grew out of America's revolutionary origins, in which an aristocracy was rejected, state and church were separated, the powers of the state were circumscribed constitutionally, property rights were enshrined, and political democracy was limited to those with a stake in society — that is, to men of property. One root was concerned with the extension of political democracy, such as the removal of property restrictions on voting, the abolition of slavery, the achievement of women's right to vote, the reduction of the voting age, and the regulation of political parties.

The second root was concerned with what T. H. Marshall (1964), in a famous essay, termed the "extension of citizenship rights," by which he meant access to the resources of the state by all citizens. This involves expanding the right to public education and increasing the various kinds of laws and governmental programs that counter deleterious effects of the capitalist market system on society. Programs inspired by this ideology include unemployment insurance, social security, the right to form unions and to bargain collectively, and labor standards legislation.

The notion of an egalitarian society traditionally, then, has had two interpretations: a narrow one associated with political democracy and a broader one emphasizing the extension of citizenship rights or, in effect, attempting to create a generous minimal quality of life for all. However, a third interpretation, associated in the popular mind with the slogan of "equal opportunity," is currently the most widely held interpretation. This is the doctrine that everyone, regardless of class origin, race, sex, or religion, should have equal access to education and job opportunities based on ability and achievement. It is an idea that fits well with America's liberal democratic tradition. It is a meritocratic doctrine that views the occupational world as a hierarchy of jobs ordered in terms of increasing technical and educational requirements and levels of responsibility, justifying a parallel hierarchy of economic and prestige rewards.

The equal opportunity ideology holds that access to the job hierarchy should be competitive, so that people of higher ability and achievement get the more highly technical and responsible jobs and, therefore, the most economically rewarding jobs. It suggests that the state should play an important role in ensuring equal opportunity by providing a range of educational institutions, by subsidizing the education of the poor, and by enforcing nondiscrimination in education and employment.

Yet, the equal opportunity ideology is an inequalitarian ideology in its implications. It does not question any inequality of result that occurs from equal opportunity. As one type of meritocratic philosophy, it is geared to encourage the very massive inequalities of wealth and power distribution in American society. (The affinity of the meritocracy principle to functionalism is relatively obvious.)

These themes can be found underlying the interests of social scientists. Mankoff (1974) has assessed what he finds to be the three social science perspectives regarding the issue of inequality in American society:

> One influential perspective which might be labeled *laissez-faire social science* and is exemplified by the work of Edward Banfield (1968), Arthur Jensen (1969), and Richard Herrnstein (1971), suggests that economic inequality is largely dependent upon the

psychological disposition or genetic endowment of the lower class. Benign neglect, population control, and intensified education and occupational tracking for the psychologically or intellectually disadvantaged seem to be the major policy implications of this school, which believes that the stratification system is both essentially just and necessary for the maintenance of our way of life (p. 20).

A second perspective Mankoff labels *conservative-liberal.* Supporters of this view — such as Daniel Bell, S. M. Lipset, and Irving Kristol — reject the biological theories of economic stratification and have advocated measures to improve the economic opportunities of the poor.[6] They point to the historical increases in material well-being and social mobility that have characterized the American experience and hope for the continuation of these historical conditions to solve the problems of inequality, especially for the poor. But, as Mankoff notes, "at the same time . . . [conservative-liberals] draw back from the policy recommendations of those such as socialists Christopher Jencks and Noam Chomsky who propose radical income leveling in lieu of what they believe to be the impossibility (and probably the limited value) of instituting equality of opportunity" (p. 20). It is this third perspective that Mankoff labels *socialist,* and it advocates "equality of result" (based on reducing income differences and curbing the power of corporations).

The first perspective, laissez-faire social science, has not been supported by the available data, which indicate that neither income nor occupational attainment bear a strong relationship to measured mental ability. Consider the analysis by Jencks et al. (1972) presented in Table 6.6. From the table it is clear that genes or biological inheritance provide a very poor explanation of income difference. The advantages due to home environment and additional education strongly suggest that the upper-middle class attempts to maintain its privileged economic position mainly by having its children receive more education than most people. Lines 4 and 5 in Table 6.6 indicate the advantage that the children of upper-middle-class fathers have because of class position alone (though

6 It is interesting to note that Mankoff lumps together the terms *liberal* and *conservative* in characterizing social scientists such as Bell and Lipset. From this mating of antithetical terms Mankoff is implying that the reform impulse of these social scientists has been considerably dampened of late. He indicates that they oppose more radical economic policies on the grounds that the traditional meritocratic principle would be violated (a moral objection), but also because they apparently fear that promotion of more radical policies of equality would meet with a great deal of opposition from important parts of the citizenry. Liberals and conservatives may differ regarding the kinds of reforms necessary, but in the short run they may agree (though for different reasons) that change is not now wise.

Table 6.6

Estimated importance of various factors contributing to the cumulative income advantage of men with high-status fathers

Source	Percent
IQ genotype	7–9
IQ advantage due to superior home environment	16–20
Extra schooling for those with equal IQs	24–29
Higher-status occupations for those with equal schooling and equal IQs	18
Higher incomes for those with equal-status occupations, equal schooling, and equal IQs	30

Source: Table 7-3 from *Inequality: A Reassessment of the Effect of Family and Schooling in America,* by Christopher Jencks et al., p. 215, © 1972 by Basic Books, Inc., Publishers, New York. Reprinted by permission of Basic Books, Inc., and Penguin Books Ltd.

Jencks does not discuss how this advantage is obtained irrespective of education, IQ, and occupational status).

Proponents of the meritocracy or equality of opportunity ideal (those whom Mankoff refers to as conservative-liberals) can be encouraged by the finding that social mobility rates have been rather high in the United States (albeit this is due more to changes in the occupational structure than to structural barriers to status inheritance). Education is the main channel to occupational attainment; and, although the amount of education that children receive is *somewhat* affected by the socioeconomic level of their parents, there still is considerable chance for educational attainment beyond that of the parents. If we examine only mobility figures, it appears that America is indeed a land that offers opportunity to a sizable minority.

However, certain social conditions are inconsistent with the equality of opportunity or meritocratic perspective. Consider the linkage of education to jobs and income in the mobility process. Since educational credentials predict job performance poorly for most kinds of work, their use in screening job applicants has the effect of discriminating against talented people, including disproportionate numbers of working-class and minority-group young people, who generally obtain less education. Jencks is able to show that a system of selection for jobs based on grades or test scores would probably produce more social mobility than would selection based on educational attainment (the procedure that increases the status link between father and son). While many people believe that the meritocratic principle operates in present-day industrial society — that there is a linear scale relating training and competence to occupational status and income as a reward — the low correlations that actually characterize the interrelations show only very weak links between the variables.

To those who prefer "equality of result," the belief in meritocracy supports inequality. While, no doubt, many progressive social policies might be designed to improve the chances of the working classes, blacks, women, and other minority youth in achieving more education and better jobs, such policies would likely lead to reducing inequality between groups, but not between individuals. As Jencks argues, equality of opportunity in effect would make inequality random, but not reduce it; it would achieve, for example, the creation of a separate black class structure that would match the one now existing in the white world (Jencks et al. 1972, chap. 6).

What is easy to overlook in examining mobility tables and regression analyses of mobility data is that the *structure* of inequality is virtually unaffected by the mobility processes going on within it. It is this that impresses proponents of Mankoff's third perspective, who are concerned with inequality of result. The American equalitarian ethic is in one sense an inequalitarian ethic, because it values the opportunity to become unequal. In advocating that everyone should have an equal starting place in the race, it accepts the legitimacy of the goals of the race. An emphasis on competition implies approval of the great discrepancies in income, power, and prestige inherent in the economic system. Social mobility, like musical chairs, rearranges the location of individuals, but it does not alter the fact that some end up privileged and others do not.

The inequalitarian implications of the equality of opportunity theme is evident in examining the social role of education. As we have seen, schools do provide the means whereby many children of blue-collar parents become white-collar professionals. Yet, while the educational institution serves as a channel whereby youngsters can get ahead, it does not challenge or disturb the basic social class alignments. More accurately, it serves the economic status quo by sorting and marking each new generation for distribution into slots in the occupational and status hierarchy. As Jencks puts it, "We suspect . . . that employers would favor educated applicants even if such applicants were not especially productive. Employers need a legitimate device for rationing privilege. Credentials are widely accepted as one of the fairest systems available for doing this" (1972, p. 183). Education, thus, is predominantly an "inequality-maintaining system" (Kreckel 1972).

For individual Americans, the presence of a certain amount of visible social mobility may serve a "cooling-out" function, dampening any sparks of class resentment in the vision that they, too, or their children may be able to share in the bounty. That income inequalities and occupational hierarchies are stable institutions, persisting relatively unchanged from generation to generation, is not so visible to them; or if visible, it is ignored. Nor are they so likely to be aware that the probability is high that their own children will occupy economic and social niches very close to their own. The belief in the equality of opportunity and the presence of a few examples around of people who have "made it" are enormously effective cultural tools for dissipating class resentment and hostility — indeed, they even help hide from conscious recognition the omnipresent influence of social stratification.

While liberal ideologies find certain strategies stimulating social mobility to be acceptable because they are consistent with belief in meritocracy and equal opportunity, such strategies will have little effect on overall economic inequality. If it is to be reduced, economic inequality must be attacked directly; this action has long been advocated by socialists. But a mounting of such an attack is not likely in America now, since few Americans consider economic inequality to be a serious social problem. "If egalitarians want to mobilize popular support for income redistribution," concludes Jencks, "their first aim should be to convince people that the distribution of income is a legitimate political issue" (1972, pp. 263–64). Reduction of occupational status differences and of the massive differences in income would clearly necessitate a move to establish a new kind of political control over the economic institutions that mold American society. Such moves toward equality would probably also require a transformation of the social consciousness, affirming the basic dignity of much socially useful work that is now held in low esteem, and the extension of political power to the less privileged, to help bring about equality of result in the long run.

7

SUBJECTIVE SUPPORTS: THE PRESTIGE HIERARCHY AND CLASS CONSCIOUSNESS

IN EARLIER CHAPTERS we have asked the question, Why do the less privileged strata go along with the system that deprives them? Why are the poor meek and the middle classes unresentful?

One possibility is that the less privileged come to believe that they are less valuable or important than the more privileged and therefore are deserving of fewer rewards. Sennett and Cobb write of how people deem themselves worthwhile only if they see themselves as "productive":

> Deference in American society has this at its root: a calculation that someone else's time is more valuable than your own, which seems to give that person the right to command your time in accordance with his needs. The most obvious example occurs in offices, where it seems right for secretaries to perform services for their superior, not because they respect him as self-sufficient or because they are awed by his abilities, but because the superior's work is considered more valuable than her typing, and so his time is more valuable than hers (1972, pp. 264–65).

The rich entrepreneurs, the powerful statesmen, the managerial experts are revered and respected, and that respect voids the anger or resentment that might otherwise be felt.

Economic and political inequalities thus are reinforced by prestige inequalities. Prestige — the attitudes of deference and honor that people carry in their heads — can be viewed as the social-psychological connection between the objective inequalities of economic and political resources, on the one hand, and the acquiescence of the less privileged to their lack of privilege, on the other. It is in this way that a hierarchy of prestige lends support and reinforcement to inequalities of resources.

An additional possibility is that people are unaware of their own inequality. In James West's study of the well-developed class structure in a small midwestern town, he frequently encountered claims from the townsfolk that classes did not exist there. "This is *one* place where ever'body is equal. You don't find no classes here" (1945, p. 115). Even those people who were aware of some differences in privilege often underestimated how great they were. Finally, most people did not perceive the degree to which differences in privilege are systematically programmed by the major institutions of society. Similar generalizations can be made about the level of awareness in the larger community. So long as people believe either that inequality does not exist or that it exists but is due to inequalities in individual ability or ambition, they will feel comfortable and accepting about it. It is to the advantage of the privileged, then, that the less privileged be unaware. Later sections of this chapter discuss what are the conditions that promote ignorance of the realities of power, wealth, and privilege.

A third answer focuses on the ideologies that people express — the pictures in their heads about how the world operates, and why, and also how it *should* operate. Ideologies can be conservative or radical. They are powerful tools of personal acceptance of the system and, on rarer occasions, of rebellion against that system.

In this chapter we investigate how these three forms of subjective supports — prestige allocation, class consciousness, and ideology — reinforce and sustain objective inequalities of wealth, income, authority, and power. Prestige concerns the patterned evaluations that people make of others. Of particular interest is the correspondence of a prestige hierarchy to other hierarchies of economic and political control. To what degree do those persons or positions that control wealth and income or wield power also receive respect and deference from others? Once identified, the prestige structure can be looked at in terms of how the individual relates to it. The study of self-identification examines how well people perceive their own position and how they feel about it. Are most people accurate observers of their own ranking, or are their estimates consistently inflated? When subjective awareness is well developed and shared, it provides the preconditions of class consciousness (the aware-ness and feeling of identity with others who are in similar economic. political, and social circumstances). Here we are interested in the stages of development of class consciousness and in the effects each stage has on group action. Crucial to the development of class consciousness is the role of ideology, that complex of doctrines, myths, and symbols that in-terprets and defines the relationship between one group and others.[1] All of these concepts help explain how subjective definitions of reality strengthen the class structure and defuse whatever potentials there are for organized protest.

Prestige

In all societies, human beings evaluate each other. In all societies, some characteristics and behaviors of people are considered to be more desirable, and others are considered to be inferior and undesirable. The emotions that accompany these evaluations range from the greatest ap-proval and admiration to disgust and revulsion. *Prestige* is the degree of respect accorded to groups, positions, or individuals based on their as-cribed characteristics or achievements. It is external to the individual or position toward which it is applied; it exists in the mental assessments of other people.

On what basis do people give respect to others? In general, prestige in any society reflects the dominating values of that society. The domi-nating values, in turn, usually are kindly to the powerful people. A warring society respects its generals; an agricultural society gives defer-ence to its landowners; an industrial society reveres its business execu-tives. Whatever the basis, in any society there are expectations governing who is granted deference and for what reasons. In a heterogeneous society such as the United States, these expectations vary somewhat by subculture. A student who takes drugs is evaluated differently by his fraternity brothers than by the city police force. Yet, even in a complex society there tends to exist a general consensus on the relative prestige of basic positions, such as occupations. The images of the doctor, the engineer, and the business executive tend to call up positive reactions, whereas the thief, the pimp, and the executioner are negatively viewed.

It is useful to distinguish between the respect given to positions or statuses and that given to the individuals in those positions. For example, the people in a community may think that brain surgeons are important in general, but that Dr. Jones, a drunkard who made several operating

---

[1] There are a number of definitions of ideology. Most of them stress that ideologies interpret the group, its history, its goals, its relationship to other groups, and its future. See Dolbeare et al. 1973; Parsons 1964, p. 349; or Johnson 1960, pp. 587–88.

mistakes, is a scoundrel. K. Davis (1949, p. 93) suggested that the term *prestige* be reserved to refer to the evaluation of a position or status and that the evaluation of a specific individual be termed *esteem*. Sometimes a person holds a position of high prestige but enjoys little esteem, or vice versa. Usually, however, the prestige of a position is consistent with the esteem given to persons occupying that position, and they expect to receive the deference attached to the occupation they are in. If it is one of high prestige, then they are insulted if they do not receive the respect they feel is deserved, as when an M.D. is mistaken for a chiropractor or a professor.

Prestige affects self-concept and, therefore, motivation. People evaluate others, but they also evaluate themselves. Their feelings about how they stand are often intense. The desire to be respected is so common that some theorists — W. I. Thomas (1923), for one — have listed it as a universal basic need. This is perhaps an overstatement, because research conducted since Thomas's time has indicated that the strength of a "need for approval" varies among individuals and is socially created. Nevertheless, it is quite common in a competitive society stressing accomplishment. Even people who are without hope for a rewarding occupation and who are held in contempt by the larger society strive to receive respect. The low-income urban males of *Talley's Corner* repeatedly failed to achieve by any of society's major standards. Still, Liebow indicates,

> the desire to be a person in his own right, to be noticed by the
> world he lives in, is shared by each of the men on the street corner.
> Whether they articulate this desire . . . or not, one can see them
> position themselves to catch the attention of their fellows in much
> the same way as plants bend or stretch to catch the sunlight. . . .
> Sea Cat cuts his pants legs off at the calf and puts a fringe on
> the raggedy edges. Tonk breaks his "shades" and continues to wear
> the horn-rimmed frames minus the lenses. Richard cultivates a
> distinctive manner of speech. Lonny gives himself a birthday party.
> And so on (1967, pp. 60–61).

Likewise, for the newly rich, the desire to increase their prestige by displaying their possessions is a powerful motivation. It was Veblen's contention that

> the possession of wealth presently assumes the character of an
> independent . . . basis of esteem. . . . Those members of the com-
> munity who fall short of this . . . degree of . . . property suffer in
> the esteem of their fellow-men; and consequently they suffer also
> in their own esteem, since the usual basis of self-respect is the
> respect accorded by one's neighbours (Mitchell 1936, pp. 222–26).

215

The high personal relevance of the prestige ranking has several effects. For many, to gain respect becomes a goal. It becomes a source of meaning and motivation. In competitive societies, for example, prestige standards encourage people to find meaning in accomplishment or acquisition of goods. A second, more subtle effect is that a stable prestige structure legitimates any coexisting economic and political inequality (Lipset and Bendix 1951, pp. 249–50). Because the powerful, the educated, and the wealthy are respected by the community at large, their advantage comes to be viewed as natural and desirable. The disprivileged accept it. If, instead, it were believed that all people are equally worthy of respect, then how could great differences in wealth and power be tolerated? By denying that people are equal in value, a prestige pattern justifies economic and political disparity.

In summary, prestige is a subjective support of objective inequality. It exists in the minds of people and reflects their socially derived values. It is a source of great interest, satisfaction, and motivation for many people and a source of pain and self-derogation for others. It legitimates disparities in economic and political well-being. The guilt of the privileged is diminished. A prestige hierarchy squares the facts of inequality with the ideology of equality.

THE MEASUREMENT OF PRESTIGE

Most of what we know about prestige in general, and about the American prestige hierarchy in particular, comes from research conducted since 1940, when the methods devised by what came to be known as the "Warner school" stimulated a great deal of research by sociologists. The techniques and concepts developed by William Lloyd Warner and his associates were enormously influential, although they eventually came under strong criticism. Warner based his work on the study of social class in small communities. Using informants, he outlined social inequality as it is perceived by the members of the community.

At about the same time, work of another kind was being developed. National surveys asked Americans to rate the importance of hundreds of occupations. The researchers were surprised to discover that there is a high consensus about which occupations are more "important" and which are less. Similar studies conducted in other countries produced the same results. The stability of the rankings of occupations encouraged the eventual development of refined measures of occupational status, which are widely used today as indicators of social class location.

These two major types of studies — the identification of community prestige through reputational methods and the ranking of occupational prestige in national surveys — are important not only because they created measures of prestige, but also because they led to a number of empirical findings about prestige and its relationship to economic stratification. In the next two sections, we describe some of the major discoveries.

COMMUNITY PRESTIGE STUDIES

Imagine yourself to be a social scientist back in the 1930s, interested in studying in a systematic way something as vague and elusive as prestige. The scholars before you, such as Marx, Weber, and Veblen, had given their insights about it, sometimes in global terms, but had not become involved in empirical tests of their ideas. How would you proceed? How would it be possible to quantify, or in some other way to codify, people's evaluations of each other so that they could be examined carefully and related to other phenomena, such as economic inequality?

You might decide that the best course would be to ask Jones what he thought of Smith, and Smith what he thought of Jones, and Clark what he thought of both Smith and Jones, and so on. If Jones were not well respected by the other people in the community and Smith were, then you would begin to discern the shape of a prestige hierarchy. You could assign scores to the resulting rankings. But what if Jones is rated low by Smith and high by Clark? What if Clark does not know Jones?

These are some of the problems that faced William Lloyd Warner, an anthropologist interested in applying "the techniques and ideas which have been developed by social anthropologists in primitive society in order to obtain a more accurate understanding of an American community" (Warner and Lunt 1941, p. 14). Convinced that prestige inequality is the prime causal determinant in a stratification system, Warner became the first to measure prestige in any systematic way. He established the concept of prestige as a measurable entity and thus seemed to promise that the study of social stratification could proceed on a more scientific basis. In subsequent years, Warner's work came under a great deal of criticism, discussed below, but that did not mar the heuristic value of his approach in encouraging a new line of analysis and investigation.

THE WARNER STUDIES   William Lloyd Warner is best known for his four volumes written on "Yankee City," which actually was Newburyport, Massachusetts, a city of seventeen thousand conveniently located within commuting distance of Harvard. He also is known for his study of "Jonesville," a small midwestern community. Warner chose Yankee City as the initial community because it seemed relatively stable, it was a "well-integrated" community without serious conflicts, and it was predominantly old American, but also contained a number of ethnic groups. The project was one of the most intensive, exhaustive, and expensive surveys ever made of a small American city. It took five years and required the services of thirty research assistants. The research, reported in five volumes consisting of more than 1,700 pages, with 208 tables, charts, and maps, was conducted between 1930 and 1935 by a team of investigators.

Warner's first step was to establish rapport with the most prestigious individuals in the community:

> It seemed highly advisable to secure the consent and cooperation of the more important men in the community lest we later find it impossible to obtain certain vital information. We finally selected one prominent and, it later developed, much-trusted individual who, we knew, was important in the town. . . . he agreed to help us in any way he could. We then asked him to introduce us to some of his friends who were leaders in the city's activities. This he did, and from his friends we received other introductions which shortly spread our sources of information from the top to the bottom of the city (Warner and Lunt 1941, pp. 41–42).

From the interviews with people across the town, he began to develop an idea of the prestige system. In a later study, to make his work more systematic, he also developed two indexes of social class: *evaluated participation* (E.P.), which was designed to uncover the subjective aspect of prestige reputation, and the *index of status characteristics* (I.S.C.), which measured the objective aspects. Because Warner's entire analysis rests upon the validity of these two instruments, it is important to examine them more closely.

Warner based his initial depiction of the class structure on the method of evaluated participation. Its use assumed that the groups a person belongs to and the activities he or she is involved in are known and evaluated by other people. It consisted of six separate steps for rating an individual's social class position, of which we will describe the three most important. First, in rating by matched agreements, informants indicated what were the social classes that they recognized. For example, a professional man in Jonesville talked about "the society class" or "the 400 class," "the fringe of society," "the upper-middle class," "the working class," and the "lulus." While Warner found that people were not always agreed on how many classes existed, he aligned the various descriptions to each other as well as he could until he was satisfied that an overall picture of the class hierarchy had emerged. Then names of people in the community were given to other people, who assigned the names to one class or another.

In the second step, rating by symbolic placement, individuals are rated as being in a particular class when they are identified with certain superior or inferior symbols by informants. Expressions such as "the Cabot-Lowell family," the "low-down John Doe tribe," and "the wrong side of the tracks" became indicative of a person's prestige standing. As Warner explained it, "Such statements as 'Smith is a Nob Hiller, but he does not live on Nob Hill' or 'Jones lives on Nob Hill, but is *not* a Nob Hiller' tell their own symbolic story about status" (Warner et al. 1949, p. 73).

The third step is rating by institutional membership. In this procedure, subjects are assigned to a particular class when informants indicate they are members of certain institutions that are ranked as superior or inferior. The institutions include churches, athletic societies, and fraternal organizations. For instance, if a man belongs to the country club, the Episcopal church, and the Rotary Club, he may be tentatively assigned to the upper class.

In addition to these three techniques, individuals are also assigned to a class when informants say that they have a reputation for possessing certain superior or inferior traits, when they are compared to others whose positions have been previously determined, or when an informant directly states that they belong in that class. Using these techniques, Warner believed that he was able to classify most of the people in the community into a six-class scheme. Not foreseeing the extensive criticism that later would challenge these parts of his methodology, Warner then proceeded to measure the objective dimensions of class through the use of the index of status characteristics.

Once the perceptions of class had been determined by use of the E.P., Warner became interested in the correspondence of those perceptions to economic stratification. To measure the latter, he devised the I.S.C., which gives four scores to each individual on the basis of occupation, source of income, house type, and dwelling area (Warner et al. 1949). An individual's scores on the four scales are weighted and summed, resulting in an overall score.

When Warner compared the class placements of individuals by the E.P. method to those by the I.S.C. method, he found a very high correlation ($r = .97$). People who were well thought of tended to have more money and to live in the better parts of town. This may seem elementary to today's reader, but the finding had an important methodological implication for social scientists in the 1940s. It suggested that a multiple-item objective index can be used as a proxy for subjective class placement. One does *not* have to go through the laborious process of interviewing everyone in the community to find the prestige hierarchy. This was a useful realization, because it is easier to find out a person's occupation, type of income, and address than his or her community reputation. It was this finding of Warner's, as well as the creation of the two measurement techniques, that made Warner's methodology so popular with later researchers. However, his influence involved his substantive generalizations as well.

WARNER'S FINDINGS   Several of the conclusions that Warner came to were widely accepted by other social scientists for a while, and some are still accepted. Six are particularly important.

One of the most outstanding conclusions was that the basis of stratification is prestige. Warner did not start out with this assumption. Initially he assumed that the basis of class is economic position. The first interviews seemed to support his hypothesis. Gradually, however, he began to accumulate evidence that some people were placed higher or lower than their incomes would warrant. Several doctors received higher community evaluations than other doctors; other discrepancies were found in the ranking of ministers, lawyers, and bankers. Warner concluded that social evaluation and ranking are the basis of the class system. In taking this position, Warner (1949, p. 129) pitted himself against the economic determinism of Marx.

Warner's second conclusion was that there were a number of criteria used by townsfolk in ranking each other and, thus, forming the basis of prestige inequality. These included education, occupation, wealth, income, family, intimate friends, clubs, and fraternities, as well as manners, speech, and general outward behavior. The members of the community tended to use similar criteria in evaluating each other, although the possession of money seemed more important to poorer persons, while family background, manners, and taste were more important to the affluent.

Third, Warner found that the single criterion most highly correlated with an individual's prestige position is occupation, followed in order by amount of income, source of income, house type, dwelling area, and education (1949, p. 168). Having already rejected a Marxian interpretation of class, Warner did not really explore the relevance of his finding that the most important three correlates of prestige happen to be measures of economic resources. Neither did the decade of sociologists who followed him and were influenced by him. They did, however, eagerly adopt the finding that occupation is the single most important criterion of class. They recognized the convenience of using occupation as the social class indicator, since it is easy and nonprovoking to find out a person's occupation, which is not so true of income or status reputation. Warner's finding was the beginning of a long period of refinement of occupational indexes.

Fourth, Warner did caution, however, that social class is most accurately measured when using *several* measures (1949, p. 168). This generalization has been verified by later research (Haer 1957; Lawson and Boek 1960). Consequently, today the most widely used indexes of social class do employ several measures, usually occupation and income or occupation and education.

Fifth, Warner concluded that members of the community can be placed into one of five or six classes according to their reputations, the groups they belong to, the location of their homes, and their economic standing. Briefly, their characteristics can be summarized as follows:

The upper-upper class (about one percent of the population) consisted of an aristocracy of birth and wealth. This was the "old family" class, composed of families who have lived in the community for at least three generations. The wealth, gained in business and finance, had existed in the family for a long time. Since family heritage was the crucial mark of upper-upper status, the members of this class took an extraordinary interest in genealogy and kinship relationships. There was considerable intermarriage within the group and a tendency to behave as a biological kinship group even when there actually was no such kinship. This re-affirmed the social proximity among members of the upper-upper class and their social distance from those in other classes. Lines between the upper-upper class and the lower strata were fairly rigidly maintained.

The lower-upper class, also about one percent of the population, was similar to the upper-upper class in wealth, occupation, visiting patterns, housing, and club memberships, but their wealth was new and they lacked a socially superior family lineage. Even though they tended to be slightly wealthier than the upper-upper class, the nouveaux riches had not fully learned the life style of the class above them. The result was that psychologically they felt less secure. The desire to exhibit their newly ac-quired wealth led them to purchase expensive material objects.

The upper-middle class, about 10 percent of the population, was com-posed of prominent, substantial business and professional people. They lived in comfortable homes in the better residential areas, participated ex-tensively in community activities, and provided the active front in civic affairs for the classes above them. They believed in money and material comforts, and most members strove for high status. Since they were con-cerned with bettering their station in life, they became oriented toward accomplishment.

The lower-middle class, about 28 percent, was composed of clerks and other white-collar workers, small tradesmen, and a few skilled workers. They were concerned with "morals" as well as money. Their small, but neat homes were located on side streets. More of them tended to be re-ligious, and their moral values tended toward Puritan fundamentalism. They wanted to be proper and conservative, "being careful with their money, saving, farsighted, forever anxious about what their neighbors think, and continually concerned about respectability" (Warner 1953, p. 76).

Members of the upper-lower class, about one-third of the total popu-lation, were the "poor but honest" semiskilled workers, operatives, and service workers. They were the most difficult to distinguish from adjacent classes, Warner believed. They lived in small houses in medium condition located near a mill or a business district. They prided themselves on be-ing more respectable than the lower-lower class, and they attempted to "raise their children right." Their material standards were low, but their ambitions were high, at least for their children. Education was the means of realizing these ambitions, they believed.

The lower-lower class, one-fourth of the total, had a bad reputation among those who were socially above them. It was believed that they were lazy, shiftless, promiscuous, sexually immoral, and improvident. Actually, many of them were guilty only of being poor and lacking the ability to get ahead. They lived in the worst sections of town and contributed the highest proportion of members to the relief rolls. They were unskilled workers and "had little interest in education, thrift, and ambition."

Warner's final conclusion, which seems obvious today, but was not as widely accepted in his time, was that class is a very important force in community life:

> Members of a class tend to marry within their own order....
> A class system also provides that children are born into the same status as their parents. A class society distributes rights and privileges, duties and obligations, unequally among its inferior and superior grades (Warner and Lunt 1941, p. 82)

Warner's focus was on prestige rather than power and on description rather than causal analysis. He was not interested in social mobility or in the forces that bring it about. His influence on other researchers was enormous, and a number of similar studies followed his lead.[2] Flourishing in the 1940s and early 1950s, these investigations stimulated a great deal of subsequent research on a number of issues and provided a rich source of information on the class system. They made a number of assumptions about class, however, and reflected a particular point of view. It was not long before they were heavily criticized.

THE CRITIQUE OF THE WARNER SCHOOL   Criticism of Warner mounted slowly but steadily, reaching a peak of attention in the mid-1950s. Three major points can be provided in summary.

First, the Warner emphasis on prestige as the basic determinant of class overlooks the important causal role of economic and political stratification. Investigators who define class in economic or political terms actually end up studying different things (Pfautz and Duncan 1950). Further, the Warner approach inhibits the systematic examination of the relationships between prestige, economics, and power (Montague 1963). These critics disagree with Warner's claim that "class is what people say it is" — that is, an entirely subjective social structure based on a prestige ranking. They counterclaim that Warner has described not the overall class system, but only the system of prestige classes; his view cannot be considered as an alternative approach to class, but offers only a complementary approach (Kornhauser 1953, p. 245). They argue that Warner should have paid more, not less, attention to the influence of economic

2 See Davis et al. 1941; Dollard 1937; Drake and Clayton 1945; Hollingshead 1949; Kaufman 1944; Lenski 1935; and West 1945. Other community studies of the period that differ in theoretical focus and method include A. W. Jones 1941; Lynd and Lynd 1929 and 1937; and Mills 1946.

differentiation on stratification; a correlation of .97 between the I.S.C. and the E.P. shows the importance of economic position even for prestige stratification (Kornhauser 1953, p. 246; Chinoy 1950, pp. 259–60). Several critics suggested that Warner and his followers emphasized prestige and ignored economic inequality because an emphasis on prestige conforms to basic American myths (Bottomore 1966; Montague 1963; Pease et al. 1970).

Second, criticism was directed at Warner's statement that the classes he found in Yankee City and Jonesville represent the overall class structure of America. Warner and associates had written:

> The Jonesvilles, Smithtowns, Greenfields, and all the other -villes, -towns, and -fields of America are essentially alike. Sometimes the road signs at their entrances say Dallas, Seattle, or maybe Indianapolis or Buffalo, . . . but no matter what the signs say or how the alphabetical letters are arranged, they still spell Jonesville. . . . Jonesville has been our laboratory for studying Americans (1949, pp. xiv–xv).

Yet, other community researchers have not always turned up the same number of classes. James West (1945) found only two main classes in Plainville; the Lynds (1929, 1937) first found two and later six; Centers (1949) found four; Hollingshead (1949), five; Warner (1941, 1949), six and five; and so forth. Obviously, these investigators could not all be describing the same class system.

The basic problem is that the communities Warner picked to study were small and homogeneous and quite different from highly urbanized America. In a large city, some have argued, prestige classes based on personal acquaintance cannot exist because the inhabitants are strangers to each other. They interact mainly on the basis of their major statuses, such as occupation. Most social contacts are impersonal. Further prohibiting the development of familiarity among a city's population is the fact that it is criss-crossed by a number of divisions — racial, ethnic, and religious, for example. This suggests that in the large urban environment the study of power hierarchies and interest groups is a more productive area of inquiry into stratification. Further, the range of class differences is greater in a large city; the upper class of Yankee City or Jonesville would not be generally comparable to the upper class in such cities as New York City or San Francisco.

A third, related criticism accuses Warner of failing to describe accurately the class structure of even the small town, describing it instead as it exists in the eyes of the upper-middle- and upper-class residents. Recall that Warner indicated that his first step was to search out an influential man in the community. Other community studies (West 1945; A. Davis et al. 1941) confirmed that upper-class informants tend to make finer and subtler class distinctions than those in lower classes. The reported structure differs depending on who is looking at it.

Members of all class groups recognize the classes above or below them. But the greater the social distance from the other classes, the less clearly are fine distinctions made (A. Davis et al. 1941). Furthermore, although individuals know that there are social groups immediately above or below their own, they do not usually perceive the social distance that actually exists between their own and these adjacent groups. In addition, it was observed, individuals visualize less clearly those class groups above them than those below them. This is true in part because many people have been socially mobile from lower classes and in part because there is a tendency to identify with "superiors," not recognizing the social distance that does exist. Consequently, upper-class individuals are more likely to make the finest classifications, while distinctions are made with decreasing precision as the social position becomes lower. Finally, not only does the perspective of the stratification system vary by class, but the criteria used vary also. Upper-class individuals put prime importance on the past and the length of time that the family has had upper-class status. The middle class emphasizes wealth, morality, self-improvement, and community improvement. Lower-class people view the structure as a hierarchy of wealth.

These generalizations of the early community researchers have been confirmed by a number of investigations (Alexander 1972; L. S. Lewis 1964; Stone and Form 1953). The problem with Warner's work, then, is that it is "actually a composite version of the prestige hierarchy which is built from the varied perspectives of the local residents. It is basically a construction of the researcher rather than the consensus of the community" (Chinoy 1950, p. 259).

In summary, the major defects of the Warner school are several: it ignores economic and political sources of inequality; it assumes a consistency of perception of class that does not exist; it claims greater objective validity for its five- or six-class system than has been found to exist in other research; and it is descriptive rather than analytic. On the other hand, the Warner school established that there *is* a prestige hierarchy in small communities, even when people are not aware of it; that prestige is related to the other institutions in the community; and that people with professional and managerial jobs, high incomes, and residence in high-status areas are likely to be well respected. Perhaps the outstanding historical significance of Warner's work is the effect it had in generating new studies of prestige. It was probably the impetus given by Warner's work, more than any other single source, that caused the field of social stratification to burgeon so rapidly in the 1940s and 1950s. In that development were studies of a different type, those of occupational prestige, which have had widespread applicability since Warner's time and continue to do so at present.

OCCUPATIONAL PRESTIGE

The second major technique that has been developed to study social prestige is the occupational prestige scale. This technique is different from the community study in that it is most commonly based on national samples rather than samples of informants in small communities. It is easily applied to the study of prestige in other countries, and thus it provides an easier method of making cross-cultural comparisons than does the Warner technique.

When we find out peoples' occupations, we are really finding out many other things about them as well. Their probable level of educational attainment, the authority and autonomy they have on the job, the economic return they probably get (and thus the quality of their living conditions), their child-rearing practices, their friendships, their leisure activities — all these are related to occupation. Because prestige status and occupational status are so highly correlated, we are learning if they are respected by the society at large. In a sense, we are also gaining information about their probable level of self-esteem and personal sense of mastery, because the prestige attached to major structural roles affects the self-concepts of the individuals in these roles. The extensiveness of personal items that are in one way or another related to an individual's occupation make the index of occupational prestige a very versatile measure indeed.

How do we go about measuring occupational prestige in a precise way? Although ratings of occupational prestige have been attempted since 1925,[3] the best-known and most widely used approach is one developed in a study conducted by the National Opinion Research Center in 1947 and again in 1963 (North and Hatt 1947; Hodge, Siegel, and Rossi 1966). In this research, a nationwide cross section of Americans was asked to rank ninety occupations. The respondents were given a card with the following instructions:

> For each job mentioned, please pick out the statement that best gives your own personal opinion of the general standing that such a job has:
>
> 1. Excellent standing.
> 2. Good standing.
> 3. Average standing.
> 4. Somewhat below average standing.
> 5. Poor standing.
> X. I don't know where to place that one.

The responses were translated into a scoring system that would allow a maximum of 100 points for any job receiving only "excellent" ratings, and a minimum of 20 points for those receiving only "poor" ratings. The

---

[3] See Caplow 1954, pp. 39 ff., for a discussion of the earlier works.

Table 7.1

Occupational prestige ratings, 1963

Occupation	Score	Occupation	Score
U.S. Supreme Court justice	94	Biologist	85
Physician	93	Sociologist	83
Nuclear physicist	92	Instructor in public schools	82
Scientist	92	Captain in the regular army	82
Government scientist	91	Accountant for a large business	81
State governor	91	Public school teacher	81
Cabinet member in the federal government	90	Building contractor	80
College professor	90	Owner of a factory that employs about 100 people	80
U.S. representative in Congress	90	Artist who paints pictures that are exhibited in galleries	78
Chemist	89	Author of novels	78
Diplomat in the U.S. Foreign Service	89	Economist	78
Lawyer	89	Musician in a symphony orchestra	78
Architect	88	Official of an international labor union	77
County judge	88	County agricultural agent	76
Dentist	88	Electrician	76
Mayor of a large city	87	Railroad engineer	76
Member of the board of directors of a large corporation	87	Owner-operator of a printing shop	75
Minister	87	Trained machinist	75
Psychologist	87	Farm owner and operator	74
Airline pilot	86	Undertaker	74
Civil engineer	86	Welfare worker for a city government	74
Head of a department in a state government	86	Newspaper columnist	73
Priest	86		
Banker	85		

Source: Condensed from Table 1 in Robert W. Hodge, Paul M. Siegel, and Peter H. Rossi, "Occupational Prestige in the United States, 1925–1963," *American Journal of Sociology* Vol. 70, No. 3 (November 1964). Copyright © 1964 by The

occupations included a wide range, enabling the identification of between two-thirds and three-fourths of gainfully employed workers. The sample of 2,920 adults was well chosen, and a number of techniques were used in administering the study to ensure accuracy (for instance, several occupations were included twice under different names to see if they would receive similar ratings regardless of the label; they did). The results are shown in Table 7.1. As it turned out, the highest ratings were given to governmental officials and to professionals. At the top was Supreme Court justice, followed by physicians and scientists. Unskilled, low-paid, and "dirty" jobs received the lowest ratings — shoe shiner, street sweeper, and garbage collector.

Occupation	Score	Occupation	Score
Policeman	72	Fisherman who owns his own boat	58
Reporter on a daily newspaper	71	Clerk in a store	56
Bookkeeper	70	Milk route man	56
Radio announcer	70	Streetcar motorman	56
Insurance agent	69	Lumberjack	55
Tenant farmer—one who owns livestock and machinery and manages the farm	69	Restaurant cook	55
		Singer in a nightclub	54
Carpenter	68	Filling station attendant	51
Local official of a labor union	67	Coal miner	50
Manager of a small store in a city	67	Dock worker	50
		Night watchman	50
Mail carrier	66	Railroad section hand	50
Railroad conductor	66	Restaurant waiter	49
Traveling salesman for a wholesale concern	66	Taxi driver	49
Plumber	65	Bartender	48
Automobile repairman	64	Farmhand	48
Barber	63	Janitor	48
Machine operator in a factory	63	Clothes presser in a laundry	45
Owner operator of a lunch stand	63	Soda fountain clerk	44
Playground director	63	Sharecropper—one who owns no livestock or equipment and does not manage farm	42
Corporal in the regular army	62	Garbage collector	39
Garage mechanic	62	Street sweeper	36
Truck driver	59	Shoe shiner	34

The biggest surprise of the 1947 study was the degree of consensus among the respondents. People in different socioeconomic categories agreed on which jobs had the most and which had the least standing. Even those employed in the occupations receiving little respect agreed that those jobs were less important! There were no significant differences in the rankings made by respondents in different regions and sizes of communities or of different ages or sexes.

Slight variations that did not appreciably affect the rank order of prestige were found according to occupation and education. An individual tended to rate his or her *own* occupation higher than did others. People who had a college education or were prosperous tended to rate professional, scientific, and artistic occupations slightly higher than did the rest of the sample, whereas skilled jobs and operative work were rated higher by persons with only a grammar school education and by the poorer economic groups.

The consensus was found to exist over time. The 1963 replication conducted by Hodge, Siegel, and Rossi (1964) showed very clearly that the relative prestige of occupations had changed little between 1947 and 1963 (r = .99). Changes that did occur were slight: Scientific, professional, and blue-collar occupations rose in prestige, whereas managerial, clerical and sales, and farming occupations declined. Hodge, Siegel, and Rossi (1966) also compared the NORC rankings with those reported by George S. Counts (1925) in 1925 and by Mapheus Smith (1943) in 1940. Counts had asked high school and college students to rank forty-five occupations according to their "social standing"; Smith had asked students how far away incumbents of different occupations should sit from the guest of honor at a dinner honoring a celebrity. (In those days, students were the main sources of survey data.) The correlation of the rankings made by the 1925 students and those of the NORC's 1963 national sample was .93; that of Smith's students to the NORC sample was .97. The authors concluded: "There have been no substantial changes in occupational prestige in the United States since 1925" (1966, p. 329).

Stability of occupational prestige rankings exists cross-culturally, also, as we mentioned in Chapter 2. Hodge, Treiman, and Rossi (1966) compared the rankings found in twenty-four countries, both industrialized and nonindustrialized. They were all very similar, the average "coefficient of determination" being 0.83 (ranging from a low of 0.62, between the United States and Poland, to a high of 0.95, between the United States and New Zealand). There was greater consensus on the relative standing of white-collar occupations than of blue-collar occupations. Even so, the coefficient of determination for blue-collar occupations was as high as .69.

The consistency of occupational prestige hierarchies across subgroups and nations was the first important finding of the research of the 1950s and 1960s. The second equally important (but less surprising) finding was that the prestige that an occupation has runs hand in hand with the income that the occupation commands and with the educational attainments of its members. As Warner found for his measure of prestige, the NORC occupational prestige rankings are closely correlated with objective indexes of socioeconomic status, three of which have been independently developed by Duncan (1961), Bogue (1969), and the U.S. Census Bureau (Nam 1963). All three of these indexes assign scores ranging from 0 to 100 to specific occupations on the basis of the average income and education of their incumbents. Those working in an occupation scoring in the 90s, for example, tend to be educated, well-paid people. When the NORC occupational prestige scores are compared to the "socioeconomic" scores developed by Duncan, Bogue, and the U.S. Census Bureau, correlations of .91, .89, and .88, respectively, occur (Duncan 1961, p. 124). Such high correlations, accounting for over 77 percent of the variation in prestige, suggest the great interdependence of occupational training and rewards and of social evaluation.

WHAT DO THESE FINDINGS MEAN? THE FUNCTIONALIST EXPLANATION Functionalists maintain that the high consensus on occupational prestige reflects a reward system ensuring that those occupations which are more important for the general welfare of the society will attract able personnel. High government posts are important because they coordinate the activities of the society, an essential function. Top industrial positions are important because they are responsible for the success of the economic enterprise. Top professions contribute to health and happiness (Abrahamson et al. 1976, pp. 195–96). People realize that these kinds of occupations are more important, so they respect them more. In trying to explain the observed similarity between the 1947 ratings of occupational prestige and the 1965 ratings, Hodge, Siegel, and Rossi invoked such an interpretation:

> First the educational requirements, monetary rewards, and even the nebulous "functional importance" of an occupation are not subject to rapid change in an industrial society. Second, any dramatic shifts in the prestige structure of occupations would upset the dependency that is presumed to hold between the social evaluation of a job, its educational prerequisites, its rewards, and its importance to society (1964, p. 294).

Another functionalist explanation of the close fit between prestige, income, and education (see Chapter 2) is that prestige and income serve to motivate individuals to enter and perform occupational roles of complexity and difficulty. In this view, both prestige and income inequities serve as rewards that distribute people of different backgrounds and talents into jobs of different requirements and responsibilities.

WHAT DO THESE FINDINGS MEAN? THE CONFLICT THEORY EXPLANATION The interpretation given by conflict theory, on the other hand, argues that prestige follows from and is dependent on power inequities. People see that certain occupations are powerful or economically rewarding, and they place those occupations in awe. Their views become adaptations to the facts of power (Gusfield and Schwartz 1963, p. 241; Lenski 1966, p. 431).

For example, a study of attitudes toward dentists (Kriesberg 1962) indicated that there is not a particularly high relationship between the amount of prestige that individuals believe an occupation has and their own perception of its importance. Rather — in the case of dentists, at any rate — prestige was related more to the benefits that respondents received from dentists than to their perception of the importance of dentists' work, the scarcity of personnel able to do the work, or the dentists' possession of valued attributes.

Some conflict theorists suggest that the process is more subtle than the simple exchange of deference for power. They maintain that the values underlying a prestige hierarchy have been developed and communicated by the upper and upper-middle classes through the major agencies of socialization that they control (education, science, and mass communication, for example). The values, thus, are compatible with the desires and interests of those classes. "It is not the moral evaluations of the population at large which give rise to the status system, but mainly the evaluations of the dominant class members" (Parkin 1971, p. 42).

Certain criteria by which positions are ranked become accepted as relevant for ranking purposes, while other criteria are defined as irrelevant. In this process, the criteria favoring the dominant classes are usually adopted. "If, for example, occupational prestige were allocated on the basis of the physical effort, or danger, or dirtiness of the tasks performed, it would result in a quite different status order from that in which technical expertise, skill, or responsibility were held to be the relevant rank criteria" (Parkin 1971, p. 42). In American society, the latter criteria are used rather than the former, giving professional occupations and political positions a higher rating than manual occupations.

It is plausible that income, education, and prestige of occupations are all directly or indirectly determined and established by the dominant strata to serve their own self-interest. The process by which the needs of the dominant strata are served, in this line of reasoning, involves four sequences of action (Vanfossen 1973): (1) Those occupations which are characteristic of the dominant classes are set to bring higher monetary rewards. This might be done by such techniques as self-determination of salary, as is the case with top-level managers of private corporations; or creation of greater demand through professional limiting of entrants, as in the case of medical and legal training and certification; or by restriction of the supply by setting up difficult and arbitrary tasks to be completed for certification, as, for example, the requirement that psychiatrists receive full medical training. (2) High levels of formal education then are prescribed as prerequisites for entering those occupations. (3) But, the process of acquiring such formal education is structured in such a way that children of the dominant strata are more likely to complete the many steps. (4) Finally, prestige evaluations that are taught by the major socialization agencies legitimate the economic inequality by defining dominant-class occupations as more deserving of monetary rewards. Thus, high correlations between an occupation's income, education, and prestige scores come to exist as a result of the influence and power of the superordinate classes, not as a result of the inherent superior value of the occupational role itself. The occupations that the dominant groups choose to monopolize, elevate in rewards, and fill might be those jobs which are more desirable because they are more powerful, interesting, challenging, exciting, pleasant, or clean, and so forth. This would account for the cross-cultural similarity in occupational ratings.

Proponents of both the functional and the conflict theories muster defenses of their positions. Perhaps the empirical validity of their arguments is yet to be established. What we can be certain of are several of the implications of the occupational prestige studies. As Warner similarly found, occupational prestige inequality is a highly patterned and stable component of social stratification in general. It is not ephemeral or elusive, but, rather, is well entrenched and pervasive. Further, as Warner found, it is highly correlated with economic and educational inequality. In this fact lies the source of its legitimating function. Regardless of its causes, an occupational prestige hierarchy bearing an almost one-to-one correspondence to the inequality of incomes and educational levels of the incumbents of those occupations lends an aura of rightness to that inequality.

To this point, in looking for the subjective underpinnings of social stratification, we have dealt primarily with the prestige structure. Additional subjective factors include the individual's perception of a class structure and of his or her position in it. The following sections define class consciousness and investigate its prevalence among Americans.

The Role of Class Consciousness

The main problem of this chapter is, Why do the less privileged strata acquiesce to a system that deprives them? Why do they not rise up in rebellion and, through force of numbers, take those scarce and desired things that are denied to them? An implied corollary question is, When change has occurred — when there *is* a redistribution of wealth, land reform, or class revolution — what were the conditions that promoted the political action for change?

We have argued so far that the prestige hierarchy is a supportive structure, because by giving honor to the privileged, it persuades others of the moral legitimacy of that privilege. In this section we deal with another set of subjective supports — those having to do with class consciousness. How sensitive a population is to class inequalities and how likely it is to feel resentful about them are important intervening variables. In the following sections, we examine the concept of class consciousness, the degree to which Americans are aware of their own stratum location, the uses of ideology in promoting or inhibiting change, and the conditions favorable to the development of class consciousness.

CLASS CONSCIOUSNESS

Here we need to define concepts and outline paradigms. Class consciousness exists when an individual perceives a common interest with others who share economic and social circumstances. Three conditions must exist for there to be a clear state of class consciousness: (1) individuals must identify themselves with the class or stratum to which they belong by objective definition; (2) they must identify with others in the same stratum; and (3) they must feel separate or distinct from those in other strata (Rosenberg 1953). Class consciousness is similar to racial, ethnic, and religious consciousness (even though the latter often exist across classes and, thus, diminish the awareness of class).

Theories about class consciousness have been highly influenced by Marx, who predicted the increasing polarization of society into two classes, the bourgeoisie and the proletariat. Marx contended that members of the various classes tend to develop a strong identification with other members of their class. Although in many historical periods, most people are unaware of their "true" class interests, the result being a "false class consciousness," in certain circumstances people do realize where their interests lie. Class consciousness then provides the psychological foundations for revolutionary activity. This process occurs only after the class members go through a series of social-psychological transformations, from the point at which they are aware of similar interests with other members of the class (*Klasse an sich*) to the point at which they are willing to organize collectively and fight for their group interests (*Klasse für sich*). In the early stages of this transition, workers are dependent on the ruling class for the satisfaction of their basic needs. Such a relationship could stabilize indefinitely. The transformation to *Klasse für sich,* according to Marx, occurs following an increase in economic insecurity, the development of extreme contrasts in wealth, the concentration of workers, and the development of unionization. Only at the final stages are the workers able to break the bonds of dependency, a stage that is particularly likely to occur if the growing class consciousness is accompanied by increased channels of communication, the development of leadership, and an activist ideology.

Morris and Murphy in 1966 further codified the various stages in the development of class consciousness and political action (also see Leggett 1964a). First is the situation in which people do not even perceive status differences. They are like the Plainvillian who claimed, "'You don't find no classes here!" In the second stage, people are at least aware of continuous status ranges, and they can place themselves and others in that range. They recognize that some people are more privileged than others.

In the third stage, people perceive *discrete* ranked categories. The conception of classes, as distinct entities, appears. In the fourth stage, they join status-related groups — workers' unions or professional groups, for example. In the fifth stage, they not only identify with stratum interests and ideologies, but actually become committed to those interests. In the final stage, they take action on behalf of these interests and ideologies.

As these models have indicated, to be aware of the existence of class does not ensure that a person will be in sympathy with the interests of the stratum to which he or she belongs. In recognition of this, a further distinction has been made (Laumann and Senter 1976, p. 1309; MacIver and Page 1949, pp. 358–64; Westie 1959; Nisbet 1959). In one kind of class consciousness, individuals believe that their own life chances depend on the actions and success of the class as a whole with which they identify: *corporate class consciousness*. In the other, individuals believe that their life chances depend on their own personal effort and resources in competition with other individuals in the society: *competitive class consciousness*. In both cases, people are aware of the status hierarchy, but their views differ on how they could improve the economic parameters of their lives.

A person whose views could be labeled corporate class-conscious is likely to favor the elevation of the class as a whole. For example, she might support or join a labor union. Another person, whose views are consistent with competitive class consciousness, would be more likely to try to maximize his own prestige or economic gain vis-à-vis his stratum cohorts. He would feel competitive to them and might feel content when his personal possessions, such as color television sets or powerboats, are more elaborate than his neighbors. Unlike the individual who works for collective improvement, a person who has developed a competitive class consciousness does not challenge the basic stratification order. Rather, he is an active participant in it, reinforcing its legitimacy by striving for its symbols of honor.

Challenge of the status quo depends on the development of corporate class consciousness. It begins with a group's perceptual breakthrough, a recognition that change is possible. The American auto industry sit-down strikes in the 1930s destroyed the idea that the authority of employers over workers is absolute, and the Montgomery bus boycott in 1955 provided a similar change in expectation for blacks. The process is accelerated when individuals project the sources of their difficulty on the social or political structure rather than on their own deficiencies or on the supernatural. Portes's (1971) study of Chilean slum dwellers, for example, found that radical leftism develops *only* after individuals have adopted an attitude of "structural blame" that locates the cause of their frustration in social structural arrangements rather than in fate.

These theories of class consciousness all suggest that its development is a complicated process dependent on a number of historical and structural circumstances. Before we analyze the specific historical conditions affecting class consciousness in the United States, however, it is first useful to know how aware of class is the American population. Are Americans on the verge of militant class action, or are they settled into contented acceptance?

SELF-IDENTIFICATION

The earliest attempt to find out how Americans view their own position in the stratification system was a nationwide survey by Roper for *Fortune* in the early 1940s. Americans were asked whether they belonged to the "upper," "middle," or "lower" classes. The fact that 79 percent responded "middle" was widely interpreted to mean that Americans perceive of themselves as a middle-class nation.

But this conclusion was challenged shortly thereafter by another nationwide survey conducted by Richard Centers. Starting from the theoretical position that "social classes . . . can be characterized as psychologically or subjectively based groupings defined by allegiance of their members," Centers developed the "interest group theory of social classes," which maintains that people in similar economic circumstances will develop a similar sense of values on political and economic issues (1949, p. 210). Centers's rephrasing of his identification question (adding a "working class" category) elicited quite different responses from those found in the *Fortune* survey. Fifty-one percent of the respondents picked "working class"; only 43 percent claimed that they belonged to the "middle class," while a miniscule 1 percent chose "lower class." People do not like to label themselves as belonging to the lower class, and if given only the three alternatives of "upper," "middle," and "lower," most of them will pick "middle." When the more acceptable label "working class" is added, a large proportion will choose that term.

Centers found a considerable correlation between self-identification and objective position. When the respondents were grouped by occupational role, for example, nearly three-fourths of all business, professional and white-collar workers identified themselves with the middle and upper classes, while four-fifths of the manual workers identified with the working and lower classes. So far, so good. Most people seemed to be aware (correctly, as judged by occupational data) of their relative position in the stratification structure.

These conclusions were challenged, however, by a survey in Minneapolis analyzed by N. Gross (1953; also see Kahl 1957, pp. 167–71; Manis and Meltzer 1963, p. 31). Before asking the respondents to select one of a list of labels, he gave them an unstructured open-ended question: "What class do you belong to?" The respondents answered as follows:

Upper class	1
Middle class	31
Working class	11
Lower class	3
Don't know, or no response	25
No classes in Minneapolis	14
Miscellaneous names, such as the "employer class," "common class," etc.	15

In brief, less than half chose "middle" or "working," while over one-third disclaimed any class membership at all or did not know. Class imagery did not seem to loom centrally in their minds. However, when the respondents were asked to identify themselves as "upper," "middle," or "lower," 76 percent picked "middle," similar to the respondents of the *Fortune* survey thirteen years earlier. Finally, Gross asked them to pick a label from "upper," "middle," "working," and "lower." Now, the responses were arranged as in Centers's study: 42 percent said they were "middle," and 45 percent picked "working."

Gross's research clearly shows the effect of question design on survey results. The responses to his first open-ended question indicate that a substantial minority of the population were not even class-conscious enough to have a name for themselves. This point is supported by the finding that when people are asked to write an essay on "Who am I?", less than 1 percent include social class designations (Mulford and Salisburg 1964). In addition, the reader will recall, community prestige studies have cast considerable doubt on the assumption that Americans can explicitly agree on how many classes there are (Lenski 1953; Sargent 1953; Manis and Meltzer 1963, pp. 31–32). About one-fifth of Americans either do not know what classes are or deny their existence (Kahl and Davis 1955; Haer 1957; and Manis and Meltzer 1954).

It is probable that surveys of the *Fortune* and Centers type underestimate the vagueness that many Americans have about the stratification system. In a society in which the prevailing ideology minimizes the significance of class differences, self-identification through polling questions is one of the least reliable methods of determining class awareness.[4] Some individuals "will claim a class position or identification which represents only wish-fulfillment or fantasy" (Gordon 1958, p. 197). (For instance, 18 percent of the unskilled workers in Centers's sample claimed membership

[4] For similar results in Great Britain see Abrams 1968 and Runciman 1966; in Switzerland, Willener 1957; in Germany, Mayntz 1958 and Popitz et al. 1961; and in Denmark, Svalastoga 1959. For a recent summary of data on working-class identification in the United States, see Schreiber and Nygreen 1970.

in the middle class. On the other hand, 7 percent of the businessmen and 10 percent of the professionals identified themselves as working-class.)

But we should not carry this line of reasoning too far. As Tucker (1967) points out, we cannot ignore the fact that there is a consistent pattern of statistical relationships between "subjective social class" and other variables. In his own study, as shown in Table 7.2, he found strong correlations between a person's class self-identification and education, occupation, income, urban residence, and prestige rank (Tucker 1967, pp. 11–12). Recent path analyses and multiple regression analyses (Jackman and Jackman 1973; Vanneman and Pampel 1977) similarly conclude that subjective social class is correlated with objective socioeconomic status (occupation, in particular). All of the studies indicate that the majority of Americans *do* recognize the existence of great differences in wealth, power, and prestige (Williams 1960, p. 134). It would be difficult to understand if they did not in a society that not only emphasizes the importance of success, but also constantly bombards its members with advertisements, mass communications, and success stories playing up the importance of achieving symbols of status.

The significant fact, (developed more fully in the following section), however, is that people tend to perceive these differences not so much as *class* differences, but as *individual* differences, resulting from lucky breaks or from the application of talent and will. They have a well-developed competitive class consciousness. If we use the Morris and Murphy schema

Table 7.2

Occupational position and subjective self-identification for males, 1963

Subjective social class	General occupational category			
	Professional and technical (N = 66)	Clerical and sales (N = 62)	Craftsmen, operatives, and service workers (N = 219)	Laborers (N = 39)
Upper and upper-middle	44%	19%	10%	5%
Middle	45	52	38	23
Lower-middle	5	11	10	15
Lower and working	6	18	42	57
Total	100	100	100	100

Source: From Charles W. Tucker, "A Descriptive Analysis of Subjective Social Class in the United States, 1963," paper presented to the Midwest Sociological Society Meetings, Des Moines, Iowa (April 1967), Table V. Reprinted by permission.

presented earlier, it seems clear that Americans are in the second or third stages of class consciousness. They recognize that some people are more privileged than others, and they tend to locate themselves somewhat accurately within the middle-class/working-class distinction (Vanneman and Pampel 1977). Yet, they do not see their own level of privilege or disprivilege as being dependent on the economic or political resources of the class stratum in which they are located. A feeling of identity with others in one's own "class," combined in a struggle and conflict with competing classes, is noticeably absent.

IDEOLOGY

The role of ideology is crucial in shaping the type and extent of class consciousness that an individual will adopt. It can effectively prevent people from developing an action-oriented view of the world. It also can encourage them to do so. Ideology consists of emotionally held ideas that explain the social world and indicate what actions should be taken relative to it. Primary effects of ideologies are the elevation of the group's sense of self-worth and the justification of its programs of action. When workers see their class as being exploited by management, for example, not only are they placing the blame for their inferior economic position on others, but they are also encouraging action oriented to change, such as strikes or labor organization. In the same vein, when the wealthy and powerful believe that their superior advantage is due to their own talent and hard work or that it is a just reward for their service to humanity, then they have reduced guilt for using and increasing their wealth and power. When the middle class asserts that its norms and values are inherently superior, then it gathers momentum for imposing them on the other classes (for example, in the passage of blue laws, property laws, and public school regulations).

Class ideologies can be conservative or radical. When a traditional, conservative ideology prevails, a common attitude of the lower classes toward the higher is one of respect and subservience, while the upper portrays condescension and patronage toward the lower. On the other hand, when a radical ideology exists, usually in a time of social change and class struggle, the lower classes tend to resent the higher ones, while the upper classes become more concerned about control and subjugation. The dominant American ideology historically falls more in the former category than in the latter.

EGALITARIANISM IN THE UNITED STATES As American ideology has evolved over the last two centuries, abstract sentiments about stratification have maintained a pervasive egalitarian emphasis. Americans tend to believe that everyone should, and does, have an equal opportunity to get ahead. The strength of such a belief is revealed when a comparison is made between the United States and capitalist Europe, where conscious skepticism about social mobility is more developed (Parkin 1971, p. 98; Ossowski 1963). European ideology evolved out of a feudalistic structure — a relatively closed system in which the nobility and peasantry were perpetuated through family inheritance over a relatively long period of time. Even when European industrialism replaced feudalism and when social mobility increased drastically, the awareness and accentuation of class differences lingered on. In the popular images, the capitalists and financiers came to replace the nobility, while the working class replaced the peasants. Among French workers, for example, resentment about limited opportunities and the belief in a closed class system are viable elements of a pervasive class consciousness (Lipset and Bendix 1964, p. 77). In England, recent changes in the distribution of wealth and the presence of social mobility have not been sufficient to overcome the popular images of "a plutocratic reality," combined with "the sentimental aromas of an aristocratic legend," as Tawney puts it (1964, p. 57).

In the United States, by contrast, ideology is dominated neither by class antagonism nor by references to an aristocratic legend, and it is hardly sympathetic to the principle of inherited privilege. As Lipset and Bendix suggest, "Americans have rarely been exposed to persons whose conduct displays a belief in an inherited and God-given superiority" (1964, pp. 72–73). Perhaps one reason for the disapproval of pedigreed superiority, and for the optimism about mobility opportunities in the United States, is the fact that the United States never developed a feudalistic system or a landed aristocracy. Rather, American ideology had its roots in the Enlightenment of the eighteenth century and was importantly affected by the values of freedom and equality that spurred the French Revolution going on at that time.

Nevertheless, American egalitarian sentiments have a superficial flavor to them. The eighteenth-century ideal that "all men are created equal" has been reinterpreted to mean that all individuals should have equal *opportunity* (to become unequal). Most Americans would not be in favor of true equality, if this would mean that all people would possess similar economic and political resources (Lane 1959). As a textile worker told an interviewer:

> It's better this way. Everyone will push and try to get up a little higher than he is now. Otherwise, people wouldn't have ambition, wouldn't work (Manis and Meltzer 1963, p. 35).

Equality to him, as to many Americans, means the opportunity to become more privileged. The dominant ideology honors achievement, mainly those kinds of achievements characteristic of the upper-middle and upper strata, and it encourages everyone to compete for success. It claims that there is great opportunity for social mobility, that anyone can succeed, that people get what they deserve, and that anyone can move from the bottom to the top if only he or she has the ambition and talent. This is a form of what we earlier referred to as competitive class consciousness, according to which people recognize inequality, but want to gain a few more of the benefits themselves. In the final analysis, it gives substantial moral support to that inequality.

Like all ideologies, the dominant American ideology contains both value preachments and factual assertions. It preaches that individuals *should* work hard and strive to succeed in competition with others and asserts that, when they do, they *will* in fact be rewarded with success. The astounding feature of these beliefs is that most of them are contrary to the facts of social life. Opportunity is not equal. It is restricted by racial, religious, ethnic, and sexual barriers, as well as by class differentials. Rags to riches is rare, and most mobility is minor. Intelligence is not related to income, nor is industriousness. Many jobs, particularly in the working class, are dead-end; there are no avenues for advancement. One large group, women, are not even considered to be in the race. Another substantial minority, blacks, occupy a semicaste status. Yet the ideology defines success as a result of character and failure as a result of personal inadequacy.

In this instance, the competitive class consciousness characteristic of Americans hinges on the belief that success is based on individual ambition or talent. Conversely, an absence of success (poverty) must be due to individual deficiencies or laziness. The reasoning goes like this: If it is true that poor people are poor because they do not try, then they have no one to blame but themselves — which means that we more affluent folks need feel no guilt about their poverty or our privilege. The effect of the idea is the legitimation of inequality.

That such a rationalization is used to justify stratification while reaffirming belief in equal opportunity was demonstrated by Feagin (1975; also see Huber and Form 1973). He asked a cross section of Americans to evaluate the importance of the "reasons some people give to explain why there are poor people in this country." The reasons he selected were paraphrases of explanations given in pretest interviews conducted in the Los Angeles area. They fell into three broad categories: (1) individualistic explanations, which place the responsibility for poverty primarily on the poor themselves (see items 1–4 in Table 7.3); (2) structural explanations, which blame external social and economic forces (items 6–10); and (3) fatalistic explanations, which cite such factors as bad luck and illness (items 5 and 11). As Feagin predicted, individualistic explanations received the greatest emphasis, as half of the sample listed lack of thrift, laziness, and loose morals as *very* important reasons for poverty. Much less emphasis was given to structural factors, ranging from the 42 percent who saw low wages as a very important cause of poverty to the 27 per-

Table 7.3

Importance of reasons for poverty, as rated by 1,017 adult Americans, 1969

Reasons for poverty	Percentage replying				
	Very important	Somewhat important	Not important	Uncertain	Total
Lack of thrift and proper money management by poor people	58%	30%	11%	2%	101%
Lack of effort by the poor themselves	55	33	9	3	100
Lack of ability and talent among poor people	52	33	12	3	100
Loose morals and drunkenness	48	31	17	4	100
Sickness and physical handicaps	46	39	14	2	101
Low wages in some businesses and industries	42	35	20	3	100
Failure of society to provide good schools for many Americans	36	25	34	5	100
Prejudice and discrimination against blacks	33	37	26	5	101
Failure of private industry to provide enough jobs	27	36	31	6	100
Being taken advantage of by rich people	18	30	45	7	100
Just bad luck	8	27	60	5	100

Source: From Joe R. Feagin, *Subordinating the Poor: Welfare and American Beliefs,* © 1975, p. 97. Reprinted by permission of Prentice-Hall, Inc., Englewood Cliffs, New Jersey.

Note: Some lines do not add to exactly 100% because of statistical rounding procedures.

cent who stressed the failure of private industry and the 18 percent who emphasized exploitation by the rich.

Who was most likely to advance the individualistic explanations? Those with higher incomes, older people, the middle-educated, those who were white Protestants or Catholics. Structural explanations were selected more often by the poor, the young, the less well educated, blacks, and Jews. In other words, those who were favored by the system were more likely to believe that poverty is the fault of the poor. They also were more likely to support conservative public policies toward the poor. For example, they opposed jobs and minimum family incomes guaranteed by the government or a radical equalization of incomes.

Feagin discovered how entrenched are individualistic explanations among people in the middle and working strata. Many of the beliefs they held, particularly those concerning welfare and welfare recipients, were simply inaccurate. Yet, he found a strong resistance to evidence to the contrary:

> In a pilot study in a city in central Texas we found a strong reluctance among average citizens to change their misconceptions about welfare, even when contrary evidence was directly presented to them in an interview setting. We also found substantial ignorance in regard to the details of public assistance programs (Feagin 1975, p. 122).

Feagin concludes that the majority of rank-and-file Americans are characterized by false consciousness and by a focus on the diversionary issues of welfare, coupled with a weak consciousness of their own class interests and their own economic oppression.

In summary, the dominant ideology regarding social stratification in the United States encourages people to try to change their own particular position in the hierarchy, but not to challenge the legitimacy of that hierarchy. It interprets inequality to be the result of individual differences in talent and motivation. It promises reward for effort. The acceptance of the dominant ideology is widespread, particularly among the more affluent members of the society. The disprivileged strata are more inclined to believe that stratification is the result of exploitation by the rich, but their ideology lacks the institutional support and coverage that the dominant ideology receives. The ideology of the poor is articulated in homes and informal social gatherings, but the ideology of the privileged receives endorsement by mass communications media, public officials, business leaders, education, and social science.

This section's answer to the question — Why do the less privileged acquiesce to a system that deprives them? — has two parts. First, many of the less privileged (particularly the middle and working classes) believe an ideology that legitimates their disprivilege. Second, those who do not believe it are not organized for change or protest. This brings us to the topic of the next section, the circumstances that not only promote a corporate class consciousness, but also encourage the development of the group structure (leadership, organization, and mobilization) necessary for class action.

STRUCTURAL PRECEDENTS OF CORPORATE
CLASS CONSCIOUSNESS

As we have seen, corporate class consciousness (the identification of individual interests with class interests) is not well developed among the general American population. This raises the question, Exactly what *are* the necessary and sufficient preconditions to a militant class consciousness? Only recently has this question received any critical empirical attention. Marx, it will be recalled, stressed the necessity for the increased isolation of workers, the development of leadership, and the emergence of channels of communication that lead to organization. He believed that resistance to capitalist interests will develop only as the workers become increasingly destitute and miserable. Modern students of revolution disagree with the latter assumption of the role of misery. They contend, instead, that it is during times of rapid economic improvement that discontent increases. Spurred by rising standards of living, the expectations of the workers soon outstrip their gains. What these theorists call the "revolution of rising expectations" itself becomes a source of unrest, often leading to social movements. If the period of rising expectations is followed by a short period of sharp reversal in objective welfare, the discontent becomes volatile (Davies 1962). Historians of various periods, including eighteenth-century France and twentieth-century Russia, claim that there is a tendency for discontent to be low during times of hardship and to rise as opportunity is seen to increase and as the disadvantaged groups gain in wealth and/or prestige (Tocqueville 1955; Pelling 1953).

Several conditions are particularly likely to bring about rising expectations, among them war, increased communication, and economic prosperity (Runciman 1966, pp. 24–25). The most effective resistance among American blacks, to cite one example, came not when they were in a destitute slave status nor when they were effectively subordinated in the semicaste position in the 1920s and 1930s, but when they began to make the rapid political and social advances of the 1950s and 1960s, followed by disillusionment in the late 1960s. As the gap grows between what people want and what they get, so does the frustration.

These theorists have focused on *structural* conditions. In the United States, a listing of the characteristics of American structure that have *inhibited* the development of corporate class consciousness include the following:

1. Relatively high rates of social mobility, which obscure the boundaries between strata and reduce the impact of identification of the mobile individual with a particular stratum;
2. Significant divisions of a society along other dimensions, such as religious, racial, or ethnic group membership, introducing competing bases of identification (Rosenberg 1953, p. 25; Leggett 1968, p. 129);
3. Complexity and segmentation of the occupational structure as well as the existence of numerous occupational hierarchies, which limit identification to a narrow structure and discourage class awareness across hierarchies (Form 1973);

4. The presence of political parties not standing for specific class interests, which prohibits the emergence of political symbols representing particular classes (Rosenberg 1953, p. 24; Selznick and Steinberg 1969, pp. 216–26);
5. Mass consumption and the availability of common products to a large proportion of the population, which impedes the development of distinctive styles of life commonly found in the highly class-conscious society (Hamilton 1964, pp. 53–57; Form 1973, p. 709);
6. Finally, an ideology that minimizes the relevance of class distinctions.

In addition, some authors focus on the *group* conditions that *encourage* the development of class consciousness:

1. Abrupt collective reversals of a previously improving economic situation;
2. Irregularity of income and employment;
3. Sharp social differentiation and isolation of workers from other elements of the community;
4. Recent entrance into urban industrial life;
5. Blocked mobility;
6. An ideology with a structural blame component.

Most of these conditions have been absent in American society (Williams 1960, p. 150). Exceptions occur among those occupational groups which are relatively isolated and have distinctive work styles. The isolation of longshoremen, fishermen, stevedores, and lumberjacks, for instance, has contributed to their traditional radicalism. Among blue-collar workers in Detroit, Leggett (1964a) found that marginal economic position linked with blocked mobility is related to the higher level of verbalized militant class consciousness of southern-born Negroes, Polish-Americans of European background, and recent migrants from rural areas. In contrast to workers who were "prepared," the inadequately skilled, "uprooted" workers experienced both a frustration of rising expectations and a sense of relative deprivation: "The situation of the uprooted has these consequences, in part, because workmen are able to compare their present economically insecure positions with (1) their original optimistic expectations developed prior to movement to the industrial community and (2) the relatively high standard of living maintained by the middle class and much of the working class as well" (Leggett 1963, p. 688).

The American workers, Leggett concluded (1964b, pp. 246–47), do not form a homogeneous population unable to develop class standards or to vote in a manner consistent with their interests. Many of them are militant, and their class views have predictable political consequences. Yet, others are anything but aggressive in their class opinion and approximate the popular image of the American workingman. The working class

243

is heterogeneous, both in social background and in class views. A corporate class consciousness can be found among certain subgroups, in spite of powerful structural and group forces operating against its emergence.

Subjective Supports: Summary and Conclusions

All stratification systems are reinforced by a prestige hierarchy, the patterned evaluations and rankings people make of each other. The prestige hierarchy closely corresponds to economic and educational inequalities. At the top stand those positions which are the most powerful; at the bottom are those with little bargaining clout. The existence of differential prestige justifies inequality by presenting the more powerful positions as more worthy of reward and respect than others.

Early community research of the Warner school established the reality of prestige rankings; indicated the integration of prestige inequality with major social institutions and with other forms of inequality; showed that highly respected people tend to have more money, professional or managerial jobs, and homes in high-status areas; and discovered the usefulness of occupational scales in measuring prestige.

National surveys of occupational prestige revealed that most people in many nations evaluate occupations similarly. Functionalists claim this reveals the cross-cultural similarity in functions that different occupations serve, although conflict theorists argue that it reveals the cross-cultural similarity in economic and power resources that they control.

A well-developed corporate class consciousness among a populace promotes challenge of the status quo by the disprivileged. Competitive class consciousness, on the other hand, or the total absence of class consciousness legitimates stratification. Most Americans recognize the existence of differences in wealth, power, and prestige. These are perceived, however, not as class differences, but as individual differences, resulting from the application of ambition and talent. American ideology reinforces competitive class consciousness by asserting the existence of equal opportunity of all for the achievement of success. Poverty is viewed as the result of personal inadequacy. The ideology is most strongly held by the privileged, but has become the dominant ideology subscribed to by the middle classes. The conservative impact of the ideology is possible because in the United States many of the structural conditions that encourage a corporate class consciousness are absent.

Why do the less privileged strata (the middle and poor classes) go along with this system, which deprives them? They do, in part, because of their subjective orientations. Some of them believe that they are less valuable and important than the privileged, that the deprivation experienced by them and others is their own fault, that equality of opportunity really does exist. The others, those who do not believe that their own disprivilege is morally just, are relatively unorganized and therefore power-less to alter their situation. The weak development of a corporate class consciousness discourages their perception of class interests, and they are often unaware of how their disprivilege ensues from broader institutional processes. How those subjective orientations which promote the privilege of the more affluent strata are communicated and propagandized is the subject of the following chapter.

SOCIALIZATION SUPPORTS: SCHOOLS AND FAMILIES

MANY PEOPLE BELIEVE that the way to get ahead is to get an education. Go to school, Johnny, and make something of yourself. Schools, in the common view, provide the opportunity for all — rich and poor, black and white alike — who are willing to try to climb the ladder of occupational success. Clearly, this is true, the man down the street is likely to explain, because he knows a poor immigrant family whose son became a doctor and a shantytown kid who became an engineer, and all because they did well in school. Even sociological studies, at first glance, suggest this: The amount of education people attain has great influence on the kind of jobs they can get and thus on their adult social status (Blau and Duncan 1967, p. 430).

As we look at studies of the very processes that the man down the street is talking about, however, nagging doubts begin to emerge. We begin to suspect that education reinforces society's basic economic and social inequalities. While appearing to benefit the common person's efforts to get ahead, it seems in reality to be vitally involved in stabilizing the stratification structure. Its effectiveness as a conservator of privilege and disprivilege seems to be enhanced by the widespread belief that it is not.

Consider three processes by which education reinforces stratification in the United States. First, it gives moral support to economic inequality by indoctrinating students to compatible values. The economic institution is characterized by bureaucratic organization, hierarchical lines of authority, job fragmentation, and unequal pay. From the employer's point of view, it is essential that the products of the educational system (students) accept these undemocratic and unequal aspects of the workaday world (Bowles and Gintis 1976, p. 104). Workers must have been trained to respect the authority and competence of their supervisors and to accept their own position in production. The entry of the student into a hierarchical work structure is facilitated by the meritocratic ideology that schools teach. Such an ideology maintains that the hierarchical division of labor is technically necessary and that job assignment is objective and efficient (and therefore just and egalitarian). Unequal incomes are necessary, it suggests, because they motivate people to work. Besides, people who are more educated deserve greater reward because they have worked harder to get where they are. The meritocratic ideology was not created by the schools; it is merely perpetuated and reinforced by them.

Second, while some children become socially mobile by gaining more education than their parents, most children do not. Social inheritance through educational attainment is the newer form of class reproduction. The system appears open and democratic, but the way it works favors the interests of the more powerful strata. There is a great gap between the ideal that education should serve the people and the reality of what schools do to and for the children of the poor. Most poor children become poor adults. The children of the affluent get the best grades and the best jobs. It is they who can afford college and who know to which college to go. At every step of the route from kindergarten to postgraduate work, the disprivileged children are more likely than the privileged to fall by the wayside. Not all of them do, however, and it is these exceptions who provide the visible examples that the myth of educational equality needs to maintain its persuasion.

Third, the schools shape the personalities of children to conform to the needs of industry. Many are trained to be obedient and docile workers — orderly, law-abiding, and tractable to industrial discipline (Katz 1971). Employers want hard-working, but compliant workers who will accept the wages they are paid. Schools foster the development of a worker personality that is compatible with the relations of dominance and subordination in the economic sphere. At the same time, a small number of children are shaped to be self-assured, independent, and decisive, and they then become suited for managerial and elite professions.

At the end of their schooling, most students slip into economic slots at one level or another with hardly a whimper. Educational processes thus

247

help to defuse and depoliticize the potentially explosive class relations of the production process (Bowles and Gintis 1976, pp. 10–13). Schools integrate youth into the labor force, rewarding them and promoting them until they are ready to be allocated to distinct positions in the occupational hierarchy.

As Bowles and Gintis suggest (1976, p. 13), these processes do not take place because the school is consciously trying to reinforce inequality. Teachers and administrators would be appalled if they believed that. Rather, the schools train students for inequality by replicating in their day-to-day routine the kinds of interactions that govern in the work place. For example, the relationships of authority and control between administrator and teachers, or between teachers and students, replicates the hierarchical division of labor dominating the work place. The motivational system of the school, utilizing grades and the threat of failure, mirrors closely the role of wages and the possibility of unemployment. The degree of authority, which differs by grade level, corresponds to differences in autonomy by occupational level. The rule orientation of the high school reflects the close supervision of low-level workers, while the freedom from constant supervision in the elite colleges reflects the social relationships of upper-level white-collar work.

To many people, this seems a disturbing, and therefore not quite believable, picture of the role of education. Yet, it is suggested by a number of empirical findings. The remainder of the chapter presents what research has shown about the effects of the educational institution on social stratification and about the role the family plays in the process. Further, it explains how that research can most accurately be interpreted. We look at two aspects of the socialization process: first, how the families and schools affect and shape individuals as they grow up; second, how they legitimize economic and occupational inequalities through supportive values and practices.

Educational Achievement and Social Status of the Adult

Education in the United States has increasingly come to play an important role in the placement of children in the occupational hierarchy. More people are attending school now than in earlier generations; they are staying in school longer; and they are attending a higher percentage of their classes (G. D. Squires 1977). Increasingly, the amount of education that they acquire affects the kind of job they can get and, thus, their adult social status (Blau and Duncan 1967, p. 430). This generalization is intuitively supported by glancing at Table 8.1, which shows that men and women with less than four years of high school tend to be operatives, craftsmen, or service workers, while men and women with college degrees

Table 8.1

Occupations of employed persons, by schooling, 1974

| Occupation group and sex | Total | Not high school graduate | High school graduate | | |
			No college	1 to 3 years of college	4 years or more of college
Male, 25 to 64 years	99.8%	100.1%	100.0%	100.0%	100.0%
Professional, technical, and kindred workers	15.7	0.9	6.3	17.1	54.1
Farmers and farm managers	2.9	5.7	3.2	1.6	1.0
Managers and administrators, except farm	16.2	5.5	15.5	24.2	26.3
Clerical and kindred workers	6.1	2.9	8.3	10.0	3.1
Sales workers	5.9	1.3	5.9	10.6	8.3
Craft and kindred workers	22.6	25.4	29.4	18.7	3.9
Operatives, including transport workers	17.3	29.7	19.3	8.9	1.1
Service workers	6.7	10.6	7.3	6.4	1.6
Farm laborers and supervisors	1.2	4.7	0.6	0.4	0.2
Laborers, except farm	5.2	13.4	4.2	2.2	0.4
Female, 25 to 64 years	100.0	100.2	99.9	100.0	100.1
Professional, technical, and kindred workers	17.1	1.0	1.6	22.5	71.4
Farmers and farm managers	0.3	0.5	0.2	0.3	0.3
Managers and administrators, except farm	6.0	2.9	5.2	7.7	6.8
Clerical and kindred workers	32.6	6.5	19.0	46.8	13.5
Sales workers	6.2	3.7	7.4	5.0	3.0
Craft and kindred workers	1.9	2.7	3.0	1.2	0.5
Operatives, including transport workers	14.1	35.1	27.9	4.4	1.3
Service workers	19.9	42.9	33.0	11.0	3.1
Farm laborers and supervisors	1.1	3.5	1.1	0.4	0.2
Laborers, except farm	0.8	1.4	1.5	0.7	—

Source: U.S. Bureau of the Census 1974, Table D.

Note: Some columns do not add to exactly 100% because of statistical rounding procedures.

tend to be professionals or managers. It also emerges from more rigorous statistical tests, particularly those of regression analysis, which indicate that the correlation between a white man's educational attainment and his occupational status is around .65 (Jencks et al. 1972, p. 181) and that between 16 and 25 percent of the variation in the occupational status of men is related to their differences in education attained when other variables are controlled (Blau and Duncan 1967, p. 170; Sewell et al., 1970). Men and women who get a lot of education are likely to end up in high-status occupations, even if their father worked in low-status occupations. Table 8.1 shows, for example, that over half of college graduates end up in professional jobs, whereas less than 6 percent of high school graduates do so. The educational institution is an important part of the allocation process that distributes individuals into the stratification system.

Educational attainment is much less related to adult income. Only around 7 percent of the variation in adult income is "due to" variations in education (Mincer 1974, p. xiv; Jencks et al. 1972; Sewell and Hauser 1975). Education affects income mainly as it influences what kind of job the graduate can get. Jobs in turn affect income.

Educational Achievement and Social Origin of the Child

While educational credentials occasionally create for an individual the major avenue for social mobility, by and large the educational institution instead functions to maintain the class system. One student rises out of the working class into a white-collar position while three of his buddies enter the factory. These opposing outcomes occur simultaneously. They are one source of the contradictions inherent in American education. Even though the majority of Americans support the value of equal educational opportunity for all, the institution designed to achieve that equality actually allocates individuals into the occupational structure in close proportions to the ways in which their parents were distributed in it.

Thus, the higher the social origin of the student, the more education he or she is likely to gain. The educational level of a student's parents, the occupation of the head of the household, and the family's income are all highly related to whether or not he or she graduates from high school and college (Sewell 1971; Jencks et al. 1972, p. 138). In 1967, for example, 82 percent of those whose fathers were college graduates went on to college, compared to only 22 percent of those whose fathers had not completed elementary school (U.S. Bureau of the Census, no. 1969b 185). One of the ways that economically successful parents try to help their children retain privilege is by making sure their children get a good education (Jencks et al. 1972, p. 138). In concrete terms, this means that upper-middle-class children will average four years more of schooling than lower-class children.

The influence of socioeconomic background extends to college performance. The results of a longitudinal study of the careers since 1957 of nine thousand Wisconsin high school students is illustrative (Sewell et al. 1970; Sewell and Shah 1968a; Sewell and Hauser 1975). This study established that high school graduates from less affluent backgrounds are (1) less likely to go to college immediately after high school graduation, (2) much less likely to attend or to be graduated from high-quality colleges, (3) more likely to drop out of college if they enter, (4) less likely to return if they drop out, and (5) more likely to have their college careers interrupted by military service (Sewell 1971, p. 796). Despite the spectacular increase in numbers attending college in the last several decades, there is no evidence that socioeconomic differentials in opportunity for higher education have altered appreciably (Sewell 1971, p. 797). Education is indeed one of the most important means to upward mobility. Yet, by and large, schools do not serve a democratizing function, because persons from a low socioeconomic background are not as likely to attain as much education as those from a more privileged background.

The Process of Educational Attainment

The scenario just described accounts for two seemingly contradictory facts. On the one hand, social mobility rates have been relatively high in the United States. On the other hand, children of high-status parents are considerably more likely than less privileged children to succeed at every level in the educational process and to secure attractive jobs at the end.

Why is the system not completely open? What are the reasons that children of economically successful parents get more credentials than those with unsuccessful parents? Jencks et al. offer several answers:

> First, they are more likely to have a home environment in which they acquire the intellectual skills they need to do well in school. Second, they are more likely to have genes that facilitate success in school. Third, they seldom have to work or borrow money to attend college. Fourth, they may feel that they ought to stay in school, even if they have no special aptitude for academic work and dislike school life. Fifth, they may attend better schools, which induce them to go to college rather than to drop out (1972, p. 138).

While some of these may be involved, Jencks's list does not exhaust the reasons that privileged children tend to do better in school. In the following section, the ways in which the educational system plays a gate-keeping role are described.

251

BARRIERS BASED ON CLASS-BIASED
CHARACTERISTICS OF STUDENTS

Students do not come to school equally prepared to cope with its demands for success. The criteria used to determine who will be successful are influenced by the societal structure of domination (Weber 1968, pp. 926–39), and they thus give greater advantage to the children of the privileged. An important activity of the school is to teach particular status cultures. As Collins (1971, p. 1919) suggests, the real goal of schools is not to impart technical knowledge, but to teach vocabulary and inflection, styles of dress, aesthetic tastes, and values and manners. This is accomplished in part by the emphasis on sociability and athletics that is at the core of the status culture propagated by the schools. In addition, those schools which have a more academic or vocational emphasis are reproducing a particular status culture, providing sets of values, materials for conversation, and shared activities for the children of status groups that make claims to a particular degree of privilege. The important point here is that students come to school unequally developed to respond to the status-group learnings of the school ssytem. Several ways in which children from working-class backgrounds are systematically handicapped in becoming successful in school have been documented.

One of the more obvious handicaps relates to language patterns. It is much easier to get good grades and impress teachers if you can use the language of the status group that is being taught. Most IQ tests, formal tests of academic performance, and grades on classwork are affected by children's ability to understand and use a standard upper-middle-class language form. Their performance is enhanced if they can use a large vocabulary, construct elaborate sentences based on "proper" grammar, and perceive subtleties in the written word. There is increasing evidence that middle-class and working-class people use different language forms, affecting not only their ease of communication, but also their modes of cognitive functioning (B. Bernstein 1964; Lawton 1968; Hess and Shipman 1965).

The exact nature of the class differences in language usage is still unclear. However, Bernstein asserts that working-class and lower-class people are more likely to use a "restricted" form of language that is concerned more with subjective observation than analysis, to have a more limited vocabulary, and to be more egocentric in the sense that the speaker is less aware of the perspective of the listener. Middle-class people are more likely to use an "elaborated" form of language that is concerned with relationships among objects and ideas, is more complicated in sentence structure, and employs a larger vocabulary (B. Bernstein 1964). Hess and Shipman (1965, p. 885), in a summary of research, suggest that the working-class youth grows up in a cognitive environment in which behavior is controlled by rules rather than by attention to the individual characteristics of a specific situation: "This environment produces a child who relates to authority rather than to rationale, who, although often compliant, is not reflective in his behavior."

Other authors (Chandler and Erikson 1968) claim that the use of restricted or elaborated forms of language is not as highly related to social class as Bernstein suggests. A number of studies have indicated that black American English, for example, is just as complex, highly structured, and conducive to abstract thought as white American English (Birren and Hess 1968; Dillard 1972; Labov 1973; and Stewart 1969). It is not that the children of the poor and minority parents are nonverbal — they are very verbal, but not in the language and ways of thinking that the middle class is used to.

So long as the school system reflects middle-class standards, children who come into it with a language form that differs from these standards are going to encounter additional difficulties in meeting performance requirements. The significance of the language differences among the socio-economic strata lies in the relationship of language to academic testing. Ability in symbolization and the "proper" use of words is a main determinant of IQ scores and other measures of classroom performance. Such tests in turn affect success in school.

MEASURED MENTAL ABILITY

That children who score well on tests of mental performance, such as IQ tests, have a greater likelihood of doing well in school seems obvious to today's reader. The "facts" back up the common-sense notion. A number of recent studies of educational attainment have found that measured mental ability is quite predictive of academic performance (Duncan et al. 1972; Jencks et al. 1972). For example, in a follow-up study of Wisconsin high school seniors, Sewell et al. (1970) found that mental ability is directly related to one-third of the variance in academic performance. The effect is not surprising because, in the American culture, tests of intelligence are designed to measure the kinds of performances that are relevant to success in academic pursuits (Duncan et al. 1972, pp. 78–79).

A less obvious finding of the educational attainment research is that the influence of mental ability on how far the child goes in school is affected by his or her social origin. "Bright" children are found at all socio-economic levels, as are the children who do not score well on IQ tests, but high-scoring children from less advantaged homes are less likely to go far in school. That measured mental ability and social origin have an interacting influence was first found in Kahl's 1950 study of 3,300 high school students. His data on the educational aspirations of working-class and lower-middle-class youth showed that both measured intelligence scores and the occupations of the fathers help to predict educational ambitions (Kahl 1953). Prediction is particularly easy when applied to the extremes of both variables. For example, 89 percent of the boys from the upper-middle-class backgrounds who also were among the top quintile of measured intelligence planned to go to college, compared to only 9 percent of those from the lowest socioeconomic category and the bottom quintile of intelligence. In the middle, however, prediction breaks down. A boy from the top quintile of intelligence scores whose father is a minor white-collar worker or skilled laborer has only a fifty-fifty chance of aiming at a college career.

Most of the research completed since Kahl's exploratory study has found a similar relationship between mental ability and socioeconomic background (Bordua 1960; Sewell and Shah 1967; McDill and Coleman 1965; Coleman et al. 1966). This becomes clear to see in Table 8.2, which gives the percentage of high school seniors with various levels of measured intelligence and social origin who actually have attended college (Sewell and Shah 1968b). Practically all of those of high intelligence scores and high social origin attended college, and even 58 percent of those high-status individuals who had low intelligence scores did so. In fact, a greater proportion of this latter group, less qualified in ability, went to college than did those who had high intelligence but low social origin. Obviously, considerable talent in the lower social strata remains undeveloped, in spite of the positive correlation between intellectual capacity and achievement ambitions. The influence of social origin can also be seen in another way: only 16 percent of all high school seniors with low intelligence attended college, but 58 percent of high-status seniors with low intelligence did so. (It is interesting to note in another table provided in Sewell and Shah's article that 25 percent of the students of

Table 8.2

Percentage of 9,007 Wisconsin high school students who attended college, by measured intelligence and social origin

Social origin	Intelligence			
	High	Middle	Low	Total
High	91.1	78.9	58.0	84.2
Middle	64.9	43.3	24.0	46.8
Low	40.1	22.9	9.3	20.8

Source: From William H. Sewell and Vimal P. Shah, "Parents' Education and Children's Educational Aspirations and Achievements," *American Sociological Review,* Vol. 33, 1968, Table 3, p. 199. Reprinted by permission of the American Sociological Association. Social origin is measured by education of father and mother; intelligence is measured by the Henmon-Nelson Test of Mental Ability.

high social origin, but low measured intelligence actually were able to graduate from college!)

The figures in the table indicate that a number of things are going on within the schools that discourage working-class youth from attaining the education of which they are capable. One important influence comes from those people who are important to the child — his or her parents, friends, and, to a lesser extent, teachers.

"SIGNIFICANT OTHERS": THE INFLUENCE OF PARENTS, FRIENDS, AND TEACHERS

How important are peers and teachers in influencing a child to stay in school? How does their influence compare to that of parents? [1] An early study by Kahl suggested that in the earliest years of school, children perform more or less according to ability (Kahl 1957, p. 284). If their native ability is good, they are more likely to be successful and to enjoy the activities of school. If it is limited, they are more likely to find school to be frustrating and representative of failure. After the third or fourth grade, the values of the peer group begin to take precedence. Upper-middle-class children learn from their parents and receive reinforcement from their peer groups that grades are important, that entrance into college is expected, and that school is a pleasant, cooperative, rewarding place. Children from lower-status homes, on the other hand, begin to learn that academic progress and grades are irrelevant, that a high school diploma is the most one should expect, and that dropping out of high school to get a job will enable them to become independent. Even working-class youth of high ability tend to accept this value system.

But not all working-class youth drop out of school. Kahl was interested in what are the influences that encourage some working-class boys to head for college. To explore this problem, he interviewed twenty-four boys, half of whom planned to go to college and half of whom did not. All of them received IQ scores in the top quintile, and all had fathers in petty white-collar, skilled, or semiskilled occupations. The most striking difference between these two groups, Kahl found, was the degree to which the parents urged their sons to strive. Of the twelve boys who aspired to go to college, eight of them had parents who applied pressure for their son's upward mobility. Of the twelve boys who were not interested in college, only one had parents who applied similar pressure.

In the cases Kahl studied, intellectual ability interacted with family values. Most of the parents in Kahl's sample, those who were satisfied with their status, tended to accept their class position. Their view was that they were ordinary people who were respectable, but unimportant;

[1] For a review of the literature on this issue, see Kandel and Lesser 1969, pp. 213–23.

who were decent, but powerless; who lived comfortably, but lacked the fun of conspicuous consumption; and who, in comparison to the middle class, had inadequate income, education, understanding, and social skills. Most of them accepted their place in the social scheme, believing that it was justified and morally legitimate. They considered people like themselves who were not overly bright or ambitious to have a certain style of life that was deserved. Some of them even rejected the middle-class way of life as being too competitive.

But a minority of the parents, including the eight sets who urged their sons to get ahead, felt that they had not risen quite as high on the social scale as they should have, and they used the middle class as one of their reference groups. They were disappointed in their own failure to acquire more education, attributing the success of those in the hierarchy above them to superior training. They often felt vaguely guilty because they accepted the middle-class value of getting ahead, but they knew they had not gotten ahead; consequently, they believed themselves to be somewhat inadequate. To compensate, they encouraged their sons to take school seriously and to aim for college. The boys, in turn, reflecting the pragmatic viewpoint of the parents, considered education to be primarily a step toward a better job rather than an end in itself. Their orientation was practical and not particularly intellectual.

The data on Wisconsin high school seniors by Sewell et al. (1970) back up Kahl's exploratory study of twenty-four boys. Consider the path diagram in Figure 8.1. The influence of "significant others" — people who are subjectively important to the youth — on that youth's aspirations and, ultimately, his attainments is sizable. In the Sewell study, influence of significant others was measured by recording the respondent's perception of the parental encouragement that he had received to attend college, of the encouragement of teachers, and of his friends' college plans. Figure 8.1 suggests that the encouragement to attend college is greater if the son comes from a higher socioeconomic background. Encouragement also becomes greater with higher measured mental ability or better academic performance. The significant others play a strong role in influencing his aspirations and his educational attainments.

A further breakdown by types of the significant others confirms that the effects of parents' encouragement and of the educational plans of friends on the son's educational attainment tend to be consistent with what others in the son's class are doing. The parents and peers of the working-class son are not particularly likely to urge him to go on to college. Encouragement from teachers, however, is affected more by the boy's academic ability and performance than by his social origin.

Indeed, teachers are not perceived to engage in direct socioeconomic discrimination, as parents and peers apparently do, but

Figure 8.1

Influence of socioeconomic background and social-psychological variables on occupational attainment, male Wisconsin high school graduates, 1957

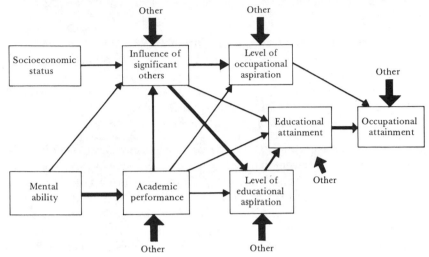

Source: William Sewell, Archibald O. Haller, and George Ohlendorf, "The Educational and Early Occupational Status Attainment Process: Replication and Revision," *American Sociological Review,* Vol. 35 (1970), p. 1023, Fig. 2. Used by permission of the American Sociological Association.

Note: This path diagram was constructed by Sewell and associates to portray the many influences affecting the status of the occupations that male high school graduates enjoyed eight years after they graduated. The heavier the line, the greater the influence. The diagram shows that the amount of education received after high school very strongly affects occupational status. How much education is attained is in turn influenced by how much education the boy wanted when he was still in high school, by what grades he received, and by whether the boy was encouraged by parents, teachers, and friends to go on. These characteristics were influenced by the person's socioeconomic background and measured mental ability. While the causal chain portrayed in Sewell's diagram indicates many of the antecedents of occupational status attainment, thare are other determinants that are undiscovered. The arrows marked "other" indicate such unknown influences.

rather depend mainly on judgments of the student's academic ability as it is validated by school performance.... Far from reflecting overt or covert discrimination, teachers' expectations appear to be based on ability and performance and, as such, make a fundamental though modest contribution to the equalization of education opportunities (Sewell and Hauser 1975, pp. 104–05).

Parents and peers are apparently about equal in their influence on the son, but either one is two to three times as influential as the son's teachers. These findings are consistent with those of another study of 600,000 children in 4,000 schools, popularly known as the Coleman Report (Coleman et al. 1966). It found that the socioeconomic background of the child is the single most important variable affecting school performance; the second is the social class composition of the student's peers. As Coleman put it:

> Altogether, *the sources of inequality of educational opportunity appear to lie first in the home itself and the cultural influences immediately surrounding the home; then they lie in the schools' ineffectiveness to free achievement from the impact of the home, and in the schools' cultural homogeneity which perpetuates the social influences of the home and its environs* (1966, p. 74).

The implications are clear: The social class background of children's parents exert a very strong influence on their achievement in school. This influence is reinforced by the (usually) similar class origins of their peers. True, in those cases in which children from an educationally deficient background are able to interact with peers from more advantageous backgrounds, their achievement is likely to increase. The higher is the social class of the other students, the higher is any given student's achievement. Yet, peer heterogeneity is minimized in the high school student subculture. Even at early ages, peer associations tend to be social-class-related. When asked who they would like to "sit near" or "invite to a birthday party," children in the first, fourth, sixth, and eighth grades are more likely than not to choose social class equals (Stendler 1949). By the eighth grade, children have fully adopted the class perceptions of adults. By high school, they are usually fully entrenched in class-homogeneous cliques.

That one's peers tend to be from a similar social origin was demonstrated by Hollingshead (1949), who coded 1,248 "'clique ties" among high school youth of Elmtown. Three of five clique bonds were between boys and girls of the same prestige class, two of five were between adolescents who belonged to adjacent classes, and only one in twenty-five involved persons who belonged to classes twice removed from one another. This means that a typical clique of five people is composed ordinarily of three adolescents from one class and two from adjacent classes. Hollingshead found no clique ties at all between the top and bottom classes.

By the time children reach high school, the influence of their peers has become very powerful. They measure themselves by comparison to others. The values learned from their parents are reinforced as they receive support and elaboration from their peers. Their friends make strong judgments about their clothing, mannerisms, speech, personality style, goals, and attitudes. They stabilize a self-concept as their image as reflected in the opinion of others.

The peer group may strengthen existing values, establish new ones, or weaken those which are in conflict with peer group values. This phenomenon accounts for the general tendency of peer groups to support the existing class system. However, the peer group sometimes is an instrumental agent of change in those cases of upward mobility in which an individual of lower status is accepted by a higher-status group.

What can we now conclude about the effects on educational attainment of class-biased characteristics of students themselves? Social origin does indeed affect how much education children will get. It influences what grades they earn, how they use their mental capacities, and what others expect of them. It has additional direct effects (not measured by the models employed to date; see Sewell and Hauser 1975, p. 103, for discussion). All of these influences exist in spite of a societal ideal of equality of educational opportunity. The majority of children enter the school system relatively undifferentiated at the age of six, and emerge many years later ready to replicate the conditions of inequality experienced by their parents. But the reasons for this class reproduction process in the schools should not entirely, or even mainly, be blamed on the students themselves. The educational system itself creates patterns that help to distribute children into adult class roles similar to those of their parents.

The Stratification Effects of Educational Practices

One of the amazing and disturbing findings of the Coleman study (1966) was that the below-average performance scores of elementary children from poorer economic backgrounds tend to get even lower, the longer the children are in school (also see Douglas 1968; and Harlem Youth Opportunities Unlimited 1964). The children from more affluent strata, at the same time, spurt ahead and increasingly perform well. Social class effects are accentuated and magnified by what happens to children while they are in school. What do poor children experience that would cause them to do more and more poorly? The reader probably does not need to be reminded that since performance is one basis of admission to privilege, these processes are important in determining the conditions under which the students will act out their adult lives. Among the patterns found within schools and created by schools that have been identified as reinforcing social inequality are teacher expectations, tracking, and curriculum.

TEACHER EXPECTATIONS

In a well-publicized study conducted in the 1960s, Rosenthal and Jacobson (1968) offered evidence that the expectations teachers have of pupils' performance have a strong effect on that performance. After giving an intelligence test to more than five hundred elementary students,

259

Rosenthal and Jacobson gave teachers the lists of students who supposedly would become intellectual "spurters" or "bloomers" during the following year. In fact, the alleged spurters were a 20-percent random sample of the children. By the end of the school year, nevertheless, those students who had been identified as potential bloomers had in fact performed better than the other students. Rosenthal and Jacobson suggested that the expectations that the teacher has of the child create a self-fulfilling prophecy.

The Rosenthal and Jacobson research has been criticized (Snow 1969; Taylor 1970; Thorndike 1968, 1969), and in one case a replication of it failed to turn up similar findings (Claiborn 1969). Nevertheless, the current status of the debate implies that teacher expectations are *sometimes* self-fulfilling (Rist 1977, p. 299). In a three-year longitudinal study of a segregated elementary school in the black community of St. Louis, Rist (1970, 1972, 1973) found that expectations that teachers hold for students can be generated as early as the first few days of the school year and then remain stable for many months. In the kindergarten he observed, for example, after only eight days the teacher made permanent seating arrangements based on what she assumed to be variations in academic capacity, even though no formal evaluations of ability had taken place. Rather, the placement of the children reflected their social class origins — the poor children from public welfare families all sat at one table, the working-class children at another, and the middle class at a third. The teacher then spent differing amounts of time with the three tables, gave different degrees of praise and control, and allowed different levels of autonomy. The next year, another teacher carried on the three groupings, calling the top group the "Tigers"; the middle group, the "Cardinals"; and the lowest group, the "Clowns." Rist suggests that "what had begun as a subjective evaluation and labeling by the teacher took on objective dimensions as the school proceeded to process the children on the basis of the distinctions made when they first began" (1977, p. 298).

Teachers form their expectations on a number of criteria. One is the grades and test scores of a student (Sewell and Hauser 1975). These are usually unreflectively assumed to be valid indicators of a child's ability. Other observable traits of the child may affect the teacher's judgment. Race and sex can be immediately surmised, and socioeconomic background can be inferred from grooming, style of dress, need for free lunches, home address, and visits by parents. It has been well documented that teachers expect less of lower-class children than of middle-class children (Becker 1953; Deutsch 1963; Leacock 1969; Rist 1970, 1973; and Stein 1971) and less of certain races and ethnic groups than of others (Brown 1968; Davison and Lang 1960; Jackson and Cosca 1974; and Rubovits and Maehr 1973). Rowe (1969) found that teachers wait longer for an answer from a student they believe to be a high achiever. Brophy and Good (1970) reported that teachers are more likely to give high-achieving students a second chance to respond and to praise them more for success and criticize them less for failure.

Although, apparently, the expectations of teachers do not always result in consistent student performance, they often do. Good and Brophy (1973, p. 75) summarize the process: The teacher expects specific behavior and achievement from particular students and, because of these expectations, behaves differently toward different students. The teacher treatment in turn affects the children's self-concept, achievement motivation, and level of aspiration. If the teacher treatment is consistent over time, and if the students do not in one way or another resist it, it will tend to shape their achievement and behavior. With time, the students' achievement will conform more and more closely to that originally expected of them. This does not, however, *always* happen, because the teacher may not have a clear-cut or consistent expectation about a particular student. In addition, the student might prevent the expectations from becoming self-fulfilling by overcoming them or by resisting them in a way that makes the teacher change them.

Yet, the struggle is unequal between the teacher (and the institution that a teacher represents) and the student (Rist 1977, p. 301). Children are vulnerable to the dictates of adults in positions of power over them, and consequently the tags of evaluative definitions are more often than not left in the hand of the powerful. Resistance is often viewed as truancy, hostility, unruliness, intellectual apathy, sullenness, or withdrawal, and the process is ready to be repeated.

Teacher expectations sometimes are reinforced by the more formal methods of differential treatment, such as tracking or curriculum assignment, which also communicate to students how they are viewed by the institution.

TRACKING

Tracking is the grouping of students into homogeneous instructional classes on the basis of performance, aspiration, or personal qualities. It includes grouping by tests of ability, such as reading or math tests or IQ tests, and by post-high-school aspirations. The latter, commonly called curriculum tracking, also is frequently based on ability tests as well as college aims.

The first recorded example of tracking was introduced in St. Louis in 1867. During the 1920s and 1930s, when large numbers of foreign immigrants needed to be incorporated into the labor force, tracking increased greatly (Persell 1977, p. 85). Then it fell into disuse until the late 1950s, when it was revived in response to the Russian launching of Sputnik. That was also a period when large numbers of southern blacks, Puerto Ricans, and Mexican Americans migrated to northern cities. It has been suggested that the rise and ebb of tracking practices are correlated with the ethnic composition of urban schools (Persell 1977, p. 85).

Tracking is a very common practice in American schools. The National Educational Association reported in 1968 that 85.4 percent of all secondary schools group students extensively by ability. Large schools employ tracking more frequently than do small schools. Although the effects of tracking are not all positive, it is clear that teachers prefer homogeneous grouping and that most prefer teaching average or high-quality students.

Once a student is placed in a track, he or she tends to stay there. Schafer and Olexa (1971, p. 36) report that only 7 percent of the students whom they studied shifted from a non-college-prep track to a college-prep track or vice versa. The rationale sometimes encountered, that tracking enables poorer students to become prepared to shift into a higher track, appears unjustified. Schafer and Olexa (1971) suggest that the track system is a virtual caste system with a high degree of closure and formal segregation.

Is tracking related to social class origin? Early critiques suggested that pupils are assigned to tracks on the basis of their class origin. This interpretation is too simple, apparently. A study of thirty thousand ninth- and twelfth-graders in forty-eight schools found that the principal determinant of track placement is not father's education or occupation, but rather verbal achievement test scores (Heyns 1974).[2] Yet, as we have already seen, there is a high correlation between socioeconomic origin and performance on standardized tests of ability and achievement. Esposito suggests that "a grouping practice which separates children according to performance on such measures predetermines the placement of a disproportionate number of children of non-white and lower socio-economic status to the lowest homogeneous ability groups" (1973, p. 269). A number of studies (Kariger 1962; Mehl 1965; and McPartland 1968) have indeed found that tracking reinforces and perpetuates the separation of children along ethnic and socioeconomic lines. This tendency is particularly true of the high- and low-ability groups, while the greatest variety of class origins is found in the middle-ability tracks.

Track placement has been found to affect the quality of instruction and interaction in the classroom. Two studies found that with lower

[2] In the language of path analysis: "The importance of verbal ability in predicting curriculum placement is immediately apparent, with a direct effect of .44. The unique effect of verbal ability on curriculum placement explains 17.6% of the variance, or slightly less than 65% of the total variance explained. The unique effects of social class explain 3.2% of the total variance in curriculum placement. The joint effects of verbal achievement and social class are somewhat larger, accounting for nearly 25% of the total variance explained. The total effect of socioeconomic status, however, is still less than the unique effects of tested verbal ability" (Heyns 1974, p. 1440).

tracks, teachers tend to use dull, unimaginative instructional approaches that stress basic skills and facts and that use drill a great deal (Heathers 1967; Squires 1966). In higher tracks, they emphasize conceptual learning and encourage independent projects. A third study reported that teachers give more empathy and praise to students in the higher tracks and more criticism and less direction to students in the lower tracks (Freiberg 1970).

The literature on the *effects* of ability grouping have been contradictory. Research completed before the 1960s suggested that grouping improved performance (compare Billett 1932; Ekstrom 1959). An NEA review (1968, p. 42) of the results of the fifty best-controlled studies published since 1960 showed that for every study exhibiting a net gain in achievement, a comparable study recorded a net loss, for all ability levels except the lowest, which had slightly more losses than gains. Careful research conducted since that review (Goldberg, Passow, and Justman 1966; Rosenbaum 1975), however, suggests that performance scores tend to rise in the high-ability groups, but to decline in the average- or low-ability groups (Borg 1966; Heathers 1969; Findley and Bryan 1971; Esposito 1973; Persell 1977). The direct result is academic differentiation of pupils in schools with ability grouping (Persell 1977, p. 93).

An additional effect of tracking is its influence on self esteem. It tends to elevate the self-esteem of children assigned to high-ability groups and to reduce that of children of average- or low-ability groups (Findley and Bryan 1970). Stigma often goes along with the non-college-prep track or the low-ability track. A former delinquent interviewed by Schafer and Polk illustrates the feeling:

> It really don't have to be the tests, but after the tests, there shouldn't be no separation in the classes. Because, as I say again, I felt good when I was with my class, but when they went and separated us — that changed us. That changed our ideas, our thinking, the way we thought about each other and turned us to enemies toward each other — because they said I was dumb and they were smart (1967, p. 241).

A boy discussing the initial pride he felt when entering junior high school commented:

> But then you go up there and the teach say — "well, so and so, you're in the basic section, you can't go with the other kids." The devil with the whole thing — you lose — something in you — like it just goes out of you. (Did you think the other guys were smarter than you?) Not at first — I used to think I was just as smart as anybody in the school — I felt it inside of me. . . . I wanted to get a diploma and go to college and help people and everything.

263

> I stepped into there in junior high — I felt like a fool going to school — I really felt like a fool. . . . I started losing faith in myself — after the teachers kept downing me, you know. You hear "a guy's in basic section, he's dumb" and all this. Each year — "you're ignorant — you're stupid" (Schafer and Polk 1967, pp. 241–42).

Additional effects relate to the development of middle-class social skills. Schafer and Olexa (1971, p. 42) found that students in a college-prep course are more likely than non-college-prep students to participate in extracurricular activities. (This holds true even when they are compared to non-college-prep students of the same IQ, social origin, and previous achievement.) The non-college-bound become progressively more alienated from school because they are not only on the bottom, looking up academically, but also on the outside, looking in socially. They miss out on the long-run benefits of participating in extracurricular affairs, such as learning social roles, setting up and maintaining social organizations, and developing skills sought by white-collar employers.

Schafer and Olexa (1971, p. 45) maintain that tracking encourages rebellion and misbehavior. In their two samples, non-college-prep students, who made up 29 percent of the graduating class, comprised 53 percent of all students who had misbehaved with sufficient seriousness to have been sent to the vice-principal at least once. The non-college-prep students also were more likely to become delinquent during their high school years. Controls for father's occupation, IQ, and previous achievement did not eliminate the difference between the non-college-prep and the college-prep students (although it did reduce it somewhat). As suggested by A. K. Cohen (1955), delinquency may be largely a rebellion against the school and an attempt to promote self-esteem in non-school-related ways.

Finally, enthusiasm for schooling apparently is affected by tracking. Even when controlling for social class origin, IQ, and previous achievement, non-college-prep students dropped out of school in considerably greater numbers than did college-prep students (19 versus 4 percent) in Schafer and Olexa's samples (1971). Track placement was particularly important for low-achievers. Fifty-seven percent of non-college-prep students who failed to achieve dropped out, but only 19 percent of low-achieving college-prep students did so.

CLASS AND THE HIERARCHY OF COLLEGES AND UNIVERSITIES

There was a time when the employer, wishing to hire a manager or a professional, was not concerned whether the job applicant had a college degree. That time is no more (Collins 1969). For the more valued occupations, employers increasingly insist that the candidate have a diploma in order to be even considered for a vacancy. Correctly or not, employers assume that college graduates have demonstrated the kinds of habits of thought, attitudes, and special skills that they are looking for (Lenski 1966, pp. 389–95; Blau and Duncan 1967, pp. 401–41; Miller and Roby 1970, pp. 119–41). Employers sometimes even look for college graduates to fill blue-collar and lower-level white-collar occupations. Because of the increased requirement of college experience for hiring into the better-paying jobs,[3] the fact that children of privileged parents are the most likely to attend college shows one way in which the educational system is used to perpetuate class inequalities across generations. Higher education confers increased chances for income, power, and prestige on people who are fortunate enough to obtain it (Sewell 1971, p. 793). Privileged parents are most concerned that their children obtain the college credentials, and they are most likely to possess the economic resources to ensure it.

The stratifying of young people does not end the moment they do or do not enter the ivory towers. Colleges and universities are themselves stratified. The more prestigious institutions of higher education lead more directly to the higher-prestige graduate and professional schools and to the better-paying employers. Here again, privileged parents are more likely to send their children to the colleges that will benefit them occupationally or professionally (Folger et al. 1970, p. 312). Who goes on to college and what type of college they attend have some effect on who becomes more privileged. Not surprisingly, then, the stratifying of college attendance strongly reveals the influence of social origin. Table 8.3 shows the distribution of students in various kinds of colleges according to their father's occupations. Community colleges have the fewest children of professionals and managers (16 percent) and the most of blue-collar workers (55 percent). Private universities, on the other hand, the most prestigious of the categories and the institutions leading students most directly into graduate and professional schools, have nearly half of their students from professional and managerial backgrounds and less than one-fifth from blue-collar backgrounds. (Students from middle-level occupations are found evenly distributed in all categories of colleges.)

As the reader is probably already aware, what kind of college a student attends is affected by his or her family's income (Spaeth and Greeley 1970, p. 154). Hansen and Weisbrod (1969) examined the family incomes of college students at public institutions of higher education in California. They found, as we expect, that students at the better institutions come from richer families (see Table 8.4). The table also shows that the

---

[3] Considerable research shows that those with advanced education enjoy much higher annual and lifetime earnings than those with lesser education. See, for example, Schultz 1963; Morgan and David 1963; Becker 1964; Weisbrod and Karpoff 1968; and Bowman 1971.

Table 8.3

Type of college or university entered, by father's occupational classification

Type of college or university	Father's occupational classification			
	Skilled, semi-skilled, unskilled	Semi-professional, small business, sales and clerical	Professional and managerial	Total
Public two-year college	55%	29%	16%	100%
Public four-year college	49	32	19	100
Private four-year college	38	30	32	100
Public university	32	33	35	100
Private university	20	31	49	100

Source: L. L. Medsker and J. W. Trent, "The Influence of Different Types of Public Higher Institutions on College Attendance for Varying Socioeconomic and Ability Levels," monograph (Berkeley, Calif.: Center for Research and Development in Higher Education, Berkeley, Calif., 1965).

state's expenditure on education is more helpful to the wealthier families. Children from more affluent families are advantaged not only because their parents can afford to help in the financial costs of their attendance at a higher-prestige college, but also because the state spends more than the share of taxes that their parents paid on those higher-prestige colleges. Children of poorer families attend the less expensive, but also less beneficial, colleges, on which the state spends less than the share of taxes that their parents paid.

That there is a relationship between social origin and type of college attended would be irrelevant to our basic question — How does the educational institution facilitate stratification? — if type of college had no effect on adult social status. But it does. The prestige of the school, its type and quality, its expense to the student — all are related to the eventual income that the graduate receives.[4] Havemann and West, for example, examined the incomes of nine thousand male college graduates by the type of school they had attended. Although their ranking is now some-

[4] A number of studies have documented the association between college prestige and adult occupational attainment. For further information, see Smigel 1964, pp. 39, 73–74, 117; Havemann and West 1952, pp. 179–81; Ladinsky 1967; Hargens and Hagstrom 1967; Reed and Miller 1970; Wolfle 1971; G. Pierson 1969; Spaeth 1968; Folger et al. 1970. Some studies have found only a weak association: Spaeth and Greeley 1970; Sharp 1970.

Table 8.4

Average family incomes, average higher education subsidies received, and average state and local taxes paid by families, by type of institution that children attend, California, 1964

	All families	Families without children in California public higher education	Families with children in California public higher education			
			Total	Junior college	State college	University of California
Average family income	$8,000	$7,900	$9,560	$8,800	$10,000	$12,000
Average higher education subsidy per year	—	0	880	720	1,400	1,700
Average total state and local taxes paid	620	650	740	680	770	910
Net transfer (line 2 minus line 3)	—	−650	+140	+40	+630	+790

Source: W. Lee Hansen and B. A. Weisbrod, *Benefits, Costs and Finance of Public Higher Education.* Copyright © by Markham Publishing Company. Reprinted by permission.

what out of date, it is still illustrative. Men who graduated from "The Big Three" (Harvard, Yale, Princeton) had the highest median incomes. The overall ordering of incomes (1947 data) by type of college was as follows (1952, pp. 178–79):

The Big Three:	$7,365
Harvard, Yale, Princeton	
Other Ivy League:	6,142
Columbia, Cornell, Dartmouth, Pennsylvania	
Seventeen technical schools:	5,382
California, Carnegie, Case, Detroit, Drexel, Georgia, Illinois, Massachusetts, and Stevens Institutes of Technology; Rensselaer, Rose, Virginia, and Worcester Polytechnic Institutes; Clarkson College of Technology; Cooper Union; Polytechnic Institute of Brooklyn; Tri-State College	
Twenty famous eastern colleges:	5,287
Amherst, Bates, Bowdoin, Brown, Clark, Colby, Franklin and Marshall, Hamilton, Haverford, Hobart, Lafayette, Lehigh, Middlebury, Rutgers, Swarthmore, Trinity, Tufts, Union, Wesleyan of Connecticut, Williams	
The Big Ten:	5,176
Chicago, Illinois, Indiana, Iowa, Michigan, Minnesota, Northwestern, Ohio State, Purdue, Wisconsin	
All other midwestern colleges	4,322
All other eastern colleges	4,235

The differences in earnings of graduates of the colleges listed above are not accounted for by the occupations entered by the men, because there were no differences in the graduates' occupational fields (except for graduates of the "all other" colleges, who disproportionately entered the low-paying fields of teaching and the clergy). Nor are they explained by ability, because even the poorest students from the Ivy League had higher incomes than the best students from other schools. "What all this amounts to is that the differences in earning power between graduates of rich and famous schools and those from small and obscure schools are so great they override everything else" (Havemann and West 1952, p. 180). The latter conclusion is only partially corroborated by a more recent study of the career success of engineering graduates. Perrucci and Perrucci (1970) found that while the prestige of the college is directly related to the graduate's salary and level of technical responsibility (especially for those students from more privileged family backgrounds), so also are college grades. According to their data (1970, Table 4), for example, a student from low social origins who makes high grades in college has a greater chance of receiving a high income in his adulthood than a low-grade student from high social origins, regardless of the prestige of the college they attend. But the high-grade student from low social origins who goes to a high-prestige college is more likely to receive a high adult income than a similar student who goes to a low-prestige college (see Table 8.5). Social origins, grades, college prestige — all are related to adult occupational success.

For those students who do not go directly into the job market after college, but rather enter graduate school, the effect of college quality is similar. Spaeth (1968) looked at the factors affecting graduate school choices of eight thousand men. He found that the variables most closely connected with graduate school quality are college quality and college grades. He comments, "A substantial part of the advantage of coming from an affluent family is gaining entrance to a good college" (Spaeth 1968, p. 347). The relationship between the quality of the college and the quality of the graduate school, Spaeth goes on to note, is probably *not* because graduates of good colleges learn more than graduates of poor ones. (As Astin [1968] found by looking at Graduate Record Examination scores, how much students learn is unrelated to the prestige of the college they attend.)

The reasons that college quality affects graduate school quality are not entirely clear. Perhaps the student at a college of higher prestige is influenced by the expectations of others to go to a higher-prestige graduate school. It has also been suggested that admissions officials in graduate schools prefer and look for the graduate from certain colleges. In effect, a flow pattern from colleges to graduate schools of similar prestige is maintained by the graduate school (Berelson 1960; Folger et al. 1970).

Regardless of the reasons, what is clear is that the hierarchy of colleges leads to a hierarchy of graduate schools and of incomes; students' social origin is one of the factors influencing the kind of college they attend, which in turn influences the kind of professional training they will get and their eventual income.

But what of those young people coming from lower social origins, or those whose grades in high school were not superlative, or those who cannot afford to attend a higher-prestige college? How do they cope psychologically with a lower adult placement in the occupational hierarchy? One of the functions of the community college, it has been suggested, is to shape and prepare those students for their labor force entry.

"COOLING OUT": THE ROLE OF THE COMMUNITY COLLEGES

The dominant American ideology portrays the United States as the land of opportunity, where anyone can get ahead if he or she is ambitious enough. Education is seen as the means to upward mobility, and its acquisition is encouraged. The community college was designed to

269

Table 8.5

Social origins, college grades, college selectivity, and percentage attaining highest career mobility

Social origins:	High				Medium				Low			
College grades:	High		Low		High		Low		High		Low	
College selectivity:	High	Low	High	Low	High	Low	High	Low	High	Low	High	Low
Annual salary of $16,000+	41.3	13.8	14.1	7.0	38.8	26.2	17.3	9.4	35.6	21.0	14.0	6.3
Monthly salary of $1,200+	59.4	28.9	23.9	14.8	56.9	38.3	31.7	21.2	48.9	34.8	27.2	12.5
High technical responsibility	54.9	34.1	27.8	14.2	49.0	38.3	30.4	20.1	35.9	38.6	20.1	17.8
High supervisory responsibility	17.2	12.9	14.4	10.9	26.1	21.9	13.1	13.6	18.4	12.7	11.1	8.5
High involvement in professional activities	29.2	15.7	8.5	5.3	24.0	17.7	8.2	6.6	15.9	17.2	8.2	4.5

Source: Adapted from C. C. Perrucci and R. Perrucci, "Social Origins, Educational Contexts, and Career Mobility," *American Sociological Review*, Vol. 35, 1970, Table 4. Reprinted by permission of the American Sociological Association.

promote equality of educational opportunity by providing a low-cost college that working-class children could afford to attend. Indeed, social mobility aspirations are very high among students in community colleges. Some two-thirds hope to enter managerial and professional occupations (Cross 1968, pp. 41–46). Yet, community colleges, composed of the lowest classes, show the highest dropout rate of all colleges (Karabel 1972, p. 531). In fact, attending a community college *increases* the chance that a student will drop out (Astin 1972). Unrealized educational aspirations, linked to a desire for upward mobility, reach genuinely massive proportions among community college students (Karabel 1972, p. 536).

How are the unrealized ambitions of these students handled? How are their frustrations mollified, their disappointments blunted? The process of phasing students out of the educational progression is what Burton Clark (1960), in a classic case study of San Jose City College, called "cooling out." According to Clark, the community college has three types of students: terminal, transfer, and latent terminal. The latent terminal student, the one who would like to transfer but is unlikely to qualify, poses a problem for the junior college. As Karabel (1972) notes: "The crux of the dilemma is how to gently convince the latent terminal student that a transfer program is inappropriate for him without seeming to deny him the equal educational opportunity that Americans value so highly." The process of cooling out begins before the students arrive on campus. Pre-entrance tests cast doubt on the lower-scoring students' promise. These students meet with a counselor who, in view of the test scores and the students' high school records, tries to assist them in choosing a realistic program. An orientation course places an emphasis on "unrealistic ambitions." If the students begin to receive low grades, they are sent "need for improvement notices," which are recorded in their permanent records, and which require them to go to the counselor again. Finally, the students are placed on probation, which status encourages them to switch away from a transfer-preparatory curriculum. "The real meaning of probation," Clark observes, "lies in its killing off the hope of some of the latent terminal students" (1960, p. 75).

The purpose of the cooling-out process is not to coerce students into dropping out, but rather to persuade them to decide on their own to switch out of the transfer program. It convinces students to blame themselves rather than the system for their dropping out. In order to be successful, the process must be invisible to the student; otherwise, it would not be effective. "The realization that the junior college is a place where students reach undesired destinations would turn the pressure for college admissions back on the 'protected' colleges" (B. Clark 1960, p. 165).

Clark sees the "situation of structured failure" to emerge out of a conflict between the rigorous academic standards of higher education and the nonselective open door. Karabel, carrying the analysis one step further, argues that academic standards, rather than expressing an objective ivory-tower concept, actually serve to justify the university as a means of distributing privilege and of legitimating inequality. "'Indeed, what appears to Clark to be a conflict between professors committed to standards and students who do not 'measure up' is, in a wider sense, a conflict between low-status students demanding upward mobility and a system unable to fully respond to their aspirations because it is too narrow at the top" (Karabel 1972, p. 539). Academic standards serve as the covert mechanism that enables the university to "do the dirty work for the rest of the society" (Rothbart 1970, p. 174). The cooling-out process is thus seen as an expression not only of academic conflict, but also of submerged class conflict. It is part of the process of preparing young people to enter the occupational world without resentment or challenge.

The Preparation of the Child for Dominance Hierarchies

A dominance hierarchy, such as that found in modern bureaucracies, is pyramidal: There are a few people at the top who give orders, and many people near the bottom who take orders. In between is a fairly large middle group that both takes orders from superiors and gives orders to inferiors. From the employer's point of view, there is a need for workers of three different personality types to perform these three kinds of functions. Some workers must be predisposed to follow orders without grumbling or questioning; some must be able to make good decisions resulting in commands to others; and some must be flexible and adaptable enough both to give and to receive orders.

The family and the school are the main institutions in bureaucratic societies that shape the child's personality to conform to the demands of dominance hierarchies for suitable workers. An emerging body of research is beginning to show that both the family and the school do this by encouraging in the children those personality traits which their parents have found to be suitable in their own jobs. Parents who themselves work in the middle or upper levels of a dominance hierarchy tend to encourage their children to become independent, achievement oriented, and autonomous, because these attributes contribute to professional and managerial career success. Working-class parents, on the other hand, and some of the parents in clerical and lower-level management jobs place more stress on obedience, conformity, and propriety, because these likewise relate to the nature of working-class occupations. Both types of parents place high value on control, but they differ on the source of the control: Middle-class parents attempt to instill *self*-control, while lower-class parents are oriented toward control by *others* (conformity and obedience).

272

These patterns were explored by Kohn (1959, 1969) and Pearlin (1972; Pearlin and Kohn 1966), who firmly established that there are important class differences in child rearing. In a 1956 survey of parents of fifth-graders (Kohn 1969, 1969), it was found that working-class parents want their children to be obedient, neat, and clean, to conform to the demands of external authority, and to respect and please adults. They wish to see their children grow up to be what they define as "respectable." In contrast, the child-rearing values of middle-class parents are more "developmental" (Duvall 1946). They want their children to be self-directive, self-reliant, independent, and eager to learn (curious). These class differences were found to exist also in Italy (Pearlin 1972; Pearlin and Kohn 1966).

The significant point of this series of researches is that the attributes desired in children are consistent with the personalities required by the occupational roles of the two classes. In particular, three characteristics of the parents' jobs — how closely they are supervised; whether they work with things, people, or ideas; and how self-reliant they must be to perform their jobs — seem to affect the kind of personality that they want their children to adopt. Those parents who are closely supervised, who work with things, and who need little self-reliance for successful performance of their work tasks are far more likely to value obedience in their children; those parents who have greater degrees of freedom in the work situation, who work with people or ideas, and who must make independent judgments on the job are more likely to value self-control. These connections are class related because midddle-class occupations, in contrast to those of the working class, require the manipulation of interpersonal relations, ideas, and symbols. Work with ideas or with people involves both mental creativity and the ability to get along with others. Thus, for upper-level jobs, getting ahead is somewhat dependent on one's initiative, thought, and judgment. Working-class occupations, by contrast, deal more with the manipulation of things and are more subject to standardization and direct supervision. A skilled laborer who is willing to follow directions and submit to authority is considered by his or her employer to be a good worker. In this case, getting ahead — when it occurs — comes about mainly through collective action, such as union activity.

The Kohn-Pearlin findings about personality characteristics desired in the work place are similar to those found by Edwards (1972, as cited in Bowles and Gintis 1976, p. 135), who compared supervisor ratings of worker performance to personality ratings (of the workers by their peers). In a sample of several hundred Boston workers, Edwards found a cluster of three personality traits that strongly predict the supervisor's ratings of the workers. "Rules orientation" — the willingness to follow orders — was important at the lowest levels of the hierarchy of production. "Dependability" — the capacity to operate without continuous and direct supervision — was important at the middle levels. "Internalization of norms" — the tendency to accept the goals of the enterprise — was predominant at the highest level.

Bowles and Gintis (1976), commenting on the Edwards research, suggested that what Kohn-Pearlin had called "self-direction" is better expressed in Edwards's term, "internalized norms."

> That is, the vast majority of workers in higher levels of the hierarchy of production are by no means autonomous, self-actualizing, and creatively self-directed. Rather, they are probably supersocialized so as to internalize authority and act without direct and continuous supervision to implement goals and objectives relatively alienated from their own personal needs. This distinction must be kept clearly in mind to avoid the error of attributing "superior" values and behavior traits to higher strata in the capitalist division of labor (Bowles and Gintis 1976, p. 145).

Bowles et al. (1975) and Brenner (1968) explored the degree to which the personality traits compatible with dominance hierarchies are encouraged by the schools as well as by the parents. They found that those high school students who are rewarded (given higher grades) are the ones who are rated by peers or teachers as being dependable, persevering, consistent, understanding of what other people want, and punctual. Those who are not rewarded are rated as being independent, creative, and aggressive.

The schools' efforts to teach obedience to working-class children begin as soon as they walk through the school doors. Wilcox and Moriarty (1976) observed 166 hours of classroom activity in an upper-middle-class school and in a working-class school. They wanted to see if there are any differences in how teachers respond to or direct children. They found that teachers in *both* schools gave orders that required the children to comply with their authority. Typical statements were:

> You have an assignment. Sit down and get busy.
>
> You have a responsibility to get that paper done and I want it done now.

But, in the upper-middle-class school, teachers *also* treated the children as self-directed persons capable of managing a process in an independent way and choosing the consequences of their activity. Examples were:

> Tommy, talk to yourself quietly and tell yourself where you are and what's expected of you.
>
> You really goofed off. Why do you do this to yourself?
>
> Our fifteen minutes are up. Have you used them wisely?

274

The authors concluded that while children at both schools were socialized to respond to external behavioral standards, only the children in the upper-middle-class school were taught that they were personally responsible for maintaining the quality of their academic work.

Apparently, colleges also are involved in personality training. Binstock (1970) analyzed the rules, regulations, and norms published in fifty-two college handbooks. She found that those colleges which enroll working-class students emphasize "followership and behavioral control." They have a stricter academic structure, more regulations governing personal and social conduct, and more control over the activities of students than do the more elite colleges, which emphasize "leadership and motivational control."

That personality training is the service that colleges perform for employers is suggested by a number of authors (Squires 1977; Thomas 1956, pp. 326–37; Drake, Kaplan, and Stone 1972; Keyser 1974; Ma 1969). In a series of twenty-five discussions that G. D. Squires held with recruiters at Michigan State University, typical comments volunteered were the following:

> College graduates are more productive retail sales representatives not because of the information learned in school but because of the social interaction skills developed in school. . . . the content of most courses is irrelevant to the outside world. . . . a bachelor's degree is an important indicator of the kind of employee we are seeking because the degree indicates a tendency on the part of an individual to complete a program. . . .
>
> College graduates are sought (for sales, managerial, and junior executive positions) because a person develops a sense of maturity in college. . . .
>
> We like our engineers to have a college degree not because of the specific knowledge learned in school, but for the social skills developed in school (1977, p. 445).

Squires suggests that employers are as concerned with the noncognitive, behavioral characteristics of their employees as with the technical abilities they possess, because they are concerned with maintaining social control within the organization.

Conclusions

It has become clear that education is highly important to adult occupational placement in industrialized societies, and it thus occupies a central place in the analysis of social stratification. It is also clear that social origin affects how much education each child will complete. Children from low-income families do not, on the average, do as well as children from more affluent homes, by any measure. Because they do not, they are hampered in adulthood in acquiring employment, income, and power.

Why is this so? A number of propositions have been offered by social scientists. By oversimplifying a little, we can group these propositions into two familiar theoretical camps, as Collins (1971) has done: the "technical-functional theory of education" and the "conflict theory of education." The technical-functional theory of education may be stated as follows: (1) The skill requirements of jobs in industrial society constantly increase due to technological change. That occurs because the proportion of jobs requiring low skill decreases and the proportion requiring high skills increases. In addition, the same jobs are upgraded in skill requirements. (2) Formal education provides the training, either in specific skills or in general capacities, that equips young adults for the more highly skilled jobs. (3) The result is that educational requirements for employment constantly rise, and increasingly larger proportions of the population are required to spend longer and longer periods in school.

Why do students from lower social origins not do as well in this kind of system? The technical-functional theory posits that differences in the characteristics of individuals going through the school system account for their adult stratification. There are several variations on the theme. One maintains that it is the genetic deficiencies of lower-class individuals (Eysenck 1971; Herrnstein 1973) or of blacks (A. Jensen 1969) that cause them to do poorly. They are not equally equipped to compete. Another variation, the cultural-deficit theory, assumes that it is the deprived cultural, family, cognitive, and attitudinal backgrounds of certain children that cause them to be unable to learn.

An appealing theory because of its close connection to the dominant conventional ideology, the technical-functional theory of education runs into empirical difficulties when it is researched, as Collins (1971) and G. D. Squires (1977) have suggested. First of all, consider the proposition that educational requirements of jobs in industrial societies increase because the proportion of jobs requiring low skill decreases and the proportion requiring high skill increases. While it appears to be true that a minor amount of educational upgrading of jobs has occurred, that does not seem to be the case for the major part of change. Folger and Nam (1964) calculate that 15 percent of the increase in education of the U.S. labor force during the twentieth century can be attributed to shifts in the occupational structure. Most educational upgrading (85 percent), however, has occurred *within* job categories.

Secondly, consider the proposition that formal education provides required job skills. Berg (1971, pp. 85–176) found that in terms of productivity, turnover, absenteeism, supervisors' ratings, and rates of promotion, education is frequently *negatively* related to job performances. Among samples of factory workers, maintenance men, department store clerks, technicians, secretaries, bank tellers, engineers, industrial research scientists, military personnel, and federal civil service employees, the better-educated employees were not generally more productive. Two other studies (Diamond and Bedrosian 1970; Horowitz and Herrnstadt 1969) found no differences in job performance that could be explained by differences in education. Of course, there are certain jobs, particularly professional jobs, that do utilize the training gained in school. For example, doctors, lawyers, and teachers of philosophy employ in their occupations certain knowledges picked up in their professional training. But even here, the facts are not clear-cut. A number of practicing engineers lack college degrees (Soderberg 1963, p. 213), suggesting that even those skills can be learned on the job. Evidence is not available for other professions. Where education is required for admission to practice, as is true of medicine and law, a comparison group of noneducated practitioners is not available.

Where, then, do employees learn the skills and knowledges needed to do their jobs competently? In 1963 the Labor Department conducted the only nationwide survey of how workers learn jobs (U.S. Department of Labor 1964). Only 30 percent of those workers who had less than three years of college (constituting 86 percent of the civilian labor force) said that they used their formal training in performing their jobs. Those with more than three years of college, unfortunately, were asked a different set of questions, so we do not know how many of them used their college training in their work. But another survey of college graduates working in two large corporations asked about the relationship between academic training and job needs (Rawlings and Ulman 1974, pp. 208–12). Forty-one percent of the respondents saw little or no relationship between their college education and their work. Seventy percent of the nontechnical employees felt that there was a strong possibility that they could perform adequately without any specialized education. It was only the technical employees who were inclined to say that they needed their college training.

The genetic explanation of why students from lower origins do not do as well in school as more affluent students likewise runs into empirical trouble. Still a controversial issue, the genetic explanation is challenged by studies that find that the relationship between ethnicity and achievement disappears when certain economic and social factors are controlled (Mayeske 1972, cited in Persell 1977, p. 2); that socioeconomic status is more important for academic attainment than is IQ (Bowles and Gintis 1976, p. 31); that the achievement gap between high- and low-status students appears to increase over time (Coleman et al. 1966); and that some lower-status children gain in IQ after they have been taught intensively (Bereiter 1967; Hawkridge et al. 1968; Heber 1972). The cultural-deficit explanation, although still a popular explanation, also has been challenged. As we discuss in Chapter 11, there is strong evidence that poor people do not carry a "culture of poverty," but rather are people with middle-class values that are impossible to live up to.

These empirical problems with the technical-functional theory of education lead to examination of a competing theory that the reader is already familiar with: the "conflict theory of education." One variant of this theory (Collins 1971) suggests that employers use education to select employees who have been socialized into the dominant status culture. For their managerial employees, they want persons who have adopted the elite culture. For their lower-level employees, they want workers who have learned an attitude of respect for the dominant culture and the elite group that carry it. This requires evidence that schools provide either training for the elite culture or respect for it and that employers use education as a means of selection for cultural attributes. Thus, in the conflict view, formal education has expanded to meet the rising social control problems generated by industrialization and urbanization in the United States by imparting noncognitive traits of obedience, discipline, and respect for authority in students (G. D. Squires 1977, p. 437). The primary function of education is to socialize workers into the socioeconomic status of their parents and perpetuate the class structure. Educational credentials are used to rank workers rather than measure their level of skills, to allocate workers to existing unequal slots within the occupational structure, and to restrict access to more desirable jobs.

In a similar vein, Persell (1977) maintains that the societal structures of dominance (the wealth, occupational, and racial structures) are legitimated largely by an ideology of merit, competition, and social mobility. The ideology is so pervasive that it obscures the existence of vast inequalities of wealth and justifies racial and occupational inequalities. It stresses that the role of education is to provide equal opportunity for all to prove their competence and to attain a high-status occupation. It assumes that a person's talent and effort are directly related to success, both in school and beyond. Persell further suggests that in order to support the societal structures of dominance, educational practices — tracking, the hierarchy of schools, testing, curricular placement, counseling, teacher expectations, and grading — shape children so that the elite offspring are considerably more likely to end up in elite jobs in adulthood.

We have already looked at the evidence on a number of the issues that the conflict theorists raise. Social origin does affect educational attainment, which does affect occupational status. While a meritocratic theory of education is supported by studies of ability as measured by grades and IQ tests (which indicate that people with high scores tend to do better in school), other studies indicate that educational outcomes are affected by social class origin, *independently* of the ability of the child. The reward of merit in the school is limited. The idea that schools teach discipline, obedience, and respect for authority to the average child has received some empirical support. That elite children learn to be autonomous but loyal to the aims of a larger group also is suggested by studies of educational processes.

Although valuable insights can be gained from both theories, it seems to us that the conflict theory is more applicable to the realities of American education. Schools do teach skills necessary for the performance of jobs in an industrial society, particularly basic reading and math skills. But they do many other things as well. They socialize children in such a way that children have increased probability of ending up in socioeconomic niches similar to those of their parents. They legitimate basic dominance hierarchies by promoting a sympathetic ideology and by replicating in miniature the authority relations to be found in the larger society. They support the interests of the more privileged groups by putting the privileged children into the elite positions and by providing a docile labor force willing to work for the privileged stratum at minimal wages without significant discontent.

While this perspective needs to be modified by the recognition of the exceptions — the poor child who does well in school and becomes a manager or professional in adulthood; the wealthy child who is unable to make it in school and who slips down the socioeconomic hierarchy; the numbers of working-class children who do not grow up accepting the dominant ideology of their own inferiority and who form the potential base of a radical social movement — it nevertheless is a powerful theory for explaining why and how the social origin of the child is reinforced by the educational system and how the educational system provides support for broader structures of inequality.

Three

The Correlates and Consequences of Inequality

CONSEQUENCES OF INEQUALITY: THE PRIVILEGED AND MANAGERIAL CLASSES

HAVING TRACED THROUGH the institutional determinants and supports of stratification, we come naturally to the question, What are the effects of these differences in wealth, power, and prestige on the life course of the individual? How do they affect his or her health and leisure, values and goals, and sense of well-being? What patterns of behavior do people with similar degrees of access to the important economic, political, and social rewards of society develop in response to their class position? It is an important scientific question — the extent to which a system of stratification influences the actions and values of a category of people. It is also a question of considerable human interest, as we try to understand the actions and values of those whom we meet every day. This chapter and the next two attempt to document how and to what extent individual behavior is structured and limited by social stratification.

We are also interested in the role each stratum plays vis-à-vis the other strata. How do the various classes intermesh? What are the exchanges between them and the relationships of dominance and coercion? We want to know, for instance, if the interests of middle- and high-income families are served by the existence of poor people, as some suggest. We want to know how the upper class is able to maintain its dominance. We need to look at the interrelating of social classes to see their mutual effects.

There are several conceptual problems to be encountered immediately in approaching these tasks. The first concerns the discrimination of categories of strata. How shall we divide people into groupings convenient for analysis? It has already become evident that clearly distinct social classes do not exist at all levels in the United States. The upper class seems to be fairly clearly differentiated, as does the professional and managerial class and the poverty class. But the middle levels of the stratification structure seem to fit more accurately a continuum model, which posits that people are subtly differentiated among themselves by economic and status inequalities. Where the lines should be drawn to break up the middle continuum into manageable analytical parts is arbitrary. Some suggest three class categories: the upper-middle, the lower-middle, and the working classes; but others think a three-part division is too gross and that a fourth stratum, "middle-middle," should be added to the classification. The dubiousness of any specific division is amplified by the fact that discussions in journalistic sources as well as in social science literature employ varying class labels. Some describe the lower-middle class as consisting almost exclusively of higher-level, skilled blue-collar workers, but others include white-collar workers such as clerks and salespeople as well, and still others eliminate the blue-collar workers entirely. The composition of the classes varies according to the analyst.

For the sake of consistency the categorization used in this and the next two chapters follows the breakdown generally employed in the early community studies of the 1940s. The "upper class" refers to those few families who are privileged to possess great wealth, power, and prestige. The "white-collar" stratum includes two subcategories: the "upper-middle class" of college-educated professionals and managers who direct the affairs of the major institutions; and the "lower-middle class" of white-collar semiprofessionals, salespersons, clerks, and lesser managers who carry out the directives of the upper-middle class. In the blue-collar stratum, we include the "working class" of skilled and semiskilled laborers who perform the physical work of the economy. In the "underprivileged class" are the unskilled and service workers who labor, but who receive minimal incomes, and the unemployed. This delineation of classes and their corresponding labels are used for the ease of analysis, yet the underlying continuous nature of stratification should be kept in mind.

A further conceptual difficulty relates to the fact that human behavior is variable, even when it is patterned. Not all male members of the upper-middle class think career is important, although most of them do. We must rely on constructed ideal types — abstracted general tendencies that

283

in reality are qualified by time, location, and particular circumstances. Generalizations indicate common patterns of a particular stratum, not behavioral laws to which all families or individuals conform. The descriptions to follow represent the modal conditions and styles of life of different strata. They are ideal types abstracted from a variety of field investigations employing a variety of methodologies.

The Social Elite: The Upper Class

Most research reports indicate that the upper class in the United States contains somewhere from 0.5 percent to 1 percent of the population (Warner et al. 1949, p. 14; Domhoff 1967, p. 7; Hodges 1968, pp. 18–19). The 1 million to 2 million Americans so indicated by these estimates do *not* include all powerful members of the functional elite (persons of influence who stand at the top of the major social institutions). There is some overlap of membership between the upper class and the functional elite of the United States, but the groups are not identical in constituency. The upper class, rather, consists of families

> whose members are descendants of successful individuals (elite members) of one, two, three or more generations ago. These families are at the top of the social class hierarchy; they are brought up together, are friends, and are intermarried one with another; . . . they maintain a distinctive style of life and a kind of primary group solidarity which sets them apart from the rest of the population (Baltzell 1958, p. 7).

Upper-class privilege thus rests upon two characteristics: the possession of enormous resources of wealth and power and the inheritance of social preeminence. It is this richness of resources controlled by the upper class that most dramatically and importantly differentiates members of the upper class from those of the middle and underprivileged classes.

It is useful to look at the behavioral patterns of the upper class in light of its unique possession of wealth and social standing. To maintain upper-class status, these assets must be protected and nourished. Wealth must be kept from disappearing, as it is wont to do, and hopefully even increased. Prestige must be protected from competition by the aggressive and capable nouveaux riches and from the challenges made by an egalitarian class ideology. Resources must be acquired, retained, and deployed. We may suspect that some of the important subcultural distinctiveness of upper-class families — their child-rearing practices, educational backgrounds, social clubs, value orientations, and exclusivity rites — have developed to buttress and support economic and political privilege. When we look at upper-class employment of economic advisers, the flexible shifting of investments as the economic environment changes, the training of upper-class-male children in money management, or the marriage of upper-class offspring into new wealth, we see typical ways of protecting wealth holdings. When we look at upper-class rejection of the newly rich, the endogamous intermarriage of upper-class children, or the upper-class reverence for family background, we see ways of reinforcing status claims. New wealth may be co-opted through marriage to increase the family resources, but it must be done in a way that does not threaten the status position of the old, established families of the upper class. The interweaving of privilege maintenance and life style will become evident if we look in greater detail at the institutional patterns of the upper class.

MAJOR SOURCES OF DATA

Although sociological studies of the upper class are much fewer in number than studies of the poor, there have been several attempts to search out the inner workings of this tiny, somewhat invisible segment of American society. The sociologist E. Digby Baltzell, himself raised as a member of the upper class, in his works on the upper class relied heavily on the *Social Register*. One of the most readily available indexes to membership in the national social elite, the *Social Register* is a series of volumes of reputed upper-class social status covering twelve major cities — New York, Chicago, Boston, San Francisco, Buffalo, Philadelphia, Baltimore, Washington, Pittsburgh, Cleveland, Cincinnati-Dayton, and St. Louis. First published in 1887, the *Social Register* by 1940 listed thirty-eight thousand conjugal family units, or about 0.1 percent of the families in the country, as members of "high society" (Baltzell 1958, p. 29). In order to be included, a family must make a formal application to the Social Register Association of New York and provide several endorsements of their social acceptability by persons already listed. Although the *Social Register* is the most reliable of available indexes, its usefulness is limited by the exclusion of southern, small-city, and Jewish elites; in addition, some members of the social elite decline having their names listed.

G. William Domhoff, a psychologist who has written several books on the upper class (1967, 1970), used the following main criteria as evidence of membership in a national upper class: (1) listing in the *Social Register;* (2) attendance at certain private preparatory schools; (3) membership in certain gentlemen's clubs; (4) offspring of a millionaire entrepreneur or corporate executive making more than $100,000 a year and attendance at a private school or membership in an exclusive club; and (5) marriage to a member of the upper class.

A third study of upper-class marriages used a listing of wedding announcements in the Sunday *New York Times*. In their sample of 370 wedding announcements, Blumberg and Paul found that 45 percent of the principals were listed in the *Social Register* and another 23 percent attended one of Domhoff's listed private boarding schools (1975, p. 63).

Some of the families so identified are well known as financiers and industrialists even to the average schoolchild: the Du Ponts, Mellons, Fords, Rockefellers, and Vanderbilts. Others are prominent political families: the Roosevelts, Tafts, Dulleses, and Lindsays.

In addition to these major studies, further information is gained from ethnographic community studies of the class structure (Warner and Lunt 1941; Lynd and Lynd 1929, 1937; Hollingshead and Redlich 1958; Hunter 1953; Hodges 1968, for example), studies of wealth distribution (see Chapter 4), and *Fortune*'s listing of rich families (Louis 1968).

ECONOMIC CONDITIONS

The upper class, a hereditary social class based on a tradition of business power and wealth, had its origins in the leadership structure of early American society. It flowered to its fullest form during the nineteenth century, when capitalist entrepreneurs amassed great wealth and fortune. The industrial boom of the late 1800s, accompanied by an increasing centralization of business power, resulted in the accumulation of great wealth in the hands of a few newly rich families. These families were in time incorporated into the aristocratic structure (Baltzell 1966). More recently, broad trends of the twentieth century have moderated the power and pervasiveness of the social elite. By 1940, its influence had already been considerably compromised by new centers of control in corporate and governmental bureaucracies and by a greater fragmentation of power among other hierarchies.

However, the influence of the upper class is far from having been extinguished. The continuing vitality of an upper class based on tradition and wealth is shown by several recent studies of the economic importance of the upper class. Domhoff examined the backgrounds of the corporate directors of the top fifteen American banks, the top fifteen insurance companies, and the top twenty industrial companies. He found that *53 percent* of the 884 individuals were drawn from the American upper class (Domhoff 1967, p. 51). (Also see Dye 1976, pp. 152–53, whose estimate is 30 percent.) When we recall that around 1 percent of the population belongs to the upper class, it is apparent that there is a disproportionate tendency for upper-class individuals to be in top positions of business leadership. Domhoff found similar percentages in banking (62 percent of bankers are rated as upper-class by Domhoff), insurance companies (44 percent), and industrial firms (54 percent) (1967, pp. 53–55). The influence of the upper class on the economy is increased through the device of interlocking directorates, whereby many individuals sit on the boards of more than one company or bank or financial institution.

The Blumberg and Paul study (1975) found that one-third of the fathers listed in the upper-class wedding announcements that they studied were company presidents or vice-presidents. Their positions were concentrated in the central institutions of wealth and power in America, the manufacturing corporations and financial institutions — banking and insurance, as well as security, brokerage, and investment companies. Two-thirds were corporate executives. In his study of Philadelphia's upper class, Baltzell likewise found that the Philadelphia upper class is a *business* aristocracy: "through banks, the law, and through directorships, a relatively small primary group passes on control from one generation to the next" (1958, p. 39).

It hardly need be pointed out that these statistics are indicators of a class stratum that has access to great resources of capital and economic control. *Fortune* in 1975 surveyed 800 people — the top executives of the 500 biggest industrial corporations and the 50 biggest banks and insurance firms. Almost one-third owned more than a million dollars' worth of their company's stock, and three-fourths owned at least $100,000 worth. They reported that their average yearly income was $209,000 (Burck 1976). Altogether, members of the upper stratum own over three-fourths of the corporate stock, and these tend to be concentrated among the larger, more powerful corporations (Lampman 1963).

THE POLITICAL AND ECONOMIC POWER OF THE UPPER CLASS

To what degree does the American upper class dominate the national economic and political arenas of action? While most observers agree that there are a few individuals and families in the United States who own great wealth, fill occupational positions of strategic importance, and receive great deference from others, there is significant disagreement in the literature concerning the degree to which the people who run society come from a hereditary upper class.

One side argues that increasingly the elites of the United States occupy their positions of managerial power because of their expertise and technical competence, and thus they increasingly have middle-class origins (Keller 1963; *Fortune* 1976; Baltzell 1958; Bell 1958). The United States, in this view, is moving toward a meritocratic society (rule on the basis of merit). Thus, according to Keller, the emergence of elites that acquire their position because of managerial competence rather than inherited class status has occurred in America because the increasing size and complexity of industrial society requires a meritocratic leadership. Membership in these elites is related to the achievement of high educational qualifications, specialized training, and technical excellence, although original wealth and high social status are quite advantageous (Keller 1963, p. 261).

The other side argues that this is an illusion, that the real decision-making power belongs to the upper class, as shown by its network of affiliations in important organizations and by its influence over the subordinate functionaries, the upper-middle class. The argument is made that upper-class status is not based on merit, but rather on the luck of birth into a high-status family (Domhoff 1970; C. Anderson 1974). Mills writes: "The men of the higher circles are not representative men; their high position is not a result of moral virtue; their fabulous success is not firmly connected with meritorious ability. Those who sit in the seats of the high and the mighty are selected and formed by the means of power, the sources of wealth, the mechanics of celebrity, which prevail in their society" (1956, p. 361).

What are we to make of these opposing assertions by scholars of the elite? Evidence has been difficult to gather, partly because identifying the elites poses problems and partly because the exercise of power is largely invisible. Several valuable investigations have been made, however. Baltzell (1958) attempted to document the extent of overlap between the social upper class and a managerial elite by looking at accomplishment. He compared the names in the *Social Register* with names in *Who's Who in America,* a publication stressing achievement and leadership position. Nationwide, 23 percent of those who were included in *Who's Who* in 1940 were also listed in the *Social Register.* Thus, the social elite (less than 1 percent of the population) is disproportionately represented among the functional elite, although it does not predominate. Members of the social elite did, however, constitute the majority in certain occupations, and, further, they were more likely to be concentrated in the most powerful positions (see Table 9.1). In his more detailed analysis of Philadelphia's elite, Baltzell found that 75 percent of the *Who's Who* bankers, for instance, are listed in the *Social Register;* 60 percent of the 532 directorships of industrial and financial institutions reported by Philadelphians are held by *Social Register* listees; and while only 51 percent of *Who's Who* lawyers are members of the social elite, over 80 percent of the partners of the six leading firms in Philadelphia are members of the social elite. The social upper class is thus disproportionately located in decision-making positions, particularly in business and finance. It is less dominant in the political, military, public relations, communications and entertainment, education, and religious hierarchies.

Baltzell further grouped the occupations listed in Table 9.1 according to their presumed function. The "goal-integrating" functions are performed by those who decide the *ends* that a social structure will strive to attain. "In Philadelphia in 1940, the goal-integrating function was performed by the business elite, which includes businessmen, bankers, lawyers, and engineers. Although differing in technical training, all these men perform essentially similar functions: the exercise of power over other men in making the decisions which shape the ends of a predominantly business-oriented social structure" (Baltzell 1958, p. 35). Forty-nine percent of the business elite were listed in Philadelphia's *Social Register.*

288

Table 9.1

Philadelphia achievers by social class, origin, and occupation

Occupation listed in *Who's Who*	Social class		Total (N)
	Percentage listed in *Social Register*	Percentage not listed in *Social Register*	
Bankers	75%	25%	32
Lawyers	51	49	39
Engineers	45	55	22
Businessmen	42	58	125
Architects	42	58	24
Physicians	37	63	43
Museum officials	35	65	14
Authors	32	68	44
Graphic artists	21	79	39
Public officials	21	79	33
Educators	16	84	178
Opinion makers[a]	13	87	53
Musical artists	12	88	16
Church officials	10	90	80
Total			742

Source: Adapted from E. Digby Baltzell, *Philadelphia Gentlemen: The Making of a National Upper Class,* Table 3, p. 33. Copyright © 1958 by The Free Press, a Corporation. Reprinted by permission.

[a] Public relations, advertising, radio, editors.

Baltzell maintained that potential goal-integrating functions are performed by public officials and opinion-makers. The members of this elite are trained in the arts of propaganda and influencing the emotions of people. While they often serve the ends of the business elite, they are also potential leaders in organizing the social structure around social welfare goals rather than profit goals. Sixteen percent of these individuals came from Philadelphia's upper class. The third type of elite — technicians such as physicians and architects — provides the knowledge and means through which the ends are achieved. Thirty-nine percent of the technical elite originated in Philadelphia's upper class. Finally, "intellectual" functions, which deal with values, morals, and ideas, are performed by the clergy, educators, artists, and authors — 18 percent of whom had upper-class backgrounds.

Baltzell's study suggests that nearly half of the business elite have upper-class origins. The other achievers are more likely to come from the middle classes. These findings are consistent with the calculations of Domhoff (1967, see pp. 53–55), who found disproportionate upper-class dominance in business, industry, banking, and insurance, and of the

Blumberg and Paul report, which found that the occupations of the males of prominent families are likely to be top executives in manufacturing and finance.

Tentatively, we can conclude that between 40 and 70 percent of elite bankers, lawyers, and businessmen have upper-class origins; that while politicians tend to come from affluent upper-middle class families (Dye 1976, p. 152), high proportions of certain categories of the political elite, such as Supreme Court justices and diplomats (Keller 1963, pp. 297–303) and members of the Cabinet (Domhoff 1967, pp. 97–103) are from "socially advantaged" families; and that elites in other fields (science, religion, education, and communications, for example) are predominantly from the middle classes. There is substantial overlap between the upper class and the managerial elite in the major economic and, to a lesser extent, political institutions — those which we term "determinative" — but not in those institutions we term "supportive." The upper class is influential in deciding the *ends* that a social structure will attain, but the upper-middle class provides the means of knowledge and expertise through which these goals are attained.

MANAGEMENT OF THE UPPER-CLASS ESTATE

A strong value of the established upper class is that capital funds must not be squandered. Each generation should live on income only and should add to the capital by prudential management (Hollingshead and Redlich 1958, p. 71). The concern over generational continuity is not unfounded. In a study of 61 families that were prominent in Ontario five generations ago, only 60 percent had prominent sons, 26 percent had prominent grandsons, and 10 percent had prominent great-grandsons (Tepperman 1972). Only 5 percent of the prominent families developed into "dynasties." (Yet, if there were no controls by the elite over the entry of families into elite positions, the percentage of those original prominent families that would develop into dynasties would be only .004.) Tepperman concludes that the process of ensuring a continuity of elite family status involves not only that fathers secure their sons' status, but also that sons must make some use of elite "supports" provided by prominent kin: "In this sense, the family, indeed the extended family, or an even more extended family-and-friendship clique is the efficient operator in securing the status of its members, and therefore the family rather than the individual, is . . . the appropriate unit of analysis in studies of stratification and mobility" (1972, p. 128).

The training of the sons for management of the estate is an important part of child socialization. As Kahl suggests,

> The capital must be wisely managed if it is to survive through the constant changes in our industrial system; it must be transferred

from buggies to automobiles to airplanes as the situation demands. Consequently, the families who maintain a top position for several generations must have some members adroit in finance to keep the fortune intact and help it grow — a complete disdain for the market place would spell doom (1957; pp. 190–91).

Consistently, upper-class sons prepare themselves in college for the important wealth-preservation function. Nearly all of the grooms studied by Blumberg and Paul had gone to college. Nearly half listed their occupations as businessmen, and another 43 percent were professionals, particularly lawyers. Although male members are expected to manage their own and their wives' fortunes, estate managers may be employed for counsel and advice. The newly rich are incorporated, through intermarriage and co-optation, to revitalize the fortunes of the old rich.

The prominence of the American social elite is not based on the possession of land, as was true of England's aristocracy for so many centuries, but rather on the possession of capital and the occupancy of leadership positions in the corporation. Whereas the private schools and elite universities in England throughout the eighteenth and nineteenth centuries managed to bring together the sons of the old landed gentry and the sons of the new-rich manufacturers to produce an aristocracy that was committed to noblesse oblige and leadership service and that provided many government, religious, and military leaders, the sons of the elite of the United States are predominantly oriented toward the economic sphere and much less toward governmental positions of responsibility. "American prep schools have, therefore, graduated many successful corporation lawyers, few Supreme Court justices; many Wall Street investment bankers, few Secretaries of the Treasury; many minstrels of Madison Avenue, but only a handful of bishops; many executives of General Foods, General Mills, and General Motors, but no Generals of the Army" (Birmingham 1958, p. 68). Franklin D. Roosevelt, a Groton alumnus, was the first American president to have graduated from a prep school, and John F. Kennedy, Choate, was the second. Whereas the traditional function of the landed gentry was as much to serve as leaders of rather large political domains as it was to control its property, the American social elite has had to be more concerned with conservation of its wealth.

EDUCATION: THE OLD SCHOOL TIE

The education of the children of the upper class is unlike that of the vast majority of American children. Formal schooling after the eighth grade is almost always received in a private institution patterned after the English public school (Blumberg and Paul 1975, pp. 67–68). These are not the Catholic parochial and other church-related institutions that comprise 85 percent of private schools in America. Rather, they are a small set of select non-church-related independent day or boarding schools. Male children tend to be sent to prestigious private boarding schools of the "St. Grottlesex" type — St. Paul's, St. Mark's, St. George's, Groton, Middlesex, Choate, Phillips Exeter, Phillips Andover, Deerfield, Kent, or Taft — where they associate with other boys of upper-class status, forming contacts of considerable advantage to them in later life, and where they receive education in upper-class culture as well as in traditional subjects (Baltzell 1958; Birmingham 1964; Gutwillig 1960). (The percentage of students who are sons of alumni at any time ranges from 18 for Middlesex to 30 for Groton [Kirstein 1968, p. 77].) Girls may go to such schools as Foxcroft, Miss Porter's, Westover, Springside, Madeira, Dobbs Ferry, Ethel Walker, or Chatham Hall. The country day and boarding schools are staffed either by headmasters and headmistresses of approved upper-class background or by upwardly mobile individuals who have identified with the upper-class value system.

Mills, Domhoff, Baltzell, and others have all stressed the stratification supports of these institutions. The boarding school has taken over many of the socializing functions formerly carried on by the upper-class family. As Baltzell puts it, "the vital role which schools such as Groton have played in creating an upper-class subculture on almost a national scale in America is best understood if they are seen as *surrogate families* whose latent function is that of status ascription in an increasingly individualistic and centralized society" (1958, p. 303). The boarding school also assimilates and integrates the children of the newly rich and small-city elite with those of the older large-city elite. Finally, the elite private school functions as "an antechamber to the upper-class marriage market" (Blumberg and Paul 1975, p. 68).

By tradition, many upper-class families have adopted particular schools as their own. Thus, St. Mark's became the favorite school of the Cabots, Hotchkiss of the Fords, Choate of the Mellons, Taft of the Tafts, and St. Paul's of the Vanderbilts (Birmingham 1968, p. 64). Schools became polarized around certain cities and also oriented toward certain colleges. St. Paul's, serving the Philadelphia elite, for many years sent boys to Yale, Princeton, or Pennsylvania; Phillips Exeter boys have gone to Harvard, Phillips Andover graduates to Yale. As late as 1940, three-fourths of Princeton graduates were products of private schools (Baltzell 1958, p. 329). But, in spite of clannish traditions, the private schools have been changing rapidly. Whereas formerly they were rather rigid in their exclusiveness, often maintaining unwritten quotas limiting Jews and lower socioeconomic groups, they have recently come under financial pressure to develop more heterogeneous student bodies, recruiting not only from broader geographical regions, but also from diverse economic, racial, and ethnic groups. And they no longer serve as an automatic admission ticket to the higher-prestige colleges. The percentage of undergraduates at Harvard and Yale who are "preppies" has declined from 60 to 40 in the last ten years. In addition, there has been some shift from prep schools to coeducational, private day schools among the children of the upper class, although this may be only a temporary manifestation of student unrest during the 1960s (Blumberg and Paul 1975, pp. 68–69).

Within the upper class, colleges are likewise socially stratified. It is more advantageous to have graduated with a low academic standing from an elite college than to have been a Phi Beta Kappan at a less prestigious college. Of the 476 top executives in the Warner and Abegglen study, 86 had received their training at Yale, Harvard, and Princeton alone (1955, p. 51). Of 513 higher politicians studied by Mills, 44 percent of those who went to college went to top-notch eastern schools (1956, p. 402). Gene Hawes's study of the New York *Social Register* showed that 67 percent of its adult men who had attended college had received degrees from Harvard, Yale, or Princeton (1963, pp. 68–71). Upper-class women may be sent to Smith, Vassar, and Radcliffe. As is true on the private-school level also, however, the social elite have recently become less concentrated in their selection of a university. While 67 percent of adult New York social elites attended Harvard, Princeton, or Yale, only 45 of those currently attending a university were at one of the Big Three (Hawes 1963; Blumberg and Paul 1975, p. 70).

CLUB MEMBERSHIPS

At least until recently, an intricate system of exclusive college clubs served to insulate the members of the upper class from the rest of the students. As late as 1940, the private school boys at Harvard, with their accents, final clubs, and Boston debutante parties — about one-fifth of the student body — stood aloof and apart from the ambitious, talented, and less polished students from public high schools (Baltzell 1958, pp. 329–30). The most prestigious clubs at Harvard have been Porcellian and A.D., followed in order by Fly, Spee, Delphic, and Owl (Amory 1947, p. 300). At Yale, the Fence Club (Groton and St. Paul's), Delta Kappa Epsilon (Exeter and Andover), and Zeta Psi were the most exclusive clubs; at Princeton it was the Ivy Club (Baltzell 1958, pp. 330–31).

The importance of college clubs in establishing prestige and social contacts is surpassed by that of the exclusive "gentlemen's clubs" of major metropolitan areas. In most cities there are one or two distinguished men's clubs whose members dominate the social and economic life of the community. The better-known include the Links and Knickerbocker in New York, the Duquesne in Pittsburgh, the Philadelphia and Rittenhouse in Philadelphia, the Piedmont Driving Club in Atlanta, the Somerset and Union in Boston, the Chicago in Chicago, and the Pacific Union in San Francisco. Below the level of these is a hierarchy of lesser clubs, including the alumni clubs, such as the Harvard, Princeton, and Yale in New York, and the Union League clubs. As a family becomes socially established over time, the prestige of its club memberships rises. Thus, for instance, John D. Rockefeller, Sr., belonged to the Union League Club, John D. Rockefeller, Jr., to the University Club, and John D. Rockefeller III to the Knickerbocker Club. Most gentlemen-businessmen of any stature belong to clubs in more than one city. J. P. Morgan listed thirteen club memberships in his 1940 *Who's Who* biography, including the Union and Knickerbocker in New York, the Somerset in Boston, the Metropolitan in Washington, and the Athenaeum, Garrick, and White's in London (Baltzell 1958, p. 340).

Upper-class women tend to be equally active in voluntary associations. The Colony Club and Cosmopolitan Club in New York, the Chilton in Boston, the Acorn in Philadelphia, and the Franciscan in San Francisco are open only to women of upper-class status, and the Junior League, although felt by some oldsters to be overpopulated by the newly rich, is a nationwide organization of the female social elite. Upper-class wives are likely to serve also on boards of philanthropic organizations, of social services such as hospitals and welfare organizations, and of cultural societies, such as symphony orchestras and art museums. These activities tie in well with the sense of obligation toward those less fortunate, the noblesse oblige, which is a well-established value of the upper class. Both men and women spend hundreds of hours each year running welfare and cultural organizations.

A primary function of the clubs is ascription of upper-class status. To this end, they blend new men of achieved upper-class status with those of ascribed upper-class status to maintain a continuity of control over important positions in the business world. Of the Philadelphia Club members listed in *Who's Who* in 1940, two-thirds were engaged in finance, law, or business (Baltzell 1958, p. 349). In addition, the clubs not only initiate newcomers into the mores of the social elite and provide a point of contact for elites visiting from other cities, but they also constitute a place in which imporant executive decisions can take place. The corporate elite is well integrated into the club system. As one old-timer in the Duquesne Club remarked, "The way to tell if a fellow's getting along in any Pittsburgh company is to see if he's yet a member of the Duquesne. As soon as his name goes up for membership, you know he ought to be watched. He's a comer" (Elliott 1959, p. 164).

Any organization that contains informal decision making within its walls and that facilitates the flow of information so essential to the decision-making process would constitute a power barrier to those who are barred. Not only are people of lesser prestige excluded from the metropolitan clubs, but so also — until most recently — are Negroes and Jews of upper-class status. Women are still excluded in most. Cleveland Amory comments, "Unhappily few Christians seem to have the slightest conception, recognition or even curiosity about the Jewish Aristocracy, which is as firmly founded as the Christian and probably more forward-looking" (1960, p. 226). Partly as a result of the clubs' caste-like requirement of nominal Christian affiliation of its members, some corporations have been loath to promote talented Jewish personnel to the higher executive levels. "In city after city, the admissions policies of the top clubs are increasingly causing our national corporations to bar some of their best-qualified men from top leadership positions" (Baltzell 1958, p. 367). In recent years, however, there have been slight movements in the direction of easing the caste barriers: New York's Century, Cosmopolitan, River, and Regency clubs all have Jewish members, as do most of the college clubs. The Harvard and Cosmopolitan clubs have a Negro member; and in a widely publicized move in 1961, George Lodge, Angier Biddle Duke, Attorney General Robert Kennedy, Assistant Attorney Geenral Burke Marshall, and Oren Rool all resigned from the Metropolitan Club because it excluded Negroes. However, such eminent clubs as Union, Knickerbocker, and the Links are still dominated by what Baltzell calls "the ideals of cast exclusion" (1964, p. 368). The younger generation has become somewhat more disenchanted with anti-Semitism (Baltzell 1964, p. 369). Partly for this reason, the active club life that marked the male side of upper-class society has gone into a steady decline since the war. As Amory puts it, "never have clubs, as clubs, seemed more forbidding than to the younger generation of the 1960's. The matter of the blanket anti-Semitism prevailing in so many clubs is an excellent example of this inhibition" (1960, p. 226).

MARRIAGE AND THE FAMILY

The social elite of America consists of a group of families whose ancestors accumulated wealth and power. To a considerable degree, they form a self-conscious entity: they are brought up together, learn a common subculture, intermarrry, and maintain a distinctive style of life and primary group solidarity that sets them apart from the rest of the population. Thus, they are the closest approximation to a real social class that can be found within the American stratification structure.

Because lineage is used to differentiate the old upper class from recently wealthy families, ethnic background is an important ascribed status. "The core group ascribes a different and lower status to persons from disapproved ethnic backgrounds — Jews, Irish, Italians, Greeks, Poles, and others from southern and eastern Europe. Core group members tend to lump these national origin groups together; all are undesirable" (Hollingshead and Redlich 1958, p. 72). The core group traces its ancestry to the colonial period and then to England, Scotland, and the Netherlands or to French Huguenot refugees. In the New Haven upper class, these backgrounds are held by almost two-thirds of the stratum. Another 11 percent have Irish and Catholic origins, and 13 percent are Jewish (Hollingshead and Redlich 1958, p. 72).

Because ancestry and relatives are more important than present achievements in the perpetuation of upper-class status, mate selection for the children is crucial and highly controlled. Marital mates from among other old families are desired in an exceptionally large proportion of the cases, or, alternatively, mates are sought from a newly rich family whose wealth contributes to the capital accumulation of the old stock. The degree to which intermarriage is a prominent pattern is illustrated by the following quotes (reported by Domhoff 1970, p. 77):

> First Families in Boston have tended toward marrying each other in a way that would do justice to the planned marriages of European royalty (Amory 1947, p. 20).
>
> Through marriage the Auchinclosses are now kin, in addition to Rockefellers, Sloans, Winthrops, Jenningses, Saltonstalls, and Smedbergs, to such other redoubtable families as the Frelinghuysens, the Van Rensselaers, the Cuttings, the Reids, the du Ponts, the Grosvenors, the Truslows, the Tiffanys, the Bundys, the Adamses, the Ingrahams, the Burdens, the Vanderbilts, and, of course, the Kennedys (Birmingham 1968, p. 327).

The kinship network of the family is highly important. Children are valued as carriers of the family's elite status, and, accordingly, the number of children per family is considerably higher than in the middle class. The nuclear family belongs to a well-integrated network of kinship among the extended family members. The solidarity of the kin group results in a very stable marital pattern with divorces being less frequent than is true of any other stratum. (This is not so true of the much more divorce-prone newly rich family, which lacks the solidifying effects of an extended kinship, is peopled by persons of high initiative and individualism, and is characterized by some social insecurity.)

The upper-class family is largely male-dominated and patriarchal. The wives are expected to be intelligent, but not necessarily well educated or career-minded; such orientations would interfere with their primary roles of running a large household, participating in civic, cultural, and philanthropic activities, and entertaining graciously (Baltzell 1958, p. 53). According to one survey, there is a threshold of family income beyond which the wife's participation in the labor force becomes markedly reduced. In middle-class income brackets, 40 percent of the wives were employed; but at higher income levels less than 10 percent were (Barlow et al. 1966, pp. 147–48). Domhoff writes of three primary functions of the upper-class wives: (1) they protect upper-class institutions by organizing social events, at which members of the upper class get to know each other, and by providing the setting wherein intermarriage can be arranged; (2) they set "cultural" standards (in dress, music, and art) for the rest of the population; and (3) they counterbalance the absence of caring for human needs characteristic of a profit-oriented business system through their own involvement in welfare movements (1970, pp. 34–35).

Families participate in an intricate web of exclusive associations, perpetuating upper-class solidarity and tradition (Baltzell 1958, p. 54). It is considered important to belong to the correct clubs, and to appear at fashionable balls, weddings, and funerals. Exclusiveness in residence, memberships, and leisure activities symbolizes superior-status position; its promotion is one way to solidify and enhance status privilege.

Social intermingling and cohesion are developed in a number of formal and informal institutions, such as clubs, balls, boarding schools, resorts, teas, and receptions. That there is considerable internal upper-class interaction has been concluded by a number of observers. For example, after looking at patterns of intermarriage, school attendance, club memberships, resort patronage, and acquaintanceship, Domhoff comments:

> The picture that emerges for me from these various types of evidence for in-group interaction within the upper class is one of overlapping social cliques that have a considerable amount of intermarriage and social interaction among them. It is quite clear that everyone does not know everyone else, but it is also highly probable that everyone has friends and relatives who interact in one way or another with one or more persons in other cliques (1970, p. 87).

In part, the function of social interaction within a class is to provide a primary group organization through which the informal norms of social control operate, to maintain control over important positions in the world of affairs, and to socialize the younger generation.

VALUES AND LIVING STYLE

The predominant value of the upper class is one that reveres the past. Tradition and conservatism, as symbolized in such wide-ranging patterns as political behavior, dress, home furnishings, and wedding ceremonies, are the hallmarks of the upper class. The past is important in part because the elitism of members of the upper class rests upon the past accomplishments of their ancestors. History, genealogy, and biography are of particular interest (Hodges 1968, p. 29).

Very rarely do upper-class members purchase and consume material goods in a conspicuous manner. The showy limousines, glittering jewels, and expensive debuts are more likely to be characteristic of the newly rich. To the secure upper class these behaviors represent the stigmata of the *arriviste*. Publicity, particularly of the sensationalistic variety, is shunned by the social elite, attitudes are quietly conservative, and mate-

297

rial possessions are just as likely to be restrained and subdued as flashy and glittering — baggy tweeds, basic black dresses, old cars, small and private parties are the norm rather than the exception. The "conspicuous consumption" of the nouveaux riches, satirized by Thorstein Veblen (1899) in his discussion of late nineteenth-century America, is no longer typical of the upper-upper class, which is secure in its established and well-known position.

Yet, money is readily spent on large fine homes (even though the sumptuous mansions of the early twentieth century are no longer particularly popular), a staff of domestics or servants, extensive travel abroad, philanthropic enterprises, and sometimes expensive leisure trappings such as yachts, second or third homes, horses, ski lodges, and so forth. Residential patterns reflect the luxury of resources held by the upper class. There may be a number of different estates, homes, and apartments for an extended family. (An example of what Lundberg calls the "multiple-dwelling arrangement" is the Rockefeller estate, Kykuit, of 4,180 acres at Pocantico Hills, New York. All the brothers have large houses on this estate. There are buildings for maintenance and the housing of a large staff, and a million-dollar playhouse with bowling alleys, tennis courts, swimming pool, and squash court. In addition, the Rockefeller brothers have residences in New York City. John III and his wife share a large duplex apartment on the Upper East Side; Nelson and his family have a triplex penthouse on Fifth Avenue; David, Laurance, Rodman C., and Winthrop all have separate residences on the Upper East Side. Additional residences are scattered around: Nelson owns a large ranch in Venezuela; Laurance has a plantation in Hawaii; and Winthrop has an estate in Arkansas (Lundberg 1968, chap. 16). The interiors of upper-class residences "are often [of] palacelike proportions with the marble walls covered by expensive paintings and tapestries. Rare Oriental draperies and rugs, entire imported paneled rooms from European chateaux and expensive bric-a-brac and furniture are in most places strictly *de rigueur*" (Lundberg 1968, p. 854). Works of art not only enhance the interior, but also make good investments and may be donated, inheritance-tax-free, to children. Residential segregation serves to preserve the style of life of a particular subculture. Upper-class neighborhoods tend to be very exclusive and thus reinforce the social distance between the upper class and other strata. Segregation is one form of status protection.

In addition to wealth and lineage, "good breeding" is considered to be an important ingredient of upper-class status. Sincerity in manner, "personal grooming," "character," graciousness of style, and evidence of "culture" are all part of the desired personality syndrome (Hollingshead and Redlich 1958, p. 84). One upper-class informant said to Domhoff: "UC individuals certainly do recognize one another, by many variations of 'the old school tie'; accent; understatement in dress and behavior frequently; common assumptions and values; maintenance of standards of behavior; and by a characteristic sense of 'noblesse oblige' which is really a *sine qua non* . . ." (1970, p. 96).

Upper-class status encourages the development of a secure self-concept and a favorable self-image among the elite (Bonjean 1966). In contrast to middle- and lower-income persons, those at the top of the inequality structure tend to believe that rich people are rich because they as individuals possess desirable personality characteristics such as self-discipline, motivation, ability, and willingness to work hard and to assume responsibility (Huber and Form 1973, Chap. 6). Also in contrast to poorer people, upper-income individuals do not tend to worry about money or to think that it is very important (Huber and Form 1973, pp. 84–88).

Coles (1978) suggests that the rearing of upper-class children puts them through a process of "entitlement," by which the class-bound prerogatives of money and power are integrated psychologically by privileged children and become part of their assumptions about themselves and the world. A major result is a strong and sometimes lifelong emphasis on self. In addition, Coles suggests, privileged children learn early in life to recognize class differences and to appreciate the power that wealth bestows. "The task of their childhood is to reconcile this, to learn to live with it and to justify it" (quoted in Woodward and Malamud 1977). Thus, in one vignette, a boy comments: "If my father weren't a grower and didn't have migrants, then they wouldn't have anything to do."

THE INTERMESHING OF UPPER-CLASS CULTURE AND ITS LEADERSHIP-DOMINANCE ROLE

The above-mentioned secure and favorable self-concepts of the upper class grow out of a pervasive class climate that orients its members to governance. Stephen Birmingham illustrates the upper-class attitude toward its own dominant position:

> Mr. Lewis cites the example of his late wife, Annie Burr Auchincloss, who, when the Second World War was declared, put down her needlepoint and her interest in collecting eighteenth-century prints, and went to work for the Red Cross and other wartime services. No previous education or training — no provisional year with the Junior League doing volunteer work — had prepared her for this. She simply *was* prepared, and did what needed to be done, providing leadership.
>
> "In other words," asked a friend, "there is something to be said for aristocratic values?"
>
> Mr. Lewis looked briefly alarmed. "Oh, yes!" he said quickly, "But of course you must never call them that. An aristocrat would

299

never *call* them that. The minute you use that *word,* the hackles rise" (1958, pp. 338–39).

And:

> Mrs. Tree speaks of her family as "The people who built and administered the schools, universities, boys' clubs and hospitals. They were the sinews of society. . . . they believed that if you tried hard enough, you could make the world a better place. And you *must* try" (1958, p. 340).

Some sociologists, too, following functionalist theory, maintain that there must be an elite group that provides the expertise needed to lead a complex, industrial society. Baltzell writes: "all complex societies . . . are oligarchical in that the few rule the many. . . . [An] empirical test of democracy is whether the . . . oligarchy is both *accountable* to the rest of the population and drawn from *all social levels* and not solely from the ranks of a few privileged families" (1958, p. 4). Later, he says, "A strong and autonomous upper class . . . is one of the important bulwarks of freedom against an all-inclusive totalitarian power" (1958, p. 63). Keller, speaking not only of an upper class, but also of functional elites, similarly argues that these elites are "responsible for keeping the organized system, society, in working order, functioning so as to meet and surpass the perennial collective crises that occur. . . . the destinies of industrial societies depend upon the actions and ideas of their *strategic* elites" (1963, pp. 22–23). Following Parsons, Keller maintains that the functions of the elite are to organize the attainment of general social purposes, to develop the means to achieve these goals, to articulate general moral standards and beliefs, and to contribute to the general morale of the members of society (1963, p. 260).

Other sociologists are not quite so approving in their views, maintaining that the most outstanding function of the upper class is the perpetuation of its own wealth and power, regardless of the interests of society. Mills calls this the "higher immorality": "In the corporate era, economic relations become impersonal — and the executive feels less personal responsibility . . . and the higher immorality is institutionalized. . . . it is a feature of the corporate rich" (1956, p. 343). It is possible because of the power amassed by the organizations that they head: "the men of the higher circles benefit from the total power of the institutional domains over which they rule. For the power of these institutions, actual or potential, is ascribed to them as the ostensible decision-makers" (Mills 1956, p. 357). Mills's theme has been echoed by more recent writings. Matras, for example, suggests that while the upper class may be interested in providing insight, leadership, and example for the larger community, it also is quite interested in (1) preserving its status, privilege, and power and defending them against erosion; and (2) avoiding being penalized or paying too high a price for its status and privilege (1975, p. 146). In spite of the differing evaluative tones that come across in these disparate views, most observers agree that the chief function of an upper class is to exercise power, not to pursue social exclusiveness and leisure (C. Anderson 1974, p. 229). As Baltzell puts it, "power over people is the indispensable mark of high social status, and the primary function of an upper class is the exercise of power" (1958, p. 60).

As suggested early in this chapter, because wealth and power are desired but scarce resources, those families so privileged to have control over them must develop powerful mechanisms to maintain that control. The most obvious mechanism is the moral legitimation implicitly adopted by the upper and upper-middle classes (an ideology glorifying private property) that signifies that the exclusive control of inherited wealth by families is right and proper. Such a moral legitimation is used to buttress a second, and perhaps more basic, mechanism — the laws and practices (tax laws, government-sanctioned interest rates, rules regarding property ownership, for instance) that organize the inequalitarian distribution of wealth.

The third set of mechanisms inhere in upper-class culture. The structure of the family, the socialization of children, the interaction of the adults, and the associational membership of upper-class members — all can be seen as patterns creating a social class that is trained, motivated, and equipped to maintain its position of dominance in the economic and, to a lesser degree, political spheres of American society. The upper-class male infant, attended by nurses and maids, soon is old enough to go to private schools where he not only learns upper-class culture, but also develops friendships and contacts that help him throughout the rest of his life to be successful in his business or profession. At elite universities, he picks up the credentials that help propel him into high-status occupations. As an adult, he joins exclusive clubs, affiliates with organizations, and is appointed to boards that help to form the social nexus on the basis of which business actions can be planned and executed. He is able to extend his influence through interlocking directorships.

The upper-class female likewise is trained for several adult roles that help to solidify the cohesion and influence of the upper class. She guides the offspring into suitable marriages and maintains the social institutions forming the bulwark of upper-class solidarity. She participates on boards of civic, cultural, philanthropic, and welfare organizations, satisfying the sense of noblesse oblige held by members of the upper class, and staving off some of the latent envy and resentment held by less privileged strata. The intermeshing of the upper-class subcultural patterns and values produces a cohesive, self-conscious, and exclusive social class that exerts enormous influence over the workings of the American economy and polity and maintains substantial control of the nation's resources.

301

The control that the upper class is able to maintain would be impossible without the supporting expertise of the upper-middle class, which we next examine. The upper and upper-middle classes participate in a mutually rewarding symbiosis, and for this unconscious coalition the upper-middle class is rewarded with high incomes (but not wealth), moderate social power (over the less-privileged strata, but not over the elite), and considerable social prestige.

The Upper-Middle Class

The upper-middle class consists predominantly of college-educated professionals, scientists, and managers, highly skilled technicians, businessmen, and their families. Privileged by property and education, they are affluent and skilled. About one-fifth of the American population can be so labeled. They do not tend to have final decision-making powers, nor are they ordinarily part of a national elite; however, they do serve as active participants in carrying out policies and decisions, and their knowledge and advice are sought and employed by the decision makers. Members of the upper-middle stratum populate and run (but do not control) political organizations, community and service clubs, churches, schools, hospitals, businesses, welfare departments, criminal justice systems, and most other intermediary groups through which the individual relates to the broader society. They conduct essential services for the ruling elite. They provide the technology on which industry thrives, they administer the bureaucracies of the corporate world, they screen out the challengers to elite rule, and they train the newcomers to the upper class. Their high salaries result not only from the bargaining power that they are able to summon, but also from the desire of those who own and control economic resources to purchase their technical, managerial, and intellectual services. The high salaries of the upper-middle class constitute rewards for the performance of tasks considered essential to the economic elite; the threat of removal of the salaries, in turn, is a social control device that restrains actions deleterious to the elite.

ECONOMIC POSITION

The upper-middle class, although not possessing the enormous wealth that is at the disposal of the upper class, can still be considered, in relation to the bulk of the population, to be a privileged stratum. Making incomes that average between $20,000 and $50,000, families in this class are able to live with considerable comfort. The incomes of professionals and managers are sufficiently higher than those of other income receivers that we may speak of an income gap that sets the upper-middle class apart. The economic advantages of the upper-middle class extend beyond matters of income: Job security is high, unemployment rates are low, benefits are excellent, and advancement is common.

Affluent incomes allow the typical upper-middle-class family to purchase items of necessity, to save money, and to stay out of debt. "The affluent don't spend frivolously, but they do buy what they want when they want it. . . . The ability to spend freely without worrying, to cope with financial demands, is a huge satisfaction and — to those who are new at it — a great relief" (Main 1968). Not many upper-middle-class families spend money on jewels, furs, chauffeurs, or private schools for their children, but expenditures on travel, investments, improvements to the home, and household furnishings are considerably higher than those made by less affluent groups (Main 1968). The modal upper-middle-class living style includes the ownership of a home, several medium-cost automobiles, and an abundant set of accompanying possessions. As a 1964 survey of consumer finances found, 83 percent of upper-middle-class families owned their own homes (compared to 67 percent of lower-middle-class families and 61 percent of blue-collar families), 52 percent of which were valued at more than $20,000 (compared to 15 percent for lower-middle-class families and 18 percent for blue-collar families) (Hamilton 1972, Table 10.6). Likewise, upper-middle-class families are more likely than other groups to own two automobiles, to buy new cars, and to buy expensive cars (Hamilton 1872, pp. 384–88).

POWER AND POLITICS

Upper-middle-class individuals occupy positions of considerably greater power than do members of other strata (aside from the upper class). Most of the directors of the major institutions, the managers under the directors, and the engineers and scientists who advise the managers are part of the upper-middle class. They tend not to have final decision-making power about the ultimate goals of the institutions they run or about the rules by which society operates (a fact that is sometimes irksome to the motivated, achievement-oriented personnel in this stratum). But because they have responsibility for creating the means whereby the goals will be reached, key members of the upper-middle class do have considerable discretion in choosing among alternative courses of action. A district attorney can decide whether to prosecute white-collar corruption in the nursing home business or city prostitutes on dope; a university president can decide whether to spend college funds on intercollegiate sports or faculty salaries; a personnel manager can decide how many minority workers to employ and who should get fired in a recession.

Yet, more likely than not, the moderate amount of power that the upper-middle class does possess is subject to the control of the elite. Threat of withdrawal of the relatively high salaries or of promotions (Stouffer et al. 1949, vol. 1, p. 264) constitutes a major means of control of professionals or executives who would do damage to elite or group interests. Another source of control is an ideology that values the immersion of the individual in the group. Along this line, Whyte writes of the emergence in industrialized society of a "social ethic," stressing group cooperation, that "rationalizes the organization's demand for fealty and gives those who offer it wholeheartedly a sense of dedication in doing so" (1956, p. 6). These economic and ideological mechanisms are generally effective. Tales abound of persons who are penalized for nonconformity: teachers who are fired for expressing radical views, Pentagon engineers who are transferred for revealing overbids in military equipment requests, priests who are defrocked for ordaining women. The higher rewards of work — a feeling of accomplishment, deference from neighbors and friends, and money enough to avoid worry — constitute powerful motivational forces. Any threat of their removal is a strong lever for the inducement of conformity to the goals of an institution. It is for these kinds of reasons that the upper-middle class is basically conservative, in spite of its potential for instituting radical change.

In the political arena, as well as in the occupational world, members of the upper-middle class are effective participants. Members of Congress and local, state, and federal governmental officials overwhelmingly come from upper-middle-class backgrounds (Mathews 1954, 1960; Mills 1956; MacMahon and Millet 1939; Warner et al. 1963; Hackett 1967). The bulk of the leadership and active participants in political parties likewise are from the upper-middle class. Finally, members of the upper-middle class are more likely than members of other strata to vote, participate in public meetings, join political organizations, and seek political office (Verba and Nie 1972; Agger et al. 1964; Campbell et al. 1954, 1960; Dahl 1961; Eulau 1962).

The majority of the upper-middle class subscribes to a generally conservative economic ideology, one which favors governmental laissez-faire, anticommunism, and minimal domestic welfare aid; which avers that high status is the due result of ability and achievement; and which thereby justifies the overall composition of the system of social inequality (Huber and Form 1973; Robinson et al. 1968). Predominantly Republican in voting patterns (four-to-one among very-high-income Protestants; see Hamilton 1972, p. 198), the upper-middle class is generally conservative on political issues as well (Bendix and Lipset 1957). In 1964 approximately 70 to 80 percent of white Protestants who had incomes of $10,000 or more thought that the government should not guarantee medical care or a minimum standard of living, that the government should not support schools, and that the government is becoming too powerful (Hamilton 1972, pp. 197–98). On issues of civil liberties and civil rights, however, they are more likely to take liberal stands (Stouffer 1955).

Not all of the upper-middle class can be labeled politically conservative, however. There is within it a substratum of radical intellectuals that overlaps somewhat with educational, literary, and artistic circles and that commonly provides the leadership of radical social and political movements (Kadushin et al. 1971). Gans conceives of another substratum as well, the "liberal-professional," which, in contrast to the "conservative-managerial" substratum, is politically and economically liberal, is employed in community-centered professions such as education and social work, is more sensitive to "ideas" in the abstract and to national issues, and is the main audience for high culture (1967, p. 31). If there is any subsegment of society that can potentially serve as the leaders of a radical social movement, it is this group of liberal and radical professionals. Well-trained, self-confident, and economically secure, they are equipped to express themselves and organize others, and they are freed from the grinding obsession with survival that is so much more imperative for the less-privileged strata. Consistently, it has been found that the leaders of revolutions and social movements are disproportionately likely to come from the upper-middle class. The student leaders of the antiwar movement of the late 1960s were not actually part of a "generation gap," as was so often averred in the newspapers of the times, but rather were acting in close agreement with the radical views of their educated, politically activist, professional parents (Lipset 1968). However, this substratum of potential advocates of change is small and ordinarily impotent, while the great bulk of professionals and managers function to serve the corporations, the government, and the military. That radical social movements are rarely significant attests not only to the complexity of modern politics and the difficulty of organizing groups, but also to the resistance to radical change that privileged individuals can be expected to offer in their self-interest.

PRESTIGE STANDING

As shown in Chapter 7, the prestige accorded to the upper-middle class is consistently greater than that accorded to the rest of the population (except for the upper class). Several studies even indicate a "prestige gap" that clearly sets off the upper-middle class. The prestige standing of a modal upper-middle-class family is probably based in the last analysis on the social awe held by others of the relative power inherent in professional and managerial occupations and of the greater affluence that the upper-middle class is able to enjoy by virtue of its ability to influence the distribution of income.

The symbolic expression of the upper-middle-class expectation of deference is exemplified in the use of residential space. The suburban home, for example, functions as a stage for the "artless" display of good taste and property, and its selection is a major enterprise. It is a demonstrable and tangible symbol of success. "The Crestwooder who owns an adequate house has become a substantial member of the community and, as such, is respected and admired by his peers. The house and its furnishings; the street and the street number; the location in Crestwood — all are acquired items which make up the total property complex of the house" (Seeley et al. 1956, p. 46). These observations on a Canadian suburb are consistent with Warner's findings that next to occupation, house type and dwelling area are the most important objective characteristics in establishing the social status of a family. The homes of the upper-middle class tend to be single-family dwellings of six to eight rooms in the suburbs or respectable apartments or condominiums in the city, which are maintained by the husband and wife rather than cleaning women and gardeners. The residential areas are often kept relatively homogeneous through the use of footage and expense requirements, "gentlemen's agreements," and the cooperation of real estate dealers.

The status differentiation of the upper-middle class is enhanced by the nearly universal experience of college in the backgrounds of upper-middle-class adults. Most of them have acquired at least some college education, and many of them have received advanced graduate training. Because a college degree is so commonly used as a basic prerequisite for the more respected occupations, it tends to serve as a prestige discriminator as well. Education in a merit-oriented society becomes a major differentiating characteristic, and one may speculate that it has contributed in American society to an increasing polarization of and social separation between those who do and those who do not go to college.

PSYCHOLOGICAL WELL-BEING

The privileged position of the upper-middle class in economics, power, and status has its payoffs for the psychological well-being of its members. There is some evidence that, in general, members of the upper-middle class are more likely to have strong, favorable self-images than members of other strata and that they do not tend to be as alienated (Bonjean 1966, pp. 156–57). They feel more secure and less anxious about status than the lower-middle class, although a concern with mobility is sometimes displayed (Bonjean 1966). According to the results of one survey, only one-fifth of upper-middle-class respondents demonstrated status ambitions by stating that it was important to them to move to a higher prestige class (compared to one-fourth of the lower-middle respondents) (Pearlin 1974). They further report that they receive considerable satisfaction from their work and that their occupational roles permit relatively full expression of their individual potential as well as opportunities to expand this potential (Bonjean 1966, pp. 156–57). When the Gallup polling organization quizzes Americans on their levels of satisfaction with their standards of living, work, family income, and perceived future, professionals and business executives consistently report the greatest degree of satisfaction of all respondents (Gallup Opinion Index 1973).

VALUE ORIENTATIONS

The determining characteristics of the upper-middle class are set by the requirements of an industrial economy for a supply of professional and managerial personnel who (1) can be mobile in both space and class; (2) are motivated to become trained and to advance; and (3) are flexible and adaptable to new technologies and new situations (Seeley et al. 1956). The motivation to move, to acquire training, and to advance is instilled through a focus on career, a value that tends to be held by all family members. Career is considered to be one of the most important foci of life activities, primarily because it is the major determinant of high social status, but also because an internalization of career-oriented values takes place in the very acquisition of the skills and knowledges so required. Family life, community position, and leisure activities all tend to be subordinated to the demands of the career and, where possible, contributory to it.

A career has a beginning, and it must be learned. First, one must become trained in specific skills and knowledges and also in the means of manipulating others.

> Consequently, there are prerequisites for admission into career competition: a certain minimum of intelligence, a personality that is sufficiently outgoing and flexible, a motivation for success strong enough to lead one to work and plan and often to sacrifice for it, an appropriate education in social and intellectual skills. *Birth into a middle-class family vastly increases the chances of meeting these prerequisites, and most middle-class sons remain in their class of birth* (Kahl 1957, p. 194).

Ambition tends to be oriented in two directions: First is the achievement of monetary rewards. Money is important not only for its value in securing goods and services, but also for its symbolic indication of success in a career. The second goal is the development of competence and achievement in a given field of specialization. Consistent with the latter, identification with one's profession is an accompaniment of a career orientation. Thus, for example, chemists may be more interested in their standing with other chemists than with their prestige in the community at large. Scientists may evaluate themselves and others by the number of scholarly publications to their credit and by the professional acclaim they have received; managers, by the size and complexity of the managed group; business executives, by the amount of profits or size of enterprise. In any case, the self-concept of the career-oriented adult quite likely includes an emphasis on success at work.

307

Achievement motivations are high among people of the upper-middle class, especially achievement as it relates to career. The adult future is seen as one in which there are regular advances in responsibility, income, and prestige. Success in work becomes a measure of accomplishment and, for some, of upward mobility (getting ahead). For those who do succeed, or at least feel that they have succeeded, the psychic as well as material rewards are great. For others, problems in developing the career according to the upper-middle-class blueprint become a major source of stress. Of all strata, when things go wrong at work, it is persons in the upper-middle class who are most likely to be troubled. This is indicated in one investigation of stress by the fact that nearly one-third of upper-middle-class males feel that their greatest problems revolve around job-related matters, whereas only one-fifth of skilled and unskilled workers so report (Pearlin 1974).

As Kahl summarizes the attitudes of the upper-middle class toward career: "They stress planning for the future; . . . activity, accomplishment, practical results; they stress individualistic achievement within the framework of group cooperation and collective responsibility. . . . These are the values of the upper levels of most bureaucratic structures. . . . they may not produce great art or literature or scientific theory, but they certainly produce efficient organizations" (1957, p. 201).

An additional major value, consistent with the others, is that of self-actualization. Development of one's intellectual and psychological resources, one's creativity, one's interpersonal sensitivity and communication skills — all are examples of the ways in which self-realization is encouraged. These goals are expressed in child-rearing practices, attitudes toward college, and leisure-time activities. They are consistent with a career orientation because they encourage the development of the autonomy, initiative, and personal competence congruent with professional and managerial skills (Pearlin and Kohn 1966).

FAMILY STRUCTURE

Distinctive aspects of the family structure are related to three characteristics of the upper-middle class: (1) its high mobility rates; (2) its career orientation; and (3) the high social status of the father.

Mobility, both vertical and horizontal, is a prominent feature of upper-middle-class living. Between 70 and 85 percent of professionals and managers in 1962 had been socially mobile in their lifetimes (see Table 8.3 in Chapter 8). Likewise, rates of physical mobility are highest in this stratum. The nuclear family, removed from kin and earlier communities of residence, is found in its most isolated form. Partly due to this break with roots, the upper-middle class places value on companionship as an important ingredient of the marital relationship. In mate selection, love is desired, but love as it rests on a base of shared interests and perspectives.

A common locale for the process of mate selection is the college campus, where individuals select one another on the basis of value compatibility and psychological congruence. Since family background plays such a minor role in the establishment of upper-middle status, the social class origin of a potential mate is considered to be less important than it is in the upper class. In any case, partners can be confident that the college experience ipso facto equips the mate for entry into upper-middle-class occupations. Compatible values, including an ability or willingness to pursue or support the husband's "career," may be more relevant.

Ordinarily, one might assume that an emphasis on companionship would lead to an equalitarian relationship, and, indeed, an equalitarian norm seems to have emerged in the United States (Richmond 1976; Burgess and Locke 1963; Hawkins 1968; Baum 1971; Wolfe 1970; Goode 1963). However, research on family decision making has generally found that the husband's authority increases with his occupational prestige (Strodtbeck 1951; Bronfenbrenner 1961; Scanzoni 1970). Whether or not the husband is dominant in the family depends to a considerable extent on the resources that he can command vis-à-vis his wife (Blood and Wolfe 1960; Gillespie 1971; Scanzoni 1972). Because the upper-middle-class male is likely by virtue of his occupational position to have greater economic and status resources than his wife, he frequently becomes the dominant figure in the family. His power is less if the wife has completed as much formal education as has he, if she works outside the home, or if the occupational prestige of her job is as high as the prestige of his (Vanfossen 1977).

Many upper-middle-class wives do work outside the home. Whether or not they do so is highly related to how much education they have received. College graduates are more likely than other women to be in the labor force. In fact, in 1974 over three-fifths of female college graduates were in the labor force, regardless of their marital status (U.S. Department of Labor 1975, p. 187). They tended to be employed in professional and technical occupations. While the occupational prestige levels of such jobs are high, and the earnings are higher than those of jobs available to less educated women, the earnings still are considerably less (60 percent) than the earnings accruing to men who are similarly employed. For this reason, male marital power based on male superiority of status and economic resources may be diminished, but it is not altogether eliminated in the upper-middle marriage, even when husband and wife are similarly educated and employed.

The upper-middle wife who works in the home finds that her role is heavily influenced by the strong career orientation of her husband. A common marital expectation is that she will support her husband's career and socialize children to upper-middle class values. William H. Whyte, Jr., elaborated on the characteristics expected of the "good executive

309

wife" by corporate management. According to Whyte's interpretation (1951) of 230 interviews of corporate executives and executive wives, the ideal wife of a junior or middle-level executive is expected to be (1) highly adaptable; (2) highly gregarious; and (3) willing for her husband to belong to the corporation. Her role is partly a negative one: "the good wife is good by *not* doing things — by *not* complaining when her husband works late; by *not* fussing when a transfer is coming up; by *not* engaging in any controversial activity." She is a "stabilizer," the "keeper of the retreat, the one who rests and rejuvenates the man for the next day's battle," who listens to his problems and soothes his ego. She listens to her husband's problems and is a companion in that respect, yet she is essentially excluded from her husband's occupational world. Whyte speculates that the husband "asks for" active, intelligent listening, yet seldom wants advice. It is as though the husband has neither the patience nor the inclination to give his wife the exposition necessary for understanding.

The corporate wife is expected to be a good "mixer" and to be very adaptable, for she meets varied social conditions:

> one year she may be a member of a company community, another year a branch manager's wife, expected to integrate with the local community — or, in some cases, to become a civic leader; and frequently, as the wife of the company representative, to provide a way station on the route of touring company brass. As a rule . . . her entire behavior — including what and where she drinks — is subtly conditioned by the corporation (Whyte 1951, pp. 86–87).

These views one the problems faced in "corporate marriages" are reinforced by Kanter's more recent (1977) analysis of men and women in the corporation, which identified three phases of the corporate wife's career progression. The problem of the first phase — the "technical phase," when a husband is on the early rungs of management ladders — is one of exclusion. One wife complained: "His high at work made me angry. He was so involved there but under-involved at home. He'd be withdrawn and too democratic at home, completely abdicating any responsibility" (Kanter 1977, p. 113). The response of wives often took one of two directions: Either they developed careers similar to those of their husbands, which meant that husband and wife were able to share concerns, or they erected exclusionary barriers over their own technical domain of home and children. In the latter case, the marital distance initiated by the husband's career interests was increased by the wife's response.

The problem of the second stage, the "managerial phase," is one of striking a balance between instrumentality and sentimentality in dealings with other people. Old friendships are sometimes put aside because the organizational situation makes them inappropriate. One officer husband, for example, let his wife know that it would no longer be seemly to maintain a relationship with a couple with whom they had previously been very close, because the first husband now far outranked the second. It thus often becomes difficult to maintain anything but superficial friendships within the corporate network, and many wives report considerable loneliness.

The problem of the third stage — the "institutional phase," in which the husband is promoted near the top — is one of handling the public quality of family roles. Distinctions between work and leisure diminish, friendships fuse with business relationships, and wives are often expected to suppress private beliefs and self-knowledge in the interest of public appearance. "People entertain one another on yachts or over long, lavish lunches — all in an attempt to mutually obligate, to create personal relations that will give someone an inside track when it comes to more formal negotiations" (Kanter 1977, p. 119).

The role conflict implicit in these discussions of the upper-middle-class wife's role is presaged at the dating-mating period, when expectations of the career-oriented male that a compatible mate be intelligent, companionate, and well educated conflict with his expectations that her career ambitions and her own needs should not interfere with his. Komarovsky's study of sixty-two seniors at an Ivy League male college revealed the extent of these incompatible expectations. The campus ethos clearly demanded that the men pay lip service to liberal attitudes toward working wives. But qualifications almost negated original responses. For example, an affirmative answer to a proposition, "It is appropriate for a mother of a preschool child to take a fulltime job," was often followed by restrictions, such as "provided, of course, that the home was run smoothly, the children did not suffer, and the wife's job did not interfere with her husband's career" (Komarovsky 1973, p. 878).

One-fourth of the respondents said that they intended to marry women who would not seek outside jobs. Half favored the wife's working *after* the children were raised. Many of them wanted their future wives to "set a goal for herself and strive to achieve it," yet believed that the husband should be the superior achiever in the occupational world and the wife should be the primary child rearer. " 'It is only fair,' declared one senior, 'to let a woman do her own thing, if she wants a career. Personally, though, I would want my wife at home' " (Komarovsky 1973, p. 330). Yet, deprecating remarks about housewifery were not uncommon, even among men with traditional views of women's roles.

The degree to which the husband is able to mix a focus on family with one on career seems to be crucial. In a study of 200 British husbands and wives, Bailyn (1970) found that the "happiest" high-income families are those in which the husbands are oriented to both work and family and seek satisfaction in both spheres, regardless of the wife's career values. The "least happy" are those in which the husbands are exclusively oriented to career and the wives wish to integrate career with family life.

SOCIALIZATION OF CHILDREN

Because advanced education is the keystone to upper-middle-class position, education of the children is very important to upper-middle-class parents, who are the most likely of those of any social stratum to send their children to college, to stress achievement in the lower grades, and to express the intrinsic importance of education. Considerable achievement motivation is transmitted to the children through a number of subtle and repetitive experiences. For example, the activities of children are often judged in terms of their preparation for the child's future upper-middle role. Participation in boy or girl scouts, the high school band, extracurricular activities, athletics, and so forth are seen as experiences that enable the child to achieve social adjustment and organizational skills (important to those upper-middle-class persons who must work with others in the corporate bureaucracies) and that will develop the ability to manipulate other people. An orientation toward the control of people is stressed more than the control of things. The verbal and organizational skills developed during the training period confer on the possessor of upper-middle-class status an aura of competence that suggests a legitimacy about what he or she is doing and that may, in adult interactions, impress or intimidate those with a lesser educational background.

The child is expected to learn independence at an early age, as this quote from a study of an upper-middle-class suburb of Toronto reveals:

> The busy mother, who must run the house without the aid of a maid, entertain her husband and friends, attend meetings, and have "outside interests," is literally compelled to ration strictly her physical contacts with her child. Thus in early infancy preparation continues for achievement-in-isolation, for the individual pursuit of materialistic goals in which human relationships must often be subordinated (Seeley et al. 1956, p. 88).

Independence prepares the child for the creative approach to work that is frequently required in upper-middle-class occupations (Pearlin and Kohn 1966). It is also consistent with the upper-middle-class value placed on individual development and self-expression (Gans 1962). The purpose of education and work becomes verbalized not only in terms of the advancement in status and material well-being of the family, but also in terms of the realization of creative potentials of the worker or student.

The upper-middle-class conception of education includes higher education as a matter of course. The possession of the college degree, the first prerequisite for professional or managerial jobs, admits its holders to the more rewarding occupations. Graduation from medium- and high-prestige universities facilitates gaining the credentials necessary for the desirable jobs, while serving as a status differentiator from those who are less well educated. Privilege thus becomes reserved for people who have completed advanced schooling. The greater deference that they are likely to receive because of their educational histories makes their greater access to rewards seem more palatable to others.

It is through their child's educational attainment that upper-middle-class parents can transmit their high economic and social status. They encourage this attainment by parental insistence and support for university education and by parental transmission of career values. That the social origin of the upper-middle-class child does indeed increase the probability that he or she will later acquire upper-middle class status is demonstrated by many investigations (see Chapter 6). One particularly interesting study of intelligence and class indicated that 34 percent of high-status males who scored in the *bottom* half of the intelligence distribution actually graduated from college, while only 20 percent of sons of low-status families who scored in the *highest* intelligence quartile so graduated (Sewell and Shah 1967). A follow-up study of those graduates, seven years later, found that 60 percent of the low-intelligence sons of upper-middle-class families had retained nonmanual status, 40 percent of them being managers (Longhi and Ellegaard 1969).

ASSOCIATIONAL ROLES

Upper-middle-class individuals are more fully integrated into their neighborhoods, are more likely to visit with friends (but not with relatives), and generally have higher rates of social participation than the lower-middle and working classes (Bell and Boat 1957; Reiss 1959; Bonjean 1965, pp. 156–57; Axelrod 1956; King 1961). They are more community centered, being the most active class in voluntary associations (Komarovsky 1946; Dotson 1951; Bell and Force 1956), providing the bulk of the participating personnel in the activities of these groups and carrying on the legwork of the community projects (Havighurst and Feigenbaum 1959; Wright and Hyman 1958). But the organizations to which they belong are class-related: not the fraternal lodges or unions, but the service clubs (Rotary, Kiwanis, Lions), the professional and business societies, the political clubs, and the civic organizations (Hausknecht 1962). The upper-middle-class wives also are most active club members, filling the bulk of the offices as well as the membership of civic, community, alumnae, and women's clubs.

Upper-middle-class individuals are more likely than other persons to belong to a church (Cantril 1943; Burchinal 1959; Demerath 1964) and to attend church services (Fukuyama 1961). They tend to belong to Presbyterian, Episcopalian, or Congregational churches, in which the emphasis is ritualistic, formal, and low in emotional intensity. As indicated in Chapter 5, the churches of the upper-middle-class are more supportive of the stratification status quo than they are interested in challenging it. They are not likely, for instance, to advocate a basic restructuring of the economic system so that the poor get a greater share of the wealth.

Membership in clubs, churches, and associations serves several functions — the conferring of status and the establishing of intimate relationships are two. But one of the more interesting functions is the provision of social networks that facilitate the real task of the upper-middle-class — the administration of the corporations, research centers, governmental agencies, and other institutions that are controlled by the ruling elite and are integral to the modern capitalist system. The respect gained by those who take on leadership positions in community organizations and the contacts made with other influentials by those who maintain high levels of social participation are useful adjuncts to the administrative power that accrues to upper-middle-class occupational positions.

Competent, highly trained, gregarious, articulate, and sophisticated, a fair number of the upper-middle class are suited to administer and are highly rewarded for their efforts. Their style of life — their community activities, their family structure and socialization patterns, and their predominant values — are well integrated with their essential managerial function. For the most part confident of the legitimacy of the secondary-level power and control that they wield in the shaping of institutional activities, and only dimly conscious of the role they play in supporting the ruling elite, as a class they constitute one of the prime conservators, stabilizers, and perpetrators of the stratification system. It is to their relative advantage to do so, and they have the skills and occupy the positions essential to the task.

10 CONSEQUENCES OF INEQUALITY: THE WHITE-COLLAR AND BLUE-COLLAR WORKERS

BENEATH THE professional and managerial elites in status and income, subject to their directives, the bulk of the labor force runs the offices and operates the machines. The laboratory assistants, the secretaries, the draftsmen, the bank tellers, and the bookkeepers — all serve as mechanical technicians and social engineers processing the paperwork and organizing the procedural details of an industrial society. The salesworkers — from the peddlers of high-priced machinery in the competitive industrial markets to the five-and-dime clerks retailing combs and candles to neighborhood folk — oil the mechanisms of trade and exchange. Thousands of clerks — filing clerks, data processors, typists, stenographers, keypunchers shuffling papers or cards — handle the records and computer programs that keep in order the accounts of business transactions. These occupations are typical of what Warner and Hollingshead labeled the "lower-middle class" and C. Wright Mills referred to as "white-collar people." Possessed of a high school training and some college, intermediate in prestige standing, the white-collar people nevertheless are subject to the directives of others, are at the bottom of the white-collar status ladder looking upward, and barely bring home enough income to keep themselves out of debt. Slightly below the white-collar stratum in prestige standing, but overlapping them in income are the "blue-collar workers" — the skilled and semiskilled workers who run the machines, drive the trucks and buses, and move the materials, performing the actual physical tasks of the economy and producing the goods that form the guts of the business world.

The dividing line between the lower-middle stratum and the blue-collar is particularly muddled. In income, educational achievements, places of residence, and material consumption, the two segments overlap. Indeed, his Yankee City studies convinced Warner that skilled workers have more in common with the white-collar workers than they do with unskilled laborers, just as he similarly believed that white-collar employees have more in common with skilled workers than with the professionals.

It was not always the case that the incomes of the two categories overlapped. Around 1915, clerical workers earned more than twice as much as manual workers. But gradually, during the first half of the twentieth century, the earnings of some blue-collar workers increased to the level of the lower-white-collar workers (Burns 1954; Mayer 1956). This merging has prompted a debate among sociologists about the exact composition of the middle and working strata and about the reasons for the changes that they are undergoing. "Embourgeoisement" theorists agree with Warner that the traditional distinction between manual and nonmanual labor has been breaking down (Mayer 1956, 1963; Lenski 1961, pp. 48–49; Swados 1957; Miller and Riessman 1961a), under the assumption that the higher incomes that the skilled laborers now receive have resulted in their adoption of "middle-class" values and attitudes. A somewhat different interpretation of the convergence of white-collar and blue-collar incomes is the "proletarianization" thesis, which is consistent with Marxist predictions of the ultimate polarization of groups into either the capitalist camp or the proletarian camp. It sees the convergence as one in which the white-collar workers are adopting blue-collar culture. While it has received limited empirical support (Hamilton 1966; Vanneman 1977), most research has not confirmed either thesis (Goldthorpe et al. 1969, for example). Instead, a number of recent studies have found substantial differences between "middle-class" and "working-class" cultures.

The most common empirical pattern is one in which major differences appear between a professional-managerial category and the rest of the white-collar workers — the latter also being differentiated from the blue-collar workers. Glenn and Alston (1968), for example, looked at the attitudes and beliefs held by eight broad occupational categories in the United States. Cultural differences among the eight categories were measured by the responses given by the sample to 113 national survey questions dealing with a variety of "culture-related" topics. If the white-collar and blue-collar strata are becoming one class, we would expect them to have similar outlooks on marriage, religion, work satisfaction, minorities, and politics. Yet, as Table 10.1 shows, the response scores of clerical and sales workers tend to be closer to those of professionals and business executives than to those of the blue-collar workers. Glenn and Alston further discovered that there is a fairly wide gap in average response scores between the professionals and the business executives. But the widest gap appears between the skilled workers and the clerical-sales category — evidence that the manual-nonmanual distinction is still important. The authors conclude:

> The four cultural levels delineated by these intervals are, from highest to lowest: (1) professional and semiprofessional workers; (2) businessmen, executives, and clerical and sales workers; (3) skilled manual workers; and (4) all other manual workers, farmers, and farm managers. . . . Skilled workers differ much more from the highest category (12.9 points) than from the lowest one (7.5 points) and are closer to three of the four lower categories than to clerical and sales workers. The most appropriate dichotomy, then, is into manual and nonmanual workers, with farmers in the manual level (1968, p. 372).

In this chapter, we are interested not only in describing the life styles of the middle- and blue-collar strata, but also in (1) discovering how the strata are shaped by their location in the inequality structure — by the nature of their work, their income constraints, their prestige standings, and their control over their own fates; and (2) determining the degree to which the families in these strata perpetuate themselves through their socialization practices. Knowledge about life style is interesting, but superficial, unless its underlying relationship to the broader forces and patterns of the society are analyzed.

White-Collar Workers: A "Lower-Middle" Stratum

The category we are calling lower-white-collar is predominantly composed of the families of semiprofessionals, clerks, civil service workers, salespersons, and small proprietors. It thus includes independents, such as the owners of small businesses and real estate dealers, as well as middle-level salaried workers, such as clerks, salespeople, and lower-level technicians. The quality and nature of life is greatly affected by the conditions of their work in the larger institutions.

THE NATURE OF THE JOB

There are three major categories of work in the lower-white-collar class: clerical, sales, and small business proprietorship. The three differ

317

Table 10.1
Cultural scores for eight occupational categories, by topic

	Professional and semi-professional workers	Business executives	Clerical and sales workers	Skilled workers	Operatives and kindred workers	Service workers	Farmers and farm managers	Nonfarm laborers
Summary score	62	56	55	49	45	45	44	41
Attitudes on civil liberties[a]	53	44	41	36	30	31	30	28
Authoritarianism[b]	63	49	57	40	40	40	45	41
Attitudes toward blacks and desegregation[c]	67	58	57	50	52	53	47	39
Political values[d]	46	51	44	50	30	27	44	21
Attitudes toward labor unions[e]	46	46	42	31	30	29	47	30
Optimism about the future state of world affairs[f]	49	50	44	38	37	39	40	37
Attitudes concerning marriage and the family[g]	64	57	58	54	50	51	42	42
Drinking attitudes and behavior[h]	67	63	69	57	54	56	35	53
Level of information[i]	66	55	52	40	35	32	33	24
Attention to current events[j]	79	64	64	56	47	48	51	37
Religious beliefs and practices[k]	54	51	47	43	39	40	36	38

Source: N. D. Glenn and J. P. Alston, "Cultural Distances among Occupational Categories," *American Sociological Review*, Vol. 33, 1968, pp. 370–71, Table 1, Reprinted by permission of the American Sociological Association.

[a] High scores indicate permissive or tolerant attitudes.
[b] Low scores indicate high authoritarianism.
[c] High scores indicate tolerant attitudes. Negro respondents are excluded.
[d] High scores indicate political conservatism.
[e] High scores indicate negative attitudes.
[f] High scores indicate optimism.
[g] Low scores indicate approval of early marriage, high fertility, and government restrictions on the dissemination of contraceptive information.
[h] Low scores indicate abstinence and restrictive attitudes.
[i] High scores indicate high level of information.
[j] High scores indicate high attention.
[k] Low scores indicate fundamentalist beliefs and low frequency of attendance at religious services. Non-Christian respondents are excluded on questions pertaining to Christian beliefs.

somewhat in job conditions, yet all three require the ability to please and get along with others.

The role of secretary is illustrative. Kanter (1977) observes that within the corporation the relationship between a secretary and boss tends to be personal rather than impersonal, is based on negotiation rather than on written job descriptions, and demands loyalty and service of secretary to boss. The boss's status determines the power of the secretary, and the secretary functions as a status symbol for the boss. Secretaries are rewarded for loyalty and devotion to their bosses, for their attitudes more than for their skills, for the appearance of liking their jobs and being willing to take care of their bosses' personal needs. Among the rewards they receive are praise and flattery, access to inside information, and opportunity for contact with those in powerful positions. These are rewards in lieu of higher pay, job control, and independent recognition. As a result of the social organization of their jobs, secretaries tend to narrow their interests and involvements over time, overidentify with their bosses, become timid and self-effacing, and develop an addiction to praise. Their power is limited, and they often find that techniques of emotional manipulation are their most effective means for managing their situation.

Not all clerical work possesses the personal quality of a secretary's job. Much clerical work has become more routinized. Some suggest that white-collar work is becoming factory-like. Certainly, a large number of clerical jobs are highly regulated, depersonalized, and task-fragmented. The growth of corporate organization in the nineteenth and twentieth centuries profoundly changed the office (Stinchcombe 1965). A new, male managerial stratum took over the quasi-managerial tasks previously performed by clerks, and details were left to be attended to by a predominantly female staff of file clerks, typists, stenographers, clerical supervisors, and secretaries. Glenn and Feldberg (1977) have studied recent changes in clerical work in five companies of varying size. They found that traditional specialties such as stenography and bookkeeping, which require extensive training, have been simplified and fractured into jobs now requiring mechanical skills (operating a copying machine), lower-level skills (typing addresses), and narrower skills. The simplification of the jobs and the absence of mental activity make such jobs more demanding, in reality. There is great pressure on the worker to work quickly and accurately, and to maintain the pace set by machines. Patience is required, and a lack of ambition is inculcated. As clerical work has become downgraded and proletarianized, the relationships of workers to each other have become less involving and satisfying; those to employers, more regulated. The managers have increased their control by creating a clerical staff that is less knowledgeable, less involved, and less committed.

Similar to the job requisites for secretaries, an emphasis on social skills — personal charm and service — is frequently important for sales personnel. Sales people in modern industrialized societies tend to be employees in a bureaucratic setting whose job is to contact the anonymous public so as to present the firm's good name (Mills 1951, p. 183). Kindness and friendliness become aspects of personalized service or of public relations, rationalized to further the sale of something. Whether the job is selling real estate for a small, personalized firm, selling panty hose in a large department store, or selling multimillion-dollar computers to corporations, the salesperson is expected by employers to be friendly, tactful, physically attractive, emotionally controlled, and conversationally adept. The smile behind the counter is a commercialized lure, a mask for the often less friendly impulses of the inner self, but it has a tendency to become self-alienating (Mills 1951, pp. 183–84).

Small business proprietors — storekeepers, filling station operators, appliance dealers — are in the third most common category of white-collar workers. Mills (1951) called them the "old middle class," for proprietors were the most representative entrepreneur in rural America of the nineteenth century. Since that time, small business proprietors have experienced a slow and gradual decline in their class position (Vidich and Bensman 1968). This is primarily due, first, to the breakdown of their monopolistic position with respect to the local market and, second, to their increasingly disadvantageous reliance on goods and services supplied by large corporations. The decrease in profits has led to greater competition among themselves. Proprietors have responded to their economic situation by increasing business hours, by carrying secondary lines, and by competing intensively for "service" trade (Vidich and Bensman 1968, p. 91). Although small business proprietors would be among the first to extol the virtues of "free enterprise" and "capitalistic competition," in their position in the economic world they are not well favored to compete. They are not at the centers of initiative or economic innovation. They operate within a setting of restrictive legislation imposed by the federal government and of trade practices laid out by big business. While proprietors have more autonomy on the job than clerical or sales workers, they do not have a great deal more control over the economic forces that affect their lives.

The majority of lower-white-collar workers who work in the corporations and of small business proprietors who handle retail trade are people who perform necessary operations, but who have little control over their economic environment or over the goals of their work. They supply the huge and essential work force that performs the everyday white-collar routines of the corporation and distributes goods and services at the local level, but they are far removed from the centers of decision making in the elite board rooms. Their only contact with the transmission of power is through their immediate superiors, the higher-status and more-educated managers and professionals who direct them, or through their dealings with far more powerful centers of control in government and large business. They lack the autonomy with which to become creative about their activities, and they are prone to an alienation from work that is not so characteristic of their bosses.

In general, members of lower-white-collar families have learned that they cannot expect the same mobility opportunities that are available to the professionals and managers. Their sights may be set upward, as they aspire to the status positions in the hierarchical levels above them, and there may be some movement into the lesser managerial positions, particularly for males. However, such mobility is usually limited. In contrast to the career lines of the upper-middle class, in which many individuals experience a series of advancements over their lifetimes, the lower-white-collar workers can expect to perform the same routine tasks throughout their careers (Hamilton 1972, pp. 375–78; Mackenzie (1973, p. 30). Members of this stratum take orders from the upper-middle class and work with them on community projects and in community organizations, but any hope they might have of moving into the upper-middle stratum is difficult to realize, in part because they lack the educational qualifications for the increasingly specialized and technical managerial roles. Thus, "career" is not a salient life perspective for most white-collar employees, and they often turn instead to an emphasis on family and respectability, which they may feel differentiates them from the blue-collar stratum.

FAMILY STRUCTURE AND PATTERNS OF SOCIALIZATION

For white-collar workers, the labor market is relatively stable, and employees tend to be secure in their jobs. Yet, economically, living is somewhat difficult, particularly in that material aspirations often outreach the means. The range of typical incomes covers several thousand dollars, say, from $8,000 to $15,000 (1977 base), thus, some families are just getting by, while others achieve the minimum for a "comfortable" existence. More than half have more comfortable incomes because both spouses are working.

Around a third of families in this stratum rent apartments or live in multiple-family dwellings (Hamilton 1972, p. 383). The rest own neat, but small homes in the fringe areas of a city or in nearby suburban divisions. Lower-white-collar families are likely to own a medium-priced automobile, but they have little surplus capital to invest in productive, wealth-producing activities.

In lineage, most individuals in the lower-middle stratum can trace their ancestry to the immigrations between 1830 and 1870, and they include large numbers of Irish and northern European ethnic backgrounds. Nearly two-thirds have blue-collar origins. Church membership is high, as is membership in such community organizations as the Elks or the Masons, the chamber of commerce, and religious auxiliaries. Yet the participation in voluntary associations is not as high as that of the more affluent groups, and it is less likely to be in leadership positions.

The subculture of white-collar workers is built around the nuclear family and its desire to make its way in the larger society (Gans 1967, p. 27). The role of the husband is often seen to be the elevation of the family's welfare through increases in status and in the standard of living. Wives are likely to be expected to be good mothers, taking detailed interest in the children's health, development, and progress in school. Nevertheless, a fairly large proportion of wives hold jobs outside the home, enabling their families to escape from economic hardship. Sex roles are less segregated than in the working-class family (Gans 1967, p. 27). Husbands and wives are closer to being companions, sharing a few common interests and participating in each other's worlds. Indeed, a larger proportion of marital relationships are equalitarian in this stratum than in more privileged strata, perhaps in part because the husband's occupational status is not so outstanding that he is likely to dominate on the basis of high status (Vanfossen 1977).

Because so much of the common interest is focused in the home, family life tends to be child-centered; the home is run for both adults and children, and the children are allowed to act as children (Gans 1967). Child-rearing practices are less authoritarian than in the working class, but the permissiveness is tempered by stricter limits and by more emphasis on the rights of the parents than is typical in the upper-middle stratum (Yorburg 1973, p. 176). Education is emphasized, for it is thought to be a prerequisite to a respectable and well-paying job and a good marriage. Children attend public schools (or perhaps parochial schools), and then about two-thirds begin postsecondary education at public colleges, such as state teachers' colleges, state universities, and junior colleges, or at business and vocational colleges.

The lower-middle stratum stands out from other occupational groups in the degree to which it is considered important that children learn to get along with other people (Mackenzie 1973, p. 53). More affluent professional and managerial parents are likely to emphasize the development of individual autonomy, while the less affluent blue-collar parents emphasize obedience and docility. The desire of lower-white-collar parents that their children be sociable and gregarious reflects the demands of their own clerical and sales jobs for employees who can please both bosses and clients.

Several researchers have suggested that the dominant value held by lower-white-collar people is the approval of respectability, which is revered, it is maintained, because it is consistent with the requirements of the job (Kahl 1957; Hollingshead 1949; Gans 1967). White-collar work demands considerable effort and sacrifice, postponement of gratification of needs, and development of a reputation as an honest, hard-working, and responsible member of the community. It requires that the employee be willing to submit to orders and yet be personable enough to get along with the many people whom he or she must deal with. It is because they revere responsibility, stability, goodwill, and submission to authority that white-collar workers are able to achieve or maintain their status and to perform their occupational roles efficiently. They are not decision makers, yet they carry out the orders of others with technical competence and initiative. In the view of such researchers, then, the occupational requirement that white-collar workers be reliable and responsible explains many of the dominant values of this stratum: formal education, rationality, controlled and respectable behavior, family integrity, and hard work. Such personal virtues as cleanliness, frugality, and personal morality are touted in rhetoric and followed in practice. Stability is considered important, and stability is symbolized by job, home, neighborhood, church, and friends.

POLITICAL ORIENTATION

Several authors have argued that the concern of the lower-white-collar family for status and social placement, fueled by a righteous rage over violated moral norms, becomes a vague discontent with the trends and directions that modern society is taking, a resentment against intellectuals in their ivory towers, bureaucrats with their briefcases, and welfare recipients with their food stamps. It is maintained that the small business owner, the real estate dealer, the clerk, and the salesperson are at the core of the "middle majority" political force of the 1960s and 1970s and that they constitute the bulk of conservative opinion in the United States. Yet, the evidence does not suggest a lower-middle-class reactionary tendency. Hamilton (1972) reports that lower-middle-class voters are more likely to be Democrats than are upper-middle-class voters, particularly if one looks at urban voters rather than small-town and rural voters. Likewise, on issues of government support of medical care and living standards, the lower-middle respondents are more "liberal." Indeed, Hamilton finds that the strongest enclave of conservatism exists among the *upper*-middle-class white Protestant independent professionals. These data throw considerable doubt on the validity of the portrait of the lower-middle class as being distinctively reactionary and compulsively moralistic and suggest, rather, that the percentages of people holding particular attitudes and views, when they reflect class differences at all, range along a smooth continuum from professionals at one end to laborers at the other.

One way in which the white-collar segment does appear to stand out from the rest of the population is in their overall evaluation of their lives. Consistently, surveys reveal them to be more discontented than other segments. For example, the Gallup opinion poll indicates that more clerical and sales workers report dissatisfaction with their standards of living, their jobs, and their family incomes than either the professional and managerial group or the manual group (Gallup Opinion Index 1973). Some suggest that their dissatisfaction stems from the invidious comparisons they make between themselves and the better-paid professionals and managers for whom they must work (Hollingshead 1949, p. 95; Yorburg 1973, p. 176). Others propose that it emerges when they feel caught in a prestige squeeze between the salaried administrators on the upper side and the increasingly affluent skilled workers on the lower side (Mills 1951). Perhaps it occurs because the nature of the work itself has become more boring as a result of office mechanization (Mackenzie 1973, p. 42; Glenn and Feldberg 1977).

Dissatisfaction may come particularly from the realization that the role of the white-collar workers is to serve others without receiving substantial return for their sacrifices. As we scan the stratification hierarchy from top to bottom, we would expect that the first signs of discontent produced by such a realization would show up in the lower-white-collar segment.

White-collar workers perform necessary work activities and are essential to the running of bureaucracies. But they lack decision-making power and work autonomy. Their jobs are relatively secure, but dead-end. Their incomes are sufficient, but minimal. They have to be gregarious and sociable to please both boss and client, yet they receive little recognition for their placating functions. They teach their children to get along with others and to get an education, for it is in these two ways that they themselves moved away from their blue-collar origins. Their levels of self-esteem are higher than in the blue-collar stratum, yet they are more prone to a chronic dissatisfaction with their jobs, their incomes, and life in general. They neither prosper nor perish. They truly are the epitome of the middle classes.

It is only when we begin to look at the blue-collar stratum that we see more fully the devastating effects of economic hardship and job insecurity. While not all blue-collar families experience such hardship, it is a common experience that permeates the style of life of the stratum and bears ramifications for all aspects of living.

Blue-Collar Workers: The "Working Class"

Blue-collar people usually are either romanticized or maligned in the popular media. Images of noble and courageous coal miners are counterposed by those of bigoted and coarse hard-hats. In reality, both images are only caricatures of the many kinds of people found in the working world. Their personalities are of all kinds, blustery and sedate, strong-willed and timid, gregarious and introspective, proud and debased. They respond in a number of different ways to the external conditions imposed on them. The conditions common to the stratum — generally low wages, job insecurity, regulating constraints and rules of all kinds, minimal prestige — produce whatever general tendencies exist among the families of this stratum.

Also variously called the "working class" or the "upper-lower" class, the blue-collar stratum is predominantly composed of skilled and semi-skilled laborers — craftsmen such as mechanics, carpenters, bricklayers, and painters, and operatives such as truck drivers, attendants, brakemen, assemblers, and machine operators. Some service workers (barbers, cooks, guards, and so forth) also fall in the blue-collar class. Comprising about one-third of the population, blue-collar workers execute much of the physical work of the economic system. They operate the factories, the mills, and the shops; they build and maintain the buildings and homes; they drive the trucks, attend the automobiles, assemble the machinery, and deliver the goods. They are the bulk of the industrial work force. Yet, for large portions of the blue-collar class, incomes are limited, jobs are unexciting, health and security are unstable, and it is a struggle just to get by. The key to many of the problems faced by blue-collar families is found in the economic conditions of their lives, conditions that are fundamentally out of their control. We turn first to an examination of the nature of work and its rewards as experienced by working families.

ECONOMIC CONSEQUENCES

About half of blue-collar workers are skilled, the others being semiskilled. Skilled work requires several years of extensive training. Although some of it is repetitious, it does involve the use of initiative and responsibility. Semiskilled work, more routine and repetitious in nature, requires less on-the-job training.

In general, the period of training for both skilled and unskilled work is less than that of middle-class jobs. Because the training required to do the work is so brief, the worker is easily replaced by someone else who is willing to work for less pay. Consequently, blue-collar workers are in a less competitive position relative to job access than are the other strata. They are protected somewhat by such devices as restricted apprenticeship systems and union regulation of hiring, but they still are faced with labor competition during periods of high unemployment. Even though blue-collar workers have almost as much education as lower-level white-collar workers (eleven to twelve years of schooling versus twelve to thirteen years), it is the blue-collar workers who are laid off during recessions, while white-collar workers hardly ever lose their jobs. Concern over job security is a realistic worry of the blue-collarite.

INCOME AND SUBSISTENCE

The fact that the most highly skilled workers in the United States now frequently carry home larger paychecks than do the clerks in the lower-white-collar stratum has somehow convinced many Americans that the

325

economic differences between the blue-collar and white-collar workers have disappeared. "Everyone knows," they say, "that plumbers get $20,000 per year and that garbage collectors in New York City start at $16,000. Feel sorry for the working guy? Not on your life!" Everyone may think this, but reference back to the income figures in Table 4.5 quickly reveals the misleading nature of these beliefs. The median annual income of white male plumbers in 1970 was $8,997 and that of white male cleaning service workers was $4,679. Even when a spouse's earnings are included, in 1974 the median *family* income of all but the elite occupational categories of the blue-collar class was below the $14,333 figure given by the U.S. Department of Labor as the cost of a "moderate standard of living" for an urban family of four, as shown in Table 10.2.

Belief that blue-collar workers are well-off is encouraged by the empirical reality of the broad range of incomes among them. At the upper end, some skilled workers are pulling in more dollars than some clerical workers or salespersons. Yet, at the lower end, the depressed wages of operatives and service workers are barely above the poverty line. For most of the more affluent blue-collar families, the figures are high only because both spouses are bringing in an income. As Hamilton (1972) shows, "affluent" blue-collar families are not like equivalent middle-class families. Of the blue-collar families that were able to draw a family income of $10,000 or more (1955 data), 93 percent were families in which both

Table 10.2

Median income of males by occupation and of families by occupation of head, 1974

	Median income	
Occupation	Males	Families
Professionals	$13,230	$19,483
Managers and proprietors	14,559	19,835
Clerical	9,734	12,991
Sales workers	10,263	16,230
Craftsmen	11,042	14,561
Semiskilled operatives	8,595	12,383
Service workers	5,695	10,507
Laborers	5,406	10,460
Farm laborers	2,940	6,581
Private household workers	—[a]	3,798

Source: From U.S. Bureau of the Census, 1976a, Tables 45 and 69
[a] Base too small for computation.

spouses worked outside the home; in only 31 percent of the white-collar families of similar incomes was this the case.

About one-fourth of this class is quite poor. For these people, life is a struggle to pay the bills for rent, groceries, the car, and repairs. Interviews readily reveal an economic concern that is characteristically absent in the middle class. Rubin asked the 100 working-class people whom she interviewed, "Would you fantasize for a minute about what you'd do if you suddenly inherited a million dollars?" She observed: "After the first surprised silence, both women and men answer with a regularity that quickly becomes predictable. 'I'd pay off my bills,' is the first thought that comes to 70 percent; for another 25 percent, it is the second thought" (1977, p. 165). Some of her sample said they would buy some small services not now possible, whereas others said they would get needed medical attention or do something special for their children.

To keep ahead of the specter of poverty, blue-collar workers change jobs frequently, accept unpleasant but better-paying shift work, and "moonlight" at a second and sometimes even a third job. On the average, manual laborers work longer hours than clerical and sales workers and have less vacation time (U.S. Bureau of Labor Statistics 1967).

The financial problems that blue-collar families experience are exacerbated by the fear of unemployment. Operatives and service workers are concerned with job security because, next to the unskilled, their unemployment rates are the highest of any occupational category (Shostak 1969, p. 7). The highly skilled blue-collar workers fare better, but even they are susceptible to unemployment, shift work, and occupational hazards.

THE MEANING OF WORK

A problem of many people in the blue-collar stratum is that their work tasks are often tedious, unpleasant, and boring. Levison describes a job on the assembly line:

> It took me about fifteen minutes to learn the job at the can manufacturing factory. I was stationed between two machines. The machine behind me cut long sheets of aluminum into rectangles the size of paperback novels and deposited piles of them in eight little trays. The machine in front automatically rolled them into cylinders and passed them through a furnace which sealed one edge to the other. My job was to take each pile of aluminum rectangles from the trays where they fell behind me, straighten them out like a deck of cards, and put them in the tray in front of me, which automatically fed them to the machine. . . .
>
> The machine in front of me operated continuously and, if there weren't any aluminum sheets in the feeder, a light would auto-

matically "fink" on you. . . . it's the rhythm you have to catch. At first you fight it and try to beat the machine. You try to lift two piles at once or find a better way than the one the foreman showed you. But finally you stop trying to beat the machine and go along with it. . . . Can factories are among the worst for noise because there are several thousand cans banging together on a half dozen conveyor belts that run overhead. The clattering doesn't recede into the background the way some other factory noises do. . . . A lot of the workers wore ear plugs to block out all sound (1974, pp. 56–57).

Levison (1974, pp. 54–55) argues that many people in the middle class do not fully realize how alienating factory work can be. He suggests that those professors who believe that professional work, such as college teaching, is as estranging as blue-collar work should imagine having to type the same single paragraph from 9 A.M. to 5 P.M., having to ask permission to go to the bathroom or to use the telephone, having salaries cut from $16,000 to $8,000 and vacations reduced to two weeks a year, and being ordered to work overtime at the discretion of the company or lose their job.

That work is less enjoyable to people doing manual labor than to the professionals, and therefore is far less meaningful to them, is pointed up by the responses to several survey questions. A sample of people in Chicago were asked if they expect to get much pleasure out of work (Pearlin 1974). The percentage who indicated they did not ranged from 0 for the professionals to 57 for the unskilled laborers. (From 22 to 42 percent of skilled and semiskilled workers did not expect to enjoy their work.) Clearly, blue-collarites are much less likely than white-collar workers to find pleasure in what they are doing for eight hours a day. Many do not find their work challenging or ennobling, and they withdraw commitment or interest in it. The significant part of life, aside from the often rewarding primary relationships on the job, comes to be defined in terms of family and neighborhood involvements. The job is valued for the goods that it can bring for the family. Thus, a prominent reason for sticking with it anyway is that they want the income. When asked if the most important thing about their job is that it provides the things they need in life, a sizable 80 to 87 percent of the blue-collar workers said yes (compared to 46 percent of the professionals). Finally, the adjustment made to unenjoyable work frequently is passive resignation. About half of the blue-collar workers believed that they had to accept their jobs, because there is nothing they can do to change them. By contrast, only 15 percent of the professionals took such a passive stance. These and other statements suggesting a pervasive alienation from work in the blue-collar stratum are presented in Table 10.3.

Table 10.3

Percentage of 1,257 Chicagoans who agree with various statements about work, by occupation, 1972

Statements	Higher executives and major professionals	Managers and lesser professionals	Small businessmen and sem-professionals	Clerical and sales	Skilled laborers	Semiskilled laborers	Unskilled laborers
	(N = 62)	(N = 157)	(N = 183)	(N = 367)	(N = 199)	(N = 198)	(N = 93)
I don't really expect to get much pleasure out of work.	0%	6%	14%	22%	23%	42%	57%
My job does not bring out the best in me.	11	22	24	31	37	41	61
The most important thing about my job is that it provides me the things I need in life.	46	56	67	71	80	87	88
I have to accept my job as it is, because there's nothing I can do to change it.	15	21	25	41	44	59	72
I can put up with a lot on my job as long as the pay is good.	47	49	51	62	70	75	79
As soon as I leave work, I put it out of my mind.	29	36	43	63	64	79	78

Source: Leonard C. Pearlin, "Social Origins of Stress," Unpublished study, National Institute of Mental Health, 1974, Washington, D.C.

BLUE-COLLAR ARISTOCRATS

Significant exceptions to the generalizations presented about work alienation and economic worry must be made when we look at the most highly skilled workers within the blue-collar stratum. Two studies in particular provide noteworthy examples. In 1967 in Providence, Rhode Island, Mackenzie interviewed bricklayers, cabinet makers, electricians, and toolmakers — craftsmen representing the elite in skill of the manual laborers. From two-thirds to four-fifths indicated that they found their jobs very interesting and stimulating. An electrician who volunteered that his work was challenging said: "'Challenging to see a forest, then houses, it's fabulous. Storeys, buildings, grow and you know you've been a small part in it" (1973, p. 37). A toolmaker said, "You make different kinds of tools. It isn't monotonous — everything's different. Sometimes you have to plan out your own work — it's a challenge" (1973, p. 37). In terms of the several aspects of the work situation that have been found to be important in influencing job satisfaction (Blauner 1966) — control over the use of one's time and physical movement, control over the pace of the work process, control of the technical and social environment, freedom from hierarchical authority, and membership in an integrated work group — highly skilled workers clearly are more privileged than the semiskilled workers.

Similar observations were made by Le Masters, who did a two-year participant observation study of "blue-collar aristocrats" who frequented a family-type tavern in Wisconsin. The workers who attended this bar seemed to derive considerable satisfaction from their work. A comment by a carpenter is typical:

> I tell you, Lee, I get a hell of a kick when I drive around town and see a building I helped to put up. You know that Edgewater Hotel down by the lake? I worked on that sonofabitch fifteen years ago and she's still beautiful. I did the paneling in that dining room that looks out over the water. Sometimes I drive down there just to see the damn thing — do you think I'm nuts or something? (Le Masters 1975, p. 23).

Le Masters (1975, pp. 20–25) indicates there are several reasons for lower levels of alienation from work among highly skilled workers: Supervision is light, the individuals have freedom to move around on their jobs, the work is not monotonous, it is easy to see the results of one's labor, the fringe benefits are good, and the workers believe that they are contributing to the welfare of society.

In the main for the blue-collar class, however, work is not very interesting; it is often difficult, exhausting, dangerous, and disagreeable; and the pay does not really compensate for the unpleasantness of the tasks.

On top of that, hard-working blue-collar workers do not even receive respect from society for their labors. Prestige is given to the professionals and managers, the business executives and politicians, not to the operatives and machinists. Empirical research has begun to establish the profound consequences that social devaluation of one's work has on individual self-evaluation. As indicated in the next section, the stereotypes and expectations of others exert a definitional pressure that is hard to ignore.

PRESTIGE CONSEQUENCES

Many working-class families do not need to see the NORC occupational prestige scale to know that blue-collar jobs inspire less respect in the eyes of others than do white-collar jobs. They do not need to read the surveys or community studies to be aware that Americans value life circumstances that they do not have — steady employment at high wages, mobility opportunities, occupations with status.

A major consequence of prestige inequality is diminution of the sense of self-worth. Society's evaluations become translated into self-evaluations. Based on personal interviews with workers, Sennett and Cobb discuss the process by which this translation takes place:

> people felt that an educated, upper-middle-class person was in a
> position to judge them, and that the judgment rendered would
> be that working-class people could not be respected as equals;
> to this fear people responded in one of two ways — either by
> trying to show that the position they held in society was not per-
> sonally their fault, or that it was wrong in general for people to
> make judgments of other people based on social standing. . . .
> the emotional impact of the class difference here is a matter of
> "impudent snobbery," of shaming, of putdown (1972, pp. 38–39).

Recall the data on income and self-esteem presented in Table 1.1, which suggested that the less privileged the socioeconomic stratum, the more likely it is that people in it will lack a sense of self-worth. Not all members of a working-class stratum suffer from low self-esteem, these data show. Some maintain dignity by redefining success so that it is more compatible with their modest accomplishments, and they accumulate possessions as the visible symbols of their achievements and status. But often that is not enough, and it does not work (Rubin 1976, p. 36). The problem of self-worth for those whose life conditions command less respect is that they receive little social reinforcement for whatever positive evaluations they make of their own activities. They see their own work as valuable because it is working with things, producing objects, or moving materials; yet it is the more educated people — those who sit around — who receive society's admiration.

The attitude of blue-collarites toward those who have more education and have secured white-collar jobs is ambivalent, to say the least. Education is seen as the key to gaining control over one's fate, to moving toward a position in which the world can be dealt with in some controlled, emotionally restrained way (Sennett and Cobb 1972, pp. 22–23). For this reason, the educated person still gets a begrudging respect. Yet, while workers recognize the advantages and privileges that white-collar people have, they do not really respect the products of white-collar work. They are not inclined to view white-collar work as real work, but rather as "pushing papers," as being nonproductive (Sennett and Cobb 1972, pp. 20–21).

In spite of the ambivalence toward the more educated, it is difficult for blue-collar men, women, and children to escape recognition of the general societal devaluation of their own lives. They see that there are no factory workers or truck drivers who are heroes of television shows. They see that teachers and mortgage lenders and welfare workers are contemptuous of their struggles to persist. Recognizing the devaluation of them by those who are more privileged makes it difficult to escape its damaging effect on self-esteem. The costs of inequality are borne in particular by working-class families, whose total existence is shaped by their economic struggles and their striving for personal dignity.

THE LIFE CYCLE OF BLUE-COLLAR FAMILIES

A drive through blue-collar residential areas typically reveals frame houses placed fairly close together, with well-trimmed lawns and small backyards and occasionally, a camper or boat in the driveway. A bare majority of blue-collarites live in stable ethnic enclaves within a large city, where life is highly social and personal. They own or rent houses or live in apartments in what used to be large single-family homes. Some blue-collar families have moved to the suburbs (an option open only to the better-off semiskilled and skilled workers), where the way of life of the ethnic city neighborhood may be transplanted as much as possible.

A fairly large proportion of the adults who live in working-class areas are themselves children of blue-collar workers, for the working class is one of the least socially mobile classes in America. About four-fifths were born to manual (skilled and unskilled) workers (Hamilton 1964, p. 43). This fact, coupled with a tendency to reside in the same community as the parents and even in the same neighborhood, means that there is considerable transmission of working-class culture from generation to generation.

The backgrounds of blue-collar people have a highly ethnic flavor. Large numbers either were born in a foreign country or had parents who were. Especially represented are Italian, German, Canadian, Polish, Russian, and English ethnic stocks. The influence of these ethnic cultures has not totally dissolved, contrary to "melting pot" theorists, and an ethnic ethos continues to permeate working-class culture. Related to the white

332

ethnic origins in southern and eastern Europe is the disproportionate number of Catholics. Although only about one-fourth of the total population is Roman Catholic, over two-thirds of blue-collar workers claim Catholic affiliation, while 30 percent claim to be Protestant and 7 percent to be Jewish (Hollingshead and Redlich 1958, p. 190). Home ownership is often a symbol of respectability. A thirty-nine-year-old welder living in a city slum remarked: "We're all working for one purpose, to get ahead. . . . My next step is a nice little modern house of my own. That's what I mean by bettering yourself — or getting ahead" (Chinoy 1955, p. 126). A blue-collar home owner ordinarily spends a greater proportion of his or her time than does a white-collar home owner in repairing and improving the house, which represents a permanent and satisfactory dwelling place, a symbol of full participation in American society, and an escape from subordination to a landlord (Handel and Rainwater 1964).

The purchase of material goods also, for many, becomes a symbol of that getting ahead. Although the limited incomes do not allow the families to buy everything that they might be persuaded by advertising to want — color television–stereo combinations, tractor lawnmowers, and yellow refrigerators — an occasional surplus in the family budget makes the business of shopping, comparing store items, and becoming acquainted with the newest goods a highly enjoyed leisure-time and weekend activity that often involves the whole family.

CHILDHOOD SOCIALIZATION

Growing up in a blue-collar family is frequently difficult, particularly when the family experiences economic hardship. One of Rubin's respondents describes her childhood:

> Life was mean and hard. My parents didn't have a lot to give us, either in things or emotion. [Guiltily.] I don't blame them; they couldn't help it. They did their best, but that's just the way it was. They were young, and their lives weren't any fun either. They were stuck together by their poverty and their five kids. [Twenty-seven-year-old beautician, second from the youngest in a family of five.] [1]

Family instability of some kind, such as divorce, desertion, or alcoholism, is not uncommon. In fact, Rubin (1976, p. 29) found in her sample of 100 blue-collar men and women that some 46 percent of them acknowledged having grown up in families with some elements of instability. All of them mentioned growing up poor.

[1] Excerpted from *Worlds of Pain: Life in the Working-Class Family,* p. 23, by Lillian Breslow Rubin, © 1976 by Lillian Breslow Rubin, Basic Books, Inc., Publishers, New York. Reprinted by permission.

333

In such a situation, planning for a child's future is difficult. Parents lack the conviction that individuals can have control over their own fate, and they do not have the economic resources necessary to plan for their children's extended education. In addition, as blue-collar children are being socialized, they do not receive the vocational guidance, see the role models in prestigious occupations, or acquire the personal contacts to help push along a career that are so likely to be experienced by the child growing up in an upper-middle professional home.

What happens is that about 40 percent of blue-collar youth drop out of high school shortly before the senior year (S. M. Miller 1964, p. 123). The lack of formal education is one of the prime reasons for the immobility of the average worker and also accounts for the only slight increase in earnings over his or her lifetime. Many working-class sons are not particularly interested in school, and they tend not to see or consider the relationship of formal education to job advancement. School for many of them is the locus of a deep-seated class rivalry between the ambitious college-oriented middle-class crowd and the less ambitious blue-collar kids with their limited occupational aspirations (Friedenberg 1964). Reacting to the "putting down" by the dominant group (middle-class children and teachers) and being unwilling to engage in the "upwardly mobile" behavior involved in pleasing teachers (Sexton and Sexton 1971, p. 252), blue-collar youth are more likely to encounter problems in school. Those who do leave before graduating may find that they can earn almost as much as their fathers after only a few months on their first job.

It is not until they marry and have children that blue-collar youth begin to realize the dead-end character of most blue-collar jobs. By this time, however, they have already made decisions that limit the alternatives open to them. Ambition must be channeled toward the limited goals of advances in pay or of a more desirable job within the factory. A few may dream of "going into business" or of achieving more education or training, but the number who actually manage this is slight. The majority of non-college-goers, realizing the lack of opportunity for vocational and personal advancement in factory jobs, regret that they had not entered college (Trent and Medsker 1968).

Young girls likewise are likely to limit their adulthood ambitions to marriage and family goals. For many of them, marriage is the singularly acceptable means for escaping from an oppressive family situation and into a respected social status (Rubin 1976, p. 41; Komarovsky 1962, pp. 24–26). The alternatives — taking an unpleasant job or remaining in a dependent relationship within the family — are not cherished. For the girls, as well as for their brothers, there are few role models available of women who do interesting or rewarding work. Advice given at school and by teachers is likely to perpetuate the common ambitions. One woman recalls her high school experiences:

> I used to dream about wanting to be a teacher. . . . I actually
> was in college prep in high school, even though my counselor
> didn't think it was such a good idea because there was nobody to
> help me through college. . . .
>
> Then, when I was going into the twelfth grade, my father got
> sick and went to the hospital. My counselor told me then that she
> didn't think I would have the strength to go through with going
> to college all by myself. So she got me a scholarship, it wasn't
> much of a scholarship; it was to a beauty college instead of to a
> real college.[2]

While sons are expected to work at a young age (to help support the
family, to earn pin money, and to learn work habits), daughters are much
less likely to find outside jobs, in part because it is believed that their future revolves around marriage and domestic duties.

FAMILY ROLES

Blue-collar youth marry, then, at a relatively young age — to establish
their adult status, to escape from families, and to find happiness. But the
early years of marriage are quickly disillusioning. We have already seen
the figures on income for blue-collar workers. Except for the most skilled
workers, blue-collar incomes are barely sufficient to keep a family out of
poverty. Young men are often intermittently employed at low-paying jobs,
and supporting a wife and baby is difficult. The young women very soon
find themselves struggling with managing a family and household on a
limited income. Some of these young families find that they have to go
on welfare or return to living with their parental families.

Economic concerns often shape all other aspects of family life, intrud-
ing in particular on the relations between husband and wife. Although
blue-collar couples are more likely than couples in other strata to verbal-
ize an ideology of male superiority, the blue-collar man finds it more difficult than the white-collar man to demonstrate any superiority. For the
blue-collar worker, self-esteem is on the line every time he brings home a
paycheck that is inadequate to meet the bills or fails to bring home one
at all. The wife of an unemployed man revealed to Rubin:

> I couldn't understand how he couldn't get a job. I knew I could
> get a job any time I really wanted one, but I had to stay home
> with the baby. It seemed like he was just dumb or something that
> he couldn't find a good, steady job. And you know, no woman likes
> to think she's smarter than her husband. But I've got to admit,

[2] Excerpted from *Worlds of Pain: Life in the Working-Class Family,*
p. 44, by Lillian Breslow Rubin, © 1976 by Lillian Breslow Rubin, Basic
Books, Inc., Publishers, New York. Reprinted by permission.

I did, and he didn't like it one bit. Neither did I. [Twenty-nine-year-old cashier, mother of two, married nine years.] [3]

It is early in the marriage that the young couple works out its pattern of division of labor. In contrast to white-collar families, blue-collar families tend to have a patriarchal, adult-centered family structure in which sex roles are sharply separated. Traditional ideals are the norm. Men are expected to be the providers; women, the keepers of the home. Although these norms are often not realized (men have difficulty in providing; women often seek paid employment), their desirability is widely expressed. Roles within the home split accordingly along traditional lines even when the wife works.

A consequence of the sharp division of labor is that there tends to be greater isolation and distance between husband and wife than in middle-class families. First, there is a distinct separation in the sex roles considered appropriate to men and women and in the sex identities from which they derive their concepts of self. Second, there is a deemphasis of spouse companionship. It is not expected that husband and wife should share each other's company or pursue many common interests. If relatives and close friends are available, this presents fewer problems for the couple; in the case of the mobile pair, however, isolation and loneliness on the part of the wife and boredom on the part of the husband may be the result (Komarovsky 1962, p. 335). Third, there is a separation of social activities. The husband's friends are more likely to be other men; the wife's, other women. Entertaining other nonrelated couples at home is done far less frequently than in the middle class, over one-third never do (Komarovsky 1962, chap. 14).

The wives tend to be more or less excluded from the husband's world of work. In some families, the sharp separation of activities leads to a lack of communication between husband and wife (Komarovsky 1962, p. 155). When speaking of television to Komarovsky's interviewers, for example, typical comments were " 'We both see it, why talk about it,' and 'What's there to talk about other than to say it's good or bad.' In more general terms, one woman put it this way: 'We tell each other things, but I don't know as how we talk about them. He'll tell me or I'll tell him something has happened, but there ain't nothing much to say' " (Komarovsky 1962, pp. 155–57). In comparison, the middle-class family may experience more tension in marriage (from ambiguous definitions of rights and duties, ethical inconsistencies, mental conflict over too many choices, conflicting loyalties and standards, or strain from the sheer volume of stimuli), but they also are likely to experience greater happiness and more

[3] Excerpted from *Worlds of Pain: Life in the Working-Class Family*, p. 91, Lillian Breslow Rubin, © 1976 by Lillian Breslow Rubin, Basic Books, Inc., Publishers, New York. Reprinted by permission.

rewards from a momentary feeling of closeness, the excitement of hope, or a fleeting triumph of achievement.

In the middle years of blue-collar marriage, work is slightly steadier, wages are slightly higher, responsibilities seem slightly lighter. It is then that the blue-collar husband becomes more comfortable with his marriage — it is a place of refuge, a place to retreat from the pressures and annoyances of the day. For the wife, however, time works the other way. She increasingly becomes dissatisfied with the constraints of her existence and the unbroken schedule of work, with having no regular time off in which to develop her own interests and activities, no night out she can count on, and, perhaps most important, no way to defy her husband's authority and dicta about what she may or may not do with her life (Rubin 1976, pp. 95–96). Again and again, Rubin's female respondents spoke of the control wielded by husbands.

> I begin to worry what's going to happen to me after the kids are grown up. I don't want to be like my mother, just sort of hanging around being a professional mother and grandmother. So I thought I could go to school — you know, take a few courses or something, maybe even be a teacher eventually. But he says I can't and no matter how much I beg, he won't let me.[4]

The ideology of male dominance, which is particularly strong in the working class (Vanfossen 1977), is related in several ways to social stratification. First of all, it reflects the relationship of the family to blue-collar work. The wife's role is not integrated with the husband's. By contrast, in professional middle-class families, wives are expected to contribute to their husband's careers by cultivating an appropriate social circle and by being entertaining and charming hostesses and companions (Rubin 1976, p. 98; Papanek 1973). It is often considered helpful if they are active members of the community, interesting conversationalists, and even pursuers of their own careers (so long as it is not competitive with the husbands' careers). To be and do these things, wives must have some freedom of movement and autonomy. In the blue-collar stratum, however, the working man has no need of a wife with such accomplishments, because his work life is almost entirely within the confines of the home. He is under no pressure to encourage his wife's freedom of movement or her self-development; and she has no external supports to legitimate whatever longings she may feel (Rubin 1977, pp. 98–99).

The second way in which the structure of inequality encourages ex-

---

[4] Excerpted from *Worlds of Pain: Life in the Working-Class Family,* p. 96, by Lillian Breslow Rubin, © 1976 by Lillian Breslow Rubin, Basic Books, Inc., Publishers. Reprinted by permission.

plicit male dominance in the blue-collar family is in its denial to blue-collar men of alternative (economic) means of asserting their masculinity. In a society in which masculinity is often and powerfully equated with the dual expectations of economic success and superiority to women (David and Brannon 1976), blue-collar men may find that the most readily available expression of male superiority lies in being authoritarian in the home. Unlike the upper-middle-level professional, whose high income, prestigious occupation, and career advancement leave no question in his and his wife's eyes about his '"masculinity," the blue-collar worker faces the specter of perceived incompetence in the areas of income, status, and career. In the provider role, he is sometimes sadly deficient. Yet, he can still be king in his own home, and he tends to express and wield the ultimate power.

In both the upper-middle and the blue-collar segments of the stratification hierarchy, the power of the husband is affected by how much greater is his education, income, and occupational status than his wife's (Vanfossen 1977). In the professional and managerial classes, sex differentials in income-producing opportunities ensure that most husbands will have higher incomes and more prestigious occupations than their wives. But in the blue-collar class, the probability that the wife has as much education as her husband and can bring home just as big a paycheck is fairly high. Husbands are more likely, in these circumstances, to resort to verbal and physical demonstrations of their "superiority." A study of domestic violence, for example, found that husbands are more likely to use violence against their wives in those families in which the wife's income, education, and occupational statuses outstrip those of her husband (O'Brien 1971).

It is in large part the fear of loss of dominance, then, that prompts about one-third of blue-collar husbands to resent their wives' employment outside the home (Rubin 1976, p. 176). In spite of such sentiments, however, blue-collar wives have until the last decade been more likely to work for pay than wives in more affluent circumstances (Scanzoni and Scanzoni 1976, p. 228). The amount of money that they can bring home is less than that of more educated women (Scanzoni and Scanzoni 1976, p. 228), yet it is likely to be a larger proportion of the family income than the middle-class wife provides. Economic necessity prompts blue-collar wives to work outside the home, even though they may not wish to. The economic need influencing women in the blue-collar stratum to go to work, sometimes against their preferences, is related to the difficulty that they may face in providing satisfactory alternative child-care arrangements. Several studies have documented some small negative consequences on the marital relationships, on the self-esteem of the husband (Hoffman and Nye 1974), and on the emotional well-being of the wife (Pearlin 1975, p. 205) when the blue-collar wife with many young children must work in spite of her wishes not to do so. The same consequences are not observed for working middle-class wives, presumably because their economic situation allows them to provide more satisfactorily for child-care and domestic help, and they thus are less susceptible to the anxieties of "role overload."

At the lower-income levels, we find in these many ways that social inequality impinges strongly and pervasively on the nature of family life and on the mental worlds of family members. Society values success and accomplishment, however these might be measured, and yet the income structure is such that a large proportion of the population cannot achieve the symbols of success. Males are taught to esteem themselves in terms of how well they can provide for their families, but only small numbers of them are allowed to carry home much in the way of socially valued rewards. By their lessened respect for their husbands or fathers, women and children sometimes show that they, too, subscribe to the success values propagated in the dominant culture.

LEISURE AND SOCIABILITY

Some relief is found in the comfort of the primary group. The blue-collar family rivals the upper-class family in the importance of relatives. Unlike the middle-class family, which is more inclined to move away from parents and community of origin, grown blue-collar children maintain much closer ties with their parents — seeking their advice and companionship, visiting with them regularly, and using them as friends. The world is seen through the perspective of the family circle and viewed as beneficent or hostile in relation to its effect on the family. The family provides emotional support, security, and mutual aid in a society that frequently appears menacing and exploitative. Cynicism and distrust toward outsiders and toward authority systems over which the blue-collar worker has little control are psychologically countered by reliance on and trust in one's parents or siblings. Work, too, is viewed in terms of its relationship to the family; it becomes a means for keeping out of poverty and for providing pleasures for the family rather than an activity to be valued for its intrinsic rewards.

Couples visit with their families often, maybe several times a week, informally and without ceremony. Neighboring is also an important activity. The sociability of the neighborhood does not depend on the entertaining and party giving so characteristic of the middle class, but is more likely to be drop-in visits during the day among the women or routinized gatherings of family members and friends that take place several times a week (Gans 1962).

Blue-collar people are less likely than the middle classes to join voluntary associations. Aside from their membership in the labor unions, which include over half of blue-collar workers,[5] and in the churches,[6] most are very inactive in community organizations. Over two-thirds belong to no associations at all (compared to slightly less than half of the professionals and managers) (Hausknecht 1962, p. 25; Berger 1960, p. 59).

In leisure activities, blue-collarites, although somewhat similar to the other classes in their preferences, place slightly greater emphasis on home workshop and repair activities and much greater emphasis on visiting with relatives, fishing, hunting, observing sports, and picnicking (Shostak 1968, p. 188). Rubin reports that in her sample of blue-collar families on a typical weekday the family gathers together early for the evening meal; then the wife does the dishes while the husband watches television or takes up a do-it-yourself project (Rubin 1976, pp. 185–86). Such projects often provide strong satisfactions for people whose jobs disallow imagination or creativity.

Television watching is a major activity, for an average of sixteen hours per week is spent in front of the set (Komarovsky 1962, p. 324). For many blue-collar workers, television is important for its escape value; it serves to "block out life's painful realities and to drain off the tensions [life] produces" (Rubin 1976, p. 191). In reading matter, blue-collar people prefer newspapers that stress sports and human interest stories, home workshop and car repair magazines, exposé publications, and magazines such as *TV Guide* and *Reader's Digest*. The automobile — its purchase, repair, and upkeep — provides much pleasure and consumes considerable time and attention. Spectator sports such as football, wrestling, and baseball are popular, as well as participant sports such as bowling, boating, and poker.

Weekends provide time for shopping expeditions, which involve the whole family and take on the air of an outing, for sporting events on television, and for Sunday visits with the parents. While over one-fourth of Rubin's sample owned campers and/or boats, in reality there is relatively little time to use them. Frequently, Rubin (1976, p. 199) reports, to meet the payments for the campers or boats the men must work overtime, using up the leisure hours in which camping or boating might be engaged in. Most families do take vacation time, but they usually are unable to afford the kind of travel they dream about — to Disneyland, the Grand Canyon, Yellowstone or Glacier national parks — places and scenes within the United States.

[5] Membership in the union is high, but participation is low. Attendance at average union meetings usually varies from 2 to 6 percent of the membership (Sayles and Strauss 1953, p. 173).

[6] Although over 90 percent of the blue-collar families claim some church affiliation (Catholic, Baptist, Lutheran, Mormon), over half never attend or attend church only rarely. Baptists are the most frequent church attenders, closely followed by Catholics. See Berger 1960, chap. 4.

POLITICAL ORIENTATIONS

In political behavior, blue-collarites vote predominantly Democratic, when they vote. Ordinarily, between one-half and two-thirds of those who go to the polls select the Democratic platform (compared to one-third to one-half of the white-collarites, professionals, and business executives). However, many — perhaps one-third — do not vote at all. Political apathy is related to *anomie*, a feeling of political powerlessness, a belief that one's vote is ineffective, a belief that community leaders are indifferent to the needs of individuals. Blue-collar men and women are expressing their discouragement when they tell the pollster that the lot of the average man is getting worse and that others cannot be trusted (Meier and Bell 1959; Srole 1956; McDill 1961; Roberts and Rokeach 1956). Their stronger sense of alienation and anomie is related to their lack of access to means for the achievement of life goals. As Cook puts it, "What has been called 'political apathy' is in fact a realistic appraisal of the situation in the absence of a credible political movement for change" (1973, p. 455).

Blue-collarites in their voting patterns tend to be liberal on economic issues (such as the role of government in the economy or the value of labor unions), but negative toward civil liberties, foreign aid, racial integration, and political improvements for minorities. Many blue-collar political views are directly related to the life and problems of the laborer. Resentment against the attempts of blacks to enter skilled trades, for example, is based on a fear of the economic competition that this would bring about, while resistance to integration in housing is related to status competition (Gans 1967, pp. 373, 382; Bressler 1960, p. 33).

However, a question that has been the subject of much debate is, Is the working class "authoritarian"? Social scientists have not always been sympathetic to the "working class." In the 1940s and 1950s, essays and research began to appear in the journals, reporting that the typical blue-collar worker has "minimal social skills," an "impoverished quality of life," an "uncertain quality of mental reasoning," an "inability to take a complex view," an "underdeveloped abstraction," and a morality which is "dogmatic, absolutist, authoritarian, stereotyped, and punitive." Is this an accurate picture? Let us examine the issues.

The concept of the "authoritarian personality" was created by T. W. Adorno and his colleagues in 1950 to explain anti-Semitism. According to the concept, authoritarian persons are rigid, intolerant, suspicious, and punitive. They see the world in black-and-white terms, they are disgusted at deviants, they admire strength and toughness, and, if male, they are unsure of their own sexual potencies. Such attitudes are considered to be in large part a product of early childhood experiences, particularly of a childhood characterized by punishment, lack of love, and an atmosphere of tension and aggression.

341

The concept of the "authoritarian personality" originally was used to explain middle-class support for fascism (Lipsitz 1965). With the publication of Lipset's *Political Man* (1960), however, the concept was broadened to cover the working-class individual, who was thought to be less tolerant of racial, religious, and political minorities and less likely to support democratic rules of procedure. Lipset argued that the intolerance of the working class comes from "low education, low participation in political organizations or voluntary organizations of any type, little reading, isolated occupations, economic insecurity, and authoritarian family patterns" (1959, p. 489). The personality syndromes of working-class people, he suggested, typically are characterized by "greater suggestibility, absences of a sense of past and future, . . . inability to take a complex view, greater difficulty in abstracting from concrete experience, and lack of imagination" (1960, p. 108). They involve a characteristic distrust of strangers, feelings of hostility toward the outside world (Gans 1962, chap. 6), paranoia concerning external events (Rainwater et al. 1959, pp. 44–45), and isolation from middle-class culture.

The ensuing research reports seemed to indicate that lower-status people are indeed more "authoritarian," less supportive of civil liberties, and more prejudiced toward minority groups than those of higher status (MacKinnon and Centers 1956; Stouffer 1955; Cohen and Hodges 1963; Prothro and Grigg 1960; Hodge and Treiman 1966; Glenn and Alston 1968; Sears 1969). Given the apparent broad base of empirical support for the thesis, it is not surprising, as Hamilton (1972, p. 40) points out, that these views were widely accepted by the upper-middle-class intelligentsia. (Not so explicitly stated, but important nevertheless, was the inverse idea that it is the occupants of the upper-middle classes who are the "tolerant" ones, those who are willing to protect minority rights and are "fair" in their political attitudes. See Lipset 1964, p. 33; Lipset 1960, p. 101.)

But not all studies substantiated the Lipset thesis (see Farris 1956; Kornhauser et al. 1956; Lipsitz 1965; Janowitz and Marvick 1953, for example). For one thing, considerable research cast doubt on the validity of the fascism scale and other scales in identifying anything other than the products of education and a tendency to agree with questionnaire items.[7] Interviewers began to report that their respondents were not like the "inarticulate, simple-minded, asocial, sexually repressed, family-centered, authoritarian stereotype" (Rubin 1974, p. 316).

Other research indicated that the political and social attitudes of the

---

[7] Lipsitz 1965; Miller and Riessman 1961b; McDill 1961; Photiadis and Biggar 1962. The original study of acquiescence sets was Bass 1955. For critiques of the authoritarianism thesis, see Christie and Jahoda 1954; Simpson and Yinger 1972; Brown 1965; and Kirscht and Dillehay 1967.

blue-collar class seem to be more complex than they were originally assumed to be. Thus, for example, although a 1964 sample showed that blue-collar workers were more opposed to friendly dealings with communist nations than were white-collar workers, it also found that the blue collarites were more willing to withdraw immediately from Vietnam and to support a compromise agreement to end the war (Patchen 1970). The "tough," more aggressive attitude about the war was taken by the educated, upper- and middle-class Protestants. On race-related questions, Hamilton found evidence that working-class intolerance on civil rights issues is due not to class background but to religious and regional background (with Protestants and southerners being the least tolerant). "Were we to take the non-South white Protestant majority and exclude the Southern-reared segment, it is clear that the relationship shown . . . would be shifted in the direction of greater working-class tolerance" (Hamilton 1972, p. 408).

Even more surprising is Campbell's report (1971, pp. 49–53), from a polling of nearly three thousand whites in 1967, that a multitude of questions about attitudes on a variety of race-related issues uncover no significant differences among seven occupational groups (except for the clerical workers, who are clearly more positive in their attitudes toward race). Education, however, *is* related to attitudes, in that the small proportion of people who went to college after World War II are considerably more prone to give "tolerant" responses about racial issues than those who did not (Campbell 1971, pp. 54–67).

Finally, an examination of behavior does not always show that there is greater tolerance, flexibility, and democratic orientation among upper-middle and upper-class individuals than among those of the working class. It is the more affluent in particular who resist the movement of blacks into the suburbs, who keep Jews and blacks out of higher management positions in the nation's supercorporations, and who use "democratic procedures" to pass mortgage and tax laws benefiting the middle and upper classes. There is, in addition, some evidence that the better educated are happier with the status quo than the less educated and thus resist change more readily (De Fronzo 1973, p. 299).

The answer to our question about authoritarianism is by no means clear. It is perhaps illuminating, however, to look at the working class in a more sympathetic light — in terms of how *they* see the world and how their perceptions might affect their response to surveys and fascism scales. Along this line, Ransford (1972) notes the anger expressed by many working-class respondents in 1969 and 1970 toward the black and student movements. In fact, they were more likely than those higher in the occupational hierarchies to express punitive attitudes toward student demonstrators, to oppose granting students more power, and to feel that blacks were pushing too hard for things they do not deserve. However,

343

Ransford found several intervening variables that partly explain the anger. These are respect for authority (arising from occupational requirements, perhaps, as we saw in Chapter 8), belief in the American dream, resentment over neglect of the working class's needs, and feelings of powerlessness. The fact that these variables influence attitudes suggests that blue-collar anger, rather than being the effect of a prejudiced personality, is a rational response to tangible strains. Ransford notes: "A lack of decision-making power on the job, the fact of hard earned dollars going for tax programs to aid blacks with no comparable programs for working-class whites, a power structure unresponsive to the needs of the workingman — these stresses probably affect working class anger as much as personal prejudice" (1972, p. 345).

A similar analysis is provided by Sexton and Sexton, who present the "grievances" of the blue-collar class: (1) the fact that the blue-collar class bears more than its share of the burden of inflation and rising taxes; (2) the difficulty involved in sending children to college; (3) the disproportionate number of blue-collar youth who die in battle; (4) the unfairness of placing the responsibility for racial integration in housing and schooling on the blue-collar family; (5) the intolerance of blaming policemen for the nation's laws; (6) the inequities revealed when privileged college students can disrupt universities and live useless life styles, while blue-collar youth cannot even get into the universities; (7) the unfairness of the sympathy that the affluent feel for the poor and those on welfare when it is the blue-collar class that does the work and pays the taxes; (8) the class inequalities revealed in medical care, housing, employment practices, education, pollution, parks, cities, and war (1971, chap. 3). Blue-collarites may be more distrustful and suspicious, but their reality would indicate that the outer world is not always so benevolent. They may be passive and conformist, but this is what they have to be to keep their jobs. They may be less sophisticated and polished in their social skills, but so also are they more honest and unpretentious. They revolt less against materialism because they are still struggling for the basic necessities. They are against change, if it is the kind that benefits others and hurts them. The Sextons conclude:

> The image of blue-collar workers as racist and conservative is a gross stereotype. The worker who thinks that dissenters should be shot or deprived of civil liberties exists, but he is not typical. The same variety of bigoted and reactionary responses is prevalent in other groups. The worker has been maligned, assaulted, ignored. . . . Aside from economic issues, perhaps nothing grieves the worker so much as the contempt universally displayed in our society for his culture. His anguish is intensified by the fact that he has no articulate defenders or champions (1971, p. 259).

344

Summary

It is in the lower-middle and blue-collar strata that the personally negative consequences of inequality for men and women begin to show up. As a man's income, occupational prestige, and autonomy drop, so too do his self-esteem, sense of control over fate, and marital harmony. He attempts to compensate — for low income by working longer and harder, for lesser prestige by becoming authoritarian in the home, for political impotence by political withdrawal. Women in these circumstances also overwork, often adding the labor of outside employment to the labor of managing a large household. They may blame their husbands for the economic hardship. They, too, experience low self-esteem and often see life as hard and drab.

Children are brought up to be obedient and respectful of their elders, and parents attempt to protect their children from the harsh realities of life by imposing strict discipline. While rebellion is the response mode adopted by some of the children, many more develop into pliable and docile workers as adults. Childhood socialization often does not encourage children to plan for college, and, getting into a pattern of working at an early age to help support the family, they are less likely than middle-class youth to pursue higher education. Early marriage and early childbearing exacerbate the ensuing economic problems.

Only dimly — if at all — aware of the role that occupational markets and income structures play in their own personal troubles, blue-collar workers are likely to blame themselves for their lack of success and their continuing material need. Other groups and classes benefit from the workers' acquiescence in performing the physical labor of the economy in return for low wages. So long as workers subscribe to the American dream and believe that their own personal inadequacies are responsible for their dilemmas, they pose no power threat to the elite or to the more affluent upper-middle class. They continue attempting to cope within the confines of their family and neighborhood.

11 CONSEQUENCES OF INEQUALITY: THE UNDERPRIVILEGED CLASS

THE CONSEQUENCES OF INEQUALITY are most dramatically revealed when we compare the fates of the very wealthy and the very poor. Two incidents concerning dogs that the newspapers reported inadvertently did just that. In one, Lady Beaverbrook wished to transport her dog by plane from London to Halifax. Miffed by the regulation of the commercial airlines that dogs must ride in the baggage compartment, the lady hired a jet plane for $17,000 to carry herself, her sister, and two small dogs across the Atlantic (*Toronto Globe and Mail* 1976). In the other incident, Ms. Bashold, a welfare recipient who had just given birth to a baby conceived during a rape, left her baby in her unfurnished apartment to retrieve the money she had left behind at the hospital. When she returned, she discovered that her German Shepherd dog, which had had no food for several days, had eaten the baby (*New York Times,* September 7, 1976, p. 66; October 8, 1976, p. 5; October 15, 1976, p. 26). Charges of negligent homicide against Ms. Bashold were eventually dropped.

Such incidents remind us that the poverty of a Ms. Bashold can coexist quite easily unnoticed with wealth of the kind possessed by Lady Beaverbrook. Obviously, the presence of great wealth in a society does not ensure that all members of that society will make a living. Periodically, journalists or humanitarian interests rediscover the coincidence of affluence and poverty. In the 1960s, for example, as the gross national product passed the $800-billion mark in the United States, when employment incomes were high and agricultural production so healthy that soil banks were used to control the surpluses, public attention turned to the fact that large numbers of people — some 36 million — still lived in poverty conditions (see, for example, Harrington 1962; Bagdikian 1964; and Conant 1961).

Some of the cases uncovered were dramatic. To check out the health conditions in rural South Carolina, for example, Senator Hollings and a medical party in 1970 toured Beaufort and Jasper counties. They discovered rickets, pellagra, scurvy, rotting teeth, sores, infection, and scarlet fever among the people. It was found that two-thirds of the children had parasites in the digestive tract, and some regularly vomited up or defecated foot-long roundworms (*New York Times,* April 1, 1977, p. 12). A nationwide wave of publicity resulted in action of sorts. Although Senator Rivers of South Carolina said that he was against anything remedial because he had "no intention of immortalizing poverty or dishing out food stamps," the federal government nevertheless responded by setting up health agencies in Jasper and Beaufort counties. These agencies not only treated diseases, but also attempted preventive care by installing plumbing facilities in homes so that children would not ingest worm eggs, by screening houses to cut down on the transmission of scarlet fever by flies, by altering diet to counteract rickets and scurvy, and by weatherproofing houses to prevent pneumonia. One hundred ninety septic tanks were built; 72 cluster wells were drilled; 257 houses were repaired. Eventually, however, the political climate in Washington shifted, funds for poverty health care were cut, and now federal money supports only treatment of the most serious diseases, not their prevention. At the same time, the existence of the wealthy resort island, Hilton Head, immediately off the coast has done little to elevate the per capita income of Jasper County, which recently dropped from $2,000 to $1,500 when a small furniture plant moved out of the area.

Such incidents and news reports raise the question, Why are there so many on welfare, unemployed, and destitute in a society that has so much abundance? Some conclude that those at the bottom of the income heap are there because they are lazy and unambitious; they are getting a free ride on welfare, supported by the tax dollars of people who are hardworking and industrious. Others, in an extension of the "noble savage" concept, counter that it is the rich, acting in their self-interests, who oppress the poor. Some point out that the poor in the United States are

347

well-off compared to the starving poor of India or Africa. Yet, the fact that there is a substantial segment of people who live on less than $5,500 a year in a society that annually spends billions of dollars on cigarettes, movies, and war is disturbing to others. Consider, for example, the value position taken by Galbraith:

> Poverty — grim, degrading, and ineluctable — is not remarkable in India. For a few the fate is otherwise. But in the United States the survival of poverty is remarkable. We ignore it because we share with all societies at all times the capacity for not seeing what we do not wish to see. Anciently this has enabled the nobleman to enjoy his dinner while remaining oblivious to the beggars around his door. In our own day it enables us to travel in comfort through south Chicago and the South. But while our failure to notice can be explained, it cannot be excused. "Poverty," Pitt exclaimed, "is not a disgrace but it is damned annoying." In the contemporary United States it is not annoying but it is a disgrace (1958, p. 258).

In an industrial age, it is the contradiction and challenge that poverty poses for the affluent society that makes it a particularly absorbing subject to study. In this chapter, we are concerned with the causes of poverty, the processes by which individuals become poor, and the consequences when they do. We approach the assessment of the competing theories about poverty by first gaining a knowledge of the basic facts.

Extent of Poverty in America

Because common ideas about poverty are so stereotyped, the first step in developing an understanding is the determination of exactly how many people and what kinds are poor. Most estimates of the size of the American poverty class range between 10 and 25 percent of the population (Roach 1961, p. 69; Sneden 1970, p. 6), the differences among them depending on exactly where the line between poor and nonpoor is drawn. The most recent definition of poverty used by the Bureau of the Census assumes that families with incomes below the poverty threshold cannot be expected to eat even the minimal diet necessary to provide adequate nutrition and still have enough left over to pay for all other living essentials (Orshansky 1964, p. 4). (The census definition reflects the different food consumption requirements of families based on their size, number of children, sex and age of the family head, and farm-nonfarm residence. The poverty thresholds are updated every year to reflect changes in the consumer price index. Thus, an urban family of four was considered to be in poverty in 1975 if its income was below $5,500. This income figure represents the upper extreme; the median income of those classified as poor is usually about half.) According to the census bureau's

definition, the number of people living in poverty in the United States in
1975 was 25.9 million, or one-eighth of the total population (U.S. Bureau
of the Census 1976). This represented a decline from the 1959 figure of
39 million, a decrease from about 22 percent to 12 percent of the total
population.

Some subgroups within the poverty class have been more successful in
leaving it than others (see Figure 11.1). Whites, rural residents, and
families headed by males of working age have found it easier to flee from
poverty. But families headed by females, unsupported mothers, black
families, and old people have been less successful in escaping being poor.
They now constitute the hard core of the poverty class. A family that
combines two or more of these characteristics is particularly liable to
economic hardship.

According to estimates put out by the Twentieth Century Fund, the
United States is sufficiently affluent to do away with poverty at the budget-
ary level of "minimum subsistence," though not to make every family
"minimally comfortable" (Ornati 1966). In 1971, using the census bureau's definition of poverty, a total investment of $9.6 billion would have
been sufficient to raise the incomes of all families and individuals to the
poverty threshold level (U.S. Bureau of the Census 1971, Table 38). Yet,

Figure 11.1

*Persons below the poverty level by sex and race of head of
household, 1959–1968*

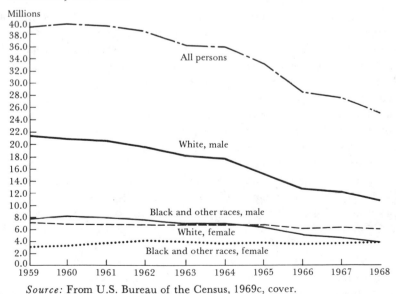

Source: From U.S. Bureau of the Census, 1969c, cover.

in spite of this, the low-income classes have benefited in only a token way from the general improvement in American life styles; some, being almost entirely outside the economy, have not benefited at all.

The Kinds of People Living in Poverty

Further analysis of the census data show that stereotypes about the poor ignore the diversity of people within the category. Although the composition of this one-eighth of the society is patterned, it is heterogeneous. Poverty is found among white urban slum residents, ghetto blacks, rural migrant workers, southern Appalachian farmers, tenant farmers, American Indians, and the disabled. It is not evenly distributed among the population, but tends, as we have seen, to be concentrated among certain especially vulnerable groups. Two-thirds of the low-income population in 1974 were black, Spanish in origin, or elderly or lived in families headed by women.

The census data also belie the popular stereotype that poor people are predominantly people who are too lazy to work or who do not want steady work. There are several problems with this idea. First of all, some poor families do receive part or all of their income from earnings (Carcagno and Corson 1977). The heads of 35 percent of poor families in 1978 worked part- or full-time.

Second, many poor people are incapable of working or they are not expected by society to work. Of the 24.3 million persons living below the poverty line in 1974, 8 million were under fourteen years of age and thus were too young to work (U.S. Bureau of the Census 1975). Of the remaining 16 million, around 15.4 million were (1) already working, but earned too little to bring them above the poverty level; (2) married to such men; (3) disabled; (4) obliged to stay home because of very small children; (5) too old to work; or (6) still going to school. That left only 624,000 adults (or only about 2.6 percent of all poor people) who could partcipate more fully in the job market. Of these, many were looking for work, but were hampered by a lack of skills and qualifications. For most male workers in the poverty class it is not current joblessness that is the cause of poverty, but rater an erratic series of short-term jobs or a spell of uninterrupted employment at low pay, coupled with a large number of people to be supported out of the family income (Orshansky 1965, p. 21). Indeed, several recent studies have found that the commitment to work is as strong among the unemployed and the poor as it is among the middle and working classes (Goodwin 1972; Kaplan and Tausky 1972).

The occupations of people who are poor are predominantly semiskilled and unskilled labor, service work, and farm labor (Hollingshead and Redlich 1958). Their jobs demand little skill and offer low pay, often in nonunionized industries, and may require strenuous physical exertion.

350

Many are so seasonal or cyclical that they involve long periods of unemployment or underemployment. In fact, underemployment may be the more critical source of poverty. In low-income neighborhoods, the "subemployment" rate is two and one-half times greater than the unemployment rate (National Advisory Commission on Civil Disorders 1968, p. 257). The unskilled workers' employment is tenuous, as they are often the last to be hired and the first to be fired in periods of economic recession. Some economists write of a dual labor market composed of a "primary" market, which offers high wages, good working conditions, job security, and chances for advancement, and of a "secondary" market, which offers low wages, poor working conditions, harsh discipline, and little opportunity to advance (Piore 1971; Doeringer and Piore 1971; Gordon 1972, chap. 4). The poor, particularly the urban poor, are confined to the latter.

Educational levels are low. Most unskilled workers left school at an early age, often before finishing the eighth grade. Those who are male enter the work market at dead-end jobs such as car washers, stock boys, janitors, messenger boys, lumbermen, or whatever they can get. Advancement in pay or prestige is minimal throughout the life of a poor worker. Most of the women who work become semiskilled factory workers or unskilled laborers such as cleaning women. Wages for both sexes start low and remain at about the same level. Because of high rates of unemployment and illness, there are periods of "hard times," during which income occasionally has to be supplemented by unemployment compensation, state aid, and welfare. Saving is difficult and small in amount when it does occur. Money for the necessities of life is an ever present problem and often is consumed more rapidly than it is earned, leading to a perpetual state of debt.

Poor families are likely to be large families. Although the birth rate of poor families is declining, it still is higher than that for the middle classes. This is not because poor people desire larger families; to the contrary, several studies have found that low-income parents ideally want fewer children than do middle-income parents (Jaffe 1964). The greater excess of unwanted children among poor people is in part due to the earlier age of marriage of unskilled workers and in part due to lack of availability of and ignorance about contraceptive methods. (For instance, according to a 1967 Gallup poll, only 39 percent of the people with no more than a grade school education believed that birth control pills are effective, compared to 77 percent of those who finished college). Many low-income adults would appreciate and utilize birth control techniques if they knew about them and had ready access to them. The "brood sow" myth — the idea that welfare mothers want to become pregnant in order to receive larger welfare payments — which is widely subscribed to by key policy makers in welfare economics (Placek and Hendershot 1974,

351

pp. 658–60) as well as by the general public, does not stand up to empirical investigation. One study of 300 welfare mothers found that additional pregnancies were in fact undesired and that the women were *more* likely to use contraceptive devices than women not on welfare (Placek and Hendershot 1974).

Poor families are somewhat likely to be broken families. While the majority have both parents present, a sizable 45 percent consist of a mother and her children (U.S. Bureau of the Census 1975b). Most of these families are headed by a mother who is divorced or widowed (Ross and Sawhill 1975). This indicates not that poor families fall apart, but rather that female-headed families become poor. Women who attempt to support a family face many handicaps: difficulty in caring for small children while working full-time, lower incomes, and discrimination against women in hiring and wage levels. Women are more likely than men to be poor for two reasons (Rytina and Huber 1974). First, full-time female workers earn only about 58 percent of what full-time male workers earn. Second, women are often obliged to support children if the father is dead or absent. One-parent families headed by a male are rare. Black women, in particular, are likely to have a rough time supporting a family. They typically can command only four-fifths the income of white women, who themselves receive less than three-fifths the income of white men for full-time work (U.S. Bureau of the Census 1972a, Table 44).

When they are aged, people are more likely to be poor (U.S. Bureau of the Census 1969c, Table B). Although some elderly persons in American society are able to live on savings, most of the aged depend on social security, public assistance, or other transfer payments. A large proportion of them have very limited resources to fall back on in case of emergency; about 30 percent have no liquid assets whatever, and another 20 percent have less than $1,000 (H. P. Miller 1964, p. 87). Most of the assets are tied up in their homes or in life insurance.

The disability of these characteristics is compounded if the individual is a member of a minority group. (Eight percent of whites were classified as poor in 1973, compared to 31 percent of nonwhites.) Blacks are the obviously disadvantaged minority group, but other segments — Mexican American farm laborers, Puerto Ricans in the cities, and American Indians — also have substantial numbers of poor persons. People are inclined to believe that the greater prevalence of poverty among these groups is due to their lower levels of education and training, yet careful study shows that far more important is institutionalized discrimination. Upgrading the employment of blacks to make their occupational distribution identical with that of the labor force as a whole would have a tremendous impact on their socioeconomic status (National Advisory Commission on Civil Disorders 1968, p. 254). Increased education is not the answer. When a black man gets more formal schooling, his income and employment chances advance far less than is true for a white man who has become similarly educated (Harrison 1971, p. 190). Many educated blacks have low incomes because they are concentrated in the lowest-skilled and lowest-paying occupations.

These statistics, brief as they are, offer some clues to the sources of poverty in an affluent society. The basic one inheres in the fact that in a highly interdependent property-based capitalist economy, a person who does not receive sufficient money income from participation in the division of labor cannot secure essential material resources (unless they are provided by governmental programs or charity). But the division of labor itself does not provide a place for everyone. Children, the aged, female heads of households — these people are excluded from wage-producing activities.

In addition, the changing structure of employment and educational demands has prevented unskilled and semiskilled workers whose trades or muscles have become obsolete from advancing in affluence along with the rest of society. As the nature of work has become more highly industrialized, the need for unskilled labor has been sharply curtailed by mechanization and automation. For example, the switch from manual labor to machine labor in the cotton industry of the South resulted in the economic displacement of millions of southern blacks and rural whites. Across the nation, the transformation from small-scale farming to large, complex agricultural enterprises dislocated many marginal farmers, who migrated to the cities only to find that their lack of training made them singularly unequipped for urban employment. Old skills become outdated, resulting in unemployment of many workers. Changing economic needs are a basic source of much poverty within the context of a property-based capitalist economy, wherein those who are unable to work or are prevented from working cannot make a living.

Consequences of Poverty

In comparison to the American middle class, the American poor have to deal with lower incomes, inadequate diets, lower levels of physical and mental health, shorter life expectancies, higher birth rates, and economic problems associated with consumption. The consequences invade every aspect of living. Take the more obvious example of economic problems. The low wages, subemployment, and unemployment of people who are poor characteristically lead to an absence of savings and a shortage of cash. This results in such economic adaptations as borrowing at high rates of interest, establishing informal credit devices requiring no interest among neighbors, and purchasing secondhand clothing and furniture. In a study of the consumption patterns of low-income families in New York City, for example, the following conclusions were reached: Some 80 per-

353

cent of the families used credit to buy durables; over 60 percent had outstanding consumer debts, but only 27 percent had at least $100 in savings; 20 percent had experienced legal pressures because of missed payments; shopping was confined to the immediate neighborhood; and the prices paid for appliances were higher than average, though the merchandise was shoddier (Caplovitz 1964).

Many of these actions represent the only ways in which people with limited incomes can purchase commodities. Consider the retail prices paid for food and other staples by residents of low-income urban neighborhoods, for example. These are often higher because poor people lack the transportation necessary to shop in the larger chain stores rather than in small local stores (U.S. Bureau of Labor Statistics 1966). When they run out of money, they are forced into accepting high-interest loans because banks are not interested in giving out low-interest loans to people who are poor. In many ways the economic behavior of people in poverty results from that poverty.

Consequences are also apparent if we look at housing conditions. The living quarters of the poverty class are typically more deteriorated than the dwellings of the nonpoor (Coward et al. 1974). In the city, they may be apartments in tenement buildings in poor repair that were built sixty to eighty years previously and house ten to fifty families. Sanitation is a problem, for there may be only two toilets in a twenty-family dwelling (Hollingshead and Redlich 1958, p. 120), roaches and rats are common (Bernton 1965, pp. 122–24), and diseases are quickly communicated. In rural areas, single-family dwellings are often constructed of salvaged materials — combinations of clapboard, tarpaper, used brick, and cement blocks. Privies or septic tanks provide the sewage. According to data collected by the U.S. Census Bureau in the 1956 housing inventory, between 40 and 60 percent of the dwellings occupied by families with incomes below $2,000 were seriously unsound and substandard; just over half had plumbing facilities.

Consequences show up in the realms of physical and mental health. Poor people get sick more often than the nonpoor, their illnesses are more likely to be chronic, and they are more likely to have a multiplicity of chronic illnesses (Richardson 1964; U.S. National Health Survey 1964). They are less likely to seek out the care of physicians and hospitals, and while in the hospitals they receive poorer care (Bergner and Yerby 1968; Bierman 1961; Linden 1967). They die at an earlier age (Antonovsky 1972; English 1968; Mechanic 1968, Table 7.2). Dental care is underutilized; more than two-thirds of the children of low-income families have never been to a dentist (Bergner and Yerby 1968; Porter 1968; Bierman 1961). Forty percent of the poor have serious medical problems because of malnutrition (Wiley 1971, p. 2077).

Poor people are less likely to say they "are happy" (Bradburn and

Caplovitz 1965; Gurin et al. 1960) and to think well of themselves
(Kohn and Schooler 1969). They are more likely to suffer from "psy-
choses" than are the more affluent strata,[1] and when they do, they are
more likely to be treated at a public, rather than a private, hospital or
to receive no treatment at all (Hollingshead and Redlich 1953, p. 169;
1958). What treatment they do receive is more likely to consist of organic therapies — such as shock therapy, lobotomies, or drug treatment
— than the individualized psychiatric therapy that more affluent patients
receive. Lack of income not only deprives the poor of luxuries; it strikes
at the core of their physical and emotional well-being.

The list of consequences could continue. Schools in low-income areas
tend to be of lowest quality; highways constructed through such areas
impose heavy relocation costs on the residents; the welfare system discourages self-improvement by its nearly 100-percent de facto tax on
earned income; poor neighborhoods tend to receive the lowest quality of
such city services as garbage collection and police protection; legal practices penalize low-income residents through discriminatory police, bail,
and incarceration practices (Downs 1970). The list could go on, but, at
this point, documentation of the consequences becomes less interesting
than the consideration of why poverty exists.

Theories of Poverty

Who is to blame for the fact that in the richest country in the world
one-eighth of the population has too few resources to take care of even
basic physical needs? The poor themselves or the affluent power elite? Indeed, is anyone? Perhaps it is inevitable. Among sociologists, three points
of view have developed to explain poverty: "culture of poverty" theories,
"situational" theories, and "structural" theories. The policy implications
of the three are widely divergent. The first suggests that the poor must
change their values before they can survive. The second suggests training
programs and better employment opportunities. The third suggests redistribution of wealth. Let us examine them in detail.

THE CULTURE OF POVERTY THEORY

Some writers assert that poor people grow up in a culture of poverty
— a subculture transmitted from generation to generation, which softens
the struggle for existence and respect, but which also perpetuates self-

[1] Hollingshead and Redlich 1958, p. 230. Hollingshead and Redlich's
findings are given added support by the Midtown Manhattan studies
(covering a representative sample of a total population), which found that
"probable psychotic types" are overrepresented among low-status groups
while "probable neurotic types" are overrepresented among high-status
groups. See Langner and Michael 1963, p. 154; Brenner et al. 1967, pp.
311–84; and Dunham 1964.

defeating behavior patterns. Poverty is caused by the subculture; and before poverty can be eliminated, the values and behavior patterns of the poor must be changed.

An early version of the thesis was advanced by Allison Davis (1946), who claimed that the lower classes have fewer deferred gratification patterns than the middle classes:

> The habits of "shiftlessness," "irresponsibility," lack of "ambition," "absenteeism," and of quitting the job, which management usually regards as a result of the "innate" perversity of underprivileged white and Negro workers, are in fact *normal responses* that the worker has learned from his physical and social environment. These habits constitute a system of behavior and attitudes which are realistic and rational in *that environment* in which the individual of the slums has lived and in which he has been trained (p. 86).

Later, in the 1950s, some hypothesized that juvenile delinquency emerges out of a delinquent subculture that repudiates legitimate channels of success in the face of inability to utilize them (A. Cohen 1955; W. B. Miller 1958). But it was in the 1960s that the theory became widely publicized, particularly by the writings of Oscar Lewis (1966). Lewis proposed that a culture of poverty crosscuts societies and constitutes a worldwide life style of poverty, emphasizing apathy, failure, discontent, and anguish. This viewpoint was picked up by Michael Harrington (1962) and Thomas Gladwin (1967) in their popular paperbacks. The idea was that the culture of poverty originates in the economic circumstances of the poor, but it is transmitted from generation to generation through socialization. Although it moderates the harshness of the struggle for existence, it creates a "design for living" that perpetuates self-defeating habits and orientations. Children learn values, attitudes, and behavior patterns that ensure their adult position in the unskilled group. Particularly important is the emphasis on the present, which prevents the poor from taking those actions which would be beneficial in the long run. Adolescents drop out of high school before graduating, even when they possess the intellectual capabilities to graduate. Young boys, because they grow up in a female-based household, have little contact with male role models emphasizing responsible work motivations and habits. In addition, the peer group of the street corner society reinforces antieducation and antiwork values. Residential segregation of the poor, in combination with limited horizons of perception, isolates the lowest-income groups from the norms and expectations of the general population. Lack of motivation, hope, and incentive militates against upward mobility.

The culture of poverty explanation itself was most prominently advanced by Oscar Lewis in *Five Families* (1959), *The Children of Sanchez* (1961), and *La Vida* (1966). Lewis hypothesized that the lower classes of different industrial countries show more similarity to each other than to the affluent classes of their own societies. He mentioned a number of economic, psychological, and social characteristics that he believed distinguish the poor. Among the economic traits are unemployment and underemployment, the struggle for survival, low wages, unskilled occupations, the absence of savings, the shortage of money, the absence of food reserves in the home, the borrowing from local moneylenders at high rates of interest, informal credit devices organized by neighbors, the pawning of personal goods, and the use of secondhand clothes and household goods. He also wrote of resultant social and psychological traits: crowded living, little privacy, gregariousness, a high rate of alcoholism, a frequent use of violence in settling quarrels and training children, wife beating, early initiation into sex, consensual marriages, high rates of abandonment of mothers and children, mother-centered families, a strong predisposition to authoritarianism, a strong present-time orientation with relatively little ability to defer gratification and plan for the future, a sense of resignation and fatalism based on the realities of their difficult life situation, a belief in male superiority, a corresponding martyr complex among women, and a high tolerance for psychological pathology of all sorts (O. Lewis 1961).

Other writers have supported Lewis's descriptions. Several have portrayed the family structure of the urban Negro poor as disorganized (Frazier 1939, p. 245; Glazer and Moynihan 1963, p. 50). As Moynihan stated it in his controversial, but influential 1965 report on the black family, "at the center of the tangle of pathology is the weakness of the family structure. . . . it [is] . . . the principal source of most of the aberrant, inadequate, or anti-social behavior that . . . serves to perpetuate the cycle of poverty and deprivation. . . . the answer is clear. . . . the cycle can be broken only if these distortions [of family structure] are set right" (pp. 30, 47). Others spoke of the poor as being helpless, apathetic, despairing, prone to break laws written by others, impulsive, present-oriented, and contemptuous of self, and as having large numbers of illegitimate children or overly large families and absent fathers.

The writers on this subject often display a strong moralism and middle-class bias, as in Allison Davis's early passage (1946) concerning the lower-class individual who "spends a great deal of his nights in sexual exploration, since he does not have to go to work the next day. He lives in a social world where visceral, genital, and emotional gratification is far more available than it is in the middle-class world" (p. 103). Another study by Schneider and Lysgaard (1953, p. 144) characterized the "impulse-following" of the lower class as "relative readiness to engage in physical violence, free sexual expression (as through intercourse), minimum pursuit of education, low aspiration level, failure of parents to identify the class of their children's playmates, free spending, little em-

phasis on being 'well-mannered and obedient,' and short-time dependence on parents." Banfield (1970) asserted that poor people can never
rise above the poverty level because they lack the ability to discipline
themselves and to postpone immediate gratification in favor of future
rewards. He suggested that money should not be given to the poor, because they would waste it by spending it.

The culture of poverty theory became very popular during the 1960s.
Its theme provided the rationale for various antipoverty programs (Marris and Rein 1969), and it was enunciated in major governmental publications, such as Chilman's *Growing Up Poor* (1966) and Moynihan's
Negro Family (1965). It was the dominant social science perspective
during the "war on poverty" years of the 1960s. The culture of poverty
thesis has been a popular one in part because it is compatible with widely
held negative attitudes toward the poor in American society. The average
American is more apt to concentrate on the assumed shiftlessness and
immorality of the poor than their plight. Feagin has collected representative quotes (1975, pp. 8–11). A Chicago cab driver is not shy about
saying:

> What do I think about the welfare? It ought to be cut back. The
> goddamn people sit around when they should be working and then
> they're having illegitimate kids to get more money. You know, their
> morals are different. They don't give a damn. Stop it. That's what
> I say.

President Nixon also believed that people on welfare do not want to
work, and he advocated work incentives in the welfare program:

> I say that instead of providing incentives for millions of more
> Americans to go on welfare, we need a program which will provide
> incentives for people to get off welfare and get to work.

To check the extent of such attitudes in a more systematic way,
Feagin (1972) conducted a survey of attitudes toward the poor. He
found that over half of his respondents — a half that tended to be older,
white, middle-to-high-income, and middle-educated — said that lack of
thrift, lack of ability, and loose morals on the part of poor people are the
most important reasons for poverty. Only a minority — particularly the
young, Jews, blacks and poor themselves — saw poverty as the result of
social and economic conditions, blaming it on low wages in business,
scarcity of jobs, lack of good schools, and exploitation by the rich.

According to the dominant middle-American point of view, then,
nothing much can be done about poverty. Because the poor are lazy, their
poverty is due to their own weak motivational structure, and it is up to
them to improve their own circumstances. It would be detrimental, in

fact, to give money to the poor, according to this line of reasoning, because this would keep them from ever developing any ambition or responsible habits. What can be done? Three-fourths of Feagin's respondents favored governmental programs to create jobs for the poor, but only if these programs would not raise their own taxes. Sixty-one percent were opposed to a guaranteed income of $3,000 for every family, arguing that this would constitute handouts and that people would stop working, lose ambition, and waste their money. Only a tiny minority of the respondents favored complete income redistribution.

While the concept of culture of poverty has persuasive qualities, critics have pointed out serious problems with the accuracy of some of its propositions, with its light treatment of other causes of lower-class behavior, and with the policy implications of its vulgarized version, which leads to attitudes favoring the status quo. It ignores the many threads of middle-class values held by low-income people while overestimating the homogeneity of cultural systems found among the poor, they say. It influences one to adopt an unrealistic "they-can't-be-helped" attitude (S. M. Miller et al. 1964; S. M. Miller and Riessman 1968; Roach and Gursslin 1967; Rainwater 1967). Let us examine the ideas of the critique one by one.

A first major criticism is that certain characteristics ascribed to the poor by the culture of poverty thesis can be empirically challenged. The evidence suggests that basically poverty is *not* an intergenerational phenomenon passed from parent to child through a restraining culture. Most poor people are *not* poor for life. As we saw in Chapter 6, the Blau and Duncan study (1967) of thirty thousand males indicated that while there is some occupational inheritance between fathers and sons, the correlations are so low that they are incompatible with the idea that sons of poor parents are highly likely to be poor themselves. Children of unskilled workers are not likely to be unskilled, and some sons of high-status fathers experience downward mobility.

A study by Kriesberg (1970) of low-income mothers in Syracuse, New York, came to similar conclusions. National data show that two-thirds of poor people come from families in which the father was uneducated and unskilled (Morgan et al. 1962, p. 207). But Kriesberg found no differences in socioeconomic background between those families who were *quite* poor and those who had at least the minimum amount of income necessary to get by (1970, p. 176). Kriesberg suggests that falling into direct poverty is somewhat fortuitous. Coming from a poor family reduces the chances of becoming affluent, but the relationship between the socioeconomic status of the family of origin and one's current economic status is not so great that being in poverty can be accounted for simply by the fact that one was raised in poverty. These reports indicate that it is more accurately the case that a large proportion of the American population

359

slips back and forth across the poverty line in their lifetimes as economic conditions fluctuate or, for women, as their marital statuses change.

The evidence is equally shaky and unsupportive regarding deferred gratification patterns (DGP). Some studies find no evidence of a class difference in DGP (Shybut 1963), while others find that differences are situationally relevant and/or dependent on expectations of reliable outcomes (S. M. Miller et al. 1968, pp. 429–31; Seagull 1964). Some studies find only minor differences (Schneider and Lysgaard 1953). The idea that the poor are unable to defer gratification and have a present-time orientation is the academic parallel to the common-sense notion that the poor are poor because they are shiftless and irresponsible (Davidson and Gaitz 1974, pp. 229–30). Yet, recent reports suggest that the poor have as strong a work motivation as anyone (Goodwin 1972; Kaplan and Tausky 1972; Davidson and Gaitz 1974).

Challenge has also been hurled at the statements about the family structure: The home of the poor is commonly broken; matricentric families abound; families are unstable and disorganized. It is true, according to census data (U.S. Bureau of the Census 1975b, Figure 3), that more poor families exist without a male head than nonpoor families (45 percent compared to 9 percent). Yet, because the majority of poor families (55 percent) are stable families with two parents, any generalization would have to indicate that the home of the poor is uncommonly unbroken.

In addition, we must note that a sizable proportion of the broken families became poor as a *result* of the departure of the husband, not as a prelude. Many women were brought up to believe that the feminine role is to get married, become mothers, and be supported by their husbands. If their husbands desert or divorce them, they often lack the experience or training to support themselves (Komisar 1977, p. 141). Since children rarely go with the husbands, these wives must support not only themselves, but children as well. Although divorce laws are designed to ensure that divorced men will share in the costs of rearing their children, the legal settlements do not work well in practice. One of the few studies of this question found that within one year of divorce, 42 percent of fathers had made no court-ordered child support payments, and after ten years the proportion rose to 79 percent (Ross and Sawhill 1975, p. 47). An American Bar Association study in 1965 found that alimony was awarded in only a very small percentage of all cases (Citizens' Advisory Council on the Status of Women 1972). Two-thirds of the people in poverty and almost all the adults on welfare are women. It is not too surprising that in a society in which women are underpaid and child-care facilities are rare, women alone cannot earn enough to support their families.

Another criticism is leveled against the assertion that poor families are "strife-ridden." Such statements are frequently based on the fact that divorce and desertion rates are higher in the lowest socioeconomic brackets. However, critics point out that divorce and desertion rates are not a good measure of marital strife. For instance, Cuber and Harroff found in their study of "successful" upper-middle-class couples, who had lived together for ten or more years and had never considered divorce, that a major habitual mode of interaction is conflict: "In this association there is much tension and conflict . . . private quarreling, nagging, and 'throwing up the past'" (1965, p. 44). Until accurate cross-class comparisons of "strife rates" are made, we cannot assume that poor families are more strife-ridden.

The tendency of the poor to use violence in their parental and marital strife also is questionable. Erlanger (1974, p. 73) finds in a review of the research that, contrary to popular belief, poorly educated parents have the highest rate of outright rejection of spanking of children. Comparing all classes, he concludes that there is a slight correlation between social class and the use of physical punishment on children, but it is "probably not strong enough to be of great theoretical or practical significance" (1974, p. 81). Recent data on wife beating lead to similar conclusions. It is not the poorest and least educated husbands who are likely to use physical violence on their wives, but those of middle occupational and income status (Gelles 1972, Tables 12–14, 16). In fact, it is the more educated Americans who are most likely to approve of slapping one's spouse on "appropriate occasions" (Harris poll). Consistently, in a survey conducted by the National Opinion Research Center, a larger percentage of educated women than uneducated women reported that they had been punched or beaten in their adulthoods (Vanfossen 1977).

Another criticism disputes the claim that lower-class individuals are sexually promiscuous and loose, a claim usually supported by a reference to Kinsey (see Kinsey et al. 1948). Schneider and Lysgaard (1953, p. 143), for example, cite the Kinsey reports to support their observation that lower-class persons have higher rates of premarital intercourse. A careful reading of Kinsey actually leads to a different interpretation concerning the degree of inhibition of sexuality among the classes, however (S. M. Miller et al. 1968, pp. 426–27). For example, Kinsey reports that middle-class males pet, masturbate, engage in fellatio and cunnilingus, have intercourse nude, make love with the lights on, and experience homosexual acts to a greater extent than do lower-class males. Furthermore, Kinsey's finding of greater premarital intercourse among the less educated was based on statistics on males. He found no such differences by educational level among the females (Kinsey et al. 1953).

Likewise, the idea that poor people do not want to work does not hold up empirically. Goodwin (1972) and others (Kaplan and Tausky 1972; Hodgson 1971, p. 31) have found that work motivation is just as strong among people who are poor as those who are not. Although the poor are

361

more likely to be unemployed, this is largely related to health disability (Osmond and Grigg 1975) and to the absence of employment opportunities. Even female heads of household are just as likely, or more so, to work as male heads and as middle-class females, yet they average much lower incomes (Treiman and Terrell 1975), increasing their probability of being poor.

Evidence from several controlled experiments designed to measure the work effort of people who receive financial assistance revealed that the work effort of male heads of household declined by only 5 to 10 percent (Peckman and Timpane 1975; Hollister, forthcoming). This misconception about the attitude of the poor toward work has encouraged the exclusion of the working poor from coverage by the cash welfare system.

In a survey of 271 poor and nonpoor black respondents in a southwestern city, Coward et al. (1974) found little empirical support for the culture of poverty theory, especially as it is advanced by Oscar Lewis. They did not find that the poor ranked high on measures of powerlessness or normlessness, although feelings of "social isolation" were more characteristic of the poor. They found no support for Lewis's argument that consensual or common-law marriages are widespread among the very poor. They did find a larger proportion of "broken" families among the poor than among the nonpoor, but over half of these had been broken by the death of a parent. The findings on parental "authoritarianism" were mixed. Poor parents were more likely to advocate the use of physical punishment in disciplining children, but they had no more explicit behavioral rules for their children than did the nonpoor parents. The survey responses of the poor did not support Lewis's contention that poor people are more suspicious and distrustful of institutions and more apathetic in general than the nonpoor. They tend to participate in church activities just as much as the nonpoor.

The study by Coward et al. did find striking differences between the poor and nonpoor in housing quality, crowding, and economic circumstances. The poor were more likely to be segregated at work, to be in unskilled jobs, to have unemployment in the family, to have serious money problems, to have secondhand furniture, and to have less in the way of education. They also were less likely to have voted in the last presidential election. The authors concluded that the four traits that did distinguish the poor from the nonpoor are better viewed as *conditions* of poverty than as *solutions* to poverty arising out of the cultural innovations of poor people.

Other research studies tend to come to similar conclusions. Kriesberg (1970) interviewed a cross section of families in four low-income public housing projects in Syracuse, New York. He was particularly interested in the process by which "fatherless families" become poor, a state that typifies about half of the fatherless families in the United States. His study is relevant to generalizations about poverty because a sizable proportion (two-fifths) of poor families are headed by females. He found that a single mother is not likely to be poor if she can earn a decent income; or has adequate insurance, alimony payments, or investments; or has relatives or friends who can support the family. Without these assistances, however, she and her children are likely to become wholly or partly dependent on public assistance, which generally provides only a subsistence income.

Kriesberg was interested in the adjustments that poor female-headed families make to their lack of economic support. The choice faced by most husbandless mothers is to earn money or accept public assistance. What are the factors that influence this choice? Whether the mother needs to work or to go on welfare is affected, first of all, by how much *secure* income she has. If the former husband earned a high income, the family he has left — by death or divorce — is likely to be decently provided for. But most husbandless mothers are not this fortunate. While 55 percent of the widows in Kriesberg's sample reported receiving insurance benefits, only 20 percent of the separated and 30 percent of the divorced mothers and none of the few unwed mothers received alimony or support payments from the departed fathers. As we might expect, whether or not the divorced or separated mothers received support payments from their former husbands was related to the husbands' income. If the husbands made over $4,000, about 39 percent of the wives received some support income, compared to 20 percent of the wives whose former husbands made less than $4,000. A man earning very little money is unable and unlikely, it seems, to make any substantial contribution to his former family's maintenance.

Given the probability of inadequate support, the husbandless mother must choose employment or public assistance. If she has *some* secure support income, the earnings she can make by working can often be combined with the support income to yield more money than public assistance benefits would supply. Thus, even some secure income encourages employment, rather than dependence on public assistance.

The number and age of the children also influence the mother's choice. Having several children or a preschool child makes employment difficult (Kriesberg 1970, p. 145). Since public assistance benefits rise with each child but job earnings do not, a mother of many children would have to earn much more than a mother of one or two children to make employment as economically rational.

Some have argued that having many children is part of the subculture of poverty and that husbandless mothers bear additional children in order to receive additional welfare benefits (Feagin 1975, pp. 6–7). However, as Kriesberg (1970, pp. 146–47) points out, this appears to be another myth that the available evidence does not support. For example, if children were desired in order to increase assistance benefits, then one would expect mothers to remain on the welfare rolls for a very long time. Actually, the median length of time that welfare payments are received is two to three years (Levitan et al. 1972, p. 50; Burgess and Price 1963, p. 51; Greenleigh and McCalley 1960, p. 15). Further, there seems to be no evidence that mothers desire to have illegitimate children (Greenleigh and McCalley 1960, p. 19). Shostak (1965, p. 51) indicates that about 90 percent of mothers who had illegitimate children would have preferred to have had their pregnancies terminated. Rather, husbandless mothers tend to want independence from welfare when circumstances make this possible, and the number and age of children are important circumstances in this regard.

Only several of the many research reports on the issue of the culture of poverty have been presented here. Most of those not reported lead to similar conclusions, however. After an extensive review of research concerning poor people, Rossi and Blum concluded that

> the empirical evidence from our review of the literature does not support the idea of a culture of poverty in which the poor are distinctly different from other layers of society. Nor does the evidence from intergenerational-mobility studies support the idea of a culture of poverty in the sense of the poor being composed largely of persons themselves coming from families living in poverty (1968, pp. 43–44).

A second major criticism rejects the inference of the culture of poverty theorists that poor people are homogeneous in values and behavior. This is a strong point that the critics make. As pointed out in an earlier section of this chapter, poverty actually is found among urban slum residents, rural migrant workers, southern Appalachian farmers, ghetto blacks, tenant farmers, American Indians, the disabled, and others. The specific historical reasons that each of these categories has a low income vary tremendously. The exact proportion of the poor that could be characterized as displaying qualities of a culture of poverty is difficult to determine. Even Oscar Lewis (1969), with whose name the concept is most commonly associated, estimates the subculture of poverty to be found in only 20 percent of the families who live below the poverty level. Likewise, most other authors admit, when pressed, that their conceptions of the culture of poverty are meant to apply only to a certain proportion of poor people. The practical problem, then, lies in the widespread disregard of this qualification in the literature on the subject and in the application of the culture of poverty thesis by interpretative writers, government agencies, or other establishment personnel to *all* poor individuals. Indeed, if only 20 percent of poor people can be said to hold the characteristics designated by the theory, then the theory would seem to be relatively inapplicable as an explanatory device. How about a theory or theories to explain the other 80 percent?

A third major point brought out by critics, related to the above questions, is that many characteristics of the poor are actually shared by middle- and upper-class families. Recent studies indicate that a number of the characteristics of the poor are found in other classes. Of those variables which *do* seem to differentiate the poor from the nonpoor, rates often fall along a continuum. That is, rates for poor people are not much different from rates for working-class people, which are not much different from rates for middle-class people (Blum and Rossi 1968, p. 345). For example, a study by Schneider and Lysgaard (1953, p. 144), which portrayed lower-class children as having low aspiration levels while middle-class children had high aspiration levels, was based on the finding that 80 percent of middle-class children — compared to 70 percent of lower-class children — plan to go to college. Or consider the finding that 25 percent of lower-class adults are authoritarian, in comparison to 15 percent of middle-class adults. Does a 10-percent difference in percentags that are low, even if it is "statistically significant," constitute sufficient evidence of a culture of poverty or justify the conclusion that the culture of poverty produces authoritarian tendencies?

The culture of poverty thesis has suggested that poor people are poor because they do not know how to spend their money. In fact, studies of the expenditures of poor families show no unusual patterns (Carcagno and Corson 1977, p. 260). Compared to more affluent individuals, low-income people spend relatively more of their total income on food, clothing, and housing, as one might expect. The evidence indicates that the poor are neither more nor less wise in their spending than everyone else.

And a final criticism is that alternative explanations of poverty that are equally plausible have been ignored and overlooked. These alternatives present different perspectives on the sources of poverty, and correspondingly, they lead to different solutions.[2] Because of the importance of perspective to policy, the choice of a theoretical paradigm has consequences far beyond its effects on scientific conclusion. The two major competing theories are the situational and the structural, which we now examine in detail.

THE SITUATIONAL THEORY OF POVERTY

Although the culture of poverty theory is perhaps currently most popular among academics and nonacademics alike, a second theory that has

[2] For a similar presentation of three models of poverty, see Valentine 1968, pp. 141–44. For an interchange between Valentine and other scholars concerning the culture of poverty thesis, see *Current Anthropology* 10 (1969): 181–200.

emerged as an alternative explanation is the situational theory of poverty. According to this theory, people who are poor are responding to the situations and opportunities available to them and adjusting their behavior accordingly. Many of the actions of low-income people can be seen as pragmatic responses to the stresses and deprivations of life (Gans 1968, p. 206; H. Lewis 1967). It is not that low-income persons have failed to learn middle-class (typical) attitudes and behaviors, but rather that certain of these attitudes and behaviors are inappropriate to living in poverty. Hyman Rodman writes of a "lower-class value stretch," which allows the lower-class person to develop an alternative set of values without rejecting the general cultural norms of the society:

> Without abandoning the values placed upon success, such as high income and high educational and occupational attainment, he stretches the values so that lesser degrees of success also become desirable. Without abandoning the values of marriage and legitimate childbirth he stretches these values so that a non-legal union and legally illegitimate children are also desirable. The result is that the members of the lower class, in many areas, have a wider range of values than others within the society. They share the general values of the society with members of other classes, but in addition they have stretched these values, or developed alternative values, which help them to adjust to their deprived circumstances (1963, p. 209).

Socialization of the poor, according to this view, is not substantially different; the problem is that the conditions of lower-class life are basically inconsistent with realization of the middle-class model. The poor do share many values with the dominant strata, but they must accept alternative ideals when the contradictions between cultural ideals and situational conditions are too sharp (Valentine 1968, p. 130). For instance, the middle-class ideal of a stable two-parent family structure (still the dominant type among poor families) is more difficult to attain when the husband is unable to earn enough to support a family or when he is frequently unemployed. Although the conventional two-parent family is preferred, broken families may be more adaptive at certain stages in the lifetime of the adults: "Consensual unions provide a flexible adaptation that is functional under conditions in which fluctuating economic circumstances, actual or threatened incarceration, and other external conditions often make it advisable for cohabiting pairs to separate either temporarily or permanently and contract alternative unions, again either temporary or lasting" (Valentine 1968, p. 132).

Many of the distinctive aspects of the low-income style of living are mere reflections of what one must do if he or she falls into poverty. The poor cannot save money, because there is little money to save;[3] they buy more expensive goods at neighborhood stores because transportation to faraway shopping centers is too costly or unavailable; they get hooked into high interest rates by loan sharks because banks will not offer them low-interest loans; they have a strong present orientation because they realistically surmise that the chances for substantial improvement of their socioeconomic status are not great or because they lack the resources to take the needed actions to bring about improvement.

In general, this theory maintains that inequities in the opportunity structure constrain the behavior of the poor and that opening up the opportunity structure would allow the expression of underlying middle-class motivational and behavioral patterns (Davidson and Krackhardt 1975). Without focusing on the overall system of inequality, the situational theory clearly takes the blame away from the poor person (Ryan 1971) and places it on the pattern of opportunities. The poor are unskilled and uneducated persons who would not be poor if they had skills needed by the labor market. Better schools and more job-training programs, federal employment programs oriented toward the unskilled, and a healthy thriving economy that reduces unemployment rates to low levels would go a long way toward eliminating poverty.

What is overlooked by the situational theory is that better schools and job-training programs would help only a small percentage of the poor — not the aged, the low-paid, or the mothers. The fact that the poor include those who are unable to become employed has led some social scientists to adopt a perspective that focuses on the total economic system.

THE STRUCTURAL THEORY OF POVERTY

The structural theory sees poverty to be an integral and inherent part of the social structure, the economic system, the distribution of wealth and income, and the supporting institutions. It cannot be eliminated without radical changes, because the dominant groups in the society, acting in their own self-interest, prohibit any significant redistribution of wealth. In this view, poverty is continued not only because affluent people refuse to decrease their own intake of wealth, but also because the existence of a poverty class is useful in other ways to both the upper and middle classes (Baran and Sweezy 1966, pp. 265–66; Wachtel 1971). The dominant classes, which control the means of production and occupy the positions of power, set their own rewards, and they set them high. We have already examined the tools of power — the use of the legal system, the regulatory agencies, the mass media, and the schools — that the dominant classes have used to perpetuate an inequality system from which they benefit. The economist Sackrey vividly expresses this theory:

[3] What saving is done may be focused more toward defensive savings than for status ascent. See McConnell 142, pp. 144 ff.

> The capitalists . . . will define an adequate income for themselves as distinctly higher than an adequate income for workers, no matter how crude, selfish, or greedy the capitalists' efforts are which lead to the income. And further, if the capitalists, or those in control of the legislatures and the newspapers, see fit to define one particular race, or one of the sexes, or certain foreigners as inferior to the rest, there arise in labor markets certain jobs which are held in safekeeping for those inferiors to fill. There will arise "colored jobs," "women's work," and other categories of labor for which a relative pittance will be paid, for it is accepted by the public — whose ideas are shaped by the flow of communication from the capitalist press and TV — that such jobs are not worthy of higher incomes. How else . . . does one explain the $800,000 paid annually to the head of General Motors for leading the corporation whose products are helping to ruin our cities and countryside, as compared to the $4,000 paid to the public employee who cleans up the cities' debris (1973, pp. 33–34).

Sackrey's reference to the use of differential job markets to reward certain categories of people at the expense of others is in agreement with analyses of the labor market emerging from industrial sociology and economics. As we saw in Chapter 4 there are a number of institutional conditions affecting the distribution of income, one of which is the occupational market structure. Poor people tend to operate within the "free market," where wages and skill levels are low, where wages reflect supply and demand, and where union organizations are nonexistent. Sackrey continues with the implications of these forces for the poor:

> In this kind of analysis, therefore, poverty is nothing more than the condition of those whose efforts have been described as worthless by those who make the rules. We could pass a law today which would take all the *property* income (in the form of rent, interest, stockholder profits, and capital gains) from the rich, for which most presently do nothing, and, hypothetically, total output would remain the same.
>
> . . . the old woman living in low-income housing, who feeds herself and her three motherless grandchildren with wages from working in a laundry, though she is paid less income, is not necessarily less productive than her suave young landlord, whisking around town in a sportscar purchased by the rents paid him by poor people. The fact that he is paid more than she is but one result of a quaint and unfortunate social custom regarding money payments for services rendered in the economy (1973, pp. 34–36).

Poverty, in this view, is functional to the more affluent segments of society. It is functional in several senses — economically, politically, and psychologically. Along these lines, Gans (1972) makes a not quite satiric formulation of the functions that poverty serves for richer Americans:

1. The existence of poverty makes sure that "dirty work" is done — work that is physically dirty and dangerous, temporary, dead-end and underpaid, undignified, and menial.
2. The poor subsidize many activities that benefit the affluent; for example, they subsidize the economy by virtue of the low wages they receive and the higher share of taxes they pay.
3. Poverty creates jobs for a number of occupations: penologists, police, the numbers rackets, drug dealers, faith healers, prostitutes, pawn brokers, and the peacetime army.
4. The poor buy goods that others do not want and thus prolong their economic usefulness, such as day-old bread, secondhand clothes, and deteriorating automobiles and buildings. They also provide jobs for doctors, lawyers, teachers, and others who are too old, poorly trained, or incompetent to attract more affluent clients.
5. The poor can be identified and punished as alleged or real deviants in order to uphold the legitimacy of dominant norms. The defenders of hard work, thrift, honesty, and monogamy need people who can be accused of being lazy, spendthrift, dishonest, and promiscuous to justify these norms.
6. The poor who are disabled or suffering from bad luck provide the rest of the population with the emotional satisfactions of compassion, pity, and charity.
7. Poverty helps to guarantee the status of those who are not poor. Since people need to know where they stand, the poor function as a reliable and permanent measuring rod for status comparison, particularly for the working class.
8. The poor serve as symbolic constituencies and opponents for several political groups. The revolutionary left could not exist without the poor, particularly now that the working class can no longer be perceived as the vanguard of the revolution; conversely, the political groups of conservative bent need the "welfare chiselers" and others who "live off the taxpayer's hard-earned money."
9. The poor, being powerless, can be made to absorb the economic and political costs of change and growth in American society. During the nineteenth century, they did the work that built the cities; today, they are pushed out of their neighborhoods to make room for middle-class stores in the city and for expressways to enable suburbanites to commute downtown. The poor have also paid a large share of the human cost of the growth of American power overseas, for they have provided many of the foot soldiers for Vietnam and other wars.
10. The poor have played an important role in shaping the American po-

litical process; because they vote and participate less than other groups, the political system has been free to ignore them, thus making American politics more centrist than would otherwise be the case, but also adding to the stability of the political process.

According to Gans, these are the functions of poverty. He goes on to ask, Are there functional alternatives; could we eliminate poverty and still have these functions performed? In some cases, yes; in some cases, no. Society's dirty work could be done without poverty by paying the workers who do it decent wages, a gesture that would cleanse such work considerably. Nor is it necessary for the poor to subsidize activities through their low-wage jobs, for many of these jobs are important enough that they would exist even if wages were raised. Alternatives for the deviance-connected social functions could be found relatively easily and cheaply. Other groups — entertainers, hippies, and adolescents in general — could serve as deviants to uphold traditional morality. The blind and disabled could serve as objects of pity and charity.

The status and mobility functions of the poor would be more difficult to replace, however. In a hierarchical society some people must be considered to be inferior to everyone else, and the poor perform this function more adequately than others. But they need not be as poverty-stricken as they are, and Gans suggests that a stratification system in which the people below the federal "poverty line" would receive 75 percent of the median income, rather than 40 percent or less, would still provide a poor group to be last in the pecking order. This, of course, would require income redistribution, an improbable prospect. Replacing the functions served by poverty could be done, but only at higher costs to other people, particularly more affluent ones. When the elimination of poverty through functional alternatives generates dysfunctions for the affluent, poverty will continue to persist; thus, poverty can be eliminated only when it either becomes sufficiently dysfunctional for the affluent or when the poor can obtain enough power to change the system of social stratification.[4]

According to the structural theory, poverty exists because it is useful for those who control or influence the distribution of wages and wealth. That there is so little protest from those who must work for nonliving wages attests to the success of the controls — ideological, institutional, and physical — that the more affluent members of the society are able to impress on the poor. Subordinate and deprived groups are not inevitably acquiescent to their lack of privilege. Protest and rebellion, conflict and

[4] Yet, as Roach and Roach (1973) point out in their commentary on Gans's idea, the fact that some groups benefit from poverty does not sufficiently explain its persistence. To do this, one must also identify the means through which such groups can and do contribute to the persistence of poverty.

objection are ever present potentials. The problem of control looms for the more privileged, who ultimately stand to lose if a subordinated group is successful in its protest.

It is the thesis of Piven and Cloward (1971) that control is facilitated by the welfare system, which historically has been used to appease mass disorder arising from unemployment. While in subsistence economies everyone works, under capitalism there are continual changes and shifts in labor requirements. At any given moment, some people are left unemployed. When mass unemployment leads to outbreaks of turmoil, as happened during the Great Depression, relief programs are initiated or expanded to absorb and control enough of the unemployed to restore order; then as turbulence subsides, the relief system contracts, expelling those who are needed to populate the low-wage labor market. The treatment of those who are left on the relief rolls is so degrading and punitive as to instill in the laboring masses a fear of the fate that awaits them, should they relax into pauperism (Piven and Cloward 1971, p. 3). Yet, the alternative to relief for many people is work that pays such low wages that a family cannot be supported. From the point of view of the employer, low welfare payments foster a steady stream of workers who are desperate for jobs, even those that pay very little. Relief lessens the bargaining power of unskilled workers and absorbs labor when it is not needed. At the same time, it quiets the outcries of the underprivileged.

Control also is facilitated by the ideologies and myths that every society perpetuates to justify and legitimate its system of social stratification. Control of the disprivileged is both more efficient and easier if they accept their position as natural, just, and right. In the United States, the legitimating ideologies are compatible with capitalism. The concepts of freedom and private property rights, for example, rationalize the accumulation of great amounts of wealth by capitalists. The concepts of equal opportunity (to become unequal) and individual initiative uphold the role that educational credentials play in creating barriers to entry into middle-income jobs and in promoting the economic differentiations among the middle classes. The belief that those who work hard and are talented shall be rewarded with success and money is well entrenched. It forms the basis of the correlative judgment that those who are poor must be lazy or unintelligent or both. Its academic counterpart can be found in the popularity of functionalist and culture of poverty theories. The belief that the poor are responsible for their own fate prohibits the emergence of the important political support that must exist before change in structural conditions can take place.

The structural theory of poverty does not lead easily to policy recommendations for the elimination of poverty. Such suggestions as are made emphasize the need to alter structural conditions. Job-training programs are not considered adequate because for many categories of poor people (blacks, Puerto Ricans, women) it does not matter how much training is acquired; income is still low (Kershaw 1970, p. 22; Mangum 1969, p. 52; Lampman 1971, p. 128). For other categories (the disabled, the old, the young), work is inappropriate. These groups are systematically channeled into subsistence-level participation in the economic system. The structuralist is more likely to advocate changes in the distribution of wealth or the guarantee of a minimum family income.[5]

Conclusion

As the evidence against the culture of poverty thesis mounts, it becomes increasingly clear that it is inadequate for depicting either the causes or the nature of poverty. It neither describes accurately the processes by which people enter an impoverished condition nor gives a realistic picture of their motivations and resources once they are poor. Given its empirical distortions, one wonders why it became such a popular theory during the 1960s and why it provided the dominant philosophy behind the war on poverty programs of that period. Several critics of the culture of poverty thesis have suggested that it is popular because it rationalizes the status quo and thus provides an ideological support for the current stratification system. If one "blames the victim" (Ryan 1971) for his or her own dire state, it seems unnecessary to look for alternative explanations and systemic solutions (Valentine 1971, p. 216). By concentrating on the internal deficiencies in the culture and personalities of poor people, one may ignore structural sources of poverty. The unavailability of decent-paying jobs for many of the aged, minorities, women, and the uneducated; the prevalence of jobs that pay too little for family support; the benefits to the affluent of a permanent lower class — all are issues remaining unexamined by the culture of poverty advocate. The ways in which dominant groups are able to use their wealth and power to preserve the same and to control the state, the educational system, and a discriminatory job market go unnoticed.

As other explanations of poverty have begun to supplant the culture of poverty thesis, several generalizations emerge. The poor in the United States are a heterogeneous group, but certain common features exist. A number of them are not participants in the employment structure (because they are children of poor parents, the aged, the unemployed of

[5] Some of the arguments for income maintenance programs are that cash transfer payments do remove people from poverty (Lampman 1971, pp. 108, 119); a guaranteed annual income program would cover most of the poor, as other programs do not (Ozawa 1971, p. 316); it would encourage families to remain intact (Domestic Council 1971, p. 9); it would reduce perceptions of stigma, and the total cost to the economy would be zero (Kershaw 1970, p. 126; Tobin 1968, p. 103).

working age, or single mothers with small children). They tend to be less educated. If they are of working age, they tend to be employed in low-paying (unskilled) jobs, and they have some probability of belonging to groups that experience economic discrimination in the United States (blacks, women, American Indians). They do not tend to be people holding values considered deviant by the mainstream of American life, nor are they people who eschew work. They are beset by a variety of troubles resulting from their economic deprivation, and many of their distinctive characteristics (absence of savings, borrowing at high interest rates, living in crowded and substandard quarters, for example) can be viewed as adjustments to their meager economic resources.

The consequences of low income that they experience go beyond mere economic problems. The poor apparently participate less than other strata in social relationships, they are more isolated, and they have lower self-esteem. Their health and health care are affected, and their sense of mastery, their feeling of control over their world, is diminished. To be at the bottom of a stratification system that stresses achievement for all is psychologically punishing (Rossi and Blum 1968, p. 49). Poor people are likely to be aware that they are evaluated negatively by others, first, because the dominant culture is decidedly middle-class, and second, because the discrimination manifest in the treatment of the poor by schools, stores, banks, law enforcement agencies, medical personnel, and landlords communicates it. The society in general looks down on them and blames them for their own condition.

The relationship between the economic straitjacket of the low-income family and the larger economic environment is pivotal to an understanding of poverty. The fact that three-fifths of the heads of all poor families are either working or looking for work is a central fact. Huber comments: "That a sizable proportion of American jobs pay such low wages that a grown man or woman supporting two or three children can live only at the poverty level says a great deal about the structure of society.... The sociological question is why, in the richest nation in the world, do such jobs exist?" (1974, p. 103). This question is most directly addressed by the structural theory, which claims that the existence of poverty in an affluent society is a product of the economic relations among groups and of the way in which wealth and income are distributed. In the capitalistic industrial economy of the United States, concentrations of wealth are protected from dispersion to the total population by property and tax laws. The bulk of the population possesses little wealth, but survives on wages and incomes, which are determined and ranked within several labor markets. Those who have little access to the wealth or to living wages constitute the poor.

What are the potentials for change? About this, there is little agreement. Indeed, it has been only in the last several hundred years that anyone has assumed that it might even be possible to eliminate poverty. The secularization of human societies and the dramatic effects of scientific and technological innovations have prompted the optimism that human fates can be affected by human design. This faith, coupled with an egalitarian political philosophy, causes many Americans to believe that poverty per se is undesirable. The reformer looks for "adjustments" (job-training programs, compensatory education, the creation of new jobs), the radical looks for revolution, and the conservative continues to believe that nothing much can be done. An underlying pessimism in all three groups stems from an awareness of the difficulty of bringing about purposive change. In general, people who are not poor do not exert much effort to change the conditions leading to poverty. They are more inclined, rather, to resist attempts to improve the economic condition of the poor. Members of the elite are against drastic redistribution of wealth because they wish to protect their own wealth holdings. The middle classes are against transfer payments because their own economic efforts and struggles are rationalized by a belief in the justice of the prevailing wage system. The competitiveness among the middle- and lower-income groups, focused on the small available proportion of overall economic resources remaining after the wealth has been concentrated, reduces intergroup sympathies and cohesion. For separate reasons, the various subgroups of the nonpoor unconsciously coalesce to preserve the conditions that result in poverty or near-poverty for a substantial minority of the population. While the ruling elite, with the help of the middle classes, constitutes the prime conservators, stabilizers, and perpetrators of the stratification system, the poor — essentially powerless, penniless, and deprived of clout of any sort — take the brunt and bear the costs of an inequalitarian social structure.

12
STRUCTURED
SOCIAL INEQUALITY
AND POLICY
IMPLICATIONS

THERE COMES A TIME when it is wise to step back from the act of describing in what ways the rich are rich and the poor are poor and from the difficult task of searching for why this is so. When we are able to construct an overview of what it all means, to build the composite picture of structured social inequality as it exists and is maintained in various kinds of societies, then we can turn to questions of value. What aspects of stratification are good for the life of a people, and what aspects are harmful? Should, and can, the structure of social inequality be shaped and modified by conscious manipulation? What features of inequality are inevitable and, therefore, resistant to change? The distended bellies of the children suffering from malnutrition and intestinal roundworms found by Senator Hollings in rural South Carolina, the sleek appearance and pampered egotism of the children of the elite found by Coles — are these unavoidable outcomes of an inevitable differential allocation of material and spiritual resources? If they are not unavoidable, then what aspects of inequality can and should be altered? Alterations always have a cost for someone. Who loses, and what is the cost? Who benefits, and with what overall outcomes? The current chapter explores the policy implications of sociological knowledge concerning inequality that we have been able to accumulate to date. To begin, let us summarize the most important insights presented in earlier chapters.

An Overview

A system of social stratification (structured social inequality) consists of institutionalized power arrangements that perpetuate intergenerational patterns of economic, political, and prestige inequalities. It develops when an economic system has become sufficiently productive that it produces a sizable surplus of goods beyond those needed for bare survival. The surplus is distributed on the basis of power.

The greatest extremes of inequality are reached in agrarian societies, where power resides in ownership of land and control of the military. Inequality is lessened somewhat in industrial societies, because the overall productivity is so great that elites can make economic concessions to encourage worker cooperation without losing in absolute terms. In addition, middle-level technicians and professionals have increased importance and, thus, greater bargaining power. Nevertheless, inequalities still are enormous. In the United States, for example, the richest 20 percent of families and individuals possesses 76 percent of the wealth and receives 41 percent of all family income, while the poorest 20 percent owns 0.2 percent of the total wealth and receives 6 percent of the total income. The concentration of wealth has been relatively stable over time and is protected by property laws and taxation. One-eighth of the population is so destitute that its families cannot secure a minimally adequate food supply.

Variations among complex societies in the degree of inequality are related to differences, first, in the extent to which surpluses are unequally distributed and, second, in the extent to which government spending on nondefense purposes redistributes wealth and income from the rich to the poor. Both of these are in turn related to the degree to which corporate interests are effectively opposed by other interests, such as those of workers, consumers, and the powerless.

There are strong and influential pressures in an industrial society leading to a high level of structured inequality. The authority hierarchies that direct and coordinate large numbers of people in performing complicated tasks provide the opportunity for the ruling segments to utilize power in their own interests and to increase and solidify their own advantage. Economic inequality through ownership of property leads to power inequities because owners have been given the right to control the use of things. Political inequality based on a socially legitimated right of some people to set public policy governing other people is enhanced by the control of military and police groups, which monopolize the weapons of force, and by the cooperation of the socialization institutions, which exert moral and ideological persuasion. In addition, the bureaucratic organizations that are created to conduct activities in all institutions extend and rigidify inequalitarian structures.

The acquiescence of the people who benefit only moderately or not at all from the stratification system is problematic to the more privileged. Compliance of the subordinated is not automatically ensured. In periods of stability, however, compliance is induced by effective socialization of the less privileged to believe that inequality is desirable. The idea, for example, that privilege is a just reward for valued performance may be sufficient to convince the poor that they deserve no more than what they have. The visibility of a few cases of individual social mobility may also lead people to accept inequality in the hopes that they or their children may eventually become part of the privileged strata. A competitive class consciousness — according to which people recognize the existence of differences in wealth, power, and prestige, but define them as being the product of differences in individual ability, worth, or performance — tends to legitimate social stratification.

Selection devices for sorting each new generation into available slots in the inequality structure also are problematic. Traditional, agrarian societies most commonly use family lineage as the criterion. One is born into a serf position or into nobility. Industrial societies, which require more flexibility of worker mobility, shift to other criteria. Objectified tests, scores, grades, or diplomas become the certifying ticket of admission to many jobs and thus to a socioeconomic level. Schools do a major job of distributing students into various levels of educational completion, which then are used by employers as evidence in the first round of selectivity. There are a number of other devices as well. Labor unions sometimes control hiring, but admission to the union is restricted. Professional associations limit certification of aspirants. Employers divert the flow of broad categories of people — the aged, women, minorities — away from the more desirable jobs, increasing their willingness to work in the less desirable jobs. To be effective as sifting devices, these mechanisms must receive at least minimal legitimation from the public in general. They must be tied into a dominant ideology. In the United States, they are said to be measures of quality, or worth, and thus they seem consistent with the dominant ideology of individualism and competition.

Sources of resistance to social stratification do exist. While the dominant ideology may favor the privileged strata, alternative competing ideologies often have substantial vitality (Turner and Singleton 1978). Resistive groups occasionally emerge, more or less challenging specific features of the distribution of wealth or power. These are particularly likely to be groups that have developed class consciousness, internal communication networks, an ideology of "system blame," and a leadership structure. While the changes instigated as a result of challenging groups are limited in scope by economic constraints, they are sufficient to create a variation of degrees of inequality among nations of the same economic form. Industrialized nations do differ, for example, in the economic power of middle-income groups, the distribution of power across governmental branches, the degree to which the state is willing to spend money on non-military programs, and the proportion of seats in the national legislature held by socialists — all of which affect levels of inequality (Rubinson and Quinlan 1977; Hewitt 1977: Jackman 1975).

Policy Implications

In this text we have examined the nature of structured social inequality — its universality and variability, the forms that it takes and the processes that lead to it. Using a conflict perspective, we have interpreted how and why a population is stratified by wealth, income, power, occupational status, and prestige; what are the consequences of inequality for different strata; how schools and families reinforce the status quo; and how class origin affects family life, group behavior, and mental health.

In all of this we have avoided any direct confrontations with questions of value. Yet, value questions are the really important ones. How much inequality is desirable? What kind of a system leads to the highest quality of life? Is stratification by ability (or inheritance or luck or wealth and so on) desirable, and if so, what of those who have only their humanity? Should the distribution of wealth be changed, by how much, and to whose benefit? Is the emphasis on competition good when it requires that so many "fail"?

To answer these questions, we must step out of the traditional scholarly stance, which presents explanations but makes no recommendations. We must take a position that makes judgments of value, states choices, and establishes preferences. Here the ground to be covered becomes rough, because choices about what *should* be social policy are necessarily influenced by beliefs concerning what *can* be — that is, by beliefs about what is politically feasible. To deal with that concern, we can only speculate. But let us begin, nevertheless.

To start, it is clear that certain consequences of inequality are harmful to large numbers of people. To take the most extreme category, even in the most productive societies, people who are poor do not have sufficient economic resources to survive. Sometimes they starve, or they may merely have inadequate nutrition for sound physical growth and prevention of disease and infirmity. Compared to the better-off, the poor get sick more often, have more chronic illnesses, lack adequate medical and dental care, and die at younger ages. The poor are unable to save money to tide themselves over in times of trouble. They are faced by high job insecurity and frequent unemployment. They work long hours, at boring or unpleasant jobs, for low pay. To little avail — they struggle to cope with a constant, complex stream of economic problems.

Income is not the only stratified commodity. Many of the important resources for living are more available to privileged groups than to the poor — adequate health care, decent housing, transportation, quality education, leisure time, satisfying work, personal autonomy, political clout, and social status, for example. These objective inequalities spill over into subjective consequences. People who lack money are, first of all, likely to suffer from low self-esteem, the feeling of being unimportant and not worthwhile. Even more damaging are frequent feelings of discouragement. The poor and the nearly poor are usually overworked, but they have a difficult time becoming not poor. The poor are more prone to depression, the statistics show, but the statistics do not convey the pain that is thereby indicated — feelings of helplessness, despair, lack of hope. The depression is sometimes mixed with anger — futile, undirected, hopeless anger, but debilitating in its bitterness and cynicism. The subjective quality of life, the emotional tone of the very act of living, is debased by poverty.

Inequality can be seen to be the cause of the poor's deprivation, for at the other end of the scale the rich have far more economic resources than they could ever hope to utilize (even if they used their entire lifetimes merely to spend money on themselves), enough political advantages to look after their interests when there is a conflict with the interests of others, and enough social honor to feel superior to others and, thus, good about themselves. A more equitable distribution of the economic resources of a society would alleviate the economic deprivation of the poor, and it would go a long way toward making more equitable the distribution of power. It has been estimated for the United States, for example, that dividing up the total personal income equitably would give *every* family of four an annual income of $16,850 (1970 figures; see Gross 1972). Dividing up wealth as well as income would elevate the well-being of the majority of the population substantially.

Not only the poor suffer from inequality. There are negative consequences for middle-income families as well. Forced to compete with others for small income and status advantages, middle-income people, as we saw in Chapter 10, often strive unsuccessfully to define themselves as socially superior to their neighbors. Brought up to believe in an ethic that emphasizes individualism and competition over others rather than collective group goals, many middle-income people are prone either to a pervasive status striving or to a sense of failure. Their status anxiety makes them hard workers, but unsatisfied human beings who resent the status accomplishments of those more privileged and who resist social welfare for those who are less privileged. The ideology of competitiveness blinds them to their common concerns and collective material interests.

A second implication for policy making is that there are certain consequences of inequality that we might define as positive. The following are the most obvious. First, an authority hierarchy is a relatively efficient organizational structure for coordinating large numbers of people to perform difficult tasks. Six hundred thousand workers could not make automobiles if there were no overall command structure for getting people to be at the right place at the right time to do the work. As Gans (1974, p. 66) has suggested, if power were completely equalized, it is doubtful that any decisions could be made and any public activities could proceed. Moreover, the society would have to be "heavily regimented to prevent new inequalities from arising, and it would have to be static, straining toward a totally egalitarian end-state above all else" (Gans 1974, p. 66).

Second, a division of labor is essential for the survival of any complex economic system. Yet, because differences in power are inherent in differences in occupational roles, political inequality is a result.

And third, unequal reward for work performance is one means for motivating people. How many would choose to work in a steel mill if wages were not offered? (However, notice that there are many alternative value systems for motivating people. Throughout most of history, money did not exist, nor did other forms of wealth; people worked nevertheless.)

VALUE JUDGMENTS

With these considerations in mind, we can make several judgments. The first is that in any society that is sufficiently productive to care for all its population, every person has a right to sufficient resources for survival and for full participation in the society. No person should go without nutritious food and medical care, for example. When a society can afford to support its total population, it should do so. Poverty instills suffering of the most dire and drastic kind and should be eliminated. Poverty is bad for children, as well as for adults. It stunts growth and chokes potential. While it is beneficial for certain more affluent groups by ensuring the presence of workers willing to labor for low wages, the benefit is limited to only certain categories and thus cannot be used as a criterion to be employed in making choices for all the people.

Second, inequality should exist to the degree that it substantially contributes to the overall productivity of the society. Or, as the philosopher John Rawls concluded, inequality is justified only when it leads to greater equality of the disadvantaged. Thus, "social and economic inequalities are to be arranged so that they are both (a) reasonably expected to be to everyone's advantage, and (b) attached to positions and offices open to all" (1971, pp. 60–61). As Gans (1974, p. 67) suggests, we need to ask what degree of income is compatible with the division of labor and with the necessity of economic efficiency in general. We need to consider what degree of political inequality is inherently tied to a large heterogeneous society that must be run by bureaucracies. Power differences perhaps must exist, but we can question the degree to which these must result in differences in privilege.

The more productive an economy is, the easier it is to provide the resources necessary for everyone's existence. This fact leads to a third value judgment: A more productive society is better than a less productive one. In today's world, this probably means that industrialization is the preferred economy. To accept that judgment, we must reject back-to-the-earth solutions and, instead, hold goals compatible with an industrial economic framework. (This does not mean that an industrial society cannot support a certain percentage of its population who prefer to live in rural communes or on farm homesteads, but only that such living arrangements cannot be considered to be the economic solution for the majority of the population.) In making this judgment, we also accept a number of determinants of at least minimal inequality: a complicated division of labor, authority hierarchies, and the need for political coordination at a high level. Inequality is part and parcel of these structures. By choosing industrialization, we thus have already limited ourselves in the degree to which we can pursue equalitarian goals.

Because political inequality operates hand in hand with economic inequality, any desire to improve the condition of the underprivileged must take the matter of power into account. So, in our fourth judgment, we agree with the suggestion made by Gans (1975, p. 69): No person should be so powerless that he or she has no control whatsoever over his or her own life, and no person should be so powerful that he or she can force others to do his or her bidding without taking these others into account. In a society of 200 million people, it is difficult to envision the situation in which every person has say-so about his or her own destiny. Forces external to the individual control most of human existence in the modern world. Yet, individuals should have some degree of choice, at least about their occupations, life styles, and living conditions.

These judgments suggest that inequality such as exists in the United States should be diminished, but that we cannot reasonably expect it to disappear altogether. Making these judgments has been easy compared to the difficulty of the next logical issue: How can inequality be decreased? Suggestions of strategies for bringing about social and political change to this end have been quite varied, but generally fall into three categories.

MEANS OF DIMINISHING INEQUALITY

IT CANNOT BE DONE A very popular assessment, this point of view recognizes the enormity of the forces maintaining stratification. In particular, it recognizes the power of economic and political elites to preserve an inequitable status quo. The point is well expressed by Dye and Ziegler in their book, *The Irony of Democracy* (1975), in which they suggest that inequalities among people are inevitable because people are not born with the same abilities. (But we have seen that this is not a particularly valid argument, because inequality does not bear much relationship to ability in the first place.) Political equality is not the answer, Dye and Ziegler further point out, because mass democracy, the most extreme example, is not feasible. In a society of 200 million people, it is inevitable that any one person's wishes are going to be quite unimportant. Dye and Ziegler recognize that one strategy sometimes suggested is that the powerless force the elites to pay attention through mass action. But they argue that protests such as those offered recently by students and blacks are futile, because they are not viewed with favor by either the elites or the masses. The elites tend to be repressive, and the masses tend to be antidemocratic.

The sociologist Krauss (1976, pp. 484–85) makes a similar assessment. He points in particular to the great power of the corporations and their tie-in with the government. Any widespread class conflict that seriously would threaten existing institutional arrangements, especially the concept of private property, he expects would be put down vigorously. Under conditions of threat, the ruling elite would form coalitions with the elites of other institutions (the supportive institutions, in our terminology) and would be able to fight attempts at redistribution of social goods. The socialization of the mass of the population to inefficiency makes it fail to use its numbers as a force for its own benefit.

Is any change at all politically feasible in the American case? It probably is not possible, as pessimists suggest, to eliminate inequality altogether. No society that has been successful enough to support a complex division of labor and to produce a surplus of goods beyond those needed for group survival has existed without some degree of economic and political inequality. Inequality is inherent in the division of labor, which requires a power hierarchy for coordination purposes. Organization inevitably results in some degree of oligarchy, as Michels (1949) pointed out. In addition, political equality in the broader sense is unlikely, too, because it is impossible for a mass to govern; governing responsibilities must be delegated to representatives, but delegation of authority creates a governing elite.

Liberals maintain, however, that it probably is possible to diminish somewhat the extent of economic and political inequality in America. The United States is not the most egalitarian of modern industrialized nations, they point out. For example, Sweden, Denmark, and Norway have accomplished more in eliminating poverty. While these nations are still characterized by social stratification, all families can receive free medical care and free preschool care for children. There is virtually no unemployment. In Sweden, for example, the government maintains a job service, provides moving expenses, and assists the unemployed with grants until they are reemployed. Families receive a cash payment for each child at birth, and a tax-free yearly allowance until the child is 16. Incomes are similar for 90 percent of the families. The result is that most Scandinavians are well fed and healthy. It is such examples which lend credence to reformist strategies.

IT CAN BE DONE ONLY THROUGH REFORMIST EVOLUTION A second category of strategies are those suggested by the judgment that inequality can and should be mollified and by the belief that a drastic revolution is not possible. Those who advocate reform maintain that evolution of economic and political forms to a closer approximation of equality is the only reasonably feasible strategy. Gans (1974, pp. 24–26) argues that Americans are not ready for the collectivist solutions put forth by socialists, who call for the replacement of private institutions by public control of the allocation of resources. Any American equality model, he maintains, must be individualistic rather than collectivistic, because Americans are not ready to stop competing for material or nonmaterial gain, and they would not allow the government to bring about equality through the collective ownership of all resources. Because of this, Gans suggests that greater economic equality could come about not by nationalizing industry, but by redistributing stock ownership and income through taxation. Gans's model would not call for everyone to get the same income. Rather, it would enable people to maximize their earnings through their own efforts and then would create more equality through tax and subsidy policies, as Sweden and England have attempted.

According to this strategy, no one would receive less than about 70 to 80 percent of the median (middle) income, which has been estimated to be the cost of a minimal level of subsistence (Jencks et al. 1972). The cost should be borne by those who earn the highest incomes; consequently, an income ceiling would have to be imposed, based on the lowest maximum at which people would continue to be willing to do unpleasant or highly responsible work or to take needed investment and other risks. Some suggest that this figure, which would ultimately have to be based on empirical research, might be at the level of a 75- to 80-percent tax on the incomes of the very rich. In addition, taxes would need to be imposed on the incomes of the top fifth of the population as well. Left out of these equations, but important nevertheless, are considerations of the wealth of private corporations and the wealth holdings of families, which also could be redistributed to benefit a greater proportion of the population.

Other liberal strategies call for larger pensions, creation of a public national medical insurance program, elimination of federal subsidies of the rich, publicly financed low-income housing, government subsidization of public transportation, elimination of credentialism, dispersal of stock ownership to workers, job-training and retraining programs, government employment programs that deliver quality services and pay union wages, greater federal regulation of corporations, worker participation in work management, and transfer of military funds to civilian production (Sexton and Sexton 1971, pp. 285–311; Gans 1974; Farmer 1971). Reformists suggest that corporations must become accountable to the public and consumers and must be required to shoulder the social costs (such as pollution) of their activities. Stock ownership must be dispensed. Taxes must be made progressive. Government subsidies should be used to benefit the poor, not the rich. Unemployment and underemployment should be eliminated (Gans 1974, p. 29).

Providing a minimum income would be expensive, Gans argues, but it would also give a tremendous boost to the economy by releasing the purchasing power of the poor. The political feasibility of a guaranteed income for the poor is more problematic. The affluent would fight any inroads into their privilege; some of the middle class would be fearful as well and would resist the idea that the poor would not have to work as hard as they themselves do. Yet the idea of a minimum family income has been discussed widely. It was a campaign plank in the 1972 presidential election, and Nixon even suggested such a plan (which, however, offered very low benefits). Gans suggests that whether or not such changes can be made depends on at least three factors: the health of the American economy, the reaction of the politically dominant to the demands for equality, and the decision of middle America as to which side it will be on.

To counteract political inequality, Gans (1974, p. 29) notes that the American political-bureaucratic complex must be restructured to attend to demands of ordinary citizens and not just to those who are more politically effective. Minorities should be persuaded or required to vote, and their vote not be gerrymandered or in other ways nullified. Noting that a majoritarian democracy almost always acts against the interests of minorities, Gans (1974, p. 139) suggests that a more egalitarian democracy "would require systems of proposing and disposing that took the needs of minorities into consideration." Thus, when majority rule has serious negative consequences, out-voted minorities would be able to achieve their most important demands and would not be forced to accept tokenism or to resort to despair or disruption. Cabinet offices and departments for minority interests could be established in Washington, and other departments might be reorganized to look after the concerns of patients, students, slum dwellers, welfare recipients, and so forth.

The responsiveness of government could be increased by extending the "one person, one vote" principle to all levels of government and to the political parties. The seniority system in all legislative bodies could be abolished, and the power of committee chairs, who may represent only a small number of voters, to block legislation wanted by a larger number could be eliminated (Gans 1974, p. 141). Administrative agencies and their bureaucracies could become more accountable by replacing appointive officers with elective ones or by requiring such bodies to be run by elected boards of directors. Election campaigns could be funded by the government to discourage the near-monopoly that wealthy individuals now have on becoming candidates. Equal amounts of free television time could be given to all candidates, even from third, fourth, and fifth parties, to better represent the diversity of the population in the electoral process. Gans (1974, p. 142) further suggests that the nation's 12 percent who are poor, for example, now have no representatives in Congress. Methods by which the citizenry communicates with its elected representatives could be fostered, perhaps by postage-free forms available for people who want to write letters to their representatives or by independently run public opinion polls on every major issue, so that government officials could obtain adequate feedback from a sample of their constituents.

Reformist strategies are advocated by many people. In the United States, they are the most likely strategies to be adopted by the liberal segment of the upper-middle class, by professionals and intellectuals, and by liberal politicians. However, some members of these groups, like the more pessimistic, are convinced that the conservative forces of the dominant elites are nearly overwhelming. The judgment that they make is that change cannot be merely reformist; it must be more radical.

IT CAN BE DONE ONLY THROUGH RADICAL RESTRUCTURING OF BASIC INSTITUTIONS   The third category of strategies is radical, suggesting that the conservative forces of privilege are so strongly entrenched that reform will not work. The only solution is radical restructuring of basic institutions. Those which have been suggested are really quite diverse, ranging from proposals of socialism founded through peaceful evolutionary changes to proposals of violent revolution, unpleasant as that may be, as the only way to bring about substantial change. Radicals sometimes maintain that the underprivileged — minorities, poor, blacks, and so forth — should themselves bring about change by making it so uncomfortable for the privileged that they have to accede to demands. Saul Alinsky, who is well known for his successful organization of black communities in the 1960s, used a model of community disruption resting on this belief. Others believe that small groups should organize — community groups, cells, status groups — and that as they organize all over the country, eventually the power elite will be overwhelmed by their size and power. A few argue that the only way to go is through violent revolution, because the conservative forces are so entrenched.

The most common radical proposals are those of the socialists, who start from the position that the reforms suggested by the reformists are impossible to achieve because they will be killed by the ruling elite, who would stand to lose by their passage. Anderson states the position clearly: As long as the seats of economic power are privately held and as tenaciously controlled as they are in the United States, only liberal reforms in the interests of the ruling class will be maneuvered.

> The United States has slight chance of building the kind of people-oriented welfare state found in Scandinavia or even West Germany; corporate power is simply too overwhelming. . . . The capitalist class in the United States holds such enormous powers over the governmental process that the introduction of any measures which would *fundamentally* alter the balance of power and wealth would never be allowed passage in anything but watered-down form at all (1974, p. 327).

What Anderson and others envision as desirable and ultimately achievable goals are (1) state ownership and social control of all of the largest corporations; (2) workers' control of the production process, stressing autonomy in innovation, initiative, and operation, while linking together individual operations through a democratically designed general national plan; and (3) elimination from production goals of all waste expenditures designed to increase private profit and, instead, increase in the production of goods and services that serve necessary human and social needs. State ownership and control of all basic industries, including advanced science-based industries (such as computers, electronics, chemicals, transport, utilities, and finance), is considered necessary because this is the only way in which they can be made to serve the common, public good, and not just the good of the corporate elite.

Medical care, for example, should be considered as fully a part of the public domain as is education. But look what has happened to it in the hands of private capitalists. It has been allowed to become the most profitable of industries and to include the most affluent of professions. One socialist goal, among many, is "to put an end to the exploitation of human suffering" (Anderson 1974, p. 328). For another example, the profit-oriented private ownership of agrobusiness has resulted in the taxpayer's paying for "soil bank" land, storage, and subsidies to the tune of millions of dollars that lead to higher profits for the big agrobusiness interests.

To bring about the socialist state is not easy, for it is not characteristic of ruling classes to step aside gracefully. There are two main methods advocated to promote change: (1) via the legislative process, by virtue of cycles of economic crisis and progressive radicalization of the electorate in its unwillingness to tolerate further disruptions; and (2) via the direct revolt of the working class (variously defined, sometimes to include the middle and the poorest classes, as well as skilled laborers) and the institution of industrial democracy, which then carries over into restructuring of the governmental and legislative process (Anderson 1974, p. 331; Hacker 1966, pp. xii–xiii). High levels of production and material well-being are crucial to the attainment of any new social order, and so also is the development of new social values that elevate human needs over private profit.

Epilogue

All three perspectives share the orientation that challenge of a system of structured inequality is difficult, although the reformist orientation is somewhat more optimistic. What they all suggest is that the forces of inequality cannot be counteracted by individuals acting alone. This is because the forces of inequality are put into operation by powerful elite groups that operate in conjunction with each other when necessary and are more or less able to write the rules, create the mythologies, and control the processes leading to their own political and economic preeminence. Institutions become organized in such a way that elite interests are promoted. To change institutional patterns, other groups must also become powerful. Desire is not enough; the challenging groups must become sophisticated in political technique and knowledgeable about institutional procedures, including knowledge about economics, law, and class psychology.

There are three weak points in the control wielded by elites and, thus, three places of attack: (1) their control is dependent on the willingness of a vast substructure of scientists, technicians, and executives to carry out their wishes — the role of the upper-middle class is crucial, for its members possess the expertise, skill, and hierarchical authority to direct others; (2) their control is dependent on the blindness and disorganization of the far more numerous middle and working classes, which perform the productive work of the society; (3) their control is dependent on the reinforcement offered by the supportive institutions — the law, the courts, the media, education, and the church, for example. Challenge of an inequality system could be mounted at any and all of these three points. While it is probably true that challenge of an inequality system must ultimately be directed at the economic and political hegemony of the ruling elite, which is basically determinative, it is probably also true that the reinforcement provided by the supportive institutions must be eroded before challenge of the determinative ones can be successful.

What kind of restructuring of institutions in industrialized society would be possible and would lead to more equality? From the reformists, we select the idea of a floor and a ceiling on incomes and wealth. Income inequality should not be altogether eliminated, but it should be cut off in the extremes. Like the socialists, we recognize that the nationalization of certain industries and services would eliminate the control of essential activities by profit-oriented and narrow interests. Like both the reformists and the radicals, we agree that monopoly capitalism should be made more socially accountable. And we emphasize the desirability of significant democratization of the work place through worker participation in work management and of greater political democratization through protection of minority interests and greater accountability of political agencies.

Like the pessimists, we recognize the difficulty of instituting these changes. Sometimes the obstacles appear overwhelming. Those who say that inequality cannot be diminished or that it can be diminished only through radical revolution make strong points when they suggest that corporate and governmental elites are powerful enough and so inclined to put down any serious threat to existing institutional arrangements. Nevertheless, convincing as these arguments may be — and we are nearly persuaded by both their logic and empirical support — it is true that social institutions are created by human beings and can be altered by human beings. Such alteration requires a political and sociological consciousness on the part of the middle and working classes that transcends the generally conservative folk wisdom of tradition and the equally conservative myths constructed by elitist interests. As Birnbaum pointed out, "If men make their history, they do so because they possess sufficient political vision to alter their circumstance" (1972, p. 152). The pessimists would no doubt respond that not all men and women are equal in economic and political power, and it is the wishes of the more powerful that generally prevail. Still, economic and political changes have occurred in history, often as a result of economic and technological transitions, but often, too, as the result of challenge to a ruling group by another class or segment. The challenge by the bourgeoisie in the fifteenth, sixteenth, and seventeenth centuries resulted in the fall of feudal monarchy, for example. It has been done before, and it is perhaps consistent with historical facts to think beyond a denial that it can be done again.

REFERENCES

Aberle, D. F.; A. K. Cohen; A. K. Davis; M. J. Levy, Jr.,; and F. X. Sutton. 1950. "The Functional Prerequisites of a Society." *Ethics* 60: 100–11.

Abrahamson, M. 1973. "Functionalism and the Functional Theory of Stratification: An Empirical Assessment." *American Journal of Sociology* 78:1239–46.

Abrahamson, M.; H. Mizruchi; and C. A. Hornung. 1976. *Stratification and Mobility.* New York: Macmillan.

Abrams, M. 1968. "Some Measurements of Social Stratification in Britain." In *Social Stratification,* ed. J. A. Jackson, Cambridge: Cambridge University Press.

Acker, J. 1973. "Women and Social Stratification: A Case of Intellectual Sexism." *American Journal of Sociology* 78:936–45.

Ackerman, F.; H. Birnbaum; J. Wetzler; and A. Zimbalist. 1971. "Income Distribution in the United States." *Review of Radical Political Economics* 3:20–34.

Adorno, T. W.; E. Frenkel-Brunswik; D. J. Levinson; and R. N. Sanford. 1950. *The Authoritarian Personality.* New York: Harper & Row.

Agger, R. E.; D. Goldrich; and B. E. Swanson. 1964. *The Rulers and the Ruled: Political Power and Impotence in American Communities.* New York: Wiley.

Alcorn, S., and P. R. Knights. 1975. "Most Uncommon Bostonians: A Critique of Stephan Thernstrom's *The Other Bostonians."* *Historical Methods Newsletter* 8:98–114.

Alexander, C. N., Jr. 1972. "Status Perceptions." *American Sociological Review* 37:767–73.

Alford, R. R. 1975. "Paradigms of Relations between State and Society. In *Stress and Contradiction in Modern Capitalism: Public Policy and the Theory of the State,* ed. Colin Crouch and Claus Offe, Lexington, Mass.: Heath.

Allen, M. 1976. "Management Control in the Large Corporation: Comment on Zeitlin." *American Journal of Sociology* 81:885–94.

Almond, G., and S. Verba. 1963. *The Civic Culture.* Princeton: Princeton University Press.

References

Almquist, E. M. 1977. "Women in the Labor Force." *Signs* 2:843–55.

American Almanac. 1970. New York: Grosset and Dunlap.

——. 1972. New York: Grosset and Dunlap.

Amory, C. 1947. *The Proper Bostonians.* New York: Dutton.

——. 1960. *Who Killed Society?* New York: Harper & Row.

Anderson, C. H. 1974. *The Political Economy of Social Class.* Englewood Cliffs, N.J.: Prentice-Hall.

Anderson, H. 1935. "The Educational and Occupational Attainments of Our National Rulers." *Scientific Monthly* 40:511–18.

Antonovsky, A. 1972. "Social Class, Life Expectancy, and Overall Mortality." In *Patients, Physicians and Marital Status,* ed. E. G. Jaco, pp. 5–31. New York: Free Press.

Apter, D. E. 1964. "Ideology and Discontent." In *Ideology and Discontent,* ed. D. E. Apter, pp. 15–46. New York: Free Press.

Aron, R. 1968. *Main Currents in Sociological Thought.* Vol. 1. Translated by Richard Howard and Helen Weaver. Garden City, N.Y.: Doubleday Anchor.

Astin, A. W. 1972. *College Dropouts: A National Profile.* American Council on Education Research Reports, vol. 7, no. 1. Washington, D.C.: American Council on Education.

Astin, A. W. 1968. "Undergraduate Achievement and Institutional Excellence." *Science,* August 16, pp. 661–68.

Atkinson, A. B. 1975. *The Economics of Inequality.* Oxford: Clarendon.

Atkinson, J. W. 1958. "Thematic Apperception Measurement of Motives within the Context of a Theory of Motivation." In *Motives in Fantasy, Action, and Society,* ed. J. W. Atkinson, pp. 596–616. Princeton: Van Nostrand.

Axelrod, M. 1956. "Urban Structure and Social Participation." *American Sociological Review* 21:14–18.

Bachrach, P., and M. S. Baratz. 1963. "Decisions and Non-Decisions." *American Political Science Review* 57:632–42.

——. 1970. *Power and Poverty: Theory and Practice.* New York: Oxford University Press.

Bagdikian, B. H. 1964. *In The Midst of Plenty.* Boston: Beacon.

Bailyn, L. 1970. "Career and Family Orientations of Husbands and Wives in Relation to Marital Happiness." *Human Relations* 23:97–113.

Baltzell, E. 1958. *Philadelphia Gentlemen: The Making of a National Upper Class.* Glencoe, Ill.: Free Press.

——. 1964. *The Protestant Establishment: Aristocracy and Caste in America.* New York: Random House.

Baltzell, E. D. 1966. " 'Who's Who in America' and 'The Social Register.' " In *Class, Status, and Power: Social Stratification in Comparative Perspective,* ed. R. Bendix and S. M. Lipset, pp. 266–75. 2nd edition, New York: Free Press.

Banfield, E. C. 1968. *The Unheavenly City: The Nature and Future of Our Urban Crisis.* Boston: Little, Brown.

——. 1970. *The Unheavenly City Revisited: The Nature and Future of Our Urban Crisis.* Boston: Little, Brown.

Baran, P., and P. Sweezy. 1966. *Monopoly Capital.* New York: Monthly Review Press.

Barber, B. 1957. *Social Stratification.* New York: Harcourt, Brace.

Barlow, R.; H. E. Brazer; and J. N. Morgan. 1966. *Economic Behavior of the Affluent.* Washington, D.C.: Brookings Institution.

Baron, H. M., and B. Hymer. 1971. "The Dynamics of the Dual Labor Market." In *Problems in Political Economy: An Urban Perspective,* ed. David M. Gordon, pp. 94–101. Lexington, Mass.: Heath.

Bartell, G. D. 1971. *Group Sex.* New York: Peter H. Wyden.

Bass, B. M. 1955. "Authoritarianism or Acquiescence?" *Journal of Abnormal and Social Psychology* 51:616–23.

Baster, N. 1970. *Distribution of Income and Economic Growth: Concepts and Issues.* Geneva: United Nations Research Institute for Social Development.

Baum, M. 1971. "Love, Marriage and the Division of Labor." *Sociological Inquiry* 41:107–17.

Bayley, D. H., and H. Mendelsohn. 1972. "The Policeman's World." In *Race, Crime, and Justice,* ed. C. E. Reasons and J. L. Kuykendall, pp. 206–18. Pacific Palisades. Calif.: Goodyear.

Beals, R. L., and H. Hoijer. 1965. *An Introduction to Anthropology.* 3d ed. New York: Macmillan.

Becker, H. S. 1953. "Social Class Variations in the Teacher-Pupil Relationship." *Journal of Educational Sociology* 25:451–65.

Bell, D. 1958. "The Power Elite—Reconsidered." *American Journal of Sociology* 64:238–50.

——. 1973. *The Coming of Post-Industrial Society.* New York: Basic Books.

Bell, W., and M. D. Boat. 1957. "Urban Neighborhoods and Informal Social Relations." *American Journal of Sociology* 62:391–98.

Bell, W., and M. T. Force. 1956. "Urban Neighborhood Types and Participation in Formal Associations." *American Sociological Review* 21:25–34.

Bendix, R., and S. M. Lipset. 1957. "Political Sociology: An Essay and Bibliography." *Current Sociology* 6:79–169.

Benoit-Smullyan, E. 1944. "Status, Status Types, and Status Interrelations." *American Sociological Review* 9:151–61.

Bensman, J. 1972. "Status Communities in an

Urban Society: The Musical Community." In *Status Communities in Modern Society: Alternatives to Class Analysis*, ed. H. R. Stub, pp. 113–30. Hinsdale, Ill.: Dryden.

Bentley, A. F. 1949. *The Process of Government: A Study of Social Pressures*. Bloomington, Ind. Principia Press.

Bereiter, C. 1967. *Acceleration of Intellectual Development in Early Childhood*. Urbana, Ill.: Illinois University. Arlington, Va.: Educational Resources Information Center, Document No. 014332.

Berelson, B. 1960. *Graduate Education in the United States*. New York: McGraw-Hill.

Berg, I. 1971. *Education and Jobs: The Great Training Robbery*. Boston: Beacon.

Bergel, E. E. 1962. *Social Stratification*. New York: McGraw-Hill.

Berger, A. S., and W. Simon. 1974. "Black Families and the Moynihan Report: A Research Evaluation." *Social Problems* 22:145–61.

Berger, B. 1957. "Sociology and the Intellectuals: An Analysis of a Stereotype." *Antioch Review* 17:275–90.

———. 1960. *Working-Class Suburb*. Berkeley and Los Angeles: University of California Press.

Bergmann, B. 1971. "The Effect on White Incomes of Discrimination in Employment." *Journal of Political Economy* 79:294–313.

Bergner, L., and A. S. Yerby. 1968. "Low Income and Barriers to Use of Health Services." *The New England Journal of Medicine* 278:541–46.

Bernstein, B. 1964. "Elaborated and Restricted Codes: Their Social Origins and Some Consequences." In *The Ethnography of Communication*, ed. J. J .Gumpery and D. Hymes, special issue of *American Anthropologist*, vol. 66, pt. 2, pp. 55–69.

Bernstein, M. H. 1972. "Independent Regulatory Agencies: A Perspective on Their Reform." In "The Government as Regulator," *Annals of the American Academy of Political and Social Science* 400:14–26.

Bernton, H. S. 1965. "The Approach of the Cockroach to Allergy." *Medical Annals of the District of Columbia* 34:122–24.

Bettelheim, B., and M. Janowitz. 1950. *The Dynamics of Prejudice*. New York: Harper & Row.

Bibb, R., and W. H. Form. 1977. "The Effects of Industrial, Occupational, and Sex Stratification on Wages in Blue-Collar Markets." *Social Forces* 55:974–96.

Bierman, P. 1961. "Meeting the Health Needs of Low-Income Families." *Annals of the American Academy of Political and Social Science* 337:103–13.

Bierstedt, R. 1950. "An Analysis of Social Power." *American Sociological Review* 15:730–38.

Billett, R. O. 1932. *The Administration and Supervision of Homogeneous Grouping*. Columbus: Ohio State University Press.

Binstock, J. 1970. "Survival in the American College Industry." Ph.D. diss., Brandeis University.

Birmingham, S. 1958. *The Right People*. Boston: Little, Brown.

Birnbaum, N. 1972. "Late Capitalism in the United States." In *The Revival of American Socialism: Selected Papers of the Socialist Scholars Conference* ed. G. Fischer, pp. 133–53. New York: Oxford University Press.

Birren, J. E., and R. Hess. 1968. "Influences of Biological, Psychological and Social Deprivations on Learning and Performance. In *Perspectives on Human Deprivation*, pp. 91–183. Washington D.C.: Government Printing Office.

Blum, Z. D., and P. H. Rossi. 1968. "Social Class Research and Images of the Poor: A Bibliographic Review." In *On Understanding Poverty: Perspectives from the Social Sciences*, ed. D. P. Moynihan, pp. 343–97. New York: Basic Books.

Blau, P. M. 1973. *The Organization of Academic Work*. New York: Wiley.

Blau, P. M., and O. D. Duncan. 1965. "Some Preliminary Findings of Social Stratification in the United States." *Acta Sociologica* 9:4–24.

———. 1967. *The American Occupational Structure*. New York: Wiley.

Blau, P. M.; M. V. Heydebrand; and R. E. Stauffer. 1966. "The Structure of Small Bureaucracies." *American Sociological Review* 31:179–91.

Blauner, R. 1966. "Work Satisfaction and Industrial Trends in Modern Society." In *Class, Status and Power*, 2d ed., ed. R. Bendix and S. M. Lipset, pp. 473–87. New York: Free Press.

Blishen, B. R. 1958. "The Construction and Use of an Occupational Class Scale. *Canadian Journal of Economic and Political Science* 24:519–31.

Blood, R. O., and R. L. Hamblin. 1958. "The Effect of the Wife's Employment on the Family Power Structure." *Social Forces* 36:347–52.

Blood, R. O., and D. M. Wolfe. 1960. *Husbands and Wives*. New York: Free Press.

Blumberg, P. M., and P. W. Paul. 1975. "Continuities and Discontinuities in Upper-Class Marriages." *Journal of Marriage and the Family* 37:63–77.

Bogue, D. J. 1963. *Skid Row in American Cities*. Chicago: Community and Family Study Center.

———. 1969. *Principles of Demography*. New York: Wiley.

Bonjean, C. M. 1966. "Mass, Class, and the Industrial Community: A Comparative Analysis of Managers, Businessmen, and Workers." *American Journal of Sociology* 72:149–62.

Bordua, D. J. 1960. "Educational Aspirations and Parental Stress on College." *Social Forces* 38:262–69.

Borg, W. R. 1966. *Ability Grouping in the Public Schools.* 2d ed. Madison, Wis.: Dembar Educational Research Service.

Bose, C. E. 1973. *Jobs and Gender: Sex and Occupational Prestige.* Baltimore: Johns Hopkins University, Center for Metropolitan Planning and Research.

Boskin, M. J. 1972. "Unions and Relative Real Wages." *American Economic Review* 62:466–72.

Bottomore, T. B. 1966. *Classes in Modern Society.* New York: Vintage Books.

————. 1968. "Marxist Sociology." In *International Encyclopedia of the Social Sciences,* vol. 10, ed. David L. Sills. New York: Macmillan and Free Press.

Boulding, K. E. 1964. *The Meaning of the Twentieth Century.* New York: Harper & Row.

Bowles, S., and H. Gintis. 1974. "IQ in the United States Class Structure." In *The New Assault on Equality: IQ and Social Stratification,* ed. A. Gartner, C. Greer, and F. Riessman, pp. 2–84. New York: Harper & Row.

————. 1976. *Schooling in Capitalist America: Educational Reform and the Contradictions of Economic Life.* New York: Basic Books.

Bowles, S.; H. Gintis; and P. Meyer. 1975. "The Long Shadow of Work: Education, the Family, and the Reproduction of the Social Division of Labor." *Insurgent Sociologist* 5:3–22.

Bowman, M. J. 1971. "Economics of Education." In *Financing Higher Education: Alternatives for the Federal Government,* ed. M. D. Orwig, pp. 37–70. Iowa City: American College Testing Program.

Bradburn, N. M., and D. Caplovitz. 1965. *Reports on Happiness.* Chicago: Aldine.

Bressler, M. 1960. "The Myers Case: An Instance of Successful Racial Invasion." *Social Problems* 8:126–42.

Brinton, C. 1955. *The Anatomy of Revolution.* New York: Vintage Books.

Brenner, M. H. 1968. "Use of High School Data to Predict Work Performance." *Journal of Applied Psychology* 52:29–30.

Brenner, M. H.; W. Mandell; S. Blackman; and R. M. Silverstein. 1967. "Economic Conditions and Mental Hospitalization for Functional Psychosis." *Journal of Nervous and Mental Disease* 145:371–84.

Bronfenbrenner, U. 1961. "The Changing American Child: A Speculative Analysis." *Journal of Social Issues* 17:6–18.

Brophy, J., and T. Good. 1970. "Teachers' Communications of Differential Expectations for Children's Classroom Performance: Some Behavioral Data." *Journal of Educational Psychology* 61:365–74.

Brown, B. 1968. *The Assessment of Self-Concept among Four Year Old Negro and White Children: A Comparative Study Using the Brown IDS Self-Concept Reference Test.* New York: Institute for Developmental Studies.

Brown, M. B. 1970. *What Economics Is About.* London: Weidenfeld and Nicolson.

Brown, R. 1965. *Social Psychology.* New York: Free Press.

Brzezinski, Z., and S. P. Huntington. 1964. *Political Power: USA/USSR.* New York: Viking Press.

Buckley, W. 1958. "Social Stratification and the Functional Theory of Social Differentiation." *American Sociological Review* 23:369–75.

Burchard, W. W. 1959. "The Status of 'Status.'" Paper presented to Midwest Sociological Society, Lincoln, Nebraska.

Burchinal, L. G. 1959. "Some Social Status Criteria and Church Membership and Church Attendance." *Journal of Social Psychology* 49:53–64.

Burck, C. G. 1976. "A Group Profile of the Fortune 500 Chief Executive." *Fortune* 93:172–77, 308–12.

Burgess, E., and D. Price. 1963. *An American Dependency Challenge.* Chicago: American Public Welfare Association.

Burgess, E. W., and H. J. Locke. 1963. *The Family: From Institution to Companionship.* 3d ed. New York: American.

Burnham, J. 1941. *The Managerial Revolution.* New York: Day.

Burns, R. K. 1954. "The Comparative Economic Position of Manual and White Collar Employees." *Journal of Business* 27:257–67.

Campbell, A. 1971. *White Attitudes Toward Black People.* Ann Arbor: Institute for Social Research.

Campbell, A.; P. Converse; W. Miller; and D. Dokes. 1960. *The American Voter.* New York: Wiley.

Campbell, A.; G. Gurin; and W. Miller. 1954. *The Voter Decides.* Evanston, Ill.: Row, Peterson.

Cantril, H. 1943. "Educational and Economic Composition of Religious Groups." *American Journal of Sociology* 48:574–79.

Caplovitz, D. 1964. "The Problems of Blue-Collar Consumers." In *Blue-Collar World,* ed. A. B. Shostak and W. Gomberg, pp. 110–20. Englewood Cliffs, N.J.: Prentice-Hall.

Caplow, T. 1954. *The Sociology of Work.* New York: McGraw-Hill.

Carcagno, G. J., and W. S. Corson. 1977. "Welfare Reform." In *Setting National Priorities: The 1978 Budget,* ed. J. A. Pechman, pp. 249–81. Washington, D.C.: The Brookings Institution.

Cassell, F. H., and S. I. Doctors. 1972. *A Three Company Study of the Intrafirm Mobility of Blue-Collar and Lower Level White-Collar Workers.* Chicago: Northwestern University.

Cavala, W., and A. Wildavsky. 1970. "The Political

Feasibility of Income by Right." *Public Policy* 18:321–54.

Centers, R. 1948. "Occupational Mobility of Urban Occupational Strata." *American Sociological Review* 13:197–203.

———. 1949. *The Psychology of Social Classes.* Princeton: Princeton University Press.

Chamberlain, N. W. 1965. *The Labor Sector.* New York: American Elsevier.

Chambliss, W. J., 1973. *Sociological Readings in the Conflict Perspective.* Reading, Mass.: Addison-Wesley.

Chandler, B. J., and F. D. Erickson. 1968. *Sounds of Society: A Demonstration Program in Group Inquiry.* Washington, D.C.: Government Printing Office.

Charles, E. 1948. *The Changing Size of the Family in Canada.* Census Monograph no. 1, 8th Census of Canada. Ottawa: The King's Printer and Controller of Stationery.

Chenoweth, L. 1974. *The American Dream of Success.* North Scituate, Mass.: Duxbury Press.

Chilman, C. S. 1966. *Growing Up Poor.* Washington, D.C.: Government Printing Office.

Chinoy, E. 1950. "Research in Class Structure." *Canadian Journal of Economics and Political Science* 16:225–63.

———. 1955. *Automobile Workers and the American Dream.* Garden City, N.Y.: Doubleday.

Christie, R., and M. Jahoda. 1954. *Studies in the Scope and Method of the Authoritarian Personality.* Glencoe, Ill.: Free Press.

Citizen Advisory Council on the Status of Women. 1972. "The Equal Rights Amendment and Alimony and Child Support Laws." Washington, D.C.

Claiborn, W. L. 1969. "Expectancy Effects in the Classroom: A Failure to Replicate." *Journal of Educational Psychology* 60:377–83.

Clark, B. R. 1960. *The Open Door College: A Case Study.* New York: McGraw-Hill.

———. 1962. *Educating the Expert Society.* San Francisco: Chandler.

Clark, C. 1952. *Conditions of Economic Progress.* Rev. ed. New York: Macmillan.

Clark, J. J., and R. H. Woodward, eds. 1966. *Success in America.* Belmont, Calif.: Wadsworth.

Clark, T. N., ed. 1968. *Community Structure and Decision-Making: Comparative Analyses.* San Francisco: Chandler.

Cohen, A. K. 1955. *Delinquent Boys: The Culture of the Gang.* Glencoe, Ill.: Free Press.

Cohen, A. K., and H. M. Hodges, Jr. 1963. "Characteristics of the Lower Blue-collar Class." *Social Problems* 10:303–34.

Cohen, J.; L. E. Hazelrigg; and W. Pope. 1975. "De-Parsonizing Weber: A Critique of Parsons' Interpretation of Weber's Sociology." *American Sociological Review* 40:229–41.

Cohen, P. S. 1968. *Modern Social Theory.* New York: Basic Books.

Cohn, W. 1960. "Social Status and the Ambivalence Hypothesis: Some Critical Notes and a Suggestion." *American Sociological Review* 25:508–13.

Coleman, J. S. 1966. "Equal Schools or Equal Students?" *Public Interest* 4:70–75.

Coleman, J. S., et al. 1966 *Equality of Educational Opportunity.* Washington, D.C.: U.S. Office of Education.

Coles, R. 1978. *Children of Crisis.* Vol. 5. Boston: Little, Brown.

Collins, R. 1969. "Education and Employment." Ph.D. diss., University of California at Berkeley.

———. 1971. "Functional and Conflict Theories of Educational Stratification." *American Sociological Review* 36:1002–19.

———. 1975. *Conflict Sociology: Toward an Explanatory Science.* New York: Academic Press.

Conant, J. B. 1961. *Slums and Suburbs: A Commentary on Schools in Metropolitan Areas.* New York: McGraw-Hill.

Cook, R. M. 1973. "Review Essay: A View From an I-Beam." *American Journal of Sociology* 79: 444–58.

Cooley, C. H. 1909. *Social Organization: A Study of the Larger Mind.* New York: Charles Scribner's.

Coser, L. A. 1956. *The Functions of Social Conflict.* London: Free Press of Glencoe.

Coult, A. D., and R. W. Habenstein. 1965. *Cross Tabulations of Murdock's World Ethnographic Sample.* Columbia, Mo.: University of Missouri Press.

Counts, G. S. 1925. "The Social Status of Occupations: A Problem in Vocational Guidance." *School Review* 33:16–27.

Coward, B. E.; J. R. Feagin; and J. A. Williams, Jr. 1974. "The Culture of Poverty Debate: Some Additional Data." *Social Problems* 21:621–34.

Crockett, H. J., Jr. 1962. "The Achievement Motive and Differential Occupational Mobility in the United States." *American Sociological Review* 27:191–204.

———. 1966. "Psychological Origins of Mobility." In *Social Structure and Mobility in Economic Development,* ed. N. Smelser and S. M. Lipset, Chicago: Aldine.

Crockett, N. L., ed. 1970. *The Power Elite in America.* Lexington, Mass.: Heath.

Cross, K. P. 1968. *The Junior College Student: A Research Description.* Princeton: Educational Testing Service.

Cuber, J. F., and P. B. Harroff. 1965. *The Significant Americans: A Study of Sexual Behavior among the Affluent.* New York: Appleton-Century-Crofts.

Cuber, J. F., and W. F. Kenkel. 1954. *Social Stratification in the United States.* New York: Appleton-Century-Crofts.

Curtis, R. F. 1959. "Occupational Mobility and Urban Social Life. *American Journal of Sociology* 65:296–98.

———. 1963. "Differential Association and the Stratification of the Urban Community." *Social Forces* 42:68–77.

Cutright, P. 1965. "Political Structure, Economic Development, and National Social Security Programs." *American Journal of Sociology* 70:537–50.

Dahl, R. A. 1958. "A Critique of the Ruling Elite Model." *American Political Science Review* 52:463–69.

———. 1961. *Who Governs?* New Haven: Yale University Press.

Dahrendorf, R. 1958a. "Out of Utopia: Toward a Reorientation of Sociological Analysis." *American Journal of Sociology.* 64:115–27.

———. 1958b. "Toward a Theory of Social Conflict." *Journal of Conflict Resolution* 2:170–83.

———. 1959. *Class and Class Conflict in Industrial Society.* Stanford, Calif.: Stanford University Press.

Das, M. S. 1971. "Economic Aspects of Caste in India and the United States." *Social Science* 46:232–37.

David, D. S., and R. Brannon, eds. 1976. *The Forty-Nine Percent Majority.* Reading, Mass.: Addison-Wesley.

Davidson, C., and C. M. Gaitz. 1974. "Are the Poor Different? A Comparison of Work Behavior and Attitudes among the Urban Poor and Nonpoor." *Social Problems* 22:229–45.

Davidson, H. H., and G. Lang. 1960. "Children's Perceptions of Teachers' Feelings toward Them." *Journal of Experimental Education* 29:107–18.

Davidson, L., and D. Krackhardt. 1975. "Structural Change and the Disadvantaged: An Empirical Test of Culture of Poverty/Situational Theories of Hard-Core Work Behavior." Paper presented to annual meeting of the American Sociological Association, San Francisco.

Davidson, P. E., and H. Anderson. 1937. *Occupational Mobility in an American Community.* Stanford, Calif.: Stanford University Press.

Davies, J. C. 1962. "Toward a Theory of Revolution." *American Sociological Review* 27:5–19.

Davis, A. 1946. "The Motivation of the Underprivileged Worker." In *Industry and Society,* ed. W. F. Whyte, pp. 84–106. New York: McGraw-Hill.

Davis, A. 1949. "Child Rearing in the Class Structure of American Society." In *The Family in a Democratic Society,* anniversary papers of the Comunity Service Society of New York, pp. 56–69. New York: Columbia University Press.

Davis, A.; B. Gardner; and M. R. Gardner. 1941. *Deep South.* Chicago: University of Chicago Press.

Davis, D. B. 1966. *The Problem of Slavery in Western Culture.* Ithaca, N.Y.: Cornell University Press.

Davis, K. 1948. *Human Society.* New York: Macmillan.

Davis, K., and W. E. Moore. 1945. "Some Principles of Stratification." *American Sociological Review* 10:242–49.

Dean, D. 1961. "Alienation: Its Meaning and Measurement." *American Sociological Review* 26:753–58.

De Fronzo, J. 1973. "Embourgeoisement in Indianapolis?" *Social Problems* 21:269–83.

De Jong, P. Y.; M. J. Brawer; and S. S. Robin. 1971. "Patterns of Female Intergenerational Occupational Mobility: A Comparison with Male Patterns of Intergenerational Occupational Mobility." *American Sociological Review* 36:1033–42.

Demerath, N. J., III. 1964. *Social Class in American Protestantism.* Chicago: Rand McNally.

Deutsch, M. 1963. "The Disadvantaged Child and the Learning Process." In *In Education in Depressed Areas,* ed. H. Passow, pp. 163–79. New York: Teachers College Press.

Diamond, D. E., and H. Bedrosian. 1970. *Hiring Standards and Job Performance.* Washington, D.C.: Government Printing Office.

Dillard, J. L. 1972. *Black English.* New York: Random House.

Doeringer, P., and M. J. Piore. 1966. "Internal Labor Markets, Technological Change, and Labor Force Adjustment." Mimeographed. Cambridge, Mass.: Harvard University.

———. 1971. *Internal Labor Markets and Manpower Analysis.* Lexington, Mass.: Heath.

Dolbeare, K. M.; P. Dolbeare; and J. Hadley. 1973. *American Ideologies: The Competing Political Beliefs of the 1970s.* Chicago: Markham.

Dollard, J. 1937. *Caste and Class in a Southern Town.* New Haven: Yale University Press.

Domestic Council, Executive Office of the President. 1971. *Workfare: Reforming the Welfare System.* Washington, D.C.: Government Printing Office.

Domhoff, G. W. 1967. *Who Rules America?* Englewood Cliffs, N.J.: Prentice-Hall.

———. 1970. *The Higher Circles: The Governing Class in America.* New York: Random House.

———. 1974. "State and Ruling Class in Corporate America." *Insurgent Sociologist* 4:3–16.

———. 1978. *Who Really Rules? New Haven and Community Power Reexamined.* Santa Monica, Calif.: Goodyear.

Dotson, F. 1951. "Patterns of Voluntary Association

among Urban Working-Class Families." *American Sociological Review* 16:687–93.

Douglas, J. W. B. 1968. *All Our Future*. London: MacGibbon.

Douvan, E. 1956. "Social Success and Success Striving." *Journal of Abnormal and Social Psychology* 52:219–33.

Douvan, E., and J. Adelson. 1958. "The Psychodynamics of Social Mobility in Adolescent Boys." *Journal of Abnormal and Social Psychology* 56:31–44.

Downs, A. 1970. *Who Are the Urban Poor?* Supplementary paper no. 26. New York: Committee for Economic Development.

Drake, L. R.; H. R. Kaplan; and R. A. Stone. 1972. "How Do Employers Value the Interview?" *Journal of College Placement* 32:47–51.

Drake, S. C., and H. R. Clayton. 1945. *Black Metropolis*. New York: Harcourt, Brace.

D'Souza, V. S. 1962. "Social Grading of Occupations in India." *Sociological Review* 10:145–59.

Duncan, O. D. 1961. "A Socioeconomic Index for All Occupations." In *Occupations and Social Status*, ed. A. J. Reiss, Jr., et al., pp. 109–38. New York: Free Press.

————. 1968. "Inheritance of Poverty or Inheritance of Race?" In *On Understanding Poverty*, ed. D. P. Moynihan, pp. 85–110. New York: Basic Books.

Duncan, O. D.; D. L. Featherman; and B. Duncan. 1972. *Socioeconomic Background and Achievement*. New York: Seminar Press.

Duncan, O. D., and R. W. Hodge. 1963. "Education and Occupational Mobility: A Regression Analysis." *American Journal of Sociology* 68:629–44.

Dunham, H. W. 1964. "Social Class and Schizophrenia." *American Journal of Orthopsychiatry* 34:634–42.

Durkheim, E. 1950. *The Rules of Sociological Method*. New York: Free Press.

Duvall, E. M. 1946. "Conceptions of Parenthood." *American Journal of Sociology* 52:193–203.

Dye, T. R. 1976. *Who's Running America? Institutional Leadership in the United States*. Englewood Cliffs, N.J.: Prentice-Hall.

Dye, T. R., and L. H. Zeigler. 1975. *The Irony of Democracy: An Uncommon Introduction to American Politics*. 3d ed. North Scituate, Mass.: Duxbury Press.

Dynes, R. R.; A. C. Clarke; and S. Dinitz. 1956. "Levels of Occupational Aspiration: Some Aspects of Family Existence as a Variable." *American Sociological Review* 21:212–15.

Edwards, A. M. 1943. *Comparative Occupational Statistics for the United States, 1870 to 1940*. Washington, D.C.: Government Printing Office.

Edwards, R. C. 1972. "Alienation and Inequality: Capitalist Relations of Production in a Bureaucratic Enterprise." Ph.D. diss., Harvard University.

Edels, K., et al. 1951. *Intelligence and Cultural Differences: A Study of Cultural Learning and Problem-Solving*. Chicago: University of Chicago Press.

Eitzen, D. S. 1974. *Social Structure and Social Problems*. Boston: Allyn and Bacon.

Ekstrom, R. B. 1959. *Experimental Studies of Homogeneous Grouping*. Princeton: Educational Testing Service.

Elder, G. 1969. "Appearance and Education in Marriage Mobility." *American Sociological Review* 34:519–32.

Elliott, O. 1959. *Men at the Top*. New York: Harper & Row.

Ellis, E. 1952. "Social Psychological Correlates of Upward Mobility among Unmarried Career Women." *American Sociological Review* 17:558–63.

Ellis, R. A. 1970. "Some New Perspectives on Upward Mobility." *Urban and Social Change Review* 4:15–17.

Ellis, R. A., and W. C. Lane. 1963. "Structural Supports for Upward Mobility." *American Sociological Review* 38:743–56.

————. 1967. "Social Mobility and Social Isolation: A Test of Sorokin's Dissociative Hypothesis." *American Sociological Review* 28:743–56.

English, J. T. 1968. "The Poor Get Sicker and the Sick Get Poorer." *Roche Medical Image* 10.

Erlanger, H. S. 1974. "Social Class and Corporal Punishment in Childrearing: A Reassessment." *American Sociological Review* 39:68–85.

Esposito, D. 1973. "Homogeneous and Heterogeneous Ability Grouping: Principal Findings and Implications for Evaluating and Designing More Effective Educational Environments." *Review of Educational Research* 43:163–79.

Eulau, H. 1962. *Class and Party in the Eisenhower Years*. New York: Free Press.

Eulau, H., and D. Koff. 1962. "Occupational Mobility and Political Career." *Western Political Quarterly* 15:507–21.

Eysenck, H. J. 1971. *The I.Q. Argument*. Freeport, N.Y.: Library Press.

Fallers, L. A. 1966. Review of G. Lenski. *Power and Privilege. American Sociological Review* 31:718.

Farmer, M. 1971. "Strategies for the '70s: A Ten-Point Public Service Program." *Social Policy* 2:3–5.

Farnsworth, C. H. 1976. "In France, the Income Disparity Is Great." *New York Times,* September 10.

Farris, C. D. 1956. "Authoritarianism as a Political Behavior Variable." *Journal of Politics* 18:61–82.

References

Feagin, J. R. 1972. "Poverty: We Still Believe That God Helps Those Who Help Themselves." *Psychology Today* 5:101–10.

———. 1975. *Subordinating the Poor: Welfare and American Beliefs*. Englewood Cliffs, N.J.: Prentice-Hall.

Featherman, D. L., and R. M. Hauser. 1975 "Sexual Inequalities and Socioeconomic Achievement in the U.S., 1962–1973." Paper presented to annual meeting of the Population Association of America, Seattle, Wash.

———. 1976. "Sexual Inequalities and Socioeconomic Achievement in the U.S., 1962–1973." *American Sociological Review* 41:462–83.

Federal Reserve System. 1966. *Survey of Financial Characteristics of Consumers, 1962*. Washington, D.C.: Government Printing Office.

Feierabend, I. K.; R. L. Feierabend; and B. A. Nesvold. 1969. "Social Change and Political Violence: Cross-National Patterns." In *Violence in America,* ed. H. D. Graham and T. R. Gurr, pp. 632–87. New York: Bantam Books.

Findley, W. C., and M. M. Bryan. *Ability Grouping: 1970*. Athens, Ga.: Center for Educational Improvement, University of Georgia.

Finley, M. J. 1960. *Slavery in Classical Antiquity*. Cambridge: W. Heffer and Sons.

Fletcher, R. 1956. "Functionalism as a Social Theory." *Sociological Review* 4:31–46.

Folger, J. K.; H. S. Astin; and A. E. Bayer. 1970. *Human Resources and Higher Education*. New York: Russell Sage Foundation.

Folger, J. K., and C. B. Nam. 1964. "Trends in Education in Relation to the Occupational Structure." *Sociology of Education* 38:19–33.

Form, W. M. 1973. "The Internal Stratification of the Working Class: System Involvements of Auto Workers in Four Countries." *American Sociological Review* 38:697–711.

Fortune. 1940. "The People of the U.S.A.—A Self Portrait." Vol. 21, p. 14.

———. 1975. "The Fortune Directory of the 500 Largest Industrial Corporations." Vol. 91, pp. 208–35.

———. 1976. "The Fortune Directory of the 500 Largest U.S. Industrial Corporations." Vol. 93, pp. 316–17.

Frank, A. G. 1973. "Functionalism and Dialectics." In *Sociological Readings in the Conflict Perspective,* ed. W. J. Chambliss, pp. 62–73. Reading, Mass.: Addison-Wesley.

Frazier, E. F. 1939. *The Negro Family in the United States*. Chicago: University of Chicago Press.

Freeman, L. C.; T. J. Fararo; W. Bloomberg, Jr.; and M. H. Sunshine. 1963. "Locating Leaders in Local Communities: A Comparison of Some Alternative Approaches." *American Sociological Review* 28:791–98.

Freiberg, J. 1970 "The Effects of Ability Grouping on Interactions in the Classroom." Arlington, Va.: Educational Resources & Information Center, Document No. 053194.

Fried, E. R.; A. M. Rivlin; C. L. Schultze; and N. H. Teeters. 1973. *Setting National Priorities: The 1974 Budget*. Washington, D.C.: Brookings Institution.

Friedenberg, E. Z. 1964. *Coming of Age in America: Growth and Acquiescence*. New York: Random House.

Friedl, E. 1975. *Women and Men: An Anthropologist's View*. New York: Holt, Rinehart and Winston.

Friedman, M. and S. Kuznets. 1954. *Income from Independent Professional Practice*. New York: National Bureau of Economic Research.

Friend, I.; J. Crockett; and M. Blume. 1970. *Mutual Funds and Other Institutional Investors: A New Perspective*. New York: McGraw-Hill.

Fuchs, V. R. 1971. "Differences in Hourly Earnings between Men and Women." *Monthly Labor Review* 94:9–15.

Fukuyama, Y. 1961. "The Major Dimensions of Church Membership." *Review of Religious Research* 2:154–61.

Fusfeld, D. R. 1972. "The Rise of the Corporate State in America." *Journal of Economic Issues* 6:1–22.

Galbraith, J. K. 1952. *American Capitalism: The Concept of Countervailing Power*. Boston: Houghton Mifflin.

———. 1958. *The Affluent Society*. Boston: Houghton Mifflin.

———. 1973. *Economics and the Public Purpose*. Boston: Houghton Mifflin.

Gallup Opinion Index. 1967. Report No. 20. Princeton: Gallup International.

———. 1973. Report No. 102. Princeton: Gallup International.

Gans, H. J. 1962. *The Urban Villagers*. New York: Free Press.

———. 1967. *The Levittowners: Ways of Life and Politics in a New Suburban Community*. New York: Random House.

———. 1968. "Culture and Class in the Study of Poverty: An Approach to Anti-Poverty Research." In *On Understanding Poverty,* ed. D. P. Moynihan, pp. 201–28. New York: Basic Books.

———. 1972. "The Positive Functions of Poverty." *American Journal of Sociology* 78:275–89.

———. 1974. *More Equality*. New York: Vintage Books.

Geis, G. 1977. "The Heavy Electrical Equipment Antitrust Cases of 1961." In *White-Collar Crime: Offenses in Business, Politics, and the Professions,* rev. ed., ed. G. Geis and R. F. Meier, pp. 117–32. New York: Free Press.

Gelles, R. 1972. *The Violent Home*. Beverly Hills, Calif.: Sage.

Gerth, H. H., and C. Wright Mills, trans. and eds. 1946. *From Max Weber: Essays in Sociology.* New York: Oxford University Press.

Giddens, A. 1973. *The Class Structure of the Advanced Societies.* New York: Barnes and Noble.

Gillespie, D. L. 1971. "Who Has the Power: The Marital Struggle." *Journal of Marriage and the Family* 33:445–58.

Gladwin, T. 1967. *Poverty U.S.A.* Boston: Little, Brown.

Glazer, N., and D. P. Moynihan. 1963. *Beyond the Melting Pot.* Cambridge, Mass.: M.I.T. Press and Harvard University Press.

Glenn, E. N., and R. L. Feldberg. 1977. "Degraded and Deskilled: The Proletarianization of Clerical Work." *Social Problems* 25:52–64.

Glenn, N. D. 1968. "Social Security and Income Redistribution." *Social Forces* 46:538–39.

Glenn, N. D., and J. P. Alston. 1968. "Cultural Distances among Occupational Categories." *American Sociological Review* 33:365–82.

Goldberg, M. L.; A. H. Passow; and J. Justman. 1966. *The Effects of Ability Grouping.* New York: Teachers College Press.

Goldhamer, H., and E. A. Shils. 1939. "Types of Power and Status." *American Journal of Sociology* 45:171–82.

Goldstein, T. 1978. "Closing the Ring around White-Collar Criminals." *New York Times,* January 29.

Goldthorpe, H. H.. D. Lockwood, F. Beckhoffer, and J. Platt. 1969. *The Affluent Worker in the Class Structure.* Cambridge: Cambridge University Press.

Good, T., and J. Brophy. 1973. *Looking in Classrooms.* New York: Harper & Row.

Goode, W. 1963. *World Revolutions and Family Patterns.* New York: Free Press.

———. 1964. "The Meaning of Class Differences in the Divorce Rate." In *Readings on the Family and Society,* ed. W. J. Goode, pp. 204–06. Englewood Cliffs, N.J.: Prentice-Hall.

Goodwin, L. 1972. *Do the Poor Want to Work? A Social-Psychological Study of Work Orientations.* Washington, D.C.: Brookings Institution.

Gordon, D. M., 1971. *Problems in Political Economy.* Lexington, Mass.: Heath.

———. 1972. *Theories of Poverty and Underemployment.* Lexington, Mass.: Heath.

Gordon, M. 1963. *Social Class in American Sociology.* New York: McGraw-Hill.

———. 1964. *Assimilation in American Life: The Role of Race, Religion, and National Origins.* New York: Oxford University Press.

Gordon, M. M. 1958. *Social Class in American Sociology.* Durham, N.C.: Duke University Press.

Grandjean, B. D., and F. D. Bean. 1975. "The Davis Moore Theory and Perceptions of Stratification: Some Relevant Evidence." *Social Forces* 54:166–80.

Greenleigh, A., and H. S. McCalley. 1960. "Facts, Fallacies and Future: A Study of the Aid to Dependent Children Program of Cook County, Illinois." Mimeographed. New York: Greenleigh Associates.

Greenleigh Associates. 1962. *Factual Data: Report to the Moreland Commission.* New York: Greenleigh Associates.

Gross, B. 1972. "A Closer Look at Income Distribution." *Social Policy* 3:61.

Gross, N. 1953. "Social Class Identification in the Urban Community." *American Sociological Review* 18:398–404.

Gupta, S. K. 1968. "On Caste Stratification in a Village of Uttar Pradesh." *Eastern Anthropologist* 21:87–94.

Gurin, G., Veroff, J., and Feld, S. 1960. *Americans View Their Mental Health.* New York: Basic Books.

Gurr, T. R. 1970. *Why Men Rebel.* Princeton: Princeton University Press.

Gusfield, J. R., and M. Schwartz. 1963. "The Meanings of Occupational Prestige: Reconsideration of the NORC Scale." *American Sociological Review* 28:265–71.

Gutwillig, R. 1960. "The Select Seventeen: A Guide to Upper-Class Education." *Esquire* 54: 162ff.

Hackett, B. M. 1967. *Higher Civil Servants in California: A Social and Political Portrait.* Berkeley and Los Angeles: University of California Press.

Haer, J. L. 1957. "An Empirical Study of Social Class Awareness." *Social Forces* 36:117–21.

Haller, A. O., and A. Portes. 1973. "Status Attainment Processes." *Sociology of Education* 46:51–91.

Hamilton, R. 1964. "The Behavior and Values of Skilled Workers." In *Blue-Collar World: Studies of the American Worker,* ed. A. B. Shostak and W. Gomberg, pp. 42–59. Englewood Cliffs, N.J.: Prentice-Hall.

———. 1966. "The Marginal Middle Class: A Reconsideration." *American Sociological Review* 31:192–200.

———. 1972. *Class and Politics in the United States.* New York: Wiley.

Handel, G., and L. Rainwater. 1964. "Persistence and Change in Working Class Life Style." *Sociology and Social Research* 48:281–88.

Hansen, W. L., and B. A. Weisbrod. 1969. *Benefits, Costs, and Finance of Public Higher Education.* Chicago: Markham.

Hargens, L. L., and W. O. Hagstrom. 1967. "Sponsored and Contest Mobility of American Academic Scientists." *Sociology of Education* 40:24–38.

Harlem Youth Opportunities Unlimited. 1964. *Youth in The Ghetto.* New York: Harlem Youth Opportunities.

Harrington, M. 1962. *The Other America: Poverty in The United States.* New York: Macmillan.

———. 1975. "The Big Lie about the Sixties." *New Republic* 173:15–19.

Harrison, B. 1971. "Education and Underemployment in the Urban Ghetto. In *Problems in Political Economy: An Urban Perspective,* ed. D. M. Gordon, pp. 181–90. Lexington, Mass.: Heath.

Hauco, G. A. 1963. "A Logical Analysis of the Davis-Moore Theory of Stratification." *American Sociological Review* 28:801–04.

Hauser, R. M.; J. Dickinson; H. P. Travis; and J. N. Koffel. 1975a. "Structural Changes in Occupational Mobility among Men in the United States." *American Sociological Review* 40:585–98.

Hauser, R. M., and D. L. Featherman. 1973. "Trends in the Occupational Mobility of U.S. Men, 1962–1970." *American Sociological Review* 38:302–10.

Hauser, R. M.; D. L. Featherman; and D. P. Hogan. 1974. "Race and Sex in the Structure of Occupational Mobility in the United States, 1962." Paper presented at the 9th World Congress of Sociology, Toronto, Ontario, Canada.

Hauser, R. M.; J. N. Koffel; H. P. Travis; and P. J. Dickinson. 1975b. "Temporal Change in Occupational Mobility: Evidence for Men in the United States" *American Sociological Review* 40:279–97.

Hausknecht, M. 1962. *The Joiners: A Study of Voluntary Associations in the United States.* New York: Bedminster Press.

———. 1964. "The Blue-Collar Joiner." In *Blue-Collar World: Studies of the American Worker,* ed. A. B. Shostak and W. Gomberg, pp. 207–14. Englewood Cliffs, N.J.: Prentice-Hall.

Havemann, E., and P. S. West. 1952. *They Went to College: The College Graduate in America Today.* New York: Harcourt, Brace.

Havens, E. M., and J. C. Tully. 1972. "Female Intergenerational Occupational Mobility: Comparisons of Patterns?" *American Sociological Review* 37:774–77.

Havighurst, R. J. 1958. *Education and Social Mobility in Four Countries.* Human Development Bulletin. Chicago: University of Chicago, Committee on Human Development.

Havighurst, R., and K. Feigenbaum. 1959. "Leisure and Life Style." *American Journal of Sociology* 64:396–404.

Havighurst, R. J., R. R. Rodgers. 1952. "The Role of Motivation in Attendance at Post-High School Educational Institutions." In *Who*

Should Go to College, ed. B. S. Hollingshead, pp. 136–64. New York: Columbia University Press.

Hawes, G. 1963. "The Colleges of America's Upper Class." *Saturday Review of Literature* 46:68–71.

Hawkins, J. L. 1968. "Association between Companionship, Hostility, and Marital Satisfaction." *Journal of Marriage and the Family* 30:647–50.

Hawkridge, D. G., A. B. Chalupsky, and A. O. Roberts. 1968. *A Study of Selected Exemplary Programs for the Education of Disadvantaged Children, Part II.* Palo Alto, Ca.: American Institutes for Research. Arlington, Va.: Educational Resources Information Center, Document No. 023777.

Hazelrigg, L. E. 1974. "Cross-National Comparisons of Father-to-Son Occupational Mobility." In *Social Stratification: A Reader,* ed. J. Lopreato and L. S. Lewis, pp. 469–93. New York: Harper & Row.

Heathers, G. 1967. *Organizing Schools Through the Dual Progress Plan.* Danville, Ill.: Interstate.

———. 1969. "Grouping." In *Encyclopedia of Educational Research,* 4th ed., ed. R. L. Ebel, pp. 559–70. New York: Macmillan.

Heber, R. 1972. "An Experiment in the Prevention of Cultural-Familial Mental Retardation." *Environment, Intelligence and Scholastic Achievement: A Compilation of Testimony to the Senate Committee on Equal Educational Opportunity.* Washington, D.C.: U.S. Government Printing Office, pp. 478–93.

Heilbroner, R. L. 1968. "Who's Running This Show?" *Psychiatry and Social Science Review* 2:15–16.

Heller, C. S., ed. 1969. *Structured Social Inequality: A Reader in Comparative Social Stratification.* New York: Macmillan.

Henle, P. 1972. "Exploring the Distribution of Earned Income." *Monthly Labor Review* 95:16–27.

Henry, A. 1978. "The Bottom of the Heap: Measuring the Socioeconomic Status of Women and Occupations." Unpublished paper, Washington, D.C.

Herrnstein, R. 1971. "IQ." *Atlantic Monthly* 228:43–64.

———. 1973. *IQ in the Meritocracy.* Boston: Little, Brown.

Hertzler, J. O. 1952. "Some Tendencies toward a Closed Class System in the United States." *Social Forces* 30:313–23.

Hess, R., and V. Shipman. 1965. "Early Experience and the Socialization of Cognitive Modes in Children." *Child Development* 36:869–86.

Hetzler, S. 1953. "An Investigation of the Distinctiveness of Social Classes." *American Sociological Review* 18:493–97.

Hewitt, C. 1977. "The Effect of Political Democracy and Social Democracy on Equality in Industrial Societies: A Cross-National Comparison." *American Sociological Review* 42:450–64.

Heyns, B. 1974. "Social Selection and Stratification within Schools." *American Journals of Sociology* 79:1434–51.

Himes, J. S., Jr. 1952. "The Factor of Social Mobility in Teaching Marriage Courses in Negro Colleges." *Social Forces* 30:439–43.

Hodge, R. W.; P. M. Siegel; and P. H. Rossi. 1964. "Occupational Prestige in the United States." *American Journal of Sociology* 70:286–302.

———. 1966. "Occupational Prestige in the United States: 1925–1963." In *Class, Status and Power,* 2d ed., ed. R. Bendix and S. M. Lipset, pp. 322–34. New York: Free Press.

Hodge, R. W., and D. J. Treiman. 1966. "Occupational Mobility and Attitudes toward Negroes." *American Sociological Review* 31:93–102.

Hodge, R. W.; D. J. Treiman; and P. H. Rossi. 1966. "A Comparative Study of Occupational Prestige." In *Class, Status and Power,* 2d ed., ed. R. Bendix and S. M. Lipset, pp. 309–21. New York: Free Press.

Hodges, H. M., Jr. 1968. "Peninsula People: Social Stratification in a Metropolitan Complex." In *Permanence and Change in Social Class,* ed. W. C. Lane, pp. 5–36. Cambridge, Mass.: Schenkman.

Hodgson, J. D. 1971. *Social Security Amendments of 1971.* Hearings, Senate Finance Committee, July 27.

Hoerning, K. H. 1971. "Power and Social Stratification." *Sociological Quarterly* 12:3–14.

Hoffman, L. W., and F. I. Nye. 1974. *Working Mothers.* San Francisco: Jossey-Bass.

Hollingshead, A. B. 1949. *Elmtown's Youth.* New York: Wiley.

———. 1956. "Two Factor Index of Social Position." Dittoed. New Haven: Yale University Press.

Hollingshead, A. B., and F. C. Redlich. 1953. "Social Stratification and Psychiatric Disorders." *American Sociological Review* 18:163–69.

———. 1958. *Social Class and Mental Illness: A Community Study.* New York: Wiley.

Hopkins, A. 1973. "Political Overconformity by Upwardly Mobile American Men." *American Sociological Review* 38:143–47.

Horowitz, I. L. 1962. "Consensus, Conflict, and Cooperation." *Social Forces* 41:177–88.

Horowitz, M. A., and I. L. Herrnstadt. 1969. *The Training of Tool and Die Makers.* Boston: Department of Economics, Northeastern University.

Huber, J. 1974. "Mechanisms of Income Distribution." In *The Sociology of American Poverty,* ed. J. Huber and H. P. Chalfant, pp. 103–23. Cambridge, Mass.: Schenkman.

Huber, J., and W. H. Form. 1973. *Income and Ideology: An Analysis of the American Political Formula.* New York: Free Press.

Huber, R. M. 1971. *The American Idea of Success.* New York: McGraw-Hill.

Hunt, M. P., and L. E. Metcalf. 1943. *Teaching High School Social Studies: Problems in Reflective Thinking and Social Understanding.* New York: Harper & Row.

Hunter, F. 1953. *Community Power Structure.* Chapel Hill, N.C.: University of North Carolina Press.

Inkeles, A., and P. H. Rossi. 1956. "National Comparisons of Occupational Prestige." *American Journal of Sociology* 61:329–39.

International Labor Organization. 1954. *I.L.O. Social Security—A Workers' Education Manual.* Geneva: International Labor Organization Office.

Ishwaran, K. I., ed. 1970. *Change and Continuity in India's Villages.* New York: Columbia University Press.

Jackman, M. R. 1972. "Social Mobility and Attitude toward the Political System." *Social Forces* 50:462–72.

Jackman, M. R., and R. W. Jackman. 1973. "An Interpretation of the Relation between Objective and Subjective Social Status." *American Sociological Review* 38:569–82.

Jackman, R. W. 1975. *Politics and Social Equality: A Comparative Analysis.* New York: Wiley.

Jackson, E. F., and H. J. Crockett, Jr. 1964. "Occupational Mobility in the United States: A Point Estimate and Trend Comparison." *American Sociological Review* 29:5–15.

Jackson, G., and C. Cosca. 1974. "The Inequality of Educational Opportunity in the Southwest: An Observational Study of Ethnically Mixed Classrooms." *American Educational Research Journal* 11:219–29.

Jaffe, F. S. 1964. "Family Planning and Poverty." *Journal of Marriage and the Family* 2:467–77.

Janowitz, M., and D. Marvick. 1953. "Authoritarianism and Political Behavior." *Public Opinion Quarterly* 17:185–201.

Jencks, C., et al. 1972. *Inequality: A Reassessment of the Effect of Family and Schooling in America.* New York: Basic Books.

Jensen, A. R. 1969. "How Much Can We Boost IQ and Scholastic Achievement?" *Harvard Educational Review* 39:1–123.

Jensen, M. C. 1978. "Tobacco: A Potent Lobby . . ." *New York Times,* February 19.

Johnson, E. H. 1957. "Selective Factors in Capital Punishment." *Social Forces* 36:165–69.

Johnson, H. M. 1960. *Sociology.* New York: Harcourt, Brace.

Jones, A. W. 1941. *Life, Liberty and Property*. Philadelphia: Lippincott.

Jones, F. L. 1969. "Social Mobility and Industrial Society: A Thesis Re-Examined." *Sociological Quarterly* 10:292–305.

Jouvenel, B. de. 1967. "The Ethics of Redistribution." In *Inequality and Poverty,* ed. E. C. Budd, pp. 6–13. New York: Norton.

Kadushin, C.; J. Hover; and M. Tichy. 1971. "How and Where to Find Intellectual Elites in the United States." *Public Opinion Quarterly* 35:1–18.

Kahl, J. A. 1953. "Educational and Occupational Aspirations of 'Common Man' Boys." *Harvard Educational Review* 23:186–203.

———. 1957. *The American Class Structure*. New York: Rinehart.

———. 1965. "Some Measurements of Achievement Orientation." *American Journal of Sociology* 70:669–81.

Kahl, J. A., and J. A. Davis. 1955. "A Comparison of Indexes of Socio-Economic Status." *American Sociological Review* 20:317–25.

Kandel, D. B., and G. S. Lesser. 1969. "Parental and Peer Influences on Educational Plans of Adolescents." *American Sociological Review* 34:213–23.

Kanter, R. M. 1977. *Men and Women of the Corporation*. New York: Basic Books.

Kaplan, H. R., and C. Tausky. 1972. "Work and the Welfare Cadillac: The Function and Commitment to Work among the Hard-Core Unemployed." *Social Problems* 19:469–83.

Karabel, J. 1972. "Community Colleges and Social Stratification." *Harvard Educational Review* 42:521–62.

Karabel, J., and A. H. Halsey, eds. 1977. *Power and Ideology in Education*. New York: Oxford University Press.

Kariger, R. H. 1962. "The Relationship of Lane Grouping to the Socioeconomic Status of the Parents of Seventh-grade Pupils in Three Junior High Schools." Ph.D. diss., Michigan State University.

Karshaw, J. A. 1970. *Government against Poverty*. Washington, D.C.: Brookings Institution.

Katz, M., ed. 1971. *School Reform: Past and Present*. Boston: Little, Brown.

Kaufman, H. F. 1944. *Prestige Classes in a New York Rural Community*. Memoir 260. Ithaca, N.Y.: Cornell University Agricultural Experiment Station.

Kaufman, H., and V. Jones. 1954. "The Mystery of Power." *Public Administration Quarterly* 14:205–12.

Keller, S. 1963. *Beyond the Ruling Class: Strategic Elites in Modern Society*. New York: Random House.

Kenkel, W. F. 1952. "An Experimental Analysis of Social Stratification in Columbus, Ohio." Doctoral diss., Ohio State University.

Kessin, K. 1971. "Social and Psychological Consequences of Intergenerational Occupational Mobility." *American Journal of Sociology* 77:1–18.

Keyser, M. 1974. "How to Apply for a Job." *Journal of College Placement* 35:63–65.

King, M. B., Jr. 1961. "Sociometric Status and Sociometric Choice." *Social Forces* 39:199–206.

Kinsey, A. C.; W. B. Pomeroy; and C. E. Martin. 1948. *Sexual Behavior in the Human Male*. Philadelphia: Saunders.

Kinsey, A. C., et al. 1953. *Sexual Behavior in the Human Female*. Philadelphia: Saunders.

Kirscht, J. P., and R. C. Dillehay. 1967. *Dimensions of Authoritarianism: A Review of Research and Theory*. Lexington, Ky.: University of Kentucky Press.

Kirstein, G. 1968. *The Rich, Are They Different?* Boston: Houghton Mifflin.

Kohn, M. L. 1959. "Social Class and Parental Values." *American Journal of Sociology* 64:337–51.

———. 1969. *Class and Conformity*. Homewood, Ill.: Dorsey Press.

Kohn, M. L., and C. Schooler. 1969. "Class, Occupation, and Orientation." *American Sociological Review* 34:659–78.

Kolko, G. 1962. *Wealth and Power in America: An Analysis of Social Class and Income Distribution*. New York: Praeger.

Komarovsky, M. 1946. "The Voluntary Associations of Urban Dwellers." *American Sociological Review* 11:686–98.

———. 1962. *Blue-Collar Marriage*. New York: Random House.

———. 1973. "Cultural Contradictions and Sex Roles: The Masculine Case." *American Journal of Sociology* 78:873–84.

Komisar, L. 1977. *Down and Out in the USA: A History of Public Welfare*. New York: F. Watts.

Kornhauser, A.; H. L. Sheppard; and A. J. Mayer. 1956. *When Labor Votes*. New York: University Books.

Kornhauser, R. R. 1953. "The Warner Approach to Social Stratification." In *Class, Status and Power,* ed. R. Bendix and S. M. Lipset, pp. 224–55. Glencoe, Ill.: Free Press.

Krauss, I. 1976. *Stratification, Class, and Conflict*. New York: Free Press.

Kreckel, R. 1972. "Soziale Ungleichheit und 'Offene Gesellschaft.'" *Soziale Welt* 23:17–40.

Kriesberg, L. 1962. "The Bases of Occupational Prestige: The Case of Dentists." *American Sociological Review* 27:238–44.

———. 1970. *Mothers in Poverty: A Study of Fatherless Families*. Chicago: Aldine.

————. 1972. "The Relationship between Socio-Economic Rank and Behavior." In *Issues in Social Inequality,* ed. G. W. Thielbar and S. D. Feldman, pp. 458–82. Boston: Little, Brown.

Kuznets, S. S. 1962. "Income Distribution and Changes in Consumption." In *The Changing American Population,* ed. H. S. Simpson, pp. 21–58. New York: Institute of Life Insurance.

Labov, W. 1973. "The Logic of Nonstandard English." In *The Myth of Cultural Deprivation,* ed. N. Keddie, pp. 21–66. Hammondsworth, England: Penguin Books.

Ladinsky, J. 1967. "Higher Education and Work Achievement among Lawyers." *Sociological Quarterly* 8:222–32.

Lampman, R. J. 1962. *The Share of Top Wealth Holders in National Wealth, 1922–1956.* Prepared for the National Bureau of Economic Research. Princeton: Princeton University Press.

————. 1971. *Ends and Means of Reducing Income Poverty.* Chicago: Markham.

Land, K. C. 1970. "Path Models of Functional Theories of Stratification as Representations of Cultural Beliefs on Stratification." *Sociological Quarterly* 11:474–84.

Landecker, W. S. 1960. "Class Boundaries." *American Sociological Review* 25:868–77.

Lane, D. 1971. *The End of Inequality? Stratification under State Socialism.* Middlesex, England: Penguin Books.

Lane, R. E. 1959. "The Fear of Equality." *American Political Science Review* 53:35–51.

————. 1962. *Political Ideology: Why the Common Man Believes What He Does.* New York: Free Press.

Langner, T. S., and S. T. Michael. 1963. *Life Stress and Mental Health.* New York: Free Press.

Latham, E. 1965. *The Group Basis of Politics.* New York: Octagon.

Laumann, E. O. 1966. *Prestige and Association in an Urban Community.* Indianapolis: Bobbs-Merrill.

Lauman, E. O., and R. Senter. 1976. "Subjective Social Distance, Occupational Stratification, and Forms of Status and Class Consciousness: A Cross-national Replication and Extension." *American Journal of Sociology* 81:1304–38.

Lawson, E. D., and W. E. Boek. 1960. "Correlations of Indexes of Families' Socio-Economic Status." *Social Forces* 39:149–52.

Lawton, D. 1968. *Social Class, Language, and Education.* London: Routledge and Kegan Paul.

Leacock, E. 1969. *Teaching and Learning in City Schools.* New York: Basic Books.

Lee. R. D., and R. W. Johnson. 1973. *Public Budgeting Systems.* Baltimore, Maryland: University Park Press.

Lefever, D. W. 1959. "Review of Henmon-Nelson Test of Mental Ability." In *The Fifth Mental Measurement Year Book,* ed. O. K. Buros, pp, 470–72. Highland Park, N.J.: Gryphon Press.

Leggett, J. C. 1963. "Uprootedness and Working-Class Consciousness." *American Journal of Sociology* 68:682–92.

————. 1964a. "Economic Insecurity and Working-Class Consciousness." *American Sociological Review* 29:226–34.

————. 1964b. "Sources and Consequences of Working-Class Consciousness." In *Blue-Collar World,* ed. A. B. Shostak and W. Gomberg, pp. 235–46. Englewood Cliffs, N.J.: Prentice-Hall.

————. 1968. *Class, Race, and Labor.* New York: Oxford University Press.

Lehman, E W. 1969. "Toward a Macrosociology of Power." *American Sociological Review* 34:453–65.

Le Masters, E. E. 1975. *Blue-Collar Aristocrats: Life-Styles at a Working-Class Tavern.* Madison, Wis.: University of Wisconsin Press.

Lenski, G. 1953. "American Social Classes: Statistical Strata or Social Groups?" *American Journal of Sociology* 58:139–45.

————. 1958. "Trends in Inter-Generational Occupational Mobility in the United States." *American Sociological Review* 23:514–23.

————. 1961. *The Religious Factor.* Garden City, N.Y.: Doubleday Anchor.

————. 1966. *Power and Privilege.* New York: McGraw-Hill.

Levine, G. N., and L. A. Sussmann. 1960. "Social Class and Sociability in Fraternity Pledging." *American Journal of Sociology* 65:391–99.

Levison, A. 1974. *The Working-Class Majority.* New York: Penguin Books.

Levitan, S. A.; M. Rein; and D. Marwick. 1972. *Work and Welfare Go Together.* Baltimore: Johns Hopkins University Press.

Lewis, H. G. 1963. *Unionism and Relative Wages in the United States.* Chicago: University of Chicago Press.

Lewis, J. 1967. *Culture, Class and Poverty.* Washington, D.C.: Health and Welfare Council of the National Capital Area.

Lewis, L. S. 1964. "Class and the Perception of Class." *Social Forces* 42:336–40.

Lewis, O. 1959. *Five Families: Mexican Case Studies in the Culture of Poverty.* New York: Basic Books.

————. 1961. *The Children of Sanchez.* New York: Random House.

————. 1966. *La Vida: A Puerto Rican Family in the Culture of Poverty.* New York: Random House.

————. 1969. "Review." *Current Anthropology* 10:189–92.

References

Lieberson, S. 1971. "An Empirical Study of Military-Industrial Linkages." *American Journal of Sociology* 76:562–84.

Liebow, E. 1967. *Tally's Corner*. Boston: Little, Brown.

Linden, G. 1967. "The Influence of Social Class in the Survival of Cancer Patients." Paper presented at the annual meeting of the American Public Health Association. Miami Beach, Fla.

Linton, R. 1936. *The Study of Man*. New York: Appleton-Century-Crofts.

Lipset, S. M. 1959. "Democracy and Working-Class Authoritarianism." *American Sociological Review* 24:482–502.

———. 1960. *Political Man*. Garden City, N.Y.: Doubleday.

———. 1964. "Three Decades of the Radical Right: Coughlinites, McCarthyites, and Birchers." In *The Radical Right*, ed. D. Bell, pp. 373–446. Garden City, N.Y.: Doubleday.

———. 1968. "The Activists: A Profile." *Public Interest* 13:39–51.

Lipset, S. M., and R. Bendix. 1951. "Social Status and Social Structure: A Re-Examination of Data and Interpretations." *British Journal of Sociology* 2:150–68, 230–54.

———. 1964. *Social Mobility in Industrial Society*. Berkeley and Los Angeles: University of California Press.

Lipsitz, L. 1965. "Working-Class Authoritarianism: A Re-Evaluation." *American Sociological Review* 30:103–09.

Longhi, D., and D. Ellegaard. 1969. "Intergenerational Occupational Mobility and Social Class." Study, Department of Sociology, University of Wisconsin, as reported in R. F. Hamilton, 1972, *Class and Politics in the United States* (New York: Wiley), p. 392.

Lopreato, J. 1968. "Authority Relations and Class Conflict." *Social Forces* 47:70–79.

Louis, A. M. 1968. "America's Centimillionaires." *Fortune* 77:152–57.

Lundberg, F. 1968. *The Rich and the Super-Rich*. New York: Lyle Stuart.

Lydall, H. F. 1959. "The Long-Term Trend in the Size Distribution of Income." *Journal of the Royal Statistical Society* 122, series A.

Lynd, R. S., and H. M. Lynd. 1929. *Middletown*. New York: Harcourt, Brace.

———. 1937. *Middletown in Transition*. New York: Harcourt, Brace.

Lyons, S. 1977. "Women Locked into Certain Job Types." *Rochester Democrat and Chronicle*, April 8.

Ma, J. C. 1969. "Current Trends in Recruiting Practices." *Journal of College Placement* 29:113–14.

McClelland, D. C. 1961. *The Achieving Society*. Princeton: Van Nostrand.

———. 1963. "The Achievement Motive in Economic Growth." In *Industrialization and Society*, ed. B. F. Hoselitz and W. E. Moore, pp. 74–95. Paris: Mouton, UNESCO.

McClelland, D. C.; J. W. Atkinson; R. A. Clark; and E. A. Lowell. 1953. *The Achievement Motive*. New York: Appleton-Century-Crofts.

McClendon, M. J. 1976. "The Occupational Status Attainment Processes of Males and Females." *American Sociological Review* 41:52–64.

McConnell, J. 1942. *The Evolution of Social Classes*. Washington, D.C.: American Council on Public Affairs.

McDill, E. 1961. "Anomie, Authoritarianism, Prejudice, and Socio-Economic Status: An Attempt at Clarification." *Social Forces* 39:239–45.

McDill, E. L., and J. S. Coleman. 1965. "Family and Peer Influences in College Plans of High School Students." *Sociology of Education* 38:112–26.

MacIver, R. M., and C. H. Page. 1949. *Society*. New York: Rinehart.

Mackenzie, G. 1973. *The Aristocracy of Labor: The Position of Skilled Craftsmen in the American Class Structure*. London: Cambridge University Press.

MacKinnon, W. J., and R. Centers. 1956. "Authoritarianism and Urban Stratification." *American Journal of Sociology* 61:610–20.

MacMahon, A., and J. D. Millet. 1939. *Federal Administrators*. New York: Columbia University Press.

McPartland, J. 1968. *The Segregated Student in Desegregated Schools: Sources of Influence on Negro Secondary Students*. Baltimore: Johns Hopkins University Press.

Main, J. 1968. "Good Living Begins at $25,000 a Year." *Fortune* 77:158–61, 180–88.

Malinowski, B. 1932. *Argonauts of the Western Pacific*. London: George Routledge.

Malkiel, B. G. and J. A. Malkiel. 1973. "Male-Female Pay Differentials in Professional Employment." *American Economic Review* 63:693–705.

Mandel, E. 1969. *An Introduction to Marxist Economic Theory*. New York: Pathfinder Press.

Mandelbaum, D. G. 1970. *Society in India*. 2 vols. Berkeley and Los Angeles: University of California Press.

Mangum, G. 1969. "The Why, How and Whence of Manpower Programs." *Annals of the American Academy of Political and Social Science* 385:50–62.

Manis, J. G., and B. N. Meltzer. 1954. "Attitudes of Textile Workers to Class Structure." *American Journal of Sociology* 60:30–35.

Mankoff, M. 1970. "Power in Advanced Capitalist Society: A Review Essay on Recent Elitist and Marxist Criticism of Pluralist Theory." *Social Problems* 17:418–30.

————. 1974. "Toward Socialism: Reassessing Inequality." *Social Policy* 4:20–31.

Marriott, M., ed. 1955. *Village India: Studies in the Little Community*. Chicago: University of Chicago Press.

Marris, P., and M. Rein. 1969. *Dilemmas of Social Reform*. New York: Atherton Press.

Marshall, T. H. 1964. *Class, Citizenship, and Social Development*. Garden City, N.Y.: Doubleday.

Marx, K. 1961. *Selected Writings in Sociology and Social Philosophy*. Translated by T. B. Bottomore and M. Rubel. London: Watts.

————. 1967. "The Holy Family." In *Writings of the Young Marx on Philosophy and Society*, ed. L. Easton and K. Guddat, pp. 361–98. New York: Doubleday Anchor.

Marx, K., and F. Engels. 1962. *Selected Works*. Vol. 2. Moscow: Foreign Language Publishing House.

————. 1964. *The Communist Manifesto*, ed. J. Katz. New York: Washington Square Press.

Mathews, D. R. 1954. *The Social Background of Political Decision-Makers*. New York: Random House.

————. 1960. *U.S. Senators and Their World*. Chapel Hill, N.C.: University of North Carolina Press.

McClelland, D. C. 1963. "The Achievement Motive in Economic Growth." In *Industrialization and Society*, ed. B. F. Hoselitz and W. E. Moore, pp. 74–95. Mouton: UNESCO.

Matras, J. 1975. *Social Inequality, Stratification, and Mobility*. Englewood Cliffs, N.J.: Prentice-Hall.

Mayer, A. J., and T. F. Hoult. 1955. "Social Stratification and Combat Survival." *Social Forces* 34:155–59.

Mayer, K. B. 1955. *Class and Society*. New York: Random House.

————. 1956. "Recent Changes in the Class Structure of the United States." *Transactions of the 3d World Congress of Sociology* 3:66–80.

————. 1963. "The Changing Shape of the American Class Structure." *Social Research* 30:458–68.

Mayer, K. B., and W. Buckley. 1970. *Class and Society*. 3d ed. New York: Random House.

Mayeske, G. W. 1972. "On the Explanation of Racial-Ethnic Group Differences in Achievement Test Scores." In *Environment, Intelligence, and Scholastic Achievement: A Compilation of Testimony to the Select Committee on Equal Educational Opportunity, United States Senate*, pp. 542–56. Washington, D.C.: U.S. Government Printing Office.

Mayeske, G. W., C. E. Wisler, A. E. Beaton, F. D. Weinfield, W. M. Cohen, T Okada, J. M. Proshek, and K. A. Tabler. 1972. *A Study of Our Nation's Schools*. Washington, D.C.: U.S. Government Printing Office.

Mayntz, R. 1958. *Sociale Schichtung und Sozialer Wandel in Einer Industriegemeinde*. Stuttgart: Ferdinand Enke.

Meade, J. E., and C. J. Hitch. 1967. "How Should Income Be Distributed?" In *Inequality and Poverty*, ed. E. C. Budd, pp.1–5. New York: Norton.

Means, G. C. 1970. "Economic Concentration." In *American Society, Inc.*, ed. M. Zeitlin, pp. 3–16. Chicago: Markham.

Mechanic, D. 1968. *Medical Sociology*. New York: Free Press.

Medsker, L. L., and J. W. Trent. 1965. "The Influence of Different Types of Public Higher Institutions on College Attendance from Varying Socioeconomic and Ability Levels." Berkeley, Calif.: Center for Research and Development in Higher Education.

Mehl, R. F., Jr. 1965. "A Study of Relationships between Homogeneous Grouping in the School and the Social Class Structure in an Up-State New York Community." Ph.D. diss., State University of New York at Albany.

Meier, D., and W. Bell. 1959. "Anomia and Differential Access to the Achievement of Life Goals." *American Sociological Review* 24:189–202.

Meisel, J. H. 1957 *The Myth of the Ruling Class: Gaetano Mosca and the Elite*. Ann Arbor: University of Michigan Press.

Merton, R. K. 1938. "Social Structure and Anomie." *American Sociological Review* 3:672–82.

————. 1949. *Social Theory and Social Structure*. Glencoe, Ill.: Free Press.

Michaelson, E. J., and W. Goldschmidt. 1971. "Female Roles and Male Dominance among Peasants." *Southwestern Journal of Anthropology* 27:330–52.

Michels, R. 1949. *Political Parties: A Sociological Study of the Oligarchical Tendencies of Modern Democracy*. New York: Free Press.

Miliband, R. 1969. *The State in Capitalist Society*. New York: Basic Books.

Miller, A. 1954. "The Problem of Class Boundaries and Its Significance for Research into Class Structure." *Transactions of the Second World Congress of Sociology* 2:343–52.

Miller, D. C., and W. H. Form. 1964. *Industrial Sociology*. New York: Harper and Row.

Miller, H. P. 1955. *Income of the American People*. New York: Wiley.

————. 1964. *Rich Man, Poor Man*. New York: Crowell.

————. 1966. *Income Distribution in the United States*. Washington, D.C.: Government Printing Office.

Miller, S. M. 1960. "Comparative Social Mobility." *Current Sociology* 9:81–89.

————. 1964. "The Outlook of Working-Class Youth." In *Blue-Collar World,* ed. A. B. Shostak and W. Gomberg, pp. 122–34. Englewood Cliffs, N.J.: Prentice-Hall.

Miller, S. M., and F. Riessman. 1961a. "Are Workers Middle Class?" *Dissent* 8:507–13, 516.

————. 1961b. "The Working Class Subculture: A New View." *Social Problems* 9:86–97.

————. 1968. *Social Class and Social Policy.* New York: Basic Books.

Miller, S. M.; F. Riessman; and A. A. Seagull. 1965. "Poverty and Self-Indulgence: A Critique of the Non-Deferred Gratification Pattern." In *Poverty in America,* rev. ed., ed. L. Ferman, J. Kornbluh, and A. Hager, pp. 285–302. Ann Arbor: University of Michigan Press.

Miller, S. M., and P. A. Roby. 1970. *The Future of Inequality.* New York: Basic Books.

Miller, W. B. 1958. "Lower Class Culture as a Generating Milieu of Gang Delinquency." *Journal of Social Issues* 14:5–19.

Mills, C. W. 1946. "The Middle Classes in Middle-Sized Cities." *American Sociological Review* 11:520–29.

————. 1951. *White Collar: The American Middle Classes.* New York: Oxford University Press.

————. 1956. *The Power Elite.* New York: Oxford University Press.

Mincer, J. 1970. "The Distribution of Labor Incomes: A Survey with Special Reference to the Human Capital Approach." *Journal of Economic Literature* 8:1–26.

————. 1974. *Schooling, Experience, and Earnings.* New York: National Bureau of Economic Research; dist. by Columbia University Press.

Mincer, J., and S. Polachek. 1974. "Family Investments in Human Capital: Earnings of Women." *Journal of Political Economy* 82:S76–S108.

Mirfin, D., ed. and trans. 1966. *Vilfredo Pareto: Sociological Writings.* New York: Praeger.

Mitchell, W. C. 1936. *What Veblen Taught.* New York: Viking Press.

Mizruchi, E. H. 1964. *Success and Opportunity.* New York: Free Press.

Montague, J. B., Jr. 1963. *Class and Nationality.* New Haven: College and University Press.

Moore, W. E. 1963a. "But Some Are More Equal Than Others." *American Sociological Review* 28:13–18.

————. 1963b. "Rejoinder to Tumin." *American Sociological Review* 28:26–28.

Morgan, J. N., and M. H. David. 1963. "Education and Income." *Quarterly Journal of Economics* 77:423–37.

Morgan, J. N., M. H. David; W. G. Cohen, and H. E. Brazer. 1962. *Income and Welfare in The United States.* New York: McGraw-Hill.

Morris, R. T., and V. Jeffries. 1970. "Class Con-

flict: Forget It!" *Sociology and Social Research* 54:306–20.

Morris, R. T., and R. J. Murphy. 1966. "A Paradigm for the Study of Class Consciousness." *Sociology and Social Research* 50:297–313.

Mosca, G. 1884. Teorica dei Governi e Sui Governo Parlamentare. Turin.

Moynihan, D. P. 1965. *The Negro Family.* Washington, D. C.: U. S. Department of Labor.

Mueller, W. F. 1970. "Recent Changes in Industrial Concentration and the Current Merger Movement." In *American Society, Inc.,* ed. M. Zeitlin, p. 7–25. Chicago: Markham.

Mulford, H. A., and W. W. Salisburg II. 1964. "Self Conceptions in a General Population." *Sociological Quarterly* 5:35–46.

Murdock, G. P. 1959. Africa: *Its People and Their Culture History.* New York: McGraw-Hill.

Nader, L., and D. Serber, 1976. "Law and the Distribution of Power." In *The Uses of Controversy in Sociology,* ed. L. A. Coser and O. N. Larsen, pp. 273–91. New York: Free Press.

National Advisory Commission on Civil Disorders. 1968. *Report of the National Advisory Commission on Civil Disorders.* New York: Dutton.

National Education Association, Research Division. 1968. *Ability Grouping.* Research summary 1968–S3. Washington, D.C.: National Education Association.

National Opinion Research Center. 1947. "Jobs and Occupations." *Opinion News,* September 1, pp. 3–13. Reprinted in *Class, Status and Power,* ed. R. Bendix and S. M. Lipset. Glencoe, Ill.: Free Press, 1953, pp. 411–426.

————. 1973. *National Data Program for the Social Sciences: Codebook for the Spring 1973 General Social Survey.* Chicago; University of Chicago.

————. 1975. *National Data Program for the Social Sciences: Codebook for the Spring 1975 General Social Survey.* Chicago; University of Chicago.

Newsweek. 1969. Vol. 74, October 6.

Nicholls, D. E., and J. Van Til. 1973. "The Magnitude of Inequality." In *Privilege in America: An End to Inequality,* ed. A. B. Shostak, J. Van Til, and S. B. Van Til, pp. 9–32. Englewood Cliffs, N.J.: Prentice-Hall.

Nicolaus, M. 1970. "Proletariat and Middle Class in Marx: Hegelian Choreography and Capitalist Dialect." In *For a New America,* ed. J. Weinstein and D. Eakins, pp. 253–83. New York: Vintage Books.

Nisbet, R. 1959. "The Decline and Fall of Social Class." *Pacific Sociological Review* 2:11–17.

North, C. C., and P. K. Hatt. 1947. "Jobs and Occupations: A Popular Evaluation." *Opinion News* 9:3–13.

Oaxaca, R. 1973. "Male-Female Wage Differentials in Urban Labor Markets." *International Economic Review* 14:693–709.

O'Brien, J. E. 1971. "Violence in Divorce Prone Families." *Journal of Marriage and the Family* 33:691–98.

Oh, J. C. H. 1969. Review of G. Domhoff, *Who Rules America?* and A. Rose, *The Power Structure. Sociological Quarterly* 10:401.

Oppenheimer, V. 1970. *The Female Labor Force in the United States: Demographic and Economic Factors Governing Its Growth and Changing Composition. Population Monograph Series,* No. 5 Berkeley: University of California.

Organization for Economic Co-operation and Development. 1972. *Expenditure Trends in OECD Countries: 1960–1980.* Paris: OECD Publications.

Ornati, O. 1966. *Poverty Amid Affluence.* New York: Twentieth Century Fund.

Orshansky, M. 1965a. "Counting the Poor: Another Look at the Poverty Profile." *Social Security Bulletin,* 1 (January) 28:3–29.

———. 1965b. "Who's Who among the Poor: A Demographic View of Poverty." *Social Security Bulletin,* 4 (April) 28:3–32.

Osmond, M. W., and C. M. Grigg. 1975. "Family Linked Characteristics of Poverty." Paper presented to American Sociological Association, San Francisco.

Ossowski, S. 1963. *Class Structure in the Social Consciousness.* Translated by Sheila Patterson. New York: Free Press.

———. 1966. "Different Conceptions of Social Class." in *Class, Status and Power,* 2d ed., ed. R. Bendix and S. M. Lipset, pp. 86–96. New York: Free Press.

Ozawa, M. 1971. "Family Allowances and a National Minimum of Economic Security." *Child Welfare* 50:313–21.

Page, C. H. 1969. *Class and American Sociology: From Ward to Ross.* New York: Schocken Books.

Papanek, H. 1973. "Men, Women, and Work: Reflections on the Two-Person Career." *American Journal of Sociology* 78:852–72.

Parkin, F. 1971. *Class Inequality and Political Order.* New York: Praeger.

Parsons, T. 1951. *The Social System.* Glencoe, Ill.: Free Press.

———. 1953. "A Revised Analytical Approach to the Theory of Social Stratification." In *Class, Status and Power,* ed. R. Bendix and S. M. Lipset, pp. 92–128. Glencoe, Ill.: Free Press.

———. 1954. *Essays in Sociological Theory.* Rev. ed. Glencoe, Ill.: Free Press.

———. 1964. *The Social System.* New York: Free Press.

———. 1975. "Response." *American Sociological Review* 40:666–70.

Patchen, M. 1970. "Social Class and Dimensions of Foreign Policy Attitudes." *Social Science Quarterly* 51:649–67.

Paukert, F. 1973. "Income Distribution: A Survey of the Evidence." *International Labour Review* 108:97–125.

Pearlin, L. I. 1972. *Social Class and Family Life.* Boston: Little, Brown.

———. 1974. "Social Origins of Stress." Study, National Institute of Mental Health, Washington, D.C.

———. 1975. "Sex Roles and Depression." In *Life-Span Developmental Psychology: Normative Life Crises,* ed. N. Datan, pp. 191–207. New York: Academic Press.

Pearlin, L. I., and M. L. Kohn. 1966. "Social Class, Occupation, and Parental Values: A Cross-National Study." *American Sociological Review* 31:466–79.

Pease, J., W. H. Form, and J. H. Rytina. 1970. "Ideological Currents in American Stratification Literature." *American Sociologist* 5:127–37.

Pechman, J. A. 1969. "The Rich, the Poor, and the Taxes They Pay." *Public Interest* 17:21–43.

———. 1971. *Federal Tax Policy.* New York: Norton.

Pechman, J. A. and B. A. Okner. 1972. "Individual Income Tax Erosion in Income Classes." In *The Economics of Federal Subsidy Programs,* a compendium of papers submitted to the Joint Economic Committee, 92d Cong., 2d sess., pt. 1, pp. 13–40.

———. 1974. *Who Bears the Tax Burden?* Washington, D.C.: Brookings Institution.

Pechman, J. A., and P. M. Timpane. 1975. *Work Incentives and Income Guarantees: The New Jersey Negative Income Tax Experiment.* Washington: Brookings Institution.

Pelling, H. 1953. *The Origins of the Labour Party, 1880–1900.* Oxford: Clarendon Press.

Penceval, J. H. 1974. "Relative Wages and Trade Unions in the United Kingdom." *Economica* 41:194–210.

Penn, R. 1975. "Occupational Prestige Hierarchies: A Great Empirical Invariant?" *Social Forces* 54:352–64.

Perrucci, C. C., and R. Perrucci. 1970. "Social Origins, Educational Contexts, and Career Mobility." *American Sociological Review* 35:451–63.

Persell, C. H. 1977. *Education and Inequality: A Theoretical and Empirical Synthesis.* New York: Free Press.

Pfautz, H. W. 1953. "The Current Literature on Social Stratification: Critique and Bibliography." *American Journal of Sociology* 58:391–418.

Pfautz, H. W., and O. D. Duncan. 1950. "A Critical Evaluation of Warner's Work in Community Stratification." *American Sociological Review* 15:205–15.

Photiadis, J., and J. Biggar. 1962. "Religiosity, Education, and Social Distance." *American Journal of Sociology* 67:666–72.

Pierson, F. C. 1959, *The Education of American Businessmen: A Study of University-College Programs in Business Administration.* New York: McGraw-Hill.

Pierson, G. W. 1969. *The Education of American Leaders.* New York: Praeger.

Pigou, A. C. 1967. "Capitalism, Socialism and the Distribution of Wealth and Incomes." In *Inequality and Poverty,* ed. E. C. Budd, pp. 134–39. New York: Norton.

Piore, M. J. 1971. "The Dual Labor Market: Theory and Implications." In *Problems in Political Economy: An Urban Perspective,* ed. D. M. Gordon, pp. 90–94. Lexington, Mass.: Heath.

Piven, F. F., and R. A. Cloward. 1971. *Regulating the Poor: The Functions of Public Welfare.* New York: Random House.

Placek, P. L., and G. E. Hendershot. 1974. "Public Welfare and Family Planning: An Empirical Study of the 'Brood Sow' Myth." *Social Problems* 21:658:–73.

Polanyi, K. 1944. *The Great Transformation.* New York: Rinehart.

Polsby, N. W. 1962. "Community Power: Some Reflections on the Recent Literature." *American Sociological Review* 27:838–41.

———. 1963. *Community Power and Political Theory.* New Haven: Yale University Press.

Popitz, H., H. P. Bahrdt; E. A. Jures; and H. Kesting. 1961. *Das Gesellschaftsbild des Arbeiters.* 2d ed. Tubingen: J. C. B. Mohr.

Porter, J. 1965. *The Vertical Mosaic: An Analysis of Social Class and Power in Canada.* Toronto: University of Toronto Press.

Porter, S. 1968. "The Health Gap." *New York Post,* January 29, p. 48.

Portes, A. 1971. "On the Logic of Post-Factum Explanations: The Hypothesis of Lower-Class Frustration as the Cause of Leftist Radicalism." *Social Forces* 50:26–44.

President's Commission on Higher Education. 1947. *Higher Education for American Democracy.* Vol. 2. Washington, D.C.: Government Printing Office.

Prewitt, K., and A. Stone. 1973. *The Ruling Elites: Elite Theory, Power, and American Democracy.* New York: Harper & Row.

Projector, D. S., and J. Bretz. 1975. "Measurement of Transfer Income in the Current Population Survey." In *The Personal Distribution of Income and Wealth,* ed. J. D. Smith, pp. 377–447. New York: National Bureau of Economic Research, Columbia University Press.

Projector, D. S., and G. Weiss. 1966. *Survey of Financial Characteristics of Consumers.* Washington, D.C.: Federal Reserve System.

Prothro, J. W., and C. M. Grigg. 1960. "Fundamental Principles of Democracy: Bases of Agreement and Disagreement." *Journal of Politics* 22:266–94.

Pryor, F. L. 1968. *Public Expenditures in Communist and Capitalist Nations.* Homewood, Ill.: Richard D. Irwin.

Putnam, R. D. 1976. *The Comparative Study of Political Elites.* Englewood Cliffs, N.J.: Prentice-Hall.

Quinney, R. 1970. *The Social Reality of Crime.* Boston: Little, Brown.

Rainwater, L. 1967. "The Lessons of Pruitt-Igoe." *The Public Interest* 8:116–26.

Rainwater, L., R. Coleman, and G. Handel. 1959. *Workingman's Wife: Her Personality, World and Life Style.* New York: Oceana Publications.

Rainwater, L., and K. K. Weinstein. 1960. *And the Poor Get Children.* Chicago: Quadrangle Books.

Ransford, H. E. 1972. "Blue Collar Anger: Reactions to Student and Black Protest." *American Sociological Review* 37:333–46.

Rawlins, V. L., and L. Ulman. 1974. "The Utilization of College Trained Manpower in the United States." In *Higher Education and the Labor Market,* ed. M. S. Gordon. A Report of the Carnegie Commission on Higher Education. New York: McGraw-Hill.

Rawls, J. 1971. *A Theory of Justice.* Cambridge, Mass.: Harvard University Press.

Rawls, W. Jr., 1977. "Indictments on Rise for Public Officials." *New York Times,* February 11.

Reed, R. H., and H. P. Miller. 1970. "Some Determinants of Variation in Earnings for College Men." *Journal of Human Resources* 5:177–90.

Rees, A., and G. P. Shultz. 1970. *Workers and Wages in an Urban Labor Market.* Chicago: University of Chicago Press.

Reiss, A. J. 1959. "Rural-Urban and Status Differences in Interpersonal Contacts." *American Journal of Sociology* 65:182–95.

———.1961. *Occupations and Social Status.* New York: Free Press.

Reissman, L. 1959. *Class in American Society.* Glencoe, Ill.: Free Press.

Richardson, W. C. 1964. *Dimensions of Economic Dependency.* Health Administration Perspectives no. A4. Chicago: Center for Health Administration Studies.

Richmond, M. L. 1976. "Beyond Resource Theory: Another Look at Factors Enabling Women to Affect Family Interaction." *Journal of Marriage and the Family* 38:257–66.

Riesman, D. A. 1950. *The Lonely Crowd.* New Haven: Yale University Press.

Rinehart, J. W. 1971. "Affluence and the Embourgeoisement of the Working Class: A Critical Look." *Social Problems* 19:149–62.

Rist, R. C. 1970. "Student Social Class and Teachers' Expectations: The Self-fulfilling

Prophecy in Ghetto Education." *Harvard Educational Review* 40:411–50.

———. 1972. "Social Distance and Social Inequality in a Kindergarten Classroom: An Examination of the 'Cultural Gap' Hypothesis." *Urban Education* 7:241–69.

———. 1973. *The Urban School: A Factory for Failure*. Cambridge, Mass.: M.I.T. Press.

———. 1977. "On Understanding the Processes of Schooling: The Contributions of Labeling Theory." In *Power and Ideology in Education,* ed. J. Karabel and A. H. Halsey, pp. 292–306. New York: Oxford University Press.

Roach, J. L. 1965. "Sociological Analysis and Poverty." *American Journal of Sociology* 71:68–75.

Roach, J. L.; L. Gross; and O. R. Gursslin. 1969. *Social Stratification in the United States*. Englewood Cliffs, N.J.: Prentice-Hall.

Roach, J. L., and O. R. Gursslin. 1967. "An Evaluation of the Concept 'Culture of Poverty.'" *Social Forces* 45:384–92.

Roach, J., and J. Roach. 1973. "Commentary." *American Journal of Sociology* 78:1499–1507.

Roberts, A. H., and M. Rokeach. 1956. "Anomie, Authoritarianism, and Prejudice: A Replication." *American Journal of Sociology* 61:355–58.

Robinson, J. P.; J. G. Rusk; and K. B. Head. 1968. *Measures of Political Attitudes*. Ann Arbor: Survey Research Center, Institute for Social Research.

Rodman, H. 1963. "The Lower-Class Value Stretch." *Social Forces* 42:205–15.

Rogoff, N. 1953. *Recent Trends in Occupational Mobility*. Glencoe, Ill.: Free Press.

———. 1973. "Patterns of Female Intergenerational Occupational Mobility: A Comment." *American Sociological Review* 38:806–07.

Rokeach, M. 1970. "A Mighty Fortress: Faith, Hope and Bigotry." *Psychology Today* 3:33–37.

Rose, A. M. 1958. "The Concept of Class in American Sociology." *Social Research* 25:53–69.

———. 1967. *The Power Structure*. New York: Oxford University Press.

Rosen, B. 1956. "The Achievement Syndrome: A Psychocultural Dimension of Social Stratification. *American Sociological Review* 21:203–11.

———. 1959. "Race, Ethnicity, and the Achievement Syndrome." *American Sociological Review* 24:47–60.

Rosenbaum, J. E. 1975. "The Stratification of Socialization Processes." *American Sociological Review* 40:48–54.

Rosenberg, M. 1953. "Perceptual Obstacles to Class Consciousness." *Social Forces* 32:22–27.

Rosenfeld, R. A. 1978. "Women's Intergenerational Occupational Mobility." *American Sociological Review* 43:36–46.

Rosenthal, R., and L. Jacobson. 1968. *Pygmalion in the Classroom*. New York: Holt, Rinehart, and Winston.

Ross, E. A. 1924. *Social Control: A Survey of the Foundations of Social Order*. New York: Macmillan.

Ross, H. L., and I. V. Sawhill. 1975. *Time of Transition: The Growth of Families Headed by Women*. Washington, D.C.: Urban Institute.

Rossi, P. H. 1976. "Conventional Wisdom, Common Sense, and Empirical Knowledge: The Case of Stratification Research and Views of American Society." In *The Uses of Controversy in Sociology,* ed. L. A. Coser and O. N. Larsen, pp. 30–50. New York: Free Press.

Rossi, P. H., and Z. D. Blum. 1968. "Class, Status, and Poverty." In *On Understanding Poverty,* ed. D. P. Moynihan, pp. 36–63. New York: Basic Books.

Rothbart, G. S. 1970. "The Legitimation of Inequality: Objective Scholarship vs. Black Militance." *Sociology of Education* 43:159–74.

Rowe, M. 1969. "Science, Silence and Sanctions." *Science and Children* 6:11–13.

Rubin, L. 1974. Quoted in *Behavior Today*. December 2, p. 316.

———. 1976. *Worlds of Pain: Life in the Working-Class Family*. New York: Basic Books.

Rubin, Z. 1968. "Do American Women Marry Up?" *American Sociological Review* 33:750–60.

Rubinson, R., and D. Quinlan. 1977. "Democracy and Social Inequality: A Reanalysis." *American Sociological Review* 42:611–23.

Rubovits, P., and M. L. Maehr. 1973. "Pygmalion Black and White." *Journal of Personality and Social Psychology* 2:210–18.

Runciman, W. G. 1966. *Relative Deprivation and Social Justice*. Berkeley and Los Angeles: University of California Press.

Ryan, W. 1971. *Blaming the Victim* New York: Random House.

Rytina, J. H.; W. H. Form; and J. Pease. 1970. "Income and Stratification Ideology: Beliefs about the American Opportunity Structure." *American Journal of Sociology* 75:703–716.

Rytina, N., and J. Huber. 1974. "The Demography of Poverty: Trends in the Sixties." In *The Sociology of American Poverty,* ed J. Huber and H. P. Chalfant, pp. 90–102. Cambridge, Mass.: Schenkman.

Sackrey, C. 1973. *The Political Economy of Urban Poverty*. New York: Norton.

Sahlins, M. 1958. *Social Stratification in Polynesia*. Seattle: University of Washington Press.

Sampson. W. A., and R. H. Rossi. 1975. "Race and Family Social Standing." *American Sociological Review* 40:201–14.

Sanday, P. R. 1973. "Toward a Theory of the Status of Women." *American Anthropologist* 75:1682–1700.

407

Sargent, S. S. 1953. "Class and Class-Consciousness in a California Town." *Social Problems* 1:22–27.

Sayles, L. R., and G. Strauss. 1953. *The Local Union: Its Place in the Industrial Plant.* New York: Harper & Row.

Scanzoni, J. H. 1970. *Opportunity and the Family.* New York: Free Press.

———. 1972. *Sexual Bargaining: Power Politics in the American Marriage.* Englewood Cliffs, N.J.: Prentice-Hall.

Scanzoni, L., and J. Scanzoni. 1976. *Men, Women, and Change: A Sociology of Marriage and Family.* New York: McGraw-Hill.

Schafer, W. E., and C. Olexa. 1971. *Tracking and Opportunity: The Locking-Out Process and Beyond.* Scranton Pa.: Chandler.

Schafer, W. E., and K. Polk. 1967. "Delinquency and the Schools." In *Task Force Report: Juvenile Delinquency and Youth Crime,* ed. President's Commission on Law Enforcement and Administration of Justice, pp. 222–77. Washington, D.C.: Government Printing Office.

Schatzman, L., and A. Strauss. 1955. "Social Class and Modes of Communication." *American Journal of Sociology* 60:329–38.

Schlegel, A. 1972. *Male Dominance and Female Autonomy: Domestic Authority in Matrilineal Societies.* New Haven: Human Relations Area Files.

Schneider, L., and S. Lysgaard. 1953. "The Deferred Gratification Pattern: A Preliminary Study." *American Sociological Review* 18:142–49.

Schreiber, E. M., and G. T. Nygreen. 1970. "Subjective Social Class in America: 1945–68." *Social Forces* 48:348–56.

Schultz, T. W. 1963. *The Economic Value of Education.* New York: Columbia University Press.

Schulze, R. O., and L. U. Blumberg. 1957. "The Determination of Local Power Elites." *American Journal of Sociology* 63:290–96.

Schwartz, R. D. 1959. "Functional Alternatives to Inequality." *American Sociological Review* 24:772–82.

Seagull, A. A. 1964. "The Ability to Delay Gratification." Doctoral diss., Syracuse University.

Sears, D. O. 1969. "Political Behavior." In *The Handbook of Social Psychology,* 2d ed., vol. 5, ed. Gardner Lindzey and E. Aronson, pp. 315–458. Reading, Mass.: Addison-Wesley.

Seeley, J. R.; R. A. Sim; and E. W. Loosley. 1956. *Crestwood Heights: A Study of the Culture of Suburban Life.* New York: Basic Books.

Selznick, G. J., and S. Steinberg. 1969. "Social Class, Ideology, and Voting Preference." In *Structured Social Inequality,* ed. C. Heller, pp. 216–26. New York: Macmillan.

Sennett, R., and J. Cobb. 1972. *The Hidden Injuries of Class.* New York: Random House.

Serber, D. 1975. "Regulating Reform: The Social Organization of Insurance Regulation." *Insurgent Sociologist* 5:83–105.

Sewell, W. H. 1971. "Inequality of Opportunity for Higher Education." *American Sociological Review* 36:793–809.

Sewell, W. H.; A. O. Haller; and G. W. Ohlendorf. 1970. "The Educational and Early Occupational Status Attainment Process: Replication and Revision." *American Sociological Review* 35:1014–27.

Sewel, W. H., and R. M. Hauser. 1975. *Education, Occupation, and Earnings: Achievement in the Early Career.* New York: Academic Press.

Sewell, W. H., and V. P. Shah. 1967. "Socioeconomic Status, Intelligence, and the Attainment of Higher Education." *Sociology of Education* 40:1–23.

———. 1968a. "Social Class, Parental Encouragement, and Educational Aspirations." *American Journal of Sociology* 73:559–72.

———. 1968b. "Parents' Education and Children's Educational Aspirations and Achievements." *American Sociological Review* 33:191–209.

Sexton, P. C., and B. Sexton. 1971. *Blue Collars and Hard Hats.* New York: Random House.

Sharp, L. M. 1970 *Education and Equipment.* Baltimore: Johns Hopkins University Press.

Shostak, A. B. 1965. "Birth Control and Poverty." In *New Perspectives on Poverty,* ed. A. B. Shostak and W. Gomberg, pp. 50–57. Englewood Cliffs, N.J.: Prentice-Hall.

———. 1969. *Blue-Collar Life.* New York: Random House.

Shybut, J. 1963. "Delayed Gratification: A Study of Its Measurement and Its Relationship to Certain Behavioral, Psychological and Demographic Variables." Master's thesis, University of Colorado.

Siegel, P. M. 1971. "Prestige in the American Occupational Structure." Ph.D. diss., University of Chicago.

Simmel, G. 1956. *Conflict and the Web of Group Affiliation.* Translated by Kurt H. Wolff. Glencoe, Ill.: Free Press.

Simpson, G. E., and J. M. Yinger. 1972. *Racial and Cultural Minorities: An Analysis of Prejudice and Discrimination.* 4th ed. New York: Harper & Row.

Simpson, R. 1956. "A Modification of the Functional Theory of Stratification." *Social Forces* 35:132–37.

———. 1962. "Parental Influence, Anticipatory Socialization, and Social Mobility." *American Sociological Review* 27:512–22.

Sio, A. A. 1965. "Interpretations of Slavery: The Slave Status in the Americas." *Comparative Studies in Society and History* 7:289–308.

Skolnik, A. M., and S. R. Dales. 1974. "Social Welfare Expenditures, 1972–1973." *Social Security Bulletin* 37:3–18, 43.

Smelser, N. J., and S. M. Lipset, eds. 1966. *Social Structure and Mobility in Economic Development.* Chicago: Aldine.

Smigel, E. O. 1964. *The Wall Street Lawyer.* New York: Free Press.

Smith, J. D., and S. D. Franklin. 1974. "The Concentration of Personal Wealth, 1922–1969." *American Economic Review, Papers and Proceedings* 64:162–67.

Smith, M. 1943. "An Empirical Scale of Prestige Status of Occupations." *American Sociological Review* 8:185–92.

Smolensky, E. 1971. "The Past and Present Poor." In *A Reinterpretation of American Economic History,* ed. S. Engerman, pp. 84–96. New York: Harper & Row.

Snow, R. E. 1969. "Unfinished Pygmalion." *Contemporary Psychology* 14:197–99.

Soderberg, C. R. 1963. "The American Engineer." In *The Professions in America,* ed. K. S. Lynn, pp. 203–30. Boston: Beacon.

Solow, R. M. 1960. "Income Inequality Since the War." In *Postwar Economic Trends in the United States,* ed. R. E. Freeman, pp. 91–138. New York: Harper & Row.

Sorokin, P. A. 1927. *Social Mobility.* New York: Harper & Brothers.

———. 1959. *Social and Cultural Mobility.* New York: Free Press of Glencoe.

Spaeth, J. L. 1968. "The Allocation of College Graduates and Professional Schools." *Sociology of Education* 41:342–49.

Spaeth, J. L., and A. M. Greeley. 1970. *Recent Alumni and Higher Education: A Survey of College Graduates.* New York: McGraw-Hill.

Spinrad, W. 1966. "Power in Local Communities." In *Class, Status and Power,* 2d ed., ed. R. Bendix and S. M. Lipset, pp. 218–30. New York: Free Press.

Squires, G. D. 1977. "Education, Jobs and Inequality: Functional and Conflict Models of Social Stratification in the United States." *Social Problems* 24:436–50.

Squires, J. R. 1966. "National Study of High School English Programs: A School for All Seasons." *English Journal* 55:282–90.

Srole, L. 1956. "Social Integration and Certain Corollaries: An Exploratory Study." *American Sociological Review* 21:709–16.

Stark, R.; B. D. Foster; C. Y. Glock; and H. Quinley. 1970. "Sounds of Silence." *Psychology Today* 3:38–41, 60–61

Stein, A. 1971. "Strategies for Failure." *Harvard Educational Review* 41:158–204.

Stendler, C. B. 1949. *Children of Brasstown.* University of Illinois Bulletin, vol. 46, no. 59,

Bureau of Research and Service of the College of Education.

Stevenson, M. H. 1975. "Relative Wages and Sex Segregation by Occupation." In *Sex, Discrimination, and the Division of Labor,* ed. C. B. Lloyd, pp. 175–200. New York: Columbia University Press.

Stewart, W. A. 1969. "Linguistic and Conceptual Deprivation—Fact or Fancy?" Paper presented at the annual meeting of the Society for Research in Child Development, Santa Monica, Calif.

Stiglitz, J. E. 1973. "Approaches to the Economics of Discrimination." *American Economic Review, Papers and Proceedings* 63:287–95.

Stinchcombe, A. L. 1963. "Some Empirical Consequences of the Davis-Moore Theory of Stratification." *American Sociological Review* 28:805–08.

———. 1965. "Social Structure and Organizations." In *Handbook of Organizations,* ed. J. G. March, pp. 142–93. Chicago: Rand McNally.

Stolzenberg, R. M. 1975. "Education, Occupation and Wage Differences between White and Black Men." *American Journal of Sociology* 81:299–324.

Stone, G. P., and W. H. Form. 1953. "Instabilities in Status: The Problem of Hierarchy in the Community Study of Status Arrangements." *American Sociological Review* 18:149–62.

Stouffer, S. A. 1955. *Communism, Conformity, and Civil Liberties: A Cross-Section of the Nation Speaks Its Mind.* Garden City, N.Y.: Doubleday.

Stouffer, S. A., et al. 1949. *The American Soldier: Adjustment during Army Life. Studies in Social Psychology in World War II.* Vol. 1. Princeton: Princeton University Press.

Strauss, A. L. 1971. *The Contexts of Social Mobility: Ideology and Theory.* Chicago: Aldine.

Strodtbeck, F. L. 1951. "Husband-Wife Interaction over Revealed Differences." *American Sociological Review* 16:468–73.

Stub, H. R. 1972. "The Concept of Status Community." In *Status Communities in Modern Society: Alternatives to Class Analysis,* ed. H. R. Stub, pp. 92–107. Hinsdale, Ill.: Dryden.

Suter, L., and H. Miller 1973. "Income Differences between Men and Career Women." *American Journal of Sociology* 78:962–74.

Sutherland, E. H. 1940. "White-Collar Criminality." *American Sociological Review* 5:1–12.

———. 1977. "White-Collar Criminality." In *White-Collar Crime: Offenses in Business, Politics, and the Professions,* rev. ed., ed. G. Geis and R. F. Meier, pp. 38–49. New York: Free Press.

Svalastoga, K. 1959. *Prestige, Class and Mobility.* Copenhagen: Gyldendal.

References

———. 1964. "Social Differentiation." In *Handbook of Modern Sociology,* ed. R. E. L. Faris, pp. 530–75. Chicago: Rand McNally.

Swados, H. 1957. "The Myth of the Happy Worker." *Nation,* no. 185 (August 17), pp. 65–68.

Tanter, R., and M. Midlarsky. 1967. "A Theory of Revolution." *Journal of Conflict Resolution* 11:264–80.

Tausky, C. 1965. "Parsons on Stratification: An Analysis and Critique." *Sociological Quarterly* 6:135–36.

Taussig, F. 1928. *Principles of Economics.* 3d ed. New York: Macmillan.

Taussig, F. W., and C. S. Joselyn. 1932. *American Business Leaders.* New York: Macmillan.

Tawney, R. H. 1964. *Equality.* 4th ed. London: Allen and Unwin.

Taylor, C. 1970. "The Expectations of Pygmalion's Creators." *Educational Leadership* 28:161–64.

Tepperman, L. 1972. "The Natural Disruption of Dynasties." *Canadian Review of Sociology and Anthropology* 9:111–33.

Tepperman, L., and B. Tepperman. 1971. "Dynasty Formation in Eight Imaginary Societies." *Canadian Review of Sociology and Anthropology* 8:121–41.

Thernstrom, S. 1964. *Poverty and Progress: Social Mobility in a Nineteenth Century City.* Cambridge, Mass.: Harvard University Press.

———. 1973. *The Other Bostonians: Poverty and Progress in the American Metropolis, 1880–1970.* Cambridge, Mass.: Harvard University Press.

———. 1975. "Reply." *Historical Methods Newsletter* 8.

Thomas, L. 1956. *The Occupational Structure and Education.* Englewood Cliffs, N.J.: Prentice-Hall.

Thomas, R. M. 1962. "Reinspecting a Structural Position on Occupational Prestige." *American Journal of Sociology* 67:561–65.

Thomas, W. I. 1923. *The Unadjusted Girl.* Montclair, N.J.: Patterson Smith, 1969.

Thorndike, R. L. 1968. Review of *Pygmalion in the Classroom. Educational Research Journal* 5:708–11.

———. 1969. "But Do You Have to Know How to Tell Time?" *Educational Research Journal* 6:692.

Thurow, L. C. 1961. *The Impact of Taxes on the American Economy.* New York: Praeger.

———. 1969. *Poverty and Discrimination.* Washington, D.C.: Brookings Institution.

———. 1970. *Investment in Human Capital.* Belmont, Mass.: Wadsworth.

Thurow, L. C., and R. E. B. Lucas. 1972. *The American Distribution of Income: A Structural Problem.* Washington, D.C.: Government Printing Office.

Tiryakian, E. A. 1958. "The Prestige Evaluation of Occupations in an Underdeveloped Country: The Philippines." *American Journal of Sociology* 63:390–99.

Tobias, A. 1975. *Fire and Ice.* New York. Morrow.

Tobin, J. 1968. "Raising the Incomes of the Poor." In *Agenda for the Nation,* ed. K. Gordon, pp. 77–116. Washington, D.C.: Brookings Institution.

Tocqueville, A. de. 1955. *The Old Regime and the French Revolution.* Garden City, N.Y.: Doubleday.

Toronto Globe and Mail. 1976. "Some Dog's Life." October 8, 1976:11.

Treiman, D. J. 1976. "A Comment on Professor Lewis Coser's Presidential Address." *American Sociologist* 11:27–33.

———. 1977. *Occupational Prestige in Comparative Perspective.* New York: Academic Press.

Treiman, D. J., and K. Terrell. 1975. "Sex and the Process of Status Attainment: A Comparison of Working Women and Men." *American Sociological Review* 40:174–200.

Trent, J. W., and L. L. Medsker. 1968. *Beyond High School.* San Francisco: Jossey-Bass.

Truman, D. 1951. *The Governmental Process.* New York: Knopf.

Tucker, C. W. 1967. "A Descriptive Analysis of Subjective Social Class in the United States: 1963." Paper presented to the Midwest Sociological Society meetings, Des Moines, Iowa.

Tumin, M. M. 1953. "Some Principles of Stratification: A Critical Analysis." *American Sociological Review* 18:387–94.

———. 1963. "On Inequality." *American Sociological Review* 28:19–26.

———. 1967. *Social Stratification: The Forms and Functions of Inequality.* Englewood Cliffs, N.J.: Prentice-Hall.

Turner, J. 1974. *The Structure of Sociological Theory.* Homewood, Ill.: Dorsey Press.

Turner, J. H., and R. Singleton, Jr. 1978. "A Theory of Ethnic Oppression: Toward a Reintegration of Cultural and Structural Concepts in Ethnic Relations Theory." *Social Forces* 56:1001–18.

Turrittin, A. H. 1974. "Social Mobility in Canada: A Comparison of Three Provincial Studies." *Canadian Review of Sociology and Anthropology,* special issue August 1974, Vol. 11, pp. 163–86.

Tyree, A., and J. Treas. 1974. "The Occupational and Marital Mobility of Women." *American Sociological Review* 39:293–302.

U.S. Bureau of the Census. 1956. *National Housing Inventory.* Washington, D.C.: Government Printing Office.

———. 1963. *Methodology and Scores of Socioeconomic Status.* Working Paper no. 15. Washington, D.C.: Government Printing Office.

————. 1964a. "Lifetime Occupational Mobility of Adult Males, March 1962." *Current Population Reports,* ser. P–23, no. 11. Washington, D.C.: Government Printing Office.

————. 1964b. "Socioeconomic Characteristics of the Population: 1960." *Current Population Reports,* ser. P–23, no. 12. Washington, D.C.: Government Printing Office.

————. 1964c. *Statistical History of the United States.* Stamford, Conn.: Fairfield.

————. 1969a. "Educational Attainment: March 1968." *Current Population Reports,* ser. P–20, no. 182. Washington, D.C.: Government Printing Office.

————. 1968a. "Annual Mean Income, Lifetime Income, and Educational Attainment of Men in the United States, for Selected Years, 1956 to 1966." *Current Population Reports,* ser. P–60, no. 56. Washington, D.C.: Government Printing Office.

————. 1968b. *Statistical Abstract of the United States: 1968.* 89th ed. Washington, D.C.: Government Printing Office.

————. 1969b. "Factors Related to High School Graduation and College Attendance: 1967." *Current Population Reports,* ser. P–20, no. 185. Washington, D.C.: Government Printing Office.

————. 1969c. "Poverty in the United States: 1959 to 1960." *Current Population Reports,* ser. P–60, no. 68. Washington, D.C.: Government Printing Office.

————. 1971. "Characteristics of the Low-Income Population, 1971." *Current Population Reports,* ser. P–60, no. 86. Washington D.C.: Government Printing Office.

————. 1972a. "Educational Attainment: March 1972." *Current Population Reports,* ser. P–20, no. 243. Washington, D.C.: Government Printing Office.

————. 1972b. "Money Income in 1971 of Families and Persons in the United States." *Current Population Reports,* ser. P–60, no. 85. Washington, D.C.: Government Printing Office.

————. 1973a. "Voting and Registration in the Election of November 1972." *Current Population Reports,* ser. P–20, no. 253. Washington, D.C.: Government Printing Office.

————. 1973b. "Money Income in 1972 of Families and Persons in the United States." *Current Population Reports,* ser. P–60, no. 90. Washington, D.C.: Government Printing Office.

————. 1973c. "Household Ownership of Cars and Light Trucks: July 1972." *Current Population Reports,* ser. P–65, no. 44. Washington, D.C.: Government Printing Office.

————. 1974. "Educational Attainment in the United States: March 1973 and 1974." *Current Population Reports,* ser. P–20, no. 274. Washington, D.C.: Government Printing Office.

————. 1975a. "Money Income in 1973 of Families and Persons in the United States." *Current Population Reports,* ser. P–60, no. 97. Washington, D.C.: Government Printing Office.

————. 1975b. "Characteristics of the Low-Income Population: 1973." *Current Population Reports,* ser. P–60, no. 98. Washington, D.C.: Government Printing Office.

————. 1975c. *Statistical Abstract of the United States.* 96th ed. Washington, D.C.: Government Printing Office.

————. 1976a. "Money Income in 1974 of Families and Persons in the United States." *Current Population Reports,* ser. P–60, no. 101. Washington, D.C.: Government Printing Office.

————. 1976b. "Money Income and Poverty Status of Families and Persons in the United States: 1975 and 1974 Revisions." *Current Population Reports,* ser. P–60, no. 103. Washington, D.C.: Government Printing Office.

U.S. Bureau of Labor Statistics. 1966. *A Study of Prices Charged in Food Stores Located in Low and Higher Income Areas of Six Large Cities, February 1966.* Prepared for the U.S. National Commission on Food Marketing. Washington, D.C.: Government Printing Office.

————. 1967. *Handbook of Labor Statistics, 1967.* Washington, D.C.: Government Printing Office.

————. 1970. *Employment and Earnings.* Vol. 17. Washington, D.C.: Government Printing Office.

U.S. Department of Labor. 1964. *Formal Occupational Training of Adult Workers.* Washington, D.C.: Government Printing Office.

————. 1971. "Fact Sheet on the Earnings Gap." Washington, D.C.: U.S. Government Printing Office.

————. 1975. *1975 Handbook on Women Workers.* Washington, D.C.: Government Printing Office.

U.S. Internal Revenue Service. 1968. *Statistics of Income, 1966: Individual Income Tax Returns.* Washington, D.C.: Government Printing Office.

————. 1972. *Statistics of Income, 1969: Supplemental Report, Personal Wealth.* Washington, D.C.: Government Printing Office.

U.S. National Center for Health Statistics, 1965. "Chronic Conditions and Activity Limitation, United States, July 1961–June 1963." Ser. 10, no. 17. Washington, D.C.: Government Printing Office.

U.S. National Health Survey. 1964. *Medical Care, Health Status, and Family Income, United States.* Ser. 10, no. 9. Washington, D.C.: Public Health Service.

U.S. Office of Management and Budget. 1973. *Social Indicators, 1973.* Washington, D.C.: Government Printing Office.

Valentine, C. A. 1968. *Culture and Poverty: Critique and Counter-Proposals.* Chicago: University of Chicago Press.

————. 1971. "The 'Culture of Poverty': Its Scientific Significance and Its Implications for Action." In *The Culture of Poverty: A Critique,* ed. E. B. Leacock, pp. 193–225. New York: Simon & Schuster.

Van den Berghe, P. 1963. "Dialectic and Functionalism: Toward a Theoretical Synthesis." *American Sociological Review* 28:695–705.

Vanfossen, B. E. 1960. "A Theoretical Analysis of 'Status' and Status-Oriented Behavior." Ph.D. diss., Emory University.

———. 1969. "Reasons for Social Inequality: The Evidence of Economic Data." *International Review of History and Political Science* 6:110–31.

———. 1973. "Twentieth-Century Stratification Theory: The Sociological Justification of Inequality." Paper presented to Society for the Study of Social Problems, New York.

———. 1977. "Sexual Stratification and Sex Role Socialization." *Journal of Marriage and the Family* 39:563–74.

Vanfossen, B. E., and R. I. Rhodes. 1974. "Commentary." *American Journal of Sociology* 80:727–32.

Vanneman, R. 1977. "The Occupational Composition of American Classes: Results from Cluster Analysis." *American Journal of Sociology* 82:783–807.

Vanneman, R., and F. C. Pampel. 1977. "The American Perception of Class and Status." *American Sociological Review* 42:422–37.

Veblen, T. 1899. *The Theory of the Leisure Class.* New York: Macmillan.

Verba, S., and N. H. Nie. 1972. *Participation in America: Political Democracy and Social Equality.* New York: Harper & Row.

Vidich, J., and J. Bensman. 1968. *Small Town in Mass Society: Class, Power and Religion in a Rural Community.* 2d ed. Princeton: Princeton University Press.

Villemez, W. J. 1977. "Male Economic Gain from Female Subordination: A Caveat and Reanalysis." *Social Forces* 56:626–36.

Vorwaller, D. J. 1970. "Social Mobility and Membership in Voluntary Organizations." *American Journal of Sociology* 75:481–95.

Wachtel, H. 1971. "Looking at Poverty from a Radical Perspective." *Review of Radical Political Economics* 3:1–19.

Wachtel, H. M., and C. Betsey. 1972. "Employment at Low Wages." *Review of Economics and Statistics* 54:121–29.

Walton, J. 1971. "A Methodology for the Comparative Study of Power: Some Conceptual and Procedural Applications." *Social Science Quarterly* 52:39–60.

Warner, W. L. 1962. *American Life: Dream and Reality.* Rev. ed. Chicago: University of Chicago Press.

Warner, W. L., and J. C. Abegglen. 1955. *Occupational Mobility in American Business and In-dustry.* Minneapolis: University of Minnesota Press.

Warner, W. L., and Associates. 1949. *Democracy in Jonesville: A Study in Quality and Inequality.* New York: Harper & Row.

Warner, W. L., and P. S. Lunt. 1941. *The Social Life of a Modern Community.* New Haven: Yale University Press.

Warner, W. L.; M. Meeker; and K. Eels. 1949. *Social Class in America.* Chicago: Science Research Associates.

Warner, W. L.; P. P. Van Riper; N. H. Martin; and O. F. Collins. 1963. *The American Federal Executive: A Study of the Social and Personal Characteristics of the Civilian and Military Leaders of the United States Federal Government.* New Haven: Yale University Press.

Warshay, L. H. 1975. *The Current State of Sociological Theory: A Critical Interpretation.* New York: McKay.

Weber, Max. 1946. *From Max Weber: Essays in Sociology.* Translated and edited by H. Gerth and C. W. Mills. New York: Oxford University Press.

———. 1947. *The Theory of Social and Economic Organization.* Translated by A. M. Henderson and T. Parsons. New York: Oxford University Press.

———. 1958. *The Protestant Ethic and the Spirit of Capitalism.* Translated by T. Parsons. New York: Scribner's.

———. 1968. *Economy and Society.* Edited by G. Roth and C. Wittich. New York: Bedminster Press.

Weinstein, J. 1969. *The Corporate Ideal in the Liberal State: 1900–1918.* Boston: Beacon.

Weisbrod, B. 1962. "Education and Investment in Human Capital." *Journal of Political Economy, supplement,* 70:106–23.

Weisbrod, B. A., and P. Karpoff. 1968. "Monetary Returns to College Education, Student Ability, and College Quality." *Review of Economics and Statistics* 50:491–510.

Weiss, L. 1966. "Concentration and Labor Earnings." *American Economic Review* 56:96–117.

Werner, S. A., Jr. ed. 1970. *The American Dream in Literature.* New York: Scribner's.

Wesolowski, W. 1962. "Some Notes on the Functional Theory of Stratification." *Polish Sociological Bulletin* 5–6:28–38.

West, J. [C. Withers.] 1945. *Plainville, U.S.A.* New York: Columbia University Press.

Westie, F. R. 1959. "Social Distance Scales." *Sociology and Social Research* 43:251–58.

White, L. 1943. "Energy and the Evolution of Culture." *American Anthropologist* 45:335–56.

Whyte, W. H., Jr. 1951. "The Wives of Management." *Fortune* 44:86–213.

———. 1956. *The Organization Man.* New York: Simon & Schuster.

Wilcox, K., and P. Moriarty. 1976. "Schooling and Work: Social Constraints on Equal Educational Opportunity." *Social Problems* 24:204–13.

Wiley, G. A. 1972. *Social Security Amendments of 1971*. Hearings, Senate Finance Committee, February 1.

Williams, Robin. 1960. *American Society*. 2d ed. New York: Knopf.

———. 1966. "Some Further Comments on Chronic Controversies." *American Journal of Sociology* 71:717–21.

———. 1970. *American Society: A Sociological Interpretation*. 3d ed. New York: Knopf.

Willener, A. 1957. *Images de la Société et Classes Sociales*. Bern.

Wolfe, D. M. 1959. "Power and Authority in the Family." In *Studies in Social Power*, ed. D. Cartwright, pp. 99–117. Ann Arbor: Research Center for Group Dynamics. Institute for Social Research.

Wolfgang, M. E., and B. Cohen. 1970. *Crime and Race: Conception and Misconceptions*. New York: Institute of Human Relations Press.

Wolfinger, R. 1960. "Reputation and Reality in the Study of Community Power." *American Sociological Review* 25:636–44.

Wolfle, D. 1971. *The Uses of Talent*. Princeton: Princeton University Press.

Woodward, K. L., and P. Malamud. 1977. "Understanding Rich Kids." *Newsweek*, August 29, p. 51.

Wright, C. R., and H. H. Hyman. 1958. "Voluntary Association Memberships of American Adults: Evidence from National Sample Surveys." *American Sociological Review* 23:284–94.

Wright, E. O., and L. Perrone. 1975. "Marxist Class Categories and Income Inequality." Paper presented to American Sociological Association, San Francisco, Calif.

Wrong, D. H. 1959. "The Functional Theory of Stratification: Some Neglected Considerations." *American Sociological Review* 24:772–82.

———. 1964. "Social Inequality without Social Stratification." *Canadian Review of Sociology and Anthropology* 1:5–16.

Wyllie, I. G. 1966. *The Self-Made Man in America*. New York: Free Press.

Yorburg, B. 1973. *The Changing Family*. New York: Columbia University Press.

Zeigler, H. 1965. "Interest Groups in the States." In *Politics in the American States*, ed. H. Jacob and K. Vines, Boston: Little, Brown, pp. 101–47.

Ziegler, H., and W. Peak. 1970. "The Political Functions of the Educational System." *Sociology of Education* 43:115–42.

Zeitlin, I. 1967. *Marxism: A Reexamination*. New York: Van Nostrand.

Zeitlin, M. 1974. "Corporate Ownership and Control: The Large Corporation and the Capitalist Class." *American Journal of Sociology* 79:1073–1119.

Zeitlin, M.; K. A. Lutterman; and J. W. Russell. 1973. "Death in Vietnam: Class, Poverty, and the Risks of War." *Politics and Society* 3:313–28.

Zweigenhaft, R. 1975. "Who Represents America?" *Insurgent Sociologist* 5:119–30.

NAME INDEX

Abegglen, J. C., 289
Abrahamson, M., 32
Acker, J., 180
Ackerman, F. H., 97–98
Adams family, 292
Adorno, T. W., 337
Alinsky, Saul, 381
Alston, J. P., 312–313
Amory, Cleveland, 290–291
Anderson, C. H., 43, 75–76, 382
Aquinas, Thomas, 15
Aristotle, 15, 21
Aron, R., 36, 49
Astin, A. W., 267
Auchincloss, Annie Burr, 295
Auchincloss family, 292

Bailyn, L., 307
Baltzell, E. D., 281, 283, 284–285, 288, 291, 296, 297
Banfield, Edward, 205–206, 354
Baran, P., 127
Barber, B., 5n1, 7n2, 52

Bean, F. D., 27, 29
Beaverbrook, Lady, 342–343
Bell, Daniel, 73, 206, 206n6
Bendix, R., 196–197, 198, 236
Berg, I., 274
Bernstein, B., 250
Betsey, C., 119, 129
Bibb, R., 119, 125, 128, 130
Binstock, J., 273
Birmingham, Stephen, 295
Birnbaum, N., 384
Blau, Peter, 181–189, 193, 195, 199, 355
Blum, Z. D., 360
Blumberg, P. M., 281, 282, 286, 287
Bogue, Donald J., 81–83, 226–227
Bottomore, T. B., 17, 30
Bowles, S., 76–77, 246, 272
Bradburn, N. M., 3
Brenner, M. H., 272
Brophy, J., 259
Buckley, W., 5n1, 7n2
Bundy family, 292
Burchard, W. W., 8

SUBJECT INDEX